Land Ro
Series II
Bonneted Control
Parts Catalogue

Part No RTC 9840CC

April 1987

LAND ROVER PARTS LTD

LAND ROVER COMMENCING VEHICLE NUMBERS
PETROL MODELS, 2¼ LITRE 4 CYLINDER SERIES IIA

Home, RH Stg)	24100001A	Home, RH Stg)	25100001A
Export, RH Stg)	24200001A	Export, RH Stg)	25200001A
Export, RH Stg,CKD) 88	24300001A	Export, RH Stg,CKD) 109	25300001A
Export, LH Stg)	24400001A	Export, LH Stg)	25400001A
Export, LH Stg,CKD)	24500001A	Export, LH Stg,CKD)	25500001A

Home, RH Stg)	31500001B*	Home, RH Stg)	26100001A
Export, RH Stg) 88	31600001B*	Export, RH Stg) 109	26200001A
Export, RH Stg, CKD) Station	31700001B*	Export, RH Stg, CKD) Station	26300001A
Export, LH Stg) Wagon	31800001B*	Export, LH Stg) Wagon	26400001A
Export, LH Stg, CKD)	31900001B*	Export, LH Stg, CKD)	26500001A

* From March, 1965 onwards. Vehicle numbers prior to this date are the same as for 88

PETROL MODELS, 2.6 LITRE 6 CYLINDER SERIES IIA

Home, RH Stg)	34500001D	Home, RH Stg)	35000001D
Export, RH Stg)	34600001D	Export, RH Stg)	35100001D
Export, RH Stg, CKD) 109	34700001D	Export, RH Stg, CKD) 109	35200001D
Export, LH Stg)	34800001D	Export, LH Stg) Station	35300001D
Export, LH Stg, CKD)	34900001D	Export, LH Stg, CKD) Wagon	35400001D

DIESEL MODELS 2¼ LITRE 4 CYLINDER SERIES IIA

Home, RH Stg)	27100001A	Home, RH Stg)	27600001A
Export, RH Stg)	27200001A	Export, RH Stg)	27700001A
Export, RH Stg, CKD) 88	27300001A	Export, RH Stg, CKD) 109	27800001A
Export, LH Stg)	27400001A	Export, LH Stg)	27900001A
Export, LH Stg, CKD)	27500001A	Export, LH Stg, CKD)	28000001A

Home, RH Stg)	32000001B*	Home, RH Stg)	28100001A
Export, RH Stg)	32100001B*	Export, RH Stg)	28200001A
Export, RH Stg, CKD) 88	32200001B*	Export, RH Stg, CKD) 109	28300001A
Export, LH Stg) Station	32300001B*	Export, LH Stg) Station	28400001A
Export, LH Stg, CKD) Wagon	32400001B*	Export, LH Stg, CKD) Wagon	28500001A

* From March, 1965 onwards. Vehicle numbers prior to this date are the same as for 88

Distributed by Brooklands Books Ltd., PO Box 146, Cobham,
Surrey KT11 1LG, England Phone: 01932 865051 Fax: 01932 868803
E-mail: sales@brooklands-books.com
www.brooklandsbook.co.uk

ISBN: 9781855202757   Part No. RTC9840CC   Ref: LR22PH   2253

CONTENTS

GROUP A   GENERAL EXPLANATION

Some of the information in this Publication is based on illustration and script type of presentation and the remainder is part-numbered illustrations with no script.

As the list covers both Home and Export models, reference is made throughout to the 'left-hand' (LH) and 'right-hand' (RH) sides of the vehicle, rather than to 'near-side' and 'off-side'. The 'left-hand side' is that to the left hand when the vehicle is viewed from the rear, similarly, 'left-hand steering' (LH Stg) models are those having the driving controls on the left-hand side, again when the vehicle is viewed from the rear.

The part numbers quoted are common to all Land Rover models, unless otherwise stated, either against the part number or in the remarks section on the page or illustration, as applicable.

Script and illustrations

Assemblies are printed in capitals, and all the parts comprising that assembly are shown by indenting the alignment of the description column, the indentation reverting to the original alignment when the assembly is complete. The indentation is clearly shown by the numbers 1, 2, 3, 4 at the top of each page.

It will be seen that the 'ROCKER COVER, TOP, ASSEMBLY' lC 10, includes the 'tappet clearance plate' and 'drive screw fixing plate' (indentation 1), while the 'joint washer', by reverting to alignment with 'ROCKER', is excluded from the assembly.

In all cases where the entire assembly is required, quote only the assembly number.

Part - numbered illustrations

A new presentation of parts information is used for certain parts of this Publication. That is, part numbered illustrations with no description, this gives a quicker look-up time and obviates the need for Parts Catalogue translation.

Information about assemblies and the components which comprise an assembly together with part numbers of gasket sets etc. will be found at the bottom of the illustration.

Figures in brackets represent the quantity used per vehicle.

No longer serviced

The code 'NLS' against an existing part number denotes that this part is no longer serviced

GROUP A   OBSERVATIONS GENERALES

Pour une partie de ce catalogue nous utilisons des illustrations accompagnées d'un texte, tandis que le reste est constitué par des illustrations auxquelles les références ont été incorporées.

Vu que cette fiche est valable bien pour les véhicules destinés au marché intérieur que pour ceux prévus pour l'exportation, nous avons recours à la spécification gauche et droite, droite et gauche étant définis par rapport au véhicule, lorsque celui-ci est examiné de l'arrière.

Sauf avis contraire, toutes les références sont valables pour tous les modèles Land-Rover. Toute exception sera indiquée soit au bas de la page, soit sur la gravure même.

Texte et illustrations

Les ensembles sont imprimés en lettres majuscules et toutes les pièces comprises dans un ensemble sont indiquées en déplaçant la désignation de ces pièces d'une colonne vers la droite par rapport à la position qu'occupe la désignation de l'ensemble. La désignation de la pièce suivante non comprise dans l'ensemble est ramenée a l'alignement des désignations et clairement montrée par les numéros 1, 2, 3 et 4 en haut de chaque page.

Par example, l'on remarquera que l'ensemble 'ROCKER COVER, TOP, ASSEMBLY' lC 10, comprend la 'tappet clearance plate' et la 'drive screw fixing plate' (colone 2), tandis que le 'joint washer' est exclu de l'ensemble, la désignation de celle-ci étant ramenée à la colonne 1, en ligne avec 'ROCKER'.

Lorsqu'un ensemble complet est requis, il suffira d'indiquer le numéro de l'ensemble.

Illustrations numérotées

Certaines parties du catalogue sont présentées sous une nouvelle form. C'est-à-dire, les références sont incorporées aux illustrations sans en utiliser une désignation, ce qui permet de rechercher une pièce plus rapidement. Ainsi, aucune traduction du catalogue de pièces détachées s'imposera.

Tous les détails au sujet des ensembles et de leurs pièces constituantes sont donnés en bas de la page avec les références des pochettes de joints.

Les chiffres entre parenthèses indiquent la quantité requise par véhicule.

GROUP A

1C 02 to 1C 14 — 2¼ litre Petrol	1D 02 to 1D 18 — 2.6 litre Petrol
1E 02 to 1E 15 — 2¼ litre Diesel	1F 02 to 1F 10
1G 02 to 1G 13	1H 02 to 1H 13
1H 14 to 1H 15	1H 16

1B 07

ALLGEMEINE ERKLAERUNGEN

Ein Teil dieses Kataloges ist in der bisherigen Aufmachung gehalten, d.h. die Abbildung auf der einen und der Text auf der gegenüberliegenden Seite, d.h. die Textseite fällt weg und die Ersatzteilnummern sind direkt in der Abbildung enthalten.

Das Transparent hat für Fahrzeuge für den Binnen- und Exportmarkt Geltung. Es wird deshalb stets auf die linke oder rechte Fahrzeugseite Bezug genommen. Unter der linken oder rechten Seite ist diejenige Seite zu verstehen, wenn das Fahrzeug von hinten her betrachtet wird. Bei einem linksgesteuerten Fahrzeug ist das Lenkrad demnach auf der linken Fahrzeugseite angeordnet, wenn dieses von hinten betrachtet wird.

Falls dies nicht anderweitig angegeben ist, haben alle aufgeführten Teilnummern für alle Land-Rover Modelle Geltung. Allfällige Abweichungen sind entweder am Fuss der Seite oder in der Abbildung selbst angegeben.

Text und Abbildung

Die Baugruppen sind in Grossbuchstaben gedruckt. Alle in der Baugruppe enthaltenen Teile sind eingerückt. Der Schluss der Baugruppe wird durch das Vorrücken an den Rand angegeben. Die Einrückung wird am oberen Seitenrand durch die Zahlen 1, 2, 3 und 4 angezeigt.

So umfasst die Baugruppe 'ROCKER COVER, TOP, ASSEMBLY' 1C 10, die 'tappet clearance plate' und die 'drive screw' (eingerückt), während der 'joint washer' in der Baugruppe nicht eingeschlossen ist, und wieder an den Rand vorgerückt wird.

Wo die ganze Baugruppe benötigt wird, ist ausschliesslich die Teilnummer dieser Baugruppe aufzuführen.

Abbildungen mit Teilnummern

Ein gewisser Teil dieses Kataloges ist in der neuen Aufmachung dargestellt. Bei dieser Darstellung sind die Teilnummern in der Abbildung eingetragen. Auf eine Bezeichnung der abgebildeten Teile wird verzichtet, um ein rascheres Auffinden der Teile zu ermöglichen. Mit dieser Methode erübrigt sich auch das Uebersetzen der Ersatzteilliste.

Die entsprechenden Angaben über Baugruppen und die darin enthaltenen Teile sind jeweils mit den Teilnummern für Dichtungssätze, etc. am Fuss der Seite aufgeführt.

Die in Klammern aufgeführten Zahlen geben die pro Fahrzeug benötigte Anzahl an.

1B 05

GROUP A   PICTORIAL INDEX, TABLE DES MATIERES ILLUSTREE, VERZEICHNIS DER ABBILDUNGEN.

2F 03 to 2F 13 2G 02 to 2G 08	2F 14 to 2F 16 2G 09 to 2G 11 2H 02 to 2H 10
2I 02 to 2I 05	2I 02 to 2I 05
2I 06 to 2I 15	2J 02 to 2J 07
2K 02 to 2K 16 2L 02 to 2L 17	

One Ton Model

1B 08

GROUP A   PICTORIAL INDEX, TABLE DES MATIERES ILLUSTREE, VERZEICHNIS DER ABBILDUNGEN.

1I 02 to 1I 08	1J 02 to 1J 14 1K 02 to 1K 10
1L 02 to 1L 18 1M 02 to 1M 12 1N 02 to 1N 10	1N 11 to 1N 15
1O 02 to 1O 05	2C 02 to 2C 15
2D 02 to 2D 15 2E 02 to 2E 08	2F 02

1B 07

ALPHABETICAL INDEX

GROUP A

GROUP A

GROUP A

GROUP A

GROUP B
ENGINE - Cylinder Block, 2¼ litre Petrol

525497 (1)
250840 (2)
524765 (2)
587628 (2)
Alternatives

536577
243959
512412
527269
52124
ERC5086(2

273166
243968

602915
513272(2)
525428 (3)
252621
NRC2938
WH600081(4)
212430 (4) Alternativ

608327
Early type fixing
252622 (3)
516133
247965
247861
247127
514527
213700 (2)
247758 (6)
247755 (6)
501593 (6)
504006 (6)
504007 (6)
SH608081(3)
SH608091(1)
Plain type
Waisted type
Alternatives

New engine assy 7:1 C/R, RTC2379N Optional from vehicle suffix 'G' onwards
New engine assy 8:1 C/R, 607303N Standard from vehicle suffix 'G' onwards
Rebuilt engine assy 7:1 C/R RTC2379R
Rebuilt engine assy 8:1 C/R RTC2352R
Short engine assembly RTC2663 8:1 C/R

Engine assemblies do not include ancillaries

Decarbonising gasket set GEG162   Engine overhaul gasket set 608124
Stud kit for cylinder block 600245   Cylinder liner 527351 (4)

1C 02

GROUP A

Glossary of American-English Automotive Part Terms listed under the following sub-headings:
Body parts, brake parts, chassis parts, electrical equipment, instruments, motor and clutch parts, rear axle and transmission parts, steering parts, tools and accessories, transmission parts and tyres.

U S A	ENGLISH
Body parts	
Bumper guard	Overrider
Cowl	Scuttle
Dashboard	Facia panel
Door post	Door pillar
Door stop	Check strap
Door vent	Quarter light
Fender	Wing
Firewall	Bulkhead
Hood	Bonnet
License plate	Number plate
Rear seat back or backrest	Rear seat squab
Rocker panel	Valance
Skirt	Apron
Tailgate	Tailboard
Toe pan	Toe board
Top	Hood
Trunk	Boot
Windshield	Windscreen
wheelhouse or housing	Wheelarch
Brake parts	
Parking brake	Hand brake
Chassis parts	
Muffler	Exhaust silencer
Side rail	Side member
Spring clamp	U-bolt
Electrical equipment	
Back up lamp	Reverse lamp
Dimmer switch	Dip switch
Dome lamp	Roof lamp
Gas pump or fuel pump	Petrol pump
Generator	Dynamo
Ignition set	Ignition harness
Parking lamp	Side lamp
Rear lamp	Tail lamp
Spark plug	Sparking plug
Turn signal	Trafficator
Voltage regulator	Control box
Instruments	
Tachometer	Rev-counter

U S A	ENGLISH
Motor and clutch parts -	Engine and clutch parts
Carburetor	Carburetter
Clutch throwout bearing	Clutch release bearing
Cylinder crankcase	Cylinder block
Hose clamp	Hose clip
Pan	Sump
Piston or wrist pin	Gudgeon pin
Rear axle and transmission parts	
Axle shaft	Half shaft
Drive shaft	Propeller shaft
Grease fitting	Grease nipple
Ring gear and pinion	Crown wheel and pinion
Steering parts	
Control arm	Wishbone
King pin	Swivel pin
Pitman arm	Drop arm
Steering idler	Steering relay
Steering knuckle	Stub axle
Steering post	Steering column
Tie bar or track bar	Track rod
Tools and accessories	
Antenna	Aerial
Crank handle	Starting handle
Wheel wrench	Wheel brace
Wrench	Spanner
Transmission parts -	Gearbox parts
Auxiliary gearbox	Transfer box
Counter shaft	Layshaft
Gear shift lever	Gear lever
Output shaft	Main shaft
Parking lock	Parking brake
Shift bar	Selector rod
Transmission casing	Gearbox housing
Tyres	
Tire	Tyre
Tread	Track

18 03

527164(4)

519440(8)

ERC1029(8)
(273390)(8)

528004(4)

Standard   RTC2410   (4)
0.020 in O/S RTC241020 (4)
0.040 in O/S RTC241040 (4)

255169(4)

265175(8)

Standard 6o8255S (4)
0.020in   OS 597501(4)
0.040in   OS 597503(4)

RTC1730 Std   US
RTC1730/10   US
① RTC1730/20 US

① Engine set

1RE 99

1C 03

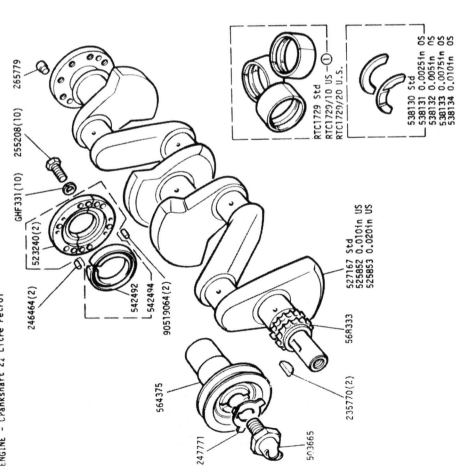

265779

255208(10)

GHF331(10)

523240(2)

246464(2)

542492

542494

90519064(2)

568333

235770(2)

564375

503665

247771

527167 Std
525852 0.010in US
525853 0.020in US

RTC1729 Std
RTC1729/10 US ──①
RTC1729/20 U.S.

538130 Std
538131 0.0025in OS
538132 0.005in OS
538133 0.0075in OS
538134 0.010in OS

011 Seal and Retainer Assy 542494 and 011 Seal Assy 542492 includes 1oz tube silicone grease 270656
① Engine set

1RE 103

1C 03

GROUP B   ENGINE - Oil Pump, 2¼ litre Petrol

PLATE REF.	DESCRIPTION	QTY.	PART No.	REMARKS
	OIL PUMP ASSEMBLY	1	513640	
1	Oil pump body	1	513641	
2	Spindle for idler gear	1	90502209	
3	Oil pump gear, driver	1	240555	
4	Oil pump gear, idler	1	278109	
5	Bush for idler gear	1	214995	
6	Steel ball	1	3748	
7	Plunger	1	273711	For oil pressure release valve
8	Spring	1	564456	For oil pressure release valve
9	Washer, inside dia 55/64"	1	243970	Alternatives.
9	Washer, inside dia 49/64"	1	232044	Alternatives.
10	Plug	1	549909	
11	Oil pump cover	1	513639	
12	Set bolt (5/16" UNF x 5/8")	4	255227	Fixing cover to body
13	Spring washer	4	GHF332	Fixing cover to body
14	Oil filter for pump	1	247664	
15	Sealing ring	1	244488	Fixing oil filter to oil pump
16	Lockwasher	1	244487	Fixing oil filter to oil pump
17	Drive shaft for oil pump	1	511680	
18	VERTICAL DRIVE SHAFT ASSEMBLY	1	503266	With split bush
19	Circlip for drive shaft	1	247742	
20	Split bush for drive shaft gear	1	247653	
21	VERTICAL DRIVE SHAFT ASSEMBLY	1	530175*	Up to engine suffix 'F' inclusive 7:1 compression ratio only — With one piece bush
21	VERTICAL DRIVE SHAFT ASSEMBLY	1	ERC6105	From Engine suffix 'G' onwards 7:1 compression ratio; Engine suffix 'A' onwards 8:1 compression ratio — With one piece bush
22	Circlip for drive shaft	1	247742	
23	One piece bush for drive shaft gear	1	522745	
24	Thrust washer for drive shaft	1	530178*	
25	Retaining ring for washer and bush	1	530179	
26	Locating screw for drive shaft bush	1	524769	
27	Set bolt (5/16" UNF x 1")	2	GHF103	Fixing oil pump to cylinder block
28	Lockwasher	2	247665	Fixing oil pump to cylinder block

* NO LONGER SERVICED

ENGINE - Oil pump, 2¼ litre Petrol

ENGINE - Camshaft and Tensioner Mechanism, 2¼ litre Petrol

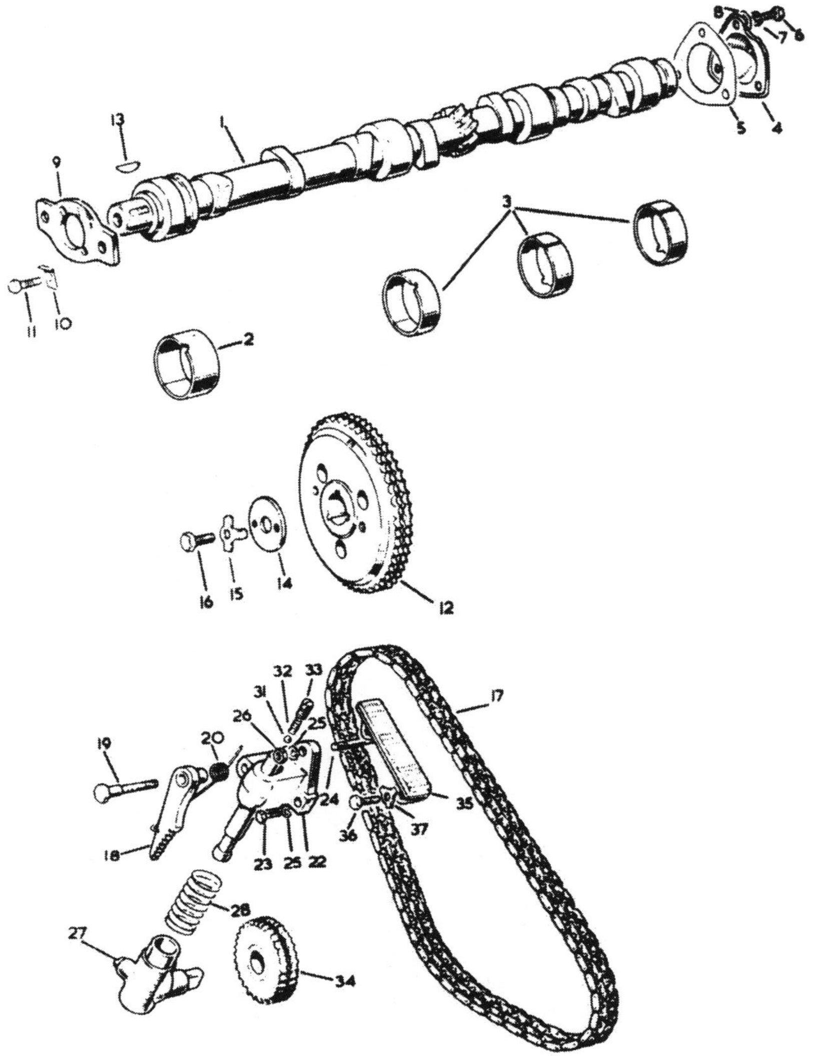

1C 05

GROUP B — ENGINE - Camshaft and Tensioner Mechanism, 2¼ litre Petrol

PLATE REF.	1 2 3 4 DESCRIPTION	QTY.	PART No.	REMARKS
1	Camshaft	1	247709	
2	Bearing complete for camshaft, front	1	90519054	
3	Bearing complete for camshaft, centre and rear	3	90519055	
4	Rear end cover for camshaft	1	538073	
5	Joint washer for cover	1	247070	
6	Set bolt (¼" UNF x ⅞")) Fixing	3	255208	) Alternative
	Set bolt (¼" UNF x ⅝")) cover	3	255206	) fixings
7	Spring washer) to	3	GHF331	
8	Plain washer) block	6	RTC840	
9	Thrust plate for camshaft	1	ERC1561	
10	Locker) Fixing thrust plate	2	2995	
11	Set bolt (¼" UNF x ¾")) to cylinder block	2	255207	
12	Chainwheel for camshaft	1	568474	
13	Key locating camshaft chainwheel	1	230313	
14	Retaining washer) Fixing	1	9093	
15	Locker) chainwheel	1	9210	
16	Set bolt (⅜" UNF x ⅞")) to camshaft	1	SH606071	
17	Camshaft chain (⅜" pitch x 78 links)	1	504375	
18	Ratchet for timing chain adjuster	1	546026	
19	Special bolt fixing ratchet and piston to block	1	247199	
20	Spring for chain adjuster ratchet	1	267451	
22	Piston for timing chain adjuster	1	90515323	
23	Set bolt (5/16" UNF x 1¼")) Fixing	1	BH605101	
24	Stud) piston to	1	247144	
25	Spring washer) cylinder	2	GHF332	
26	Nut (5/16" UNF)) block	1	GHF201	
27	Cylinder for timing chain adjuster	1	277388	
28	Spring for chain tensioner	1	233326	
31	Steel ball (7/32") for non-return valve	1	3739	
32	Spring retainer for steel ball	1	515321	
33	Plug for spring retainer	1	515325	
34	Idler wheel for timing chain	1	236067	
35	Vibration damper for timing chain	1	275234	
36	Set bolt (¼" UNF x ½")) Fixing damper to	2	255204	
37	Locking plate) cylinder block	2	557523	

1C 05

GROUP B   ENGINE – Valve Gear and Rockershafts, 2¼ litre Petrol

PLATE REF.	1	2	3	4	DESCRIPTION	QTY.	PART No.	REMARKS
1					Inlet valve	4	277593	
2					Exhaust valve	4	557967	
3					Valve spring, inner and outer	8	568550	
4					Valve spring cup	8	268292	
5					Split cone for valve, halves	16	268293	
6					Valve rocker, exhaust LH	2	512207	
7					Valve rocker, exhaust RH	2	90512208	
8					Bush for exhaust valve rocker	4	247614	
9					Valve rocker, inlet, LH	2	90512205	
10					Valve rocker, inlet, RH	2	512206	
11					Bush for inlet valve rocker	2	247614	
12					Tappet adjusting screw	8	506814	
13					Locknut for tappet adjusting screw	8	NT605061	
14					Tappet push rod	8	546798	
					Tappet, tappet guide, roller and set bolt assembly			
15					Tappet	8	507829	
16					Tappet guide	8	507026	
17					Roller	8	502473	
18					Special set bolt	8	90517429	
19					Aluminium washer for tappet guide set bolt	8	507025	
21					Valve rocker shaft	1	273069	
22					Spring for rocker shaft	4	554070	
23					Rocker bracket	5	247040	
24					Washer for rocker bracket	6	554602	
25					Locating dowel for rocker bracket	5	525389	
26					Stud in rocker bracket for rocker cover	3	277956	4 off on early models
27					Set bolt (5/16" UNF x 2⅛") } Fixing rocker bracket to cylinder head	3	502656	
28					Spring washer	5	525500	
						5	GHF332	
29					Locating screw) For rocker shaft	1	525390	2 off any early models
30					Spring washer) at bracket	1	GHF332	

1C 06

ENGINE – Valve Gear and Rockershafts, 2¼ litre Petrol

1C 06

16

ENGINE - Front Cover, Side Covers and Sump, 2¼ litre Petrol

GROUP B — ENGINE - Front Cover, Side covers and Sump, 2¼ litre Petrol

PLATE REF. 1 2 3 4	DESCRIPTION	QTY.	PART No.	REMARKS
1	FRONT COVER ASSEMBLY	1	90514451	Up to engine suffix 'G' inclusive 7:1 compression ratio only
1	FRONT COVER ASSEMBLY	1	554541	From engine suffix 'H' onwards 7:1 compression ratio. Engine suffix 'A' onwards 8:1 compression ratio
1	FRONT COVER ASSEMBLY	1	568667	With Lucas 2AC type 12-volt AC/DC generator. Up to engine suffix 'G' inclusive 7:1 compression ratio only.
1	FRONT COVER ASSEMBLY	1	554843	With Lucas 2AC type 12-volt AC/DC generator. From engine suffix 'H' onwards 7:1 compression ratio only.
2	Dowel locating front cover	2	6395	
3	Oil seal for front cover	1	213744	
4	Stud fixing water pump	5	252500	
5	Mud excluder	1	247766	
6	Hammer drive screw fixing excluder	8	AB606021	
7	Joint washer for front cover	1	538039	
8	Joint washer at water inlet	1	538038	
	Spring washer	15	GHF332	
	Bolt (5/16" UNF x 3")	7	BH605241	
	Set bolt (5/16" UNF x 3¼")	2	BH605261	
	Set bolt (5/16" UNF x 2")	3	BH605161	Fixing front cover and water pump to cylinder block
	Set bolt (5/16" UNF x 3¼")	2	BH605281	1 off with Lucas 2AC type 12 volt AC/DC generator
	Nut (5/16" UNF)	2	GHF201	With Lucas 2AC type 12 volt AC/DC generator — Up to engines suffix 'G' inclusive 7:1 compression ratio only
9	Spring washer	15	GHF332	From engine suffix 'H' onwards 7:1 compression ratio. Engine suffix 'A' onwards 8:1 compression ratio.
10	Set bolt (5/16" UNF x 3")	3	BH605241	
	Bolt (5/16" UNF x 3¼")	2	BH605261	
11	Set bolt (5/16" UNF x 2")	7	BH605161	Fixing front cover and water pump to cylinder block
	Set bolt (5/16" UNF x 3¼")	1	BH605281	when Lucas 2AC type generator is fitted
	Plain washer	1	2266	
12	Nut (5/16" UNF)	2	GHF201	when Lucas 2AC type generator is 7:1 compression ratio. Engine suffix 'A' onwards 8:1 compression ratio.

1C 07

ENGINE - Front Cover, Side Covers and Sump, 2¼ litre Petrol

1C 07

ENGINE - Front Cover, Side Covers and Sump, 2¼ litre Petrol

ENGINE - Front Cover, Side Covers and Sump, 2¼ litre Petrol

1C 08

GROUP B   ENGINE – Front Cover, Side Covers and Sump, 2¼ Litre Petrol

PLATE REF.	1 2 3 4	PART No.	DESCRIPTION	REMARKS
	1	564362	Timing pointer at front cover	From engine suffix 'K' onwards 7:1 compression ratio. Engine suffix 'A' onwards 8:1 compression ratio.
13	1	90510730	Side cover and oil filler pipe for engine, front	Not part of engine assy
14	1	529394	Baffle plate for side cover, front	
15	2	247555	Joint washer for side cover, front	
16	1	542600	SIDE COVER ASSEMBLY, REAR	
17	2	500792*	Stud for fuel pump	
18	2	4047	Plain washer	
19	2	GHF201	Nut (5/16" UNF) Fixing stud	Nut and split pin type fixing
20	2	2422	Split pin	
	2	542601	Stud for fuel pump	Plain type stud fixing
21	1	247554	Joint washer for side cover, rear	
22	6	GHF332	Spring washer	Fixing rear side cover plate
23	6	GHF103	Set bolt (5/16" UNF x 1")	
24	7	GHF332	Spring washer	Fixing front side cover plate
25	7	GHF120	Set bolt (5/16" UNF x ¾")	
26	1	529823	Crankcase sump	
27	1	536577	Drain plug for crankcase sump	
28	1	243959	Washer for drain plug	
29	1	GEG537	Joint washer for crankcase sump	
30	21	255227	Set bolt (5/16" UNF x ¾") Fixing sump	
31	22	GHF332	Spring washer	Fixing sump to cylinder block
32		GHF201	Nut (5/16" UNF) for stud	
33	1	ERC4199	Oil level rod	
34	1	532387	Sealing ring for rod	
35	1	504032	Tube for oil level rod	Alternative to one-piece type of oil level rod tube. Not part of engine assemble
36	1	236060	Double-ended union	
37	1	243958	Washer	Fixing tube to cylinder block
38	1	236408	Olive	
39	1	236407	Union nut	
40	1	541860	Tube for oil level rod	One-piece type. Alternative to tube with separate union.
41	1	546440	Oil filler cap and breather filter	

* NO LONGER SERVICED

1C 08

GROUP B
ENGINE – Thermostat and Housing, 2¼ litre Petrol

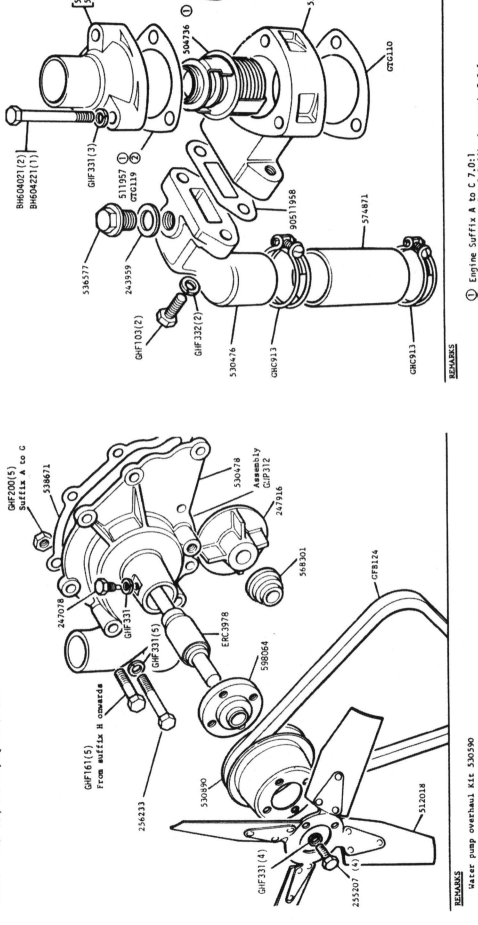

511956 ①
527109 ②

GTG109 ②

GTS109 ②

BH604021(2)
BH604221(1)

GHF331(3)

504736

516059

GTC110

511957 ①
GTG119 ②

536577

243959

90511958

574871

GHF103(2)

GHF332(2)

530476

GHC913

GHC913

REMARKS

① Engine Suffix A to C 7.0:1
② Engine Suffix D 7.0:1 Suffix A onwards 8.0:1

1C 09

GROUP B
ENGINE – Water Pump and Fan, 2¼ litre Petrol

GHF200(5)
Suffix A to G

538671

247078

GHF331

GHF331(5)

GHF161(5)
From suffix H onwards

256233

GHF331(4)

255207(4)

530890

530478

Assembly
GUP312

247916

568301

ERC3978

598064

GFB124

512018

REMARKS

Water pump overhaul Kit 530590

1C 09

19

GROUP B ENGINE – Cylinder Head, 2¼ litre Petrol

PLATE REF. 1 2 3 4	DESCRIPTION	QTY.	PART No.	REMARKS
1	CYLINDER HEAD ASSEMBLY 7:1 COMPRESSION RATIO	1	598086	with 'O' ring type seal.
1	CYLINDER HEAD ASSEMBLY 8:1 COMPRESSION RATIO	1	598089	
2	Valve guide, inlet, and sealing ring	4	500144	Up to engine suffix 'J'
3	Sealing ring for inlet valve guide	4	247186⊘	inclusive. 7:1 compression
4	Valve guide, exhaust and sealing ring	4	500145	ratio only
5	Sealing ring for exhaust valve guide	4	233419⊘	
	Valve guide, inlet,	4	568686	With lip type oil seal.
	Oil seal for inlet valve guide	4	554727⊘	From engine suffix 'K'
	Valve guide, exhaust,	4	568687	onwards 7:1 compression
	Oil seal for exhaust valve guide	4	554728	ratio. Engine suffix 'A' onwards 8:1 compression ratio
6	Core plug, ⅞" diameter	1	250830	Alternatives
	Cup plug, 15/16" diameter	1	525497	
7	Core plug, 1" diameter	4	518272	
8	Core plug, 1⅛" diameter	1	230250	
	Stud, short, for manifold	2	247144	
	Stud for manifold flange, centre	1	564574	
11	Dowel for cylinder head	2	213700	
12	Cylinder head gasket	1	GEG3308	
13	Special set bolt, short	4	279648	
14	Special set bolt, medium	9	247051	
15	Special set bolt (6.11/16" long) Fixing cylinder head to cylinder block	5	279650	
	Special set bolt (5.3/16" long)	5	554621	Up to engine suffix 'H' inclusive 7:1 compression ratio
				From engine suffix 'J' onwards 7:1 compression ratio. Engine suffix 'A' onwards 8:1 compression ratio
16	ROCKER COVER, TOP, ASSEMBLY	1	524846	
17	Tappet clearance plate	1	247634	
18	Drive screw fixing plate	4	A8606021	
19	Joint washer for top rocker cover	1	GEG431	
20	Sealing washer	3	273069	
21	Rubber washer	3	506069	
22	Cover for rubber washer Fixing top rocker cover	3	247624	
23	Special nut	3	247121	

⊘ Not included in cylinder head assembly

1C 10

ENGINE – Cylinder Head, 2¼ litre petrol

1C 10

ENGINE - Cylinder Head, 2¼ litre Petrol

GROUP B   ENGINE - Cylinder Head, 2¼ litre Petrol

PLATE REF.	1	2	3	4	DESCRIPTION	QTY.	PART No.	REMARKS
24					Lifting bracket for engine, front	1	525131	
25					Lifting bracket for engine, rear	1	ERC2686	
26					Spring washer } Fixing brackets	4	GHF332	
27					Set bolt (5/16" UNF x ½") } to cylinder head	4	GHF120	
28					Breather filter for engine	1	247631	Not part of engine
29					Sealing ring for filter	1	268887	assembly
30					Special set screw fixing breather filter	1	515291	
					Sealing washer for set screw	1	232037	
31					Joint washer } For heater valve hole	1	243959	
32					Plug (⅜" BSP) } in cylinder head	1	536577	
33					Engine oil filter	1	537229	Short type
34					Element for filter, overall length 6.13/16"	1	GFE144	For long type filter
					Element for filter, overall length 4⅛"	1	GFE130	For short type filter
35					Gasket for filter	1	272539	
					Rubber washer for centre bolt	1	269889*	
36					Joint washer for filter	1	598354	
37					Set bolt (7/16" UNF x 1½") } Fixing filter to	1	SH607101	
38					Spring washer } cylinder block	2	WM600071	
39					Oil pipe complete to cylinder head	1	275679	
40					Banjo bolt fixing oil pipe	2	597563	
41					Joint washer for banjo bolts	4	232039	
42					Plug for thermometer hole in cylinder head	1	536577	Up to engine suffix 'H' inclusive 7:1 compression ratio only
					Water temperature transmitter	1	GTR111	From engine suffix 'J' onwards 7:1 compression ratio. Engine suffix 'A' onwards 8:1 compression ratio
					Adaptor for water temperature transmitter	1	568457	
43					Joint washer for plug or adaptor	1	231577	
44					Oil pressure switch	1	GPS102	
45					Joint washer for switch	1	232039	
					Shakeproof washer for switch terminal	1	GHF321	
46					Thermostat switch for mixture warning light	1	BHA5252	
47					Joint washer for switch, 1/16" thick	1	236022	
48					Set bolt (2BA x ⅜") } Fixing	3	237119	Alternatives
					Set bolt (2BA x 7/16") } switch	3	251002	
49					Spring washer } to head	3	WM702001	
					Valve guide oil control kit	1	605761*	To convert early engines with 'O' ring type valve guide seals to lip type oil seals

* NO LONGER SERVICED

1C 11

ENGINE - Cylinder Head, 2¼ litre Petrol

1C 11

ENGINE - Manifolds, 2¼ litre Petrol

ENGINE — Manifolds, 2¼ litre Petrol

GROUP B

PLATE REF. 1 2 3 4	DESCRIPTION	QTY.	PART No.	REMARKS
	Carburetter complete	1	278163	) See row 1L 02
	Joint washer for carburetter	2	278162	) Up to engine suffix
	Packing for carburetter	1	GHF333	) 'H' inclusive 7:1
	Spring washer) Fixing	2	GHF202	) compression ratio
	Nut (¼" UNF)) carburetter	2		only
1	Carburetter complete	1	554175	) See row 1L 06
2	Adaptor for carburetter	2	252514	
3	Stud for carburetter	2	278163	
4	Joint washer for adaptor and packing piece	1	278162	) From engine suffix
5	Packing for adaptor	1	GHF333	) 'J' onwards 7:1
6	Spring washer) Fixing adaptor and packing	2	GHF202	) compression ratio
7	Nut (¼" UNF)) to inlet manifold	2	554163	) From engine suffix
8	Joint washer for carburetter	2	GHF332	) 'A' onwards 8:1
9	Spring washer) Fixing carburetter	2	GHF201	) compression ratio
10	Nut (5/16" UNF)) to adaptor Suction pipe complete, carburetter to distributor	1	527349	Up to engine suffix 'H' inclusive 7:1 compression ratio only
11	Suction pipe complete, carburetter to distributor	1	554145	From engine suffix 'J' onwards 7:1 compression ratio. From engine suffix 'A' onwards 8:1 compression ratio
12	Nipple) Suction pipe,	1	RTC607	Up to engine suffix 'H' inclusive 7:1 compression ratio only
13	Nut) carburetter end	1	3783	
	Screwed union) Suction pipe,	1	260707	From engine suffix 'J' onwards 7:1 compression ratio. From engine suffix 'A' onwards 8:1 compression ratio
	Olive) carburetter end	1	260708	
14	Rubber tube, suction pipe to carburetter	1	574878	
15	Clip for suction pipe	1	214228	Up to engine suffix 'H' inclusive 7:1 compression ratio
16	Clip, suction pipe to manifold stud	1	514580	
17	Clip, suction pipe to cylinder head stud	1	90512646	
18	Rubber grommet for clip	3	214229	
19	Bolt (¼" UNF x ½")) Fixing clip	1	255206	
20	Spring washer) to rear	1	GHF331	
21	Plain washer) lifting	1	RTC609	
22	Nut (¼" UNF)) bracket	1	GHF200	
23	INLET MANIFOLD ASSEMBLY	1	596000	
	Stud for carburetter or adaptor	2	587726	
	Plug for inlet manifold (servo connection)	1	596069	With tapping for servo
	Washer for plug	1	243958	

1C 12

ENGINE - Manifolds, 2¼ litre Petrol

1C 12

22

GROUP B   ENGINE – Manifolds, 2¼ litre Petrol

PLATE REF.	1 2 3 4	DESCRIPTION	QTY.	PART No.	REMARKS
24		Liner for inlet manifold	1	278161	
25		Exhaust manifold	1	599473	
26		Butterfly valve	1	247811*	For early type manifold
27		Spindle for butterfly valve	1	279168*	with butterfly valve
28		Counterbalance weight	1	279169	
29		Set screw (2BA x ⅜") fixing weight to spindle	1	237119	
30		Stop pin for adjusting plate	1	247819	
31		Bi-metal spring for butterfly	1	247818	
32		Adjusting plate and pin for spring	1	536646	
33		Stud (3.11/16")) For inlet	3	574048	
		Stud (3⅞")) manifold	1	530135	
34		Stud for exhaust pipe	2	BX605161	
35		Special set bolt) Fixing inlet to	2	256429 *	LH Stg
		Special set bolt) exhaust manifold	3	568664	RH Stg
36		Joint washer	2	247824	
37		Plain washer	4	RTC613	
38		Spring washer	4	GHF332	
		Nut (5/16" UNF)	4	GHF201	
39		Joint washer, inlet and exhaust manifold to cylinder head	1	GEG639	Metal and fibre type. Up to engines numbered 25283642J except Switzerland, 25282861J Switzerland
		Joint washer, inlet manifold to cylinder head	2	GEG661@	Corrugated tin plate type From engines numbered 25283643J onwards except Switzerland 25282862J onwards Switzerland
40		Clamp for manifold	2	564308	Not part of engine assembly
41		Set bolt (5/16" UNF x 2¼")) Fixing	4	BH605221	
		Set bolt (5/16" UNF x 2")) manifold	4	BH605161	
		Set bolt (5/16" UNF x 1¾")) to	2	255029	
42		Spring washer) cylinder	11	GHF332	
43		Plain washer) head	5	587405	
		Plain washer, thick	4	GHF301	
		Nut (5/16" UNF)	3	GHF201	
44		Exhaust manifold fixing kit	1	606988	

* NO LONGER SERVICED

@ With corrugated tin plate inlet manifold joint washer, the exhaust manifold and cylinder head are in metal-to-metal contact.

IC 13

GROUP B

ENGINE Mountings and Rubbers, 2¼ litre Petrol

272498 (4)
GHF105(4)
WD110061(4)
GHF333(4)
GHF202(4)

251322(4) (1)(4)   GHF233(4) (2)(4)
NRC2054(2) (2)(3)   NRC2053(2) (2)(4)

272501 (4)

2851 (1)(3)   850641 (2)(3)
GHF333(4) (1)(3)   WL110001(4) (2)(3)
WD110061(2) (1)(3)   WL110061(2) (2)(3)
2827(4) (1)(3)   GHF214(4) (2)(3)

272506 (3)
GHF105(2)
WD110061
GHF333(2)
GHF202(2)

1 BSF Fixings
2 Metric Fixings
3 Front Mounting
4 Rear Mounting

IC 14

23

GROUP B
ENGINE - Cylinder Block Fixings 2.6 Litre Petrol

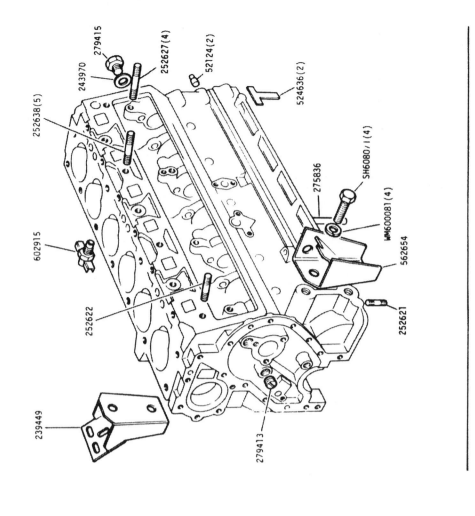

279415
243970
252627(4)
52124(2)
524636(2)
252638(5)
602915
275836
SH60801/1(4)
WM600081(4)
562654
252622
252621
239449
279413

1D 03

GROUP B
ENGINE - Cylinder Block 2.6 Litre Petrol

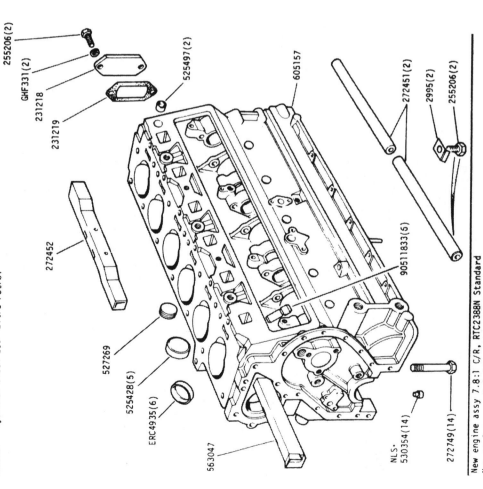

255206(2)
GHF331(2)
231218
231219
525497(2)
605157
272452
9051183(6)
527269
525428(5)
ERC4935(6)
563047
NLS.
530354(14)
272749(14)
272451(2)
2995(2)
255206(2)

New engine assy 7.8:1 C/R, RTC2388N Standard
New engine assy 7:1 C/R, RTC2407N Optional
Rebuilt engine assy 7.8:1 C/R, RTC2388R
Rebuilt engine assy 7:1 C/R, Not serviced
Engine overhaul gasket kit 605106
Decarbonising gasket kit GEG1214

Stud kit 535708
Cylinder liner 516498(6)

1D 03

ENGINE - Crankshaft, 2.6 litre Petrol

1D 04

GROUP B   ENGINE - Crankshaft, 2.6 litre Petrol

PLATE REF.	1	2	3	4	DESCRIPTION	QTY.	PART No.	REMARKS
1					CRANKSHAFT ASSEMBLY, STD	1	541910	
2					Dowel for flywheel	1	6395	
3					BEARING SET FOR CRANKSHAFT, STD	1	RTC1720	} Engine
					BEARING SET FOR CRANKSHAFT, .010" US	1	RTC172010	} set
					BEARING SET FOR CRANKSHAFT, .020" US	1	RTC172020	
4					Thrust washer for crankshaft, Std	1	600177	
					Thrust washer for crankshaft, .0025" OS	1	600174	
					Thrust washer for crankshaft, .005" OS	1	600175	} Pairs
					Thrust washer for crankshaft, .0075" OS	1	600176	
					Thrust washer for crankshaft, .010" OS	1	600178	
					Thrust washer for crankshaft, .0125" OS	1	600179	
5					Chainwheel on crankshaft	1	564463	
6					Key, front, locating vibration damper	1	542622	
7					Key, rear, locating chainwheel	1	542623	
8					Oil seal ring for crankshaft	1	541921	
9					Oil thrower on crankshaft	1	530343	
10					VIBRATION DAMPER AND PULLEY ASSEMBLY	1	ERC4182	Not part of engine assembly
11					Starting dog	1	546324	
12					Lockwasher for starting dog	1	542494	
13					Crankshaft oil retainer and seal assembly	1	542492	
14					Oil seal assembly	1	270656	
					Silicone grease	1	523240	
15					Rear bearing split seal halves	2	90519064	
16					Dowel, lower } Fixing retainer	2	246464	
17					Dowel, upper } to cylinder block			
18					Spring washer } and rear	10	GHF331	
19					Bolt (¼" UNF x ⅝") } bearing cap	10	255208	

1D 04

ENGINE - Connecting Rod and Piston, 2.6 litre Petrol

1D 05

GROUP B   ENGINE - Connecting Rod and Piston, 2.6 litre Petrol

PLATE REF.	1	2	3	4	DESCRIPTION	QTY.	PART No.	REMARKS
1					CONNECTING ROD ASSEMBLY	6	524492	
2					Gudgeon pin bush	6	273163	
3					Special bolt) Fixing connecting	12	90518100	
4					Special nut) rod cap	12	ERC1027	
5					Connecting rod bearing set, Std	1	RTC1721	
					Connecting rod bearing set, .010" US	1	RTC172110	
					Connecting rod bearing set, .020" US	1	RTC172120 *	
6					PISTON ASSEMBLY, STD, GRADE 'Z'	6	537263 *	) Engine with
					PISTON ASSEMBLY, STD, GRADE 'A'	6	537264 *	)
					PISTON ASSEMBLY, STD, GRADE 'B'	6	537265 *	)
					PISTON ASSEMBLY, STD, GRADE 'C'	6	537266 *	) 7.8:1 compression ratio
					PISTON ASSEMBLY, STD, GRADE 'S'	6	ERC2337S	)
					PISTON ASSEMBLY, .010" OS	6	537268 *	
					PISTON ASSEMBLY, .020" OS	6	537269 *	
					PISTON ASSEMBLY, .030" OS	6	537270 *	
					PISTON ASSEMBLY, .040" OS	6	537271 *	
					PISTON ASSEMBLY, STD, GRADE 'Z'	6	536267 *	) Engine with
					PISTON ASSEMBLY, STD, GRADE 'A'	6	536268 *	)
					PISTON ASSEMBLY, STD, GRADE 'B'	6	536269 *	)
					PISTON ASSEMBLY, STD, GRADE 'C'	6	536270 *	) 7:1 compression ratio
					PISTON ASSEMBLY, STD, GRADE 'S'	6	ERC2339S	)
					PISTON ASSEMBLY, .010" OS	6	536272 *	
					PISTON ASSEMBLY, .020" OS	6	536273 *	
					PISTON ASSEMBLY, .030" OS	6	536274 *	
					PISTON ASSEMBLY, .040" OS	6	536275 *	
7					Piston ring, compression, Std	12	231155 *	
					Piston ring, compression, .010" OS	12	236173 *	
					Piston ring, compression, .020" OS	12	236174 *	
					Piston ring, compression, .030" OS	12	236175 *	
					Piston ring, compression, .040" OS	12	236176 *	
8					Duaflex scraper ring, Std	6	554620 *	
					Duaflex scraper ring, .010" OS	6	554789 *	
					Duaflex scraper ring, .020" OS	6	554790 *	
					Duaflex scraper ring, .030" OS	6	554791 *	
					Duaflex scraper ring, .040" OS	6	554792 *	
9					Gudgeon pin, Std	6	264569 *	
					Gudgeon pin, .001" OS	6	267257 *	
					Gudgeon pin, .003" OS	6	267258 *	
10					Circlip for gudgeon pin	12	C3964	
11					Piston ring set, Standard	6	RTC2411	
					Piston ring set, 0.020in OS	6	RTC2411020	
					Piston ring set, 0.040in OS	6	RTC2411040	

* NO LONGER SERVICED

1D 05

ENGINE - Oil Pump, 2.6 litre Petrol

GROUP B   ENGINE - Oil Pump, 2.6 litre petrol

PLATE REF.	1	2	3	4	DESCRIPTION	QTY.	PART No.	REMARKS
					OIL PUMP ASSEMBLY	1	90564334	
1					OIL PUMP BODY ASSEMBLY	1	542396	
2					Bush for drive shaft	1	212309	
3					Oil pump gear, driver	1	240555	
4					OIL PUMP COVER ASSEMBLY	1	564335	
5					Dowel locating body	2	236257	
6					Spindle for idler wheel	1	90502209	
7					Stud for oil strainer	1	90564217	
8					OIL PUMP IDLER GEAR ASSEMBLY	1	278109	
9					Bush for idler gear	1	214995	
10					Oil pump shield	1	9225	
11					Set bolt (5/16" UNF x ⅞" long) } Fixing cover	4	255227	
					Spring washer } to body	4	GHF332	
13					Oil strainer	1	266900	
					Extension piece, strainer to oil pump	1	90564216	
14					Castle nut } Fixing strainer	1	N604041	
15					Split pin } to pump cover	1	2556	
16					DISTRIBUTOR HOUSING ASSEMBLY	1	274084	
17					Bush for drive shaft	1	521583	
18					Cork washer for distributor housing	1	52278	
19					Drive shaft for distributor	1	267829	
20					Oil pump and distributor gear and shaft assembly	1	598214	
					(phosphor-bronze gear)			
21					Steel ball } For oil	1	1035	
22					Plunger } pressure	1	245940	
23					Spring } release	1	504997	
24					Retaining cap } valve	1	504995	
25					Joint washer	1	243971	
26					Special set screw } Fixing oil pump	1	274086	
27					Locknut (5/16" UNF) } to cylinder block	1	NT605061	
28					Oil feed bolt locating distributor housing	1	274928	
29					Locker for bolt	1	2504	
30					Oil pipe to cylinder head	1	558302	
					Banjo for oil pipe	1	557782	
31					Banjo bolt fixing oil pipe to cylinder head	1	265038	
33					Joint washer for banjo bolt	2	231577	
34					Banjo bolt fixing oil pipe to cylinder block	1	233520	
35					Joint washer for banjo bolt	2	232039	
36					Oil pressure switch complete	1	GPS102	
37					Joint washer for switch	1	232039	

1D 06

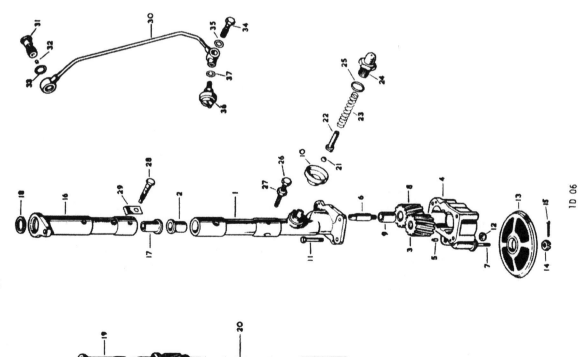

1D 06

27

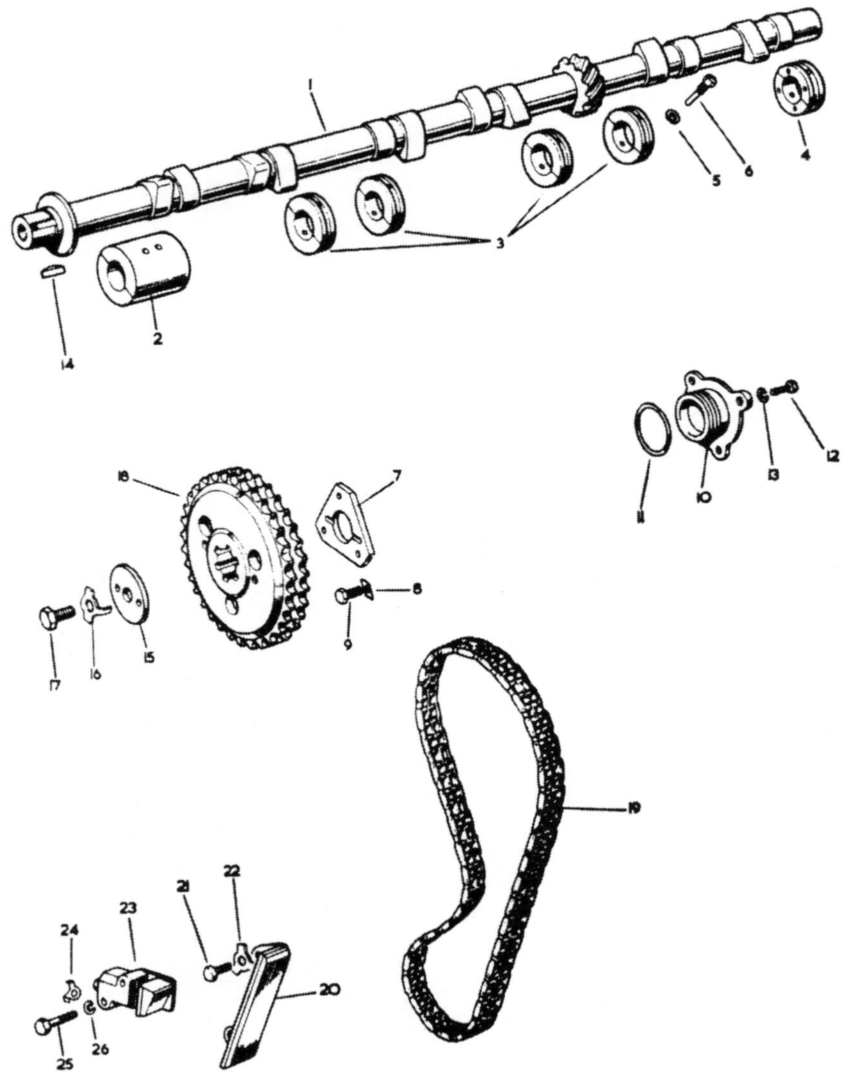

PLATE REF.	1 2 3 4 DESCRIPTION		QTY.	PART No.	REMARKS
1	Camshaft		1	523139	
2	Bearing, front	)	1	274116	
3	Bearing, intermediate	) For camshaft	4	274115	
4	Bearing, rear	)	1	274117	
5	Spring washer	) Fixing camshaft	6	GHF332	
6	Special set screw	) bearing to block	6	274118	
7	Thrust plate for camshaft		1	502266	
8	Locker	) Fixing thrust	3	2500	
9	Set bolt (¼" UNF x ⅝")	) plate to block	3	255206	
10	Sealing plate for camshaft		1	530481	
11	Joint washer for sealing plate		1	276541	
12	Set bolt (¼" UNF x ⅝")	) Fixing sealing plate	3	255206	
13	Spring washer	) to cylinder block	3	GHF331	
14	Key locating chainwheel		1	230313	
15	Retaining washer	) Fixing	1	9093	
16	Locker	) chainwheel	1	9210	
17	Set bolt (⅜" UNF x ⅞")	) to camshaft	1	SH606071	
18	Chainwheel for camshaft		1	563145@	
19	Camshaft chain		1	266662	
20	Vibration damper for timing chain		1	275234	
21	Set bolt (¼" UNF x ½")	) Fixing damper to	2	255204	
22	Locker	) cylinder block	2	557523	
23	Tensioner for timing chain		1	266661	
24	Tab washer for tensioner		1	504443*	
25	Set bolt (¼" UNF x 1⅜")	) Fixing tensioner	2	BH604111	
26	Spring washer	) to cylinder block	2	GHF331	

@ Also supplied as replacement for early type chainwheel with separate hub and fixings.

* NO LONGER SERVICED

GROUP B
ENGINE - Valves and Push Rod, 2·6 litre Petrol

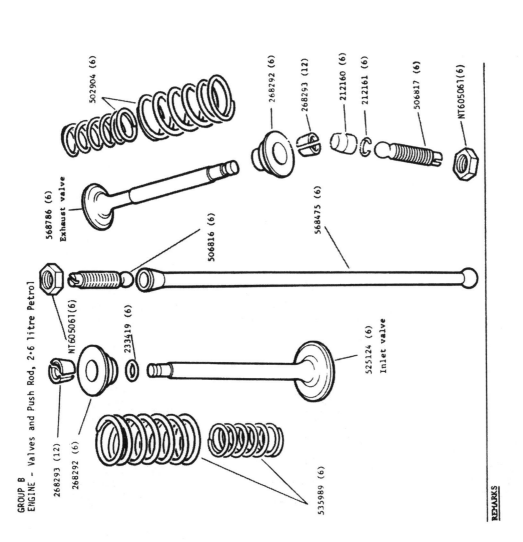

502904 (6)

268292 (6)

268293 (12)

212160 (6)

212161 (6)

506817 (6)

NT605061(6)

568786 (6)
Exhaust valve

506816 (6)

568475 (6)

NT605061(6)

233419 (6)

525124 (6)
Inlet valve

268293 (12)

268292 (6)

535989 (6)

REMARKS

1D 08

This page is intentionally left blank

GROUP B
ENGINE - Exhaust Valve Rockers, 2.6 litre Petrol

587923
231577
90500610 (6)
531874 (3)
90517429 (3)
536872 (3)
273309 (2) Thin
90517429 (3)
505597 (2)
536873 (3)
273306
90517429 (3)
27330b (2) Thick
531873 (3)
273307
90517429 (3)
AXE2070(2)
RTC1964(2)
RTC636

GROUP B
ENGINE - Inlet Valve Rockers, 2.6 litre Petrol

525910 (3)
GHF322(3)
231352 (3)
NT605061(3)
238871 (3)
231343 (3)
231349
231344 (3)
525911 (3)
230034 (6)
231348
243959
500609 (6)
536577

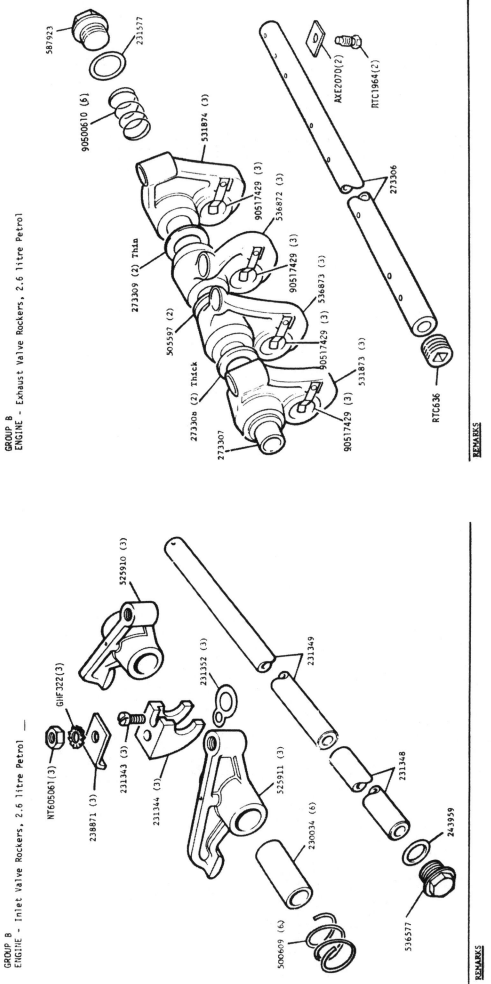

30

ENGINE - Front Cover, Side Cover and Sump, 2.6 litre Petrol

GROUP B   ENGINE - Front Cover, Side Cover and Sump, 2.6 litre Petrol

PLATE REF.	1	2	3	4	DESCRIPTION	QTY.	PART No.	REMARKS
1					FRONT COVER ASSEMBLY	1	554924	
2					Dowel locating front cover	2	6395	
3					Oil seal for front cover	1	90516028	
4					Mud excluder	1	542073	
5					Drive screw fixing excluder	8	A606021	
6					Joint washer for front cover	1	272835	
7					Spring washer	10	GHF332	} Fixing front cover
8					Set bolt (5/16" UNF x 1⅜")	10	256025	} to cylinder block
9					Timing pointer at front cover	1	564163	
10					Spring washer for timing pointer	1	GHF331	
11					Rocker cover, side, and oil filler	1	542425	
12					Joint washer for rocker cover	1	GEG433	
13					Special nut	3	274091	] Up to engines numbered 34516198B, 34600575B,
					Special union nut	1	55483	] 34516199B, 34600576B
14					Special nut	4	274091	From engines numbered 34516199B, 34600576B onwards
15					Rubber sealing washer)	4	267828	
16					Oil filler cap	1	598231	
17					Breather pipe for engine crankcase	1	541291*	] Up to engines numbered
18					Joint washer for breather pipe	1	214058*	] 34500469B
19					Spring washer	2	GHF332	] 34600024A
20					Set bolt (5/16" UNF x ½")	2	255226	} Fixing breather pipe to cylinder block
21					Filter for breather pipe	1	90518145	
22					Clip fixing filter to breather pipe	1	GHC811	
23					Steady bracket for breather pipe	1	554917*	
24					Clip for breather pipe	1	518146*	
25					Bolt (¼" UNF x ⅝")	1	255206	
26					Plain washer	2	RTC609	} Fixing breather pipe
27					Spring washer	2	GHF331	} bracket and clip
28					Nut (¼" UNF)	2	GHF200	
29					Breather pipe for engine crankcase	1	566957	] From engines numbered
30					Joint washer for breather pipe	2	214058*	] 34500470B
31					Spring washer	2	GHF332	} Fixing breather pipe 34600025A onwards
32					Set bolt (5/16" UNF x ½")	2	GHF120	} to cylinder block
33					Hose, breather pipe to flame trap	1	587105	
34					Flame trap	1	149996*	
35					Hose, flame trap to carburetter	1	587104	
36					Clip for hoses	3	554260	
37					Crankcase sump	1	564215	
38					Drain plug for sump	1	536577	
39					Joint washer for plug	1	243959	
40					Joint washer for sump	1	GEG538	
41					Set bolt (5/16" UNC x ½")	2	SH505071	} Fixing sump to
42					Spring washer	19	GHF332	} cylinder block
43					Set bolt (5/16" UNF x ½")	16	255227	
					Nut (5/16" UNF)	1	GHF201	

* NO LONGER SERVICED

1D 10

1D 10

ENGINE - Front Cover, Side Cover and Sump, 2.6 litre Petrol

1D 10

GROUP B   ENGINE - Front Cover, Side Cover and Sump 2.6 litre petrol

PLATE REF.	1	2	3	4	DESCRIPTION	QTY.	PART No.	REMARKS
44					Oil level rod	1	554834	
45					Sealing ring for oil level rod	1	532387	
46					Tube for oil level rod	1	554832	
47					Adaptor for tube	1	541266	* Up to engines numbered 34516198B, 34600575B
48					Olive } Fixing tube	1	236408	
49					Union nut (½" BSP) } to adaptor	1	236407	
50					Bracket, oil level tube to side cover	1	554833	*
51					Set bolt (¼" UNF x 9/16") } Fixing bracket to	1	255205	Up to engines numbered
52					Sealing washer } special union nut on } side cover	2	232037	34516198B 34600575B
53					Clip for oil level tube	1	554852	
54					Bolt (¼" UNF x ⅜") } Fixing	1	255206	
55					Spring washer } clip and tube	1	GHF331	
56					Nut (¼" UNF) } to bracket	1	GHF200	
					Guide tube for oil level rod	1	546584	From engines numbered 34516199B, 34600576B
					Adaptor for guide tube	1	232040	onwards.
					Washer fixing adaptor to block			

* NO LONGER SERVICED

1D 11

ENGINE - Water Pump and Thermostat, 2.6 litre Petrol

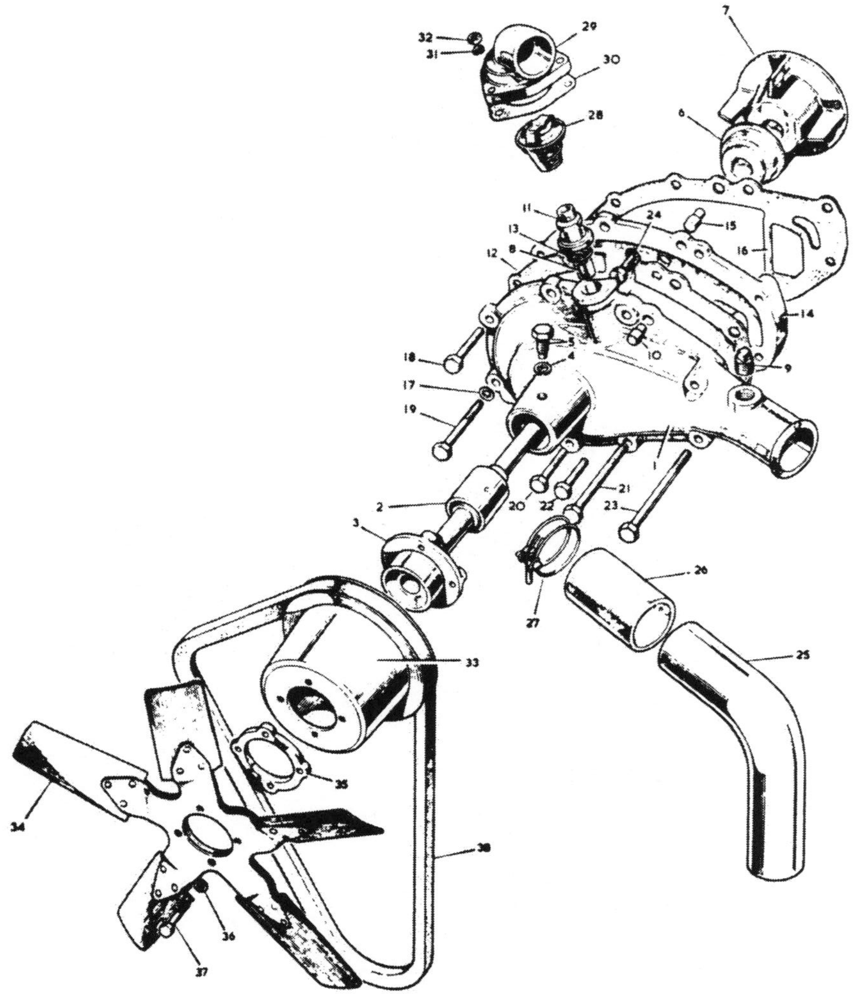

1D 12

PLATE REF.	1 2 3 4 DESCRIPTION	QTY.	PART No.	REMARKS
1	WATER PUMP ASSEMBLY	1	GWP305	
2	Spindle and bearing complete	1	ERC3978	
3	Hub for fan blade	1	564270	
4	Spring washer) Locating bearing	1	GHF331	
5	Special set bolt) in casing	1	247078	
6	Carbon ring and seal	1	568301	Not part of engine assembly
7	Impeller for pump	1	563037	
8	Tube for thermostat by-pass	1	564164	
9	Plug (⅜"BSP) for heater adaptor hole in casing	1	3291	
10	Dowel for water pump casing	2	6395	
11	Connector, by-pass to water pump	1	564165	
12	Joint washer for water pump	1	564157	
13	Rubber seal, pump to cylinder head	1	RTC1975	
14	Adaptor for water pump	1	563154	
15	Dowel for adaptor	2	6395	
16	Joint washer for adaptor	1	563038	
17	Spring washer)	10	GHF331	
18	Set bolt (¼" UNF x 1"))	3	GHF101	
19	Set bolt (¼" UNF x 1⅝")) Fixing water	1	256004	
20	Set bolt (¼" UNF x 1¾")) pump and	2	BH604091	
21	Set bolt (¼" UNF x 2¼")) adaptor to block	1	BH604181	
22	Set bolt (¼" UNF x ⅞"))	1	255208	
23	Set bolt (¼" UNF x 2¾"))	2	256410	
24	Special 'Wedgelok' screw)	3	563050	
25	Inlet pipe for water pump	1	552517	
26	Hose, water inlet pipe to pump	1	562915	Not part of engine assembly
	Clip, hose to inlet pipe	1	GHC1217	
27	Clip, hose to pump	1	50322	
28	Thermostat, wax type	1	GTS114	
29	Outlet pipe to radiator	1	587463	
30	Joint washer for water outlet pipe	1	GTG118	
31	Spring washer) Fixing pipe to	3	GHF331	
32	Nut (¼" UNF)) cylinder head	3	GHF200	
33	Pulley for fan	1	564267	
34	Fan blade	1	574044	
35	Distance piece for fan blade	1	274737	
36	Spring washer) Fixing pulley	4	GHF332	Not part of engine assembly
37	Set bolt (¼" UNF x 1¼")) and blade to hub	4	BH604101	
38	Fan belt	1	GFB189	
	Water pump overhaul kit	1	605716	

1D 12

ENGINE - Cylinder Head, 2.6 litre Petrol

GROUP B   ENGINE - Cylinder Head, 2.6 litre Petrol

PLATE REF.	1 2 3 4	DESCRIPTION	QTY.	PART No.	REMARKS
1		CYLINDER HEAD ASSEMBLY	1	564202	
2		Insert for inlet valve	6	266321	
3		Washer for valve spring	6	230062	
4		Valve guide, inlet	6	504169	
5		Rubber ring for valve guide, inlet	6	233419	
6		Core plug, 11/16" diameter	7	230251	
7		Core plug, ⅝" diameter	2	210492	
		Core plug, 1" diameter	1	518272	
8		Core plug, 1¼" diameter	2	230250	
9		Stud for water outlet pipe	3	252501	
10		Stud for carburetter	3	252515	
		Stud for carburetter relay bracket	4	252497	
11		Stud for rocker cover, long	3	506047	
13		Double-ended union for servo pipe	3	90513171	
14		Joint washer for union	1	243958	
15		Thermostat switch for choke warning light	1	BHA5252	
16		Joint washer for thermostat switch	1	236022	
17		Set bolt (2BA x 7/16") Fixing switch	3	251002	
18		Spring washer	3	WM702001	
19		Water temperature transmitter	1	GTR111	
20		Plug for heater connection hole	1	278164	
21		Joint washer for plug	1	243972	
22		Set bolt (¼" UNC x 7/16") For hole in	1	253003	
23		Joint washer for bolt } thermostat housing	1	232037	
24		'O' ring for oil return hole in cylinder head	1	532319	
25		Cylinder head gasket	6	GEG339	
26		Plain washer, small	11	MB110061	
27		Plain washer, large	6	RTC611	
28		Special set bolt (⅜" UNF x 1.29/32") } Fixing	3	274093	
29		Special set bolt (7/16" UNF x 2.17/32") } cylinder	3	90574103	
30		Special set bolt (7/16" UNF x 4.29/32") } head to	8	90574104	
31		Special set bolt (7/16" UNF x 5.5/32") } block	3	587338	
		Plain washer	3	587339	For use with bolt 587338
32		Front lifting bracket	1	568363*	
33		Rear lifting bracket at rear face	1	ERC4387	
34		Rear lifting bracket at rear side face, RH	1	564206	
35		Spring washer } Fixing	2	GHF332	
36		Set bolt (5/16" UNC x ½") } front bracket	2	SH505061	
37		Spring washer } Fixing rear bracket	2	GHF332	
38		Set bolt (5/16" UNC x ½") } at side face	2	SH505061	
39		Spring washer } Fixing bracket	2	GHF333	
40		Set bolt (⅜" UNC x ½") } at rear face	2	SH506061	

* NO LONGER SERVICED

1D 13

1D 13

ENGINE - Cylinder Head, 2.6 litre Petrol

GROUP B   ENGINE - Cylinder Head, 2.6 litre petrol

PLATE REF.					DESCRIPTION	QTY.	PART No.	REMARKS
41	1	2	3	4	ROCKER COVER ASSEMBLY, TOP	1	568725	
42					Tappet clearance plate	1	274100	
43					Hammer drive screw for plate	4	3767 *	
44					Clip for ignition wire carrier	2	566813	) Early models with
45					Drive screw fixing clip	2	AB610031	) ignition wire carrier
46					Joint washer for rocker cover	1	GEG432	
47					Sealing washer) Fixing top	3	231576	
48					Special nut) rocker cover	3	274089	
					Engine breather filter, top	1	547605	@ *)
49					Engine breather filter, top	1	546203	@@) Not part of
50					Sealing ring for breather filter	1	268887	@@) engine assembly
51					Special set screw fixing filter	1	515291	@@)
					Sealing washer for set screw	1	232037	@@)
52					Hose, top breather filter to carburetter elbow	1	568391	@@
53					Clip, fixing hose to breather filter and elbow	2	546210	@@
54					Clip, securing hose to carburetter body	1	568392	@@

@ Up to engines numbered 34500469B, 34600024A
@@ From engines numbered 34500470B, 34600025A onwards

* NO LONGER SERVICED

1D 14

ENGINE - Cylinder Head, 2.6 litre Petrol

1D 14

35

ENGINE - Oil Filter and Adaptor, 2.6 litre Petrol

1D 15

GROUP B   ENGINE - Oil Filter and Adaptor, 2.6 litre Petrol

PLATE REF.	1	2	3	4	DESCRIPTION	QTY.	PART No.	REMARKS
1					Oil filter for engine	1	9051359	Not part of engine assembly
2					Element	1	GFE111	
3					Gasket, large } For oil filter	1	516885	
					Gasket, small, lower }	1	605169	
4					Adaptor for oil filter	1	554925	
5					Joint washer, front } For oil filter adaptor	1	274609	
6					Joint washer, rear }	1	274104	
7					Set bolt (5/16" UNF x 1⅛")	2	256025	
8					Spring washer	2	GHF332	
9					Set bolt (7/16" UNF x 3") } Fixing adaptor to cylinder block	1	BH607241	
10					Set bolt (7/16" UNF x 3½") }	1	BH607281	
11					Spring washer	2	MM600071	
12					Plug (⅜" BSP) } For adaptor oil way	1	563121	] Part of adaptor
13					Joint washer }	1	231577	]
14					Joint washer	1	598354	
15					Set bolt (7/16" UNC x 1¼") } Fixing oil filter to adaptor	2	SH507101	
16					Spring washer	2	MM600071	
17					Plug (⅜" BSF) } Blanking oil pressure transmitter hole	1	557498	] Part of adaptor
18					Joint washer }	1	232039	]

1D 15

ENGINE – Exhaust Manifold, 2.6 litre Petrol

1D 16

GROUP B   ENGINE – Exhaust manifold, 2.6 litre petrol

PLATE REF.	1	2	3	4	DESCRIPTION	QTY.	PART No.	REMARKS
1					EXHAUST MANIFOLD ASSEMBLY	1	587401	
2					Stud for exhaust pipe 1¾" long	3	252623	) Alternatives
					Stud for exhaust pipe 1.13/16" long	3	596097	)
3					Joint washer for exhaust manifold	1	GEG640	
5					Clamp for manifold	5	9161	
6					Spring washer) Fixing	5	GHF333	
7					Nut (¾" UNF)) clamps	5	GHF202	
8					Spring washer) Fixing ends	2	GHF332	
9					Nut (5/16" UNF)) of manifolds	2	GHF201	

1D 16

ENGINE - Tie Rod, 2.6 litre Petrol

GROUP B   ENGINE - Tie rod 2.6 litre petrol

PLATE REF.	1	2	3	4	DESCRIPTION	QTY.	PART No.	REMARKS
1					Bracket for tie rod at bell housing	1	543254	
2					Bolt (5/16" UNF x 1¼")	2	GHF104	
3					Spring washer	2	GHF332	Fixing bracket
4					Nut (5/16" UNF)	2	GHF201	at bell housing
5					Tie rod for engine	1	504606	
6					Sleeve for engine tie rod	2	504607	
7					Rubber bush	4	509885	
8					Cup washer	4	7015	Fixing tie rod
9					Nut (5/16" UNF)	4	GHF201	
10					Locknut (5/16" UNF)	4	NT605061	
11					Bracket for tie rod at frame	1	90508339	
12					Bolt (⅜" UNF x 3¼")	1	BH606281	Fixing bracket
13					Spring washer	1	GHF333	to No.4 crossmember
14					Nut (⅜" UNF)	1	GHF202	

1D 17

38

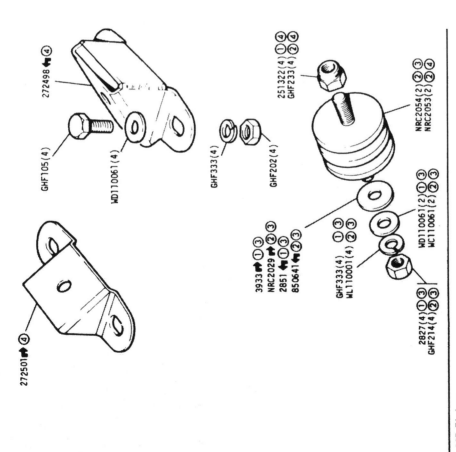

GROUP B

Engine Mountings and Rubbers, 2.6 litre Petrol

272501 ⬆ ④

272498 ⬅ ④

GHF105(4)

WD110061(4)

GHF333(4)

GHF202(4)

251322(4) ① ④
GHF233(4) ② ④

NRC2054(2) ② ③
NRC2053(2) ② ④

3933 ⬆ ① ③
NRC2029 ⬆ ② ③
2851 ⬅ ① ③
850641 ⬅ ② ③

GHF333(4) ① ③
WL110001(4) ② ③

WD110061(2) ① ③
WL110061(2) ② ③

2827(4) ① ③
GHF214(4) ② ③

① BSF Fixings
② Metric Fixings
③ Front Mounting
④ Rear Mounting

1D 18

This page is intentionally left blank

ENGINE – Cylinder Block, 2¼ litre Diesel

GROUP B
271975 ①
516133 ②

525497 (1)
250840 (2)
524765 (2)
587628 (2)
Alternatives
536577
243959
273166
243968
527269
52124 (2)
608327
596097(3)
247965
510272(2)
602915
525428 (3)
ERC5086(2)
252621 (2)
Alternatives
JM600081(4)
212430 (4)
SH608081(3)
SH608091(1)
554434 ①
577348 ②
247861
514527
247127
213700 (2)
504006 (6)
501593 (6)
504007 (6)

Short engine assembly RTC2664

Decarbonising gasket set GEG1200   Engine overhaul·gasket set 525520
Stud kit for Cylinder block 600245   Cylinder liner 527351 (4)

① When early type radiator block with metal cowl is fitted
② When late type radiator block with plastic cowl is fitted

1E 02

GROUP B
ENGINE ASSEMBLIES, 2¼ litre Diesel

New Engine Assemblies.
Standard,   PTC·2385N } Up to engine suffix 'J'
With Lucas 2AC generator   No longer serviced }
With Prestolite generator   No longer serviced
Standard   RTC1813N } Suffix 'K'
With Lucas 11AC generator - No longer serviced, use RTC1813N } onwards
With Prestolite generator - No longer serviced, use RTC1813N }

Rebuilt Engine Assemblies:
Standard   RTC 2385R } Up to engine suffix 'J'
With Lucas 2AC generator - No longer serviced }
With Prestolite generator- No longer serviced }
Standard   RTC 2353R } Suffix 'K'
With Lucas 11AC generator - No longer serviced, use RTC 2353R } onwards
With Prestolite generator - No longer serviced, use RTC 2353R }

1E 02

ENGINE - Crankshaft, 2¼ litre Diesel

GROUP B   ENGINE - Crankshaft, 2¼ litre Diesel

PLATE REF.	1 2 3 4	DESCRIPTION		QTY.	PART No.	REMARKS
1		CRANKSHAFT ASSEMBLY, STD		1	527167	
2		Dowel for flywheel		1	265779	
3		Main bearing set, Std		1	RTC1729	
5		Thrust washer for crankshaft, Std	⎫	1	538130	
		Thrust washer for crankshaft, .0025" OS	⎬	1	538131	
		Thrust washer for crankshaft, .005" OS	⎬ Pairs	1	538132	
		Thrust washer for crankshaft, .0075" OS	⎬	1	538133	
		Thrust washer for crankshaft, .010" OS	⎭	1	538134	
		REAR BEARING OIL SEAL ASSEMBLY		1	542494	
6		Rear bearing split seal halves		2	523240	
7		Oil seal complete for rear bearings		1	542492	
		Silicone grease, MS4, 1 oz tube		1	270656	
8		Dowel, lower ⎫Fixing split seal		2	90519064	
9		Dowel, upper ⎬to cylinder block		2	246464	
10		Spring washer ⎬and rear		10	GHF331	
11		Bolt (¼" UNF x ⅞" long)⎭bearing cap		10	255208	
12		Chainwheel on crankshaft		1	568333	
13		Key locating chainwheel and pulley		2	235770	
14		Crankshaft pulley		1	564375	
15		Starting dog		1	503665	
16		Lockwasher for starting dog		1	247771	

1E 03

1E 03

ENGINE - Connecting Rod and Piston, 2¼ litre Diesel

GROUP B   ENGINE - Connecting Rod and Piston, 2¼ litre Diesel

PLATE REF.	1	2	3	4	DESCRIPTION	QTY.	PART No.	REMARKS
1					CONNECTING ROD ASSEMBLY	4	527169	
2					Gudgeon pin bush	4	247583	
3					Special bolt) Fixing connecting	8	519440	
4					Special Nut) rod cap	8	ERC1029	
5					Connecting rod bearing set, Std	1	RTC1730	
6					PISTON ASSEMBLY, STD	4	ERC2342S	
					PISTON ASSEMBLY, .020" OS	4	564231	
					PISTON ASSEMBLY, .040" OS	4	564233	
7					Piston ring, compression, Std	4	568588	
					Piston ring, compression, .010" OS	4	605539	
					Piston ring, compression, .020" OS	4	605540	} Chromed
					Piston ring, compression, .030" OS	4	605541*	}
					Piston ring, compression, .040" OS	4	605542*	} Insert
8					Piston ring, compression, Std	8	90520978	
					Piston ring, compression, .010" OS	8	90520940	
					Piston ring, compression, .020" OS	8	90520941*	} tapered
					Piston ring, compression, .030" OS	8	90520942	}
					Piston ring, compression, .040" OS	8	90520943*	}
9					Oil control ring, Std	4	564226	
					Oil control ring, .010" OS	4	605047	
					Oil control ring, .020" OS	4	605048	
					Oil control ring, .030" OS	4	605049	
					Oil control ring, .040" OS	4	605050	
10					Gudgeon pin	4	50029	
11					Circlip for gudgeon pin	8	266945	
12					Piston ring set, standard	4	RTC2415	
					Piston ring set, 0.020in OS	4	RTC241520	
					Piston ring set, 0.040in OS	4	RTC241540	

* NO LONGER SERVICED

1E 04

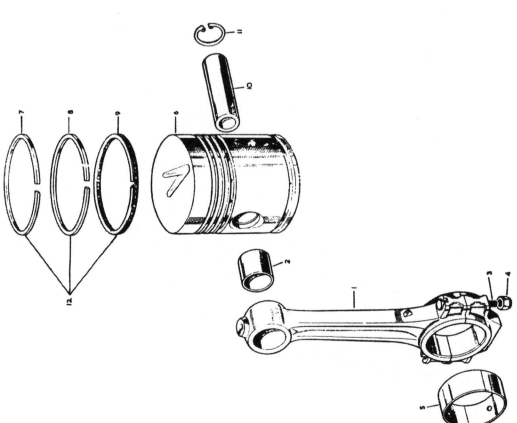

1E 04

GROUP B   ENGINE - Oil Pump, 2¼ litre Diesel

PLATE REF.	1	2	3	4	DESCRIPTION	QTY.	PART No.	REMARKS
					OIL PUMP ASSEMBLY		RTC2554	
1					Oil pump body	1	513641	
2					Spindle for idler gear	1	90502209	
3					Oil pump gear, driver	1	240555	
4					Oil pump gear, idler	1	278109	
5					Bush for idler gear	1	214995	
6					Steel ball	1	3748	
7					Plunger	1	273711	
8					Spring	1	564456	
9					Washer, inside diameter 55/64"	1	243970	For oil pressure release valve] Alternatives.
9					Washer, inside diameter 49/64"	1	232044	]
10					Plug	1	549909	
11					Oil pump cover	1	513639	
12					Set bolt (5/16" UNF x ⅞" long)	4	255227	] Fixing cover to body
13					Spring washer	4	GHF332	]
14					Oil filter for pump	1	247664	
15					Sealing ring Fixing oil filter	1	244488	
16					Lockwasher to oil pump	1	244487	
17					Drive shaft for oil pump	1	511680	
18					VERTICAL DRIVE SHAFT ASSEMBLY	1	503266	
19					Circlip for drive shaft	1	247742	
20					Bush for drive shaft gear	1	247653	
21					Locating screw for drive shaft bush	1	524769	
22					Set bolt (5/16" UNF x 1" long)	2	GHF103	] Fixing oil pump to cylinder block
23					Lockwasher	2	247665	]

1E 05

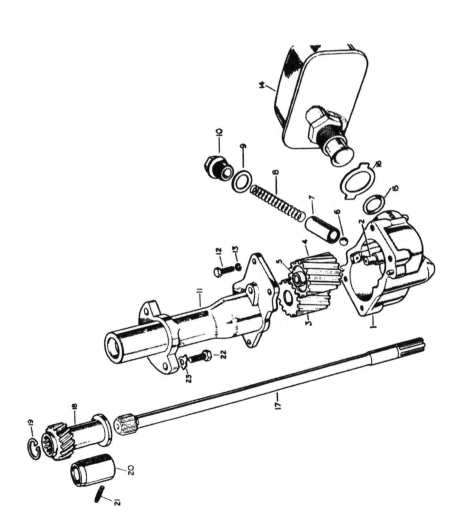

1E 05

43

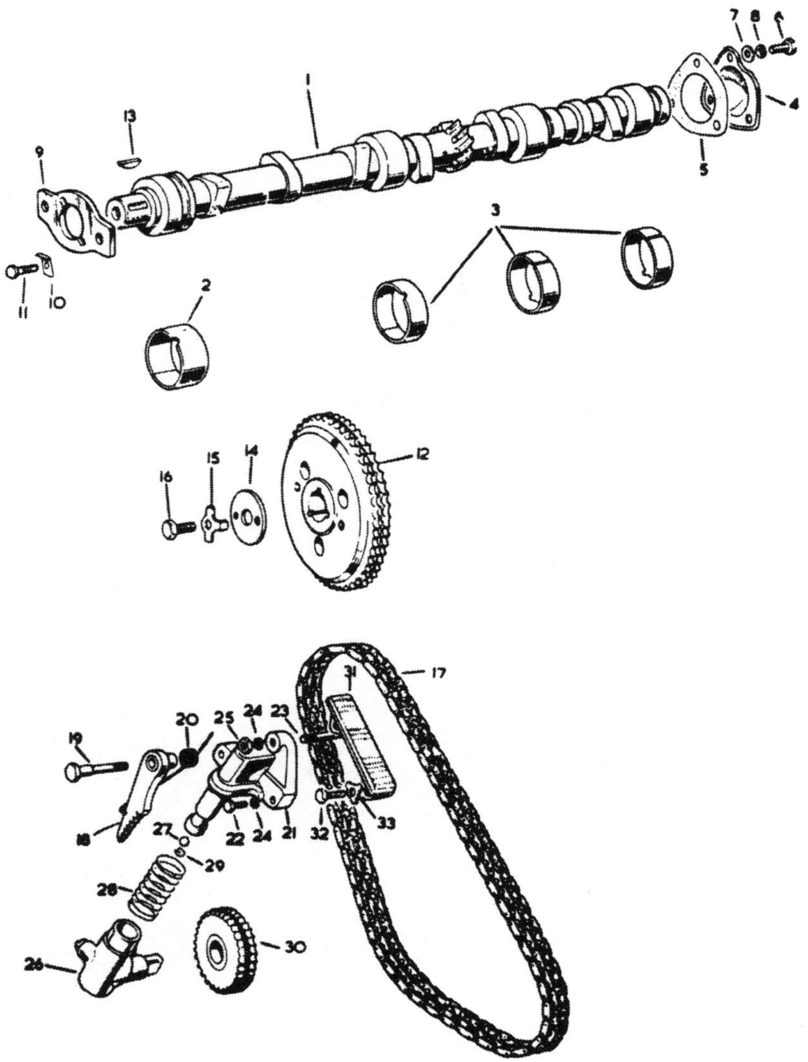

ENGINE – Camshaft and Tensioner Mechanism, 2¼ litre Diesel

GROUP B   ENGINE – Camshaft and tensioner, 2¼ litre Diesel

PLATE REF.				DESCRIPTION	QTY.	PART No.	REMARKS
1	2	3	4				
1				Camshaft	1	274711	
2				Bearing complete for camshaft, front	1	90519054	
3				Bearing complete for camshaft, centre and rear	3	90519055	
4				Rear end cover for camshaft	1	538073	
5				Joint washer for cover	1	247070	
6				Set bolt (¼" UNF x ¾" long) ⎫ Fixing cover to	3	255208	⎫ Alternative fixings.
				Set bolt (¼" UNF x ⅝" long) ⎬	3	255206	⎬
				Set bolt (¼" UNF x ½" long) ⎭ block	3	255207	⎭
7				Plain washer	4	RTC840	
8				Spring washer	3	GHF331	
9				Thrust plate for camshaft	1	ERC1561	
10				Locker ⎫ Fixing thrust plate	2	2995	4 off on early type
11				Set bolt (¼" UNF x ½" long) ⎭ to cylinder block	2	255207	thrust plate
12				Chainwheel for camshaft	1	276133	
13				Key locating camshaft chainwheel	1	230313	
14				Retaining washer ⎫ Fixing	1	9093	
15				Locker ⎬ chainwheel to camshaft	1	9210	
16				Set bolt (⅜" UNF x ⅞" long) ⎭	1	SH606071	
17				Camshaft chain (⅜" pitch x 78 links)	1	504375	
18				Ratchet for timing chain adjuster	1	546026	
19				Special bolt fixing ratchet and piston to block	1	247199	
20				Spring for chain adjuster ratchet	1	267451	
21				Piston for timing chain adjuster	1	247912	
22				Set bolt (5/16" UNF x 1¼" long) ⎫ Fixing piston to	1	BH605101	
23				Stud (5/16" UNF) ⎬ cylinder	2	247144	
24				Spring washer ⎭ block	2	GHF332	
25				Nut (5/16" UNF)	1	GHF201	
26				Cylinder for timing chain adjuster	1	277388	
27				Steel ball (7/32") for non-return valve	1	3739	
28				Spring for chain tensioner	1	233326	
29				Retainer for steel ball	1	233328	
30				Idler wheel for timing chain	1	236067	
31				Vibration damper for timing chain	1	275234	
32				Set bolt (¼" UNF x ½" long) ⎫ Fixing damper	2	255204	
33				Locking plate ⎭ to cylinder block	2	557523	

1E 06

44

GROUP B
ENGINE - Valve Gear and Rockershafts, 2¼ litre Diesel

247738 (4)
274773 (2)
247737 (4)
274774 (2)
NT605051(8)
506814 (8)
247153 (4)
GHF332
247153 (4)
525390
274775 (2)
523181 (3)
247040 (4)
BH605161(5)
274772 (2)
GHF332(5)
523181 (2)
247607 (3)
277956 (3)
554073

1E 07

GROUP B
ENGINE - Valves and Tappets, 2¼ litre Diesel

546799 (8)
507026 (8)
90517429(8)
502473 (8)
268293 (16)
268292 (8)
507025 (8)
273069 (8)
Inlet valve 527240 (4)
Exhaust valve 550198 (4)
568550 (8)

REMARKS   Tappet, tappet guide, roller and set bolt assembly 507829 (8)

1E 07

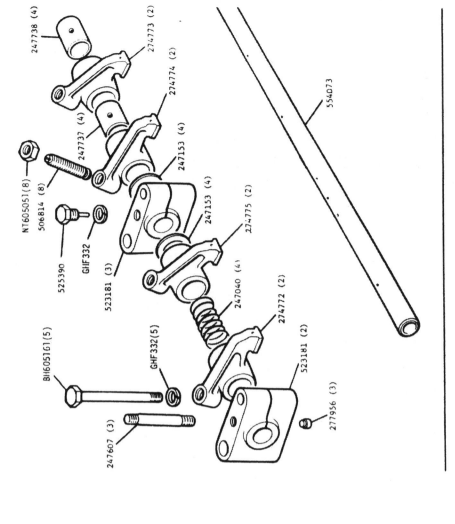

45

GROUP B   ENGINE - Front cover, side covers, sump, 2¼ litre diesel

PLATE REF.	1	2	3	4	DESCRIPTION	QTY.	PART No.	REMARKS
					FRONT COVER ASSEMBLY	1	90514451	Up to engine suffix 'F' inclusive
1					FRONT COVER ASSEMBLY	1	554541	From engine suffix 'G' onwards
1					FRONT COVER ASSEMBLY	1	568667	Models with Lucas 2 AC type 12 volt AC/DC generator. Up to engine suffix 'F' inclusive
					FRONT COVER ASSEMBLY	1	554843	Models with Lucas 2 AC type 12 volt AC/DC generator. From engine suffix 'G' onwards
2					Dowel locating front cover	2	6395	
3					Oil seal for front cover	1	213744	
4					Stud fixing water pump	5	252500	
5					Mud excluder	1	247766	
6					Drive screw fixing excluder	8	AB606021	
7					Joint washer for front cover	1	538039	
8					Joint washer at water inlet	1	538038	
9					Set bolt (5/16" UNF x 3")	7	BH605241	
10					Set bolt (5/16" UNF x 2") ⎞ Fixing front cover and water pump to cylinder block	3	BH605161	
					Set bolt (5/16" UNF x 3¼") ⎟	2	BH605281	
11					Set bolt (5/16" UNF x 3¼") ⎟	2	BH605261	
12					Set bolt (5/16" UNF x 3¾") ⎠	1	256233	
13					Spring washer	14	GHF332	
14					Nut (5/16" UNF)	2	GHF201	
					Side cover and oil filler pipe for engine, front	1	90510730	Up to engine suffix 'J' inclusive
					Side cover and oil filler pipe for engine, front	1	568542	From engine suffix 'K' onwards
16					Baffle plate for side cover, front	1	529394	Up to engine suffix 'J' inclusive
					Baffle plate for side cover, front	1	564467	From engine suffix 'K' onwards
17					Timing pointer for distributor pump	1	564470	
					Set bolt (10 UNF x 7/16") ⎞ Fixing timing pointer to baffle plate	2	257004	
					Spring washer ⎟	2	WM702001	
					Plain washer ⎠	2	4030	
18					Joint washer for side front cover	1	247555	
19					SIDE COVER ASSEMBLY, REAR	1	542600	
20					Stud for fuel pump	2	500792	
21					Plain washer	2	4047	
22					Nut (5/16" UNF) ⎞ Fixing stud	2	254911*	Nut and split pin type fixing
23					Split pin ⎠	2	2422	
					Stud for fuel pump	2	542601	Plain type stud fixing

* NO LONGER SERVICED

1E 08

1E 08

ENGINE - Front Cover, Side Covers and Sump, 2¼ litre Diesel

GROUP B ENGINE - Front cover, side covers, sump, 2¼ litre diesel

PLATE REF.	1 2 3 4	DESCRIPTION	QTY.	PART No.	REMARKS
24		Joint washer for side cover, rear	1	247554	
25		Spring washer	6	GHF332	Fixing rear side cover plate
26		Set bolt (5/16" UNF x 1" long)	6	GHF103	
27		Spring washer	7	GHF332	Fixing front side cover plate
28		Set bolt (5/16" UNF x ¾" long)	7	GHF120	
29		Crankcase sump	1	529823	
30		Drain plug for crankcase sump	1	536577	
31		Washer for drain plug	1	243959	
32		Joint washer for crankcase sump	1	GEG537	
33		Set bolt (5/16" UNF x ¾" long)	21	255227	Fixing sump to cylinder block
34		Spring washer	22	GHF332	
35		Nut (5/16" UNF)	2	GHF201	
36		Oil level rod	1	274154	
37		Sealing ring for rod	1	532387	
38		Tube for oil level rod	1	504032	Alternative to one piece type oil level rod tube
39		Double-ended union	1	236060	
40		Washer	1	243958	
41		Olive	1	236408	
42		Union nut	1	236407	
43		Tube for oil level rod	1	541860	One-piece type. Alternative to tube with separate union.
44		Oil filler cap and breather filter	1	546440	Up to engine suffix 'J' inclusive. Not part of engine assembly
45		Oil filler cap	1	598231	From engine suffix 'K' onwards

1E 09

1E 09

47

ENGINE - Water pump and Thermostat, 2¼ litre Diesel

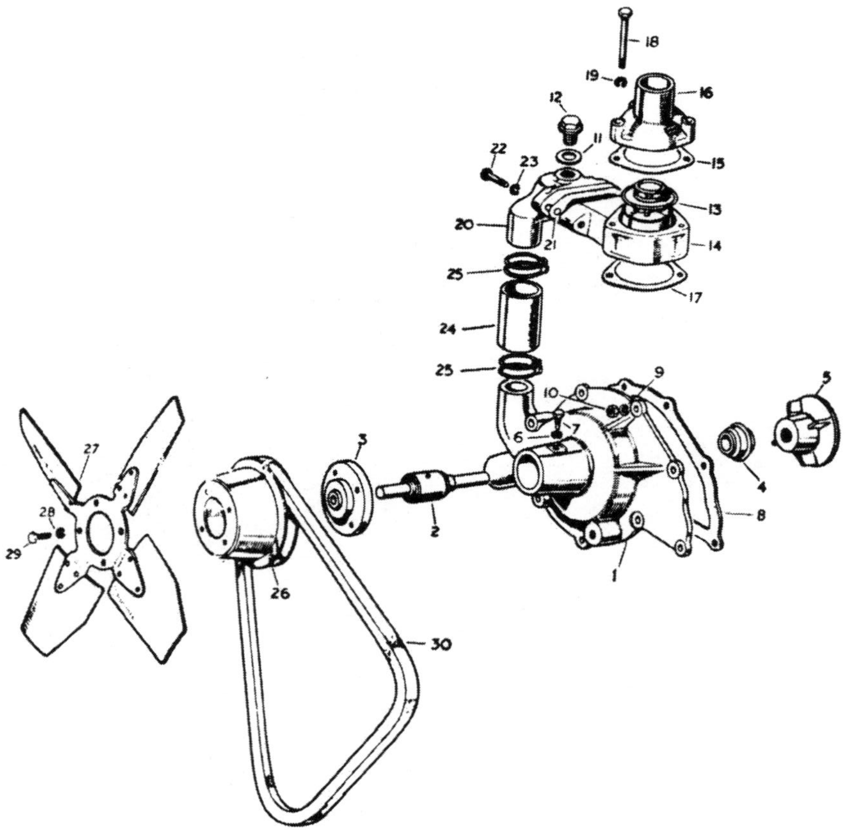

PLATE REF.	1 2 3 4 DESCRIPTION	QTY.	PART No.	REMARKS
	WATER PUMP ASSEMBLY	1	GWP312	
1	Water pump casing	1	530478	
2	Pump spindle and bearing	1	ERC3978	
3	Hub for fan	1	598064	
4	Carbon ring and seal unit	1	568301	
5	Impeller for pump	1	247916	
6	Spring washer) Locating	1	GHF331	
7	Special set bolt) bearing casing	1	247078	
8	Joint washer for water pump	1	538671	
9	Spring washer) Fixing	5	GHF331	
10	Nut (¼" UNF)) water pump to) cylinder	5	GHF200	Up to engine suffix 'F' inclusive
	Set bolt (¼" UNC x 1")) block	5	GHF161	From engine suffix 'G' onwards
11	Joint washer) For heater return in	1	243959	
12	Plug (⅜" BSP)) thermostat by-pass pipe	1	536577	
13	Thermostat, bellows type	1	504736*	Up to engine suffix 'B'
	Thermostat, wax type	1	GTS109	From engine suffix 'C' onwards
	'O' ring for thermostat	1	GTG109	
14	Thermostat housing	1	516059	
15	Joint washer for thermostat housing, upper	1	511957	Up to engine suffix 'B'
	Joint washer for thermostat housing, upper	1	GTG119	From engine suffix 'C' onwards
16	Water outlet pipe, thermostat to radiator	1	511956*	Up to engine suffix 'B'
	Water outlet pipe, thermostat to radiator	1	527109	From engine suffix 'C' onwards
17	Joint washer for thermostat housing, lower	1	GTG110	
18	Set bolt (¼" UNF x 2½")) Fixing thermostat	3	BH604201	
19	Spring washer) housing and outlet) pipe to cylinder head	3	GHF331	
20	Thermostat by-pass pipe	1	530476	
21	Joint washer for by-pass pipe	1	90511958	
22	Set bolt (5/16" UNF x 1")) Fixing by-pass pipe	2	GHF103	
23	Spring washer) to thermostat) housing	2	GHF332	
24	Hose for by-pass pipe	1	574871	
25	Hose clip for by-pass pipe	2	GHC913	
26	Fan pulley	1	530890	
27	Fan blade	1	90515090	4 blade fan
28	Spring washer) Fixing fan blade	4	GHF331	
29	Set bolt (¼" UNF x ⅜")) and pulley to hub	4	255207	
30	Fan and dynamo belt	1	GFB124	
	Fan blade	1	574044	5 blade fan
	Spring washer) Fixing fan and	4	GHF331	
	Set bolt (¼" UNF x 1¾")) pulley to hub	4	BH604111	
	Fan and dynamo belt	1	GFB124	
	Water pump overhaul kit	1	530590	

* NO LONGER SERVICED

ENGINE - Cylinder Head, 2¼ litre Diesel

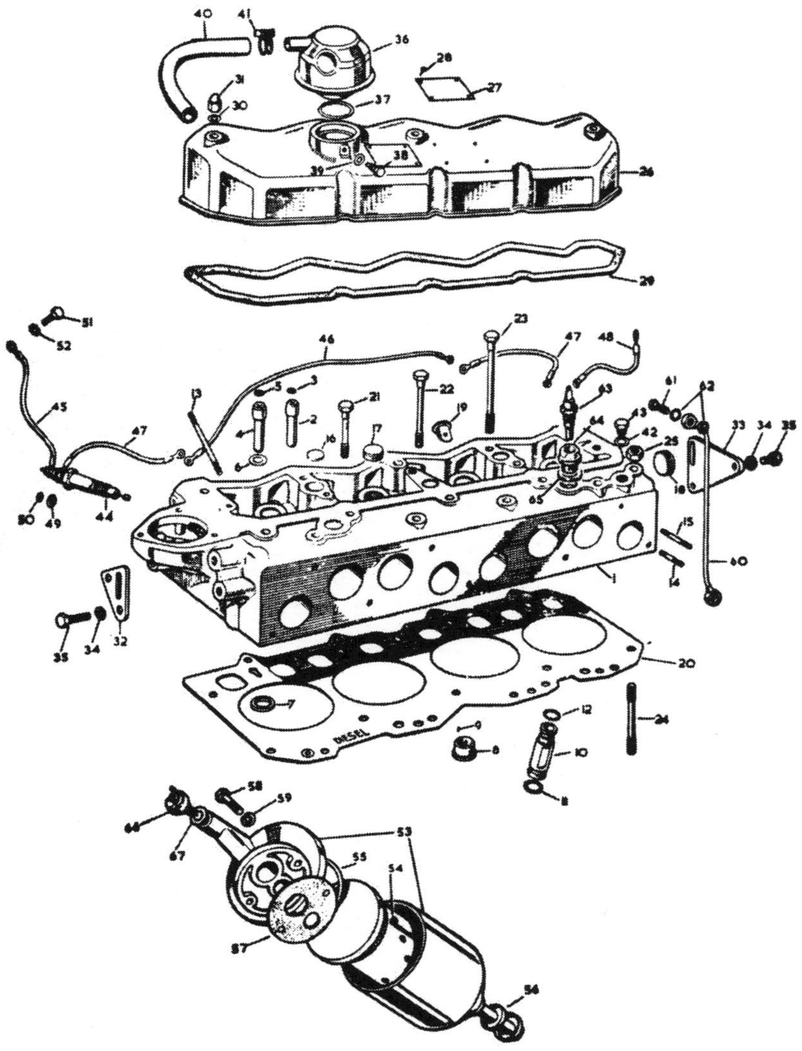

1E 11

PLATE REF.	1 2 3 4 DESCRIPTION	QTY.	PART No.	REMARKS
1	CYLINDER HEAD ASSEMBLY	1	601469	Up to engine suffix 'J' inclusive
	CYLINDER HEAD ASSEMBLY	1	RTC772	From engine suffix 'K' onwards
2	Valve guide, inlet	4	511837	
3	Sealing ring for inlet valve guide	4	247186@	With 'O' ring type seal Up to engine suffix 'J' inclusive
4	Valve guide, exhaust	4	511838	
5	Sealing ring for exhaust valve guide	4	233419@	
6	Packing washer for valve guides	20	230062	
	Valve guide, inlet,	4	568688	With lip type oil seal. From engine suffix 'K' onwards
	Oil seal for inlet valve guide	4	554727@	
	Valve guide, exhaust	4	568689	
	Oil seal for exhaust valve guide	4	554728@	
7	Insert for exhaust valve seat	4	512828	
8	Hot plug in cylinder head	4	558168	
9	Peg for hot plug	4	271881	
10	Push rod tube	8	514224	
11	'O' ring for push rod tube, large	8	515573	
12	'O' ring for push rod tube, small	8	515572	
	Stud for injector, thread length ⅞"	5	247883*	For stepped type clamping strip for injector. Up to engine suffix 'J' incl.
	Stud for injector, thread length 2½"	3	521600*	
13	Stud for injector, thread length 1.3/32"	7	531896	For plain type clamping strip for injector.
	Stud for injector, thread length 2.19/32"	1	531895	
	Stud for injector, thread length 1.3/32"	8	596097	For flanged type injector. From engine suffix 'K' onwards
14	Stud, short — For manifold	5	247144	
15	Stud, long — For manifold	4	247143	
16	Core plug, ⅞" diameter	2	250830	Alternatives
	Cup plug	4	525497	
	Core plug, ¾" diameter	2	90512413*	
17	Core plug, 1" diameter	7	518272	
18	Core plug, 1⅜" diameter	1	230250	
19	Shroud for injector bore	4	524680	
20	Cylinder head gasket	1	GEG393	
21	Special set bolt, short — Fixing cylinder head to cylinder block	2	247683	
22	Special set bolt, medium — Fixing cylinder head to cylinder block	9	247051	
23	Special set bolt, long — Fixing cylinder head to cylinder block	5	247723	
24	Stud (½" UNF) — Fixing cylinder head to cylinder block	2	90518466	
25	Nut (½" UNF) — Fixing cylinder head to cylinder block	2	NH608061	

@ Not included in cylinder head assembly

* NO LONGER SERVICED

1E 11

ENGINE - Cylinder Head, 2¼ litre Diesel

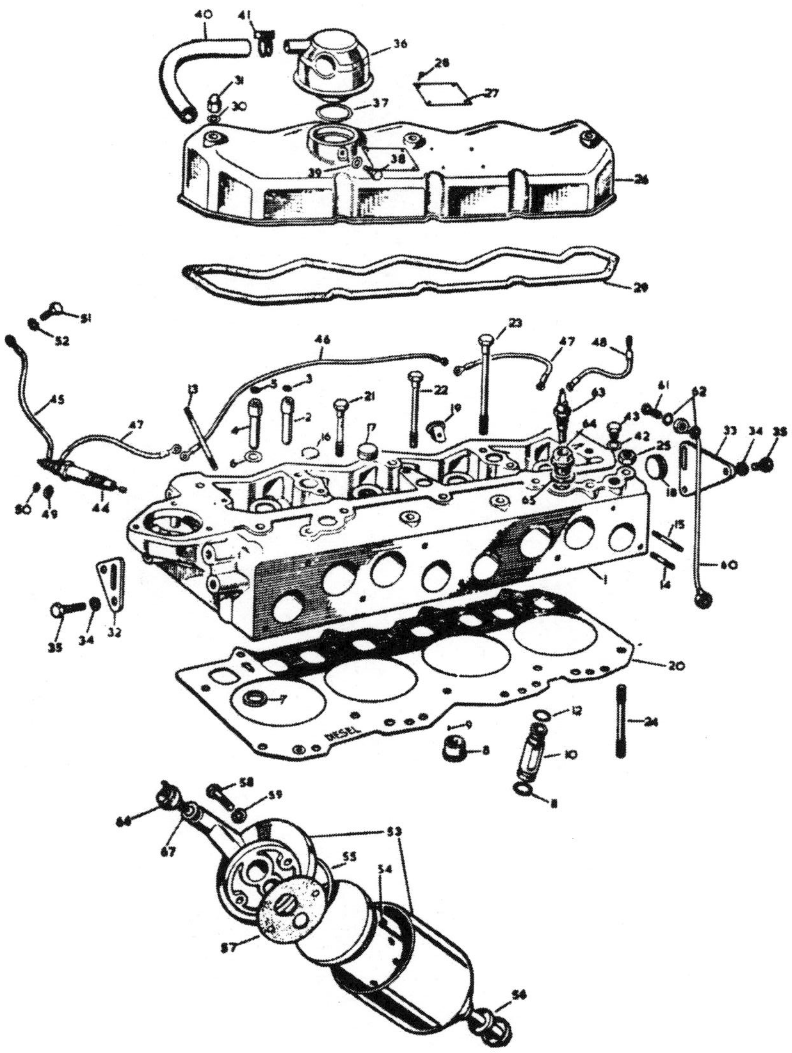

1E 12

PLATE REF.	1 2 3 4 DESCRIPTION	QTY.	PART No.	REMARKS
26	ROCKER COVER, TOP, ASSEMBLY	1	90518719	
27	Tappet clearance plate	1	247634	
28	Drive screw fixing plate	4	AB606021	
29	Joint washer for top rocker cover	1	GEG452	
30	Sealing washer) Fixing tip	3	273069	
31	Special nut) rocker cover	3	247121	
32	Lifting bracket for engine, front	1	525131	
33	Lifting bracket for engine, rear	1	ERC2686	
34	Spring washers) Fixing brackets	4	GHF332	
35	Set bolt (5/16" UNF x ¾")) to cylinder head	4	GHF120	
	Breather filter for engine	1	563180*	Up to engine suffix 'J' inclusive
36	Breather filter for engine	1	574658	From engine suffix 'K' onwards
37	Sealing ring for filter	1	268887	
38	Special set screw fixing breather filte	1	515291	
39	Sealing washer for set screw	1	232037	
40	Hose, breather filter to inlet manifold	1	90574655	From engine suffix 'K' onwards
41	Clip fixing hose	2	554260	
	Clip for hose at manifold clamp	1	574654	
42	Joint washer) For heater valve hole	1	243959	
43	Plug (⅜" BSF)) in cylinder head	1	536577	
44	Heater plug	4	568335	
45	Heater plug lead No.1 to earth	1	247953	
46	Heater plug lead No.2 to No.3	1	247952	
47	Heater plug lead No.1 to 2 and 3 to 4	2	247953	
	Heater plug lead No.4 to resistor	1	529972	For Lucar blade type resistor
48	Heater plug lead No.4 to resistor	1	541523	For terminal type resistor
49	Shakeproof washer, large) Fixing leads to	4	77626	
50	Shakeproof washer, small) heater plug	4	WE702101	
51	Bolt (⅜" UNF x ⅝")) Fixing heater earth	1	253905	
52	Fan disc washer) lead to cylinder head	1	90512305	
53	ENGINE OIL FILTER	1	537229	Short type
	Element for filter, overall length 6.13/16"	1	GFE144	For long type filter
54	Element for filter, overall length 4⅝"	1	GFE130	For short type filter
55	Gasket for filter	1	272539	
56	Rubber washer for centre bolt	1	269889	
57	Joint washer for filter	1	598354	
58	Set bolt (7/16" UNF x 1¼")) Fixing filter to	2	SH607101	
59	Spring washer) cylinder block	2	WM600071	
60	Oil pipe complete to cylinder head, length 10½"	1	275679	
61	Banjo bolt fixing oil pipe	2	597563	
62	Joint washer for banjo bolts	4	232039	

* NO LONGER SERVICED

1E 12

ENGINE - Cylinder Head, 2¼ litre Diesel

GROUP B   ENGINE - Cylinder head, 2¼ litre diesel

PLATE REF.	1 2 3 4	DESCRIPTION	QTY.	PART No.	REMARKS
		Plug for thermometer hole in cylinder head	1	278164	Up to engine suffix 'G' inclusive
63		Water temperature transmitter	1	GTR11	From engine
64		Adaptor for water temperature transmitter	1	546117	suffix 'H' onwards
65		Joint washer for plug or adaptor	1	243972	
66		Oil pressure switch	1	GPS102	
67		Joint washer for switch	1	232039	
		Valve guide oil control kit	1	605484*	To convert early engines with 'O' ring type valve guide seals to lip type oil seals

* NO LONGER SERVICED

1E 13

1E 13

51

ENGINE – Manifolds, 2¼ litre Diesel

PLATE REF.	1 2 3 4	DESCRIPTION	QTY.	PART No.	REMARKS
1		INLET MANIFOLD	1	550263	Up to engine suffix 'J' inclusive
		INLET MANIFOLD	1	574661	From engine suffix 'K' onwards
2		Connecting tube and plug, hose to manifold	1	574656	
3		Plug for inlet manifold	1	10713	Hexagon head, brass type plug
4		Joint washer for plug	1	243960	
5		Plug for inlet manifold, 25/64" outside diameter	1	524765	Cup type, steel
		Plug for inlet manifold, 1.61/64" outside diameter	1	525428	plug
6		Plug for redundant hole at manifold elbow	1	90574691	
7		EXHAUST MANIFOLD ASSEMBLY	1	247651	Up to engine suffix 'C'
		EXHAUST MANIFOLD ASSEMBLY	1	536514	From engine suffix 'D' onwards
8		Stud for exhaust pipe	4	252621	
9		Joint washer for inlet and exhaust manifold	1	GEG685	
10		Clamp for manifold	4	564308	
11		Plain washer	5	RTC613	Fixing inlet and exhaust manifold
12		Spring washer	9	GHF332	
13		Nut (5/16" UNF)	9	GHF201	

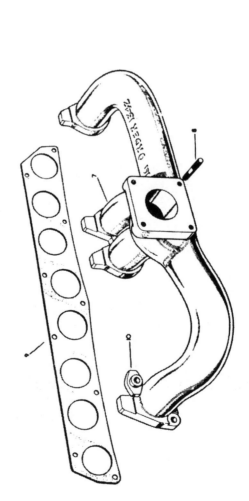

1E 14

GROUP B
ENGINE - Mountings and Rubbers, Diesel Models

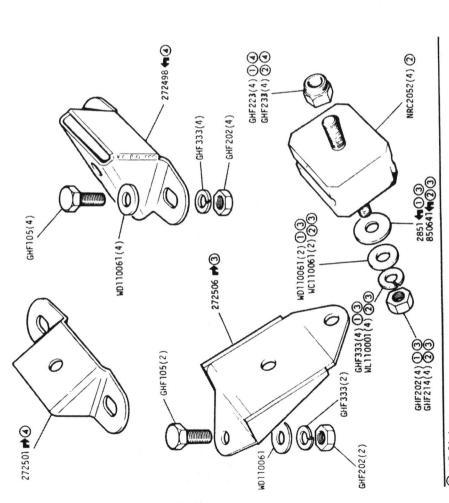

272501 ↑④

GHF105(2)

WD110061

GHF333(2)

GHF202(2)

272506 ↑③

GHF333(4)④①
WL110001(4)②③

GHF202(4)①③
GHF214(4)②③

WD110061(2)①③
WC110061(2)②③

2851 ←①③
850641←②③

GHF223(4)①④
GHF233(4)②④

NRC2052(4) ②

272498 ←④

GHF105(4)

WD110061(4)

GHF333(4)

GHF202(4)

① UNF Fixings
② Metric Fixings
③ Front Mounting
④ Rear Mounting

1E 15

This page is intentionally left blank

53

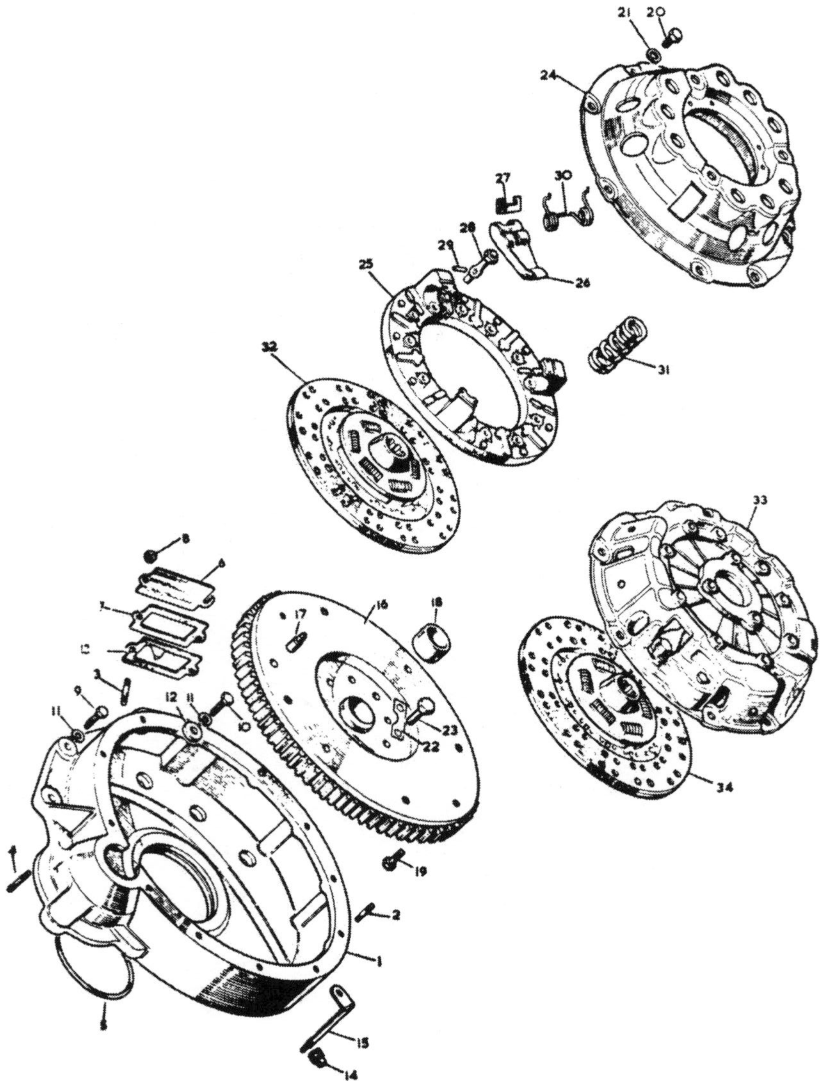

1F 02

PLATE REF.	1 2 3 4 DESCRIPTION	QTY.	PART No.	REMARKS
1	FLYWHEEL HOUSING ASSEMBLY	1	247526*	Up to engine suffix 'J' inclusive 7:1 compression ratio only
	FLYWHEEL HOUSING ASSEMBLY	1	564394	From engine suffix 'K' onwards 7:1 compression ratio. From engine suffix 'A' onwards 8:1 compression ratio
2	Stud (⅜" UNF) fixing flywheel housing to bell housing	12	247145	
3	Stud (¼" UNF) fixing inspection cover	2	247146	Up to engine suffix 'J' inclusive 7:1 compression ratio only
4	Stud (⅜" UNF) for starter motor	2	247145	
5	Sealing ring for flywheel housing	1	246169	
6	Inspection cover plate	1	56140	) Up to engine suffix 'J'
7	Joint washer for cover plate	2	50216	) inclusive 7:1 compression
8	Nut (¼" UNF) fixing cover plate	2	GHF200	) ratio only
9	Bolt (⅜" UNF x 1¾")) Fixing flywheel housing to cylinder block	2	BH606141	Up to engine suffix 'J' inclusive 7:1 compression ratio only
	Bolt (⅜" UNF x 1⅜"))	2	256040	From engine suffix 'K' onwards 7:1 compression ratio. From engine suffix 'A' onwards 8:1 compression ratio
10	Bolt (⅜" UNF x 1⅜"))	6	255248	
11	Spring washer)	8	GHF333	
12	Plain washer)	6	2219	
13	Indicator for engine timing	1	272784*	Up to engine suffix 'J' inclusive 7:1 compression ratio
14	Drain plug for housing	1	3290	
	Stowage bracket for drain plug	1	276511	
15	FLYWHEEL ASSEMBLY	1	600243	
	Ring gear for flywheel	1	506799	
16	Dowel locating clutch cover plate	2	502116	3 off on vehicles with 9½" clutch
17	Bush for primary pinion	1	8566	
18	Set bolt fixing clutch	6	255427	
19	Tab washer for set bolt	6	546197	) Alternatives
	Spring washer for set bolt	6	GHF332	)
20	Locker) Fixing flywheel	4	526161	
21	Special set bolt) to crankshaft	8	247135	

* NO LONGER SERVICED

1F 02

FLYWHEEL and CLUTCH, 2¼ litre Petrol

GROUP C   CLUTCH, 2¼ litre petrol

PLATE REF.	1 2 3 4	DESCRIPTION	QTY.	PART No.	REMARKS
		CLUTCH ASSEMBLY	1	GCC127	9" type clutch with black clutch spring
22		Cover plate for clutch	1	231888	
23		Pressure plate for clutch	1	46032	
24		Release plate for clutch	3	501211	
25		Strut for release lever	3	231884	*
26		Eyebolt and nut for release lever	2	242996	
27		Pin for release lever	3	42537	
28		Anti-rattle spring for release lever	2	231883	
29		Clutch spring (yellow and light green)	9	7H3082	For early type clutch
		Clutch spring (black)	9	7H3006	Part of GCC127 for late type clutch
30		Clutch plate complete	1	GCP109	⎫ Alternatives
		Lining package for clutch plate (Ferodo)	1	AEU1022	⎬
		Lining package for clutch plate (Mintex)	1	90517026	⎭
31		CLUTCH COVER ASSEMBLY	1	GCC112	⎫ 9½" type
32		Clutch plate complete	1	GCP129	⎪ American Dollar Area
		Lining package for clutch plate	1	605997	⎬ From engines numbered 25163284 onwards. Optional equipment for all other areas.
		CLUTCH COVER ASSEMBLY	1	GCC181	⎫ Vehicles fitted with all-synchromesh gearbox:-
		Clutch plate complete	1	GCP129	⎪ Home Market 88 and 109
		Lining package for clutch plate	1	605997	⎬ Station Wagons from vehicle suffix 'H' onwards.

* NO LONGER SERVICED

1F 03

55

FLYWHEEL and CLUTCH, 2.6 litre Petrol

GROUP C   FLYWHEEL and CLUTCH, 2.6 litre petrol

PLATE REF.	1	2	3	4	DESCRIPTION	QTY.	PART No.	REMARKS
1					FLYWHEEL HOUSING ASSEMBLY	1	541195	
2					Stud, short (⅞")) Fixing flywheel housing	12	3650	
3					Stud (5/16")) to bell housing	1	3200	
4					Stud (⅜") for inspection cover	2	3651	*
5					Drain plug for housing	1	3290	
6					Sealing ring for flywheel housing	1	246169	
7					Inspection cover plate	1	56140	
9					Nut (¼" BSF) fixing cover plate	2	3819	
10					Bolt (⅜" UNF x 1½")) Fixing flywheel	2	GHF106	
					Bolt (⅜" UNF x 1⅜")) housing to	8	255248	
12					Spring washer) cylinder block	6	GHF333	
13					Plain washer	6	2219	
					Plain washer	2	WB110061	
					Plain washer	2	4085	
15					FLYWHEEL ASSEMBLY	1	541760	
16					Ring gear for flywheel	1	506799	
17					Dowel for clutch cover plate	3	502116	
18					Bush for primary pinion	1	8566	
19					Locker) Fixing flywheel	3	534098	
					Special set bolt) to crankshaft	6	247135	
20					Set bolt (5/16" BSF x ⅞")) Fixing clutch	6	237324	
21					Locker) to flywheel	6	546197	) Alternatives
					Spring washer	6	GHF332	)
22					CLUTCH COVER ASSEMBLY	1	GCC112	
23					Clutch plate complete	1	GCP129	
					Lining package for clutch plate	1	605997	
					CLUTCH COVER ASSEMBLY	1	GCC181	) Vehicles fitted with
					Clutch plate complete	1	GCP129	) all-Synchromesh gearbox:-
					Lining package for clutch plate	1	605997	) Home Market 88 and 109

Station Wagons from vehicle suffix 'H' onwards.

* NO LONGER SERVICED

1F 04

FLYWHEEL and CLUTCH, 2.6 litre Petrol

1F 04

FLYWHEEL AND CLUTCH, 2¼ litre Diesel

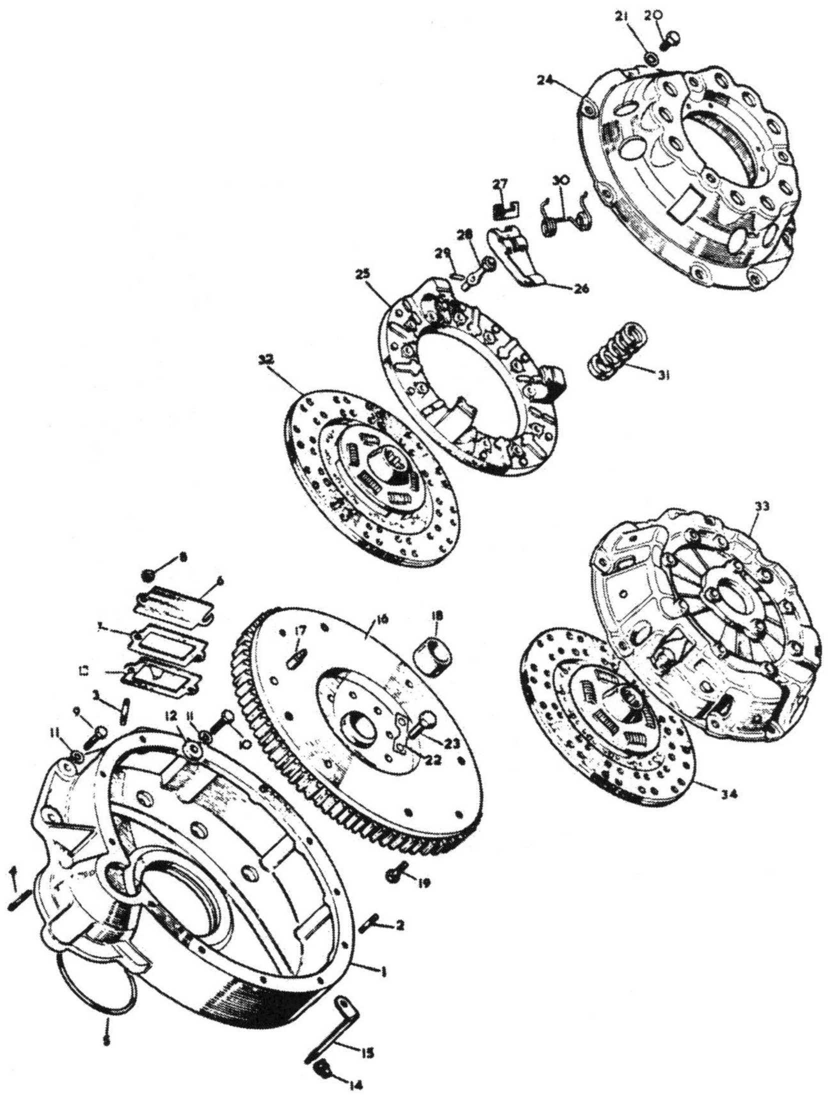

1F 05

PLATE REF.	1 2 3 4 DESCRIPTION	QTY.	PART No.	REMARKS
1	FLYWHEEL HOUSING ASSEMBLY	1	90515086	
2	Stud (3/8" UNF) fixing flywheel housing to bell housing	12	247145	
3	Stud (1/4" UNF) fixing inspection cover	2	247146	
4	Stud (7/16" UNF) for starter motor	1	277532	
5	Sealing ring for flywheel housing	1	246169	
6	Inspection cover plate	1	56140	
7	Joint washer for cover plate	2	50216	
8	Nut (1/4" UNF) fixing cover plate	2	GHF200	
9	Bolt (3/8" UNF x 1¾")) Fixing	2	BH606141	
10	Bolt (3/8" UNF x 1⅛")) flywheel housing	6	255248	
11	Spring washer) to	8	GHF333	
12	Plain washer) cylinder block	6	2219	
13	Indicator for engine timing	1	ERC2250	
14	Drain plug for housing	1	3290	
15	Stowage bracket for drain plug	1	276511	
16	FLYWHEEL ASSEMBLY	1	566851	Cast iron flywheel
	Ring gear for flywheel	* 1	510489	For steel flywheel
	Ring gear for flywheel	1	568431	For cast iron flywheel
17	Dowel locating clutch cover plate	2	502116	3 off on vehicles with 9½" clutch
18	Bush for primary pinion	1	8566	
19	Special fitting bolt fixing clutch cover plate	6	247166	For steel flywheel
20	Set bolt) Fixing clutch	6	255427	For cast iron flywheel
21	Spring washer) cover plate	6	GHF332	
22	Locker) Fixing flywheel	4	526161	
23	Special set bolt) to crankshaft	8	247135	
	CLUTCH ASSEMBLY	1	GCC127	9" type with black clutch springs
24	Cover plate for clutch	1	231888	
25	Pressure plate for clutch	1	46032	
26	Release lever for clutch	3	501211	
27	Strut for release lever	* 3	231884	
28	Eye bolt and nut for release lever	3	242996	
29	Pin for release lever	3	42537	
30	Anti-rattle spring for release lever	3	231883	
	Clutch spring (yellow and light green)	9	7H3082	For early type clutch
31	Clutch spring (black)	9	7H3006	Part of GCC127 For late type clutch

* NO LONGER SERVICED

1F 05

GROUP C   FLYWHEEL AND CLUTCH, 2¼ LITRE DIESEL

PLATE REF.	1 2 3 4	DESCRIPTION	QTY.	PART NO.	REMARKS
32		Clutch plate complete	1	GCP109	Alternatives
		Lining package for clutch plate (Mintex)	1	90517026)	
		Lining package for clutch plate (Ferodo)	1	261921)	
33		CLUTCH COVER ASSEMBLY	1	GCC112)	9½" diaphragm type
34		Clutch plate complete	1	GCP129)	American Dollar
		Lining package for clutch plate	1	605997)	Area. Optional equipment for all other areas up to engine suffix 'H' inclusive Standard equipment from engine suffix 'J' onwards.
		Self-locking nut (5/16" UNF) Fixing clutch cover plate	6	GHF242)	When steel flywheel is fitted.
		Spacer	6	90571227*)	is fitted.
		CLUTCH COVER ASSEMBLY	1	GCC181)	Vehicles fitted with all-
		Clutch plate complete	1	GCP129)	synchromesh gearbox:-
		Lining package for clutch plate	1	605997)	Home Market 88 and 109 Station Wagons from vehicle suffix 'H' onwards.

* NO LONGER SERVICED

1F 06

FLYWHEEL AND CLUTCH, 2¼ litre Diesel

1F 06

This page is intentionally left blank

GROUP C
Clutch Withdrawal Mechanism,
except All-Synchromesh Gearbox

NLS 231071   Suffix A
528707   Suffix B onwards ①
591205

90213663
528697 } Suffix B onwards

Suffix 'A'
Suffix 'B' onwards

GHB130 ①
268053 ①
594224 ①
591202 ①
231075
231321 (4)
214794 (2)
90214787
231074
219768 ①
264807
591204 ①
265969 ①
213660
213700 (2)
214793
251320 (3)
90213662
264806
GHF331(2)
90215593 (2)
213661
231943

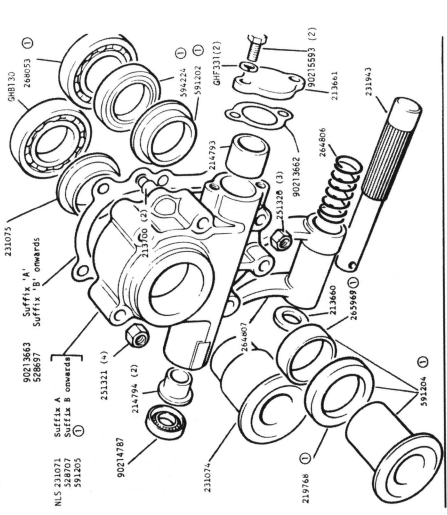

REMARKS ① With sealed clutch withdrawal unit

1F 07

59

GROUP C   CLUTCH SLAVE CYLINDER

PLATE REF.	1 2 3 4	DESCRIPTION	QTY.	PART No.	REMARKS
1		CLUTCH SLAVE CYLINDER	1	266694	
2		Bleed screw for clutch slave cylinder	1	556508	
3		Bolt (5/16" UNF x 1")	2	GHF103	
4		Bolt (5/16" UNF x 1¼") } Fixing slave	2	SH605101	When 9" type clutch is fitted
			2	544686 *	When 9½" diaphragm spring clutch is fitted
		Packing piece } cylinder to	2	GHF332	
5		Spring washer } support bracket	2	GHF201	
6		Nut (5/16" UNF)	1	537601	
7		Push rod for clutch slave cylinder	1	275199	
8		Clevis for push rod	1	GHF201	
9		Locknut (5/16" UNF) for push rod	1	GBH134	
10		Hose, pipe to clutch slave cylinder	1	233220	All RH Stg
11		Gasket for hose at slave cylinder	1	569462	Also LH Stg with 3/16" pipe
12		Mounting bracket for hose	2	234603	
13		Bolt (2BA x ¾") } Fixing	2	WM702001	
14		Spring washer } bracket	1	RTC608	
15		Nut (2BA) } to dash	1	GHF323	4 cylinder models
16		Shakeproof washer } Fixing hose	1	NT606041	All-syncromesh gearbox
17		Special nut } to bracket			
		Hose, pipe to clutch slave cylinder	1	552057	
		Adaptor, pipe to clutch master cylinder	1	139082	
		Gasket, adaptor to master cylinder	1	233220	
		Banjo, hose to slave cylinder	1	538068	
		Gasket, banjo to slave cylinder	1	233220	
		Banjo bolt } Fixing hose	1	512235	
		Gasket } to banjo	2	216914	
		Mounting bracket for hose	1	569462	
		Shakeproof washer } Fixing hose	1	90512651	
		Special nut } to bracket	1	216912	
		Bolt (2BA x ¾") } Fixing bracket to	2	234603	LH Stg with ½" pipe
		Spring washer } dash	2	WM702001	4 cylinder models
		Nut (2BA)	2	RTC608	
		Clip fixing clutch and brake pipes	2	50639	

* NO LONGER SERVICED

1F 08

CLUTCH SLAVE CYLINDER

1F 08

PLATE REF. 1 2 3 4	DESCRIPTION	QTY.	PART NO.	REMARKS
20	Spherical bearing	1	217984	
21	Housing for spherical bearing	2	217983	
22	Felt ring for spherical bearing	2	217985	
	Bolt (5/16" UNF x ¾")) Fixing	2	GHF120	4 cylinder
23	Bolt (5/16" UNF x 1")) spherical	2	GHF103	6 cylinder
	Spring washer) bearing to	2	GHF332	
24	Nut (5/16" UNF)) support bracket	2	GHF201	
25	Clevis pin, lever to fork end	1	216471	
26	Split pin for clevis pin	1	2392	
27	Connecting tube for clutch cross-shaft	1	561661	
28	Pin) Fixing tube to	2	536R03	
29	Plain washer) clutch cross and	2	RTC840	
30	Split pin) operating shafts	2	2A22*	
31	Return spring for clutch operating lever	1	278490	) Up to engine suffix 'A'
	Anchor plate for return spring at slave cylinder support bracket	1	272920*	)
	Mounting bracket for clutch jump hose	1	569462	F cylinder RH Stg only
	Clutch jump hose	1	592515	4 cylinder
	Clutch jump hose	1	NPC2130	6 cylinder
	Support plate for clutch jump hose	1	ERC2060	4 cylinder
	Support plate for clutch jump hose	1	587622	6 cylinder
	Pipe, jump hose to clutch slave cylinder	1	NRC1655	Vehicles fitted
	Clutch slave cylinder	1	591231	with all-synchromesh
	Push rod for clutch slave cylinder	1	576751	gearbox:-
	Clip fixing push rod	1	576723	Home Market
	Bleed pipe for clutch slave cylinder	1	594776	88 and 109
	Adaptor for bleed pipe	1	594922	Station Wagons
	Bracket for bleed pipe	1	593664	From vehicle
	Bolt 5/16" UNF x 1⅛") Fixing bracket	2	25F223	suffix 'H'
	Spring washer) to bell	2	GHF332	onwards
	Nut 5/16" UNF) housing	2	GHF201	
	Bleed screw	1	565508	
	Shakeproof washer) Fixing bleed screw	1	GHF322	
	Locknut ⅜" UN:) to bracket	1	NT606041	
	Clutch slave cylinder overhaul kit	1	8G8600	

* NO LONGER SERVICED

PLATE REF. 1 2 3 4	DESCRIPTION	QTY.	PART NO.	REMARKS
	Adaptor) Fixing pipe to	1	139082	
	Gasket) clutch slave cylinder	1	233220*	For early type
	Adaptor) Fixing pipe to	1	562943*	nylon pipe
	Gasket) clutch master cylinder	1	233220	
	Clip for pipe, clutch master cylinder to slave cylinder	1	562947*	Except vehicles fitted with All-Synchromesh gearbox
	Drive screw, fixing clip to dash	1	72626	
	Adaptor) Fixing hose	1	139082	
	Gasket for adaptor) to clutch	1	216914	
	Gasket) slave cylinder	1	233220	
	Hose, adaptor to pipe	1	552057	LH Stg 109
	Mounting bracket for hose	1	569462	6 cylinder models
	Shakeproof washer) Fixing hose	1	90512651	
	Special nut) to bracket	1	216912	
	Bolt (2BA x ½")) Fixing	2	234603	
	Spring washer) bracket	2	MM702001	
	Nut (2BA)) to dash	2	RTC608	
	Adaptor) Fixing pipe to clutch	1	139082	
	Gasket) master cylinder	1	233220	
	Clip, fixing brake pipe to toebox	1	AEU1581	For late type metal pipe
	Clip,) Fixing	1	50639	
	Screw (2BA x½")) clutch pipe	1	78318 *	
	Nut (2BA)) to dash	1	RTC608	
18	Support bracket for clutch slave cylinder	1	509856	Engine suffix 'A'
18	Support bracket for clutch slave cylinder	1	561242	2¼ litre Petrol and Diesel models from engine suffix 'B' onwards
	Support bracket for clutch slave cylinder	1	561922	2.6 litre Petrol models. Early type for use with straight type operating lever
	Support bracket for clutch slave cylinder	1	561762*	2.6 litre Petrol models. Late type for use with cranked type operating le`
19	Shaft and operating lever for clutch	1	273077*	Engine suffix 'A'
19	Shaft and operating lever for clutch	1	537603	2¼ litre Petrol and Diesel models from engine suffix 'B' onwards
	Shaft and operating lever for clutch	1	544980	2.6 litre Petrol models. Early type with straight lever
	Shaft and operating lever for clutch	1	537603	2.6 litre Petrol models. Late type with cranked le`

* NO LONGER SERVICED

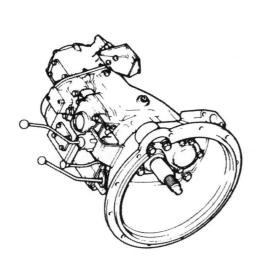

248720 (3)

622045

232604 except ③ ⑤

9021559 (2)

GHF331 (2)

512237

512238

GHF202 (12)

WB110061 (9) ③ ⑤
WB110061 (8) ③ ⑤

251324 (4)

269413 (3) except ③ ⑤

236281 Suffix A to D
553262 Suffix E onwards, except ③ ⑤

232647 Suffix A to D

277961 ①
556039 ②
576714 ③
556044 ④
576762 ⑤

REMARKS

① 2¼ litre Petrol and Diesel Suffix 'A'
② 2¼ litre Petrol and Diesel Suffix 'B' onwards, Standard Gearbox
③ 2¼ litre Petrol and Diesel, All-Synchromesh Gearbox
④ 2.6 litre Petrol, Standard Gearbox
⑤ 2.6 litre Petrol, All-Synchromesh Gearbox

1G 02

GROUP D
GEARBOX - Bell Housing

New Gearbox Assemblies		
	607125N	①
NLS	591440	② ③
	RTC1443	① ④
	FRC2000N	① ③
	607127N	①
NLS	591441	② ③
	RTC1215	① ④
	FRC2001N	① ③

2¼ Litre Petrol and Diesel

2.6 Litre Petrol

Rebuilt Gearbox Assemblies	
607125R	②
607125RR	① ③
576730R	① ⑤
607127R	②
607127RR	① ③
576761R	① ⑤

① All synchromesh
② Part synchromesh
③ With sealed clutch withdrawal, Optional
④ Less transfer box
⑤ Home Market 88 and 109 Station Wagons only from vehicle suffix 'H' onwards

1G 02

VS 1236

SIIA LAND ROVER

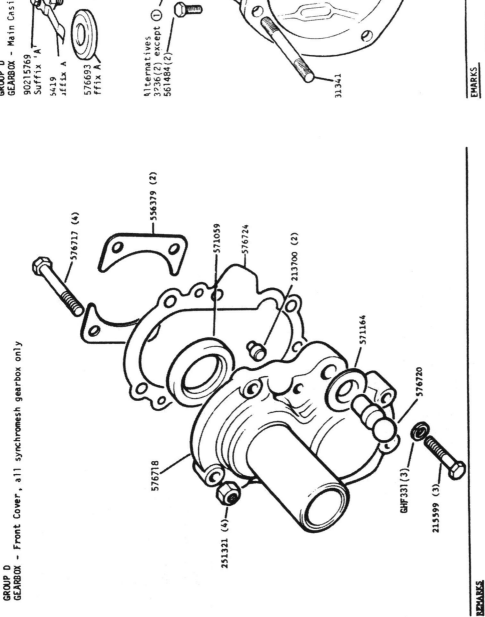

GROUP D
GEARBOX - Main Casing

9021S769 Suffix 'A'

RTC609 Suffix A

5419 ffix A

556570 Suffix B onwards

576693 ffix A

533354 Suffix A

52246(2)

5b43

2827(4)

GHF333(4)

Not supplied separately

3319(2)

55778(2)

528865 Suffix C onwards

3238(3) Suffix A and B
3238(2) Suffix C onwards

55636(2)

3291 Suffix A
3292 Suffix B onwards

NLS 269960 Suffix A and B
605933 Suffix C onwards
606881 ①

7289(2)

Alternatives
3236(2) except ①
561484(2)

515599

540870

31341

600603 Gearbox gasket kit

1RE 12

① All synchromesh, Home Market 88inch and
109inch Station Wagons, from vehicle
suffix 'H'

1G 03

REMARKS

GROUP D
GEARBOX - Front Cover, all synchromesh gearbox only

576717 (4)

556379 (2)

571059

576724

213700 (2)

571164

576720

576718

251321 (4)

GHF331(3)

215599 (3)

1G 03

REMARKS

63

GROUP D
GEARBOX – Second Speed Gears, Mainshaft and Layshaft
except All-Synchromesh Gearbox

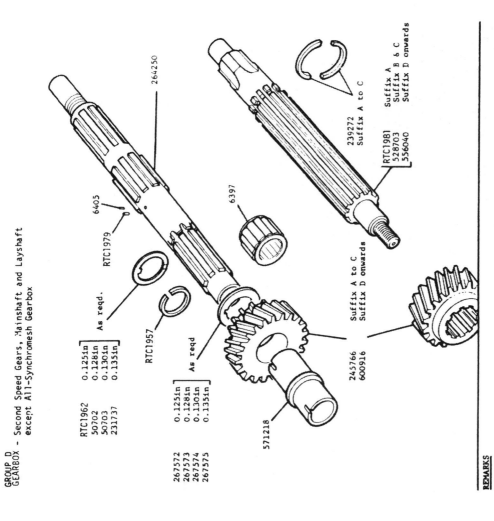

RTC1979

6405

264250

239272
Suffix A to C

RTC1981   Suffix A
528703   Suffix B & C
556040   Suffix D onwards

6397

Suffix A to C
Suffix D onwards

RTC1957

As reqd.
RTC1962   0.125in
50702   0.128in
50703   0.130in
231737   0.135in

As reqd
267572   0.125in
267573   0.128in
267574   0.130in
267575   0.135in

571218

245766
600916

GROUP D
GEARBOX – First Speed and Reverse Gears
except All-Synchromesh Gearbox

Alternatives
217811   Peg fixing
561877   Loctite fixing

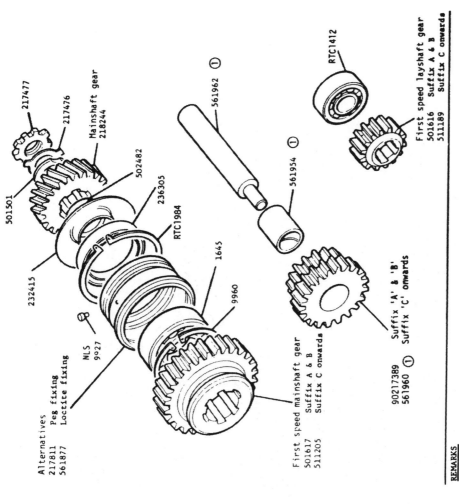

217477

217476

Mainshaft gear
218244

501501

502482

236305

232415

RTC1984

NLS
9927

1645

9960

561962 ①

561954 ①

RTC1412

First speed layshaft gear
501616   Suffix A & B
511189   Suffix C onwards

First speed mainshaft gear
501617   Suffix A & B
511205   Suffix C onwards

90217389   Suffix 'A' & 'B'
561960 ①   Suffix 'C' onwards

REMARKS

① Interchangeable as a set

Loctite Compound, Grade AVV, 10cc bottle 600303

GROUP D
GEARBOX - Primary Pinion and Mainshaft, Front
All-Synchromesh Gearbox Only

576725
591364
RTC1979
6405
RTC 1956 (3)
FRC1758
Second speed gear
591363
Thrust washer A/R
0.125" 267572
0.128" 267573
0.130" 267574
0.135" 267575
571218
Third speed gear
556010
RTC1957
6397
Primary pinion and constant gear 606880
Shims, as required
2.00 mm 594021
2.05 mm 594020
2.10 mm 594019
2.15 mm 594018
55714
571059
214795
Thrust washer, as required
0.125 in RTC1962
0.128 in 50702
0.130 in 50703
0.135 in 231737

1G 05

REMARKS

GROUP D
GEARBOX - Third Speed Gears and Primary Pinion
except All-Synchromesh Gearbox

245767
263878
RTC1956(3)
FRC1758
Distance piece for layshaft
528685 Suffix B onwards
213417 (3) Suffix A
556147 (4) Suffix E onwards
556379(2) Suffix A to D
NLS Suffix A and B
542231 Suffix C onwards ② ③
606099
90607809
NLS 214792 Suffix A
RTC1982 Suffix A
528683 Suffix B onwards
8185
528692
251321 (4) Suffix A to D
NLS 214090 (4) Suffix A to D
NLS 213666 Suffix A to D
576207 Suffix A
528701 Suffix A
213419 NLS Suffix A
528690
RTC1954
55714
RTC1963
213416

2828 (3)Suffix A
NT605061(3) Suffix A
2974 Suffix A
2766
RTC1983 Suffix A
528691 Suffix B onwards

1G 05

REMARKS

① Distance piece for layshaft

0.312in.	241649	
0.332in.	241650	As req'd Suffix A
0.352in.	241651	
0.405in.	528720	
0.425in.	528721	As req'd Suffix B onwards
0.445in.	528722	

② For gearbox with sealed clutch withdrawal unit

③ For gearboxes 607125N and 607127N only

65

GROUP D
GEARBOX - Mainshaft Rear
All-Synchromesh Gearbox Only

217477
217476
SO1501
218244
Mainshaft gea
232415
502482
RTC1984
236305
576836
1645
9960
576735
576734
First speed gear
591362
591364
608283
553084 (3) ①
503805 (3) ①
BLS108(3) ①

REMARKS ① Part of Inner and Outer Member Assembly 608283

1G 06

GROUP D
GEARBOX - Layshaft Gears and Reverse
All-Synchromesii Gearbox Only

PTC1412
576686
591519
591527
561954
576707

Primary pinion and
constant gear
606880

0.405 in 528720
0.425 in 528721
0.445 in 528722

528685
528701
528690
528683
NT605061(3)
576907
SH607101

REMARKS

1G 06

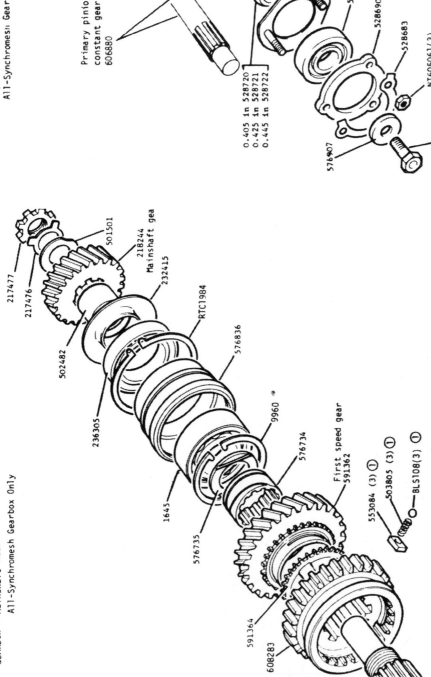

66

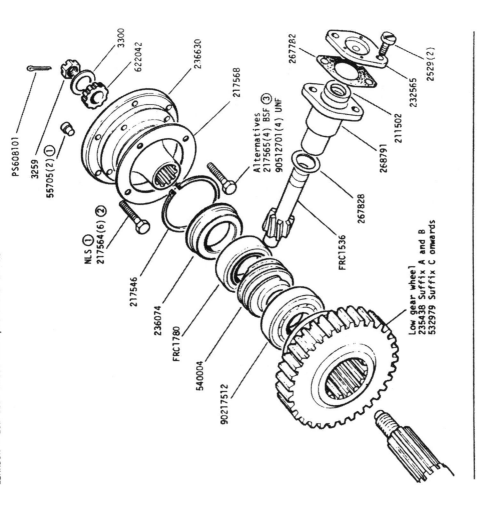

GROUP D
GEARBOX - Low Gear Wheel and Speedometer Drive

PS608101
3259
55705(2)①
3300
622042
236630
217568
NLS① 217564(6)②
217546
236074
FRC1780
540004
90217512
Alternatives 217565(4) BSF ③ 90512701(4) UNF
FRC1536
267828
Low gear wheel
235438 Suffix A and B
532979 Suffix C onwards
267782
232565
2529(2)
211502
268791

① 109 Diesel up to gearbox number 27600879
② All Petrol and 88 Diesel, also 109 Diesel from gearbox number 27600880
③ Except All-Synchromesh Gearbox.

1G 07

GROUP D
GEARBOX-Rear Output Shaft and Intermediate Gear

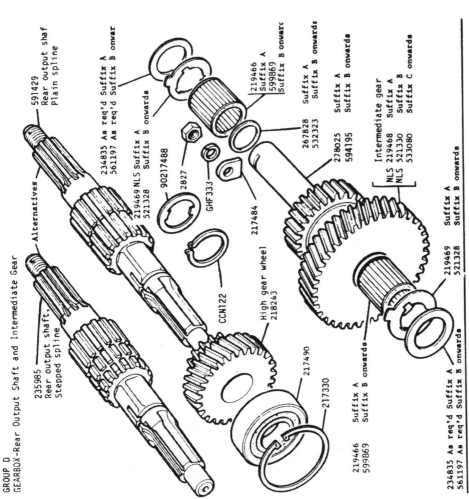

591429 Rear output shaft Plain spline
235985 Rear output shaft, Stepped spline
Alternatives
234835 As req'd Suffix A
561197 As req'd Suffix B onwar
219469 NLS Suffix A
521328 Suffix B onwards
90217488
2827
GHF333
217484
219466 Suffix A
599869 Suffix B onwards
267828
532323
278025
594195
Intermediate gear
219468 Suffix A
521330 Suffix B
533080 Suffix C onwards
NLS
NLS
Suffix A
Suffix B onwards
CCN122
High gear wheel 218243
217490
217330
219466 Suffix A
599869 Suffix B onwards
234835 As req'd Suffix A
561197 As req'd Suffix B onwards
219466 599869
Suffix A Suffix B onwards
219469 521328
Suffix A Suffix B onwards

REMARKS

1G 07

GROUP D
GEARBOX - Speedometer Pinion and Rear Mainshaft Bearing Housings

2827 (6)
GHF333(6)
GHF333(6)
2827 (6)
533731 ①
622047
217977(4)
522318
232846
217523 ①
90217843 ①
217478 ①
217523 ①
217525 ①

.003in. 235455
.005in. 217622
.010in. 217623
.015in. 217620
.040in. 549200
As required

REMARKS

① Rear mainshaft bearing housing assy. 230696

1G 08

GROUP D
GEARBOX - Transfer Box Casing

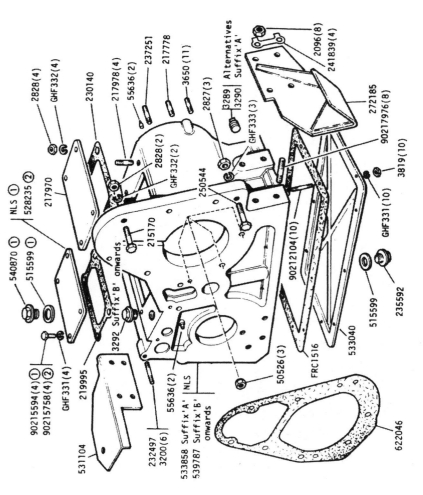

2828(4)
GHF332(4)
230140
217978(4)
237251
217778
55636(2)
3650(11)
2827(3)
3289
3290 } Alternatives Suffix 'A'
GHF333(3)
2096(8)
241839(4)
272185
90217976(8)
3819(10)
540870 ①
515599 ①
NLS ①
528235 ②
217970
2828(2)
GHF332(2)
250544
GHF331(10)
235592
515599
90217594(4)①
90215758(4)②
GHF331(4)
219995
3292 Suffix 'B' onwards
217970
215170
90212104(10)
FRC1516
533040
531104
232297
3200(6)
55636(2)
533858 Suffix 'A' } NLS
539787 Suffix 'B' onwards
50526(3)
622046

① Suffix 'A', cover plate with oil hole
② Suffix 'B' onwards, plain cover plate

90217448 Bush for shaft guide - for early type casing

1G 08

GROUP D
GEARBOX - Front Output Shaft and Housing

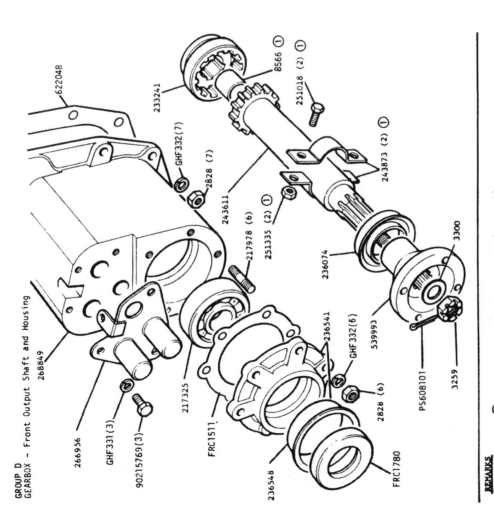

622048
268849
266956
GHF331(3)
90215769(3)
217325
FRC1511
236548
233241
GHF332(7)
2828 (7)
243611
217978 (6)
251335 (2) ①
8566 ①
251018 (2) ①
243873 (2) ①
236074
236541
GHF332(6)
2828 (6)
539993
3300
PS608101
3259
FRC1780

REMARKS   ① Part of 243611 Front output shaft assembly

1G 09

GROUP D   GEARBOX – Main Gear Change Lever

PLATE REF.	1	2	3	4	DESCRIPTION	QTY.	PART No.	REMARKS
					MAIN GEAR-CHANGE LEVER ASSEMBLY		FRC1836*RH Stg	4-cylinder models
					MAIN GEAR-CHANGE LEVER ASSEMBLY		FRC1837*LH Stg	models
					MAIN GEAR-CHANGE LEVER ASSEMBLY		622006 RH Stg	6-cylinder models
					MAIN GEAR-CHANGE LEVER ASSEMBLY		622007 *LH Stg	models
					MAIN GEAR-CHANGE LEVER ASSEMBLY		FRC1454 RH Stg	4-cylinder models
					MAIN GEAR-CHANGE LEVER ASSEMBLY		FRC1455 LH Stg	models
					MAIN GEAR-CHANGE LEVER ASSEMBLY		FRC1832 RH Stg	6-cylinder models
					MAIN GEAR-CHANGE LEVER ASSEMBLY		FRC1833 LH Stg	models
1					Gear-change lever	1	FRC1836*RH Stg	
2					Gear-change lever	1	FRC1454 RH Stg	
					Gear-change lever	1	FRC1832 RH Stg	
					Gear-change lever	1	FRC1833 LH Stg	
3					'O' ring for gear-change lever	1	540354	For early type gear change lever
					'O' ring for gear-change lever	1	FRC1387	For late type gear change lever
4					Housing for lever	1	219714	
5					Locating pin for lever ball	1	507447	
6					Spherical seat for gear lever	1	219721	
7					Retaining spring for lever	1	219723	
8					Retaining plate for spring	1	219722	
9					Circlip fixing retaining plate	1	219797	
10					Knob for lever	1	217735)	Screw-on type, for early
					Locknut (½" BSF) for knob	1	3905 *)	type gear change lever.
					Knob for lever	1	576316)	Press-on type, for late
11					Star tolerance ring	1	571661)	type gear change lever.
12					Mounting plate for gear change	1	232608	
13					Set bolt (5/16" Whit x 13/16")	4	90215647	Fixing housing
14					Locker	4	2499	to mounting plate
15					Spring washer	2	GHF331	Fixing mounting
16					Set bolt (¼" Whit x 21/32")	2	90215593	plate to bell housing
17					Reverse stop hinge complete	1	502202	
18					Adjusting screw	1	76653	For hinge
19					Locknut (2BA)	1	RTC608	
20					Bracket for reverse stop spring	1	502205	
21					Spring for reverse stop	2	231116	Fixing hinge and bracket
22					Set bolt (¼" BSF x ½")	2	237139	to reverse selector shaft
23					Locker	1	FRC2469	

* NO LONGER SERVICED

1G 10

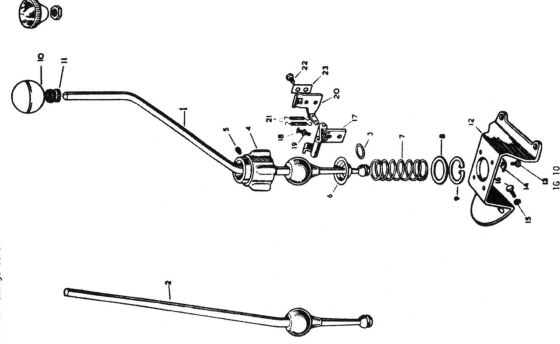

GEARBOX – Main Gear Change Lever

1G 10

GROUP D
GEARBOX-Selector Forks and Shafts
All-Synchromesh Gearbox Only

90215758(4)
GHF331(4)
5852
3649
5853
217564
55697
55638
571145
217564
1643
RTC1958
272596
576704
622281
1643
56102
3649
1643
5854
5852
217564
GHF331(4)
90215769(4)
241598 (2)
272596
272597
Reverse
576729
1st and 2nd Speed
576727
3rd and 4th speed
9213636

IG 11

GEARBOX - Selector Forks and Shafts
GROUP D except All-Synchromesh Gearbox

250693
210204
210203
90215758(4)
GHF331(4)
5853
5852
3649
1643
251018
RTC600
55697
55638
Alternatives
55775
571145
237160
RTC1958
622281
1643
56102
90217391
55638
3649
1643
6421
272596
237160(2)
5852
241598 (2)
GHF331(4)
90215769(4)
272597
272596
Reverse
502201
1st and 2nd
213637
3rd and 4th
9213636

IG 11

GROUP D
GEARBOX - Selector Rod, Four Wheel Drive

GROUP D
GEARBOX - Selector Shaft, Four Wheel Drive

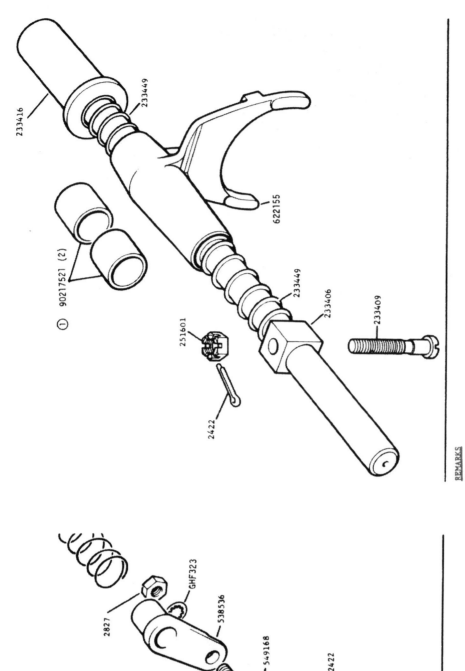

232813
3819
561221
234658
571855
3958
3619
2876
540842
230279
215808
3958
268847
230086
232464
233407
549169
266992
538536
GHF323
2827
549168
251601
2422

233416
233449
9021752i (2)
622155
233449
251601
2422
233406
233409

1G 12

1G 12

1RE17

REMARKS

① For use with early type selector fork with replaceable bushes

REMARKS

GEARBOX - Transfer Gear Change Lever

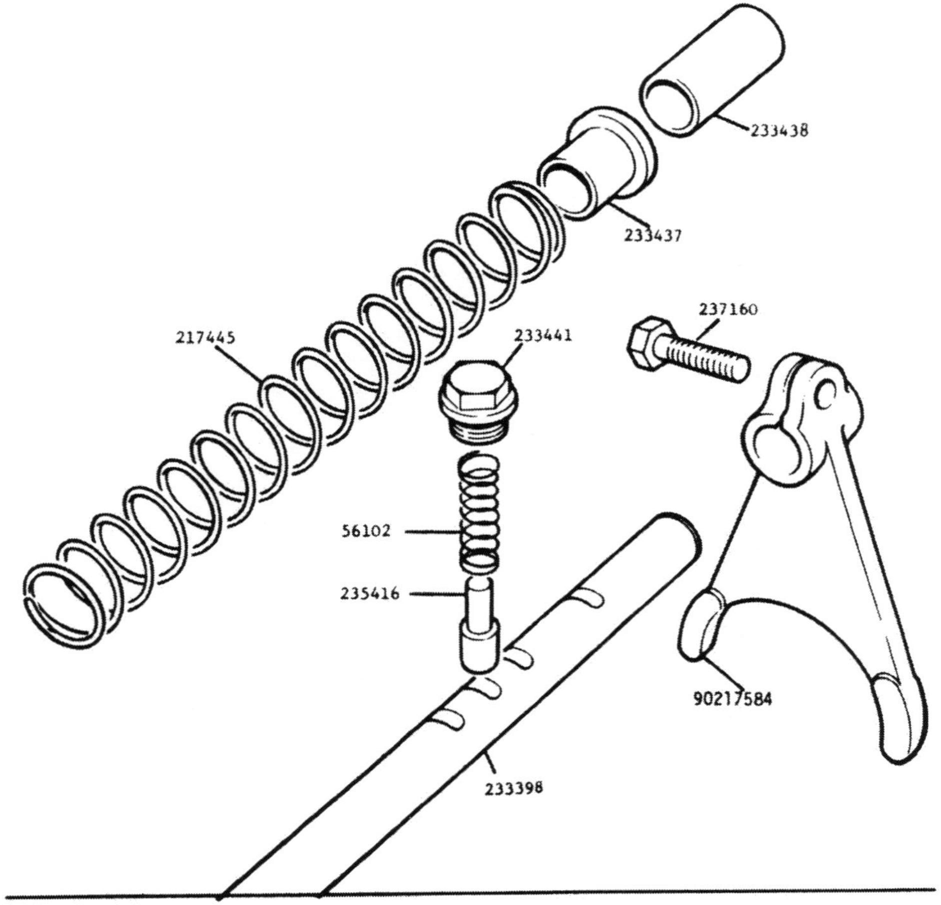

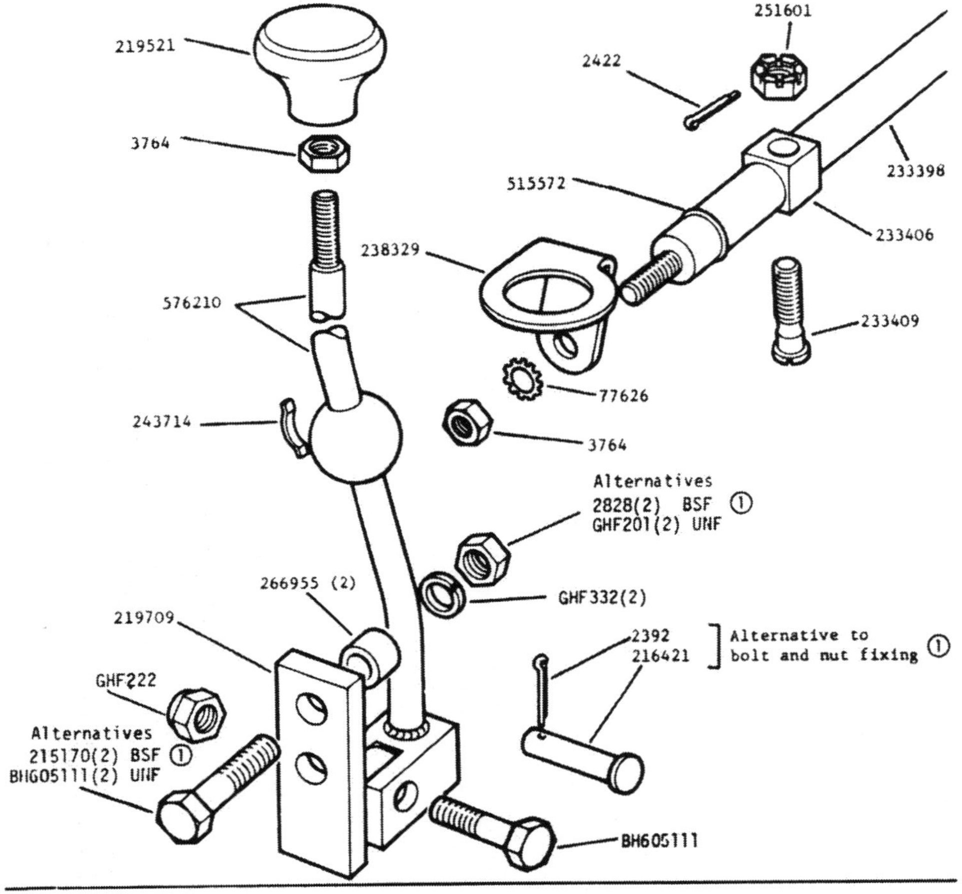

219521
3764
576210
243714
238329
515572
2422
251601
233398
233406
233409
77626
3764
Alternatives
2828(2) BSF ①
GHF201(2) UNF
GHF332(2)
266955 (2)
219709
GHF222
Alternatives
215170(2) BSF ①
BHG05111(2) UNF
2392
216421
Alternative to
bolt and nut fixing ①
BH605111

REMARKS

① Except All-Synchromesh Gearbox

1G 13

GEARBOX - Selector Fork, Transfer Gear Lever

233438
233437
217445
233441
237160
56102
235416
233398
90217584

REMARKS

1G 13

FRONT AXLE AND PROPELLER SHAFT
GROUP E

This page is intentionally left blank

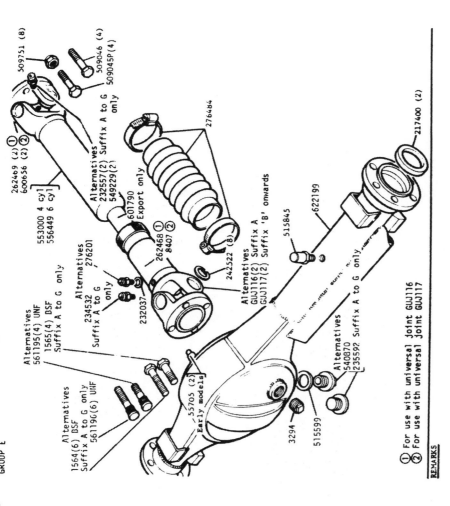

509751 (8)

509046 (4)
509045P (4)
Suffix A to G only

262469 (2) ①
600656 (2) ②

Alternatives
561195(4) UNF
1565(4) BSF
Suffix A to G only

553000 4 cyl
556449 6 cyl

Alternatives
234532 276201
Suffix A to G only

Alternatives
232557(2) Suffix A to G only
549229(2)
Export only

601790

276484

262468 ①
8407 ②

242522 (8)

232037

515845

Alternatives
GUJ116(2) Suffix A
GUJ117(2) Suffix 'B' onwards

622199

217400 (2)

Alternatives
561196(6) UHF
Suffix A to G only

1564(6) BSF

55705 (2)
Early models

Alternatives
540870
235592 Suffix A to G only

Alternatives
FRC2061 LH Stg

3294

515599

① For use with universal joint GUJ116
② For use with universal joint GUJ117

REMARKS

Front axle assembly FRC4396 RH Stg } 08"
Front axle assembly FRC2135 LH Stg
Front axle assembly FRC 2138 RH Stg } 109" 4 cyl
Front axle assembly FRC3995 LH Stg
Front axle assembly FRC 2060 RH Stg } 109" 6 cyl
Front axle assembly FRC2061 LH Stg

Front axle assemblies include differential, brakes, universal joints,
front hubs and steering track rod

1H 02

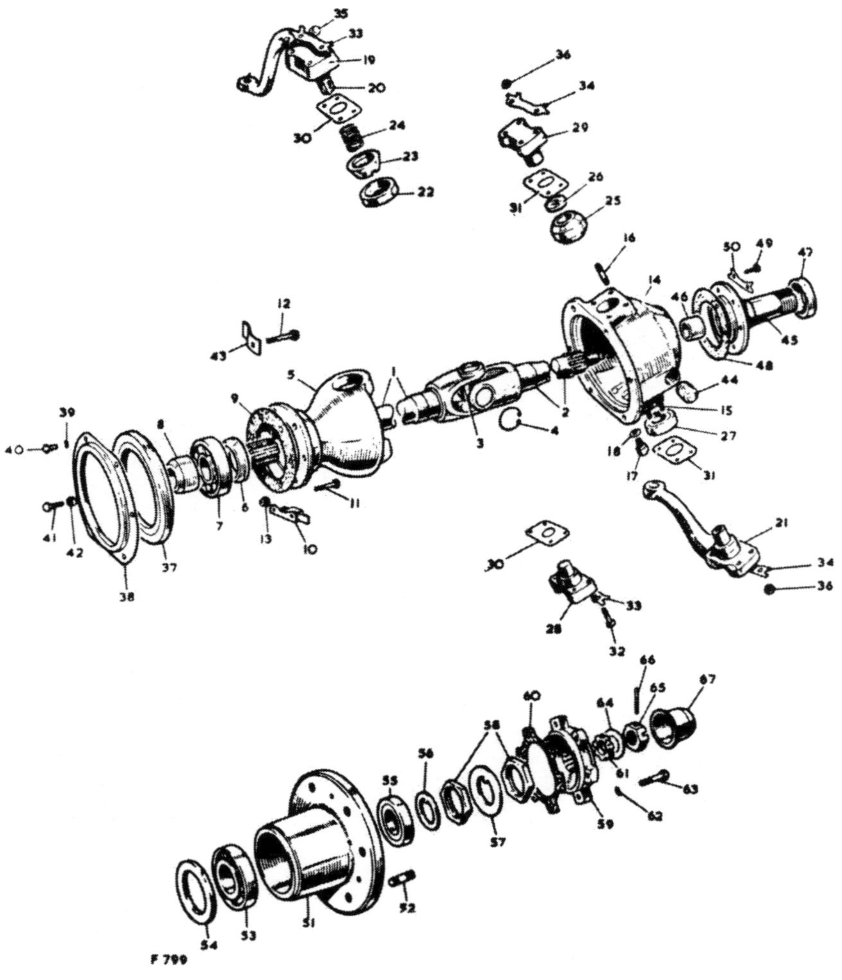

PLATE REF.	1 2 3 4 DESCRIPTION	QTY.	PART No.	REMARKS
	HALFSHAFT COMPLETE FOR FRONT AXLE, RH	1	269265	
	HALFSHAFT COMPLETE FOR FRONT AXLE, LH	1	269266	
1	Halfshaft only, RH	1	276719	
	Halfshaft only, LH	1	276720	
2	Stub shaft	2	242520	
3	Universal joint	2	GUJ118	
4	Circlip for journal	8	242522	
5	Housing for swivel pin bearing	2	539741	
6	Distance piece for bearing	2	244151	
7	Bearing for halfshaft	2	244150	
8	Retaining collar for bearing	2	90217398	
9	Joint washer for housing	2	GFG107	
10	Location stop for jack	1	90519206	
11	Bolt (⅜" BSF x 1¼")) Fixing stop	10	90576510	) For standard axle
12	Bolt (⅜" BSF x 1⅜")) and housing	2	576521	) casing
	Bolt (⅜" BSF x 1⅜")) to front	10	576521	) For reinforced axle
	Bolt (⅜" BSF x 1½")) axle	2	576522	) casing
13	Self-locking nut (⅜" BSF)) casing	12	50526	
	HOUSING ASSEMBLY FOR SWIVEL PIN, LH	1	524874*)	For axles with ⅜" steering
	HOUSING ASSEMBLY FOR SWIVEL PIN, RH	1	524875*)	lever studs
	HOUSING ASSEMBLY FOR SWIVEL PIN, LH	1	FRC2075	) For axles with 7/16"
14	HOUSING ASSEMBLY FOR SWIVEL PIN, RH	1	FRC2074	) steering lever studs
	Special stud (⅜"), for steering lever and bracket	2	90508153	) For axles with pendant
	Stud (⅜"), for steering lever	6	90508152	) type ball joints
	Special stud (⅜"), for steering lever and bracket	8	90508153	) For axles with non-
	Stud (⅜"), for steering lever	8	90508152	) pendant type ball joints) and ⅜" studs
15	Special stud, 7/16" for steering lever and bracket	4	531043	) For axles with non-pendan) type ball joints and 7/16
16	Stud 7/16", steering lever	4	531494	) studs
	Set bolt (7/16" BSF x 1⅜") fixing steering lever	8	237357	)
17	Drain plug for housing	2	236070	) Not part of assemblies
18	Joint washer for drain plug	2	230511	) 531004/5
19	Swivel pin and steering lever complete, RH	1	274145 *	RH Stg)
	Swivel pin and steering lever complete, LH	1	274147 *	RH Stg)
	Swivel pin and steering lever complete, RH	1	274146 *	LH Stg) For axles with
	Swivel pin and steering lever complete, LH	1	274148 *	LH Stg) pendant type
20	Swivel pin only	2	239017	) ball joints
	Grooved pin fixing swivel pin	2	50453	)
	Swivel pin and steering lever complete, RH	1	90502710*	RH Stg)
	Swivel pin and steering lever complete, LH	1	502711 *	RH Stg) For axles with
	Swivel pin and steering lever complete, RH	1	90502713*	LH Stg) non-pendant type
	Swivel pin and steering lever complete, LH	1	502712 *	LH Stg) ball joints and) ⅜" studs
21	Swivel pin and steering lever complete, RH	1	530988	RH Stg) For axles with
	Swivel pin and steering lever complete, LH	1	530989	RH Stg) non-pendant type
	Swivel pin and steering lever complete, RH	1	530990	LH Stg) ball joints and
	Swivel pin and steering lever complete, LH	1	530991	LH Stg) 7/16" studs
	'O' ring for steering levers	2	531433	For axles with non-pendant type ball joints

* NO LONGER SERVICED

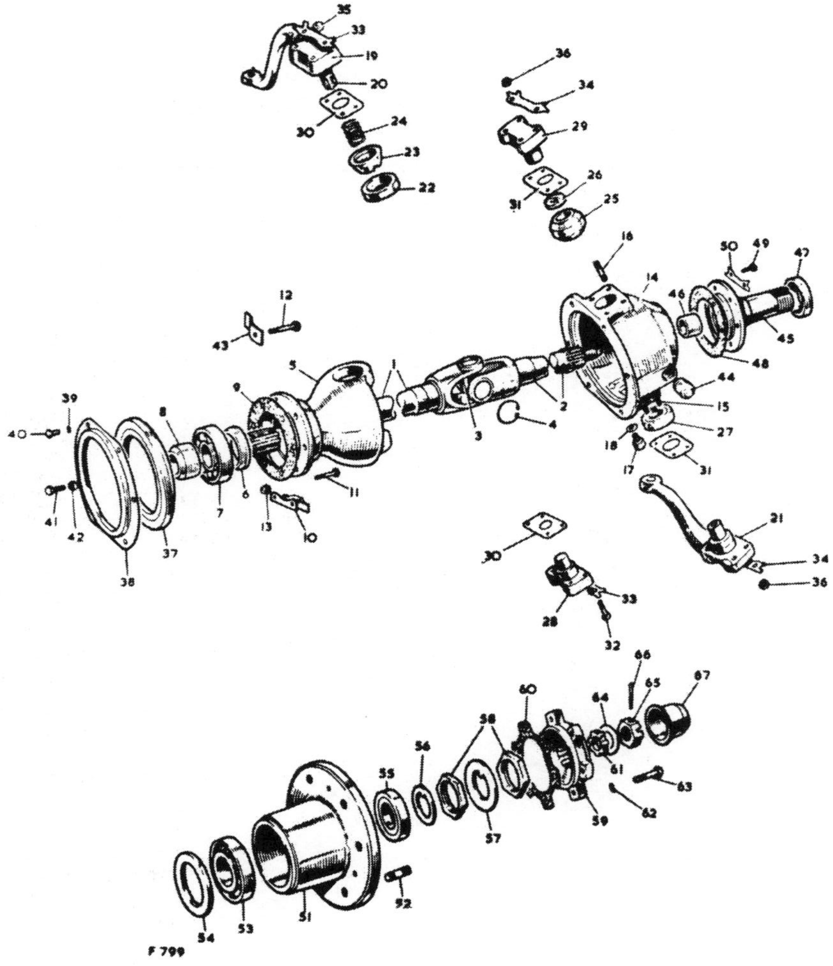

F799

PLATE REF.	1 2 3 4 DESCRIPTION	QTY.	PART No.	REMARKS
22	Cone seat for swivel pin, top	2	230858	) Cone and spring type
23	Cone bearing for swivel pin, top	2	238553	) steering damping. Up to
24	Spring for cone bearing	2	242742	) axles numbered 24109240) 88 RH Stg, 25107785 109) RH Stg, 24405088 88LH Stg,) 25404199 109 LH Stg
25	Railko bush and housing	2	539742	) Bush and thrust washer
26	Thrust washer for swivel pin	2	528702	) type steering damping.) From axles numbered) 24109241 88 RH Stg) 25107786 109 RH Stg) 24405089 88 LH Stg) 25404200 109 LH Stg onwards
27	Bearing for swivel pin, bottom	2	217268	
	Swivel pin and bracket complete	2	217421*	For axles with pendant type ball joints
	Swivel pin and bracket complete	2	90502714*	For axles with non-pendant type ball joints and ⅜" studs. Cone and spring type steering damping
28	Swivel pin and bracket complete	2	530992*	For axles with non-pendant type ball joints and 7/16" studs. Cone and spring type steering damping
29	Swivel pin upper complete	2	576583	For axles with non-pendant type ball joints and 7/16" studs. Bush and thrust washer type steering damping.
	Shim .003")	As reqd	230007	)
30	Shim .005")	As reqd	217453	) For axles with ⅜" studs
	Shim .010")	As reqd	217454	)
	Shim .030") For swivel pin	As reqd	217455	)
	Shim .003") bearing	As reqd	530984	)
	Shim .005")	As reqd	530985	) For axles with 7/16"
	Shim .010")	As reqd	530986	) Studs
	Shim .030")	As reqd	530987	)
32	Set bolt (⅜" BSF x 1⅜")) Fixing	8	576521	For axles with pendant type ball joints
	) swivel			
33	Locker) pin	8	270287	For axles with ⅜" studs
34	Locker) to	8	531001	For axles with 7/16" studs
35	Nut (⅜" BSF)) swivel	8	2827	For axles with pendant type ball joints
	) pin			
	Nut (⅜" BSF)) housing	16	2827	For axles with non-pendant type ball ioints and ⅜" studs
36	Nut (7/16" BSF))	8	594104	For axles with non-pendant type ball joints and 7/16" studs

* NO LONGER SERVICED

PLATE REF.	1 2 3 4 DESCRIPTION	QTY.	PART No.	REMARKS
37	Oil seal for swivel pin bearing housing	2	GHS1003	
38	Retainer for oil seal	2	235968	
39	Spring washer)	10	GHF331	
40	Set bolt (¼" BSF x ½"))	10	237139	
	Plain washer)	10	RTC609	
41	Adjustable lock stop bolt) Fixing	2	250696	
42	Locknut (¼" BSF) for stop bolt) retainer) to) swivel	2	3819	4 off on 109 and when 7.00 x 16, or 8.20 x 15 tyres are fitted
43	Lock stop plate) pin housing	2	508175	
44	Oil filler plug for swivel housing	2	3292	
45	STUB AXLE ASSEMBLY	2	599826	
46	Bush for driving shaft	2	217354	For early type stub axle
47	Distance piece for inner bearing	2	599698	
48	Joint washer, stub axle to swivel pin housing	2	GFG108	
49	Set bolt (⅜" BSF x 1")) Fixing stub axle to	12	237339	
50	Locker) swivel pin housing	6	277311	
51	FRONT HUB ASSEMBLY	2	561889	
52	Stud for road wheel) 9/16" BSF x 1.21/32"	10	561590	Plain] Alter-
	Stud for road wheel) overall length	10	561886	Serrated] natives
53	Bearing for front hub, inner	2	GHB162	
54	Oil seal for inner bearing	2	GHS202	
55	Bearing for front hub, outer	2	GHB163	
56	Key washer)	2	217352	
57	Locker) Fixing front hub bearing	2	217353	
58	Special nut)	4	90217355	
59	Driving member complete for front hub	2	571235	Grease-packed type
	Joint washer) For driving	2	232038	] Early models
	Oil filler plug) member	2	556204	] with oil filled hub
60	Joint washer for driving member	2	GFG106	
61	Oil seal for stub shaft	2	GHS1002	
62	Spring washer) Fixing driving	12	GHF333	
63	Set bolt (⅜" BSF x 1.19/32")) member to front) hub	12	215331	
64	Plain washer) Fixing	2	571922	
65	Slotted nut) driving member	2	3259	
66	Split pin) to driving shaft	2	PS608101	
67	Hub cap, front	2	219098	
	Swivel pin stud conversion kit	1	532329	To convert ⅜" stud to 7/16" stud on non-pendant type steering levers only
	Swivel pin conversion kit	1	532268	To convert cone and sprin steering damping to bush and thrust washer type

PLATE REF.	1 2 3 4 DESCRIPTION	QTY.	PART No.	REMARKS
	REAR AXLE ASSEMBLY	1	FRC3400	88 See note ①
	[REAR AXLE ASSEMBLY	1	591544 *	109 Rover type)
	[No longer available, replaced by:-			) Up to
	REAR AXLE CONVERSION KIT	1	RTC2464	109 2¼ litre) vehicle
	REAR AXLE CONVERSION KIT	1	RTC2465	109 2.6 litre) suffix 'H'
	REAR AXLE ASSEMBLY	1	591316 *	109 ENV type. Optional ②
1	Rear axle casing complete	1	622195	88
	Rear axle casing complete	1	622197	109 Rover type
	Rear axle casing complete	1	533567	109 ENV type. Optional
	Special bolt (⅜"BSF x 1.3/16")) Fixing	4	1565	) Bolt type)
	Special bolt (⅜"BSF x 1.11/16")) differential	16	1564 *	) fixing) Rover type
2	Special stud (⅜"UNF x 1¼")) housing	4	561195	)Stud type) axles
3	Special stud (⅜"UNF x 1⅜")) to	6	561196	)fixing)
	Set bolt (⅜" UNF x 1⅜")) axle	10	255248	)ENV type axle
	Spring washer) casing	10	GHF333	)109 Optional
4	Dowel locating differential housing	2	55705	Early type axles
5	Breather complete for rear axle	1	515845	
6	Drain plug for rear axle casing	1	235592	
7	Joint washer for drain plug	1	515599	
8	Rear axle shaft, RH	1	591378	) Rover type
9	Rear axle shaft, LH	1	591379	) axles
10	Rear axle shaft, RH	1	533579	) ENV type axle
11	Rear axle shaft, LH	1	533580	) 109 Optional
12	Rear hub bearing sleeve	2	599828	
13	Distance piece for bearing sleeve	2	599698	
14	Joint washer, bearing sleeve to axle casing	2	GFG103	
15	REAR HUB ASSEMBLY	2	561889	)Vehicle
16	Stud for road wheel) 9/16" BSF x 1.21/32"	10	561590	Plain)Alter-)suffix
	Stud for road wheel) overall length	10	561886	Serrated)natives)A to G
	REAR HUB ASSEMBLY	2	576844	)From vehicle suffix H
	Stud for road wheel 16 mm	10	576825	)onwards
17	Hub bearing, inner	2	GHB162	
18	Oil seal for inner bearing	2	GHS202	
19	Hub bearing, outer	2	GHB163	

① Also required:

Adaptor bracket for tee-piece	1	577731	
Bolt ¼" UNF x ⅜"	1	255202	
Plain washer	1	WB106041	

② For replacement of complete rear axle assy - See page 2L 06

* NO LONGER SERVICED

REAR AXLE AND PROPELLER SHAFT

GROUP E   REAR AXLE AND PROPELLER SHAFT

PLATE REF.	1	2	3	4	DESCRIPTION	QTY.	PART No.	REMARKS
20	Key washer				} Fixing	2	217352	
21	Special nut				} hub	4	90217355	
22	Locker				} bearing	2	217353	
23	Driving member for rear hub					2	571235	Grease-packed type, Rover axles
	Driving member for rear hub					2	571711	Grease-packed type, ENV axle. 109 Optional
25	Joint washer for driving member					2	GFG106	
26	Filler plug for driving member					2	556204	Early models with
27	Joint washer for filler plug					2	230380	oil filled hub
28	Oil seal for rear axle shaft					2	GHS1002	Rover type axles
29	Set bolt (⅜" BSF x 1.19/32")				} Fixing driving	12	215331	
30	Spring washer				} member to rear hub	12	GHF333	
31	Plain washer				} Fixing	2	571922	} Rover type axles
32	Slotted nut				} axle shaft to	2	3259	
33	Split pin				} driving member	2	PS608101	
34	Circlip					2	549473	ENV type axle
35	'O' ring					2	GHS1007	109 Optional
36	Hub cap, rear					2	219098	
37	PROPELLER SHAFT ASSEMBLY, REAR					1	553001	88 4-cyl } Rover
	PROPELLER SHAFT ASSEMBLY, REAR					1	553002	109 4-cyl } type
	PROPELLER SHAFT ASSEMBLY, REAR					1	556450	109 6-cyl } axles
	PROPELLER SHAFT ASSEMBLY, REAR					1	533639	109 4-cyl } ENV type axle
	PROPELLER SHAFT ASSEMBLY, REAR					1	591279	109 6-cyl } Optional
	PROPELLER SHAFT ASSEMBLY, REAR					1	591279	109 4-cyl } Salisbury type
	PROPELLER SHAFT ASSEMBLY, REAR					1	591283	109 6-cyl } axle from vehicle Suffix 'H' onwards
38	Splined stub shaft for propeller shaft					1	601790	Export only
39	Splined end				} For propeller	2	262468	For use with Universal
	Flange				} shaft	2	262469	Joint Part No. GUJ116
40	Splined end				} shaft	1	8407	For use with Universal
	Flange					2	600656	Joint Part No. GUJ117
41	Universal Joint					2	GUJ116	} Alternatives
42	Universal Joint					2	GUJ117	} Alternatives
43	Circlip for universal joint					8	242522	
	Grease nipple for universal joint, ¼" BSF					2	232557	} Alternatives
	Grease nipple for universal joint, ¼" UNF					2	549229	} Alternatives
44	Grease nipple for shaft sleeve					1	234532	Straight type. } Alter-
	Grease nipple for shaft sleeve					1	276201	Angled }natives
45	Joint washer for nipple					1	232032	type
	Bolt (⅜" UNF x 1⅜")				} Fixing	8	509045P	
46	Self-locking nut (⅜" UNF)				} propellor shaft	8	GHF273	

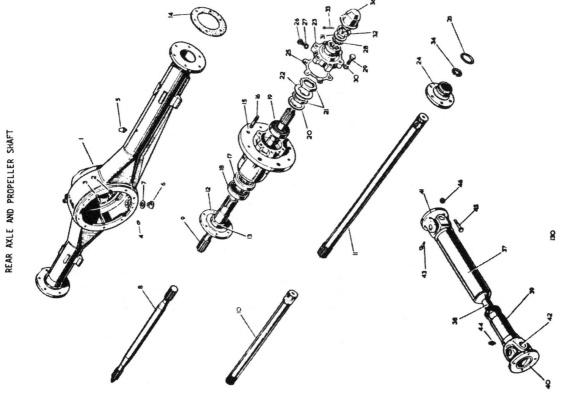

REAR AXLE AND PROPELLER SHAFT

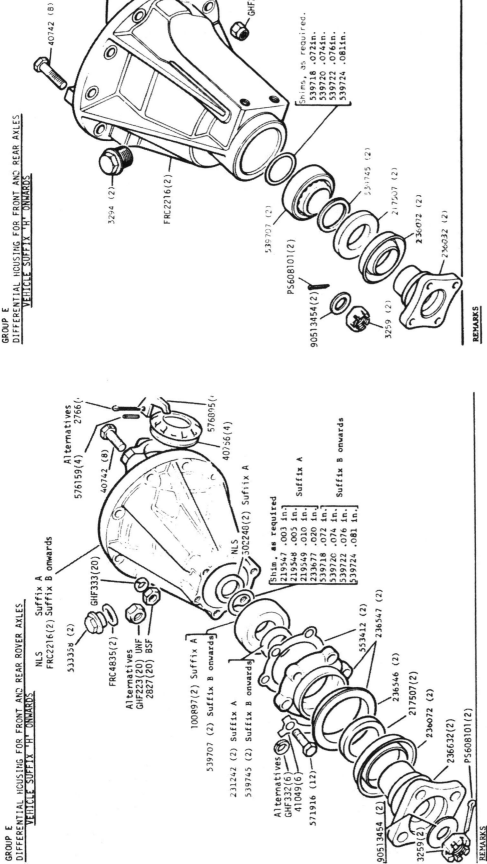

GROUP E
DIFFERENTIAL CROWN WHEEL AND BEVEL PINION FOR FRONT AND REAR ROVER AXLES.

80

This page is intentionally left blank

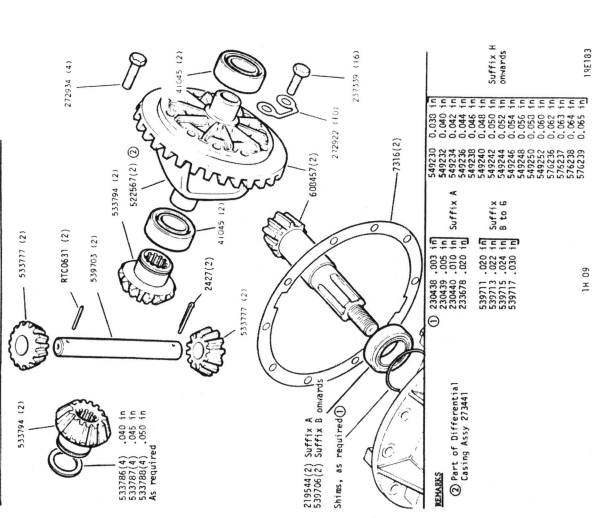

533794 (2)

272934 (4)

41045 (2)

533777 (2)

RTC0631 (2)

533794 (2)

522567(2) ②

539703 (2)

41045 (2)

2427(2)

533777 (2)

533777 (2)

608457(2)

272922 (16)

237359 (16)

7316(2)

533794 (2)
533786(4) .040 in
533787(4) .045 in
533788(4) .050 in
As required

219544(2) Suffix A
539706(2) Suffix B onwards

Shims, as required ①

①					
230438	.003 in				
230439	.005 in				
230440	.010 in	Suffix A			
233678	.020 in				
539711	.020 in				
539713	.022 in	Suffix			
539715	.024 in	B to G			
539717	.030 in				

549230	0.038 in
549232	0.040 in
549234	0.042 in
549236	0.044 in
549238	0.046 in
549240	0.048 in
549242	0.050 in
549244	0.052 in
549246	0.054 in
549248	0.056 in
549250	0.058 in
549252	0.060 in
576236	0.062 in
576237	0.063 in
576238	0.064 in
576239	0.065 in

Suffix H onwards

REMARKS
② Part of Differential
Casing Assy 273441

1H 09

19E183

DIFFERENTIAL, REAR, ENV TYPE AXLE, 109 OPTIONAL

1H 10

DIFFERENTIAL, REAR, ENV TYPE AXLE, 109 OPTIONAL

PLATE REF.	1	2	3	4	DESCRIPTION	QTY.	PART No.	REMARKS
					DIFFERENTIAL ASSEMBLY, 4.7 RATIO	1	533568	*
1					Crown wheel and bevel pinion	1	549493	
2					Differential casing	1	600901	
3					Set bolt (7/16" UNF x 1") } Fixing crownwheel to differential casing	12	SH607081	
4					Locking plate	6	549460	*
5					Set bolt (7/16" UNF x 1¼") } Fixing differential casing halves together	8	BH607141	
6					Locking plate, double tyoe	4	549464	
7					Differential wheel	2	549461	
8					Differential pinion	4	549462	
9					Spindle for pinion	1	549463	
10					Spherical differential pinion washer	4	549466	
11					Differential wheel washer	2	549465	
12					Taper roller bearing for differential	2	549457	
13					Differential bearing adjuster	2	549411	*
14					Locking plate } For bearing adjuster	2	549447	*
15					Set bolt (¼" UNC x ½") } adjuster	2	SH504041	
16					Nose piece and bearing cap complete	1	600902	*
17					Special set bolt, fixing bearing cap	4	549409	
18					Bearing for bevel pinion, nose end	1	549417	
19					Retaining washer } Fixing bearing to nose piece and bevel pinion	1	2228	
					Alum. rivet (⅜" x 1½")	1	4560	
20					Circlip	1	549419	
21					Bearing for bevel pinion	2	549420	
22					Spacer .370"	As reqd	549425	
					Spacer .373"	As reqd	549427	
					Spacer .376"	As reqd	549429	
					Spacer .379" } For pinion	As reqd	549431	
					Spacer .382" shaft	As reqd	549433	
					Spacer .385" bearing	As reqd	549435	
					Spacer .388" adjustment	As reqd	549437	
					Spacer .391"	As reqd	549439	
					Spacer .394"	As reqd	549441	
					Spacer .397"	As reqd	549443	
					Spacer .400"	As reqd	549445	
23					Bevel pinion housing complete	1	549413	
24					Oil seal for pinion	1	549412	
25					Mudshield for bevel pinion bearing housing	1	549454	
26					Mudshield for driving flange	1	549453	*
27					Driving flange for bevel pinion	1	549421	*
28					Special nut (⅞" UNF), fixing driving flange to bevel pinion	1	549448	*
29					Shim .002" } For differential bearing housing	As reqd	549414	*
					Shim .003"	As reqd	549415	
					Shim .010" } adjustment	As reqd	549416	
30					Set bolt (⅜" UNF x 1½") } Fixing pinion housing to nose piece	8	255248	
31					Shakeproof washer	8	GHF323	

* NO LONGER SERVICED

1H 10

81

DIFFERENTIAL, REAR, ENV TYPE AXLE 109 OPTIONAL

1H 11

GROUP E   DIFFERENTIAL, REAR, ENV TYPE AXLE 109 OPTIONAL

PLATE REF.	1	2	3	4	DESCRIPTION	QTY.	PART No.	REMARKS
32					Joint washer, differential to axle casing	1	533645*	
33					Set bolt (⅜" UNF x 1⅛") } Fixing differential to axle casing	10	255248	
34					Spring washer	10	GHF333	

* NO LONGER SERVICED

1H 11

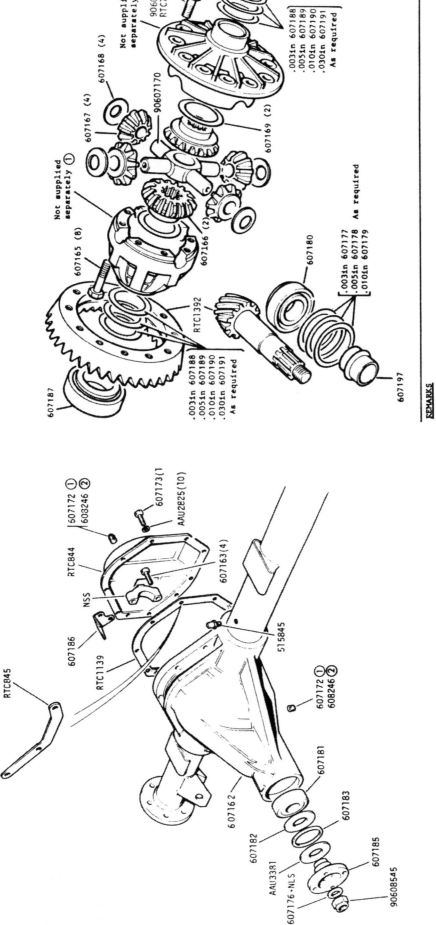

GROUP E
Rear Differential Crown Wheel and Pinion – 109inch from vehicle suffix 'H' onwards

Not supplied separately ①

90607193(12) ②
RTC773(12) ③

607168 (4)

607167 (4)

90607170

607169 (2)

607187

.003in 607188
.005in 607189
.010in 607190
.030in 607191
As required

Not supplied separately ①

607165 (8)

607166 (2)

607180

.003in 607177
.005in 607178   As required
.010in 607179

RTC1392

.003in 607188
.005in 607189
.010in 607190
.030in 607191
As required

607197

607187

REMARKS

① Differential case less gears 607164

② Course thread

③ Fine thread

1H 12

GROUP E
Rear Axle Casing – 109inch from Vehicle Suffix 'H' onwards

607172 ①
608246 ②

607173(1

AAU2825(10)

RTC844

607163(4)

NSS

607186

RTC1139

RTC845

515845

607172 ①
608246 ②

607181

607162

607183

607182

AAU3381

607176-NLS

607185

90608545

Rear axle assembly FRC4398 Salisbury type

Rear axle assembly less hubs, brake units and axle shafts 607247

① Square head | Alternatives
② Recessed head |

1H 12

83

GROUP E
SUSPENSION - Front and rear shock absorbers

GROUP E
Rear Hub and Axleshaft - 109inch from vehicle suffix 'H' onwards

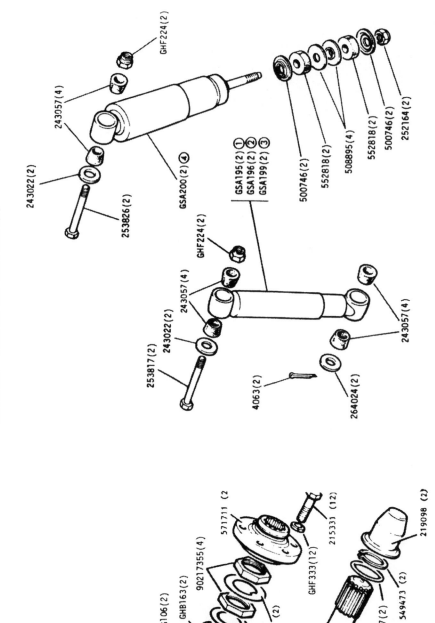

GHF224(2)
243057(4)
243022(2)
253826(2)
GSA200(2) ④

GSA195(2) ①
GSA196(2) ②
GSA199(2) ③

500746(2)
552818(2)
508895(4)
552818(2)
500746(2)
252164(2)

GHF224(2)
243057(4)
243022(2)
253817(2)
4063(2)
264024(2)
243057(4)

1H 14

571711 (2
90217355(4)
215331 (12)
GHF333(12)
GHB163(2)
GFG106(2)
217353 (2)
217352 (2)
219098 (2)
GHB162(2)
549473 (2)
576844 (2)
GHS1007(2)
599698(2)
576825 (10)
GHS202(2)
599828(2)
GFG103(2)
576767
576768

1H 13

REMARKS
① 88in Front
② 109in Front
③ 88in Rear
④ 109in Rear

GROUP E
SUSPENSION - Rear road spring

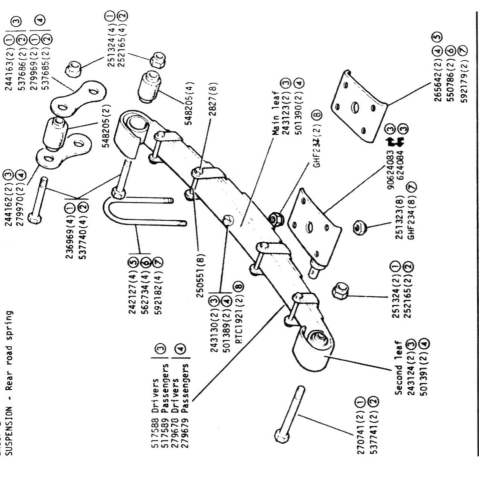

244163(2) ③
537686(2) ②
279969(2) ①
537685(2) ②
251324(4) ①
252165(4) ②

244162(2) ③
279970(2) ④
236969(4) ①
537740(4) ②
548205(2)
548205(4)
2827(8)
Main leaf
243123(2) ③
501390(2) ④
GHF232(2) ⑧
265642(2) ④
550786(2) ⑥
592179(2) ⑦
90624083
624084
251323(8)
GHF234(8) ⑧
242127(4) ⑤
562734(4) ⑥
592182(4) ⑦
250551(8)
243130(2) ③
501389(2) ④
RTC1921(2) ⑧
251324(2) ①
252165(2) ②

517588 Drivers ③
517589 Passengers
279670 Drivers ④
279679 Passengers

Second leaf
243124(2) ③
501391(2) ④

270741(2) ①
537741(2) ②

Part numbers of road springs are stamped on underside of 3rd or bottom leaf
① ¼in BSF - Vehicle suffix A
② 9/16in UNF - From vehicle suffix B onwards   ⑧ Metric
③ 88in
④ 109in
⑤ Rover type axle
⑥ ENV type axle - 109 optional
⑦ Salisbury type axle - 109 only from vehicle suffix 'H' onwards

1H 15

GROUP E
SUSPENSION - Front road spring

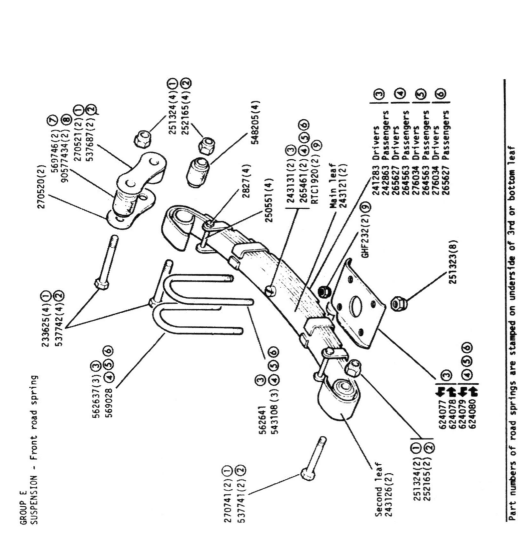

270520(2)
569746(2) ⑦
90577434(2) ⑧
270521(2) ①
537687(2) ②
251324(4) ①
252165(4) ②

233625(4) ①
537742(4) ②
548205(4)
2827(4)
250551(4)
562637(3) ③
569028 ④⑤⑥
562641 ③
543108(3) ④⑤⑥
243131(2) ③
265461(2) ④⑤⑥
RTC1920(2) ⑨
Main leaf
243121(2)
GHF232(2) ⑨

241283 Drivers ③
242863 Passengers
265627 Drivers ④
264563 Passengers
276034 Drivers ⑤
264563 Passengers
276034 Drivers ⑥
265627 Passengers

251323(8)

624077
624078
624079
624080

251324(2) ①
252165(2) ②

Second leaf
243126(2)

270741(2) ①
537741(2) ②

Part numbers of road springs are stamped on underside of 3rd or bottom leaf
① ¼in BSF Vehicle suffix A
② 9/16in UNF From vehicle suffix B onwards
③ 88in Petrol
④ 88in Diesel and 109in Petrol, 4 cyl and 6 cyl
⑤ 109in Petrol 6 cyl
⑥ 109in Diesel
⑦ All 88". 109" up to suffix G, 1.187" o/d
⑧ 109", from suffix H, 1.5" o/d
⑨ Metric

1H 15

GROUP E
TYRES

Dunlop T29A
650 X 16
750 X 16

Dunlop RK3
750 X 16
Avon Ranger
750 X 16

Michelin XZY
750 X 16

Dunlop Road
Trak Major
700 X 15
750 X 16 6 ply
750 X 16 8 ply

Goodyear
Sure Grip
600 X 16

Michelin
Sahara
750 X 16

Dunlop RK3
650 X 16

Goodyear
All Service
750 X 16

Michelin XY
750 X 16

1H 16

GROUP E
ROAD WHEEL - Tyre and Inner Tube

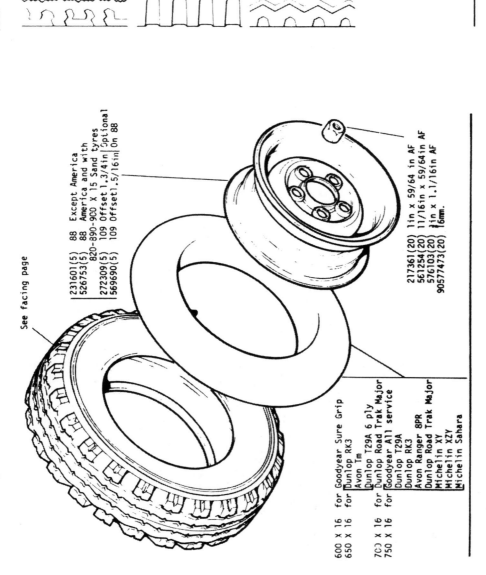

See facing page

231601(5)	88	Except America
526753(5)	88	America and with
		820-890-900 X 15 Sand tyres
272309(5)	109	Offset 1.3/4in Optional
569690(5)	109	Offset 1.5/16in On 88

217361(20) 1in x 59/64 in AF
561254(20) 11/16in x 59/64in AF
576103(20) 1in x 1.1/16in AF
90577473(20) 16mm.

600 X 16 for Goodyear Sure Grip
650 X 16 for Dunlop RK3
                Avon Tm
700 X 16 for Dunlop T29A 6 ply
750 X 16 for Dunlop Road Trak Major
                Goodyear All service
                Dunlop T29A
                Dunlop RK3
                Avon Ranger 8PR
                Dunlop Road Trak Major
                Michelin XY
                Michelin XZY
                Michelin Sahara

1H 16

GROUP F   STEERING COLUMN

PLATE REF.	1 2 3 4	QTY.	PART No.		DESCRIPTION	REMARKS
	STEERING UNIT ASSEMBLY	1	509449*	RH Stg		With centre horn push. For 5/16" diameter support bracket bolts. Up to vehicle suffix 'A'
	STEERING UNIT ASSEMBLY	1	509448*	LH Stg		
	STEERING UNIT ASSEMBLY	1	537541	RH Stg		With centre horn push. For ⅜" diameter support bracket bolts. Vehicle suffix 'B' only
	STEERING UNIT ASSEMBLY	1	537542	LH Stg		
	STEERING UNIT ASSEMBLY	1	551702	RH Stg		With centre horn push. For ⅜" diameter support bracket bolts. From vehicle suffix 'C' onwards
	STEERING UNIT ASSEMBLY	1	551703	LH Stg		
1	Steering box assembly	1	515508*	RH Stg		Dowel type. For 5/16" diameter support bracket bolts. Up to vehicle suffix 'A'
	Steering box assembly	1	515509*	LH Stg		
	Steering box assembly	1	541899	RH Stg		Dowel type. For ⅜" diameter support bracket bolts. From vehicle suffix 'B' onwards
	Steering box assembly	1	541900	LH Stg		
2	Bush for rocker shaft	1	261850			
3	Outer column, overall length 23½"	1	271364*			Models with side horn push.
	Outer column, overall length 24½"	1	600468*			Models with centre horn push. Up to vehicle suffix 'B' inclusive
	Outer column	1	600984			Models with centre horn push. From vehicle suffix 'C' onwards
4	Joint washer, steel	As reqd	261858			
5	Joint washer, paper	As reqd	261857			
	Joint washer, plastic	As reqd	271379			
	Bolt (5/16" UNC x 29/32")	4	271380			Fixing outer column
	Spring washer	4	GHF332			
6	Inner column	1	271367*	RH Stg		Models with side horn push
	Inner column	1	271368	LH Stg		
	Inner column	1	518676*	RH Stg		Models with centre horn push.
	Inner column	1	518677*	LH Stg		
	Inner column and main nut assembly	1	AEU1168	RH Stg		Vehicle suffix A and B
	Inner column and main nut assembly	1	AEU1083	LH Stg		
7	Inner column and main nut assembly	1	90577193*	RH Stg		Models with centre Horn push. From vehicle suffix 'C' onwards
	Inner column	1	90577194*	LH Stg		
	Inner column and main nut assembly	1	AEU1082	RH Stg		
	Inner column and main nut assembly	1	AEU1160	LH Stg		

* NO LONGER SERVICED

1I 02

STEERING COLUMN

1I 02

87

GROUP F   STEERING COLUMN

PLATE REF.	1 2 3 4 — DESCRIPTION	QTY.	PART No.	REMARKS
8	Bush for inner column	1	501245	Part of outer column
9	Spring ring for inner column bush	1	501246	Up to vehicle suffix 'B' inclusive
10	Bearing for inner column	1	RTC324	From vehicle suffix 'C' onwards
11	Dust shield for inner column	1*	267016	Models with side horn push
12	MAIN NUT ASSEMBLY	1	261862	RH Stg
	MAIN NUT ASSEMBLY	1	261865	LH Stg
	Set bolt (2BA x 3/8") } Fixing	2*	234603	
	Lockwasher for bolt } retainer	2*	261868	
13	Steel ball (3/8") for main nut	12	1643	
14	Roller for main nut	1	261869	
15	Adjustable ball race	2	271384	
16	Steel balls (9/32") for adjustable race	20	BLS109	
17	Rocker shaft	1	271372	
18	Adjuster screw for rocker shaft	1	261873	
19	Locknut for adjuster screw	1	261874	
20	Oil seal for rocker shaft	1	271013	
21	Washer for rocker shaft oil seal	1	271014	
22	End plate	1	271378	
23	Joint washer, steel	As reqd	261858	
24	Joint washer, paper	As reqd	261857	
	Joint washer, plastic	As reqd	271379	
25	Bolt (5/16" UNC x 29/32") } Fixing	4	271380	
26	Spring washer } end plate	4	GHF332	
27	Side cover plate	1*	272181	Plain type
	Side cover plate	1	261880	Dowel type
28	Joint washer for side cover plate	1	515848	
29	Bolt (5/16" UNC x 1.1/16") } Fixing side	4	515849	
30	Spring washer } cover plate	4	GHF332	
31	Oil filler plug	1	271382	
32	Special nut } Fixing	1	271386	
33	Lockwasher } drop arm	1	NT612061	
34	Steering drop arm	1	RTC623	
35	Rubber seal for steering column	1	595123	
36	Cover for steering column seal	1	MRC4867	
37	Screw (2BA x 3/8")	2	303997	
38	Special washer } Fixing cover and	2	77861	
39	Spring washer } seal to dash	2	303996	
40	Nut (2BA)	2	WM702001	
		2	RTC608	

* NO LONGER SERVICED

1I 03

1I 03

PLATE REF.	DESCRIPTION 1 2 3 4	QTY.	PART No.	REMARKS
41	Steering wheel	1*	90512322	Up to vehicle suffix 'B' inclusive
42	Steering wheel	1	NRC4346	From vehicle
43	Special spring washer	1	NRC3150	suffix 'C' onwards
44	Bolt (5/16" UNF x 2"))	1	BH605161	
45	Plain washer) Fixing	1	RTC613	Up to vehicle suffix 'B'
46	Nut (5/16" UNF)) steering	1	GHF201	inclusive
47	Tag washer) wheel	1	552572	From vehicle
48	Special nut)	1	552804	suffix 'C' onwards
49	Steering wheel centre cover	1*	268284	
50	Horn push bracket	1*	271496	
51	Clip for horn push bracket	1*	277560	
52	Yoke assembly for horn push bracket	1*	270724	
53	Nut (¼" BSF)) Fixing horn push	1	3819	
54	Shakeproof washer) bracket	1	78114	Models with side horn push
55	Horn push	1	90217279	
	Special screw) Fixing	2*	3279	
	Spring washer) horn push	2	WM704001	
	Nut (5BA)) to bracket	2*	4011	
56	Lead, horn push to junction box	1*	270961	
57	Horn push and centre cover for steering wheel	1	512352	Up to vehicle suffix 'B'
58	Horn push and centre cover for steering wheel	1	90575201	From vehicle suffix 'C' onwards — Models with centre horn push
59	Dust cover and horn contact	1	512359	Up to vehicle suffix 'B'
60	Dust cover and horn contact	1	552575	From vehicle suffix 'C' onwards
	Screw (2BA x 5/16"))	2*	67184	Up to vehicle
	Shakeproof washer) Fixing dust cover	2	WF702101	suffix 'B'
	Screw (2BA x ⅜")) to steering	2	77925	From vehicle
	Plain washer) wheel	2	3902	suffix 'C' onwards
61	Slip ring complete for horn contact	1	519753	
63	Cable cleat on steering column	1	240431	
	Dip switch	1	502087	Alternatives
65	Dip switch	1	RTC432	
	Screw (10 UNF x 1¼"))	2*	78316	UNF
	Spring washer)	2	WM702001	fixing
	Nut (10 UNF)) Fixing	2	HN2005	Alternatives
	Screw (2BA x ⅜")) dip switch	2*	78173	2BA
	Spring washer)	2	WM702001	fixing
	Nut (2BA))	2	RTC608	
66	Lead)	1*	514840	RH Stg 4-cylinder models — Up to vehicle suffix 'E'
	Lead)	1	531501	LH Stg
	Lead) Dip switch	1*	560533	RH Stg 6-cylinder models
	Lead) to	1*	560534	LH Stg
	Lead) junction box	1*	560968	RH Stg 4 and 6 cylinder models — From vehicle suffix 'F' onwards
	Lead)	1	531501	LH Stg

* NO LONGER SERVICED

PLATE REF.	DESCRIPTION 1 2 3 4	QTY.	PART No.	REMARKS
67	Grommet for lead in toe box floor	1	236389	
68	Clip fixing dip switch lead to floor	2	50639	
	Screw)	2	77941	5 off on LH Stg
	Spring washer) Fixing clip	2	WM702001	
	Nut (2BA))	2	RTC608	
69	Support bracket on dash	1*	302986	
	Bolt (5/16" UNF x ⅞"))	4	SH605051	
	Plain washer, small) Fixing	2	2266	
	Plain washer, large) support bracket	2	RTC604	
	Spring washer) to dash	4	GHF332	
	Nut (5/16" UNF))	4	GHF201	
70	Support bracket for steering column	1*	303701	
71	Packing piece for steering column support bracket	1*	332729	
72	Clip for steering column	1*	300715	Up to vehicle suffix 'C' inclusive
73	Rubber strip for clip	1	348747	
	Bolt (¼" UNF x ¾")) Fixing clip	2	255207	
	Spring washer) to support	2	GHF331	
	Nut (¼" UNF)) bracket	2	GHF200	
	Bolt (5/16" UNF x ⅞"))	2	255227	
	Bolt (5/16" UNF x ¾")) Fixing support	2	GHF120	
	Plain washer) bracket to	2	3966	
	Spring washer) dash bracket	4	GHF332	
	Nut (5/16" UNF))	4	GHF201	
74	Support bracket on dash	1*	348743	
	Bolt (5/16" UNF x ¾"))	4	GHF120	
	Plain washer, small) Fixing	6	3830	
	Plain washer, large) support bracket	2	RTC604	
	Spring washer) to dash	4	GHF332	
	Nut (5/16" UNF))	4	GHF201	
75	Clamp, upper, for steering column	1*	348744	
	Bolt (5/16" UNF x ¾"))	3	GHF120	From vehicle suffix 'D'
	Plain washer) Fixing upper clamp	3	3830	onwards
	Spring washer) to support bracket	3	GHF332	
	Nut (5/16" UNF))	3	GHF201	
76	Clamp, lower, for steering column	1	346715	
77	Rubber strip for clamp	1	348747	
	Bolt (¼" UNF x ⅞")) Fixing upper and	2	255208	
	Spring washer) lower clamps to	2	GHF331	
	Nut (¼" UNF)) steering column	2	GHF200	
	Support bracket, RH)	1*	277294	For 5/16" dia. steering box fixing bolts. Up to
78	Support bracket, LH) For steering box	1*	277295	vehicle suffix 'A'
	Support bracket, RH) on chassis	1*	537535	For ⅜" dia. steering box fixing bolts. From
	Support bracket, LH)	1	537533	vehicle suffix 'B' onwards
	Packing piece for support bracket	1	569522	LH Stg
79	Bolt (5/16" UNF x 3½"))	6	256233	
80	Plain washer, thin) Fixing	6	3830	
	Plain washer, thick) brackets to	6	WP185	
81	Spring washer) chassis frame	6	GHF332	
82	Nut (5/16" UNF)	6	GHF201	

* NO LONGER SERVICED

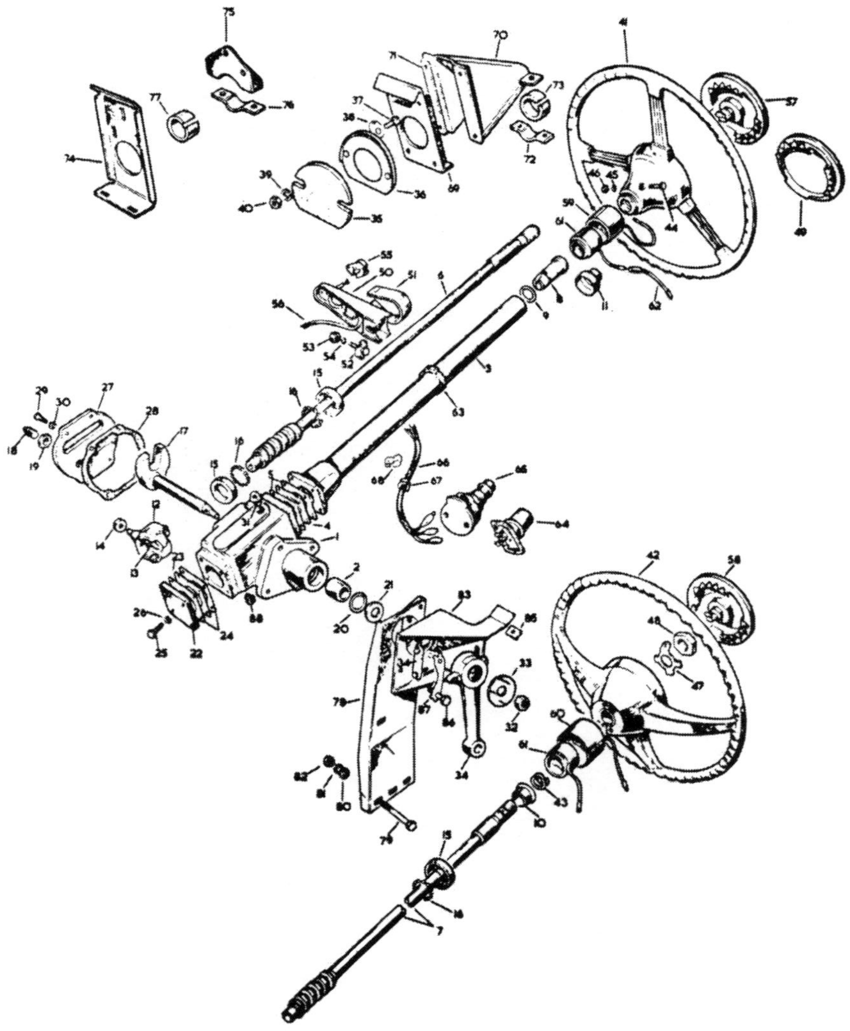

PLATE REF.	1 2 3 4	DESCRIPTION	QTY.	PART No.	REMARKS
83	Stiffener bracket	For steering box	1*	504276	RH Stg — For 5/16" diameter steering box fixing bolts. Up to vehicle suffix 'A'
	Stiffener bracket	For steering box	1*	504272	LH Stg — For 5/16" diameter steering box fixing bolts. Up to vehicle suffix 'A'
	Stiffener bracket	For steering box	1	90577264	RH Stg — For ⅜" diameter steering box fixing bolts. From vehicle suffix 'B' onwards
	Stiffener bracket	For steering box	1*	537539	LH Stg — For ⅜" diameter steering box fixing bolts. From vehicle suffix 'B' onwards
	Bolt (¼" UNF x 9/16")	Fixing stiffener bracket to front face toe box	4	255205	Alternatives to line below — RH Stg
	Plain washer	Fixing stiffener bracket to front face toe box	4	RTC609	Alternatives to line below — RH Stg
84	Bolt plate	Fixing stiffener bracket to front face toe box	2	395064	Alternative to 2 lines above — RH Stg
	Spring washer	Fixing stiffener bracket to front face toe box	4	GHF331	
	Nut (¼" UNF)	Fixing stiffener bracket to front face toe box	4	GHF200	
	Bolt (¼" UNF x 1")	Fixing stiffener bracket to top face of toe box	1	GHF101	3 off on LH Stg
	Plain washer	Fixing stiffener bracket to top face of toe box	1	RTC609	3 off on LH Stg
	Spring washer	Fixing stiffener bracket to top face of toe box	1	GHF331	3 off on LH Stg
	Nut (¼" UNF)	Fixing stiffener bracket to top face of toe box	1	GHF200	3 off on LH Stg
85	Shim washer	Fixing stiffener bracket to top face of toe box	As reqd	504279	RH Stg
	Shim washer	Fixing stiffener bracket to top face of toe box	As reqd	504275	LH Stg
	Bolt (5/16" UNF x 1⅜")	Fixing steering box to chassis support bracket	2	BH605111	5/16" fixings Up to vehicle suffix 'A' inclusive
	Set bolt (5/16" UNC x ¾")	Fixing steering box to chassis support bracket	1	SH505061	Except 109 LH Stg — 5/16" fixings Up to vehicle suffix 'A' inclusive
	Set bolt (5/16" UNC x ⅞")	Fixing steering box to chassis support bracket	1	SH505071	109 LH Stg — 5/16" fixings Up to vehicle suffix 'A' inclusive
	Locking plate	Fixing steering box to chassis support bracket	1*	517877	5/16" fixings Up to vehicle suffix 'A' inclusive
86	Set bolt (⅜" UNC x ⅞")	Fixing steering box to chassis support bracket	1	SH506071	5/16" fixings Up to vehicle suffix 'A' inclusive
87	Locking plate	Fixing steering box to chassis support bracket	1	90517878	5/16" fixings Up to vehicle suffix 'A' inclusive
88	Self-locking nut (5/16" UNF)	Fixing steering box to chassis support bracket	2	GHF242	5/16" fixings Up to vehicle suffix 'A' inclusive
	Bolt (⅜" UNF x 1⅜")	Fixing steering box to chassis support bracket	2	255050	⅜" fixings From vehicle suffix 'B' onwards
	Set bolt (⅜" UNC x ¾")	Fixing steering box to chassis support bracket	1	SH506061	Except 109 LH Stg — ⅜" fixings From vehicle suffix 'B' onwards
	Set bolt (⅜" UNC x ⅞")	Fixing steering box to chassis support bracket	1	SH506071	109 LH Stg — ⅜" fixings From vehicle suffix 'B' onwards
	Locking plate	Fixing steering box to chassis support bracket	1*	537543	⅜" fixings From vehicle suffix 'B' onwards
	Set bolt (⅜" UNC x ⅞")	Fixing steering box to chassis support bracket	1	SH506071	⅜" fixings From vehicle suffix 'B' onwards
	Locking plate	Fixing steering box to chassis support bracket	1	537544	⅜" fixings From vehicle suffix 'B' onwards
	Self-locking nut (⅜" UNF)	Fixing steering box to chassis support bracket	2	GHF243	⅜" fixings From vehicle suffix 'B' onwards

* NO LONGER SERVICED

GROUP F   STEERING RELAY AND LINKAGE

PLATE REF.	1	2	3	4	DESCRIPTION	QTY.	PART No.	REMARKS
					STEERING RELAY COMPLETE ASSEMBLY	1	NRC1269	
1					Housing for relay shaft	1	543972	
2					Shaft for steering relay levers	1	562875	
3					Split bush for housing, halves	4	537877	
4					Washer for spring	2	230760	
5					Spring for housing	1	230759	
6					Thrust washer for shaft	2	241388	
7					Distance piece for shaft	2*	230184	For early type shaft only
8					Oil seal for shaft	2	213340	
9					Retainer for oil seal	2	230294	
10					Joint washer for retainer	2	90624436	
11					Special bolt } Fixing retainer	8	544337	
12					Plain washer } to housing	8	RTC840	
13					Plug for oil hole	2	237138	For early type housing with oil plug hole
14					Joint washer for plug	2	GHF342	
15					Relay lever, upper	1	531040	
16					Bolt (7/16" UNF x 2¼") } Fixing lever	1	BX607181	
18					Self-locking nut (7/16" UNF) } to shaft	1	GHF224	
19					Bolt (5/16" UNF x 3½") } Fixing	2	BX605281	
20					Spring washer } housing to	2	564825	
21					Nut (5/16" UNF) } chassis frame	2	GHF201	
22					Flange plate for relay mounting	1	217694	
23					Set bolt (¼" UNF x ⅞") } Fixing flange plate	4	255206	
24					Spring washer } to chassis frame	4	GHF331	
25					Relay lever, lower	1	535286	
26					Bolt (7/16" UNF x 2¼") } Fixing lever	1	BX607181	
28					Self-locking nut (7/16" UNF) } to shaft	1	GHF224	
29					STEERING TRACK ROD ASSEMBLY	1	269267	For pendant type ball joints
					Steering track rod only	1	269269	
					STEERING TRACK ROD ASSEMBLY	1	608465	For non-pendant type ball joints
					Steering track rod only	1	526994	
30					BALL JOINT ASSEMBLY, RH THREAD	1	608464	Metric threads
31					BALL JOINT ASSEMBLY, LH THREAD	1	320902	
					Plain washer } Fixing	2	WC112081	
					Castle nut (12 mm) } ball joints	2	NC112041	
					Split pin } to levers	2	PS105281	
32					Rubber cover for ball joint	2	214649	
33					Spring ring, cover to body	2	214685	
34					Spring ring } Cover	2	90214684	
					Retainer } to ball	2	214662	
35					Plain washer } Fixing	2	RTC605	For early type ball joints with BSF or UNF threads
36					Castle nut (7/16" BSF) } ball joints	2	2822	Alternatives
					Castle nut (7/16" UNF) } to levers	2	276482	
37					Split pin	2	2393	
38					Clip for ball joint	2	577898	

* NO LONGER SERVICED

11 07

STEERING RELAY AND LINKAGE

11 07

91

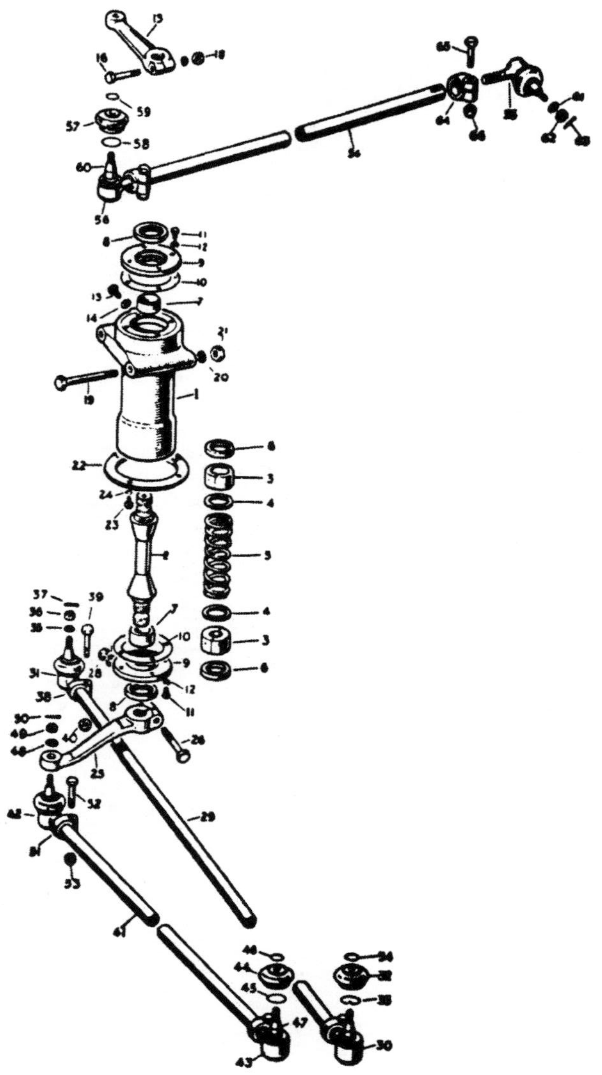

PLATE REF.	1 2 3 4 DESCRIPTION		QTY.	PART No.	REMARKS	
39	Bolt (¼" BSF x 1½")	Fixing ball joint clips	2	250517	BSF fixing	Alternatives
40	Self-locking nut (¼" BSF)		2	251320		
	Bolt (¼" UNF x 1⅞")		2	BH604161	UNF fixing	
	Plain washer		2	WB106041		
	Self-locking nut (¼" UNF)		2	252210		
41	STEERING DRAG LINK ASSEMBLY		1	RTC2547		
	Steering drag link only		1	NRC4609		
42	BALL JOINT ASSEMBLY, RH THREAD		1	608464	Metric threads	
43	BALL JOINT ASSEMBLY, LH THREAD		1	320902		
	Plain washer	Fixing ball joints to levers	2	WC112081		
	Castle nut (12 mm)		2	NC112041		
	Split pin		2	PS105281		
44	Rubber cover for ball joint		2	214649		
45	Spring ring, cover to body		2	214685		
46	Spring ring	Cover to ball	2	90214684		
47	Retainer		2	214662		
48	Plain washer	Fixing ball joints to levers	2	RTC605		For early type ball joints with BSF or UNF threads
49	Castle nut (7/16" BSF)		2	2822	Alter-natives	
	Castle nut (7/16" UNF)		2	276482		
50	Split pin		2	2393		
51	Clip for ball joint		2	577898		
52	Bolt (¼" BSF x 1½")	Fixing ball joint clips	2	250517	BSF fixing	Alternatives
53	Self-locking nut (¼" BSF)		2	251320		
	Bolt (¼" UNF x 1⅞")		2	BH604161	UNF fixing	
	Plain washer		2	WB106041		
	Self-locking nut (¼" UNF)		2	252210		
54	LONGITUDINAL STEERING TUBE ASSEMBLY		1	90608462		
	Longitudinal steering tube only		1	276784		
55	BALL JOINT ASSEMBLY, RH THREAD		1	608464	Metric thread	
56	BALL JOINT ASSEMBLY, LH THREAD		1	320902		
	Plain washer	Fixing ball joints to levers	2	WC112081		
	Castle nut (12 mm)		2	NC112041		
	Split pin		2	PS105281		
57	Rubber cover for ball joint		2	214649		
58	Spring ring, cover to body		2	214685		
59	Spring ring	Cover to ball	2	90214684		
60	Retainer		2	214662		
61	Plain washer	Fixing ball joints to levers	2	RTC605		For early type ball joints with BSF or UNF threads
62	Castle nut (7/16" BSF)		2	2822	Alter-natives	
	Castle nut (7/16" UNF)		2	276482		
63	Split pin		2	2393		
64	Clip for ball joint		2	577898		
65	Bolt (¼" BSF x 1½")	Fixing ball joint clips	2	250517	BSF fixing	Alternatives
66	Self-locking nut (¼" BSF)		2	251320		
	Bolt (¼" UNF x 1⅞")		2	BH604161	UNF fixing	
	Plain washer		2	WB106041		
	Self-locking nut (¼" UNF)		2	252210		

BRAKES, FOOT, FRONT AND REAR, 10", 88 MODELS

GROUP G BRAKES, FOOT, FRONT AND REAR, 10", 88 MODELS

PLATE REF. 1 2 3 4	DESCRIPTION	QTY.	PART No.	REMARKS
1	BRAKE ANCHOR PLATE ASSEMBLY, LH	2	515406	
	BRAKE ANCHOR PLATE ASSEMBLY, RH	2	515405	
4	Set bolt (¼" BSF x 1") } Fixing front anchor	12	237339	
5	Locker } plate to axle case	6	232416	
	Bolt (¼" BSF x 1¼") } Fixing rear anchor	12	576521	
	Self-locking nut (¼" BSF) } plate to axle case	12	251322	
6	BRAKE SHOE ASSEMBLY, AXLE SET, FRONT AND REAR	2	GBS728	For early type shoe with riveted linings.
	Lining complete with rivets	8*	241090	Riveted type lining for replacement of bonded originals
7	Linings and rivets, axle set, front and rear	2	AAU9942	Part of brake shoe
8	Spring post for brake shoe	4	232074	
9	Anchor for brake shoe	4	236993	
10	Special set screw fixing anchor	8	238542	
11	Locking plate for bolt	4	236995	
12	Pull-off spring for brake shoe	4	218983	
13	Pull-off spring for leading shoe	4	503981	
14	WHEEL CYLINDER ASSEMBLY, RH FRONT	1	GWC305	
	WHEEL CYLINDER ASSEMBLY, LH FRONT	1	GWC306	
	WHEEL CYLINDER ASSEMBLY, RH REAR	1	GWC1308	
	WHEEL CYLINDER ASSEMBLY, LH REAR	1	GWC1307	
15	Spring for piston, front	2	212919	
	Spring for piston, rear	2*	212943	
16	Washer for spring, front	4	232107	
	Washer for spring, rear	4	242117	
17	Bleed screw	4	556508	
18	Nut (5/16" UNF) } Fixing	8	GHF201	
19	Spring washer } wheel cylinder	8	WL600050	
20	Brake drum	4	591661	Chassis suffix A to G
	Brake drum	4	591039	From chassis suffix H onwards
21	Set screw fixing brake drum	12	1510	
	Wheel cylinder overhaul kit, front	1	275744	
	Wheel cylinder overhaul kit, rear	1	266687	

*NO LONGER SERVICED

1J 02

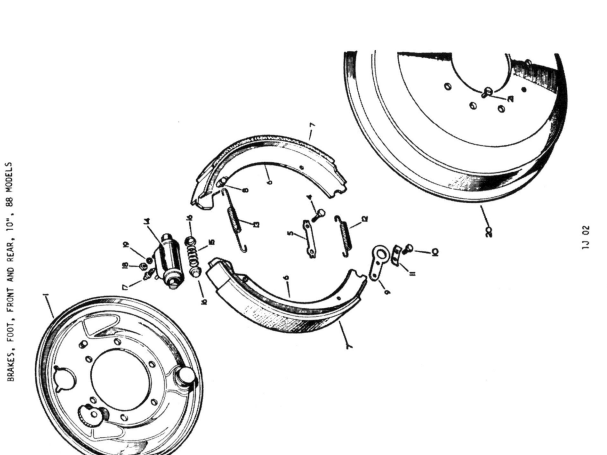

1J 02

93

GROUP G   BRAKES, FOOT, FRONT, 11" 109 4-CYLINDER MODELS

PLATE REF.	1 2 3 4	DESCRIPTION	QTY.	PART No.	REMARKS
1		Brake anchor plate, LH front	1	246565	
		Brake anchor plate, RH front	1	246566	
		Set bolt (⅜" BSF x 1")) Fixing anchor plate	12	237339	
		Locker) to axle case	6	277311	
2		Steady post and bush kit	6	607808	
4		Special nut fixing steady post	4	NT605061	
5		BRAKE SHOE ASSEMBLY, AXLE SET, FRONT			
		Lining complete with rivets	1	GBS729	For early type shoe with riveted linings
			4	246569	
6		Linings and rivets, axle set, front	1	AAU8471	Riveted type linings for replacement of bonded originals
7		Pull-off spring for brake shoe	4	234889	
8		WHEEL CYLINDER ASSEMBLY, LH FRONT	2	GWC303	
		WHEEL CYLINDER ASSEMBLY, RH FRONT	2	GWC304	
9		Spring (⅝" dia)) For	4	233211	Alternatives
		Spring (7/16" dia)) piston	4	600212	
10		Air excluder	4*	242463	Early models only with ⅝" diameter spring
11		Sealing ring for cylinder	4	505790	
12		Bleed screw	2	556508	
13		Spring washer) Fixing wheel	8	GHF332	
14		Nut (5/16" UNF)) cylinder	8	GHF201	
15		Connecting pipe for wheel cylinder	2	NRC5347	
16		Brake drum	2	516599	Chassis suffix A to G
		Brake drum	4	576973	From chassis suffix H onwards
17		Set screw fixing brake drum	6	1510	
		Wheel cylinder overhaul kit, front	1	266684	

* NO LONGER SERVICED

1J 03

K179

1J 03

94

BRAKES, FOOT, FRONT, 11" 109 6-CYLINDER MODELS

GROUP G   BRAKES, FOOT, FRONT, 11" 109 6-CYLINDER MODELS

PLATE REF. 1 2 3 4	DESCRIPTION	QTY.	PART No.	REMARKS
1	Brake anchor plate, LH front	1	600202	
	Brake anchor plate, RH front	1	600203	
	Set bolt (⅜" BSF x 1") } Fixing anchor plate	12	237339	
	Locker } to axle case	6	277311	
2	Steady post for brake shoe	4	607808	
4	Special nut fixing steady post	4	NT605061	
5	BRAKE SHOE ASSEMBLY, AXLE SET, FRONT	1	GBS730	
6	Linings and rivets, axle set, rear	1	AAU8469	
7	Pull-off spring for brake shoe	4	234889	
8	WHEEL CYLINDER ASSEMBLY, LH FRONT	2	GWC301	
	WHEEL CYLINDER ASSEMBLY, RH FRONT	2	GWC302	
9	Spring	4	600212	
10	Sealing ring for cylinder	4	505790	
11	Bleed screw	2	556508	
12	Spring washer } Fixing wheel	8	WL600050	
13	Special set bolt } cylinder	8	SH605041	
14	Connecting pipe for wheel cylinder	2	600206	
15	Brake drum	2	522593	Chassis suffix D to G
	Brake drum	2	576974	From chassis suffix H onwards
16	Set screw fixing brake drum	6	1510	
	Brake wheel cylinder overhaul kit, front	1	600210	

1J 04

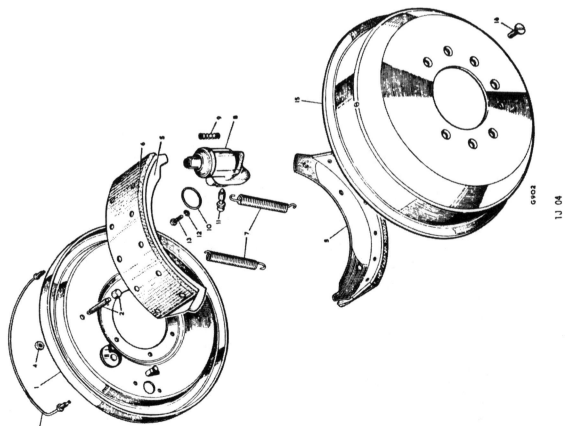

G902

1J 04

BRAKES, FOOT, REAR, 11" 109 MODELS.

GROUP G   BRAKES, FOOT, REAR, 11", 109 MODELS.

PLATE REF.	1	2	3	4	DESCRIPTION	QTY.	PART No.	REMARKS
1					Brake anchor plate, LH rear	1	531888	
					Brake anchor plate, RH rear	1	531889	
					Bolt (⅜" BSF x 1½")) Fixing rear anchor	12	576521	
					Nut (⅜" BSF)) plate to axle case	12	251322	
2					BRAKE SHOE ASSEMBLY, AXLE SET, REAR	1	GBS793	
3					Linings and rivets, axle set, rear	1	AAU8470	
4					Spring, abutment end) For brake	2	531893	
5					Spring, wheel cylinder end) shoe	2	548169	
6					WHEEL CYLINDER ASSEMBLY, RH	1	GWC305	
					WHEEL CYLINDER ASSEMBLY, LH	1	GWC306	
7					Spring for piston	2	212919	
8					Washer for spring	4	242117	
9					Bleed screw	2	556508	
10					Nut (5/16" UNF)) Fixing wheel	4	GHF201	
11					Spring washer) cylinder	4	WL600050	
12					Brake drum	2	516599	Chassis suffix A to G
					Brake drum	2	576973	From chassis suffix H
13					Set screw fixing brake drum	6	1510	
					Brake wheel cylinder overhaul kit, rear	1	275744	

1J 05

BRAKES, FOOT, REAR, 11" 109 MODELS.

K185

1J 05

GROUP G   HAND BRAKE. TRANSMISSION

Plate Ref. (1 2 3 4)	Description	Qty.	Part No.	Remarks
1	Shaft for hand brake relay lever	1	240829*	8R)
	Shaft for hand brake relay lever	1	267193*	109) Up to vehicle suffix 'C' inclusive
2	Bolt (3/8" UNF x 4"))Fixing	2	BH606321	
	Plain washer)shaft to	2	WB110061	
3	Self-locking nut (3/8" UNF))chassis frame	2	GHF223	
4	Shaft for hand brake relay lever	1	552746	From vehicle suffix 'D' onwards with welded washer plate)Alternatives
5	Self-locking nut (3/8" UNF) fixing shaft to chassis frame	1	GHF223	
	Shaft for hand brake relay lever	1	577137	With loose washer plate)
	Self-locking nut (7/16" UNF) fixing shaft to chassis frame	1	GHF224	
	Washer for hand brake relay shaft	1	577354	
	Washer plate for hand brake relay shaft	1	57713R	
6	RELAY LEVER ASSEMBLY FOR HAND BRAKE	1	238180	
7	Bush for relay lever	2	21838F	
8	Plain washer)Fixing lever	1	3299	
9	Circlip)to spindle	1	CCN112	
	Brake rod, relay to hand brake lever	1	277921	RH Stg)Up to vehicle suffix 'C' inclusive
10	Brake rod, relay to hand brake lever	1	278020*	LH Stg)'C' inclusive
10	Brake rod, relay to hand brake lever	1	552407	From vehicle suffix 'D' onwards
11	Clevis, fork end)Fixing	1	275199	
12	Clevis pin complete)brake rod	1	216421	
13	Locknut (5/16" UNF))to relay and	3	GHF201	
14	Split pin)hand brake lever	2	2392	
15	Anchor plate, transmission brake	1	515365	
16	Oil catcher for transmission brake	1	561369	
17	Joint washer for oil catcher	1	561856	
18	Spring washer)Fixing anchor plate and oil	4	GHF333	
18	Nut (3/8" BSF))catcher to speedometer housing	4	2R27	
20	BRAKE SHOE ASSEMBLY, BOXED PAIR	1 set	GBS552	
21	Lining for brake shoe	1 set	607249	10 hole type)Alternatives
	Rivet for lining	20	607250	
	Lining for brake shoe	1 set	607251	8 hole type)
	Rivet for lining	16	607252	
22	Pull-off spring, expander end)For brake	1	FRC3233	
23	Return spring, adjuster end)shoe	1	FRC3234	
24	ADJUSTER UNIT ASSEMBLY	1	37HK134	
25	Nut (3/8" UNF))Fixing	2	GHF200	
26	Tab washer)adjuster unit	1	542515	
	Repair kit for adjuster unit	1	51592A	
27	EXPANDER UNIT ASSEMBLY	1	51536F	
28	Clip retaining tappets	1	515927	
29	Brake rod, expander to relay lever	1	51592F	
	Repair kit for expander unit	1	515923	
30	Dust cover for expander unit	1	515466	
31	Packing plate)Fixing	1	515470	
32	Locking plate)expander	1	515467	
33	Retaining spring)unit	1	515468	

* NO LONGER SERVICED

1J 06

HANDBRAKE, TRANSMISSION

1J 06

GROUP G   HAND BRAKE TRANSMISSION

PLATE REF.	1	2	3	4	DESCRIPTION		QTY.	PART No.	REMARKS
34					Clevis complete	} Fixing	1	215809	
35					Clevis pin complete	} brake rod	1	216421	
36					Locknut (5/16" BSF)	} to relay	1	2828	
37					Split pin	} lever	1	2392	
38					Return spring for brake rod		1	59663	
39					Anchor for spring		1	240708	
40					Anchor for spring, on transfer box		1	267412	
41					Brake drum		1	274423	
42					Self-locking nut (5/16" BSF) fixing brake		6	251321	
					drum and damper				
43					Transmission damper at rear end of gearbox		1*	275239	109 Diesel. Up to gearbox number 27600879

* NO LONGER SERVICED

1J 07

1J 07

GROUP G   CLUTCH AND BRAKE PEDALS AND MASTER CYLINDERS
6-cylinder models up to vehicle suffix 'F' inclusive   All 4-cylinder models

PLATE REF.	1 2 3 4	DESCRIPTION	QTY.	PART No.	REMARKS
		BRAKE PEDAL AND BRACKET ASSEMBLY	1	523916	88. Up to vehicle suffix 'E' inclusive
		BRAKE PEDAL AND BRACKET ASSEMBLY	1	569054	88. From vehicle suffix 'F' onwards.
		BRAKE PEDAL AND BRACKET ASSEMBLY	1	568894	109. Up to vehicle suffix 'E' inclusive
		BRAKE PEDAL AND BRACKET ASSEMBLY	1	569084	109. From vehicle suffix 'F' onwards
		Bracket for brake pedal	1*	523695	88. Up to vehicle suffix 'E' inclusive
		Brake pedal and bushes	1*	523696	
1		Bracket for brake pedal	1	569055	88. From vehicle suffix 'F'
2		Brake pedal and bushes	1	569057	'F' onwards
		Bracket for brake pedal	1	272632	109. Up to vehicle suffix 'E' inclusive
		Brake pedal and bushes	1	568896	'E' inclusive
		Bracket for brake pedal	1	569085	109. From vehicle suffix
		Brake pedal and bushes	1	569086	'F' onwards
3		Bush for pedal	2	272714	
4		Distance piece for pedal trunion	1	269783	
5		Trunnion for pedal	1	568883	
6		Shaft for pedal	1	272712	
7		Pin locating pedal shaft	1	50446	
8		Oil plug	1	255202	
9		Joint washer for oil plug	1	GHF342	
10		Grommet for brake pedal bracket	1	90509970	88
11		Stop lamp switch, mechanical	1	13H3735	From vehicle suffix 'F'
12		Mounting bracket for stop lamp switch	1	569058	onwards

* NO LONGER SERVICED

1J 08

CLUTCH AND BRAKE PEDALS AND MASTER CYLINDERS
6-cylinder models up to vehicle suffix 'F' inclusive
All 4-cylinder models

1J 08

CLUTCH AND BRAKE PEDALS AND MASTER CYLINDERS
6-cylinder models up to vehicle suffix 'F' inclusive
All 4-cylinder models

GROUP G   6-cylinder models up to vehicle suffix 'F' inclusive All 4-cylinder models

CLUTCH AND BRAKE PEDALS AND MASTER CYLINDERS

PLATE REF. 1 2 3 4	DESCRIPTION	QTY.	PART No.	REMARKS
13	End stop } Fixing switch to	1	569117	From vehicle suffix 'F'
14	Special locknut } mounting bracket	1	BMK1903	onwards
15	Special bolt } Brake pedal	1	560223	
16	Locknut (5/16" UNF) } stop in lever	1	NT605061	
17	Switch protector plate and spring anchor	1	569201	Except Station Wagon
	CLUTCH PEDAL AND BRACKET ASSEMBLY	1	568893	RH Stg
	CLUTCH PEDAL AND BRACKET ASSEMBLY	1	568894	LH Stg
18	Bracket for clutch pedal	1	272632	
19	Clutch pedal and bushes	1	568895	RH Stg
	Clutch pedal and bushes	1	568896	LH Stg
	Bush for pedal	2	272714	
20	Distance piece for pedal trunnion	1	269783	
21	Trunnion for pedal	1	568883	
22	Shaft for pedal	1	272712	
23	Pin locating pedal shaft	1	50446	
24	Oil plug	1	255202	
25	Joint washer for oil plug	1	GHF342	
26	BRAKE MASTER CYLINDER, CB type	1	GMC314	88. Up to vehicles numbered 24131336D, 24431620 Petrol models 271086930, 274050720 Diesel models
27	BRAKE MASTER CYLINDER, CV type	1	GMC310	88. From vehicles numbered 24131337D, 24431622D Petrol models 271086940, 274050730 onwards Diesel models
	BRAKE MASTER CYLINDER, CB type	1	GMC312	109. 4-cylinder models. Up to vehicle suffix 'E' inclusive
	BRAKE MASTER CYLINDER, CV type	1	GMC311	109. 4-cylinder models.
	Packing piece for brake master cylinder	1	564944	From vehicle suffix 'F' onwards
	BRAKE MASTER CYLINDER, CB type	1	564706	109 6-cylinder models
	Spacer	1	606330	88 } For CB type
	Spacer	1	606332	109 } master cylinder
	Spacer for brake and clutch master cylinders	2	569096	88 and 109 For CV type master cylinder
28	CLUTCH MASTER CYLINDERS, CV type	1	GMC310	
29	Nut for master cylinder push rod	4	GHF201	
30	Plain washer for push rod	4	WB108051	
31	Bolt (5/16" UNF x 1½")	4	255029	2 off on 109 4-cylinder models
32	Bolt (5/16" UNF x 1½") } Fixing master	2	GHF104	109 4-cylinder models
	Plain washer } cylinder	4	3830	
33	Self-locking nut (5/16" UNF) } to	4	GHF242	
34	Bolt (¼" UNF x 1") } In bracket for	2	GHF101	
35	Nut (¼" UNF) } pedal stop	2	254810	
36	Gasket for pedal bracket too cover	2	272819	
37	Top cover for pedal bracket	1	272713	

1J 09

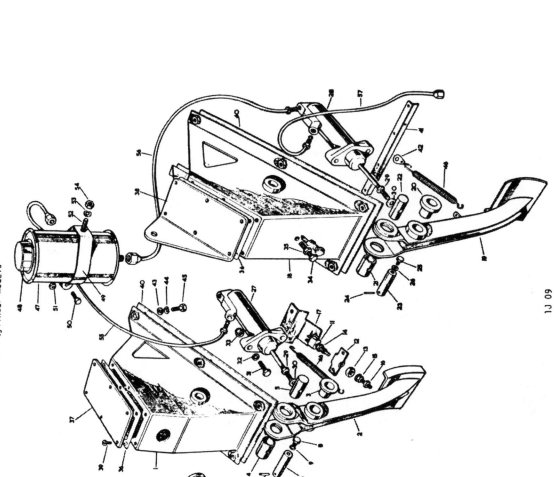

1J 09

GROUP G   CLUTCH AND BRAKE PEDALS AND MASTER CYLINDERS
6-cylinder models up to vehicle suffix 'F' inclusive All 4-cylinder models

PLATE REF. 1 2 3 4	DESCRIPTION	QTY.	PART No.	REMARKS
38	Pedal bracket top cover and reservoir tank support	1*	277840	All 109 and 88 RH Stg
	Pedal bracket top cover and reservoir tank support	1	517907	88 LH Stg
39	Drive screw fixing top cover to bracket	12	78227	
40	Gasket for pendant pedal brackets	2	562940	
41	Anchor for pedal springs	1*	272730	Early type
42	Anchor for pedal springs	2	240708	Late type. 1 off when mechanical stop lamp is fitted
43	Bolt (5/16" UNF x ⅞") } Fixing pedal	12	255227	
44	Plain washer } bracket and	10	RTC610	
	Plain washer } anchor to	3	4594	
45	Spring washer } dash	12	GHF332	
	Clutch and brake pedal return spring, 3.1/32" long	2	568866	Alternatives
46	Clutch and brake pedal return spring, 3.17/32* long	2	272729	
	Clutch and brake pedal return spring, 4" long	2	569701	
47	Clutch and brake reservoir tank	1	504105	
	Filter for clutch and brake tank	1	90518682	
48	Sealing washer for filter	1	264767	
	Filler cap for supply tank	1	500201	
49	Clip for reservoir tank	1	90217636	
50	Screw (2BA x 1") } Fixing clip	1	74838	
51	Nut (2BA) } to tank	1	RTC608	
52	Bolt (¼" UNF x ⅞") } Fixing	1	255206	
53	Spring washer } tank clip to	1	GHF331	
54	Nut (¼" UNF) } mounting bracket	1	GHF200	
55	Pipe, reservoir tank to brake master cylinder	1	504106	All 88 LH Stg 88 RH Stg up to vehicles numbered 24131336D Petro models, 27108693D Diesel models

* NO LONGER SERVICED

GROUP G   CLUTCH AND BRAKE PEDALS AND MASTER CYLINDERS
6 Cylinder models up to vehicle suffix 'F' inclusive. All 4 cylinder models

PLATE REF. 1 2 3 4	DESCRIPTION	QTY.	PART No.	REMARKS
S5	Pipe complete, reservoir tank to brake master cylinder	1	564785	88 RH Stg. From vehicles numbered 24131337D Petrol models 27108694D Diesel models
	Pipe complete, reservoir tank to brake master cylinder	1	504106	109 4-cylinder models up to vehicles suffix 'E' inclusive 109 6-cylinder models
	Pipe complete, reservoir tank to brake master cylinder	1	569147	109 4 cylinder models. From vehicle suffix 'F' (RH Stg)
	Pipe complete, reservoir tank to brake master cylinder	1	569149	onwards (LH Stg)
	Banjo	1	90216909	88 up to vehicles numbered 24431621D
	Banjo bolt } Fixing pipe to brake	1	267601	Petrol models 27405072D Diesel models. (LH Stg)
	Gasket, small } master cylinder	1	216914	109 4-cylinder models up to vehicle suffix 'E'
	Gasket, large	1	504104	inclusive 109 6-cylinder models
56	Pipe, reservoir tank to clutch master cylinder	1	277929	RH Stg
	Pipe, reservoir tank to clutch master cylinder	1	562978	LH Stg
57	Pipe, 3/16", clutch master cylinder to hose	1	277930	RH Stg } 88 and 109
	Pipe, 3/16", clutch master cylinder to hose	1	512839*	LH Stg } 4-cylinder models
	Pipe, ¼", clutch master cylinder to hose	1	569224*	LH Stg }
	Pipe, 3/16", clutch master cylinder to slave cylinder	1	562932	RH Stg } 109 6-cylinder models
	Pipe, ¼", clutch master cylinder to hose	1	568947*	LH Stg }
	Adaptor for clutch master cylinder	1	139082	Vehicles fitted with all-Synchromesh gearbox:- Home Market
	Pipe, clutch master cylinder to jumphose bracket	1	592508	RH Stg } 88 and 109 Station Wagons from vehicle suffix 'H' onwards 4-cyl.

* NO LONGER SERVICED

GROUP G   CLUTCH AND BRAKE PEDALS AND MASTER CYLINDERS
6-cylinder models up to vehicle suffix 'F' inclusive All 4-cylinder models

PLATE REF.	1	2	3	4	DESCRIPTION	QTY.	PART No.	REMARKS
					BRAKE SERVO CONVERSION KIT	1	90606892	109 2¼ litre petrol models Optional equipment
					Brake master cylinder overhaul kit	1	502333	88. For CB type master cylinder (GMC314)
					Brake master cylinder overhaul kit	1	8G8837	88. For CV type master cylinder (GMC310)
					Brake master cylinder overhaul kit	1	503754	109 4 cylinder models. For early CB type master cylinder G1 64067722
					Brake master cylinder overhaul kit	1	605127	109 4 cylinder models For late CB type master cylinder G1 64068750 (GMC31
					Brake master cylinder overhaul kit	1	90606023	109 4 cylinder models. For CV type master cylinder (GMC311)
					Brake master cylinder overhaul kit	1	605127	109 6 cylinder models
					Clutch master cylinder overhaul kit	1	8G8837	

1J 12

CLUTCH AND BRAKE PEDALS AND MASTER CYLINDERS
6-cylinder models up to vehicle suffix 'F' inclusive
All 4-cylinder models

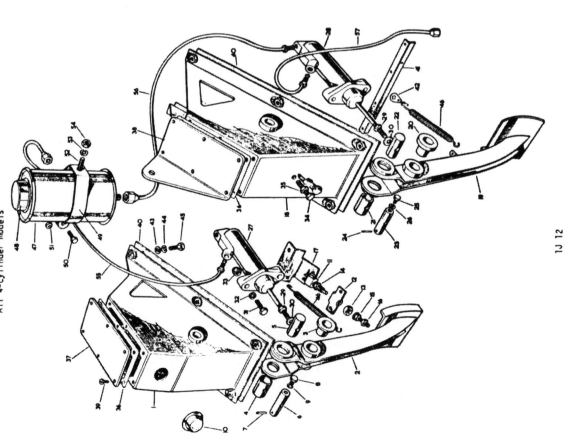

1J 12

PLATE REF.	1 2 3 4 DESCRIPTION	QTY.	PART No.	REMARKS
	BRAKE PEDAL AND BRACKET ASSEMBLY	1	569652	
1	Bracket for brake pedal	1	569601	
2	Brake pedal and bushes	1	90569611	
3	Bush for pedal	2	564816	
4	Shaft for pedal	1	564813	
5	Pin, locating pedal shaft	1	50446	
	Gasket for clutch pedal and bracket	1	562940	
	Gasket for brake pedal and bracket	1	90564832	
6	Plastic plug for oil hole in pedal bracket	1	338029	
7	Stop lamp switch, mechanical	1	575166	
8	Mounting bracket for stop lamp switch	1	569606	
9	Operating lever for switch	1*	569584	
10	Nylon bush) Fixing lever to	2	569609	
11	Split pin) mounting bracket	1	3035	
12	Split pin, lever stop	1	2427	
13	Gasket for switch mounting bracket	1	90569612	
14	Clip for switch cable	1	8885	
15	Self-tapping screw (8 UNC x 3/8") fixing mounting bracket and clip to pedal bracket	4	78905	
16	BRAKE SERVO UNIT, type 38	1	569338	
	Non-return valve and grommet for servo	1	18G8953	
17	Plug for vacuum switch hole in servo	1	90577611	
18	Pivot pin) Connecting servo	1	90564812	
19	Plain washer) operating rod to	1	RTC611	
20	Split pin) brake pedal	1	2393	
21	Plastic plug for pivot pin access hole in pedal bracket	2	338027	
22	Spring washer) Fixing servo unit	4	GHF332	
23	Nut (5/16" UNF)) to pedal bracket	4	GHF201	
24	Brake pedal return spring	2	569291	
25	Plain washer) Fixing brake	6	RTC610	
26	Spring washer) pedal bracket	6	GHF332	
27	Bolt (5/16" UNF x 3/8")) to dash	6	SH605051	
28	BRAKE MASTER CYLINDER CV TYPE	1	GMC309	
29	Filler cap for fluid unit	1	RTC253	
30	Sealing washer for filler cap	1	606404	
31	Special nut, fixing brake master cylinder to servo	2	GHF202	
	CLUTCH PEDAL AND BRACKET ASSEMBLY	1	568893	RH Stg
	CLUTCH PEDAL AND BRACKET ASSEMBLY	1	568894	LH Stg
32	Bracket for clutch pedal	1	272632	
33	Clutch pedal and bushes	1	568895	RH Stg
	Clutch pedal and bushes	1	568896	LH Stg
34	Bush for pedal	2	272714	
35	Distance piece for pedal trunnion	1	269783	
36	Trunnion for pedal	1	568883	
37	Shaft for pedal	1	272712	
38	Pin locating pedal shaft	1	50446	
39	Oil plug	1	255202	
40	Joint washer for oil plug	1	GHF342	

*NO LONGER SERVICED

PLATE REF.	1 2 3 4 DESCRIPTION	QTY.	PART No.	REMARKS	
41	CLUTCH MASTER CYLINDER, CV TYPE	1	550732		
42	Filler cap for fluid unit	1	500201		
43	Sealing washer for filler cap	1	264767		
44	Nut for master cylinder push rod	2	GHF201		
45	Plain washer for push rod	2	WB108051		
46	Bolt (5/16" UNF x 1 1/4")) Fixing clutch	2	255029		
47	Plain washer) master cylinder to	2	3830		
48	Self-locking nut (5/16" UNF) pedal bracket	2	GHF242		
49	Bolt (1/4" UNF x 1")) In bracket for	1	GHF101		
50	Nut (1/4" UNF)) pedal stop	1	GHF200		
51	Gasket for pedal bracket top cover	1	272819		
52	Top cover for pedal bracket	1	272713		
53	Drive screw fixing top cover to bracket	6	78227		
54	Anchor for clutch pedal spring	1	240708		
55	Return spring for clutch pedal	1	569701		
56	Bolt (5/16" UNF x 7/8")) Fixing clutch pedal	6	255227		
	Plain washer, thin) bracket and	5	RTC610		
57	Plain washer, thick) anchor to dash	1	4594		
58	Spring washer)	6	GHF332		
59	Pipe, 3/16", clutch master cylinder to slave cylinder	1	562932	RH Stg	
	Pipe, 1/4", clutch master cylinder to hose	1	569702	LH Stg	
	Adaptor for clutch master cylinder	1	139082		)Vehicles fitted with)all -synchromesh
	Pipe, clutch master cylinder to jump hose bracket	1	592509	RH Stg	)gearbox:- Home Mar)109 Station Wagons)from vehicle suffi)'H' onwards
	Brake master cylinder overhaul kit	1	606415		
	Clutch master cylinder overhaul kit	1	8G8837		
	Brake servo unit overhaul kit	1	18G8951		

GROUP G   BRAKE PIPES, 4-CYLINDER MODELS

PLATE REF.	1 2 3 4 DESCRIPTION	QTY.	PART No.	REMARKS
1	Bracket for junction piece	1	594938	
2	Drive screw fixing bracket	2	72626	
3	5-way junction piece for brake pipes	1	279412	Up to vehicle suffix 'E' inclusive
4	4-way junction piece for brake pipes	1*	241690	From vehicle suffix 'F' onwards
4	4-way junction piece for brake pipes	1	BH604101	
5	Bolt (¼" UNF x 1¼")	1	GHF331	⎫ Fixing junction piece
6	Spring washer	1	GHF200	⎬
7	Nut (¼"UNF)	1	560775	⎭
8	Stop lamp switch	1		Hydraulic type. Up to vehicle suffix 'E' inclusive. See 1J 08 for mechanical type
9	Brake pipe ⎫ Master cylinder to 5-way junction piece	1	508148	RH Stg ⎤ 88. Up to vehicles
9	Brake pipe ⎭	1	512838	LH Stg ⎦ numbered 241311336D Petrol, 27108693D Diesel
9	Brake pipe ⎫	1	564786	RH Stg ⎤ 88. From vehicles
9	Brake pipe ⎭	1	569223	LH Stg ⎦ numbered 241311337D Petrol, 27108694D Diesel up to vehicle suffix 'E' inclusive
9	Brake pipe ⎫ Master cylinder to 4-way junction piece	1	508148	RH Stg ⎤ 109. Up to vehicle
9	Brake pipe	1	512838	LH Stg ⎦ suffix 'E' inclusive
9	Brake pipe	1	564786	RH Stg ⎤ 88. From vehicle
9	Brake pipe	1	569223	LH Stg ⎦ suffix 'F' onwards
9	Brake pipe	1	90577165	RH Stg ⎤ 109. From vehicle
9	Brake pipe ⎭	1	577166	LH Stg ⎦ suffix 'F' onwards
10	Brake pipe, junction piece to LH front	1	592549	
11	Brake pipe, junction piece to RH front	1	277923	
12	Bracket for LH front brake pipe	1*	90508566	
	Bolt (5/16" UNF x ¾") ⎫ Fixing bracket to hose bracket on chassis frame	1	GHF120	
	Plain washer ⎪	1	3830	
	Shakeproof washer ⎬	1	GHF322	
	Nut (5/16" UNF) ⎭	1	GHF201	
13	Clip for LH front brake pipe	1*	508565	
	Bolt (2BA x ¾") ⎫ Fixing clip	1	234603	
	Plain washer (2BA) ⎬	1	3902	
	Nut (2BA) ⎭	1	RTC608	

* NO LONGER SERVICED

1K 02

BRAKE PIPES, 4-CYLINDER MODELS

1K 02

PLATE REF.	1	2	3	4	DESCRIPTION	QTY.	PART No.	REMARKS
14					Hose complete for front wheels	2	GBH134	
15					Hose complete to rear axle	1	GBH134	88
					Hose complete to rear axle	1	GBH302	109
16					Joint washer for hoses	3	233220	
17					Shakeproof washer } Fixing hose	3	GHF323	
18					Special nut } to bracket	3	NT606041	
19					'T' piece on rear axle	1	234928	Rover type axle
20					'T' piece on rear axle	1	BTB657	ENV type axle. 109 optional
21					Nut (5/16" UNF) } Fixing 'T' piece	1	GHF201	
22					Spring washer	1	GHF332	
23					Bolt (5/16" UNF x ⅞")	1	GHF120	
24					Bracket for 'T' piece	1*	537805	ENV type axle. 109 optional
					Bolt (5/16" UNF x ⅞") } Fixing	1	GHF332	
					Spring washer } bracket to	1	GHF201	
					Nut (5/16" UNF) } rear axle	1		
25					Brake pipe to rear hose	1	279418	88
					Brake pipe to rear hose	1	279452	109
26					Brake pipe, LH rear to 'T' piece	1	504517	88. Also 109 with
27					Brake pipe, RH rear to 'T' piece	1	531906	Rover type axle
					Brake pipe, LH rear to 'T' piece	1	592374	ENC type axle
					Brake pipe, RH rear to 'T' piece	1	551652	optional
					Brake pipe, LH rear to 'T' piece	1	592374	Salisbury type axle
					Brake pipe, RH rear to 'T' piece	1	592375	109 only from vehicle suffix 'H' onwards
28					Clip, brake pipes to chassis frame	As reqd	41379	
29					Clip, brake and clutch pipes to dash	As reqd	508945	LH Stg
					Clip, fixing pipe to steering box stiffener bracket	1	90513940	RH Stg
					Drive screw	As reqd	72626	
					Screw (2BA x ⅜") } Fixing clips	As reqd	77758	
					Shakeproof washer	As reqd	WE702101	LH Stg
					Nut (2BA)	As reqd	RTC608	LH Stg
30					Clip on rear axle for LH pipe	1	11820	
					Clip	4	56666	
					Rubber grommet	4	6860	
					Bolt (2BA x ⅞") } Fixing LH brake pipe	4	234603	
					Plain washer } to chassis frame	4	WC702101	
					Spring washer	4	WN702001	
					Nut (2BA)	4	RTC608	

* NO LONGER SERVICED

1K 03

BRAKE PIPES, 4-CYLINDER MODELS

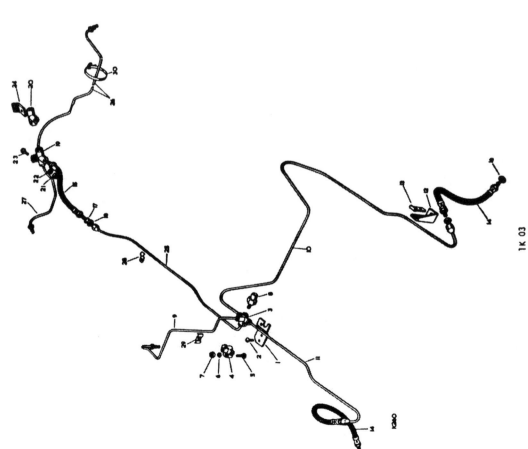

1K 03

BRAKE SERVO UNIT AND BRAKE PIPES, 6-CYLINDER MODELS
Up to vehicle suffix 'F' inclusive

1K 04

GROUP G — BRAKE SERVO UNIT AND BRAKE PIPES, 6 CYLINDER MODELS
Up to vehicle suffix 'F' inclusive

PLATE REF. 1 2 3 4	DESCRIPTION	QTY.	PART No.	REMARKS
1	BRAKE SERVO UNIT	1	562678	
2	Support bracket for brake servo	1	562675	*
3	Set screw (5/16" UNC x ⅞")) Fixing servo	2	SH505051	
4	Plain washer) to support	2	3830	
5	Spring washer) bracket	2	GHF332	
6	Bolt (5/16" UNF x ⅞"))	2	255226	
7	Plain washer) Fixing support bracket	1	3830	
8	Spring washer) to chassis frame	1	GHF332	
9	Nut (5/16" UNF)	1	GHF201	
10	Spring washer) Fixing servo to	2	GHF332	
11	Nut (5/16" UNF)) air cleaner support	2	GHF201	
12	Banjo for servo	1	538614	
13	Banjo bolt	1	538615	
14	Gasket) Fixing banjo to servo	1	538616	
15	Gasket	1	538612	*
16	Pipe complete, inlet manifold to hose	1	562666	*
17	Adaptor) Fixing servo pipe to	1	90513171	
18	Gasket) inlet manifold	1	538616	
19	Clip, fixing servo pipe to water outlet pipe	1	50642	
20	Rubber hose connecting manifold pipe to servo	1	37H8863	
21	Clip, fixing rubber hose to pipe and brake servo	2	GHC406	
22	Adaptor for servo pipe	1	538613	
23	Gasket for adaptor	1	538612	*
24	Pipe complete, master cylinder to union	1	277923	RH Stg
	Pipe complete, master cylinder to union	1	562906	LH Stg
25	Union for pipe	1	504765	*
26	Pipe complete, union to servo	1	562905	
27	Pipe complete, brake servo to junction piece	1	562908	
28	Bracket for junction piece	1	594938	
29	Drive screw fixing bracket	2	72626	
30	5-way junction piece for brake pipes	1	279412	Up to vehicle suffix 'E' inclusive
31	4-way junction piece for brake pipes	1	241690	Vehicle suffix 'F'
31	Bolt (¼" UNF x 1¼")) Fixing junction	1	BH604101	
32	Spring washer) piece to	1	GHF331	
33	Nut (¼" UNF)) support bracket	1	GHF200	
34	Stop lamp switch	1	560775	Hydraulic type. Up to vehicle suffix 'E' inclusive. See 1J 08 for mechanical type
35	Brake pipe, junction piece to LH front	1	592549	
36	Brake pipe, junction piece to RH front	1	277923	
37	Hose complete for front wheels	2	GHB134	
38	Hose complete to rear axle	1	GBH302	
39	Joint washer for hoses	3	233220	
40	Shakeproof washer) Fixing hose	3	GHF323	
41	Special nut) to bracket	3	NT606041	

* NO LONGER SERVICED

1K 04

GROUP G   BRAKE SERVO UNIT AND BRAKE PIPES, 6 CYLINDER MODELS
Up to vehicle suffix 'F' inclusive

PLATE REF.	1	2	3	4	DESCRIPTION	QTY.	PART No.	REMARKS
42					'T' piece on rear axle	1	234928	
43					Bolt (5/16" UNF x ½")	1	GHF120	} Fixing 'T' piece
44					Spring washer	1	GHF332	
45					Nut (5/16" UNF)	1	GHF201	
46					Brake pipe to rear hose	1	279452	
47					Brake pipe, LH rear to 'T' piece	1	504517	
48					Brake pipe, RH rear to "T" piece	1	531906	
49					Single clip, brake pipes to chassis frame	As read	41379	
50					Double clip, brake pipes to chassis frame	As read	233274	
					Drive screw fixing clips	As read	77626	
51					Grommet } Fixing brake servo pipe	1	6860	
52					Clip } to pedal bracket top cover	1	56666	
53					Clip, fixing brake pipe to steering box bracket	1	90513940	RH Stg
							338035	LH Stg
					Clip, fixing brake pipe to dash	3	11820	
54					Clip on rear axle to LH pipe	4	56666	
55					Clip for bush	4	6860	
56					Rubber bush } Fixing LH	4	234603	
57					Bolt (2BA x ½") } axle pipe to	4	WM702001	
58					Spring washer } chassis frame	4	RTC608	
59					Nut (2BA)	4		
					Brake servo major overhaul kit	1	600432	
					Brake servo poppet valve overhaul kit	1	600434	} Export only
					Brake servo non-return valve overhaul kit	1	600435	

1K 05

BRAKE SERVO UNIT AND BRAKE PIPES, 6-CYLINDER MODELS
Up to vehicle suffix 'F' inclusive

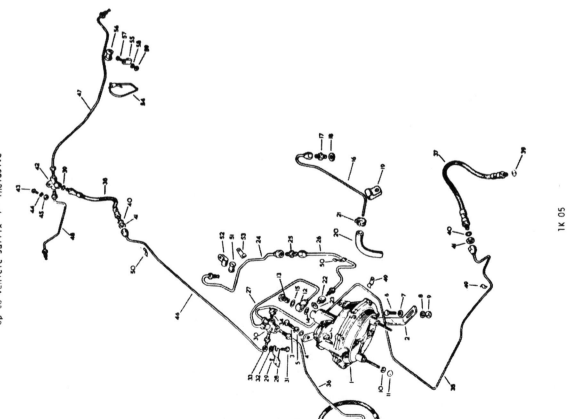

1K 05

107

BRAKE PIPES, 6-CYLINDER MODELS
From vehicle suffix 'G' onwards

GROUP G   BRAKE PIPES, 6-CYLINDER MODELS
From vehicle suffix 'G' onwards

PLATE REF.	1	2	3	4	DESCRIPTION	QTY.	PART No.	REMARKS
1					Pipe complete, inlet manifold to hose	1	569434	See 1J 13 for servo unit
2					Adaptor) Fixing servo pipe to	1	90513171	
3					Gasket) inlet manifold	1	538616	
4					Rubber hose connecting manifold pipe to servo	1	37H8863	
5					Clip, fixing rubber hose to pipe and brake servo	2	GHC406	
6					Pipe complete, master cylinder to junction piece	1	569769*	RH Stg
					Pipe complete, master cylinder to junction piece	1	569433	LH Stg
7					Bracket for junction piece	1	594938	
8					Drive screw fixing bracket	2	72626	
9					4-way junction piece for brake pipes	1	241690	
10					Bolt (¼" UNF x 1¼")) Fixing junction	1	BH604101	
11					Spring washer) piece to	1	GHF331	
12					Nut (¼" UNF)) support bracket	1	GHF200	
13					Brake pipe, junction piece to LH front	1	592549	
14					Brake pipe, junction piece to RH front	1	277923	
15					Hose complete for front wheels	2	GBH134	
16					Hose complete to rear axle	1	GBH302	
17					Joint washer for hoses	3	233220	
18					Shakeproof washer) Fixing hose	3	GHF323	
19					Special nut) to bracket	3	NT606041	
20					'T' piece on rear axle	1	234928	
21					Bolt (5/16" UNF x ¾"))	1	GHF120	
22					Spring washer) Fixing 'T' piece	1	GHF332	
23					Nut (5/16" UNF))	1	GHF201	
24					Brake pipe to rear hose	1	279452	
25					Brake pipe, LH rear to 'T' piece	1	504517	
26					Brake pipe, RH rear to 'T' piece	1	531906	
					Brake pipe, LH rear to 'T' piece	1	592374	) Salisbury type axle
					Brake pipe, RH rear to 'T' piece	1	592375	) 109 only from vehicle
								) suffix 'H' onwards
27					Single clip, brake pipes to chassis frame	As reqd	41379	
28					Double clip, brake pipe to chassis frame	As reqd	552678	
					Drive screw fixing clips	As reqd	72626	
29					Grommet) Fixing brake pipe	1	6860	
30					Clip) to pedal bracket top cover	1	56666	
31					Clip, fixing brake pipe to steering box bracket	1	90513940	RH Stg
32					Clip on rear axle for LH pipe	1	11820	
33					Clip for bush	4	56666	
34					Rubber bush	4	6860	
35					Bolt (2BA x ½")) Fixing LH	4	234603	
36					Spring washer) axle pipe to	4	WM702001	
37					Nut (2BA)) chassis frame	4	RTC608	
					Clip, fixing brake pipe to toe box	1	41379	
					Screw (2BA x ½"))	1	78177	
					Plain washer) Fixing clip	1	4034	LH Stg
					Spring washer) to toe box	1	WM702001	
					Nut (2BA)	1	RTC608	
					Clip fixing brake pipe to chassis	1	41379	
					Mounting bracket for pipe clip	1	577016	
					Drive screw fixing bracket to chassis	2	72626	
					Bolt (10 UNF x ½")) Fixing clip	1	257017	
					Spring washer) to mounting	1	WM702001	
					Nut (10 UNF)) bracket	1	HN2005	* NO LONGER SERVICED

1K 06

BRAKE PIPES, 6-CYLINDER MODELS
From vehicle suffix 'G' onwards

1K 06

This page is intentionally left blank

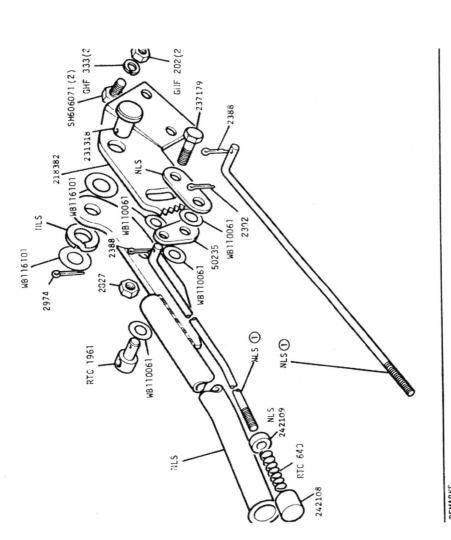

REMARKS Hand brake lever assembly 50858, NLS

① Alternatives

1K 07

HANDBRAKE LEVER, RH STG. From vehicle suffix 'D' onwards

GROUP G HAND BRAKE LEVER, RH Stg.
From vehicle suffix 'D' onwards

PLATE REF. 1 2 3 4	DESCRIPTION	QTY.	PART No.	REMARKS
	HAND BRAKE LEVER ASSEMBLY	1	624252	
1	Hand brake lever	1	543265	
2	Plunger rod, upper	1	543292	
3	Plunger rod, lower	1	543291	
4	Washer for plunger spring	1	552857	
5	Spring for plunger rod	1	RTC640	
6	Plunger	1	552856	
7	Ratchet for hand brake	1	543546	
8	Bolt (⅜" UNF x 1¼") } Fixing	1	255249	
9	Plain washer } lever to	2	WB110061	
10	Self-locking nut (⅜" UNF) } ratchet	1	GHF223	
11	Brake catch	1	50235	
12	Pin	1	559563	
13	Distance piece } Fixing catch	2	543275	
14	Plain washer } to lever	1	4574	
15	Split pin	1	2392	
16	Pin for hand brake adjuster rod	1	543281	
17	Plain washer } Fixing pin to	2	4574	
18	Split pin } hand brake lever	1	2392	
19	Fulcrum pin for hand brake lever	1	231318	
20	Plain washer } Fixing pin	3	WB116101	
21	Spring washer } to ratchet	1	* 2290	
22	Split pin } and lever	1	2974	
23	Bolt (⅜" UNF x ⅞") } Fixing hand brake	2	SH606071	
24	Spring washer } lever to	2	GHF333	
	Nut (⅜" UNF) } chassis frame	2	GHF202	

* NO LONGER SERVICED

1K 08

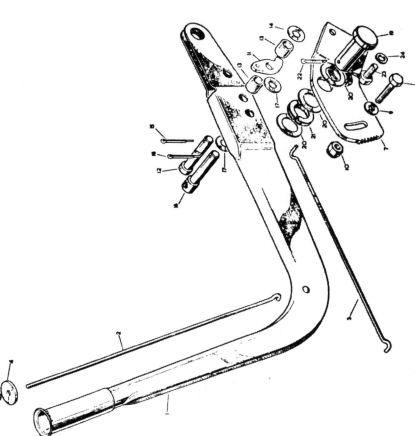

1K 08

110

90217984
90217983
237161 (2)
GHF 332(2)
217985
217985
NLS 90218410 (2)
NLS 218409
90217983
90217984
GHF 333(2)
2827 (2)
NLS
90217983
90217984
217985
90218410 (2)
217985
90217983
90217984
GHF 332(2)
237161 (2)

1K 09

90218408
2208
2392
NLS
90218402
2388
2827
RTC1061
WB110061
WB116101
NLS
NLS ①
RTC540
242109
242108
NLS ②
NLS ①
NLS
WB110061
2338
WB110061
WB110061
50235
237179
NLS
2392
GHF 202(2)
GHF 333(2)
SH606071(2)
NLS ②

1K 09

Hand brake lever assembly (508582) - NLS

① Straight type) Alternatives
② Cranked type)

HAND BRAKE LEVER, LH STG. From vehicle suffix 'D' onwards

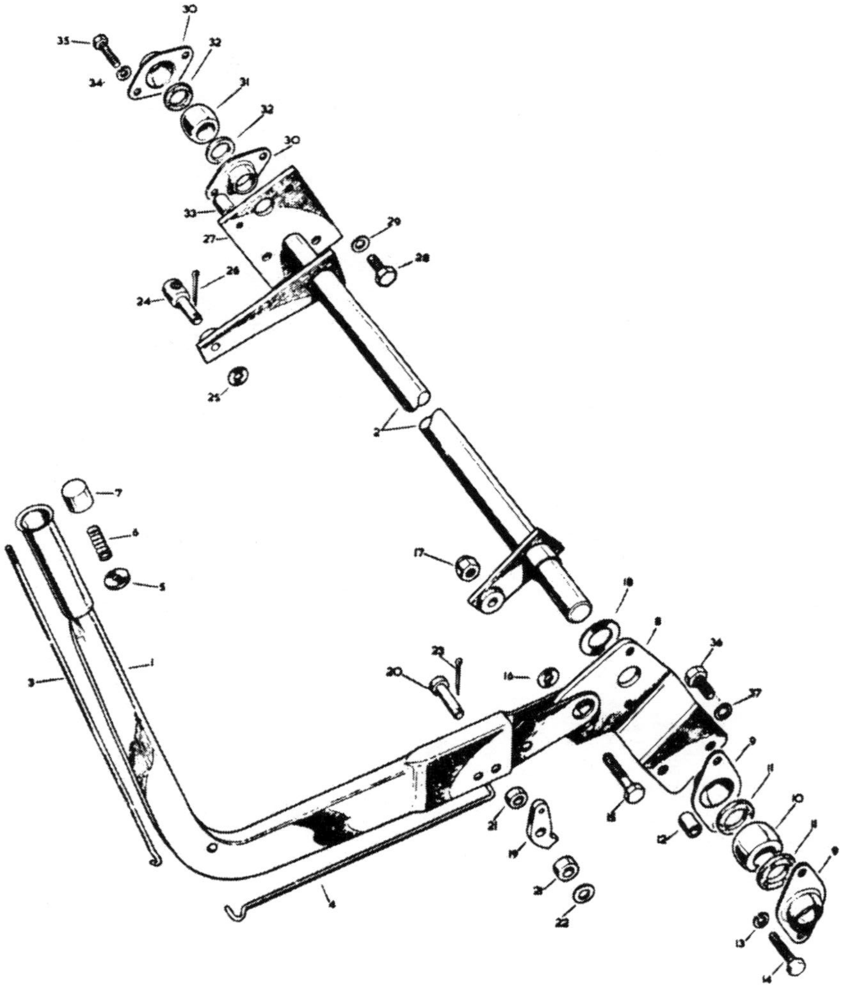

1K 10

HAND BRAKE LEVER, LH Stg
From vehicle suffix 'D' onwards

PLATE REF.	DESCRIPTION	QTY.	PART No.
	HAND BRAKE LEVER ASSEMBLY	1	624262
1	Hand brake lever	1	543265
2	Cross shaft for hand brake	1	552578
3	Plunger rod, upper	1	543292
4	Plunger rod, lower	1	543291
5	Washer for plunger spring	1	552857
6	Spring for plunger rod	1	RTC640
7	Plunger	1	552856
8	Ratchet for hand brake	1	552583
9	Housing for cross shaft bearing	2	90217983
10	Spherical bearing for cross shaft	1	90217984
11	Felt ring for bearing	2	217985
12	Distance piece) Fixing bearing	2	522805
13	Spring washer) and housing to	2	GHF332
14	Set bolt (5/16" UNF x 1¼")) ratchet	2	255029
15	Bolt (⅜" UNF x 1¾")) Fixing	1	SH606141
16	Plain washer) lever to	2	WB110061
17	Self-locking nut (⅜" UNF)) ratchet	1	GHF223
18	Plain washer between lever and ratchet	1	WB116101
19	Brake catch	1	50235
20	Pin)	1	599563
21	Distance piece) Fixing catch	2	543275
22	Plain washer) to lever	1	4574
23	Split pin)	1	2392
24	Pin for hand brake adjuster rod	1	90218408
25	Plain washer) Fixing pin to	1	2208
26	Split pin) cross shaft lever	1	2392
27	Support plate for hand brake bearing housing	1	552858
28	Bolt (⅜" UNF x ⅞")) Fixing support	2	SH606071
29	Spring washer) plate to	2	GHF333
	Nut (⅜" UNF)) chassis frame	2	GHF202
30	Housing for cross shaft bearing	2	90217983
31	Spherical bearing for cross shaft	1	90217984
32	Felt ring for bearing	2	217985
33	Distance piece) Fixing housing	2	90218410
34	Spring washer) and bearing to	2	GHF332
35	Set bolt (5/16" UNF x ⅞")) support plate	2	255227
36	Bolt (⅜" UNF x ⅞")) Fixing hand brake	2	SH606071
37	Spring washer) lever to	2	GHF333
	Nut (⅜" UNF)) chassis frame	2	GHF202

1K 10

FUEL SYSTEM - Carburetter, Solex type, 2¼ litre Petrol
Up to engine suffix 'H' inclusive
7:1 compression ratio only

GROUP H   FUEL SYSTEM - Carburetter, Solex type, 2¼ litre Petrol

Up to engine suffix 'H' inclusive 7:1 compression ratio only

PLATE REF.	1	2	3	4	DESCRIPTION	QTY.	PART No.	REMARKS
					CARBURETTER COMPLETE	1	546029 @	Without starter heater element.
					The above is no longer available use:-			
					CARBURETTER CONVERSION KIT	1	RTC2038	
					CARBURETTER COMPLETE	1	546180 @	With starter heater element Note: Identification, Lucas connection adjacent to starter unit
1					*For carburetter without starter element.	1	9051350	6*
					For carburetter with starter element.	1	528037 *	
2					Carburetter body only	1	524114	For carburetter without starter heater element.
					Throttle chamber only	1	538435 *	For carburetter with starter heater element.
					Throttle chamber only			
3					Spindle for throttle	1	503889 *	
4					Butterfly for throttle	1	503890 *	
5					Special screw fixing butterfly	2	260138 *	
6					Plate, throttle abutment	1	503891 *	
7					Special screw) For slow running	1	260140 *	
8					Spring) adjustment	1	260141 *	
9					Special screw) For throttle	1	260142 *	
10					Locknut) stop	1	260143 *	
11					Throttle lever	1	504683 *	
12					Nut fixing throttle lever	1	260159 *	
13					Lockwasher for nut	1	504485 *	
14					Special screw) For mixture	1	260146 *	
15					Spring) control	1	260141 *	
16					Screwed union) For suction	1	260707 *	
17					Olive) pipe	1	260708 *	
18					Joint washer for throttle chamber	1	503893	
19					Special screw and spring washer fixing chamber to carburetter body	4	512402 *	

@ Carburetter and fittings are not included in the engine assembly

* NO LONGER SERVICED

1L 02

1L 02

113

FUEL SYSTEM - Carburetter, Solex type, 2¼ litre Petrol
Up to engine suffix 'H' inclusive
7:1 compression ratio only

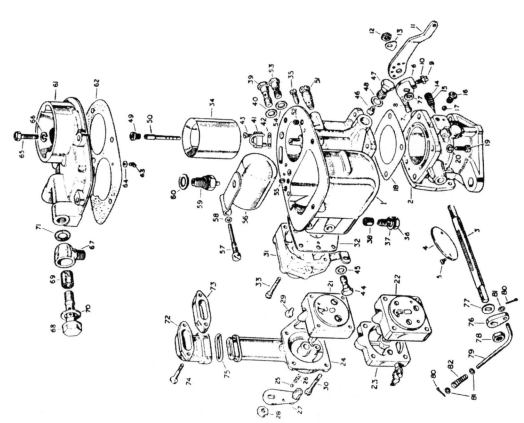

1L 03

GROUP H · FUEL SYSTEM - Carburetter, Solex type, 2¼ petrol

Up to engine suffix 'H' inclusive 7:1 compression ratio only

PLATE REF. 1 2 3 4	DESCRIPTION	QTY.	PART No.	REMARKS
21	Starter complete	* 1	503895	For carburetter without starter heater element.
22	Starter complete	1	527273	For carburetter with starter heater element.
	Starter valve complete	* 1	503896	For carburetter without starter heater element.
	Starter valve complete	* 1	528039	For carburetter with starter heater element.
23	Heater element for starter	* 1	528053	
24	Cover for starter	1	503897	
25	Ball) For	* 1	260155	
26	Spring) starter valve	1	260156	
27	Lever for starter	1	503898	
28	Nut fixing starter lever	* 1	260159	
29	Special bolt fixing starter cable	1	AAU1054	
30	Special screw fixing starter body	4	262313	For carburetter without starter heater element.
	Special screw fixing starter body	4	527272	For carburetter with starter heater element.
31	Accelerator pump complete	* 1	524115	For carburetter without starter heater element.
	Accelerator pump complete	1	528041	For carburetter with starter heater element.
32	Diaphragm assembly for pump	1	503900	
33	Joint washer for pump	* 1	503939	
34	Special screw fixing pump	4	503901	
	Choke tube (30)	* 1	503902	
	Choke tube (28)	1	512105	
	Choke tube (26)	1	542368	
35	Special screw fixing choke tube	* 1	260163	
36	Non-return valve	1	260765	
37	Fibre washer for valve	1	260734	
38	Filter gauze for non-return valve	* 1	503903	
39	Jet (65), accelerator pump	1	503904	
	Jet (50), accelerator pump	1	542640	
40	Fibre washer for jet	1	260734	
41	Pump injector	* 1	503905	
42	Joint washer for pump injector	* 1	261570	
43	Special screw fixing injector	* 1	260767	

* NO LONGER SERVICED

1L 03

GROUP H   FUEL SYSTEM - Carburetter, Solex type, 2¼ litre Petrol

Up to engine suffix 'H' inclusive 7:1 compression ratio only

PLATE REF.	1 2 3 4 DESCRIPTION	QTY.	PART No.	REMARKS
72	Elbow for top cover	1	503906	*
45	Joint washer for blank jet	1	260734	*
44	Economy jet, blank	1	503906	*
45	Joint washer for blank jet	1	260734	*
46	Main jet (135)	1	503907	*
46	Main jet (125)	1	505701	*
46	Main jet (120)	1	542639	*
47	Bolt, main jet carrier	1	260180	*
48	Fibre washer for bolt	1	260181	*
49	Correction jet (175)	1	503908	*
49	Correction jet (185)	1	90512106	*
50	Emulsion tube	1	503909	*
50	Emulsion tube, No. 10	1	260743	*
51	Pilot jet (60)	1	260216	*
51	Pilot jet (50)	1	260268	* For carburetter without starter heater element / For carburetter with starter heater element
51	Pilot jet (55)	1	260269	* For carburetter without starter heater element / For carburetter with starter heater element
52	Jet air bleed (1.5)	1	260179	*
52	Jet air bleed (blank)	1	542641	*
53	Starter jet (145)	1	503910	*
53	Starter jet, petrol (130)	1	528038	*
54	Fibre washer for jet	1	260734	*
55	Economy jet, high speed (150)	1	503911	*
55	Economy jet, high speed (100)	1	512107	*
56	Float	1	503912	*
57	Spindle for float	1	503913	*
58	Copper washer for spindle	1	503914	*
59	Needle valve complete	1	260725	*
60	Fibre washer for valve	1	601512	*
61	Top cover for carburetter	1	503915	*
62	Joint washer for top cover	1	90503916	*
63	Screw } Fixing joint washer	2	90503917	*
64	Washer } to top cover	2	90503918	*
65	Special screw fixing top cover	4	503919	*
66	Spring washer for screw	4	260714	
67	Banjo union	1	260166	* Not part of carburetter
68	Special bolt for union	1	260167	*
69	Filter gauze for union	1	260168	*
70	Fibre washer, large } For	1	260169	*
71	Fibre washer, small } union	1	260170	*

* NO LONGER SERVICED

GROUP H   FUEL SYSTEM - Carburetter, Solex type, 2¼ litre Petrol

Up to engine suffix 'H' inclusive 7:1 compression ratio only

PLATE REF.	1 2 3 4 DESCRIPTION	QTY.	PART No.	REMARKS
72	Elbow for top cover	1	503920	* For carburetter with starter heater element.
73	Distance piece, elbow to top cover	1	527275	* For carburetter without starter heater element.
74	Screw fixing elbow to top cover	2	503921	* For carburetter without starter heater element
74	Screw fixing elbow to top cover	1	260157	* For carburetter with starter heater element.
75	Rubber sealing washer, elbow to starter cover	1	503922	*
76	Lever for accelerator pump rod	1	503923	*
77	Special washer for levers	2	261410	*
78	Nut fixing lever to spindle	2	260159	*
79	Control rod for accelerator pump	1	90503924	*
80	Split pin	4	3359	*
81	Plain washer } For control rod	3	260771	*
82	Spring }	1	503925	*
	Carburetter overhaul kit	1	507687	
	Carburetter gasket kit	1	507693	
	CARBURETTER CONVERSION KIT	1	542637	* To convert early type PA 10-5A and PA 10-6 carburetters to late types with revised jet sizes
	Carburetter overhaul kit	1	605092	) For carburetter Conversion
	Carburetter gasket kit	1	605093	) Kit RTC2038

* NO LONGER SERVICED

PLATE REF.	1	2	3	4	DESCRIPTION	QTY.	PART No.	REMARKS
					From engine suffix 'J' onwards 7:1 compression ratio			
					From engine suffix 'A' onwards 8:1 compression ratio			
					CARBURETTER COMPLETE	1	ERC2886	For 7:1 or 8:1 compression ratio
1					Carburetter main body	1	601834	
2					Throttle spindle	1	601835	
3					Butterfly for throttle	1	601844	
4					Special screw fixing butterfly	2	601845	
5					Floating lever on throttle spindle	1	601842	
6					Plain washer on spindle for floating lever	1	601843	
7					Interconnecting link, throttle to choke	1	601893	
8					Split pin fixing link to levers	2	601894	
9					Relay lever, throttle to accelerator pump	1	601840	
10					Split pin fixing relay lever to floating lever	1	601841	
11					Throttle stop and fast idler lever	1	601837	
12					Special screw } Fixing throttle	1	601846	
13					Spring } stop	1	9060184?	
14					Throttle lever	1	601836	
15					Lockwasher } Fixing throttle	1	RTC166	
16					Special nut } levers	1	601838	
17					Volume control screw	1	90601848	
18					Spring for control screw	1	90601849	
19					Emulsion block	1	601851	For use with early type carburetter 554149
					Emulsion block	1	606319	For use with carburetter 574540
20					Pump jet (65)	1	601899	
21					Pump discharge valve	1	601855	
22					Plug for pump jet	1	601854	
23					Piston for accelerator pump	1	601856	
24					Ball for piston	1	601852	
25					Circlip for piston	1	601853	
26					Slow-running jet (60)	1	601897	
27					Main jet (125)	1	601895	
28					Enrichment jet (195)	1	601896	
					Enrichment jet (150)	1	606318	For use with early type carburetter 554149
29					Needle valve (1.75)	1	601900	For use with carburetter 574540
30					Special washer (2mm) for needle valve	1	601857	
31					Float	1	601858	
32					Spindle for float	1	601859	
33					'O' ring, emulsion block to body	1	601850	
34					Special screw } Fixing emulsion	1	601886	
35					Spring washer } block to body	1	601887	

1L 06

FUEL SYSTEM - Carburetter, Zenith type, 2¼ litre Petrol
From engine suffix 'J' onwards 7:1 compression ratio
From engine suffix 'A' onwards 8:1 compression ratio

1L 06

FUEL SYSTEM – Carburetter, Zenith type, 2¼ litre Petrol

PLATE REF.	1 2 3 4 DESCRIPTION	QTY.	PART No.	REMARKS
				From engine suffix 'J' onwards 7:1 compression ratio
				From engine suffix 'A' onwards 8:1 compression ratio
36	Top cover for carburetter	1	601860	
37	Gasket for top cover	1	606679	
38	Ventilation screw (3.0) for choke	1	90601898	
39	Pump lever, internal	1	601876	
40	Retaining ring for pump lever	1	601878	
41	Shakeproof washer) Fixing	1	601877	
42	Special nut) pump lever	1	601838	
43	Screw and spring washer, short) Fixing top	2	601889	
44	Screw and spring washer, long) cover to main) body	2	601888	
45	Diaphragm for carburetter	1	601879	
46	Gasket for diaphragm	2	601880	
47	Spring for diaphragm	1	601881	
48	Cover for diaphragm	1	601882	
49	Screw) Fixing diaphragm	3	601883	
50	Spring washer) cover	3	601884	
51	Spindle and pin for choke lever	1	601865	
52	Lever and swivel for choke	1	601861	
53	Screw for choke lever swivel	1	601864	
54	Circlip fixing choke lever to top cover	1	601863	
55	Spring, small) For choke	1	601866	
56	Spring, large) lever	1	601862	
57	Plain washer for choke spindle	1	601869	
58	Butterfly for choke	1	601867	*
59	Special screw fixing butterfly	2	601868	
60	Bracket and clip for choke cable	1	601870	
61	Clip for choke bracket	1	516962	
62	Special screw) Fixing choke bracket	1	601872	
63	Shakeproof washer) to top cover	1	601873	
64	Spindle and lever for accelerator pump	1	601874	
65	Spacing washer for pump spindle	1	601875	
66	Pin) Fixing relay	1	90601890	
67	Plain washer) lever to	2	601892	
68	Split pin) pump lever	1	601891	
	Carburetter overhaul kit	1	605092	
	Carburetter gasket kit	1	605093	

CARBURETTER SETTINGS WHICH MAY BE ADVANTAGEOUS FOR HIGH ALTITUDES

Main jet (120)	1	605683	5,000 to 7,000 ft	
Main jet (117.5)	1	605684	7,000 to 9,000 ft	
Main jet (115)	1	605685) 9,000 to		
Slow running jet (55)	1	605687) 12,000 ft		
Main jet (112.5)	1	605686) 12,000 to		
Slow running jet (55)	1	605687) 14,000 ft		

* NO LONGER SERVICED

1L 07

FUEL SYSTEM – Carburetter, Zenith type, 2¼ litre Petrol
From engine suffix 'J' onwards 7:1 compression ratio
From engine suffix 'A' onwards 8:1 compression ratio

1L 07

GROUP H
FUEL SYSTEM - Pump 2¼ litre petrol

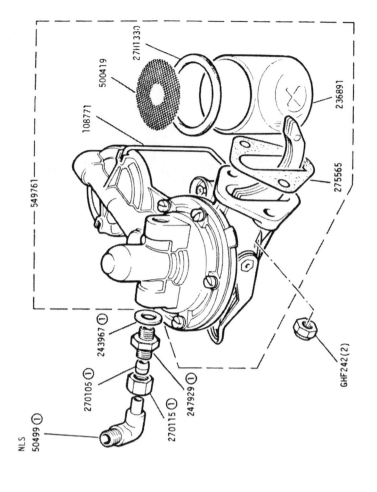

- 549761
- 108771
- 500419
- 27H1330
- 236891
- 275565
- NLS 50499 ①
- 270105 ①
- 243967 ①
- 270115 ①
- 247929 ①
- GHF242 (2)

Overhaul kit for fuel pump 18G8246
Repair kit for fuel Pump 8G2039
Fuel pump is not part of Engine assembly.
① Early type fixing only

1L 08

GROUP H
FUEL SYSTEM - Air cleaner 2¼ litre petrol

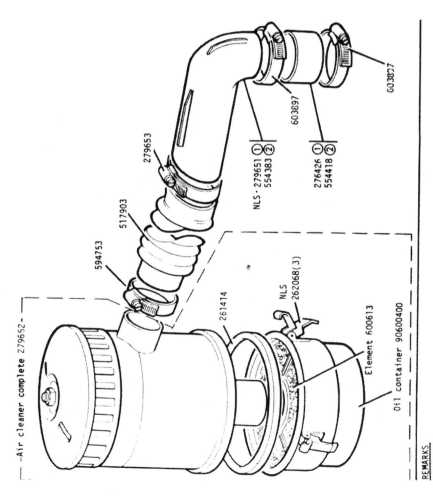

─ Air cleaner complete 279652 ─

- 279653
- 517903
- 594753
- NLS · 279651 ①
  554383 ②
- 603897
- 276426 ①
  554418 ②
- 603827
- 261414
- NLS 262068 (3)
- Element 600613
- Oil container 90600400

REMARKS

① Engine Suffix A to H
② Engine Suffix J onwards

1L 08

GROUP H

FUEL SYSTEM - Fuel Injection, 2¼ litre Diesel
Up to engine suffix 'J' inclusive

PLATE REF.	1	2	3	4	DESCRIPTION	QTY.	PART No.	REMARKS
1					FUEL PUMP, MECHANICAL	1	550324	With red diaphragm
						1	500419	For early type pump
2					Filter for bowl	1	27H1330	
3					Washer for bowl	1	236891	
4					Sediment bowl	1	108771	
5					Retainer for bowl	1	275565	
6					Joint washer, fuel pump to cylinder block	2	GHF242	
7					Self-locking nut fixing fuel pump	2	243967	⎤ Early type
8					Joint washer ⎤ For mechanical pump	2	247929	⎦ fixing
9					Union ⎦ inlet and outlet	1	56495	
10					DISTRIBUTOR PUMP	1	509009	
11					Accelerator control lever ⎤ For	1	554525	
12					Stop lever ⎥ distributor	1	AAU1053	
					Swivel for stop lever ⎥ pump	1	AAU1054	
					Clamp bolt for swivel			
13					Joint washer for injection pipe, distributor pump end	6	247802	
					Sleeve for control lever stop screw	1	546282	
14					Joint washer for distributor pump	1	247212	
15					Plain washer ⎤ Fixing distributor	3	GHF301	
16					Spring washer ⎥ pump to	3	GHF332	
17					Nut (5/16" UNF) ⎦ cylinder block	3	GHF201	
18					FUEL FILTER	1	517682	
19					Element for fuel filter	1	37H1581	
					Seal for element, small	1	AAU9903	
					Seal for element, large, top	1	AAU9902	
					Seal for element, large, bottom	1	522939	
					Special centre bolt for filter	1	522940	
					Washer for centre bolt	1	37H770	
					Seal for centre bolt	1	517689	
19					Plug for filter	1	517705	
20					Joint washer for plug	1	BH605101	
21					Bolt (5/16" UNF x 1¼" long) ⎤ Fixing	2	544389	
22					Distance plate ⎥ filter	2	GHF332	
23					Spring washer ⎥ to dash	2	3830	
24					Plain washer ⎦	2	501224	
25					Rivnut (5/16" UNF)	1	517707	⎤ Not required when addi-
26					Non-return valve for filter	1	517706	⎦ tional fuel filter is fitted
27					Joint washer for non-return valve			
28					Leak-off pipe, complete	1	548262	
29					Banjo bolt ⎤ Fixing leak-off pipe	4	273521	
30					Washer ⎦ to injector	8	273069	
31					Fuel pipe, spill return to tank	1	509909	
32					Banjo bolt ⎤ Fixing spill return	1	505805	
33					Joint washer ⎥ pipe to filter	2	51797K*	
34					Bracket for leak-off pipe	1	521584*	
35					Locknut (5/16" UNF) fixing bracket to injector stud			
36					Bolt (2BA x ¾" long) ⎤ Fixing spill	2	254881	
					Plain washer ⎥ return pipe	1	250961*	
37					Spring washer ⎥ to bracket on	1	558190	
38					Nut (2BA) ⎦ injector stud	1	WM702001	
						1	RTC608	

* NO LONGER SERVICED

FUEL SYSTEM - Fuel Injection, 2¼ litre Diesel
Up to engine suffix 'J' inclusive

1L 09

1L 09

GROUP H

FUEL SYSTEM - Fuel Injection, 2¼ litre Diesel
Up to engine suffix 'J' inclusive

PLATE REF.	DESCRIPTION	QTY.	PART No.	REMARKS
39	Clip for spill return pipe	1	525168	
	Plain washer for spill pipe clip	2	RTC840	
	Fuel pipe, mechanical pump to filter	1	552439*	Not required when additional fuel filter is fitted
	Nut] Fixing pipe	1	557531	
	Olive] to filter	1	517690	
	Olive for fuel pipe, pump end	1	530966	
	Nut] Fixing pipe to mechanical pump	1	270115	Early type fixing
	Olive]	1	270105	
40	Fuel pipe, filter to distributor pump	1	517685	
41	Nut] Fixing pipe	1	517690	
42	Olive] to filter	1	530966	
43	Banjo bolt] Fixing pipe to	1	275266	
44	Joint washer] distributor pump	2	275265	
45	Clip, fixing pipe to distributor pump	1	8885	
46	Fuel pipe, distributor pump return to filter	1	517686	
47	Nut] Fixing pipe to	1	517690	
48	Olive] filter	1	530966	
49	Clip, fixing fuel pipe to dash	1	517684*	
50	Drive screw, fixing clip	2	AB608031	
51	Double pipe clip (fixing distributor pump feed and return pipes together)	2	243395	
52	Bolt (2BA x ½")] Fixing pipes	2	234603	
53	Spring washer (2BA)] and	1	WM702001	
54	Nut (2BA)] clips	1	RTC608	
55	INJECTOR COMPLETE	4	90515552	
56	Nozzle for injector	4	247726	
57	Joint washer for injector, copper	4	247179	Part of engine assembly
58	Joint washer for injector, steel	4	272474	
59	Clamping strip for injector	4	531897	
60	Spring washer] Fixing injector	8	GHF332	
61	Nut (5/16" UNF)] to cylinder head	8	GHF201	
62	Injector pipe to No.1 cylinder	1	513926	
	Injector pipe to No.3 cylinder	1	513928	
	Injector pipe to No.4 cylinder	1	513929	
	Injector pipe to No.2 cylinder	1	513927	
63	Damper for injector pipe	4	277838*	Damper and Shroud type fixing
64	Shroud for damper	2	277839*	
63	Clamping plate for injector pipe grommet	4	541229	Clamp and grommet type fixing
64	Grommet for injector pipe	4	272512	
65	Bracket for damper shroud	1	277816*	Up to engines numbered 27105814
66	Support strap for shroud	1	278002*	
67	Steady strap for shroud	1	278021*	
68	Backplate for shroud	2	277815*	Not required with clamp and grommet type fixing

* NO LONGER SERVICED

1L 10

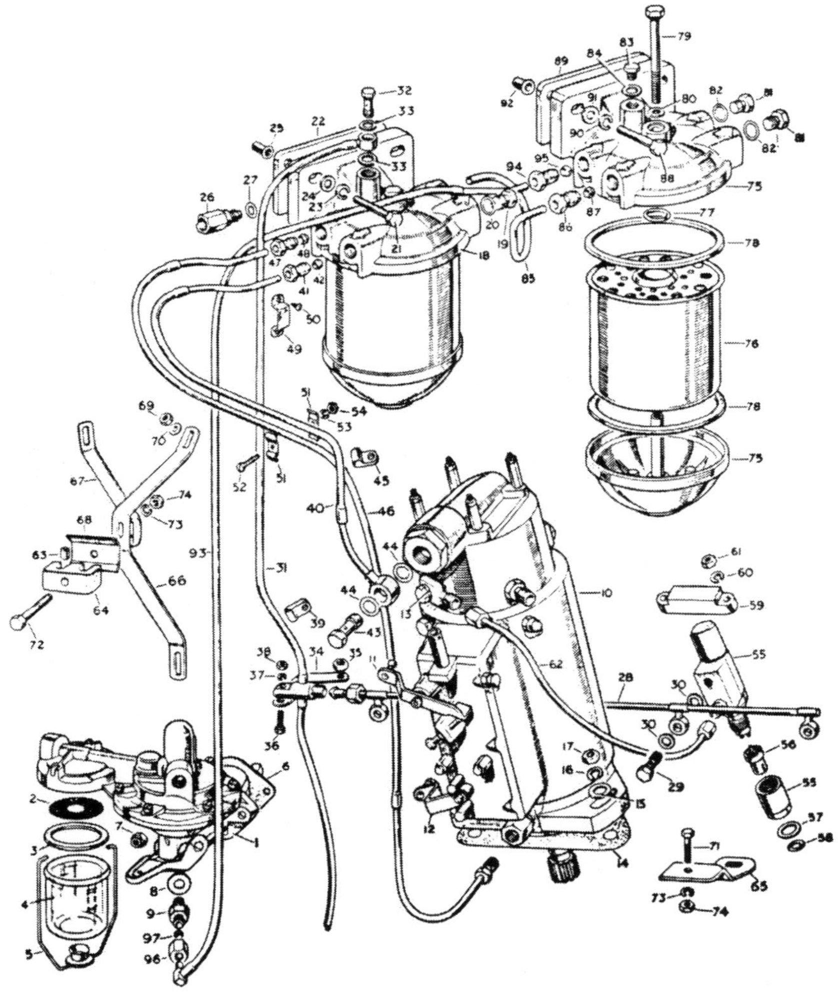

FUEL SYSTEM – Fuel Injection, 2¼ litre Diesel
Up to engine suffix 'J' inclusive

PLATE REF.	1 2 3 4	DESCRIPTION	QTY. PART No.	REMARKS
69		Locknut (5/16" UNF) — Fixing straps to injection studs	4 NT605061	
70		Plain washer	4 4047	
71		Bolt, front (5/16" UNF x 1¼") — Fixing shrouds and dampers to backplate, strap and support brkt	1 256220	Up to engines numbered
			GHF104	numbered 27105814
72		Bolt, rear (5/16" UNF x 1¼")	2 GHF332	27105814
73		Spring washer	2 GHF201	
74		Nut (5/16" UNF)	1 BH605101	From engines numbered
		Bolt (5/16" UNF x 1¼") — Fixing shrouds and dampers to backplate	2 GHF201	numbered
		Spring washer	2 255205	27105815
		Nut (5/16" UNF)	2 GHF331	onwards
		Bolt (¼" UNF x 9/16") — Fixing clamping plates and grommets	2 GHF200	} Part of engine assembly
		Spring washer	1 255204	Up to engines numbered
		Nut (¼" UNF)	GHF331	numbered
		Bolt (¼" UNF x ½") — Fixing bracket for damper shroud to oil filler pipe	2 GHF200	27105814
		Plain washer		
		Spring washer		
		Nut (¼" UNF)		

ADDITIONAL FUEL FILTER, COMPLETE ASSEMBLY

PLATE REF.	DESCRIPTION	QTY. PART No.	REMARKS
75	Fuel filter	1 522756*	
76	Element for fuel filter	1 517682*	
77	Seal for element, small	1 37H1581	
78	Seal for element, large, top	1 37H575	
	Seal for element, large, bottom	1 AAU9903	
79	Special centre bolt for filter	1 AAU9902	
80	Washer for centre bolt	1 522939	
	Seal for centre bolt	1 522940	
81	Plug for fuel filter	1 37H770	
82	Joint washer for plug	1 517689	
83	Plug for fuel filter, top, leak-off	2 517706	
84	Joint washer for leak-off plug	2 517855	
85	Transfer pipe, extra filter to basic filter	1 517976*	
86	Nut — Fixing pipe to filter	2 544391*	
87	Olive	2 517690	Early type
		530966	fixing
88	Bolt (5/16" UNF x 1¼")	1 BH605101	
89	Distance plate — Fixing filter to dash	2 544389	
90	Spring washer	2 GHF332	
91	Plain washer	2 3830	
92	Rivnut (5/16" UNF)	2 501224	
93	Fuel pipe, mechanical pump to twin filters	1 552438	
94	Olive for fuel pipe, pump end	1 557531	
95	Nut — Fixing pipe to filter	1 517690	
96	Olive	1 530966	
97	Nut — Fixing pipe to mechanical pump	1 270115	Early type
	Olive	1 270105	fixing
	Repair kit for mechanical fuel pump	1 8G8844	
	Overhaul kit for mechanical fuel pump	1 8G8845	

Standard on Export models — Optional equipment on Home models

* NO LONGER SERVICED

1L 11

FL FUEL SYSTEM – Fuel Injection, 2¼ litre Diesel
Up to engine suffix 'J' inclusive

1L 11

FUEL SYSTEM - Fuel Injection, 2¼ litre Diesel
From engines suffix 'K' onwards

1L 12

GROUP H   FUEL SYSTEM - FUEL INJECTION 2¼ LITRE DIESEL
From engine suffix 'K' onwards

PLATE REF.	1 2 3 4	DESCRIPTION	QTY.	PART No.	REMARKS
1		FUEL PUMP, MECHANICAL	1	563146	
2		Joint washer, fuel pump to cylinder block	1	275565	
3		Self-locking nut, fixing fuel pump	2	GHF242	
4		DISTRIBUTOR PUMP	1	564495	
5		Accelerator control lever	1	509009	
6		Stop lever	1	90568525	*
7		Swivel for stop lever	1	AAU1053	
		Clamp bolt for swivel	1	AAU1054	
8		Union, fuel pipe connection	1	90566617	
9		Joint washer for injection pipe, distributor pump end	6	247802	
10		Sleeve for control lever stop screw	1	546282	
11		Joint washer for distributor pump	1	247212	
12		Plain washer ⎤ Fixing distributor pump to	3	2920	
13		Spring washer ⎥ cylinder block	3	GHF332	
14		Nut (5/16" UNF) ⎦	3	GHF201	
15		Non-return valve for distributor pump	1	ERC3788	
16		Joint washer for non-return valve	1	517706	
17		FUEL FILTER	1	563190	
18		Element for fuel filter	1	90517711	
19		Seal for element, small	1	37H575	
20		Seal for element, large, top	1	AAU9903	
		Seal for element, large, bottom	1	AAU9902	
21		Special centre bolt for filter	1	522939	
22		Washer for centre bolt	1	522940	
		Seal for centre bolt	1	37H770	
23		Nylon drain plug for filter	1	605012	
24		Rubber seal for drain plug	1	605013	
25		Plug for filter	2	517689	
26		Joint washer for plug	2	517706	
27		Bolt (5/16" UNF x 1⅛" long) ⎤ Fixing	2	255029	
28		Distance plate ⎥ filter	1	544389	
29		Spring washer ⎥ to dash	2	GHF332	
30		Plain washer ⎥	2	3830	
31		Rivnut (5/16" UNF) ⎦	2	501224	
32		INJECTOR COMPLETE	4	564332	
33		Nozzle for injector	4	247726	
34		Joint washer for injector, copper	4	247179	
35		Joint washer for injector, steel	4	272474	
36		Spring washer ⎤ Fixing injectors to	8	GHF332	
37		Nut (5/16" UNF) ⎦ cylinder head studs	8	GHF201	
		Injector pipe to No.1 cylinder	1	563165	
		Injector pipe to No.3 cylinder	1	563167	
		Injector pipe to No.4 cylinder	1	563168	
38		Injector pipe to No.2 cylinder	1	563166	
39		Clamping plate for injector pipe grommet	4	541229	
40		Grommet for injector pipe	4	272512	
		Bolt (¼" UNF x 9/16" long) ⎤ Fixing clamping	2	255205	
		Spring washer ⎥ plates and	2	GHF331	
		Nut (¼" UNF) ⎦ grommets	2	GHF200	

1L 12

* NO LONGER SERVICED

PLATE REF.	1 2 3 4 Description	QTY.	PART No.	REMARKS
61	Fuel pipe, filter to leak off pipe	1	564905	
62	Banjo bolt ⎤Fixing fuel pipe	1	13H1515	
63	Joint washer ⎦to filter	*2	517976	
63	Double clip ⎤Fixing fuel pipes	*1	517684	
64	Drive screw ⎦to bulkhead	2	AB610051	
65	SEDIMENT COMPLETE ASSEMBLY	1	605560	88 and 109
	SEDIMENT COMPLETE ASSEMBLY	*	90605561	109 Station Wagon
65	Sedimentor	1	562748	
	Seal for sedimentor, top	1	AAU9903	
66	Seal for sedimentor, bottom	1	AAU9902	
67	Special centre bolt for sedimentor	1	522939	
	Washer for centre bolt	1	522940	
68	Seal for centre bolt	1	37H770	
69	Drain plug for sedimentor	1	605010	
70	Rubber seal for drain plug	1	605011	
71	Mounting bracket for sedimentor	1	569585	
	Set screw (¼" UNF x 1" long) ⎤Fixing sedimentor to mounting bracket	2	GHF105	
	Plain washer	2	WB110061	
	Spring washer	2	GHF333	
	Nut (¼" UNF)	2	GHF202	
	Screw (10 UNF x ½" long) ⎤Fixing mounting bracket to chassis	4	78384	
	Plain washer	4	WC702101	
	Spring washer	4	WM702001	
	Rivnut (10 UNF)	4	532848	
72	Fuel pipe, tank to sedimentor	1	564936	88 and 109
	Fuel pipe, tank to sedimentor	1	564963	109 Station Wagon
73	Fuel pipe, sedimentor to mechanical pump	1	564937	
	Double clip ⎤Fixing fuel pipe to chassis sidemember	1	509412	
	Drive screw	1	72626	
	Repair kit for mechanical fuel pump	1	8G8844	
	Overhaul kit for mechanical fuel pump	1	8G8845	

Remarks: Standard on Export models. Optional equipment on Home models.

* NO LONGER SERVICED

1L 14

PLATE REF.	1 2 3 4 Description	QTY.	PART No.	REMARKS
41	Leak off pipe	1	ERC4480	
42	Banjo bolt for No 1, 2 and 3 injectors ⎤Fixing leak	3	273521	
43	Banjo union for No 4 injector ⎥off pipe	3	563195	
44	Joint washers for banjo bolt ⎦to injectors	8	273069	
45	Fuel pipe, leak off return to tank	1	564907	88 and 109
	Fuel pipe, leak off return to tank	1	564962	109 Station Wagon
	Fuel pipe, tank to mechanical pump	1	564898	88 and 109 ⎤Except when sedimentor is fitted
	Fuel pipe, tank to mechanical pump	1	552436	109 Station Wagon ⎦
46	Double clip ⎤Clamping feed and return	2	243395	
	Bolt (2BA x ¾" long) ⎦pipes together	1	234603	
	Spring washer	1	WM702001	
	Nut (2BA)	1	RTC608	
	Double clip	1	509417	88 and 109
	Drive screw ⎤Fixing feed and return pipes to chassis sidemember	1	72626	
	Double clip	3	509415	109 Station Wagon
	Drive screw	3	72626	
48	Double clip for feed and return pipes	1	509412	
49	Bracket for clip ⎤Fixing clip and bracket to chassis crossmember		270297*	Alternative to 4 lines below
	Bolt (2BA x ¾" long)	3	234603	
	Plain washer	4	3902	
	Spring washer	3	WM702001	
	Nut (2BA)	3	RTC608	
	Clip for fuel pipe	1	90514721	
	Bolt (¼" UNF x ¾" long) ⎤Fixing clip to No 3 crossmember	1	255206	Alternative to 6 lines above
	Spring washer	1	GHF331	
	Nut (¼" UNF)	1	GHF200	
	Double clip	1	509412	
	Bracket for clip ⎤Fixing pipes to check strap mounting in chassis	1	NRC76	
	Bolt (2BA x ¾" long)	1	237121	109 Station Wagon
	Spring washer	1	WM702001	
	Nut (2BA)	1	RTC608	
	Fuel pipe, mechanical pump and distributor pump to filter	1	564899	
51	Banjo bolt ⎤Fixing fuel pipe	1	90568489	
52	Joint washer ⎦to mechanical pump	2	231576	
53	Nut ⎤Fixing pipe	1	517690	
54	Olive ⎦to filter	1	530966	
55	Fuel pipe, filter to distributor pump	1	564902	
56	Nut ⎤Fixing pipe	1	517690	
57	Olive ⎦to filter	1	530966	
58	Banjo bolt ⎤Fixing pipe to	1	275266	
59	Joint washer ⎦distributor pump	2	275265	
60	Clip ⎤Fixing fuel	1	8885	
	Spring washer ⎥pipe to	1	WM702001	
	Nut (10 UNF) ⎦distributor pump	1	HN2005	

* NO LONGER SERVICED

1L 13

123

GROUP H
FUEL SYSTEM - Pipes, 4 cylinder models

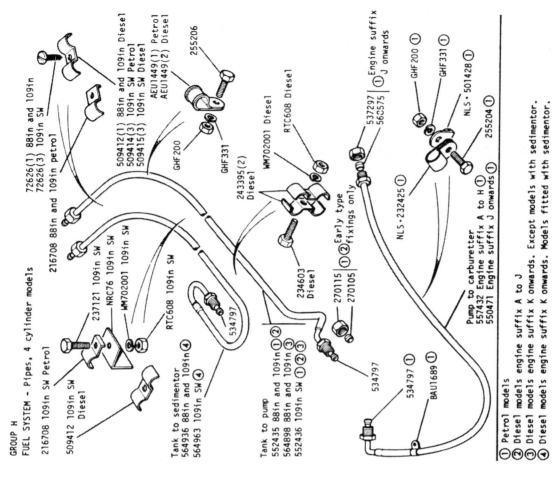

72626(1) 88in and 109in
72626(3) 109in SW

216708 109in SW

216708 88in and 109in

509412(1) 88in and 109in Diesel
509414(3) 109in SW Petrol
509415(3) 109in SW Diesel

GHF200

GHF331

AEU1449(1) Petrol
AEU1449(2) Diesel

255206

WM702001 Diesel

243395(2) Diesel

RTC608 Diesel

270115 (1)(2) Early type
270105 (1)(2) fixings only

234603 Diesel

537297 (1) Engine suffix
562575 (1) J onwards

GHF200 (1)

GHF331 (1)

NLS · 501428 (1)

255204 (1)

NLS-232425 (1)

Pump to carburetter
557432 Engine suffix A to J
550471 Engine suffix K onwards

216708 109in SW Petrol

509412 109in SW Petrol

237121 109in SW
NRC76 109in SW
WM702001 109in SW

RTC608 109in SW

509412 109in SW Diesel

534797

Tank to sedimentor
564936 88in and 109in (4)
564963 109in SW (4)

Tank to pump
552435 88in and 109in (1)(2)
564898 88in and 109in (1)(2)(3)
552436 109in SW (1)(2)(3)

534797

534797 (1)

BAU1689 (1)

REMARKS

(1) Petrol models
(2) Diesel models engine suffix A to J
(3) Diesel models engine suffix K onwards. Except models with sedimentor.
(4) Diesel models engine suffix K onwards. Models fitted with sedimentor.

1L 16

GROUP H
FUEL SYSTEM - Air Cleaner, 2¼ litre Diesel

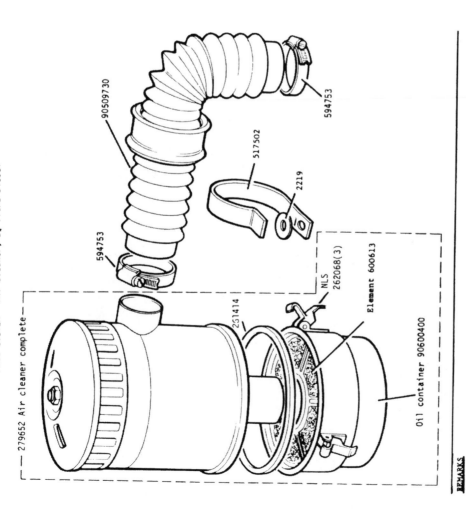

— 279652 Air cleaner complete —

90509730

594753

594753

517502

2219

NLS 262068(3)

Element 600613

251414

Oil container 90600400

1L 15

GROUP H
FUEL FILLER - 4 cylinder, 109" Station Wagon

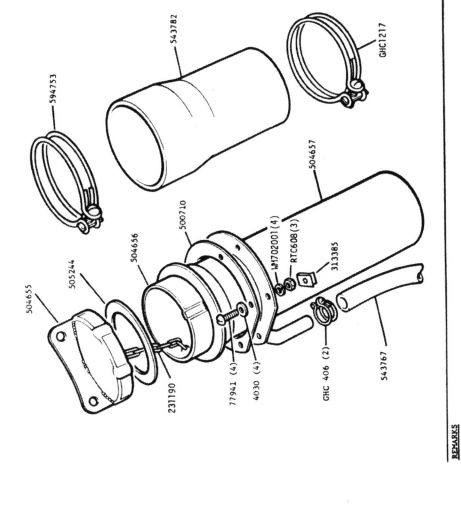

594753
543782
GHC1217
504657
500710
504656
505244
504655
WM702001(4)
RTC608(3)
313385
231190
77941 (4)
4030 (4)
GHC 406 (2)
543767

REMARKS
Telescopic filler tube complete 277259

1L 17

GROUP H
FUEL FILLER - All 4 cylinder models, except 109" Station Wagon

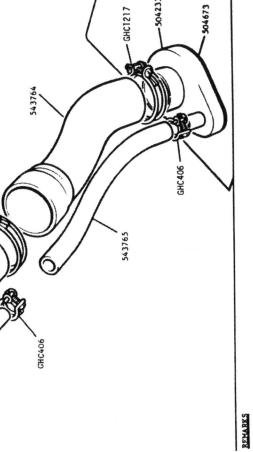

504655
505244
504656
231190
500710
GHC406
77941 (4)
4030 (4)
WM702001(4)
313385
RTC608(3)
504657
594753
GHC406
GHC1217
504233
504673
543764
543765

REMARKS
Telescopic filler tube complete 277259

1L 17

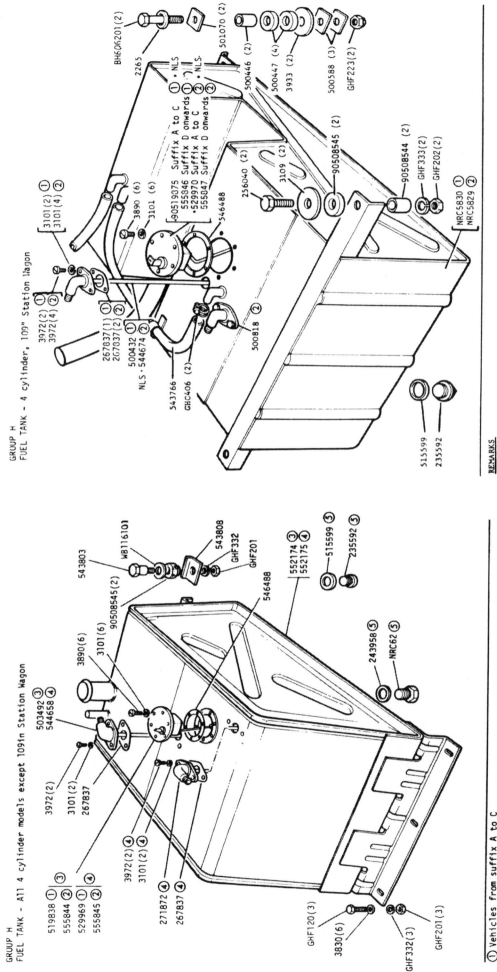

GROUP H
FUEL TANK - 4 cylinder, 109" Station Wagon

GROUP H
FUEL TANK - All 4 cylinder models except 109in Station Wagon

BH606201(2)

2265

501070 (2)

500446 (2)

500447 (4)

3933 (2)

500588 (3)

GHF223(2)

① · NLS
② · NLS
Suffix A to C
Suffix D onwards
Suffix A to C
Suffix D onwards

90519075
555846
·529970
555047

3101(2) ①
3101(4) ②

3890 (6)

3101 (6)

256040 (2)

3109 (2)

90508545 (2)

546488

90508544 (2)

GHF333(2)

GHF202(2)

NRC5830 ①
NRC5829 ②

3972(2) ①
3972(4) ②

267837(1) ①
267837(2) ②

500432 ①
NLS·544674 ②

543766

GHC406 (2)

500818 ②

515599

235592

1L 18

REMARKS

① Petrol
② Diesel

WB11610①

543803

90508545(2)

543808

GHF332

GHF201

546488

552174 ③
552175 ④

515599 ⑤

235592 ⑤

243958 ⑤

NRC62 ⑤

519838 ① ③
555844 ②
529969 ① ④
555845 ②

3972(2)
3101(2)
267837

3972(2) ④
3101(2) ④

271872 ④
267837 ④

GHF120(3)

3830(6)

GHF332(3)

GHF201(3)

503492 ③
544658 ④

3890(6)

3101(6)

1L 18

① Vehicles from suffix A to C
② Vehicles from suffix D onwards
③ Petrol
④ Diesel
⑤ Alternatives

126

GROUP H FUEL SYSTEM - Carburetter, SU type, 2.6 litre Petrol

PLATE REF.	1 2 3 4	DESCRIPTION	QTY.	PART No.	REMARKS
		CARBURETTER (HD6)	* 1	AUD247	Carburetter and fittings are not included in engine assembly. @ See footnote for applicability.
1		Carburetter body	* 1	90512458	
3		Adaptor, ignition and weakening device	1	504082	
4		Gasket for adaptor	1	AUC2014	
5		Shakeproof washer) Fixing	2	601594	
6		Screw) adaptor	2	AUC2175	
7		Union for ignition pipe	* 1	108364	
8		Union for economiser pipe	* 1	245295	
9		Suction chamber and piston complete	* 1	274954	
10		Special screw fixing suction chamber	3	AUC2175	
11		Spring for piston (yellow)	1	AUC1167	
12		Thrust washer for suction chamber	1	262492	
13		Needle, SS	** 1	245292	
14		Special screw fixing needle	1	AUC2057	
15		Oil cap complete	1	GSU320	
16		Jet complete	1	AUC8155	
17		Jet bearing	1	AUC2001	
18		Jet screw	1	AUC2002	
19		Jet spring	1	AUC2006	
20		Jet housing complete	* 1	605162	
21		Throttle spindle	* 1	512459	
22		Throttle butterfly	* 1	600351	
23		Screw for throttle butterfly	2	AUC1358	
24		Throttle stop	1	274963	
25		Taper pin for throttle stop lever	* 1	108353	
26		Gland washer for throttle spindle, brass	2	274964	
27		Spring for throttle spindle gland	2	274965	
27		Gland washer for throttle spindle, langite	2	274966	
28		Retainer cap for gland washer	2	274967	
29		Slow-running adjusting valve	1	AUC2028	
30		Gland spring for slow-running	1	AUC2027	
31		Gland washer for slow-running, rubber	1	AUC2029	
32		Brass washer for slow-running	1	AUC2030	
33		Float chamber	1	6993	
34		Bolt) Fixing	4	AUC2110	
35		Shakeproof washer) float chamber	4	601594	
36		Float	1	AUC1123	
37		Lid for float chamber	* 1	10025	
38		Joint washer for float chamber lid	1	GSU551	
39		Needle valve and seat	1	GSU102	
40		Lever for float	1	AUD2285	
41		Pin for lever	1	AUC1152	

@ All items on this page up to engines numbered 3450046 9B, 34600024A

* NO LONGER SERVICED

1M 02

FUEL SYSTEM - Carburetter, SU type, 2.6 litre Petrol

1M 02

FUEL SYSTEM - Carburetter, SU type, 2.6 litre Petrol

GROUP H FUEL SYSTEM - Carburetter, SU type, 2.6 litre Petrol

PLATE REF.	1	2	3	4	DESCRIPTION	QTY.	PART No.	REMARKS
42	Banjo					* 1	245279	@See footnote for applicability
43	Fibre washer for banjo			} On	1	AUC1928	
44	Aluminium washer for banjo			} float	1	AUC1557	
45	Cap nut fixing banjo			} chamber	1	5832	
46	Double-ended union for carburetter				* 1	245278	
47	Washer for union				1	232006	
48	Filter and spring for carburetter body				1	AUC2139	
49	Economiser union for rubber tube				* 1	245258	
50	Pipe for economiser				1	512460	
51	Union for economiser pipe				1	245266	
57	Sliding rod, roller and cam shoe				1	536796	
58	Spring for sliding rod				1	274979	
59	Top plate				1	274980	
61	Stop screw, bottom				* 1	601521	
62	Stop screw, top				1	601521	
63	Spring for stop screw				2	AUC2451	
64	Cold-start lever				* 1	513991	
65	Lever for throttle return spring				* 1	501374	
	Bolt (2BA x ⅜") } Fixing lever				* 1	WM702001	
	Spring washer } to throttle				1	250961	
	Nut (2BA) } spindle				1	RTC608	
	Throttle lever for carburetter				* 1	505796	
	Bolt (2BA x ⅜") } Fixing lever				* 1	250961	
	Spring washer } to carburetter				1	WM702008	
	Nut (2BA) } spindle				1	273964	
	Ball end for carburetter lever				1	WM702001	
	Spring washer } Fixing				1	RTC608	
	Nut (2BA) } ball end				* 1		
68	Bracket for throttle return spring				1	505787	
69	Throttle return spring				1	505786	
70	Joint washer for carburetter				1	511690	
71	Joint washer for distance piece				1	511652	
72	Liner for manifold				* 1	505612	@See footnote for applicability
73	Distance piece for carburetter				1	505613	
74	Spring washer } Fixing carburetter and distance				4	GHF332	
75	Nut (5/16" UNF)} piece to cylinder head				4	GHF201	
76	Suction pipe complete				1	501769	
77	Clip for suction pipe } On				* 1	275037	
78	Rubber grommet for clip } engine				1	214229	

@ All items on this page up to engines numbered 34500469B, 34600024A

* NO LONGER SERVICED

1M 03

1M 03

FUEL SYSTEM - Carburetter, SU type, 2.6 litre Petrol

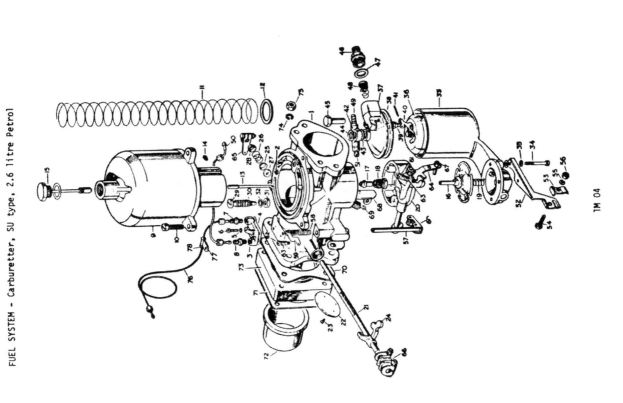

TM 04

GROUP H   FUEL SYSTEM - Carburetter, SU type, 2.6 litre Petrol

PLATE REF. 1 2 3 4	DESCRIPTION	QTY.	PART No.	REMARKS
AIR INLET ADAPTOR ASSEMBLY			557693	*
Stud) For		1	541494	*
Stud) adaptor		1	252728	*
Joint washer for adaptor		1	242375	
Locking pin for cold start cable		1	560103	
Support for cold start cable		1	563181	*
Plain washer) Fixing adaptor		1	2920	
Spring washer) and support		2	GHF332	
Nut (5/16" UNF)) to carburetter		2	GHF201	
Clip) Fixing cold start		1	41379	
Bolt (10 UNF x ½")) cable to		1	257017	
Nut (10 UNF)) support		1	257023	
Economiser hose for carburetter		1	557694	
Adaptor for economiser hose		1	242319	*
Joint washer for adaptor		1	232039	
Clip fixing hose to adaptor		1	546017	*
Clip fixing hose to adaptor and carburetter		2	50301	*
Carburetter gasket kit		1	GSU524	

* NO LONGER SERVICED

TM 04

129

FUEL SYSTEM - Carburetter, Zenith type, 2.6 litre Petrol

1M 05

GROUP H FUEL SYSTEM – CARBURETTER, ZENITH TYPE, 2.6 LITRE PETROL

PLATE REF.	1	2	3	4	DESCRIPTION	QTY.	PART No.	REMARKS
					CARBURETTER COMPLETE	1	598110	Carburetter and fittings are not included in engine assembly
1					Top cover for carburetter	1	605846	
2					Special screw and washer fixing top cover	4	605847	
3					Damper and oil cap assembly	1	605848	
4					Special washer, upper	1	605849*	
5					Special washer, lower	1	605856*	
6					Bush for damper	1	605850*	
7					Retaining ring for damper	1	90605851	
8					Air valve, shaft and diaphragm assembly	1	605844	
9					Diaphragm	1	JS499	
10					Retaining ring for diaphragm	1	605842	
11					Special screw fixing retaining ring	4	605843	
12					Return spring for air valve	1	606486	
13					Lifting pin for air valve	1	605820	
14					Spring for lifting pin	1	605821	
15					Spring clip for lifting pin	1	605822	
16					Metering needle	1	606487	
17					Locking screw for metering needle	1	605845	
18					Ignition adaptor	1	605793	
19					Throttle spindle	1	605794	
20					Butterfly for throttle	1	605800	
21					Special screw fixing butterfly	2	605801	
22					Throttle stop screw	1	605816	
23					Spring for stop screw	1	605817	
24					Throttle lever	1	605795	
25					Special nut ⎫ Fixing	1	605799	
26					Special washer ⎬ throttle	1	605797	
27					Tab washer ⎭ levers	1	RTC162	
28					Throttle stop and fast-idle lever	1	605796	
29					Special screw ⎤ For throttle stop	1	605818	
30					Locknut	1	512287	*
31					Throttle return spring	1	605802	
32					Bracket and clip for choke cable	1	605813	
33					Clip for choke bracket	1	516962	

* NO LONGER SERVICED

1M 05

PLATE REF.	1 2 3 4	DESCRIPTION	QTY.	PART No.	REMARKS
67		Joint washer for carburetter	1	568365	
68		Adaptor for carburetter	1	564446	
69		Joint washer for adaptor	1	568364	
70		Spring washer) Fixing carburetter and	4	GHF332	
71		Nut (5/16" UNF)) adaptor to cylinder head	4	GHF201	
		Suction pipe, carburetter to distributor	1	564602	For distributor with 'screw-on' connection
72		Suction pipe, carburetter to distributor	1	564603	For distributor with 'push-on' connection
73		Rubber sleeve, suction pipe to distributor	1	574878	
74		Clip for suction pipe) On	1	275037*	
75		Rubber grommet for clip) engine	1	214229	
76		Rubber sleeve, suction pipe to carburetter	1	574878	
77		AIR INLET ELBOW ASSEMBLY	1	596495	
78		Adaptor for top breather hose	1	568380	
79		Joint washer for inlet elbow	1	564447	
80		Set bolt (5/16" UNC x 2¼")) Fixing elbow	2	BH505201	
81		Set bolt (5/16" UNC x 3")) to carburetter	1	BH505241	
		Plain washer	3	RTC613	

* NO LONGER SERVICED

PLATE REF.	1 2 3 4	DESCRIPTION	QTY.	PART No.	REMARKS
34		Special screw fixing choke bracket	1	605815	
35		Cold start spindle	1	605804	
36		Special washer for starter spindle	1	605806	
37		Cold start spring	1	605805	
38		Cover for cold start) Fixing	1	605803	
39		Special screw) cover	2	605811	
40		Shakeproof washer	2	90605812	
41		Return spring for cam lever	1	605809	
42		Cam lever for cold start	1	605808	
43		Clamping screw for cam lever swivel	1	605807	
44		Spacing washer] Fixing cam	1	605810	
45		Shakeproof washer] lever to cold	1	601877	
46		Special nut] start spindle	1	601838	
47		Jet orifice	1	605827	
48		Spring	1	605828	
49		Guide bush	1	607815	
50		'O' ring For jet orifice	1	RTC165	
51		Bush	1	607815	
52		Special washer	1	512319	
53		Carrier for jet orifice	1	605830	
54		Adjusting screw for jet orifice	1	12882	
55		'O' ring for adjusting screw	1	512307	
56		'O' ring for carrier	1	512308	
57		Needle valve (1.75mm)	1	AAU1484	Late type For use with early type 2.22 mm needle valve
58		Washer for needle valve	1	605852*	For use with late type 1.75 mm needle valve
		Washer for needle valve	1	606301	
59		Float chamber	1	605836	
60		Gasket for float chamber	1	605835	
61		Special screw, long] Fixing	4	605837	
62		Special screw, short] float	2	605838	
63		Spring washer] chamber	6	605839	
64		Plain washer	6	605840	
65		Float and arm	1	605833	
66		Spindle for float	1	605834	
		Gasket kit for carburetter	1	605857	
		Overhaul kit for carburetter	1	606098	

* NO LONGER SERVICED

GROUP H FUEL PUMP, 6 - CYLINDER MODEL

PLATE REF.	1	2	3	4	DESCRIPTION	QTY.	PART No.	REMARKS
					FUEL PUMP, DOUBLE ENTRY TYPE	1	AZX1500	
1					Coil complete	2	530884	*
2					Spring for armature	2	530885	*
3					Diaphragm complete	2	WZX1712	*
4					Roller for diaphragm	22	90608241	
5					Joint washer diaphragm to body, inner	2	538499	
					Joint washer, diaphragm to body, outer	2	AUB849	
6					Screw fixing coil housings to body	12	538501	
7					Body	1	538485	
8					Special screw) For earth	1	538502	*
9					Spring washer) terminal	1	538503	*
10					'Lucar' connector	1	538510	*
11					Valve assembly	4	AUB6062	
12					Sealing washer for valve assembly	6	AUB676	*
13					Screw for valve assembly	4	538489	*
14					Filter	1	WZX1700	*
15					Unions, inlet and outlets	3	538498	*
16					Sealing ring for unions	3	AUB654	
17					Rocker and blade	2	AUB6106	
18					Dished washer	2	538507	*
19					Screw	2	538506	*
20					End plate	2	2E0585	*
21					Screw) Fixing	4	262308	
22					Spring washer) end plate	2	262303	*
23					Joint washer for dished cover	1	AUA573	
24					Dished washer) Fixing	1	538491	
25					Spring washer) dished cover	1	605322	
26					Bolt) to body	1	538493	*
27					Diaphragm for air bottle	1	AUB656	
28					Joint washer, diaphragm to housing	1	AUB795	
29					Sealing ring, for air bottle cover	1	AUB657	
30					Screw, fixing air bottle cover	4	538496	*
31					Condenser	1	AUB6179	*
32					Clip for condenser	1	245384	*
33					Terminal screw	2	262307	*
34					Spring washer for terminal	2	262303	*
35					Terminal nut	2	262306	*
36					Lead washer	2	262305	*
37					Washer for terminal screw	2	538508	*
38					Cover, black	2	538509	*
39					Shakeproof washer	2	601594	*
40					'Lucar' connector	2	538510	*

* NO LONGER SERVICED

1M 08

PETROL PUMP, 5-CYLINDER MODELS

1M 08

GROUP H   FUEL PUMP, 6-CYLINDER MODELS

PLATE REF.	1	2	3	4	DESCRIPTION	QTY.	PART No.	REMARKS
41					Terminal nut, fixing 'Lucar' connector	2	262309	*
42					Insulating sleeve for terminal	2	538511	*
43					Clamp plate	2	529141	*
44					Rubber strip } Fixing petrol pump	2	534200	*
45					Bolt (¼" UNF x ⅞") } to	2	255208	
46					Self-locking nut (¼" UNF) } support bracket	1	GHF221	*
					Support bracket for fuel pump	1	562719	
					Bolt (¼" UNF x ⅝") } Fixing support	4	255206	
					Spring washer } bracket to	4	GHF331	
					Nut (¼" UNF) } chassis frame	4	GHF200	
					Diode resistor suppressor	1	CZX1004	

* NO LONGER SERVICED

1M 09

PETROL PUMP, 6-CYLINDER MODELS

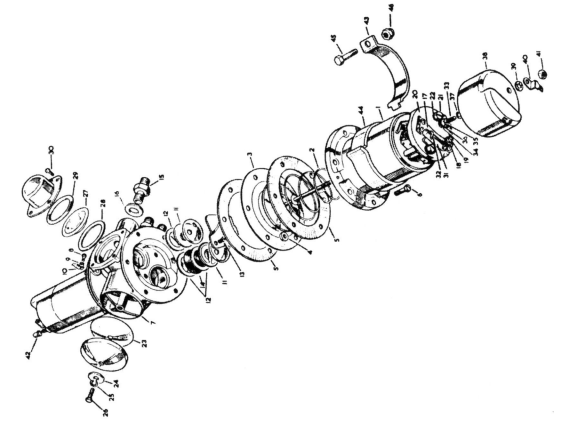

1M 09

133

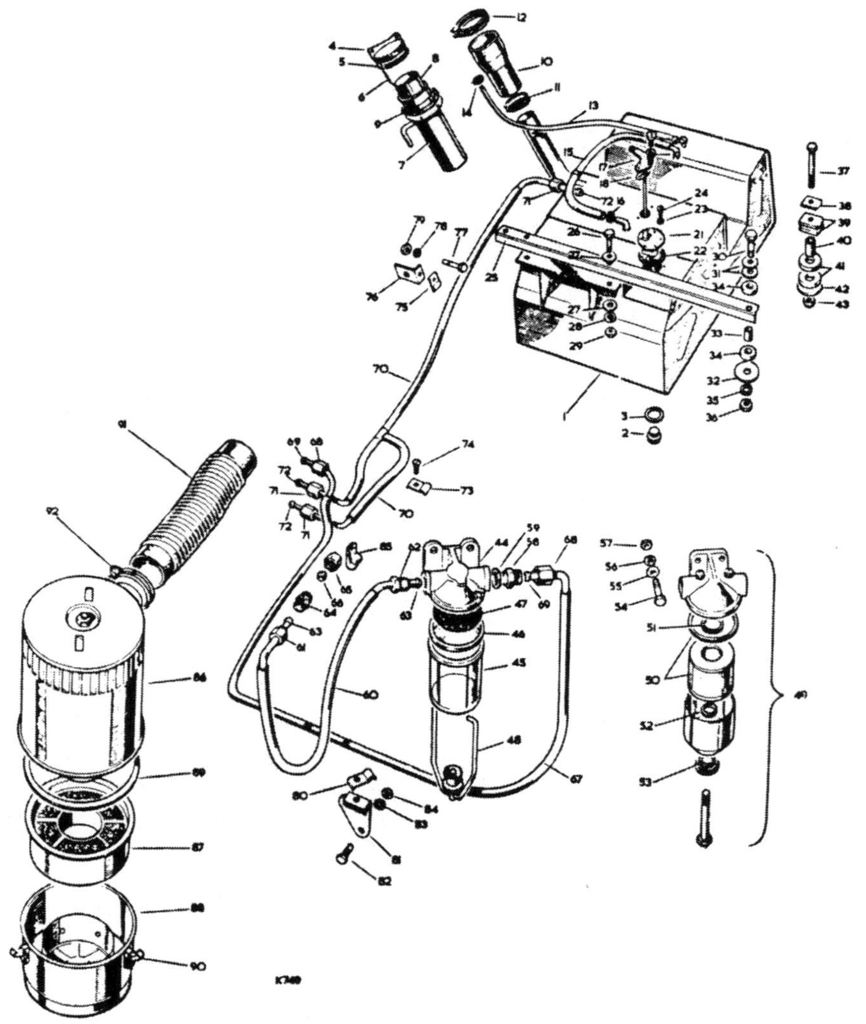

PLATE REF.	1 2 3 4 DESCRIPTION	QTY.	PART No.	REMARKS
1	FUEL TANK COMPLETE	1	90552971	Except Station Wagon
	FUEL TANK COMPLETE	1	NRC5830	Station Wagon
2	Drain plug) For	1	235592	
3	Joint washer) fuel tank	1	515599	
	TELESCOPIC FILLER TUBE COMPLETE	1	277259	
	Filler cap	1	277260	With ball valve
	Joint washer for cap	1	505244	in filler cap
	Chain for filler cap	1	231190	
	Filler tube	1	277261	
	Extension tube for filler	1	277262	
4	Filler cap	1	504655	With felt pad
5	Joint washer for cap	1	505244	in filler cap
6	Chain for filler cap	1	231190	
7	Filler tube	1	504657	
8	Extension tube for filler	1	504656	
9	Grommet for fuel tank filler	1	500710	
	Screw (2BA x 3/8"))	4	77941	
	Plain washer) Fixing	4	4030	
	Spring washer) filler to	4	WM702001	
	Special nut) body side	1	313385	
	Nut (2BA))	3	RTC608	
10	Hose, tank to filler tube	1	543782	
11	Clip for hose, bottom	1	GHC1217	
12	Clip for hose, top	1	594753	
13	Breather hose for fuel tank	1	543767	
14	Clip for breather hose	2	GHC406	
15	Air balance hose for fuel tank	1	543766	
16	Clip for air balance hose	2	GHC406	
17	Outlet elbow complete for tank	1	500432	
18	Joint washer for outlet elbow	1	267837	
19	Spring washer) Fixing elbow	2	3101	
20	Screw (3BA x 9/16")) to tank	2	3972	
21	Gauge unit for fuel tank	1	90560612	Except Station Wagon
22	Joint washer for gauge unit	1	RTC1148	
	Gauge unit for fuel tank	1	555846	Station Wagon
	Joint washer for gauge unit	1	546488	
23	Spring washer) Fixing gauge	6	3101	
24	Set screw (3BA x 3/8")) unit to tank	6	3890	
25	Support for fuel tank	1	568802	Except Station Wagon
	Bolt (1/4" UNF x 3/4"))	4	255207	1/4" UNF fixing
	Plain washer)	2	RTC609	
	Spring washer)	4	GHF331	
	Locking plate)	2	277491*	
	Square nut) Fixing support	2	277490	
	Nut (1/4" UNF)) to tank	2	GHF200	
26	Bolt (5/16" UNF x 3/4"))	2	255245	5/16" UNF fixing
27	Plain washer)	4	WD110061	
28	Spring washer)	2	GHF333	
29	Nut (5/16" UNF))	2	GHF202	

* NO LONGER SERVICED

PLATE REF.	1 2 3 4 DESCRIPTION	QTY.	PART No.	REMARKS
30	Bolt (3/8" UNF x 1 3/4"))	2	256040	
31	Plain washer, small)	4	WD110061	
32	Plain washer, large) Fixing front of fuel	2	3109	
33	Distance tube) tank to support and	2	90508544	
34	Rubber bush) chassis frame	4	90508545	
35	Spring washer)	2	GHF333	Except Station Wagon
36	Nut (3/8" UNF))	2	GHF202	
37	Bolt (3/8" UNF x 2 1/2"))	2	BH606201	
38	Distance piece)	2	501070	
39	Distance piece) Fixing rear of fuel	4	500588	
40	Distance tube) tank to support and	2	500446	
41	Mounting rubber) chassis frame	4	500447	
42	Plain washer)	2	3933	
43	Self-locking nut (3/8" UNF))	2	GHF223	
	Bolt (3/8" UNF x 1 3/4"))	2	256040	
	Plain washer) Fixing fuel	2	3109	
	Distance piece) tank to	2	90508544	
	Mounting rubber) frame at	2	90508545	
	Spring washer) front	2	GHF333	
	Nut (3/8" UNF))	2	GHF202	
	Bolt (3/8" UNF x 2 1/2"))	2	BH606201	
	Distance piece, top)	2	501070	Station Wagon
	Plain washer) Fixing	4	3933	
	Spring washer) fuel tank to	1	2265	
	Distance piece) frame at rear	2	500446	
	Mounting rubber)	4	500447	
	Distance piece, bottom)	2	500588	
	Self-locking nut (3/8" UNF))	2	GHF223	
	FUEL SEDIMENT BOWL COMPLETE	1	267494	
44	Body only	1	268793 *	
45	Bowl only	1	236891	
46	Joint washer for bowl	1	27H1330	AC Delco type
47	Gauze for bowl	1	241223	
48	Retainer for bowl	1	108771	
	Body only	1	514269 *	
	Bowl only	1	236896	
	Joint washer for bowl	1	236895	Wipac type
	Gauze for bowl	1	514270 *	
	Retainer for bowl	1	240234	
	Screw cap for retainer	1	240235 *	
49	FUEL FILTER COMPLETE	1	90577064	
50	Element and seal for filter	1	JS660	
51	Centre seal, upper	1	JS657	
52	Centre seal, lower	1	AEU1147	
53	Seal for centre bolt	1	606207	

* NO LONGER SERVICED

PLATE REF.	1 2 3 4 DESCRIPTION	QTY.	PART No.	REMARKS
	Bolt (5/16" UNF x 3/4"))	2	GHF120	
	Plain washer) Fixing sediment bowl	2	3830	
	Spring washer) to RH toe box	2	GHF332	
	Nut (5/16" UNF))	2	GHF201	
54	Bolt (1/4" UNF x 5/8"))	2	255208	
55	Plain washer) Fixing fuel filter	2	3900	
56	Spring washer) to RH toe box	2	GHF331	
57	Nut (1/4" UNF))	2	GHF200	
58	Double-ended union for filter or bowl	2	525530	1 off when Zenith type
59	Joint washer for union	2	267721	carburetter is fitted
	Petrol pipe, nylon, filter bowl to carburetter	1	559884 *	For use with
	Nut) Fixing pipe to filter	2	542845	SU type
	Olive) and carburetter	2	542846	carburetter
60	Petrol pipe, nylon, filter or bowl to carburetter	1	564581	
61	Nut, pipe to carburetter union	1	537297	
62	Nut, pipe to filter or bowl	1	524894	For use
63	Olive	2	534797	with Zenith
64	Union for petrol pipe	1	564580	type
65	Nut) Fixing union	1	537297	carburetter
66	Olive) to carburetter	1	568575	
67	Petrol pipe, nylon, pump to filter or bowl	1	559885	
68	Nut) Fixing pipe to	2	542845	
69	Olive) pump and filter	2	542846	
70	Petrol pipe, nylon, tank to pump	1	552675	
71	Nut) Fixing pipe	2	542845	
72	Olive) to pump	2	542846	
73	Clip) Fixing fuel pipe to	4	552678	
74	Drive screw) chassis sidemember	4	72626	
75	Clip)	1	552681	
76	Bracket) Fixing fuel pipe	1	NRC76	
77	Bolt (2BA x 3/8")) to body	1	237121	
78	Spring washer) support bracket	1	WM702001	
79	Nut (2BA))	1	RTC608	
80	Clip)	2	552681	
81	Bracket) Fixing fuel pipe	1	270297	
	Drive screw) to chassis	1	72626	
82	Bolt (2BA x 1/2")) crossmember	3	234603	
83	Spring washer)	3	WM702001	
84	Nut (2BA))	2	RTC608	
85	Clip fixing fuel pipe to hand brake bracket	1	589806	
86	AIR CLEANER	1	543209	
87	Element for air cleaner	1	606613	
88	Oil container	1	600401	
89	Washer for container	1	261414	
90	Toggle	3	262068 *	
91	Connection, air cleaner to carburetter adaptor or elbow	1	517903	
92	Clip, fixing connection to air cleaner and adaptor	2	594753	

* NO LONGER SERVICED

ACCELERATOR LEVER AND RODS, 2¼ LITRE PETROL

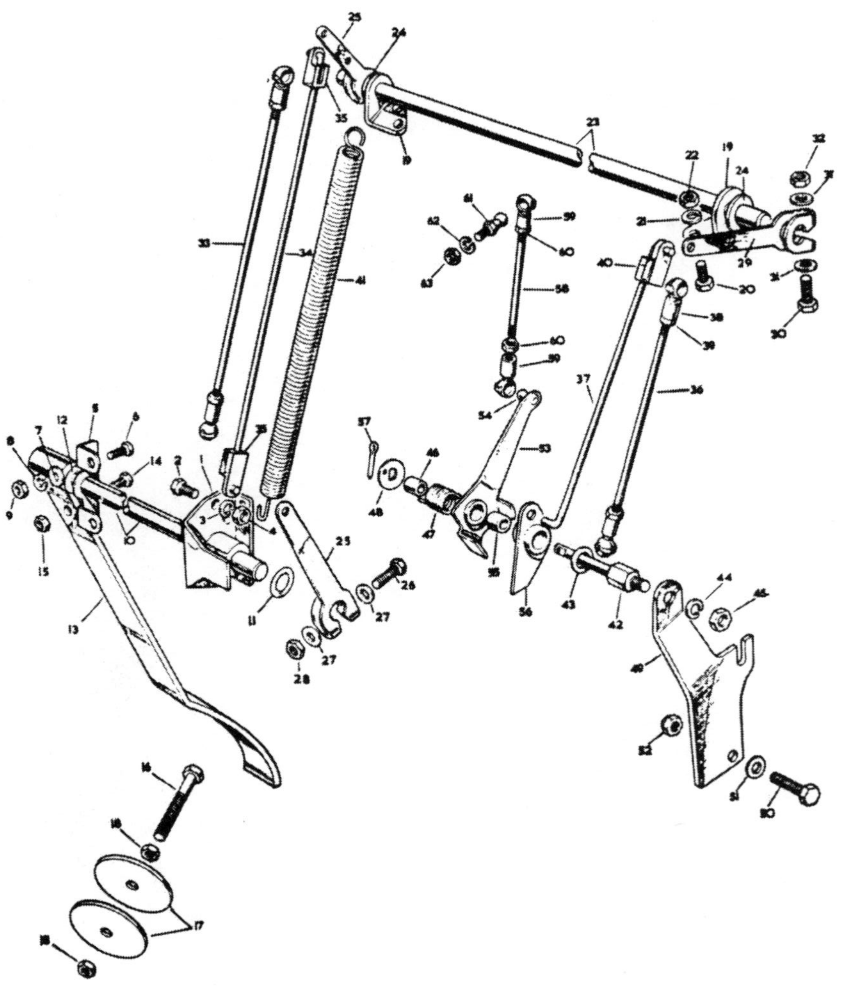

PLATE REF.	1 2 3 4 DESCRIPTION	QTY.	PART No.	REMARKS
1	Housing for accelerator shaft and pedal stop	1	277103	
2	Bolt (¼" UNF x ½")) Fixing housing	2	255204	
3	Spring washer) and pedal stop	2	GHF331	
4	Nut (¼" UNF)) to dash	2	GHF200	
5	Bracket for accelerator pedal shaft	1	272804	
6	Bolt (¼" UNF x ⅝"))	1	255206	
7	Plain washer) fixing bracket	2	WP8019	
8	Spring washer) to dash	2	GHF331	
9	Nut (¼" UNF))	2	GHF200	
10	Shaft for accelerator pedal	1	236658	RH Stg
	Shaft for accelerator pedal	1	277153	LH Stg
11	Special washer) On accelerator	1	508962	
12	Plain washer) shaft	1	RTC611	
13	Accelerator pedal	1	500257	
	ACCELERATOR PEDAL RESTRICTOR KIT	1	516057 *	88 models.
	Accelerator restrictor lever complete	1	509407 *	88 models.
	Spring, accelerator restrictor	1	264362	88 models.
	Control rod, pedal shaft to cross shaft	1	90509556	88 models.
	Control rod, relay shaft to engine	1	90509558 *	88 models.
	Stop clip for relay shaft	1	269132	RH Stg; 88 models.
	Bolt (¼" UNF x 1⅜")) Fixing clip	1	BH604091	RH Stg; 88 models.
	Nut (¼" UNF)) to shaft	1	GHF200	RH Stg; 88 models.
	Anchor plate for restrictor spring	1	240708	88 models. Up to vehicle suffix 'C' inclusive
	Bolt (5/16" UNF x ½")) Fixing anchor	1	255223	RH Stg; 88 models. Up to vehicle suffix 'C' inclusive
	Spring washer) plate to	1	GHF332	RH Stg; 88 models. Up to vehicle suffix 'C' inclusive
	Nut (5/16" UNF)) toe board	1	GHF201	RH Stg; 88 models. Up to vehicle suffix 'C' inclusive
	Bolt (¼" UNF x 1¼")) Lever stop	1	255211	88 models. Up to vehicle suffix 'C' inclusive
	Nut (¼" UNF)) on toe board	2	GHF200	88 models. Up to vehicle suffix 'C' inclusive
14	Bolt (5/16" UNF x ⅞")) Fixing pedal	1	255027	
15	Nut (5/16" UNF)) to shaft	1	GHF201	
16	Bolt (5/16" UNF x 1⅜"))	1	255029	
17	Plain washer) Pedal stop in floor	2	2258	
18	Nut (5/16" UNF))	2	GHF201	
19	Bracket for accelerator cross shaft, 'L' shaped	2	236998	Alternatives
	Bracket for accelerator cross shaft, 'U' shaped	2	236665	Alternatives
20	Bolt (¼" UNF x ⅝")) Fixing	4	255206	2 off on LH Stg
21	Spring washer) bracket	4	GHF331	2 off on LH Stg
22	Nut (¼" UNF)) to dash	4	GHF200	2 off on LH Stg
23	Cross Shaft for accelerator	1	277154	RH Stg
	Cross shaft for accelerator	1	277153	LH Stg
24	Distance washer for lever	2	RTC605	
	LEVER ASSEMBLY FOR ACCELERATOR	2	277105	Ball joint type
	Ball end for lever	2	1481	Ball joint type
25	Lever for accelerator	2	277475	Linkage clip type
26	Bolt (¼" UNF x 1¼")) Fixing	2	BH604101	
27	Plain washer) levers	4	WB106041	
28	Nut (¼" UNF)) to shaft	2	GHF200	

* NO LONGER SERVICED

PLATE REF.	1 2 3 4 DESCRIPTION	QTY.	PART No.	REMARKS
	LEVER ASSEMBLY FOR CROSS SHAFT	1	277106*	Up to vehicle
	Ball end for lever	1	1481	suffix 'A'
29	Lever for cross shaft	1	531395	From vehicle suffix 'B' onwards
30	Bolt (¼" UNF x 1¼")) Fixing	1	BH604101	
31	Plain washer) lever to	2	WB106041	
32	Nut (¼" UNF)) cross shaft	1	GHF200	
33	Control rod, pedal shaft to cross shaft	1	90509556	Ball joint type] Alterna-
34	Control rod, pedal shaft to cross shaft	1	531390	Linkage clip] tives
35	Linkage clip for control rod	2	531394	type
36	Control rod, cross shaft to engine	1	90509558*	Up to vehicle suffix 'A'
	Control rod, cross shaft to engine	1	531389 *	Linkage clip type. From vehicle suffix 'B' to suffix 'C' inclusive
37	Control rod, cross shaft to engine	1	531388	Linkage clip type. From vehicle suffix 'D' onwards
38	Ball joint socket for rods	4	AAU2003	2 off (cross shaft to engin on linkage clip type. Up
39	Locknut for socket	4	RTC608	to vehicle suffix 'A'
40	Linkage clip for control rod, cross shaft to engine	2	531394	From vehicle suffix 'B' onwards
41	Return spring for pedal	1	277455	
42	Spindle for carburetter bell crank	1	502900	
43	Plain washer)	1	WB110061	
44	Spring washer) Fixing spindle	1	GHF333	
45	Nut (⅜" UNF))	1	GHF202	
46	Spacer for spindle	1	502899	
	Torsion spring for bell crank	1	502982	Up to engine suffix 'H' inclusive
47	Torsion spring for bell crank	1	552223	From engine suffix 'J' onwards
48	Special washer for torsion spring	1	502898	
	Bracket for accelerator controls	1	503430	For 5/16" diameter bolt fixing. Up to engine suffix 'C'
49	Bracket for accelerator controls	1	537707 *	For ⅜" diameter bolt fixin From engine suffix 'D' onwards
	Bolt (5/16" UNF x 1"))	2	GHF103	RH Stg
	Plain washer) Fixing bracket	2	3830	Up to engine
	Self-locking nut (5/16" UNF)) to steering	2	GHF242	suffix 'C'
50	Set screw (⅜" UNF x 1")) column support	2	GHF105	RH Stg
51	Plain washer) bracket	2	3036	From engine
52	Self-locking nut (⅜" UNF))	2	GHF243	suffix 'D' onwards
	CARBURETTER BELL CRANK LEVER ASSEMBLY	1	504619	Up to engine suffix 'C'
	CARBURETTER BELL CRANK LEVER ASSEMBLY	1	531267 *	From engine suffix 'D'
	Ball end for lever	1	1481	to suffix 'H'
	Bush for bell crank	1	277120	inclusive
53	CARBURETTER BELL CRANK LEVER ASSEMBLY	1	552097	
54	Ball end for lever	1	1481	From engine suffix 'J'
55	Bush for bell crank	1	277120	onwards

* NO LONGER SERVICED

PLATE REF.	1 2 3 4 DESCRIPTION	QTY.	PART No.	REMARKS
	CARBURETTER RELAY LEVER ASSEMBLY	1	504621*	Up to engine
	Ball end for lever	1	1481	suffix 'C'
56	Carburetter relay lever	1	504620	From engine suffix 'D' onwards
57	Split pin fixing levers to spindle	1	2392	
	Control rod and ball joint assembly	1	ERC2533	Up to engine suffix 'C'
	Locknut (¼" UNF)	2	GHF200	
	Ball joint	2	ERC2533	For earlier type control rod, not part of ERC2533
	Spring washer) Fixing rod to bell	2	GHF331	
	Nut (¼" UNF)) crank and carburetter	2	GHF200	
58	Control rod, bell crank to carburetter	1	531439	
59	Ball joint) For	2	AAU2003	
60	Locknut (2BA)) control rod	2	RTC608	From engine suffix 'D'
61	Ball end for carburetter lever	1	535168	onwards
62	Spring washer) Fixing ball end to	1	GHF331	
63	Nut (¼" UNF)) carburetter lever	1	GHF200	

* NO LONGER SERVICED

ACCELERATOR LEVER AND RODS, 2.6 LITRE PETROL

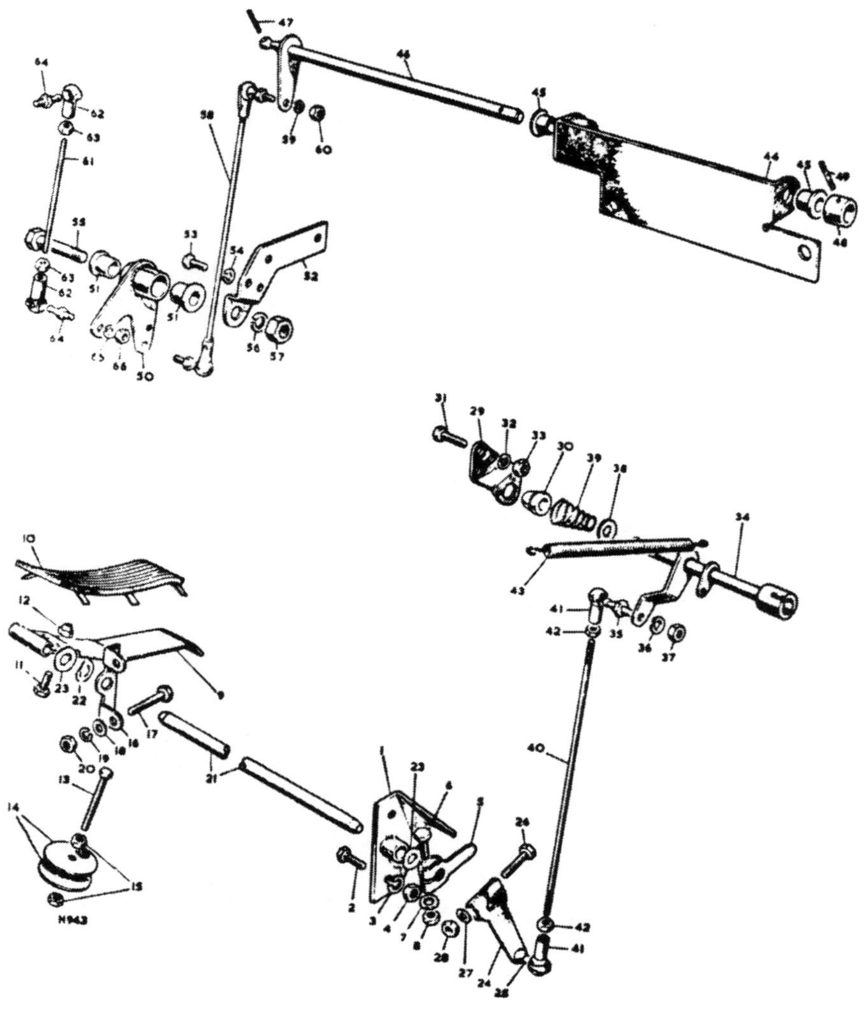

ACCELERATOR LEVERS AND RODS, 2.6 LITRE PETROL

PLATE REF.	1 2 3 4 DESCRIPTION	QTY.	PART No.	REMARKS
1	Bracket for accelerator pedal and stop	1	552975	RH Stg
	Bracket for accelerator pedal and stop	1	552520	LH Stg
2	Bolt (¼" UNF x ½")) Fixing bracket	2	255204	
3	Spring washer) and pedal stop	2	GHF331	
4	Nut (¼" UNF)) to dash	2	GHF200	
	Bolt (¼" UNF x 1¼")) Pedal stop	1	255211	
	Locknut (¼" UNF)) in bracket	1	254850	LH Stg
5	Pedal stop lever	1	230939	
6	Bolt (¼" UNF x 1¼")) Fixing lever	1	BH604101	
7	Plain washer) to	2	WB106041	RH Stg
8	Nut (¼" UNF)) pedal shaft	1	GHF200	
9	Accelerator pedal	1	500257	
10	Pad for accelerator pedal	1	GLR303	
11	Bolt (5/16" UNF x ⅞")) Fixing pedal	1	255227	
12	Nut (5/16" UNF)) to shaft	1	GHF201	
13	Bolt (5/16" UNF x 1⅜"))	1	255029	
14	Plain washer) Pedal stop in floor	2	2258	
15	Nut (5/16" UNF))	2	GHF201	
16	Bracket for accelerator pedal shaft	1	272804	
17	Bolt (¼" UNF x ⅝"))	2	255206	
18	Plain washer) Fixing bracket	2	WP8019	
19	Spring washer) to dash	2	GHF331	
20	Nut (¼" UNF))	2	GHF200	
21	Shaft for accelerator pedal	1	90562714	RH Stg
	Shaft for accelerator pedal	1	277153	LH Stg
22	Special washer) On accelerator	1	508962	
23	Plain washer) shaft	2	RTC611	
24	LEVER ASSEMBLY FOR ACCELERATOR	1	277105	Early models with SU carburetter
	LEVER ASSEMBLY FOR ACCELERATOR	* 1	90552522	Late models with Zenith carburetter
25	Ball end for lever	1	1481	
26	Bolt (¼" UNF x 1¼"))	1	BH604101	
27	Plain washer) Fixing lever to shaft	2	WB106041	
28	Nut (¼" UNF))	1	GHF200	
29	Mounting bracket for extension shaft	1	552524	
30	Bearing in mounting bracket for shaft	1	545571	
31	Bolt (¼" UNF x ⅝")) Fixing	3	255206	
32	Spring washer) mounting bracket	3	GHF331	
33	Nut (¼" UNF)) to dash	3	GHF200	
34	Extension shaft and lever	1	564793	RH Stg
	Extension shaft and lever	1	564792	LH Stg
35	Ball end for extension shaft lever	1	273964	
36	Spring washer) Fixing ball end	1	WM702001	
37	Nut (2BA)) to lever	1	RTC608	
38	Plain washer) For	* 1	4514	
39	Conical spring) extension	1	562717	RH Stg
	Conical spring) shaft	1	542861	LH Stg

* NO LONGER SERVICED

GROUP H   ACCELERATOR LEVERS AND RODS, 2.6 LITRE PETROL

PLATE REF.	1	2	3	4	DESCRIPTION	QTY.	PART No.	REMARKS
40					Control rod, pedal shaft to extension shaft	1	564797	RH Stg
					Control rod, pedal shaft to extension shaft	1	552526	LH Stg
41					Ball joint socket for control rod	2	AAU2003	
42					Locknut (2BA) fixing socket to control rod	2	RTC608	
43					Return spring, bell crank to extension shaft	1	277455	
44					BRACKET ASSEMBLY FOR ACCELERATOR CROSS-SHAFT	1	552784	
45					Bearing for cross-shaft	2	511127	
46					Accelerator cross-shaft and lever	1	552980	RH Stg
					Accelerator cross-shaft and lever	1	552989	LH Stg
47					Spiral pin for cross-shaft	1	542783	
48					Boss for cross-shaft	1	542762	
49					Spring dowel fixing boss to shaft	1	534021	
50					BELL CRANK LEVER AND BUSHES ASSEMBLY	1	598652	
51					Bush for bell crank	2	238793	
52					Support bracket for bell crank	1	562670	
53					Set bolt (¼" UNC x 9/16") ⎫ Fixing support	3	253205	
54					Spring washer ⎬ bracket to cylinder	3	GHF331	
					⎭ head			
55					Centre pin ⎫ Fixing bell crank	1	542776	
56					Spring washer ⎬ to	1	GHF332	
57					Nut (5/16" UNC) ⎭ support bracket	1	256801	
58					Control rod, cross-shaft to bell crank	2	564794	
59					Spring washer ⎫ Fixing control rod	2	WM702001	
60					Nut (10 UNF) ⎬ to levers	2	257023	
61					Control rod, bell crank to carburetter	1	531439	
62					Ball joint ⎫ For	2	AAU2003	
63					Lockut (2BA) ⎬ control rod	2	RTC608	
64					Ball end ⎭ Fixing control rod	2	273964	⎫ 1 off with
65					Spring washer ⎫ to bell crank lever	2	WM702001	⎬ Zenith type
66					Nut (2BA) ⎬ and carburetter	2	RTC608	⎭ carburetter

1N 06

ACCELERATOR LEVER AND RODS, 2.6 LITRE PETROL

1N 06

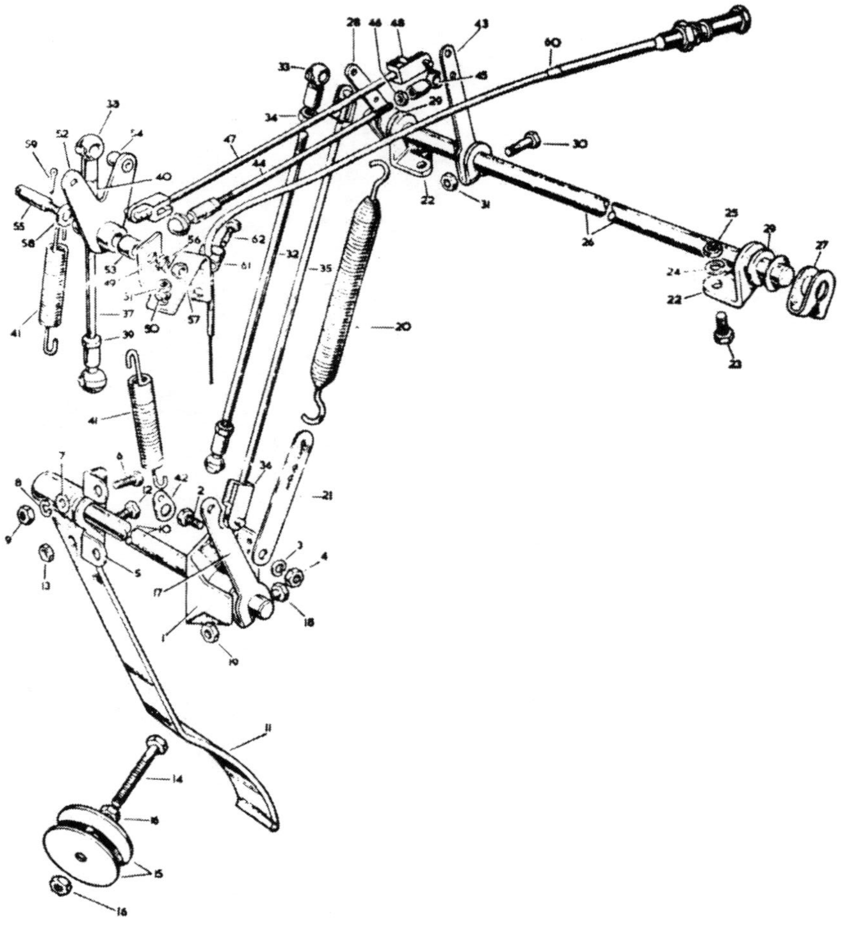

1N 07

PLATE REF. 1 2 3 4	DESCRIPTION	QTY.	PART No.	REMARKS
1	Housing for accelerator shaft and pedal stop	1	277103	
2	Bolt (¼" UNF x ½")) Fixing housing	2	255204	
3	Spring washer) and pedal stop	2	GHF331	
4	Nut (¼" UNF)) to dash	2	GHF200	
5	Bracket for accelerator pedal shaft	1	272804	
6	Bolt (¼" UNF x ⅝"))	2	255206	
7	Plain washer) Fixing bracket	2	WP8019	
8	Spring washer) to dash	2	GHF331	
9	Nut (¼" UNF))	2	GHF200	
10	Shaft for accelerator pedal	1	236658	RH Stg
	Shaft for accelerator pedal	1	277153	LH Stg
11	Accelerator pedal	1	500257	
12	Bolt (5/16" UNF x ⅞")) Fixing pedal	1	255227	
13	Nut (5/16" UNF)) to shaft	1	GHF201	
14	Bolt (5/16" UNF x 2½")) Pedal	1	SH605201	
15	Plain washer) stop in	2	2258	
16	Nut (5/16" UNF)) floor	2	GHF201	
	LEVER ASSEMBLY FOR ACCELERATOR ON PEDAL SHAFT	1	277105	] Ball joint
	Ball end for lever	1	1481	] type
17	Lever for accelerator on pedal shaft	1	277475	Linkage clip type
18	Bolt (¼" UNF x 1¼")) Fixing	1	BH604101	
	Plain washer) lever to	2	WB106041	
19	Nut (¼" UNF)) shaft	1	GHF200	
20	Return spring for pedal	1	231393	
21	Anchor for return spring	1	543498	
22	Bracket for accelerator cross shaft	2	236998	
23	Bolt (¼" UNF x ⅝")) Fixing	4	255206	
24	Spring washer) brackets	4	GHF331	
25	Nut (¼" UNF)) to dash	4	GHF200	
26	Accelerator cross shaft	1	277154	
27	Stop clip for cross shaft	1	269132	2 off on LH Stg
	Accelerator lever on cross shaft from pedal	1	277472*	Ball joint type
28	Accelerator lever on cross shaft from pedal	1	277473	Linkage clip type
29	Distance washer for cross shaft	2	RTC605	
30	Bolt (¼" UNF x 1¼")) Fixing levers and	3	BH604101	4 off on LH Stg
	Plain washer) stop clip to	6	WB106041	8 off on LH Stg
31	Nut (¼" UNF)) cross shaft	3	GHF200	4 off on LH Stg
32	Control rod, pedal shaft to cross shaft	1	90509556	] Ball
33	Ball joint socket) For	2	AAU2003	] joint
34	Locknut (2BA)) rod	2	RTC608	] type
35	Control rod, pedal shaft to cross shaft	1	531390	RH Stg] Linkage
	Control rod, pedal shaft to cross shaft	1	537792	LH Stg] clip
36	Linkage clip for control rod	2	531394	] type
37	Control rod, bell crank to accelerator lever	1	277779	Overall length 3"] Alter-
	Control rod, bell crank to accelerator lever	1	537791	Overall length 3¼"] natives
38	Ball socket)	2	AAU2003	
39	Nut (2BA)) For bell crank control rod	2	RTC608	
40	Adjuster nut)	1	277778	

* NO LONGER SERVICED

1N 07

GROUP H   ACCELERATOR LEVER AND RODS, DIESEL

PLATE REF. 1 2 3 4	DESCRIPTION	QTY.	PART No.	REMARKS
41	Return spring for accelerator and stop levers on distributor pump	2	277502	
42	Anchor for return spring	1	277565	
	Accelerator lever on cross shaft to engine	1	277612*	Ball joint type
	Ball end) Fixing	1	273964	Ball joint type
	Spring washer) ball end to	1	WM702001	
	Nut (2BA)) accelerator lever	1	RTC608	
43	Accelerator lever on cross shaft to engine	1	531395	Linkage clip type
44	Control rod, cross shaft to bell crank	1	504699*	Ball joint type
45	Ball joint) For	2	AAU2003	
46	Locknut (2BA)) control rod	1	RTC608	Ball joint type
47	Control rod, cross shaft to bell crank	1	531391	Linkage clip type
48	Linkage clip for control rod	2	531394	Linkage clip type
	Bracket for bell crank on distributor pump	2	544451	Up to engine suffix 'J' inclusive
49	Bracket for bell crank on distributor pump	1	564911	From engine suffix 'K' onwards
50	Spring washer) fixing bracket to	4	WM702001	2 off on late type bracket
51	Nut (10 UNF)) distributor pump	4	257023	type bracket
	Bell crank complete on distributor pump	1	277450	Ball joint type
52	Bell crank complete on distributor pump	1	531392	Linkage clip type
53	Bush for bell crank	1	277453	
54	Ball end for bell crank	2	1481	
55	Pin for bell crank	1	277454	
56	Shakeproof washer) Fixing pin to bell	1	78114	crank bracket
57	Nut (¼" UNF)) crank bracket	1	GHF200	
58	Plain washer) Fixing bell crank	1	2208	
59	Split pin) lever to pin	1	2390	
	'Engine stop' control	1	277478*	Up to engine suffix 'G' inclusive
60	'Engine stop' control	1	552688	From engine suffix 'H' to suffix 'J' inclusive
	'Engine stop' control	1	552689	From engine suffix 'K' onwards
61	Clip) Fixing control	1	239673	
62	Screw (2BA x ⅜")) outer cable	1	77758	Alternative to 3 lines below
	Bolt (2BA x ⅝")) to abutment	1	250962	Alternative to line above
	Spring washer) bracket on	1	WM702001	
	Nut (2BA)) distributor pump	1	RTC608	

* NO LONGER SERVICED

1N 08

1N 08

HAND CONTROL, ENGINE SPEED, DIESEL. Up to vehicle suffix 'E' inclusive

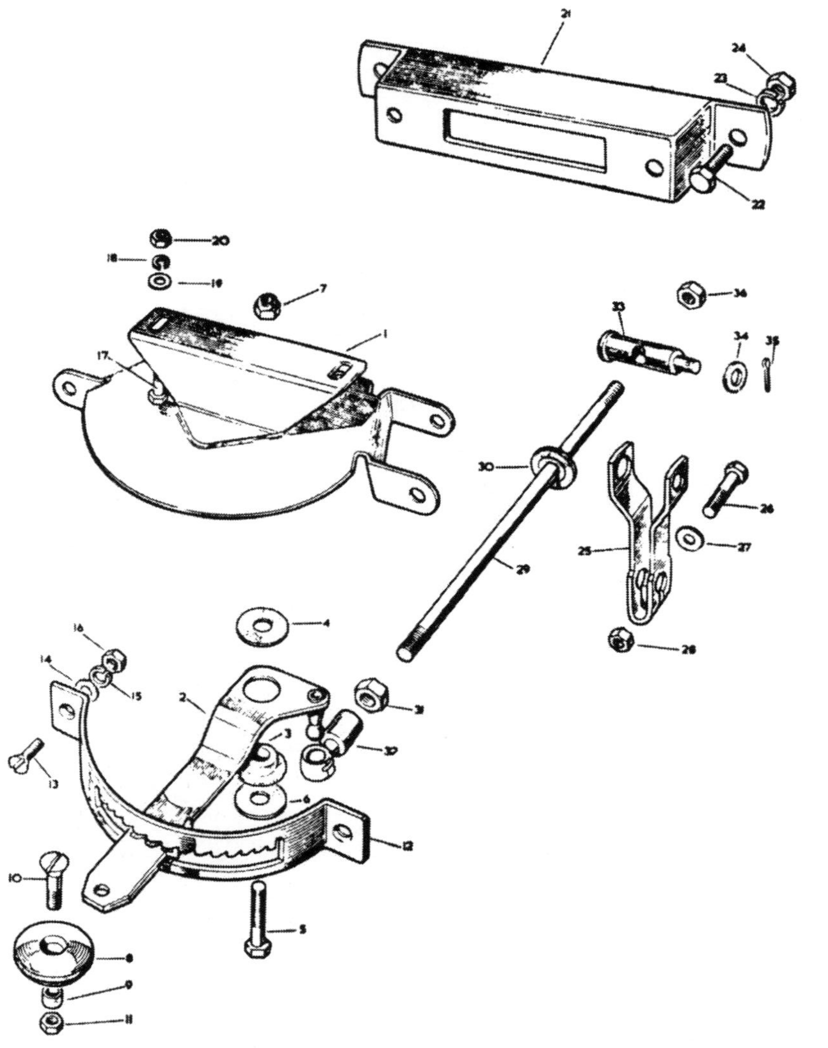

1N 09

GROUP H

HAND CONTROL, ENGINE SPEED, DIESEL
Up to vehicle suffix 'E' inclusive

PLATE REF.	1 2 3 4 DESCRIPTION	QTY.	PART No.	REMARKS
1	Housing for control quadrant	1	275706*	
2	Lever and ball end for control	1	275709*	
3	Bush for lever	1	275714	
4	Washer for lever	1	275715*	
5	Bolt (5/16" UNF x 1")) Fixing	1	GHF103	
6	Plain washer) control lever	1	RTC610	
7	Self-locking nut (5/16" UNF)) to housing	1	GHF242	
8	Knob for lever	1	552703*	
9	Nylon spacer for knob	1	552555*	
10	Special screw) Fixing knob	1	219673*	
11	Nut (2BA)) to lever	1	RTC608	
12	Quadrant plate	1	275713*	
13	Special screw)	2	278386*	
14	Plain washer) Fixing quadrant plate	2	RTC609	
15	Spring washer) to housing	2	GHF331	
16	Nut (¼" UF))	2	GHF200	
	Bolt (2BA x ½"))	2	234603	Up to vehicle suffix 'C' inclusive
	Plain washer) Fixing control	2	WC702101	
	Spring washer) to dash, upper	2	WM702001	
	Nut (2BA))	2	RTC608	
	Bolt (1¼" UNF x ½")) Fixing	2	255206	
	Spring washer) control to	2	GHF331	
	Nut (¼" UNF)) dash, lower	2	GHF200	
17	Bolt (10 UNF x ½"))	2	257017	From vehicle suffix 'D' to 'E' inclusive
18	Spring washer) Fixing control	2	WM702001	
19	Plain washer) to dash, upper	4	WC702101	
20	Nut (10 UNF))	2	257023	
21	Mounting box for hand speed control	1	338428	
22	Bolt (¼" UNF x ½")) Fixing mounting box	4	255204	
23	Spring washer) and speed control	4	GHF331	
24	Nut (¼" UNF)) to dash, lower	4	GHF200	
25	Operating lever for hand engine speed control	1	276013	
26	Bolt (¼" UNF x 1⅛")) Fixing operating	1	BH604101	
27	Plain washer) lever to accelerator	1	WB106041	
28	Nut (¼" UNF)) cross shaft	1	GHF200	
29	Control rod for engine speed control	1	276014*	
30	Grommet in dash for control rod	1	312937	
31	Nut (2BA)) For	1	RTC608	
32	Ball socket) control rod	1	AAU2003	
33	Joint pin) For	1	276015	
34	Plain washer) engine speed	1	2208	
35	Split pin) control rod	1	3958	
36	Nut (2BA) fixing control rod to joint pin	2	RTC608	

* NO LONGER SERVICED

1N 09

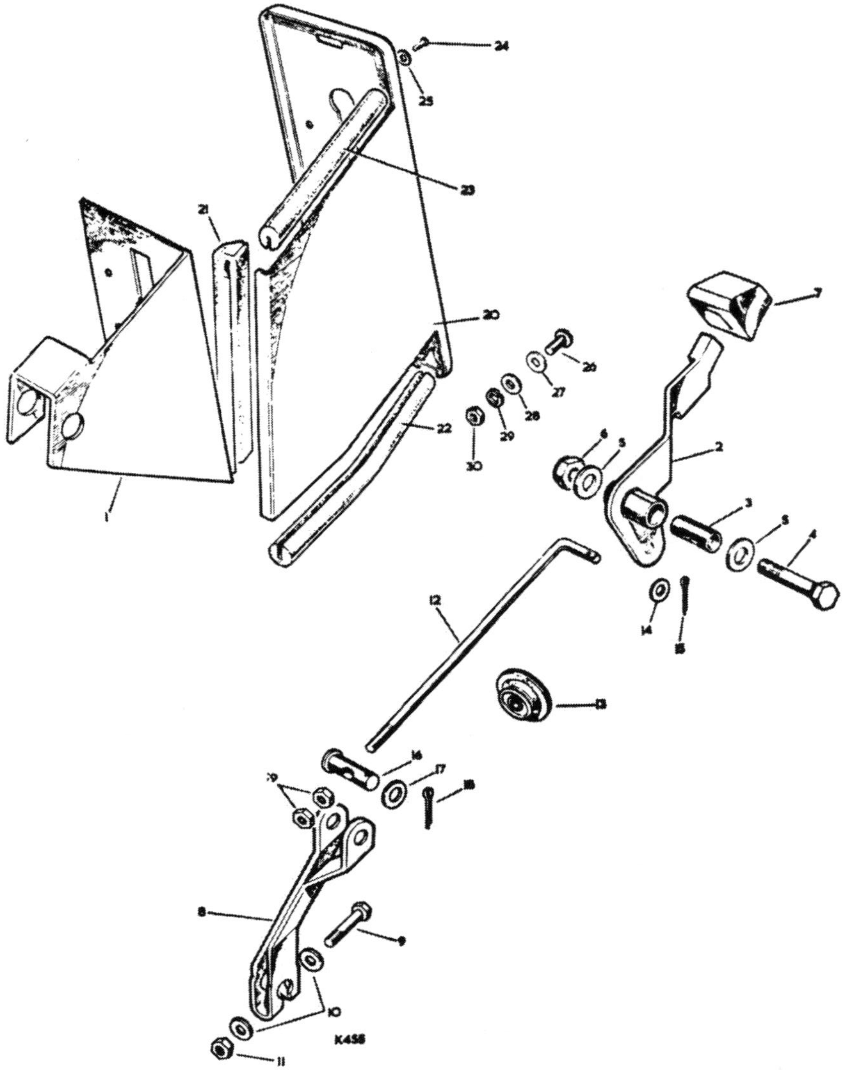

HAND CONTROL, ENGINE SPEED, DIESEL. From vehicle suffix 'F' onwards

1N 10

GROUP H   HAND CONTROL, ENGINE SPEED, DIESEL
From vehicle suffix 'F' onwards

PLATE REF.	1 2 3 4 DESCRIPTION	QTY.	PART No.	REMARKS
1	Housing and quadrant for control	1	577331	
2	Lever for control	1	90577065	
3	Distance tube for housing	1	569247	*Long type ⎤ Alter-
3	Distance tube for housing	1	577332	Short type ⎦ natives
4	Bolt (¼" UNF x 1¼") ⎤ Fixing control	1	256203	⎤ Alternatives
4	Bolt (¼" UNF x 1⅜") ⎥ lever and	1	BH604111	⎦
5	Plain washer ⎥ tube	2	RTC618	Early models
6	Self-locking nut (¼" UNF) ⎦ to housing	1	GHF221	
7	Knob for lever	1	90577060	
7	Screw (10 UNF x ¼") ⎤ Fixing knob	1	78384	
	Nut (10 UNF) ⎦ to lever	1	257023	
8	Operating lever for cross shaft	1	569250	
9	Bolt (¼" UNF x 1¼") ⎤ Fixing operating	1	BH604101	
10	Plain washer ⎥ lever to accelerator	2	WB106041	
11	Nut (¼" UNF) ⎦ cross shaft	1	GHF200	
12	Control rod for engine speed control	1	90569251	
13	Grommet in dash for control rod	1	312937	
14	Plain washer ⎤ Fixing control rod	1	3902	
15	Split pin ⎥ to control lever	1	2392	
16	Joint pin ⎦ Fixing	1	276015	
17	Plain washer ⎤ control rod to	1	2208	
18	Split pin ⎦ operating lever	1	3958	
19	Nut (2BA) fixing control rod to joint pin	2	RTC608	
20	Mounting panel, LH ⎤ For control	1	569653	* RH Stg
20	Mounting panel, RH ⎦ housing	1	569654	LH Stg
21	Rubber seal, rear ⎤ For	1	348537	
22	Rubber finisher, bottom ⎥ mounting	1	348541	
23	Rubber finisher, top ⎦ panel	1	348535	
24	Drive screw ⎤ Fixing mounting panel	6	A604021	
25	Plain washer ⎦ to control housing	6	4428	
26	Screw (2BA x ¾") ⎤ Fixing mounting	1	77869	
27	Plain washer ⎥ panel to	1	4030	
28	Packing washer ⎥ dash, lower	1	4172	
29	Spring washer ⎦	1	WM702001	
30	Nut (2BA)	1	RTC608	

*NO LONGER SERVICED

1N 10

GROUP H
EXHAUST SYSTEM - Heat Shield - all 4 cylinder petrol models

GHF120

RTC613(2)

GHF332(2)

515506

GHF201

GHF332

253029
SH505071

RTC613

SH505071 ①
SH505051 ②

GHF332

RTC613

255003 ①

GHF331 ①

RTC609 ①

515505

NLS·515331 ①

515597 ① · NLS
587095 ②

① ②

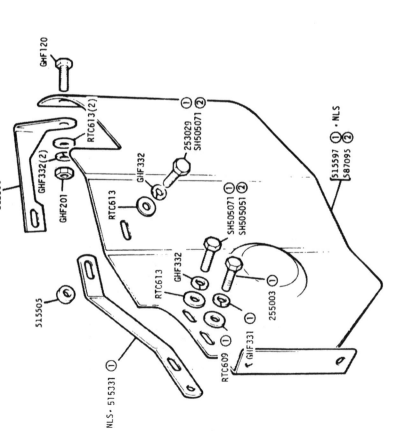

REMARKS

Heat shield assembly (Toe box) RH Stg 516496·NLS ①
Heat shield assembly (Toe box) LH Stg·NLS

① Engine suffix A to H
② Engine suffix J onwards

1N 11

GROUP H
EXHAUST SYSTEM - Front exhaust pipe 4 Cyl

GEX1369 88in Diesel
GEX1563 109in Diesel

GHF201(3)

GHF332(3)

256222(3)

GEX1372 88in Petrol

GEX1376 109in Petrol

NLS·503310 ①

GHF331(4) ①

GHF200(4) Diesel

NRC605090(4) Diesel

GHF332(4) Diesel

GEG723 Diesel

503307(2) Diesel 255208(4) Diesel

GHF331(4) Diesel

GHF200(4) Diesel

503309 Diesel

GHF332(3) Diesel

NR605090(3) Diesel

503307(2) ①

255208(4) ①

GHF332(3)

NR605090(3)

1N 11

① Diesel models up to vehicle suffix 'C' inclusive

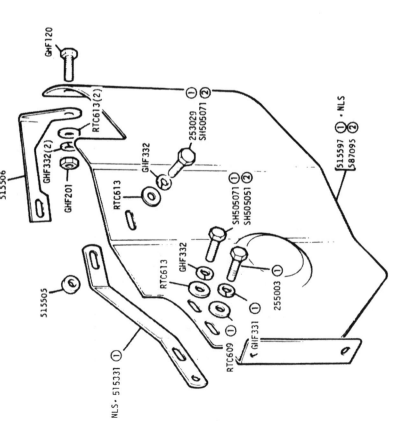

EXHAUST SYSTEM - Intermediate Pipe 109in 4 cylinder

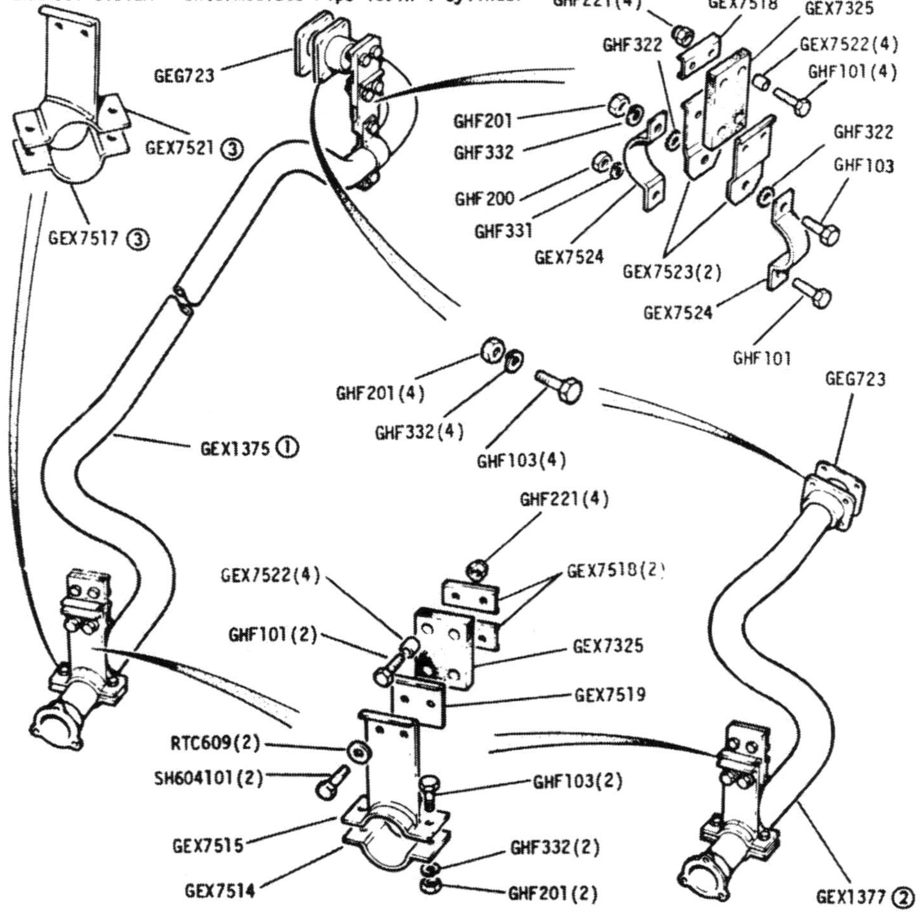

GEX7325
GEX7522(4)
GHF101(4)
GHF322
GHF103
GEX7518
GHF221(4)
GHF322
GEX7523(2)
GEX7524
GHF101
GEG723
GEX1377 ②
GHF201
GHF332
GHF200
GHF331
GEX7524
GEX7518(2)
GHF221(4)
GHF103(4)
GHF201(4)
GHF332(4)
GEX7325
GEX7519
GHF103(2)
GHF332(2)
GHF201(2)
GEX7522(4)
GHF101(2)
RTC609(2)
SH604101(2)
GEX7515
GEX7514
GEG723
GEX7521 ③
GEX7517 ③
GEX1375 ①

① Basic
② Station Wagon
③ Bracket and Saddle for alternative shaped pipe (GEX1375)

1N 12

GROUP H
EXHAUST SYSTEM - Intermediate Exhaust Pipe 88in 4 cyl

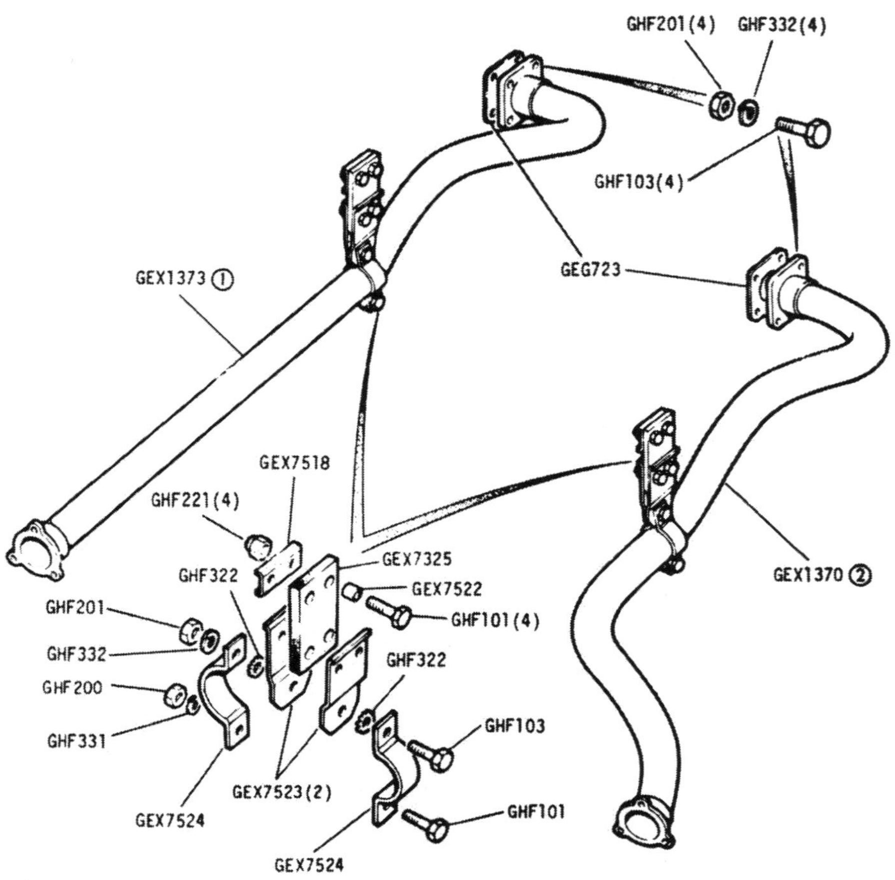

GHF201(4) GHF332(4)
GHF103(4)
GEG723
GEX1370 ②
GEX7325
GEX7522
GHF101(4)
GHF322
GHF103
GHF101
GEX7524
GEX7518
GEX7523(2)
GHF221(4)
GHF322
GEX7524
GHF201
GHF332
GHF200
GHF331
GEX1373 ①

① Petrol
② Diesel

1N 12

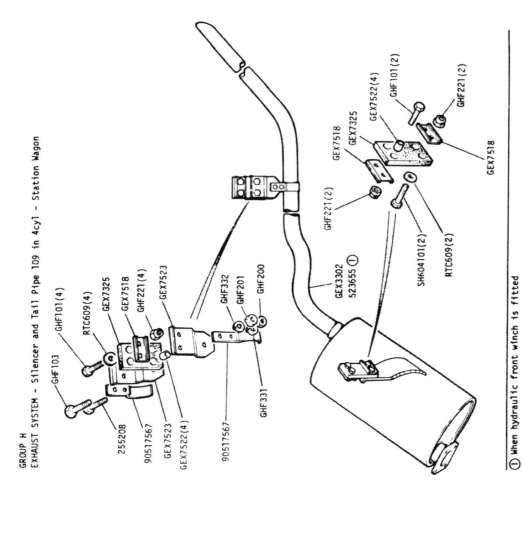

GROUP H
EXHAUST SYSTEM - Silencer and Tail Pipe 109 in 4cyl - Station Wagon

1N 13

① When hydraulic front winch is fitted

GROUP H
EXHAUST SYSTEM - Silencer and tail pipe, all 4 cylinder models, except 109 Station Wagon

1N 13

① Fixings for 88in
② Fixings for 109in
③ Required for ⊂⊙⊃ only

146

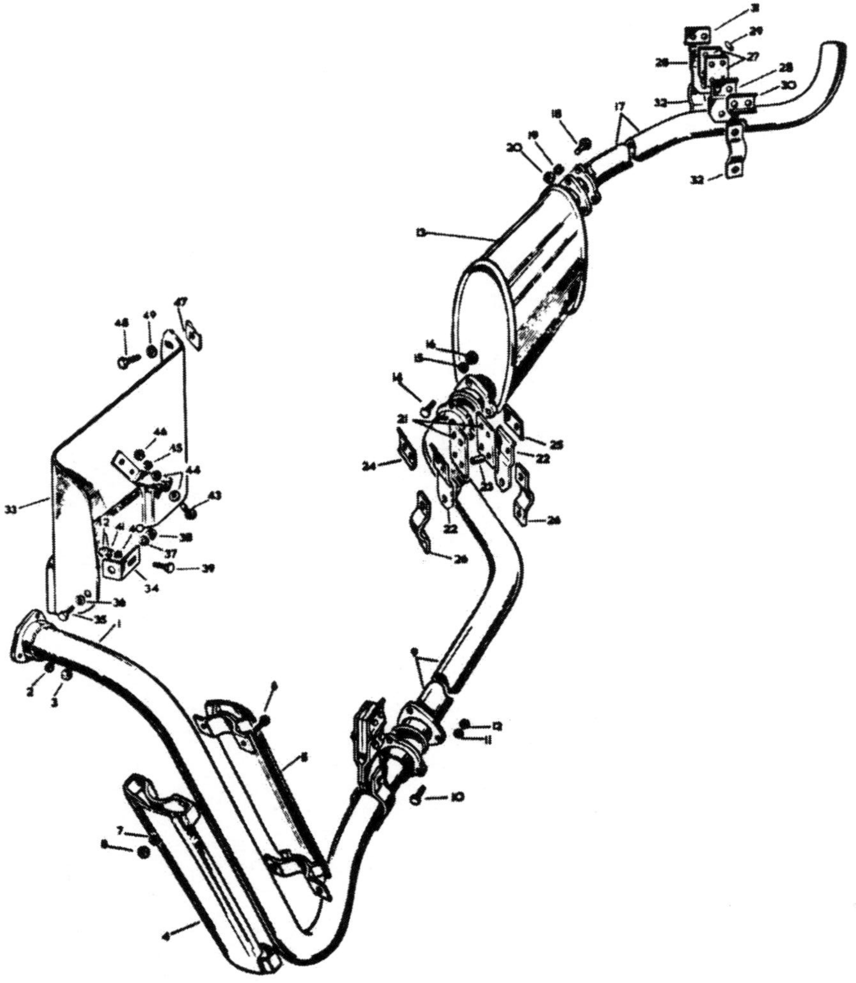

EXHAUST SYSTEM, 6-CYLINDER MODELS

1N 14

GROUP H   EXHAUST SYSTEM, 6 CYLINDER MODELS

PLATE REF.	1	2	3	4	DESCRIPTION	QTY.	PART No.	REMARKS
1					Front exhaust pipe complete	1	GEX1380	
2					Spring washer } Fixing front exhaust	3	GHF332	
3					Nut (5/16" UNF) } pipe to manifold	3	NR605090	
4					Heat shield } For front	1	552720	
5					Heat shield } exhaust pipe	1	562781	
6					Bolt (¼" UNF x ⅞") } Fixing heat shields	4	255208	
7					Spring washer } together on	4	GHF331	
8					Nut (¼" UNF) } front exhaust pipe	4	GHF200	
9					Intermediate exhaust pipe complete	1	GEX1381	
10					Bolt (5/16" UNF x 1¼") } Fixing front and	3	GHF104	
11					Spring washer } intermediate exhaust	3	GHF332	
12					Nut (5/16" UNF) } pipes together	3	GHF201	
13					Exhaust silencer	1	GEX3307	
14					Bolt (5/16" UNF x 1¼") } Fixing	3	GHF104	
15					Spring washer } intermediate pipe	3	GHF332	
16					Nut (5/16" UNF) } to silencer	3	GHF201	
17					Tail pipe complete	1	GEX1383	
18					Bolt (5/16" UNF x 1¼") } Fixing silencer	3	GHF104	
19					Spring washer } to	3	GHF332	
20					Nut (5/16" UNF) } tail pipe	3	GHF201	
21					Flexible mounting for front and intermediate pipes	2	GEX7325	
22					Plate for flexible mounting } Fixing flexible	4	GEX7523	
23					Distance piece } mounting to	8	GEX7522	
24					Clamp plate } mounting plate	2	GEX7518	
25					Packing plate } and chassis	2	GEX7516	
					Bolt (¼" UNF x 1") } frame	6	GHF101	
					Self-locking nut (¼" UNF)	6	GHF221	
26					Pipe clamp, front and intermediate exhaust	4	GEX7513	
					Bolt (5/16" UNF x 1")	4	GHF103	
					Plain washer } Fixing	4	RTC613	
					Spring washer } pipe clamp	4	GHF332	
					Nut (5/16" UNF)	4	GHF201	
27					Flexible mounting for tail pipe	1	GEX7325	
28					Plate for flexible mounting } Fixing flexible	2	GEX7523	
29					Distance piece } mounting to	4	GEX7522	
30					Clamp plate } mounting plate	1	GEX7518	
31					Packing plate } and chassis	1	GEX7516	
					Bolt (¼" UNF x 1") } frame	4	GHF101	
					Self-locking nut (¼" UNF)	4	GHF221	
32					Clamp for tail pipe	2	GEX7513	
					Bolt (5/16" UNF x 1")	2	GHF103	
					Plain washer } Fixing	2	RTC613	
					Spring washer } pipe clamp	2	GHF332	
					Nut (5/16" UNF)	2	GHF201	

1N 14

GROUP H   EXHAUST SYSTEM, 6 CYLINDER MODELS

PLATE REF.	1 2 3 4	DESCRIPTION	QTY.	PART No.	REMARKS
33		Heat shield, exhaust manifold	1	562758	
34		Support bracket for heat shield	1	562763	
35		Bolt (¼" UNF x 9/16")	1	255205	
36		Plain washer	1	WB106041	} Fixing support bracket
37		Spring washer	1	GHF331	} to heat shield
38		Nut (¼" UNF)	1	GHF200	
39		Bolt (¼" UNF x ½")	1	255245	} Fixing bracket
40		Plain washer	1	WB110061	} to dash support
41		Spring washer	1	GHF333	
42		Nut (¼" UNF)	1	GHF202	
43		Bolt (¼" UNF x 1")	1	GHF101	} Fixing
44		Plain washer	6	3831	} heat shield
45		Spring washer	1	GHF331	} to toe box
46		Nut (¼" UNF)	1	GHF200	
47		Spire nut	1	GHF713	
48		Self-tapping screw	1	78296	
49		Plain washer	1	MC702101	

TN 15

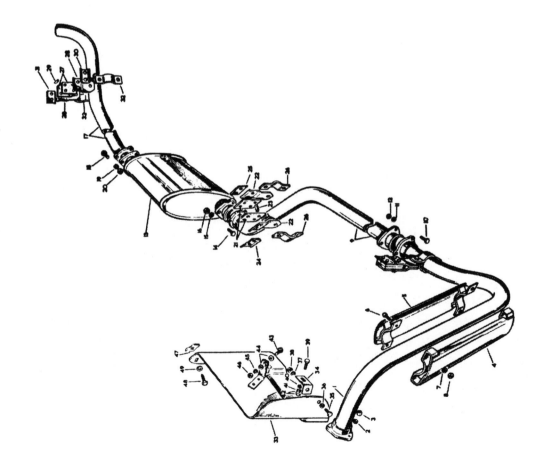

TN 15

GROUP J   RADIATOR AND FITTINGS

PLATE REF.	1 2 3 4	DESCRIPTION	QTY.	PART No.	REMARKS
1		RADIATOR BLOCK ASSEMBLY (less cowl) } With overflow bottle provision	1	577609	2¼ litre Petrol and Diesel models
		RADIATOR BLOCK ASSEMBLY (less cowl) }	1	577383	2.6 litre Petrol models
2		Cowl for fan, metal type	1	544848 *	For use with blocks 568842 or 568843 2¼ litre Petrol models
		Cowl for fan, plastic type	1	577342	For use with blocks 577382 and 577609, 2¼ litre Petrol models. Not part of radiator block assembly
		Cowl for fan, plastic type	1	562944	2.6 litre Petrol models. Not part of radiator block assembly
		Cowl for fan, metal type	1	559579 *	For use with blocks 526772 or 568845 Diesel models
		Cowl for fan, plastic type	1	568916	For use with blocks 577382 and 577609. Diesel models. Not part of radiator block assembly.
3		Drive screw fixing cowl to radiator block	10	AB606031	Early 4 cylinder models with metal type fan cowl
		Self-tapping screw } Fixing cowl to Spring washer, double coil } radiator block	9 9	562979 564741	For all plastic type fan cowls. Not part of radiator block assembly.
4		Filler cap for radiator, 10 lb pressure	1	242399 *	Diesel and 2¼ litre Petrol models Alternatives Without over-flow bottle provision
		Filler cap for radiator, 9 lb pressure	1	GRC118	
5		Chain for filler cap	1	230328*	For 10 lb pressure cap
		Chain for filler cap	1	509769	For 9 lb pressure cap
6		Retainer for chain	1	230329 *	For 10 lb pressure cap.
7		Joint washer for filler cap	1	90516914	
8		Filler cap for radiator, 9 lb pressure	1	GRC118	With overflow bottle provision
9		Joint washer for filler cap	1	564999	
10		Chain for filler cap	1	509769	

* NO LONGER SERVICED

10 02

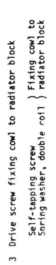

RADIATOR AND FITTINGS

10 02

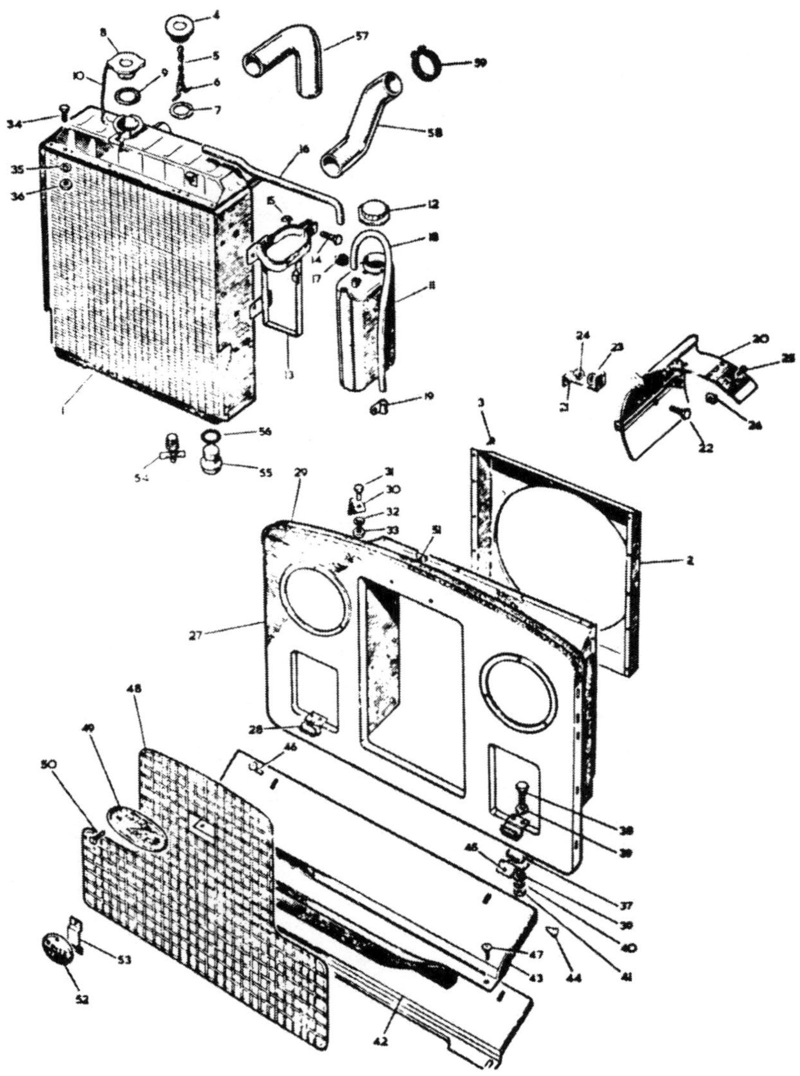

PLATE REF.	1 2 3 4 DESCRIPTION	QTY.	PART No.	REMARKS
1	Overflow bottle for radiator	1	564718	For radiator block with overflow provision
2	Cap for overflow bottle	1	564719	
3	Carrier bracket for overflow bottle	1	598531	
4	Bolt (¼" UNF x ⅞")) Clamping bottle	1	255208	
5	Self-locking nut (¼" UNF)) to carrier	1	GHF221	
6	Hose, radiator to overflow bottle	1	564720	
7	Clip, fixing hose	2	GHC304	
8	Flexible pipe, overflow bottle outlet	1	564724	
9	Clip, fixing outlet pipe	1	219677	
	Clip outlet pipe to bottle	1	90577082	
20	Shroud for fan cowl	1	551714	2¼ litre Petrol except models fitted with Lucas 2AC type 12-volt AC/DC generator
21	Steady strip for shroud	1	531332	Alternatives
	Steady strip for shroud	1	577874	
22	Bolt (¼" UNF x ⅝")) Fixing	1	255206	
	Plain washer) steady	2	RTC609	
23	Spring washer) strip	1	GHF331	
24	Nut (¼" UNF)) to shroud	1	GHF200	
	Bolt (2BA x ½"))	4	234603	
	Nut (2BA)) Fixing	4	251335	Alternative fixings
25	Drive screw) shroud	4	AB610051	
26	Spire nut)	4	78237	
	Shroud for fan cowl	1	559580	For early type radiator block fitted with metal type fan cowl. 2¼ litre Diesel. Except models fitted with Lucas 2AC type 12 volt AC/DC generator
	Drive screw)	3	AB610051	
	Spire nut)	3	78237	
	Bolt (2BA x ⅜")) Fixing shroud	1	237119	
	Spring washer)	1	WM702001	
	Nut (2BA))	1	RTC608	
	Shroud for fan cowl	1	568917	For late type radiator block fitted with plastic fan cowl 2¼ litre Diesel models
	Drive screw) Fixing	3	AB610051	
	Plain washer) shroud	3	WC702101	
	Steady strip for shroud	1	568922 *	Alternatives
	Steady strip for shroud	1	577874	
	Bolt (¼" UNF x ⅝"))	1	255206	
	Plain washer) Fixing steady strip	2	RTC609	
	Spring washer) to shroud	1	GHF331	
	Nut (¼" UNF))	1	GHF200	
	Shroud for fan cowl	1	569212	2.6 litre Petrol models
	Drive screw, fixing shroud to fan cowl	1	AB610051	
	Radiator grille panel complete	1	330950 *	Models with headlamps in grille panel. American Dollar Area up to vehicle suffix 'F' to vehicle suffix 'F' inclusive. Up to vehicle suffix 'A' for other areas.

* NO LONGER SERVICED

PLATE REF.	DESCRIPTION (1 2 3 4)	QTY	PART No.	REMARKS
27	Radiator grille panel complete	1	336466*	Models with headlamps in grille panel. From vehicle suffix 'B' to suffix 'F' inclusive. Except American Dollar Area.
	Radiator grille panel complete	1	345573*	Models with headlamps in wings. All areas from vehicle suffix 'G' onwards.
28	Support clip for grille mesh	2	330150*	
	Pop rivet, fixing clip to grille panel	4	300789	
29	Bonnet rest strip, 35" long	10	300824	
	Bifurcated rivet, fixing strip	10	68087	Alternative fixings
	Spring clip, fixing strip	1	338380	
	Protection plate for horn	1	396124	
	Special bolt) Fixing protection plate	2	303750	
	Plain washer) to radiator grille	2	3900	
	Spire nut) baffle plate RH	2	79246	
30	Protection plate for headlamp	1	348182*	From vehicle suffix 'B' to suffix 'F' inclusive
31	Bolt ($\frac{1}{4}$" UNF x $\frac{3}{8}$")) Fixing plate	1	255206	
32	Spring washer) to	1	GHF331	
33	Nut ($\frac{1}{4}$" UNF)) grille panel	1	GHF200	
34	Bolt ($\frac{1}{4}$" UNF x $\frac{3}{8}$")) Fixing	13	255206	
35	Spring washer) radiator block	13	GHF331	
36	Nut ($\frac{1}{4}$" UNF)) to grille panel	13	GHF200	
37	Spring washer) Fixing	As read	90306465	
	Rubber buffer) grille panel	3	3830	
38	Bolt (5/16" UNF x 1$\frac{1}{2}$")) and front apron	6	GHF332	
39	Plain washer) bracket to	3	GHF222	
40	Spring washer) chassis frame	3	GHF332	
41	Nut (5/16" UNF))	1	GHF201	
42	Front apron panel	1	332640*	Flat type panel
	Canvas strip for front apron panel	1	332656*	Alternative to shaped type.
43	Rivet, fixing strip	8	78226*	
	Front apron panel	1	336786*	Shaped type panel
44	Rubber buffer for front apron panel	4	310877	Alternative to flat type.
45	Securing bracket for panel	2	345192	
	Special set bolt) Fixing	2	78208	
	Plain washer) apron panel	2	3900	
	Spring washer) to	2	GHF331	Early type fixing
46	Special thread-forming screw ($\frac{1}{4}$" UNC x $\frac{1}{2}$")) securing brackets	2	78796	Late type fixing / For flat type front apron panel
	Bolt (5/16" UNF x $\frac{1}{2}$")) Fixing apron	2	GHF120	
	Spring washer) panel to chassis	2	GHF332	
	Nut (5/16" UNF)) at front	2	GHF201	Early type fixing
	Drive screw) Fixing apron	2	72628	
47	Special thread-forming screw ($\frac{1}{4}$" UNC x $\frac{3}{8}$")) panel to chassis at front	2	78795*	Late type fixing / For shaped type front apron panel / Up to vehicle suffix 'F' inclusive

* NO LONGER SERVICED

PLATE REF.	DESCRIPTION (1 2 3 4)	QTY	PART No.	REMARKS
	Front apron panel	1	395459	
	Rubber buffer for apron panel	4	310877	
	Special thread-forming screw ($\frac{1}{4}$" UNC x $\frac{1}{2}$") fixing Apron panel to securing bracket	2	78796	From vehicle suffix 'G'
	Special thread-forming screw ($\frac{3}{8}$" UNC x $\frac{3}{8}$") fixing apron panel to chassis at front	2	78795	Up to vehicle suffix 'F' inclusive
48	Grille for radiator	2	330149	
	Grille for radiator	1	345666	From vehicle suffix 'G' onwards
49	'Land-Rover' nameplate	1	332670	
50	Drive screw) Fixing nameplate and	2	GHF426	
51	Spire nut) grille to grille panel	2	7R237	
52	'Diesel' badge	1	32027F	Diesel models
53	Fixing bracket for badge	1	320333	*
	Rivet) Fixing bracket	2	7R255	*
	Lockwasher) and badge to grille	2	7R256	
54	Drain tap for radiator	1	602915	Alternatives
55	Drain plug for radiator	1	569047	
56	Joint washer for plug	1	213959	
57	Hose for radiator, top	1	GRH439	For early type radiator blocks 568842 or 568843 / 2½ litre Petrol models
58	Hose for radiator, bottom	1	GRH369	
57	Hose for radiator, top	1	GRH585	For late type radiator blocks 577382 and 577609
58	Hose for radiator, bottom	1	GRH409	
	Hose for radiator, top	1	GRH439	For radiator with straight bottom connection (568842) / 2½ litre Petrol models when Lucas 2AC type 12-volt AC/DC generator is fitted
	Hose for radiator, bottom	1	530585	
	Hose for radiator, top	1	GRH439	For radiator with angled bottom connection (568843)
	Hose for radiator, bottom	1	543F29	
	Hose for radiator, top	1	GRH530	2.6 litre Petrol models
	Hose for radiator, bottom	1	GRH531	

* NO LONGER SERVICED

GROUP J — RADIATOR AND FITTINGS

PLATE REF.	1 2 3 4	DESCRIPTION	QTY.	PART No.	REMARKS
		Hose for radiator, top	1	GRH439	For early type radiator block 568845 ⎱ Diesel models
		Hose for radiator, bottom	1	GRH369	
		Hose for radiator, top	1	GRH585	For late type radiator blocks 577382 and 577609
		Hose for radiator, bottom	1	GRH609	
59		Clip, top and bottom, for radiator hoses	2	GHC811	Early models ⎱ 2¼ litre Petrol and Diesel models
		Clip, top and bottom, for radiator hoses	2	GHC1217	
		Clip, top and bottom, for radiator hoses	4	GHC913	Late models
		Clip, top and bottom, for radiator hoses	4	GHC1217	2.6 litre Petrol models

10 06

GROUP K   ELECTRICAL - Distributor, 2¼ litre Petrol

PLATE REF.	1 2 3 4	DESCRIPTION	QTY.	PART No.	REMARKS
1		DISTRIBUTOR COMPLETE	1	ERC4110	Ducellier
2		Distributor cap	1	GDC226	
3		Brush and spring	1	AEU1428	
4		Rotor arm	1	GRA123	
5		Contact set	1	GCS125	
7		Condenser	1	GSC113	
10		Vacuum unit	1	AEU1429	

COMPONENTS FOR LUCAS TYPE DISTRIBUTORS

PLATE REF.	DESCRIPTION	QTY.	PART No.	REMARKS
2	Distributor cap	1	GDC107+	
2	Distributor cap	1	GDC103++	
3	Brush and spring	1	262703	
4	Rotor arm	1	GRA101	
6	Contact points (quickafit)	1	GCS101	
6	Contact breaker base plate (long pivot post)	1	503684	} Alternatives
7	Contact breaker base plate (short pivot post)	1	9060760?++	}
7	Condenser for distributor	1	GSC111	
8	Auto advance springs set	1	502285	* For distributor LU40609
8	Auto advance springs set	1	600476	* For distributor LU40944 and 41363
9	Auto advance weight	1	262708	* For distributor LU40609
9	Auto advance weight	1	539572	* For distributor LU40944 and 41363
10	Vacuum unit	1	608111	
11	Cam	1	245008	* For distributor LU40609
11	Cam	1	605785++	*For distributor LU40944 and 41363
12	Shaft and action plate	1	269990	* For distributor LU40609
12	Shaft and action plate	1	539575	* For distributor LU40944 and 41363
13	Bush for shaft	1	245012	* For distributor LU40609
13	Bush for shaft	1	600334+	* For distributor LU40944
13	Bush for shaft	1	606895++	* For distributor LU41363
14	Driving dog	1	513679	
15	Terminal bush and lead	1	502283	For distributor LU40609
15	Terminal bush and lead	1	600329	For distributor LU40944 and 41363
16	Clamping plate	1	245003+	For distributor LU40609 and 40944
16	Clamping plate	1	245857	* For distributor LU41363
17	Clip for cover	2	502287	*
18	Sundry parts kit	1	245015	*
18	Adaptor	1	247672	* Up to engine suffix 'F' 7:1 compression ratio. From engine suffix 'G' onwards 8:1 compression ratio.
	Adaptor	1	549610	From engine suffix 'G' onwards 7:1 compression ratio. From engine suffix 'A' onwards 8:1 compression ratio.

+ For distributor with acorn nut connections
++ For distributor with push in type connections
* NO LONGER SERVICED

2C 02

ELECTRICAL - Distributor and Starter Motor, 2¼ litre Petrol

2C 02

GROUP K   ELECTRICAL - Distributor, 2¼ litre Petrol

PLATE REF.	1 2 3 4	DESCRIPTION	QTY.	PART No.	REMARKS
19		Joint washer, adaptor to cylinder block	1	247212	
20		Plain washer) Fixing	3	3966	
21		Spring washer) adaptor	3	GHF332	
22		Nut (5/16" UNF)) to cylinder block	3	GHF201	Alternative to set bolt type fixing
		Set bolt (5/16" UNF x ⅞"))	3	255227	Alternative to stud and nut type fixing
23		Driving shaft for distributor, top	1	247806	Spline type shaft. Up to engine suffix 'F' 7:1 compression ratio only
24		Distributor drive coupling	1	549611	Blade type coupling. From engine suffix 'G' onwards. From engine suffix 'A' onwards 8:1 compression ratio
25		Cork washer for distributor housing	1	52278	
26		Plain washer) Fixing	1	WB106041	
27		Spring washer) distributor	1	GHF331	
28		Set bolt (¼" UNF x 9/16")) to adaptor	1	253205	
29		Sparking plug	4	N8	For 7:1 compression ratio engines
29		Sparking plug	4	N12Y	For 8:1 compression ratio engines
30		Joint washer for sparking plug	4	40441	
31		Suppressor for sparking plug	4	240138 *	) Alternative to 5 lines below
32		Sparking plug cover	4	214262 *	)
33		Sealing ring for plug cover	4	90213172 *	)
34		Cable nut	9	214278 *	)
35		Washer for cable nut	3	214279 *	)
36		Suppressor and cover for sparking plug	4	WCX600 *	) Alternatives to
37		Rubber boot for suppressor	4	240408 *	) 5 lines above
38		Cable nut	5	214278 *	)
39		Washer for cable nut	5	214279 *	)
40		Rubber boot for cable nut	5	507001	
		HT wire	As reqd	80K03+	
		Lead, HT, distributor to coil (nut connection for distributor, push-in connection for coil)	1	568766	
41		Distributor lead set	1	GHT173	For Ducellier distributor
41		Distributor lead set	1	GHT130++	For Lucas distributor

+ For distributor with acorn nut connections
++ For distributor with push-in type connections
* NO LONGER SERVICED

2C 03

ELECTRICAL - Distributor and Starter Motor, 2¼ litre Petrol

2C 03

ELECTRICAL - Distributor and Starter Motor, 2¼ litre Petrol

GROUP K   ELECTRICAL - Starter Motor, 2¼ litre Petrol

PLATE REF.	1 2 3 4 DESCRIPTION	QTY.	PART No.	REMARKS
42	STARTER MOTOR COMPLETE	1	GEU419	
43	End cover bracket, commutator	1	AEU1586	
44	Bracket, drive end	1	608174	
45	Armature	1	90608175	
	Bush kit	1	608172	
48	Pinion and sleeve	1	244711	
49	Pinion retaining kit	1	607932	
50	Main spring for pinion	1	7H5007	
	Retention kit, armature shaft	1	AEU1367	
53	Brush set	1	GSB112	
	Sundry parts kit	1	90608178	
	COMPONENT PARTS FOR STARTER MOTOR COMPLETE GEU411 WHICH IS NO LONGER AVAILABLE			
43	Bracket, commutator end	1	244706	
44	Bracket, drive end	1	244713	
45	Armature	1	244715	
47	Bush, commutator end	1	242958	
46	Bush, pinion end	1	244714	
48	Pinion and sleeve	1	244711	
49	Pinion retaining kit	1	607932	
50	Main spring for pinion	1	7H5007	
51	Nut for pinion	1	244709	For armature LU255463
	Cup) For armature	1	9060621?	*) For armature) LU54245913
	Circlip) shaft	1	606220	*
52	Field coil for starter	1	242961	*
53	Brush set	1	GSB103	
54	Spring set for brushes	1	601754	
55	Bolt for bracket	2	244717	*
56	Cover band	1	244705	*
57	Grease cap	1	243095	
	Sundry parts kit	1	244718	
58	Nut (⅜" UNF)) Fixing	2	GHF202	
59	Spring washer) starter motor to	2	GHF333	
	Fan disc washer) flywheel housing	1	90512305	

* NO LONGER SERVICED

2C 04

ELECTRICAL - Distributor and Starter Motor, 2.6 litre Petrol

GROUP K   ELECTRICAL - Distributor, 2.6 litre Petrol

PLATE REF.	1 2 3 4	DESCRIPTION	QTY.	PART No.	REMARKS
1		DISTRIBUTOR COMPLETE	1	541492*	Early type with side cable fixing Distributor and fittings are not included in engine assembly
		DISTRIBUTOR COMPLETE	1	ERC545	Late type with top cable fixing
2		Distributor cap	1	GDC101	For distributor 541492
3		Distributor cap	1	GDC115	For distributors 568729, 597735, ERC545
4		Brush and spring for cap	1	262703	For distributors 541492, 568729, 597735
5		Rotor arm, standard	1	GRA102	For distributor ERC545
6		Rotor arm, speed limiting	1	CRA119	For distributors 541492, 568729
		Contact points	1	GCS107	
		Contact points	1	GCS101	For distributors 597735, ERC545
7		Condenser	1	GSC111	
8		Auto advance spring set	1	608421*	For distributors 541492, 568729
		Auto advance spring set	1	RTC1019*	For distributors 597735, ERC545
9		Auto advance weight	1	539572	For distributors 541492, 597735, ERC545
10		Vacuum unit	1	539573	For distributor 568729
		Vacuum unit	1	606574*	
11		Clamping plate	1	245857*	For distributors 541492, 568729
12		Base plate for contact breaker	1	502282	
		Base plate for contact breaker	1	90607607	For distributors 597735, ERC545
13		Cam	1	539578*	
14		Shaft and action plate	1	539575*	
15		Clip for cover	1	539575*	
16		Driving dog	1	513679	
		Sealing ring	1	9938*	
17		Sundry parts kit	1	245015	
18		Cork washer for distributor housing	1	5227R	
19		Set bolt (¼" UNF x 9/16") } Fixing distributor to cylinder block	1	253205	
20		Spring washer	1	GHF331	
		Plain washer	1	WB106041	
		Distributor heat shield	1	587001	
		Bolt (¼" UNC x 9/16") } Fixing heat shield to distributor flange	1	253205	
		Plain washer	1	WB106041	
		Spring washer	1	GHF331	
		Nut (¼" UNC)	1	GHF207	

* NO LONGER SERVICED

2C 05

ELECTRICAL - Distributor and Starter Motor, 2.6 litre Petrol

2C 05

156

PLATE REF. 1 2 3 4	DESCRIPTION	QTY.	PART No.	REMARKS
21	Sparking plug	6	N5	
22	Washer for plug	6	40441	
23	Cover for sparking plug	6	214262	
24	Rubber sealing ring for plug cover	6	90213172 *	For use in conjunction with early type distributor with side cable fixing
25	Cable nut	6	214278 *	
	Rubber boot for cable nut	6	506679	
26	Washer for cable nut	6	214279	
27	Ignition wire carrier	1	231234	
28	Sparking plug lead set	1	558321 *	
29	Cable cleat securing No.1 plug lead and coil leads	1	240429	
	Cable cleat securing Nos.1, 2 & 3 plug leads to coil lead	1	240429	
30	Sparking plug lead set with integral spark plug covers	1	240429	For use in conjunction with late type distributor with top cable fixing and coil with 'push-in' connection.
31	Cable cleat } Securing plug and	1	GHT127	
32	Cable cleat } coil leads	4	240429	
		1	240428	
	Spark plug lead conversion set with integral plug covers	1	574144 @	For use in conjunction with late type distributor with top cable fixing and coil with terminal nut connection.
31	Cable cleat } Securing plug and	4	240429 @	
32	Cable cleat } coil leads	1	240428 @	

@ To enable latest type spark plug leads with integral covers to be fitted to vehicles with early type distributor and terminal nut type ignition coil, part numbers GDC115, 574144, 240429 and 240428 are required.

* NO LONGER SERVICED

PLATE REF. 1 2 3 4	DESCRIPTION	QTY.	PART No.	REMARKS
33	STARTER MOTOR COMPLETE	1	GEU419	
34	End cover bracket, commutator	1	AEU1586	
35	Bracket, drive end	1	608174	
36	Armature	1	90608175	
	Bush kit	1	608172	
39	Pinion and sleeve	1	244711	
40	Pinion retaining kit	1	607932	
41	Main spring for pinion	1	7H5007	
	Retention kit, armature shaft	1	AEU1367	
44	Brush set	1	GSB112	
	Sundry parts kit	1	90608178	

COMPONENT PARTS FOR STARTER MOTOR COMPLETE GEU411 WHICH IS NO LONGER AVAILABLE

PLATE REF. 1 2 3 4	DESCRIPTION	QTY.	PART No.	REMARKS
34	Bracket, commutator end	1	244706	
35	Bracket, drive end	1	244713	
36	Armature	1	244715	
37	Bush, commutator end	1	242958	
38	Bush, pinion end	1	244714	
39	Pinion and sleeve	1	244711	
40	Pinion retaining kit	1	607932	
41	Main spring for pinion	1	7H5007	
42	Nut for pinion	1	244709	For armature LU255463
	Cup } For armature	1	90606219 *	For armature
	Circlip } shaft	1	606220 *	LU54245913
	Field coil for starter	1	262861 *	
43	Brush set	1	GSB103	
44	Spring set for brushes	1	601754	
45	Bolt for bracket	2	244717 *	
46	Cover band	1	244705 *	
47	Grease cap	1	243095	
48	Sundry parts kit	1	244718	
49	Set bolt (⅜" Whit x 1") } Fixing starter motor	1	215703	
50	Bolt (⅜" BSF x 1¼") } to flywheel housing	1	250543	
	Spring washer	2	GHF333	
51	Nut (⅜" BSF) }	1	2827	

* NO LONGER SERVICED

GROUP K
ELECTRICAL - Starter Motor, 2½ litre Diesel
Up to engine suffix 'J' inclusive

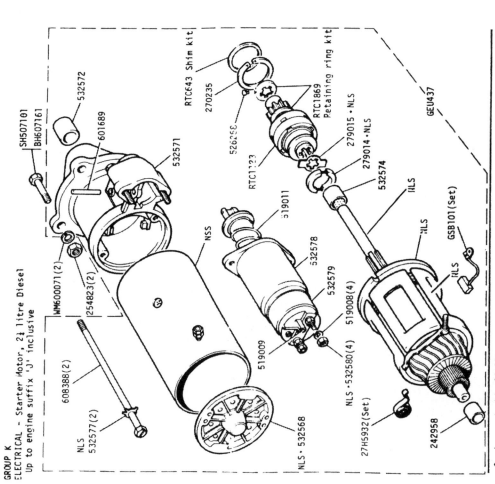

532572

SH507101
BH607161

601689

532571

WM600071(2)

(254823(2)

NLS
532577(2)

608388(2)

NSS

NLS · 532568

519011

532578

532579

519009

27H5932(Set)

NLS · 532580(4)   519008(4)

242958

RTC643 Shim kit

270235

526258

RTC1123

RTC1869
Retaining ring kit

279015 · NLS

279014 · NLS

532574

NLS

NLS

GSB101(Set)

NLS

GEU437

Sundry parts kit 270251
Starter motor complete GEU430
Terminal eyelet for starter cable 560874   Fully sealed type
Insulating boot for starter terminal 560875   Optional equipment
Clip for starter cable 575082·NLS   see 2C 09 for details
                                              of components.

This page is intentionally left blank

2C 08

ELECTRICAL - Starter Motor, 2¼ litre Diesel
From engine suffix 'K' onwards

2C 09

GROUP K   ELECTRICAL - Starter Motor. 2¼ litre Diesel

PLATE REF.	1	2	3	4	DESCRIPTION	QTY.	PART No.	REMARKS
					From engine suffix 'K' onwards.			
1					STARTER MOTOR COMPLETE	1	GEU430	Fully sealed type (see footnote)
						1	37H8531	For fully sealed starter
						1	606504	For semi sealed starter
2					Bracket, commutator end	1	608304	
2					Bracket, commutator end	1	27H5932	
3					Bush, commutator end	1	JS370	
4					Spring set for brushes	1	606505	For fully sealed starter
5					Bracket cover kit, commutator end	1	37H7618	For semi sealed starter
					Cover band or starter	1	607747	For fully sealed starter
6					Sealing ring for cover, commutator end	1	606506*	For semi sealed starter
7					Intermediate bracket kit	1	608304	
					Intermediate bracket	1	607749	For fully sealed starter
8					Bush kit for bracket	1	605621	
9					Seal kit	1	90605617	
10					Armature	1	608507*	For semi sealed starter
11					Bracket for starter, drive end	1	608304	
11					Bracket for starter, drive end	1	605615	For fully sealed starter
12					Bush kit for bracket	1	606508*	For semi sealed starter
13					Pivot pin for starter motor	1	279010*	
13					Pivot pin for starter	1	GSB101	
14					Field coil for starter	1	RTC254	
15					Brushes for starter motor, set	2	279019	For fully sealed starter
16					Drive (roller clutch) for starter	2	608388	For semi sealed starter
17					Bolt for starter motor	1	517474	
17					Bolt for starter motor	1	605658	
18					Solenoid for starter motor			
					Spindle and contact plate for starter solenoid	2	605705	
19					Special nut for starter solenoid	1	605622	
					Sundry parts kit	1	270251	
					Sundry parts kit	1	SH507101	} Fixing
20					Bolt (7/16" UNC x 1½")	1	BH607161	} starter motor
21					Set bolt (7/16" UNF x 2")	3	WM600071	
22					Spring washer	2	254823	
23					Nut (7/16" UNF)			

Footnote: Fully sealed type starter motor supplied as Service replacement for semi sealed type as fitted on Production.

* NO LONGER SERVICED

2C 09

GROUP K   ELECTRICAL - Dynamo and Fixings, 2¼ litre Petrol

PLATE REF.	1 2 3 4	DESCRIPTION	QTY.	PART No.	REMARKS
1		DYNAMO COMPLETE	1	GEU101	Type C40
		Bracket, commutator end	1	242669*	For dynamo type C39
2		Bracket, commutator end	1	514195	For dynamo type C40
3		Armature for dynamo	1	509311	
		Brushes for dynamo, set	1	261483	For dynamo type C39
4		Brushes for dynamo, set	1	GGB102	For dynamo type C40
		Spring set for brushes	1	261238	For dynamo type C39
5		Spring set for brushes	1	RTC466	For dynamo type C40
6		Field coil for dynamo	1	2K2860*	For dynamo type C39
		Field coil for dynamo	1	607141	For dynamo type C40
7		Ball bearing, front	1	529221	
8		Bush, commutator end	1	271614	
		Bracket, drive end	1	242673*	For dynamo type C39
9		Bracket, drive end	1	514190*	For dynamo type C40
		Oiler for dynamo	1	271615*	For dynamo type C39
10		Oiler for dynamo	1	514189	For dynamo type C40
11		Bolt for bracket	2	242675	
		Terminal, set	1	264436*	For dynamo type C39
12		Terminal, set	1	532566	For dynamo type C40
		Sundry parts, set	1	37H6836	
14		Pulley for dynamo	1	527913	
15		Fan for dynamo	1	554055	
16		Distance washer for fan	2	533860	
17		Woodruff key	1	1664	
		Lockwasher } Fixing pulley	1	217781	} Alternatives
		Spring washer } to dynamo	1	37H6835	
18		Special nut	1	3466	
20		Support bracket for dynamo	1	277900	
21		Steady bracket for dynamo	1	278000	
22		Spring washer } Fixing anchor or	2	GHF332	
24		Set bolt (5/16" UNF x ⅞") } support bracket	2	SH605051	
25		Locking plate for dynamo bolts	1	501198	Not required when front cover timing pointer is fitted
30		Bolt (5/16" UNF x 1¼") } Fixing dynamo	1	BXF05111	
31		Self-locking nut (5/16" UNF) } to front support	1	GHF242	

* NO LONGER SERVICED

2C 10

ELECTRICAL - Dynamo and Fixings, 2¼ litre Petrol

2C 10

160

ELECTRICAL - Dynamo and Fixings, 2¼ litre Petrol

PLATE REF.	1	2	3	4	DESCRIPTION	QTY.	PART No.	REMARKS
32					Special stud ⎫ Fixing dynamo	1	526225	
33					Plain washer ⎬ to support	A/R	WB108051	
34					Plain washer ⎭ bracket	2	RTC613	
35					Self-locking nut (5/16" UNF)	2	GHF242	
36					Locknut (5/16" UNF)	2	GHF201	
38					Adjusting link for dynamo	1	514472	
39					Special bolt ⎫ Fixing	1	SH505071	
40					Plain washer ⎬ adjusting link	1	2266	
41					Spring washer ⎭ to dynamo	1	GHF332	
44					Bolt (5/16" UNF x 3¼") ⎫ Fixing adjusting	1	BH605261	
45					Plain washer ⎭ link to front cover	1	2266	

ELECTRICAL - Dynamo, Sealed Bearing Type, 2¼ litre Petrol, 'Optional'

NLS

Cover 605056
For dynamo Lucas 22764

N.L.S.

90605057

GEU105 • NLS

550281

27H3793 Set

N.L.S.

NLS • 550336

242675 (2)

605061 Set

607141

Bracket, drive end
605063 • NLS

522913

①

1664

3466

605062

REMARKS
Sundry parts set 37H6836 ①

ELECTRICAL - Dynamo and Fixings, 2.6 litre Petrol

GROUP K   ELECTRICAL - Dynamo and Fixings, 2.6 litre Petrol

PLATE REF.	1 2 3 4	DESCRIPTION	QTY.	PART No.	REMARKS
1		DYNAMO COMPLETE	1	GEU104	
2		Bracket, commutator end	1	541313	
3		Bush for armature, commutator end	1	538628	
4		Oiler for dynamo	1	514189	
5		Springs, set, for brush tension	1	RTC466	
6		Brushes, set, for dynamo	1	GGB101	
7		Bracket, drive end	1	538629	
8		Ball bearing, drive end	1	529221	
9		Field coil for dynamo	1	538631	*
10		Armature for dynamo	1	538630	*
11		Bolt for bracket	2	538632	
		Sundry parts kit	1	37H6836	
12		Pulley for dynamo	1	546287	
13		Fan for dynamo	1	554055	
14		Distance washer for fan	2	533860	
15		Woodruff key	1	1664	
16		Special nut	1	3466	
17		Spring washer) Fixing pulley to dynamo	1	37H6836	
18		Mounting plate for dynamo	1	566761	
19		Set bolt (5/16" UNF x ⅞")) Fixing mounting	2	255426	
20		Spring washer) plate to	2	CHF332	
21		Plain washer) cylinder block	2	RTC613	
22		Anchor bracket for dynamo	1	532552	
23		Bolt (5/16" UNF X 1")) Fixing	2	255428	
24		Plain washer) anchor bracket	2	RTC613	
25		Spring washer) to	2	GHF332	
26		Nut (5/16" UNF)) mounting plate	2	GHF201	
27		Bolt (5/16" UNF x 1")) Fixing	2	255428	
28		Spring washer) dynamo to	2	GHF332	
29		Nut (5/16" UNF)) anchor bracket	2	GHF201	
30		Adjusting link for dynamo	1	564162	
31		Set bolt (5/16" UNF x 2¼")) Fixing adjusting	1	255237	
32		Spring washer) link to	1	GHF332	
33		Distance piece) cylinder block	1	4075	
34		Set bolt (5/16" UNC x ⅞")) Fixing adjusting	1	SH505071	
35		Spring washer) link to	1	GHF332	
36		Plain washer) dynamo	2	2266	

* NO LONGER SERVICED

2C 13

162

GROUP K
ELECTRICAL - Dynamo Fixings, 2¼ litre Diesel

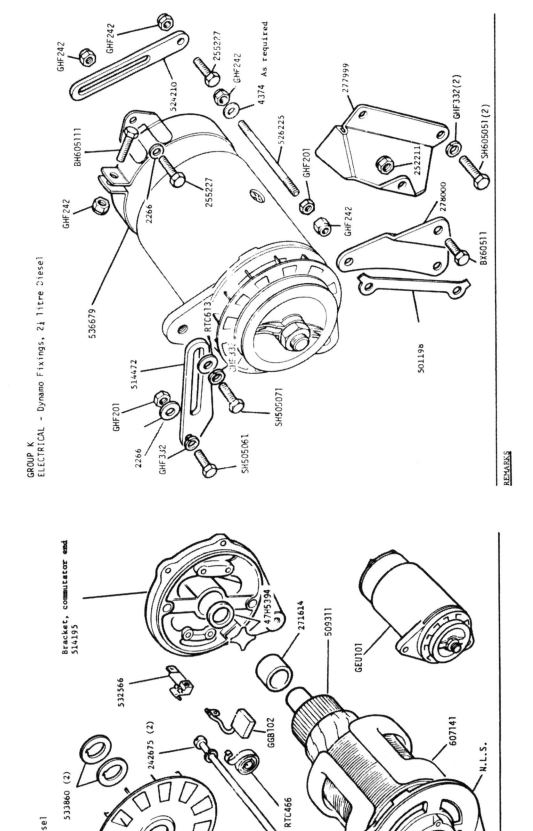

GROUP K
ELECTRICAL - Dynamo, 2¼ litre Diesel

GHF242
GHF242
524210
255227
GHF242
4374 As required
526225
GHF201
277999
GHF332(2)
SH605051(2)
BH605111
252211
255227
2266
GHF242
GHF242
278000
BX60511
536679
RTC613
GHF332
50119b
514472
GHF201
SH505071
GHF201
2266
GHF332
SH505061

Bracket, commutator end
514195
47H5394
271614
509311
GEU101
532566
GGB102
607141
N.L.S.
533860 (2)
242675 (2)
554055
RTC466
522913
1664
3466
529221
21778l
Alternatives

GROUP K
ELECTRICAL - Dynamo, Sealed Bearing Type, 2¼ litre Diesel, Optional

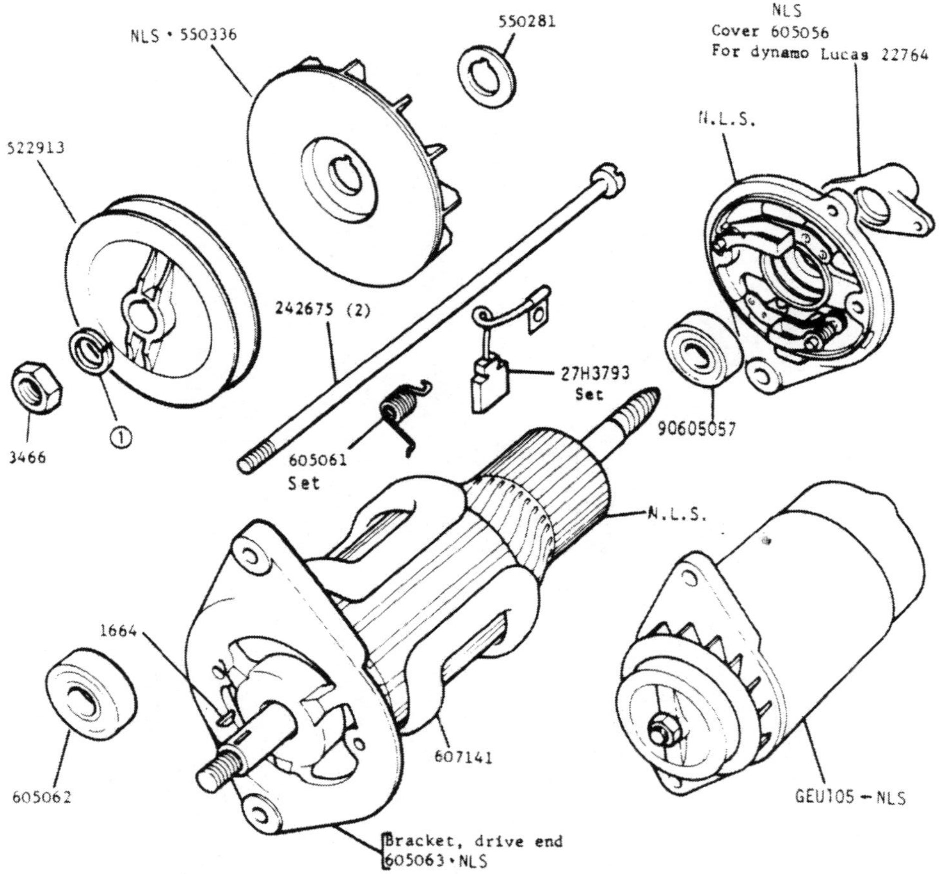

This page is intentionally left blank

NLS
Cover 605056
For dynamo Lucas 22764

N.L.S.

GEU105 — NLS

90605057

N.L.S.

27H3793
Set

550281

607141

Bracket, drive end
605063 · NLS

NLS · 550336

242675 (2)

605061
Set

522913

3466

1664

605062

REMARKS
Sundry parts set 37H6336 ①

2C 15

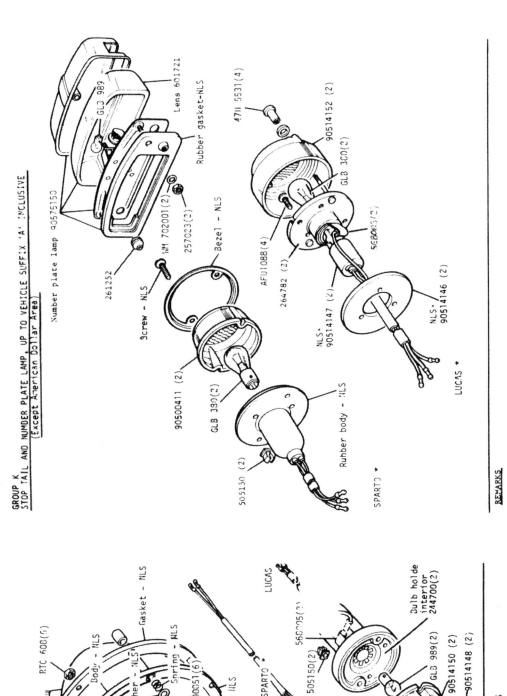

GROUP K
STOP TAIL AND NUMBER PLATE LAMP. UP TO VEHICLE SUFFIX 'A' INCLUSIVE
(Except American Dollar Area)

Number plate lamp 90575150
GL3 989
Lens 601721
Rubber gasket-NLS
261252
WM 702001(2)
257023(2)
Screw - NLS
Bezel - NLS
AFU1088(4)
264782 (2)
90514152 (2)
GLB 300(2)
56604503(2)
NLS- 90514147 (2)
90500411 (2)
GLB 380(2)
505150 (2)
Rubber body - NLS
NLS- 90514146 (2)
A711 5531(4)
SPARTO *
LUCAS *

REMARKS

* Stop tail lamp: Sparto 276317(2)·NLS] Alternatives
              Lucas 510176(2)

2D C2

GROUP K
HEAD, SIDE, TAIL AND FLASHER LAMPS. From vehicle suffix 'A'
(Except American Dollar Area)

Bulb
GL3 414(2) ①
GLB 415(2) ②
GLB 410(2) ③
GLB 411(2) ④

Light unit
7H5483(2)
262302 (2)
GLU 517(2) Early ③
GLU 513(2) Late ④
NLS

Rim - NLS
① ② ③ ④

Rubber gasket - NLS
142D01(2)
RTC 465(2)
NLS · 90500514(2)
504130(2)
90514149 (4)
Bulb holder interior - NLS
GLB 207(2)
535150(2)
SPARTO
Body NLS
505150(2)
56C005(2)
GLB 989(2)
90514150 (2)
90514148 (2)
Bulb holder interior 244700(2)
LUCAS

RTC 608(6)
Body - NLS
Gasket - NLS
Flasher - NLS
Spring - NLS
G00051(6)
WM 702001(6)
77790(6)
274378(2)
PZJ602
Spire nut - NLS

REMARKS

Headlamp Complete: ABU5794(2) ①   635070(2) ② · NLS
                   AEU1061(2) ③   RTC445(2) ④   ] Alternatives

Side lamp Complete: Sparto 5051A(2)·NLS]
                    Lucas 510179(2)   ] Alternatives

NLS - 90514149 (4)

① RH Stg Except Europe
② LH Stg Except Europe
③ RH Stg Europe except France
④ LH Stg France

2D C2

165

HEAD, SIDE, TAIL AND FLASHER LAMPS. From vehicle suffix 'B' onwards
(Except American Dollar Area)

2D 03

GROUP K   ELECTRICAL - HEAD, SIDE, TAIL AND FLASHER LAMPS
From vehicle suffix 'B' onwards. (Except America Dollar Area)

PLATE REF.	1 2 3 4	DESCRIPTION	QTY.	PART No.	REMARKS	
1		HEADLAMP COMPLETE, SEALED BEAM	2	536006*	RH Stg	
		HEADLAMP COMPLETE, SEALED BEAM	2	536111	LH Stg Except Europe	
2		HEADLAMP COMPLETE	2	536112	LH Stg Europe except France and Austria	Headlamps in radiator grille panel up to vehicle suffix 'F' inclusive
3		HEADLAMP COMPLETE	2	536113	LH Stg France only	
		HEADLAMP COMPLETE	2	90545107	LH Stg Austria only	
		Bulb for headlamp	2	GLB410	LH Stg Europe except France	
4		Bulb for headlamp	2	GLB411	LH Stg France only	
		Light unit, sealed beam	2	GLU104	RH Stg	
		Light unit, sealed beam	2	GLU133	LH Stg Except Europe	
5		Light unit, bulb type	2	GLU513	LH Stg Europe	
6		Adaptor and leads for headlamp	2	536116		
7		Rim for light unit	2	601990*		
8		Rim for headlamp, chrome	2	545149*		
9		Screw } For light unit	6	600024		
10		Spring for screw } adjustment and	6	600025		
11		Fibre washer for screw } fitting headlamp to front grille	6	600026		
		HEADLAMP COMPLETE, SEALED BEAM	2	27H8499	RH Stg	
		HEADLAMP COMPLETE, SEALED BEAM	2	27H8207	LH Stg except Europe	
		HEADLAMP COMPLETE, BULB TYPE	2	AEU1061	LH Stg Europe	Headlamps in wing From vehicle suffix 'G' onwards
		Bulb for headlamp	2	GLB410	LH Stg Europe except France	
		Bulb for headlamp	2	GLB411	LH Stg France only	
		Light unit, sealed beam	2	GLU104	RH Stg	
+		Light unit, sealed beam	2	GLU133	LH Stg except Europe	
+		This part is no longer available, use GLU513 and GLB410			France and Italy	
		Light unit, bulb type	2	GLU513	LH Stg France and Italy only	
		Adaptor and leads for headlamp	2	600226		
		Retaining rim for light unit	2	515218		
		Special screw, fixing retaining rim	6	RTC464		
		Gasket for headlamp	2	531586		
		Screw (10 UNF x ⅜") } Fixing	6	78291		
		Spring washer } headlamp to	6	WM702001		
		Nut (10 UNF) } front wing	6	257023		
		SIDE LAMP COMPLETE	2	536117	Up to vehicle suffix 'F' inclusive	
		Bulb holder and body complete	2	542037		
		Bulb for side lamp	2	GLB207		
		Lens for side lamp	2	536151		
		Special screw fixing lens	4	542038		Sparto type
		SIDE LAMP COMPLETE	2	575119	From vehicle suffix 'G' onwards	
		Bulb holder and body complete	2	606499		
		Bulb for side lamp	2	GLB207		
		Lens for side lamp	2	536151		
		Special screw fixing lens	4	542038		

* NO LONGER SERVICED

2D 03

PLATE REF. 1 2 3 4	DESCRIPTION	QTY.	PART No.	REMARKS
19	NUMBER PLATE LAMP	1	90575150	Optional equipment
20	Bulb for number plate lamp	1	GLB989	
21	Lens	1	601721	
22	Rubber grommet for wire	1	261252	
23	Rubber gasket for lamp	1	261253*	
	Spring washer	2	WM702001	
	Nut (10 UNF)	2	257023	
	STOP/TAIL AND REAR NUMBER PLATE LAMP	2	532881	SPARTO TYPE
	Base for lamp	2	532879	
	Bulb for holder complete	2	532878	
	Bulb for lamp	2	GLB380	
	Lens for lamp	2	532880	
	Special screw, fixing lens	5	542036	
	STOP/TAIL AND REAR NUMBER PLATE LAMP	2	531684	WIPAC TYPE - required for France
	Bulb holder and base complete	2	542045	
	Bulb for lamp	2	GLB380	
	Lens for lamp	2	542043	
	Special screw, fixing lens	4	542041	
24	STOP/TAIL AND REAR NUMBER PLATE LAMP	1	264782	LUCAS TYPE - Superseded by 589446
25	Bulb holder, interior	2	GLB380	
26	Bulb for lamp	2	589448	
27	Lens, stop/tail and reflex	4	551436	
28	Special screw, fixing lens	2	568005	
29	Sleeve for terminal			
	STOP/TAIL AND REAR NUMBER PLATE LAMP	2	589446	PEREI TYPE
	Bulb	2	GLB380	
	Lens	2	589444R	
	Screw and washer, fixing lens	4	608004	
	STOP/TAIL LAMP	2	541520	SPARTO TYPE
	Base for lamp	2	532879	
	Bulb holder complete	2	532878	
	Bulb for lamp	2	GLB380	
	Lens for lamp	2	541521	
	Special screw, fixing lens	4	542036	
	STOP/TAIL LAMP	2	541522	WIPAC TYPE Optional equipment
	Bulb for holder and base complete	2	542045	
	Bulb for lamp	2	GLB380	
	Lens for lamp	2	542044	
	Special screw, fixing lens	4	542041	
	Drive screw fixing lamp to rear body	6	GHF421	
30	Screw (4BA x ½") Fixing lamp to rear body	6	77899	} Alternative fixings
31	Spring washer Fixing lamp to rear body	6	WM704001	}
	Nut (4BA)	6	4023	}
	Red rear reflector	2	551595	} Optional equipment
32	Spring washer Fixing reflectors	2	WM702001	}
	Nut (2BA)	2	RTC608	}

* NO LONGER SERVICED

PLATE REF. 1 2 3 4	DESCRIPTION	QTY.	PART No.	REMARKS
	SIDE LAMP COMPLETE - Superseded by 589403	2	542049	WIPAC TYPE - Up to vehicle suffix 'F' inclusive
	Bulb holder and base complete	2	GLB207	
	Bulb for side lamp	2	589283	
	Lens for side lamp	4	542042	
	Special screw, fixing lens			
	SIDE LAMP COMPLETE - Superseded by 589403	2	9060500	WIPAC TYPE - From vehicle suffix 'G' onwards
	Bulb holder and base complete	2	GLB207	
	Bulb for side lamp	2	589283	
	Lens for side lamp	2	542042	
	Special screw, fixing lens	4	589403	} Reqd. for France
	SIDE LAMP COMPLETE	2	542042	WIPAC TYPE
	Bulb for side lamp	2	589403	
	Lens for side lamp	2	GLB989	
	Special screw, fixing lens	2	589283	
	Screw and washer, fixing lens	4	608005	
12	SIDE LAMP COMPLETE - Superseded by 589404	2	244700	LUCAS TYPE - Up to vehicle suffix 'F' inclusive
13	Bulb holder, interior	2	GLB989	
14	Bulb for side lamp	2	589284	
15	Lens for side lamp	4	600523	
16	Special screw, fixing lens	4	551430	
17	Washer for special screw	2	568005	
18	Sleeve for terminal			
	SIDE LAMP COMPLETE - Superseded by 589404	2	244700	LUCAS TYPE - From vehicle suffix 'G' onwards
	Bulb holder, interior	2	GLB989	
	Bulb for side lamp	2	589284	
	Lens for side lamp	4	600423	
	Special screw, fixing lens	4	551430	
	Washer for special screw	2	568005	
	Sleeve for terminal	2	515060	
	Grommet for cable entry			
	SIDE LAMP COMPLETE - Superseded by 589404	2	GLB989	LUCAS TYPE
	Bulb for side lamp	2	589284	
	Lens for side lamp	4	608004	
	Screw and washer, fixing lens			
	SIDE LAMP COMPLETE	2	589404	PEREI TYPE
	Bulb	2	GLB989	
	Lens	2	589284	
	Screw and washer, fixing lens	4	608004	
	Screw (4BA x ½") } Fixing	6	77899	
	Spring washer } side lamp	6	WM704001	
	Nut (4BA) } to wing	6	4023	

ELECTRICAL - HEAD, SIDE, TAIL AND FLASHER LAMPS
From vehicle suffix 'B' onwards. (Except America Dollar Area)

PLATE REF. 1 2 3 4	DESCRIPTION	QTY.	PART No.	REMARKS
	FLASHER INDICATOR COMPLETE ASSEMBLY	1	541755*	Optional equipment up to vehicle suffix 'E' inclusive. Fitted as standard on vehicle suffix 'F'
33	Flasher unit	1	GFU103	
34	Drive screw, fixing flasher unit	1	72628	
35	SELF-CANCELLING SWITCH FOR FLASHER	1	90519866	
36	Bulb for flasher switch	1	GLB643	
	Wheel for flasher switch	1	522882*	
	Feed lead for flasher switch	1	90519865	
	FLASHER LAMP COMPLETE	4	536094	PEREI TYPE - Up to vehicle suffix 'F' inclusive
	Lens	4	536152	
	Special screw, fixing lens	8	542038	
	Bulb	4	GLB382	
	Bulb holder and body complete	4	542040*	
	FLASHER LAMP COMPLETE	4	536148	WIPAC TYPE - Up to vehicle suffix 'F' inclusive
	Lens	4	542048	
	Special screw, fixing lens	8	542042	
	Bulb	4	GLB387	
37	Bulb holder and base complete - Superseded by 589409	4	542046	LUCAS TYPE - Up to vehicle suffix 'F' inclusive
38	Lens	4	AEU1058	
39	Special screw, fixing lens	8	600423	
40	Special washer, fixing lens	8	551430	
41	Bulb	4	GLB382	
42	Bulb holder, interior	4	37H5452	
	FLASHER LAMP COMPLETE	4	589409	PEREI TYPE - Up to vehicle suffix 'F' inclusive
	Lens	4	589295	
	Screw and washer, fixing lens	8	608004	
	Bulb	4	GLB382	
	Flasher unit	1	GFU116	
	Mounting clip for flasher unit	1	567959	
	Drive screw fixing clip to dash	1	GHF423	
	SELF-CANCELLING SWITCH FOR FLASHER	1	575114	
	Bulb for flasher switch	1	GLB643	
	Wheel for flasher switch	1	522882	
	Feed lead for flasher switch	1	90519865	
	FLASHER LAMP COMPLETE	4	575125	SPARTO TYPE
	Lens	4	536152	
	Special screw fixing lens	8	542038	
	Bulb	4	GLB382	
	Bulb holder and body complete	4	606501	
	FLASHER LAMP COMPLETE	4	575123	WIPAC TYPE — From vehicle suffix 'G' onwards
	Lens	4	542048	
	Special screw, fixing lens	8	542042	
	Bulb	4	GLB382	
	Bulb holder and base complete	4	606502*	

* NO LONGER SERVICED

2D 06

HEAD, SIDE, TAIL AND FLASHER LAMPS. From vehicle suffix 'B' onwards
(Except American Dollar Area)

2D 06

K854

PLATE REF. 1 2 3 4	DESCRIPTION	QTY.	PART No.	REMARKS
				LUCAS TYPE - Vehicle suffix 'G' onwards
	FLASHER LAMP COMPLETE - Superseded by 589409	4	AEU1058	
	Lens	4	600423	
	Special screw, fixing lens	8	551430	
	Special washer, fixing lens	8	GLB382	
	Bulb	4	37H5452	
	Bulb holder, interior	4	568005	
	Sleeve for terminal	4	601543	
	Grommet for cable entry	4	589409	PEREI TYPE - Vehicle suffix 'G' onwards
	FLASHER LAMP COMPLETE	4	589285	
	Screw and washer, fixing lens	8	608004	
	Bulb	4	GLB382	
	Screw (4BA x ½") } Fixing front	6	77899	
	Spring washer" } flasher lamp to	6	WM704001	
	Nut (4BA) } front wing	6	4023	
	Drive screw, fixing flasher lamp to rear body	6	GHF421	
	Earthing clip on rear chassis crossmember	2	236364	
	Clip for flasher harness on RH wing valance	2	240406	LH Stg
	Clip, fixing flasher lead to dash	1	233770	
	Clip for lamp and flasher harness to wing valance	1	4020	Diesel

2D 07

HEAD, SIDE, TAIL AND FLASHER LAMPS. From vehicle suffix 'B' onwards
(Except American Dollar Area)

2D 07

169

HEAD, SIDE, TAIL AND FLASHER LAM
(America Dollar Area)

GROUP K   ELECTRICAL - HEAD, SIDE, TAIL AND FLASHER LAMPS
(America Dollar Area)

PLATE REF.	1 2 3 4	DESCRIPTION	QTY.	PART No.	REMARKS
1		HEADLAMP ASSEMBLY, SEALED BEAM	2	27H8207	
2		Light unit	2	GLU133	
3		Rim for light unit	2	515218	
4		Rim for headlamp	2	142001	
5		Gasket for headlamp	2	531586	
6		Adaptor and leads for light unit	2	536116	
		Screw (2BA x ½") } Fixing headlamp	6	77700	
		Spring washer } to front	6	WM702001	
		Nut (2BA) } grille panel	6	RTC608	
7		SIDE LAMP COMPLETE	2		(Superseded by AAU1130)
8		Bulb	2	GLB207	
9		Bulb holder, interior	2	244700	
10		Lens	2	271931*	
11		Rim for lens	2	261640*	
12		Sleeve for terminal	2	568005	
7		SIDE LAMP COMPLETE	2	AAU1130	
8		Bulb	2	GLB989	
		Lens	2	271931*	
		Screw (4BA x ½") } Fixing	6	77899	
		Spring washer } side lamp to	6	WM704001	
		Nut (4BA) } front wing	6	4023	
13		STOP/TAIL LAMP COMPLETE	2	532809	
14		Bulb	2	GLB380	
15		Bulb holder, interior	2	264782	
16		Lens	2	37H6109	
17		Gasket for lens	2	601717*	
18		Special screw	2	601719*	
19		Special washer	4	551430	
20		Sleeve for terminal	2	568005	
21		Grommet for cable entry	2	600349	
22		NUMBER PLATE LAMP COMPLETE	1	532810*	
23		Bulb	2	GLB989	
24		Lens	1	601721	
25		Gasket for lens	1	261253*	
26		Red reflector complete	2	240542*	

* NO LONGER SERVICED

2D 08

2D 08

ELECTRICAL - HEAD, SIDE, TAIL AND FLASHER LAMPS
(America Dollar Area)

PLATE REF.	1	2	3	4	DESCRIPTION	QTY.	PART No.	REMARKS
27					Flasher unit	1	GFU103	
					Drive screw, fixing flasher unit	1	72628	
28					SELF-CANCELLING SWITCH FOR FLASHER	1	90519866	
29					Bulb	1	GLB643	
30					Wheel for flasher switch	1	522882	
31					FRONT FLASHER LAMP	2	532806	
32					Bulb	2	GLB387	
33					Bulb holder interior	2	37H5452	
34					Lens	2	37H6928	
35					Chrome rim for lens	2	261640*	
36					Sleeve for terminal	6	568005	
					Screw (4BA x ½") } Fixing front	6	77899	
					Spring washer } flasher lamp	6	WM704001	
					Nut (4BA) } to wing	6	4023	
37					REAR FLASHER LAMP COMPLETE	2	532807	
38					Bulb	2	GLB382	
39					Bulb holder interior	2	27H5452	
40					Lens	2	601720	
41					Gasket for lens	2	601717*	
42					Special screw	2	601719*	
43					Special washer	4	551430	
44					Grommet for cable entry	6	600349	

* NO LONGER SERVICED

2D 09

HEAD, SIDE, TAIL AND FLASHER LAM
(America Dollar Area)

2D 09

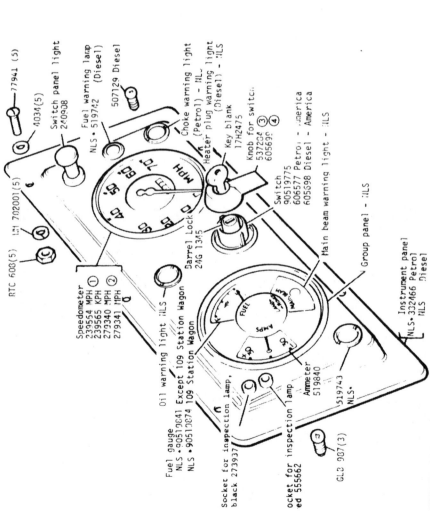

GROUP K
STARTER SWITCH AND CHOKE CONTROL, POSITIVE EARTH SYSTEM UP TO VEHICLE SUFFIX 'D' INCLUSIVE

233017 Petrol

278010 (2)

240417

241367

Speedometer cable complete
GSD 133

530571 Petrol ①
523637 Petrol ②

RTC 608(2) Petrol
WM 702001(2) Petrol

234503(2) Petrol

214223 Petrol

Choke control bracket assy
(Petrol) - NLS

433243

273370

240407

232566

WM 702001(3)

78924 (3)

239600

6860 (3)

606230 Petrol

530237 Petrol

536913 Diesel

Key blank
③ 17H2475 Diesel

Alternatives
NAU 4071 Non-barrel lock type - Diesel
575001 Barrel lock type - Diesel

REMARKS
① Must be used with Carburetter without starter heater element
② Must be used with Carburetter with starter heater element
③ For switch 575081

2D 10

GROUP K
INSTRUMENTS, POSITIVE EARTH SYSTEM, UP TO VEHICLE SUFFIX 'C' INCLUSIVE

RTC 608(5)   WM 702001(5)

77941 (5)

4034(5)

Switch panel light
240908

Fuel warning lamp
NLS • 519742 (Diesel)

507129 Diesel

Choke warning light
(Petrol) - NLS
Heater plug warning light
(Diesel) - NLS

Key blank
17H2475

Knob for switch
537234 ③
605698 ④

Switch
90519775
606577 Petrol - America
605698 Diesel - America
NLS

Main beam warning light - NLS

Speedometer
239554 MPH
239565 KPH ①
279340 MPH ②
279341 MPH

Oil warning light NLS
Fuel gauge
NLS • 90519641 Except 109 Station Wagon
NLS • 90519874 109 Station Wagon

Barrel Lock
24G 1345

Group panel - NLS

Instrument panel
NLS • 332466 Petrol
Diesel

Socket for inspection lamp,
black 273937

Socket for inspection lamp
red 555662

Ammeter
519840

519743
NLS •

GLB 907(3)

REMARKS
① 38in
② 109in also 86in when 7.50 x 16 tyres are fitted
③ For switch 90519775 and 606577
④ For switch 605698

2D 10

GROUP K   ELECTRICAL - INSTRUMENTS, NEGATIVE EARTH SYSTEM
           From vehicle suffix 'D' onwards

PLATE REF. 1 2 3 4	DESCRIPTION	QTY.	PART No.	REMARKS
1	Instrument panel	1	345052	
2	Set screw (2BA x 3")) Fixing instrument	5	77941	
3	Plain washer) panel	5	403A	
4	Spring washer)	5	WH702001	
	Nut (2BA)	2	RTC608	
5	Gauge panel complete	1	560744	
	Water temperature gauge	1	560744	
6	Fuel gauge	1	555835	
7	Warning light, charging, red	1	555837	
	Bulb for warning light	1	GLB9P7	
	Switch for panel lights	1	RTC430	Except Station Wagon
8	Nameplate for switch 'PANEL'	1	560404	) Station Wagon
	Switch for panel and interior lights	1	555877	)
9	Nameplate for switch 'PANEL/INTERIOR'	1	560405	
10	Switch for lamps	1	1H9077	
11	Nameplate for switch 'SIDE/HEAD'	1	560407	
12	Switch for wiper motor	1	555778	
13	Nameplate for switch 'WIPER'	1	560410*	Petrol models
14	Switch for ignition and starter	1	551508	)
15	Barrel lock for ignition switch	1	24G1345	)
16	Key blank	1	17H2475	
	Switch for heater plug and starter	1	575C81	) Diesel models
	Barrel lock and key for starter heater switch	1	536013	)
	Key blank	1	17H2475*	
17	Socket for inspection lamp, black	1	273937*	
18	Socket for inspection lamp, red	1	555F62	
	Bulb for panel lights	2	GLB987	
19	Warning light, fuel (blue)	1	560756	2½ litre Diesel models
20	Cold start control complete	1	555282	2½ litre Petrol models
	Cold start control complete	1	555283	2.6 litre Petrol models
	Grommet for cold start cable	1	235113	2½ litre Petrol models
21	Nameplate for control 'COLD START'	1	560411	) Petrol
22	Switch for cold start warning light	1	5F3318*	) models
	Nameplate for control 'ENGINE STOP'	1	560412	) Diesel models
23	Plug, large) For redundant	1	338016	
24	Plug, small) holes in panel	3	338013	
25	Speedometer and warning lights, miles	1	540114	) 88 models
	Speedometer and warning lights, kilometres	1	540115	)109 models. Also) 2½ litre
	Speedometer and warning lights, miles	1	540117	)on 88 models..) Petrol &
	Speedometer and warning lights, kilometres	1	540118	)when 7.50" x 16") Diesel
				)tyres are fitted) models
	Speedometer and warning lights, miles	1	559159	)
	Speedometer and warning lights, kilometres	1	559160	2.6 litre Petrol models
	Bulb for warning light on speedometer	3	GLB987	

2D 11

* NO LONGER SERVICED

INSTRUMENTS, NEGATIVE EARTH SYSTEM
From vehicle suffix 'D' onwards

H760   2D 11

173

GROUP K   ELECTRICAL – INSTRUMENTS, NEGATIVE EARTH SYSTEM
From vehicle suffix 'D' onwards

PLATE REF.	1	2	3	4	DESCRIPTION	QTY.	PART No.	REMARKS
27					Cable complete for speedometer	1	GSD133	2¼ litre Petrol and Diesel models
28					Cable complete for speedometer	1	GSD138	2.6 litre Petrol models
					Retaining plate for cable	1	232566	
					Spring washer) Fixing	3	WM702001	
					Set screw (2BA x ½")) retaining plate	3	78924	
					Felt washer for speedometer	1	241387	
29					Rubber grommet, in dash) For speedometer	1	233243	
30					Rubber grommet, on cable) cable	4	6860	5 off on 2.6 litre Petrol models
					Rubber grommet for speedometer cable at fuel pump	1	273370	
31					Clip) For	1	239600	3 off on 2.6 litre Petrol models
32					Clip) speedometer	1	240407	
					Clip) cable	1	279010	
					Clip) For speedometer cable	1	240417	
					Distance washer) at camshaft cover	6	258883)	2¼ litre Diesel models
							RTC840)	

2D 12

INSTRUMENTS, NEGATIVE EARTH SYSTEM
From vehicle suffix 'D' onwards

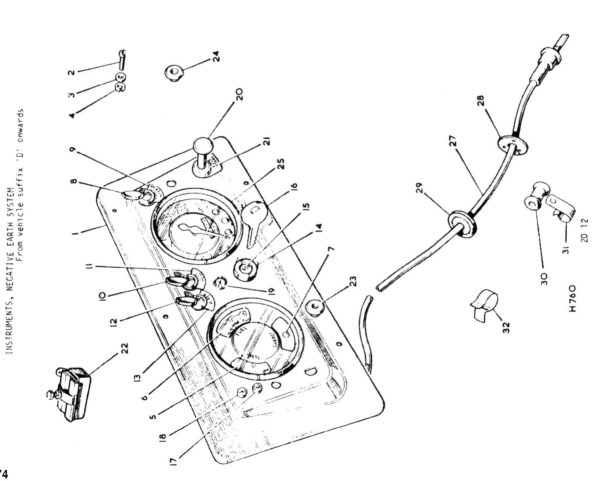

H760   2D 12

174

GROUP K
HORN AND WINDSCREEN WIPER, POSITIVE EARTH SYSTEM UP TO VEHICLE SUFFIX 'C' INCLUSIVE
4-cylinder models.

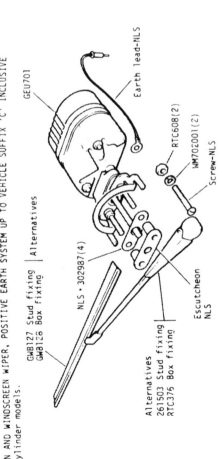

GEU701

Earth lead-NLS

RTC608(2)

WM702001(2)

Screw-NLS

GWB127 Stud fixing | Alternatives
GWB126 Box fixing

NLS · 302987(4)

Escutcheon
NLS

Alternatives
261503 Stud fixing
RTC376 Box fixing

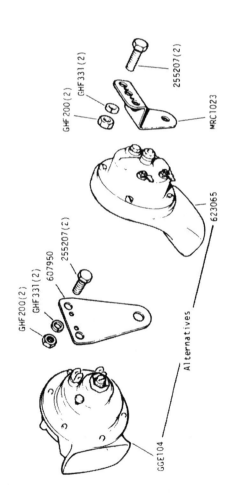

GHF331(2)
GHF200(2)

255207(2)

MRC1023

623065

GHF200(2)
GHF331(2)
607950
255207(2)

Alternatives

GGE104

Contact set 600638 for Clearhooter type horns 575191 and 600890
NLS

2D 13

This page is intentionally left blank

175

WINDSCREEN WIPER, NEGATIVE EARTH SYSTEM
From vehicle suffix 'D' to suffix 'E' inclusive

GROUP K WINDSCREEN WIPER, NEGATIVE EARTH SYSTEM
From vehicle suffix 'D' to suffix 'E' inclusive

PLATE REF.	1	2	3	4	DESCRIPTION	QTY.	PART No.	REMARKS
1					Windscreen wiper motor complete	1	GEU714	
2					Flexible drive cable	1	RTC202	
					Gear and con rod	1	90608307	
3					Wheelbox for wiper	2	551227	
4					Spindle and gear for wheelbox and wiper arm	2	605904	
5					Outer casing, motor to wheelbox	1	555754*	
6					Outer casing, wheelbox to wheelbox	1	555702*	
7					Outer casing, wheelbox end	1	575047	
8					Rubber cover for wiper motor in dash	1	338846*	
					Threaded ferrule for wiper motor	1	37H3694	
9					Arm for wiper blade, for RH side	1	37H7847	
					Arm for wiper blade, for LH side	1	37H7848	
10					Wiper blade	2	GWB12R	
11					Mounting bracket for wiper motor	1	338794*	
12					Screw (¼" UNF x ⅜")) Fixing	3	78755	
13					Plain washer) mounting	3	RTCf17	
14					Spring washer) bracket to	3	GHF331	
15					Nut (¼" UNF)) LH glove box	3	GHF200	
16					Cover plate for wiper motor	1	345079*	
17					Rubber finisher) For	1	348541	
18					Rubber seal) cover plate	1	348537	
19					Screw (2BA x ⅜")) Fixing cover	4	78177	
20					Plain washer) plate to LH	4	4030	
21					Spring washer) glove box	4	WM702001	
22					Distance washer)	4	4172	
23					Nut (2BA))	4	RTC608	

* NO LONGER SERVICED

20 14

20 14

WINDSCREEN WIPER, NEGATIVE EARTH SYSTEM
From vehicle suffix 'F' onwards

2D 15

GROUP K   ELECTRICAL - WINDSCREEN WIPER, NEGATIVE EARTH SYSTEM
From vehicle suffix 'F' onwards

PLATE REF.	1 2 3 4	DESCRIPTION	QTY.	PART No.	REMARKS
1		Windscreen wiper motor complete	1	GEU708	
2		Shaft and gear for wiper motor	1	37H2736	
3		Flexible drive cable	1	RTC202	
4		Wheelbox for wiper	2	560887	
		Spindle and gear for wheel box	2	605904	
5		Outer cable, motor to wheelbox	1	560966	
6		Outer casing, wheelbox to wheelbox	1	AAU1909	
7		Outer casing, wheelbox end	1	575047	
8		Rubber cover for wiper motor in dash	1	338846	
		Threaded ferrule for wiper motor	1	37H3694	
9		Arm for wiper blade, for RH side	1	37H7847	)Vehicle suffix 'F' only
		Arm for wiper blade, for LH side	1	37H7848	)
10		Wiper blade	2	GWB128	
		Arm for wiper blade, LH	1	RTC819	)From vehicle suffix 'G'
		Arm for wiper blade, RH	1	RTC822	)onwards
		Wiper blade	2	GWB195	)
11		Nut plate for wiper motor	1	560967	
		Mounting strap for wiper motor	1	606929	
		Mounting pad for wiper motor	1	150844	
12		Set screw (¼" UNF x ¾") fixing wiper motor to dash and nut plate	2	78898	
13		Cover plate for wiper motor	1	345079	
14		Rubber finisher) For	1	348541	
15		Rubber seal) cover plate	1	348537	
16		Screw (2BA x ¼")	4	78177	
17		Plain washer) Fixing cover	4	4030	
18		Spring washer) plate to LH	4	WM702001	
19		Distance washer) glove box	4	4172	
20		Nut (2BA)	4	RTC608	

2D 15

GROUP K
GENERAL ELECTRICAL EQUIPMENT, POSITIVE EARTH SYSTEM UP TC VEHICLE SUFFIX 'C' INCLUSIVE

4 cyl models

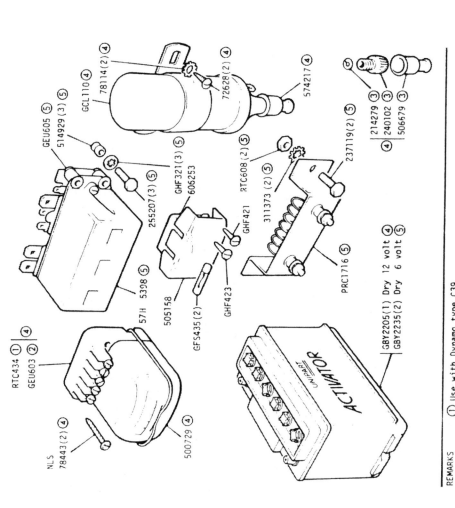

RTC434 ① | ④
GEU603 ② | ④

NLS
78443(2) ④

500729 ④

GEU605 ⑤
514929(3) ⑤

255207(3) ⑤

GHF321(3) ⑤
606253

57H 5398 ⑤

505158

GFS435(2) ④

GHF423

GHF421

GCL110 ④
78114(2) ④

72628(2) ④

574217 ④

RTC608(2) ⑤

311373(2) ⑤

237119(2) ⑤

PRC1716 ⑤

214279 ③
240102 ③
506679 ③
④ | ⑤

GBY2205(1) Dry 12 volt ④
GBY2235(2) Dry 6 volt ⑤

ACTIVATOR

UNIPART

REMARKS   ① Use with Dynamo type C39
          ② Use with Dynamo type C40
          ③ For early type Coil with terminal nut connection
          ④ Petrol models
          ⑤ Diesel models

2E 02

This page is intentionally left blank

178

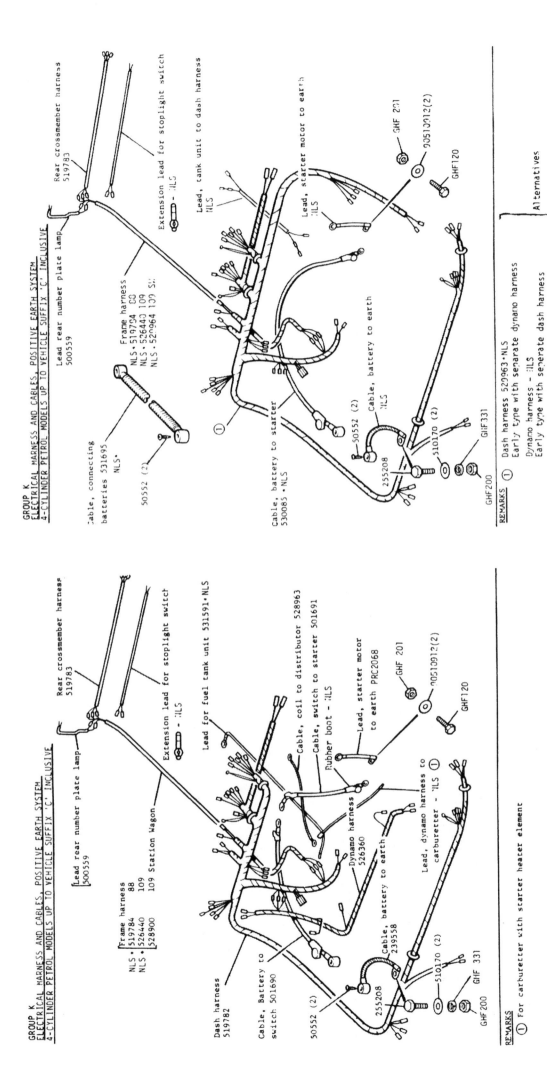

GROUP K
ELECTRICAL HARNESS AND CABLES, POSITIVE EARTH SYSTEM
4-CYLINDER PETROL MODELS UP TO VEHICLE SUFFIX 'C' INCLUSIVE

Rear crossmember harness
519783

Extension lead for stoplight switch

Lead rear number plate lamp
500559

Frame harness
NLS• 519784   88
NLS• 526440 109
      528900 109 Station Wagon

Dash harness
519782

Cable, Battery to
switch 501690

50552 (2)

GHF 200

GHF 331

510170 (2)

255208

Cable, battery to earth
239558

Cable, battery to earth

Dynamo harness
526360

Lead, dynamo harness to
carburetter - NLS ①

Lead for fuel tank unit 531591•NLS

Cable, coil to distributor 528963

Cable, switch to starter 501691

Rubber boot - NLS

Lead, starter motor
to earth PRC2068

GHF 201

90510012(2)

GHF120

REMARKS
① For carburetter with starter heater element

2E 03

GROUP K
ELECTRICAL HARNESS AND CABLES, POSITIVE EARTH SYSTEM
4-CYLINDER PETROL MODELS UP TO VEHICLE SUFFIX 'C' INCLUSIVE

Rear crossmember harness
519783

Extension lead for stoplight switch
NLS

Lead rear number plate lamp
500559

Cable, connecting
batteries 531695
NLS•

50552 (2)

Frame harness
NLS•519784   88
NLS•526440 109
NLS•520964 109 SW

①

Cable, battery to starter
530085 •NLS

Lead, tank unit to dash harness
NLS

Lead, starter motor to earth
NLS

GHF 201

90510012(2)

GHF120

Cable, battery to earth
NLS

50552 (2)

510170 (2)

255208

GHF331

GHF200

REMARKS
① Dash harness 529963•NLS
   Early type with separate dynamo harness
   Dynamo harness - NLS
   Early type with separate dash harness
   Main harness 545210•NLS
   Late type with combined dash and dynamo harness
   } Alternatives

2E 03

179

GROUP K GENERAL ELECTRICAL EQUIPMENT, NAGATIVE EARTH SYSTEM
4-cylinder models. From vehicle suffix 'D' onwards

PLATE REF. 1 2 3 4	DESCRIPTION	QTY.	PART No.	REMARKS
1	Windtone horn, low note	1	600890	Clearhooter type)Alternatives
	Windtone horn, low note	1	673065	Mixo type)natives
	Windtone horn, low note	1	GEU804	Lucas type
	Contact set for windtone horn	1	271500*	Lucas type
	Contact set for windtone horn	1	600638*	Clearhooter type
	Mounting bracket for horn	1	MRC1023	Mixo type
	Mounting bracket for horn	1	607950	Lucas type
	Bolt (¼" UNF x ½")) Fixing horn to	2	255207	
	Spring washer) battery support/	2	GHF331	
	Nut (¼" UNF)) mounting bracket	2	GHF200	
	Protector plate for horn	1	396124	
	Self-locking nut (¼" UNF) fixing protector plate to radiator grille			
2	Activator, dry, 12 volt	2	GHF221	Petrol models
	Activator, dry, 6 volt	1	GBY2205	Diesel models
		2	GBY2235	
3	Ignition coil	1	GCL110	
	Rubber boot for ignition coil) For	1	574217	
	Acorn nut) ignition	2	240102	
	Rubber boot for acorn nut) coil	1	506679	For early type coil
	Split washer	2	214279	with terminal nut
	Drive screw) Fixing coil	2	72628	connection
	Shakeproof washer) to dash	2	7R114	
4	Starter solenoid switch	1	13H5952	
	Spring washer) For solenoid	2	575014	
	Nut) terminal post	2	90575015	
	Bolt (10 UNF x ⅝")) Fixing solenoid	2	257019	
	Fan disc washer)	2	513282	
	Spring washer) to dash	2	WM702001	
	Nut (10 UNF)	1	257023	
5	Voltage regulator box	1	GEU603	
	Cover for regulator box	1	500729	
	Drive screw, fixing regulator box to dash	2	78443*	
	Current/voltage regulator box	1	GEU605	
	Cover for regulator box	1	600442	
	Screw (10 UNF x 1½")) Fixing	3	79054	
	Plain washer) regulator box	3	3902	
	Special nut (10 UNF)) to dash	3	79239	
6	Voltage regulator for instruments, 10 volt	1	BHA4602	
	Spring washer) Fixing	2	3101	
	Drive screw) regulator	2	AB606021	
7	Fuse box	1	606253	
	Cover for fuse box	1	505158	
	Fuse, 35 amp	1	GFS435	
	Drive screw, fixing fuse box	1	AB610051	
	Drive screw, locating fuse box	1	GHF421	

Petrol models

Diesel models

* NO LONGER SERVICED

2E 04

GENERAL ELECTRICAL EQUIPMENT, NAGATIVE EARTH SYSTEM
4-cylinder models. From vehicle suffix 'D' onwards

2E 04

180

GENERAL ELECTRICAL EQUIPMENT, NEGATIVE EARTH SYSTEM
4-cylinder models. From vehicle suffix 'D' onwards

PLATE REF.	1	2	3	4	DESCRIPTION	QTY.	PART No.	REMARKS
8					Resistor for heater plugs	1	PRC116	) Diesel
					Bolt (10 UNF x ¾")) Fixing resistor to dash	2	257015	) models
					Shakeproof washer) earth lead	2	311373	)
					Nut (10 UNF)	2	257023	)
9					Dash harness	1	555776	)Petrol models. Up to vehicle
					Dash harness	1	555799	)vehicle suffix 'E' inclusive
10					Dynamo harness	1	560899	)Petrol models. From vehicle
					Dash harness	1	560869*	)suffix 'F' onwards
					Engine harness			
					Dash and dynamo harness	1	559058	Diesel models. Up to vehicle suffix 'E' inclusive
					Dash harness	1	560904	Diesel models. From vehicle suffix 'F' onwards
11					Frame harness	1	519784	88 models)Up to vehicle
					Frame harness	1	526440	109 models)suffix 'E')inclusive
					Frame harness	1	528900	109 Station Wagon)Up to Petrol models)vehicle suffix 'F'
					Frame harness	1	529964*	109 Station Wagon)suffix 'F' Diesel models)inclusive
12					Rear crossmember harness	1	519783	Up to vehicle suffix 'E' inclusive
					Frame and rear crossmember harness	1	560903*	88)Petrol)From
					Frame and rear crossmember harness	1	560898*	109)models)vehicle suffix 'F'
					Frame and rear crossmember harness	1	560901*	109 Station Wagon)onwards
					Frame and rear crossmember harness	1	560977*	88)Diesel
					Frame and rear crossmember harness	1	560975	109)models
					Frame and rear crossmember harness	1	560976*	109 Station Wagon)
13					Lead for rear number plate lamp	1	500559	All America Dollar Area Optional for other areas
14					Lead, starter motor to earth	1	219640	Petrol models
					Lead, starter motor to earth	1	531672*	Up to vehicle suffix 'D' inclusive)Diesel
					Lead, starter motor to earth	1	90575183	From vehicle suffix 'E' onwards)models
15					Fan disc washer for earth lead at starter motor	1	90512305	
					Bolt (5/16" UNF x ¾"))Fixing starter	1	CHF120	
					Fan disc washer) earth lead to	2	90510912	
					Nut (5/16" UNF)) chassis frame	1	GHF201	
16					Inhibitor socket for winer motor leads	1	555722	Up to vehicle)
					Lead, winer switch to inhibitor socket	1	555800*	suffix 'E')Except
17					Lead, inhibitor socket to windscreen	1	555801*	inclusive)Station Wagon
					Lead, winer switch to earth	1	555800*	Station Wagon.Up to vehicle suffix 'E' inclusive
18					Lead, winer motor to earth	1	555801*	Up to vehicle suffix 'E'
					Fan disc washer) Fixing earth	1	90519897	inclusive
					Drive screw) lead to dash	1	AB606021	

* NO LONGER SERVICED

2E 05

GENERAL ELECTRICAL EQUIPMENT, NEGATIVE EARTH SYSTEM
4-cylinder models. From vehicle suffix 'D' onwards

PLATE REF.	1	2	3	4	DESCRIPTION	QTY.	PART No.	REMARKS
					Cable, switch to winer motor	1	560965*	From vehicle suffix 'F' onwards
19					Cable, coil to distributor, low tension	1	528963	Eyelet type)connections)
					Cable, coil to distributor, low tension	1	579203	Lucar type)Alter-)Petrol connections)natives)models
20					Cable, battery to earth	1	551318	
21					Cable, battery to solenoid switch	1	551319	
					Cable, battery to earth	1	551346	Up to vehicle suffix 'D' inclusive
					Cable, battery to starter	1	551347*	From vehicle suffix 'E' onwards
					Cable, battery to starter	1	560902*	
22					Cable, connecting batteries	1	551638	
					Drive screw, fixing battery cables	2	50552	4 off on Diesel models
					Rubber cover for battery terminal	1	263158*	
					Cable, solenoid switch to starter	1	501691	)Petrol)models
					Rubber boot for starter cable	2	500980*	
					Bolt (¼" UNF x 2"))Fixing	1	255208	)Diesel models
					Fan disc washer) battery	2	510170	
					Spring washer) earth cable	1	GHF331	
					Nut (¼" UNF)) to frame	1	GHF200	
					Warning label 'NEGATIVE EARTH'	1	348433*	
					Pop rivet, fixing label to grille panel	2	78257	
23					Lead, tank unit to dash harness	1	529966*	Diesel models)Up to vehicle suffix 'E'
					Lead for fuel tank unit	1	531691*	Petrol models)inclusive Part of frame harness on later model

* NO LONGER SERVICED

2E 06

GENERAL ELECTRICAL EQUIPMENT, NEGATIVE EARTH SYSTEM
6-cylinder models.

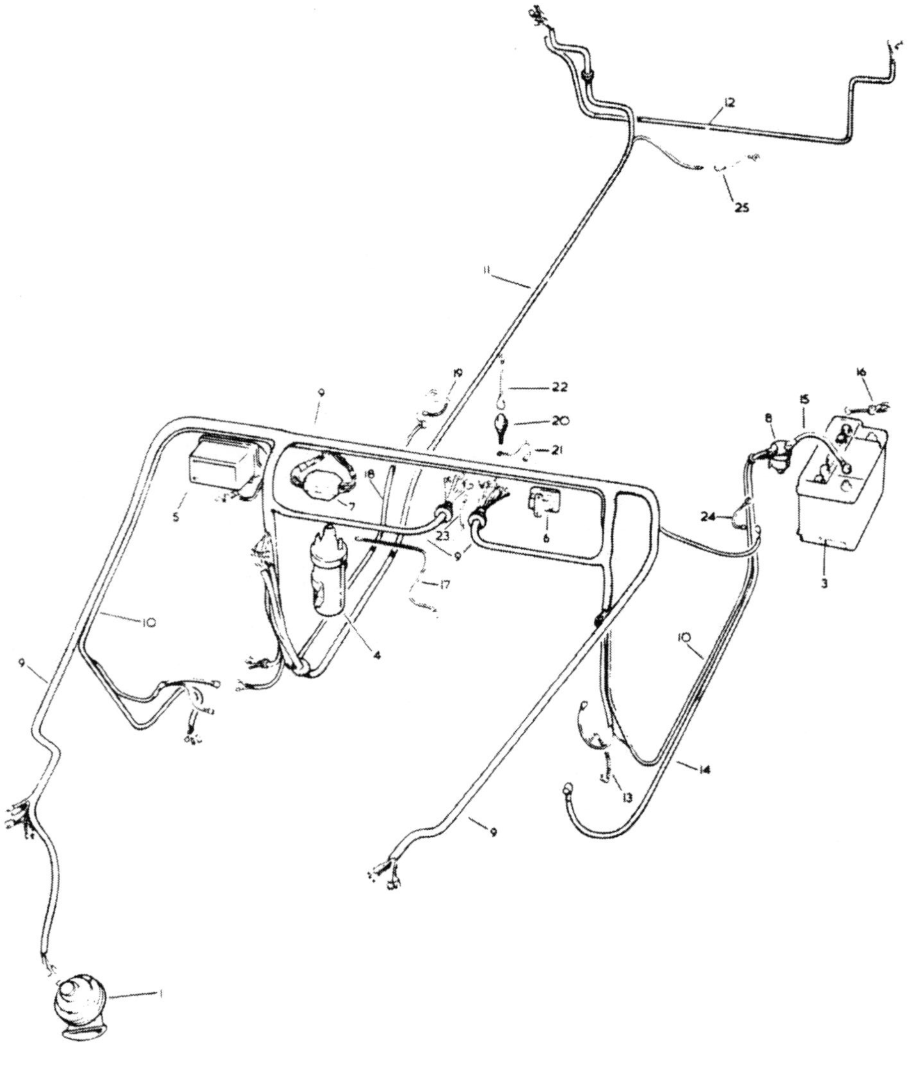

PLATE REF.	1 2 3 4 DESCRIPTION	QTY.	PART No.	REMARKS
1	Windtone horn, complete with bracekt	1	560749	
	Contact set for windtone horn	1	271500*	Lucas type
	Contact set for windtone horn	1	600638*	Clearhooter type
	Rubber grommet for horn	1	234041*	
	Bolt (¼" UNF x ⅞")) Fixing horn bracket	2	255206	
	Spring washer) to toe box or	2	GHF331	
	Nut (¼" UNF)) bridge plate	2	GHF200	
	Protector plate for horn	1	396124	
	Self-locking nut (¼" UNF) fixing protector plate to radiator grille	2	GHF221	
3	Activator, dry, 12 volt	1	GBY2205	
4	Ignition coil	1	GCL110	
	Rubber boot for ignition coil	1	574217	
	Terminal nut)	1	510237*	)
	Acorn nut) For ignition coil	1	240102	) For early type coil with
	Rubber boot)	1	506679	) terminal nut connection
	Split washer)	1	214279*	)
	Bolt (¼" UNF x ⅞"))	1	255207	
	Plain washer) Fixing coil	1	PTC609	
	Spring washer) to engine	1	GHF331	
	Nut (¼" UNF))	1	GHF200	
5	Current voltage control box	1	GEU607	
	Cover for control box	1	600442	
	Rubber seal for cover	1	507810*	
	Screw (10 UNF x 1½")) Fixing	3	79054	
	Plain washer) control box	3	3902	
	Special nut (10 UNF)) to dash	3	7999Q	
6	Voltage regulator for instruments	1	BHA4602	
	Drive screw) Fixing regulator	2	AB606021	
	spring washer) to dash	2	3101	
7	Fuse box	1	506253	
	Cover for fuse box	1	505158	
	Fuse, 35 amp	2	GFS435	
	Drive screw, fixing fuse box	1	GHF423	
	Drive screw locating fuse box	1	GHF421	
8	Starter solenoid switch	1	PTC461	
	Spring washer) For solenoid	2	575014	
	Nut) terminal post	2	90575015	
	Bolt (10 UNF x ⅞"))	2	257019	
	Spring washer) Fixing solenoid switch	2	WM702001	
	Fan disc washer) to seat base	2	513282	
	Nut (10 UNF))	2	257023	
9	Dash harness	1	560754*	Up to vehicle suffix 'E' inclusive
	Dash harness	1	560910	From vehicle suffix 'F' onwards
10	Dynamo harness	1	560532	
11	Frame harness	1	560557*	) Up to vehicle suffix 'E'
12	Rear crossmember harness	1	560555*	) inclusive
	Frame and rear crossmember harness	1	560901*	From vehicle suffix 'F' onwards

* NO LONGER SERVICED

GROUP K

GENERAL ELECTRICAL EQUIPMENT, NEGATIVE EARTH SYSTEM
2.6 litre Petrol, 6-cylinder models

PLATE REF. 1 2 3 4	DESCRIPTION	QTY.	PART No.	REMARKS
13	Lead, starter motor to earth	1	219649	
	Bolt (5/16" UNF x 2")) Fixing starter		GHF120	
	Fan disc washer) earth lead to	2	90519912	
	Nut (5/16" UNF)) chassis frame	1	GHF201	
14	Cable, solenoid to starter motor	1	559140	
15	Cable, battery to starter solenoid	1	560567	
16	Cable, battery to earth, negative	1	560566	
	Drive screw, fixing battery cables	2	50552	
17	Cable, coil to distributor, low tension	1	559163*	Up to vehicle suffix 'E' inclusive
			528963	Vehicle suffix 'F' only
	Cable, coil to distributor, low tension	1		From vehicle suffix 'G' onwards
	Lead, coil to distributor, low tension	1	570243	
18	Cable, fuel pump feed	1	90560577*	Up to vehicle suffix 'E' inclusive
	Cable, fuel pump feed	1	559150*	From vehicle suffix 'F' onwards
19	Lead, fuel pump to earth	1	559141*	
	Bolt (2BA x ¾")) Fixing earth lead	1	234603	
	Fan disc washer) to fuel pump bracket	1	513282	
	Spring washer)	1	WM702001	
	Nut (2BA)	1	RTC608	
20	Inhibitor socket for wiper motor leads	1	555762	Up to vehicle)Except
21	Lead, wiper switch to inhibitor socket	1	555800*	suffix 'E')Station inclusive)Wagon
22	Lead, inhibitor socket to windscreen	1	555801*	Station Wagon. Up to vehicle suffix 'E' inclusive
23	Lead, wiper switch to earth	1	555800*	
24	Earth lead for wiper motor	1	555801*	Up to vehicle suffix 'E' inclusive
	Drive screw) Fixing earth		ABC06021	
	Fan disc washer) lead to dash	1	90519897	From vehicle suffix 'F' onwards
	Cable, switch to wiper motor	1	560965*	
25	Earth lead for fuel tank gauge	1	239688	
	Drive screw) Fixing earth	1	72626	
	Fan disc washer) lead to body	1	90519857	
	Warning label, 'NEGATIVE EARTH'	1	348433*	
	Pop rivet, fixing label to grille panel	2	78257	

* NO LONGER SERVICED

2E 08

2E 08

183

GROUP L
CHASSIS FRAME

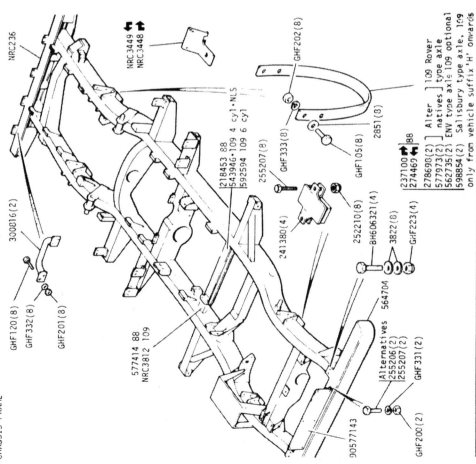

GHF120(8)

GHF332(8)

GHF201(8)

NRC236

300816(2)

NRC3449
NRC3448

577414 88
NRC3812 109

Alternatives
255206(2)
255207(2)
GHF331(2)

90577143

GHF200(2)

564704

241380(4)

252210(8)

BH606321(4)

3822(8)

GHF223(4)

218453 88
543946•109 4 cyl•NLS
592594 109 6 cyl

255207(8)

GHF333(8)

GHF105(8)

2851(8)

GHF202(8)

237100(2)
274469(4) } 88

278690(2)] Alter] 109 Rover
577973(2)] natives] type axle
562735(2) ENV type axle 109 optional
598854(2) Salisbury type axle, 109
only from vehicle suffix 'H' onwards

Chassis Frame NRC4642 88 ①
Chassis Frame NRC4355 109 4 cyl ① ① Station Wagon ①
Chassis Frame NRC4356 109 4 cyl Station Wagon
Chassis Frame 594697 109 6 cyl
Chassis Frame NRC4354 109 6 cyl Station Wagon

① When supplying for vehicles prior to vehicle 'D', the following parts must be fitted:
   Shaft for handbrake relay 552746 and Self locking nut GHF223

2F 02

GROUP L
CHASSIS - Battery Casing and Air Cleaner Support

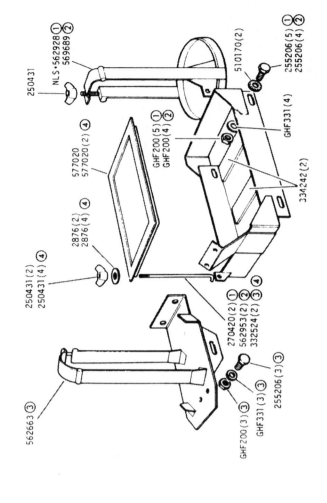

NLS•562928 ①
569689 ②

250431

577020
577020(2) ④

GHF200(5) ①
GHF200(4) ②

2876(2) ①
2876(4) ④

250431(2)
250431(4) ④

510170(2)

255206(5) ①
255206(4) ②

GHF331(4)

334242(2)

270420(2) ①
562953(2) ②
332524(2) ③
250431(4) ④

562663 ③

GHF200(3) ③

GHF331(3) ③

255206(3) ③

① 4 cylinder vehicles with integral horn protector plate
② 4 cylinder vehicles with separate horn protector plate
③ 6 cylinder
④ Diesel

2F 02

GROUP L
FRONT WINGS

330426
330427

330147 332589 338015 (2)
330436
330437

GHF200 (22)
GHF331 (22)
RTC609 (44)
255206 (22)

RTC2051 ①
RTC2052 ①
395014 ②
MRC2595 ②

255207 (6)
2215 (14)
GHF331 (9)
GHF200 (9)

3830 (3)
WM702001 (8)
NLS-78331 (8)
78393 (8)
UL2806 (8)
3830 (8)

GHF331 (2)
2215 (4)
255206 (2)
GHF200 (2)

606187 (2)

2851 (2)
GHF333 (2)
2827 (2)
562912 (2)

2827 (2)
2219 (2)

345620
345621

345623
345624

79051 (8) ②
GHF423 (8) ②
345631 (2) ②

① Suffix A to F
② Suffix G onwards

2F 03

GROUP L
Bonnet

336476

255206 (6)
GHF331 (6)
GHF200 (6)

336535
349931
336536

336474•NLS

4433•NLS

2393

MRC2479 De luxe without recess
MRC2440 De luxe with recess

347595

GHF200 (2)
GHF331 (2)
2215 (4)
255207 (2)

3830 (4) ①
GHF332 (4) ①
GHF120 (4) ①

NLS,
330540 ①
332400
332401

RTC609 (2)
255206 (2)

332625 Bolted
337969 Welded ①

REMARKS   ① For earlier type standard bonnet

2F 03

185

DASH, WINDSCREEN AND VENTILATOR

2F 05

GROUP L
COVER PANELS FOR FRONT WINGS

330333 (2)
RTC609 (4)
GHF331 (4)
GHF200 (4)
2215 (12)
GHF331 (6)
255206 (6)
255203 (6)
GHF200 (6)
330652 ③
336863 ③
345552 ④
345553 ④
345556
345557
345663
345664

255204 (8)
3817 (8)
GHF331 (3)
GHF200 (6)

332581 (2)
GHF200 (4)
GHF331 (4)
255206 (4)

255206
330445
330448
330444
330447

3900 (7)
GHF331 (4)
GHF200 (4)
78248 (4)

79246 (6)
WP6019 (6)
303750 (6)

330459 ①
330460 ②

255204
GHF300
GHF331
GHF200

330144
MN702001 (4)
RTC608 (4)
255204
GHF331
GHF200

234603 (4)
3902 (8)

330443 88 in
330534 109 in

REMARKS

① RH Strg
② LH Strg
③ Suffix A to F
④ Suffix G onwards

2F 04

186

PLATE REF.	DESCRIPTION (1 2 3 4)	QTY.	PART No.	REMARKS
1	Dash complete	1	345879*	4 cylinder models
	Dash complete	1	345611*	6 cylinder models
	Mounting bracket for control panel	1	345882	) 4 cylinder)
	Pop rivet, fixing bracket to dash	7	78257	) models) Up to
2	Panel for controls	1	332725*	Petrol models) vehicle
	Panel for controls	1	332726*	Diesel models) suffix 'C'
	Screw (2BA x ¼")) Fixing	6	77869	) inclusive
	Spring washer) panel	6	WM702001	)
	Plain washer) to	6	WC702101	)
	Nut (2 BA)) dash	3	RTC608	)
	Rubber edge finisher, outer) For dash	2	348370*	)Up to vehicle) 4 cylinder
	Rubber edge finisher, centre) top rail	1	348371*	)suffix 'C') models)inclusive)
	Finisher for dash top casing	1	345077	From vehicle suffix 'D' to suffix 'E' inclusive
	Finisher for dash top casing	1	345591	From vehicle suffix 'F' onwards
	Drive screw) Fixing	2	AB610051	) From vehicle
	Plain washer) finisher	2	4034	) suffix 'D'
	Spire extension nut) to dash	2	78237	) onwards
3	Cover panel for steering cutout	1	304111*	
	Rivet fixing cover plate	4	302222	
4	Cover plate for accelerator pedal hole	1	303990*	
	Bolt (¼" UNF x ⅜")) Fixing	2	255202	
	Spring washer) cover plate	2	GHF331	
	Nut (¼" UNF)) to dash	2	GHF200	
	Blanking plug 5/16" dia.) For accelerator	2	338029	
	Blanking plug ½" dia.) pedal hole	1	338015	
5	Cover panel for governor cutout in dash	1	306421*	))
	Bolt (¼" UNF x ⅜")) Fixing	2	255206	) Petrol) Up to
	Spring washer) cover	2	GHF331	) models) vehicle
	Nut (¼" UNF)) panel	2	GHF200	)) suffix 'C'
	Cover panel on dash for hand speed control	1	275742*	) Diesel) inclusive
	Grommet in dash for hand speed control rod	1	236389	) models)
	Blanking plate for hand throttle aperture	1	345883*	) 4 cylinder
	Pop rivet) Fixing	7	78257	) models from
	Bolt (¼" UNF x ½")) plate	3	255204	) vehicle
	Spring washer) to dash	3	GHF331	) suffix
	Nut (¼" UNF))	3	GHF200	) 'D' onwards
	Mounting box on dash for hand speed control	1	338428	)
	Grommet in dash for hand speed control rod	1	312937	)
	Bolt (¼" UNF x ½")) Fixing control	4	255204	) Diesel models. From vehicle
	Spring washer) and mounting	4	GHF331	) suffix 'D' to suffix 'E'
	Nut (¼" UNF)) box to dash	4	GHF200	) inclusive
	Pop rivet filling paint drain hole	2	78248	
6	Cover plate for pedal holes	1	330143	) 4 cylinder
	Rivet fixing plate	8	78248	) models
	Plate for brake and clutch pedals	1	338086*	RH Stg) All 4 cylinder
	Plate for brake and clutch pedals	1	338085	LH Stg) models. Also 6) cylinder models. Up) to vehicle suffix) 'F' inclusive
	Plate for brake and clutch pedals	1	345636	RH Stg) 6 cylinder models.
	Plate for brake and clutch pedals	1	345637*	LH Stg) From vehicle suffix) 'G' onwards

* NO LONGER SERVICED

PLATE REF.	DESCRIPTION (1 2 3 4)	QTY.	PART No.	REMARKS
	Rivet (3/16" Imex) fixing pedal plate to dash	12	78697	
	Cover plate for toe panel, LH	1	338091*	RH Stg
	Cover plate for toe panel, RH	1	338088*	LH Stg
	Rivet (3/16" Imex) fixing cover plate to dash	14	78687	
	Drive screw, earth point on dash	1	72628	
8	Rubber plug for redundant accelerator holes	5	307220	
9	Plastic plug, 1⅜" dia. for demister holes	2	338027	)
	Plastic plug, 1⅞" dia. for demister holes	2	338009	) Alternatives
	Plastic plug, 2" dia. for demister holes	2	338028	)
	Plastic plug, 1⅜" dia. for bridge plate	1	338027	
	Plastic plug, 11/16" dia.) For heater	2	338019	)
	Plastic plug, ⅞" dia.) pipe holes	2	338020	) Alternatives
	Plastic plug, ⅞" dia. for hand throttle hole	1	338020	Petrol models
	Plastic plug, 9/16" dia. for choke control hole	1	338017	)
	Rubber plug, 3.5/32" dia. for banjo bolt access hole	1	364584	) 6-cylinder) Petrol
	Rubber grommet, 1¼" dia. for bridge plate	1	368427	) models
	Plastic plug, ¾" dia.) For redundant windscreen	1	338015	4 cylinder models
	Plastic plug, ⅞" dia.) washer holes in dash) panel	1	338020	
	Rubber grommet for dip switch lead	1	233243	6-cylinder Petrol models
	Rubber plug, 7/16" dia. for windscreen washer holes in outer vent panel	2	338014	
10	Rubber plug, redundant accelerator stop hole	1	73198	
	Rubber plug for filling redundant clip holes	6	73198	2¼ litre Petrol models 1 off on Diesel models
	Buffer for bonnet panel on dash front	2	332647	
	Bolt (5/16" UNF x ¾")) Fixing dash to	4	255227	
	Plain washer) steering box	10	3830	
	Self-locking nut (5/16" UNF)) support brackets	6	GHF242	
12	Tie bolt (¼" UNF)) Fixing dash	2	336738	
	Plain washer) to	4	WC112081	
	Nut (¼" UNF)) chassis	2	NH608041	
	Ventilator hinge, RH	2	330060*	) For ventilator
13	Ventilator hinge, LH	2	330061	) lids with hinges
	Screw (2BA x ¼")) Fixing	8	78399*	) fixed by screws
	Spring washer) hinges	8	WM702001	) and nuts
	Plain washer) to	16	4280*	)
	Nut (2BA)) lid	8	RTC608	)

* NO LONGER SERVICED

GROUP L   DASH, WINDSCREEN AND VENTILATOR

PLATE REF. 1 2 3 4	DESCRIPTION	QTY.	PART No.	REMARKS
14	Ventilator lid and hinge for dash, RH	1	345845	
	Ventilator lid and hinge for dash, LH	1	345846	
	Hinge pin for ventilator lid	4	334121	For ventilator lid with welded hinges.
15	Sealing rubber for ventilator lids	2	330671	
16	Ventilator control mechanism complete	2	RTC2665	Quadrant type
	Knob and fixing screws for ventilator control	2	332327	For quadrant type ventilator control.
	Circlip for ventilator control knob	2	320500*	For screw type ventilator control.
	Drive screw	4	AB610051	
	Spire nut	4	7P237	
	Bolt (2 BA x ¼")	8	234603	}
	Plain washer, small	4	WC702101	} For screw type ventilator control.
	Plain washer, medium	4	4034	
	Plain washer, large	4	3862	
	Spring washer	8	WM702001	
	Nut (2 BA)	8	RTC608	
	Taptite screw (10 UNF x ½")	4	78808*	} For quadrant type) Alternatives
	Plain washer	4	WC702101	} ventilator)
	Drive screw	4	AB610051	
	Plain washer	4	4034	
	Spire nut	4	78237	
	Set bolt (2 BA x ½")	4	234603	} Fixing
	Plain washer	4	WC702101	} control to
	Spring washer	4	WM702001	} ventilator lid
17	WINDSCREEN COMPLETE ASSEMBLY, toughened glass	1	337643*	
	WINDSCREEN COMPLETE ASSEMBLY, laminated glass	1	339805*	
18	Glass for windscreen, toughened	2	337644	
	Glass for windscreen, laminated	2	MRC6526	
	Glazing strip for glass	14 ft	78150	
19	Retainer for windscreen glass, RH top	1	330668	
	Retainer for windscreen glass, LH top	1	330669	
20	Retainer for windscreen glass, side	2	330667	
21	Retainer for windscreen glass, RH bottom	1	347637	
	Retainer for windscreen glass, LH bottom	1	347638	
22	Cover for centre strip	1	330670*	Up to vehicle suffix 'C' inclusive
	Cover for centre strip	1	336422	From vehicle suffix 'D' onwards
23	Drive screw fixing retainers and covers	37	AB604031	
	Bolt (¼" UNF x 1⅜")	2	256280	} Alternatives
	Screw (¼" UNF x 1¾")	4	255288	}
	Plain washer	4	3879	} Fixing windscreen to dash
24	Turret nut (¼" UNF)	2	549043	
25	Rubber sealing strip for windscreen	1	395430	

* NO LONGER SERVICED

2F 07

DASH, WINDSCREEN AND VENTILATOR

2F 07

GROUP L   DASH, WINDSCREEN AND VENTILATOR

PLATE REF. 1 2 3 4	DESCRIPTION	QTY.	PART No.	REMARKS
	End filler for windscreen sealing strip	2	330850	
	Buffer for top of windscreen	1	332550	} Only required when
	Pop rivet fixing buffer	4	78410	} hood is fitted
	Fastener for windscreen, RH	1	338194	} Turret
	Fastener for windscreen, LH	1	338195*	} nut type
26	Wing nut for fastener (5/16" BSF)	2	303709*	
27	Wing nut for fastener (5/16" UNF)	2	338208*	Alternatives.
	Turret nut (5/16" UNF) plastic capped	2	338240	
	Set bolt (5/16" UNF x 5/8") } Fixing	4	SH605051	
	Plain washer } fasteners	4	RTC610	
	Spring washer	4	GHF332	
	CHECK STRAP ASSEMBLY	2	306677A	
28	Rod for check strap	2	332715	
29	Buffer for check strap	2	306471	
30	Plain washer } Fixing buffer to rod	4	4035	
	Spring washer	2	GHF331	
	Nut (1/4" UNF)	2	GHF200	
31	Check strap mounting bracket, RH	1	334959	
	Check strap mounting bracket, LH	1	334960	
	Bolt (1/4" UNF x 3/4" long) }	8	255706	Early models
	Plain washer } Fixing	8	GHF300	
	Spring washer } mounting bracket	8	GHF331	
	Plain washer } to dash	8	RTC609	
	Nut (1/4" UNF)	8	GHF200	
32	Clevis pin } Fixing check strap	4	3815*	
33	Plain washer } rod to	2	306564	
	Split pin } front door	2	RTC610	
34	Tie bar for dash support	1	332588	For 5/16" UNF bolt and nut fixing. Up to vehicle suffix 'A'
	Tie bar for dash support	1	346540	RH Stg } For 1/4" UNF bolt and
	Tie bar for dash support	1	346370	LH Stg } nut fixing. From vehicle suffix 'B' onwards
	Nut (1/4" BSF) fixing tie bar to dash	2	2827	} Alternative
	Nut (1/4" UNF) fixing tie bar to dash	2	GHF202	} fixings
	Bolt (5/16" UNF x 1/2") }	1	255227	} Up to vehicle suffix 'A'
	Spring washer } Fixing	1	GHF332	
	Nut (5/16" UNF) } tie bar to	1	CHF201	
	Bolt (1/4" UNF x 1/2") } support bracket	1	SH606071	} From vehicle suffix 'B'
	Spring washer } on chassis frame	1	GHF333	} onwards
	Nut (1/4" UNF)	1	GHF202	Plastic type
	Licence holder	1	544573	

* NO LONGER SERVICED

2F 08

GROUP L
FLOOR PANEL

① 79048(3)
AB610051(3)②
302533(2)
WP8019(2)
78837(3)②
79246(3)①
303828
303817
338871
330069①
303750(4)
3900(4)
79246(4)
301437
AB610051(4)
WC702101(4)
348869②
79246(4)
NLS-
348868②
320045(6)
3900(6)
79246(6)
330037 ①
330038 ①
301437
320045(13)
3900(9)
3817(4)
79246(4)
333882①
334189(2)①
78210(4)
GHF331(4)
3900(8)
320045(14)
3900(10)
3817(4)
79246(14)
GHF200(4)
78208(5)
GHF331(5)
3900(5)
345140②
348893 ②
348894 ②

① 4 cylinder
② 6 cylinder

2F 09

189

GROUP L
SEAT BASE

GROUP L
EAT BASE FIXINGS

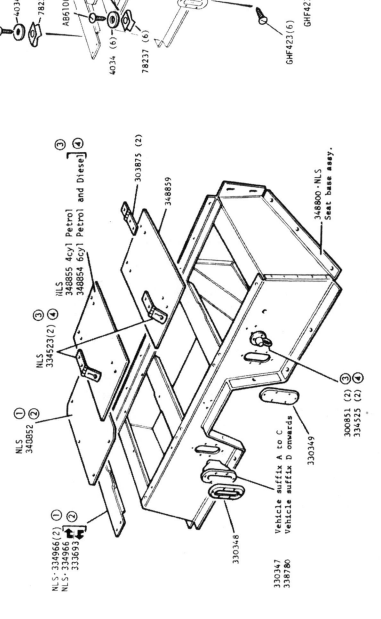

Top diagram (SEAT BASE FIXINGS):

255206 (2)
GIF331 (2)
GHF200 (2)
GHF200 (2)
GIF331 (2)
UFS1254R (2)

255207 (9)
RTC609 (9)
GHF331 (9)
GHF200 (9)

For redundant holes in rear stiffener

320045 (2)
79246 (2)
78248 (2)

78248 (6)

7o248 (2)

RTC608 (6)
UN702001 (6)
77784 (6)
78977 (6)

AB610051 (6)
4034 (6)
78237 (6)
AB610051 (6)
4034 (6)
78237 (6)
GHF423 (6)
GHF423 (6)

Alternative fixings

REMARKS

2F 10

Bottom diagram (SEAT BASE):

① ②
NLS 334966 (2)
NLS 334966
333693

NLS
340852

NLS
334523 (2) ③ ④

③ ④
NLS
348855 4cyl Petrol
348854 6cyl Petrol and Diesel

303875 (2)
348859

348800 · NLS
Seat base assy.

300851 (2) ③
334525 (2) ④

330349

Vehicle suffix A to C
Vehicle suffix D onwards

330347
338780

330348

REMARKS

① For one locker lid type seat base
② For two locker lid type seat base
③ Circular base turnbuckle
④ Semi- circular base turnbuckle

2F 10

GROUP L
SILL PANELS

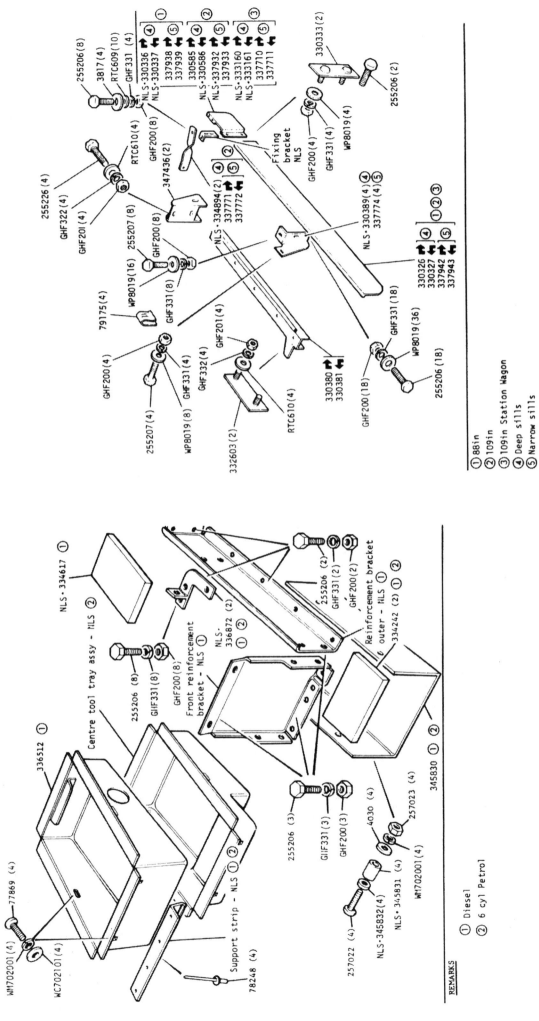

GROUP L
CENTRE TOOL TRAY

255206(8)
3817(4)
RTC609(10)
GHF331(4)

① ④ ⑤
NLS·330336
NLS·330337
337938
337939
② ④ ⑤
330585
NLS·330586
337932
337933
③ ④ ⑤
NLS·333160
NLS·333161
337710
337711

330333(2)
255206(2)

255226(4)
GHF322(4)
GHF201(4)

RTC610(4)
GHF200(8)
347436(2)

④ ⑤
NLS·334894(2)
337771
337772

② ④ ⑤

Fixing bracket
NLS

WP8019(4)
GHF331(4)
GHF200(4)

NLS·330389(4) ④
337774(4) ⑤

①②③

330326
330327
337942
337943
④ ⑤

WP8019(16)
255207(8)
GHF200(8)

GHF331(8)

79175(4)

GHF200(4)
255207(4)
WP8019(8) GHF331(4)
GHF332(4)
GHF201(4)

332603(2)
RTC610(4)

330380
330381

④ ⑤
GHF331(18)
WP8019(36)

GHF200(18)
255206(18)

2F 11

① 88in
② 109in
③ 109in Station Wagon
④ Deep sills
⑤ Narrow sills

WM702001(4)
WC702101(4)
77869 (4)

336512 ①

Centre tool tray assy - NLS ②

NLS·334617 ①

255206 (2)
GHF331(2)
GHF200(2)

Reinforcement bracket
outer - NLS ① ②

334242 (2) ① ②

255206 (8)
GHF331(8)
GHF200(8)

Front reinforcement
bracket - NLS ①

NLS·
336872 (2)
①②

345830 ① ②

Support strip - NLS ① ②

78248 (4)

257022 (4)
NLS·345832(4)

255206 (3)
GHF331(3)
GHF200(3)

4030 (4)
257023 (4)

WM702001(4)

NLS·345831 (4)

REMARKS

① Diesel
② 6 cyl Petrol

2F 11

191

GROUP L
BODY - Sidescreen for front door

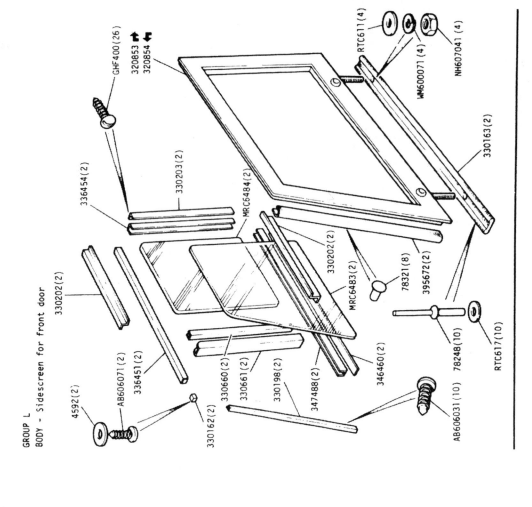

GHF400(26)
320853
320854
336454(2)
330203(2)
MRC6484(2)
330202(2)
330202(2)
MRC6483(2)
78321(8)
395672(2)
346460(2)
330660(2)
330661(2)
330198(2)
347488(2)
4592(2)
AB606071(2)
336451(2)
330162(2)
AB606031(10)
78248(10)
RTC617(10)
RTC611(4)
WM600071(4)
NH607041(4)
330163(2)

2F 12

GROUP L
BODY - Front Door

395670
395671
78321(14)
302222(8)
395529
395530
78321(18)
MRC5740(2)
78248(10)
330122
330123
346426(2)
395598
395599
78321(10)

2F 12

GROUP L
DOOR LOCKS AND HINGES

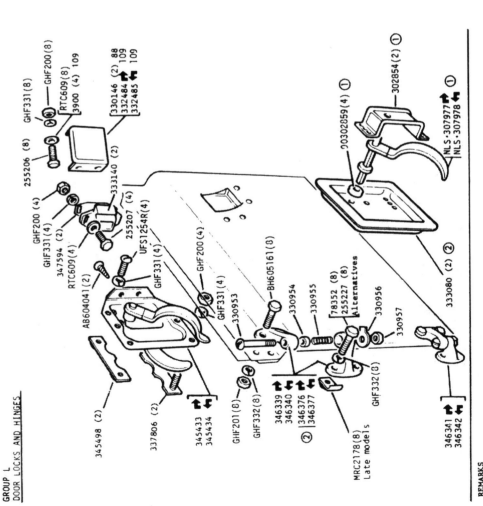

This page is intentionally left blank

345498 (2)

337806 (2)

345433
345434

GHF201(8)

GHF332(8)

MRC2178(8)
Late models

255206 (8)   GHF331(8)

GHF200 (8)

RTC609(8)
3900 (4) 109

330146 (2) 88
332484 109
332485 109

GHF200 (4)

GHF331(4)

347594 (2)

RTC609(4)

AB604041(2)

333140 (2)

255207 (4)

UFS1254R(4)

GHF331(4)

GHF200(4)

GHF331 (4)

330953

BH605161(8)

330954

330955

78352 (8)
255227 (8)
Alternatives

330956

330957

346339
346340
346376
346377

GHF332(3)

346341
346342

333080 (2)

30302859(4)

NLS·307977
NLS·307978

302854(2)

2F 13

REMARKS
① For early type lock with detachable inner handle.
② Incorporating bracket for exterior mirror. Optional.

193

REAR SIDE DOORS—109IN STATION WAGON

GROUP L   REAR SIDE DOORS—109IN STATION WAGON

PLATE REF. 1 2 3 4	DESCRIPTION	QTY.	PART No.	REMARKS
1	REAR SIDE DOOR ASSEMBLY, RH	1	320857	
1	REAR SIDE DOOR ASSEMBLY, LH	1	320858	
1	DOOR LOCK, MOUNTING AND HANDLE ASSEMBLY RH	1	395652	) With non-detachable
1	DOOR LOCK, MOUNTING AND HANDLE ASSEMBLY LH	1	395653	) inner handle
2	Mounting plate for door lock	2	333080	
3	Door handle complete, RH	1	307977	
3	Door handle complete, LH	1	307978*	) For early type
4	Bracket for door handle, outer mounting	2	302854	) lock with detachable
5	Door lock complete, RH	1	345433	) inner handle.
5	Door lock complete, LH	1	345430	
6	Sealing washer, handle to cover	2	90302850	
	Screw (2 BA x ⅜")	8	313858*	)
	Spring washer	12	MP702001	) Fixing lock,
	Nut (2 BA)	12	RTC608	) brackets and
	Plain washer	8	RTC618	) cover together
	Screw (2 BA x ⅜")	4	314203	
7	Locking catch, RH	1	333271*	
7	Locking catch, LH	1	333272	
	Screw (2 BA x ⅜")	2	313860*	
	Plain washer, large	2	4034	)
	Plain washer, small	2	3902	) Fixing catches
	Spring washer	2	MP702001	)
	Nut (2 BA)	6	RTC608	)
	Locking catch, RH	1	345435	Models with pivot type catch.
	Locking catch, LH	1	345436	Spring loaded type catch
	Rivet fixing door lock cover to outer panel	8	302222	With plunger operating inside lock case
	Screw (¼" UNF x ¾")	8	UFS1254R	Alternative to 2 lines below
	Screw retainer, RH	2	337806	) Fixing lock
	Screw retainer, LH	2	332733	) assemblies
	Spring washer	8	GHF331	) to door
	Nut (¼" UNF)	8	GHF200	) lock cover
	Drive screw, fixing lock assembly to door	2	AB604041	Alternative to line above
8	Door hinge, upper RH	1	346339	
8	Door hinge, upper LH	1	346340	
8	Door hinge, lower RH	1	346341	

* NO LONGER SERVICED

2F 14

2F 14

D594

PLATE REF.	1 2 3 4 DESCRIPTION	QTY.	PART No.	REMARKS
9	Door hinge, lower LH	1	346342	
	Bolt (5/16" UNF x 2")) Fixing	8	BH605161	
	Spring washer) door hinge to	8	GHF332	
	Nut (5/16" UNF)) door frame	8	GHF201	
10	Fixed window for sidescreen	2	MRC6485	
11	Retainer for sidescreen, fixed window	2	333033	
	Drive screw (⅜" No.6) fixing retainer to frame	10	AB606031	
12	Filler, top and bottom, for side screen	4	333081	
13	Filler, rear, for sidescreen	2	330203	
	Packing strip, for glass channel	2	333082	
14	Sliding window with knob for sidescreen	2	333089	
15	Sliding light channel, rear	2	336454	
16	Sliding light channel, top and bottom	4	347489	
	Drive screw (⅜" No.6) fixing sliding channel	28	GHF400	
17	Buffer for sidescreen sliding window at top	2	330162	
	Plain washer) Fixing	2	4592	
	Drive screw) buffer	2	AB606071	
18	Sealing rubber for sliding glass	2	330660	
19	Channel for sliding glass sealing rubber	2	330661	
20	Sliding window catch	2	332435	
	Pop rivet fixing catch	4	78248	
	Rod for check strap, RH	1	333041	
21	Rod for check strap, LH	1	333204	
22	Buffer for check strap, short	2	306295	
	Buffer for check strap, long	2	333445	
	Door check bracket, RH, for rear side door	1	MRC4753	
23	Door check bracket, LH, for rear side door	1	333096	
	Bolt (5/16" UNF x 1¼"))	4	255229	
	Bolt (5/16" UNF x 1"))	4	GHF103	
	Shakeproof washer) Fixing brackets to	8	GHF322	
	Shim) chassis frame	8	305232	
	Nut (5/16" UNF))	8	GHF201	
24	Clevis pin)	2	302828	
	Plain washer, small) Fixing door check rod	4	3947	
	Plain washer, large) to bracket	2	RTC609	
	Split pin)	2	3958	
	Bolt, top (5/16" UNF x 2¼"))	4	BH605201	
	Bolt, bottom (5/16" UNF x 3")) Fixing door	4	BH605241	
	Plain washer) hinge to 'BC' post at bottom	8	3966	4 off when nut plate is use
	Spring washer)	8	GHF332	
	Nut (5/16" UNF))	8	GHF201	4 Off when nut plate is us
	Nut plate)	2	333710	
25	Striking plate for rear side door locks	2	333140	
	Shim	2	347594	
	Bolt (¼" UNF x ¾"))	4	255207	
	Plain washer) Fixing striking plate	4	RTC609	
	Spring washer) to 'D' post	4	GHF331	
26	Nut plate)	2	346241	
	Waist moulding, rear side door RH	1	333719	
27	Waist moulding, rear side door LH	1	333720	

PLATE REF.	1 2 3 4 DESCRIPTION	QTY.	PART No.	REMARKS
	Special bolt)	16	302533	
	Plain washer) Fixing moulding to doors	16	2630	
	Spire nut)	16	79246	
	Seal retainer for rear side door, RH top	1	MRC2381	
28	Seal retainer for rear side door, LH top	1	MRC2382	
29	Rubber seal for retainer	2	333228	
	Rivet fixing seal to retainer	12	78321	
	Screw (2BA x ¼"))	8	77869	
	Plain washer) Fixing seal and	8	3902	
	Spring washer) retainer to cant rail	8	WM702001	
	Nut (2BA))	8	RTC608	
30	Door sealing rubber for upper vertical 'D' post	2	395674	
	Rivet fixing seal to 'D' post	10	78321	
	Door sealing rubber for lower vertical 'D' post, RH	1	333261	
31	Door sealing rubber for lower vertical 'D' post, LH	1	333262	
	Rivet fixing seal to 'D' post	10	78321	
32	Door sealing rubber for sloping 'D' post	2	395674	
	Rivet fixing seal to 'D' post	8	78321	
33	Door sealing rubber at rear side sills, bottom	2	333233	
	Rivet fixing seal to sill	8	78321	
34	Door sealing rubber at 'C' post	2	333229	
	Rivet fixing seal at 'C' post	22	78321	
	Door sealing rubber at 'B' post, lower, RH	1	395670	
35	Door sealing rubber at 'B' post, lower, LH	1	395671	
	Rivet fixing seal to 'B' post	12	78321	
36	Door sealing rubber at 'B' post, upper	2	395674	
	Rivet fixing seal to 'B' post	10	78321	
37	Filler piece for 'B' post seal	2	330850	
	Frame for front and rear side doors, RH	1	MRC3141	
38	Frame for front and rear side doors, LH	1	MRC6950	
	Bracket, sill channel to panel	6	330389*	
	Bolt (¼" UNF x ¾"))	12	255207	
	Plain washer) Fixing brackets	24	WP8019	
	Spring washer) to sill channels	12	GHF331	
	Nut (¼" UNF))	12	GHF200	
	Bolt plate)	2	332603	
	Plain washer) Fixing sill channels	4	RTC610	
	Spring washer) to dash pillar	4	GHF332	
	Nut (5/16" UNF))	4	GHF201	
	Bracket for sill, rear end RH	1	333259	
	Bracket for sill, rear end LH	1	333260*	
	Bolt (5/16" UNF x ⅞"))	8	255227	
	Plain washer) Fixing bracket	16	RTC610	
	Plain washer) to sill and	2	WP185	
	Spring washer) chassis frame	8	GHF332	
	Nut (5/16"UNF))	8	GHF201	
	Plug for redundant hole on 'BC' post, bottom	2	338021	

* NO LONGER SERVICED

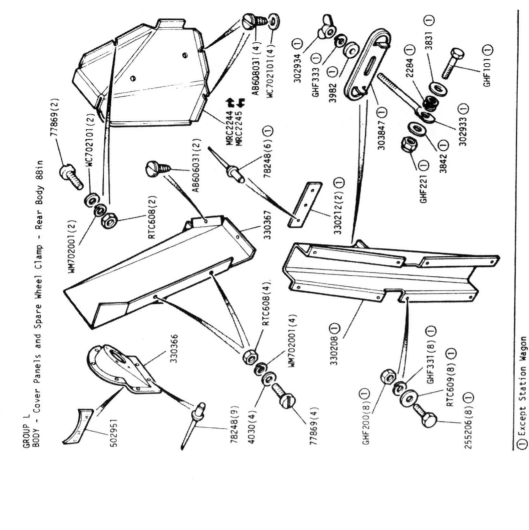

GROUP L
BODY - Cover Panels and Spare Wheel Clamp - Rear Body 88in

77869(2)
WC702101(2)
WM702001(2)
RTC608(2)
AB606031(4)
WC702101(4)
MRC2244
MRC2245
AB606031(2)
78248(6)
330367
330212(2)
302934
GHF333
3982
303847
3842
GHF221
302933
3831
GHF101
2284
RTC608(4)
WM702001(4)
330366
502951
78248(9)
4030(4)
77869(4)
330208
GHF200(8)
GHF331(8)
RTC609(8)
255206(8)

① Except Station Wagon

2G 02

GROUP L
BODY - Rear Body - 88in

330249
Rear Panel only
330248 Rear Panel only
330267
330271
332521(2)
255206(4)
78208(2)
GHF331(6)
330303
330304
GHF200(6)
301879(12)
78248(18)
Complete
330214 Side Panel Only
330295
Complete
330215 Side Panel only
330296
330265(3)
73979(12)
78248(9)
72085(2)
90508035(5)
332582(6)
21563(2)
332451
395409
GHF331(4)
GHF200(4)
RTC609(8)
255207(4)

Rear Body complete assembly 320863

2G 02

196

GROUP L
BODY - Tailboard Fixings and Rear Name Plate - 88in

Alternatives
332146(4) ①
330419(2) ①

Alternatives
333972(2) ①
337290(2) ①

332670

306407 ②

78248(2) ②

GHF400(7) ①
GHF421(13) ②

77899(4) ①

4030(4) ①

4023(4) ①

78321(10) ①

78248(2)

255206(4)

338743 ①
332565 ②

330399(2) ①

330422(4) ①

RTC609(4)

GHF200(4)

GHF331(4)

302825(2) ①

3958(2) ①

302828(2) ①

① Except Station Wagon
② Station Wagon

2G 03

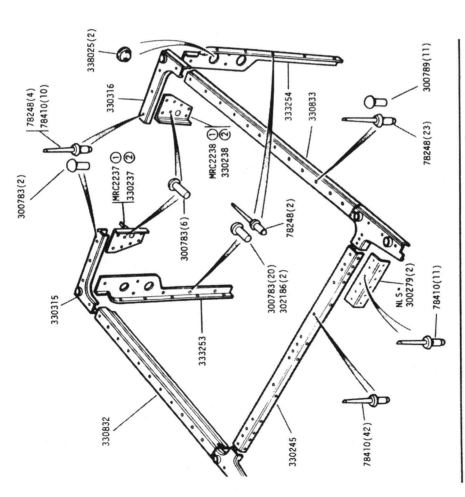

GROUP L
BODY - Cappings - 88in

338025(2)

330316

333254
330833

300789(11)

78248(4)
78410(10)

MRC2237 ①
330237 ②

MRC2238 ①
330238 ②

300783(2)

300783(6)

78248(2)

78248(23)

300783(20)
302186(2)

NLS-
300279(2)

78410(11)

330315

333253

78410(42)

330832

330245

① Except Station Wagon
② Station Wagon

2G 03

197

GROUP L
BODY - Rear Body - 109in except Station Wagon

330248 ⬆ Rear Panel only

330663 ⬆①Complete
347035 ⬆①Side panel only
348871 ⬆②Complete • NLS
348872 ⬆②Side panel only

305232 A/R 255227(16)
21563(6)②
332451(3)②
336782①
255227(16)
90510912(28)
GHF201(18)
AD604031(12)②

330468①
333159②
330249
Rear panel only

NLS
348882(3)①
NLS
347036 ⬅ Complete
347036 ⬅ Side panel only

330617①
NLS • 348874②

GHF200(2)
90510912(2)

3900(4)
255207(2)

78248(9)
332582(12)

330265(6)
90508035(5)
72085(2)
78248(9)

395404

78208(4)
255206(2)
GHF331(6)
GHF200(6)

332521(2)
NLS •
334895(2)

301879(22)
78248(36)
73979(24)

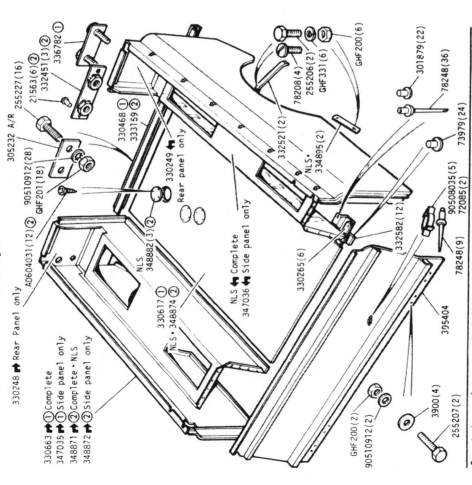

Rear body complete assembly 330958 4 Cylinder • NLS
Rear body complete assembly 320658 6 Cylinder • NLS

① 4 Cylinder
② 6 Cylinder

2G 04

GROUP L
BODY - Cover Panels - Rear Body - 109in except Station Wagon

NLS ① ②
334523 ① ③
338027(2)
78248(3) ①

300851①②
345525①③
78248(20)

78248(4) ①
303875(2) ①
304401 ①
300789(2) ①
330616

255206(2) ①
RTC622(2) ①
GHF331(2) ①
GHF200(2) ①
300783(2)
78248(20)

330602

330366 4 cyl

502951
78248(9)

347553(4)
302186(8)

78410(8)

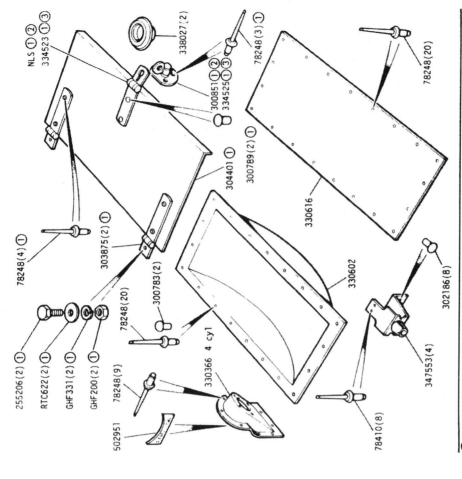

① Double quantities for 4 cylinder vehicles
② Circular base turnbuckle
③ Semi - circular base turnbuckle

2G 04

GROUP L
BODY - Cappings - 109in except Station Wagon

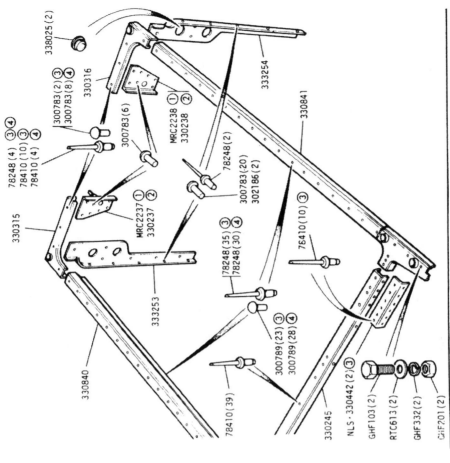

338025(2)
300783(2) ③
300783(8) ④
330316
78248(4) ③④
78410(10) ③
78410(4) ④
300783(6)
MRC2238 ①
330238 ②
78248(2)
330315
300783(20)
302186(2)
MRC2237 ①
330237 ②
78410(10) ③
333253
78248(35) ③
78248(30) ④
333254
330841
300789(23) ③
300789(28) ④
330840
78410(39)
330245
NLS·330442(2)③
GHF103(2)
RTC613(2)
GHF332(2)
GHF201(2)

① Except hard top with rear door
② Hard top with rear door
③ 4 cylinder vehicles
④ 6 cylinder vehicles

2G 05

GROUP L
BODY - Spare Wheel Mounting and Rear Lamp Cover Panels - 109in except Station Wagon

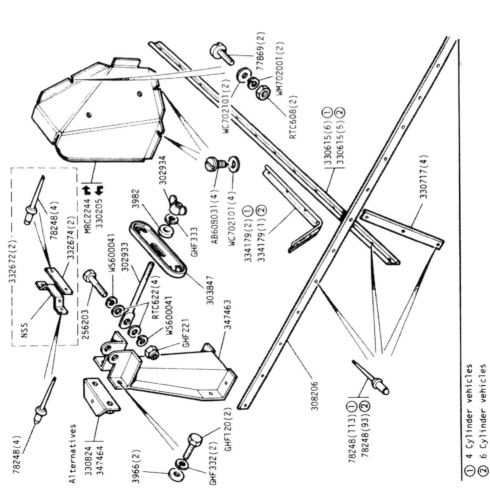

78248(4)
332672(2)
Alternatives
330824
347464
NSS
332674(2)
78248(4)
302934
MRC2244
330205
3982
GHF333
302933
WS600041
256203
RTC622(4)
WS600041
303847
GHF221
347463
3966(2)
GHF332(2)
GHF120(2)
77869(2)
WM702001(2)
WC702101(2)
RTC608(2)
AB608031(4)
WC702101 ①
334179(2) ①
334179(1) ②
330615(6) ①
330615(5) ②
330717(4)
308206
78248(113) ①
78248(93) ②

① 4 Cylinder vehicles
② 6 Cylinder vehicles

2G 05

199

GROUP L
BODY - Rear Body - 109in Station Wagon

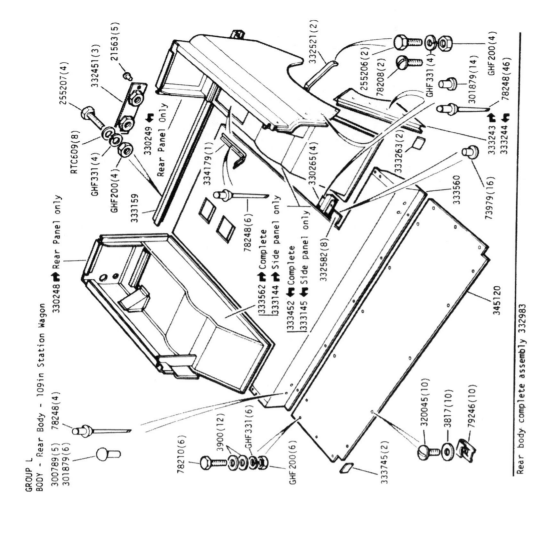

300789(5) 78248(4)
301879(6)

25520/(4)
21563(5)
332451(3)
RTC609(8)
GHF331(4)
GHF200(4)
333159

330248 ← Rear Body - 109in Station Wagon
330249 ← Rear Panel Only
← Rear Panel only

334179(1)

330265(4)
78248(6)
333562 ← Complete
333144 ← Side panel only

333452 ← Complete
333145 ← Side panel only

332521(2)
255206(2)
78208(2)
GHF331(4)
301879(14)
GHF200(4)
78248(46)

333243
333244

333263(2)
73979(16)
333560

332582(8)

345120

78210(6)
3900(12)
GHF331(6)
GHF 200(6)

333745(2)

320045(10)
3817(10)
79246(10)

Rear body complete assembly 332983

2G 06

GROUP L
BODY - Tailboard Fixings and Rear Nameplate - 109in except Station Wagon

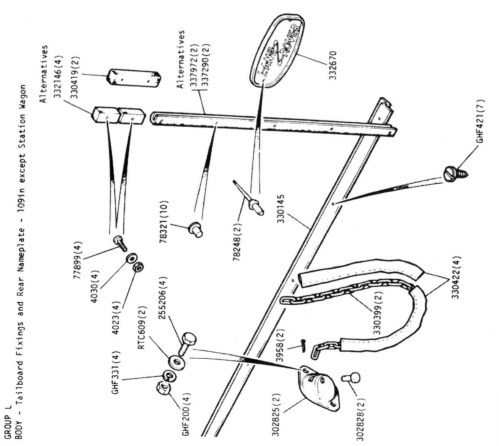

Alternatives
332146(4)
330419(2)

Alternatives
337972(2)
337290(2)

332670

77899(4)
4030(4)
4023(4)

78321(10)

78248(2)

330145

GHF421(7)

GHF331(4)
RTC609(2)
255206(4)
GHF200(4)

3958(2)

302825(2)
302828(2)

330399(2)
330422(4)

2G 06

200

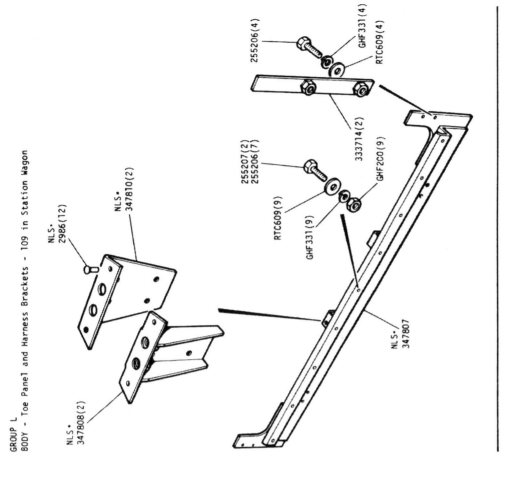

GROUP L
BODY - Toe Panel and Harness Brackets - 109 in Station Wagon

255206(4)
GHF331(4)
GHF609(4)
RTC609(4)
333714(2)
GHF200(9)
NLS.
347807
NLS.
347810(2)
NLS.
2986(12)
NLS.
347808(2)
255207(2)
255206(7)
RTC609(9)
GHF331(9)

2G 07

GROUP L
BODY - Cover Panels - Rear Body - 109in Station Wagon

78248(4)
332670
306407
320045(4)
3900(4)
79246(4)
304401
303875(2)
255206(2)
RTC622(2)
GHF331(2)
GHF200(2)
77869(2)
WC702101(2)
WM702001(2)
RTC608(2)
MRC2244
330205
AB608031(4)
WC702101(4)
333202
333201
NLS ①
334523 ②
300851 ①
334525 ②
RTC612
78248(3)
300789(2)
78248(4)

① Circular base turnbuckle
② Semi - circular base turnbuckle

2G 07

201

GROUP L
BODY - Cappings - 109in Station Wagon

333267

78248(4)
78410(4)

300783(8)

330238

330237

300783(4)
300784(2)

333266

302186(2)
300783(20)

78248(2)

333254

333235

333253

333234

300789(18)

78248(26)

2G 08

GROUP L
BODY - Tailboard Assembly

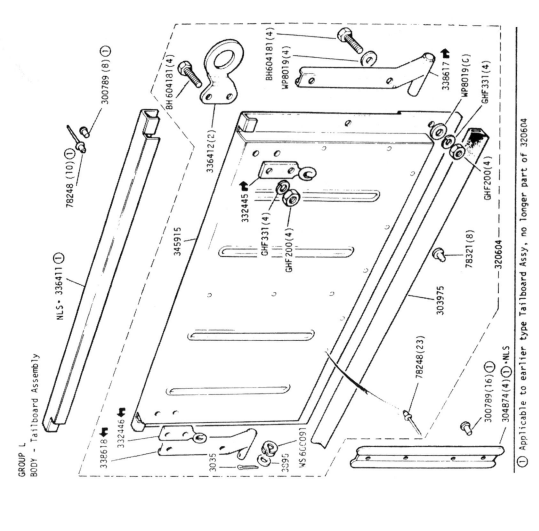

300789(8) ①

78248(10) ①

BH604181(4)

BH604181(4)
WP8019(4)

338617

WP8019(C)

GHF331(4)

GHF200(4)

336412(2)

332445

GHF331(4)

GHF200(4)

345915

NLS • 336411 ①

78321(8)

320604

303975

78248(23)

300789(16)①

304874(4)①•NLS

332446

338618

3035

3095

WS6CC091

① Applicable to earlier type Tailboard Assy, no longer part of 320604

2G 08

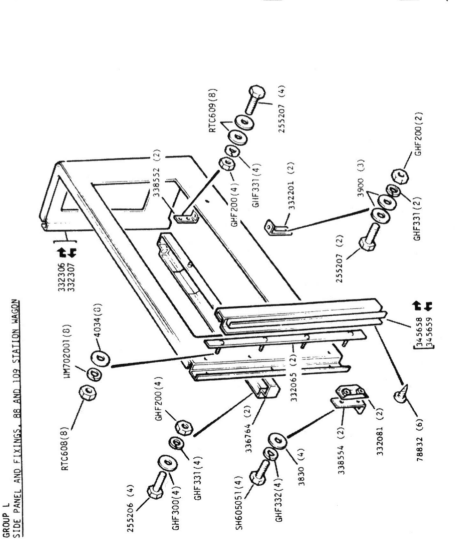

GROUP L
REAR SIDE WINDOWS, 88 AND 109 STATION WAGON

332280 / 332281
AB604031 (36)
78159 as required
MRC6493(2)
332282 (4)
332283 / 332284
348393 (2)
348394 (2)
336454
GHF421(76) 88
GHF400(76) 109
330661
MRC6490(4)
332230 (2)
78248 (28)
330848 (4)
332216 (4)
348396 (4)
336454 (2)
78401 (2) Rear
78402 (2) Front
340391 (16)
332324 (2) Front
332325 (2) Rear
332329 (4)

REMARKS

2G 09

GROUP L
SIDE PANEL AND FIXINGS, 88 AND 109 STATION WAGON

332306 / 332307
338552 (2)
RTC609(8)
255207 (4)
GHF200(4)
GHF331(4)
332201 (2)
3900 (3)
GHF200(2)
GHF331(2)
255207 (2)
UM702001(8)
4034(8)
RTC608(8)
255206 (4)
GHF300(4)
GHF331 (4)
SH605051(4)
GHF332(4)
3830 (4)
336764 (2)
332065 (2)
338554 (2)
332081 (2)
78832 (6)
345658 / 345659
GHF200(4)

REMARKS

2G 09

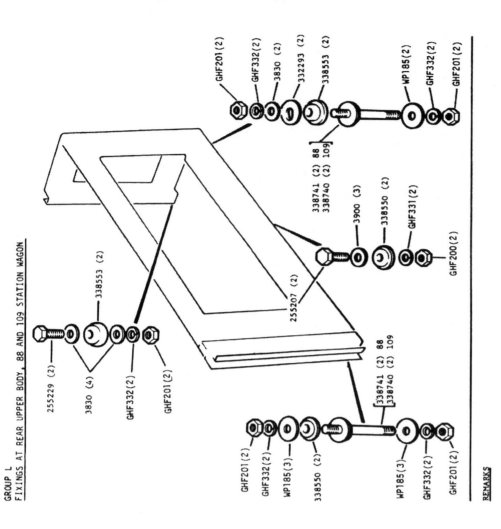

GROUP L
SEALING RUBBERS AND FIXINGS 88 AND 109 STATION WAGON

334612
334613

109 only

334615 (2)

RTC608(10)
WM702001(10)
3902 (10)
77869 (10)

330788
330789

395431

395673(2)

332215 (6)

302818(10)

395674(2)

334487 (2)

302818 (10) 88
78321 (10) 109

REMARKS

2G 10

GROUP L
FIXINGS AT REAR UPPER BODY, 88 AND 109 STATION WAGON

GHF201(2)
GHF332(2)
3830 (2)
332293 (2)
338553 (2)
WP185(2)
GHF332(2)
GHF201(2)

338741 (2) 88
338740 (2) 109

3900 (3)
338550 (2)
GHF331(2)
GHF200(2)

255207 (2)

338553 (2)

255229 (2)
3830 (4)
GHF332(2)
GHF201(2)

338741 (2) 88
338740 (2) 109

GHF201(2)
GHF332(2)
WP185(3)
338550 (2)
WP185(3)
GHF332(2)
GHF201(2)

REMARKS

2G 10

GROUP L
ROOF AND TROPICAL ROOF PANEL, 109 STATION WAGON

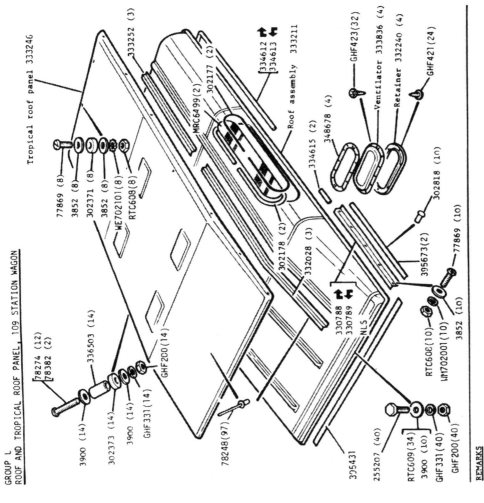

Tropical roof panel 333246

77869 (8)
3852 (8)
302371 (8)
3852 (8)
WE702101(8)
RTC608(8)

333252 (3)

78274 (12)
78382 (2)

336503 (14)

3900 (14)
302373 (14)
3900 (14)
GHF331(14)
GHF200(14)

78248(97)

302177 (2)
302178 (2)
MRC6499(2)

334612
334613

Roof assembly 333211

334615 (2)

332028 (3)

330788
330789
NLS

348678 (4)

GHF423(32)
Ventilator 333836 (4)
Retainer 332240 (4)
GHF421(24)

302818 (10)

77869 (10)

395673(2)

RTC60E(10)
VM1702001(10)
3852 (10)

395431

255207 (40)
RTC609(34)
3900 (10)
GHF331(40)
GHF200(40)

REMARKS

2G 11

GROUP L
ROOF AND TROPICAL ROOF PANEL, 109 STATION WAGON

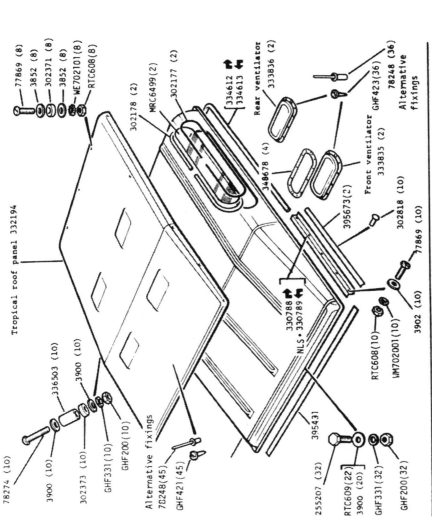

Tropical roof panel 332194

77869 (8)
3852 (8)
302371 (8)
3852 (8)
WE702101(8)
RTC608(8)

78274 (10)

336503 (10)

3900 (10)
302373 (10)
GHF331(10)
GHF200(10)

Alternative fixings
78248(45)
GHF421(45)

302177 (2)
302178 (2)
MRC6499(2)

334612
334613

Rear ventilator
333836 (2)

348678 (4)

395673(2)

Front ventilator
333835 (2)

GHF423(36)
78248 (36)
Alternative fixings

302818 (10)

77869 (10)

330788
330789
NLS

RTC608(10)
VM702001(10)
3902 (10)

395431

255207 (32)
RTC609(22)
3900 (20)
GHF331(32)
GHF200(32)

REMARKS

Roof and tropical assy 332193

2G 11

205

REAR DOOR-88IN STATION WAGON

2H 02

GROUP L   REAR DOOR, 88IN STATION WAGON

PLATE REF.	1	2	3	4	DESCRIPTION	QTY.	PART No.	REMARKS
					REAR DOOR COMPLETE ASSEMBLY	1	RTC1421	
1					Rear door	1	33778l	
2					Glass for rear door	1	333031	
3					Retainer for glass, vertical	2	333033	
4					Retainer for glass, bottom	1	333032	
5					Retainer for glass, top	1	333034	
6					Retainer for glass, corners	2	333035	
					Drive screw fixing retainers	32	AB606031	
7					DOOR LOCK, MOUNTING AND HANDLE ASSEMBLY	1	337789	Cam lever type lock with extended inner handle
8					DOOR LOCK, MOUNTING AND HANDLE ASSEMBLY	1	337801	Cam lever type lock with short inner handle
9					Mounting plate for door lock	1	333080	)For early type lock with
10					Washer, handle to cover	1	90302859	)detachable inner handle
11					Door handle with lock	1	332432*	
12					Barrel lock	1	306036*	Early type with hook catch
								Locking pillar type
13					Barrel lock	1	320609	Late type with plain catch. Cam lever type
								State key number
14					Key for barrel lock, ZENI type	1	307289	For early type lock
					Bracket for door handle	1	302854	with detachable
					Screw (2 BA x ⅜") Fixing lock	6	313858*	inner handle.
					Spring washer) together	4	WM702001	
					Plain washer	4	WC702101	
					Nut (2 BA)	6	RTC608	
					Rivet	4	302222	
					Special screw	4	UFS1254R	2 off when screw retainer is fitted
15					Screw retainer, door lock, bottom	1	337805	
					Nut retainer	1	345498	
					Spring washer	4	GHF331	
					Nut (⅜" UNF)	4	GHF200	
16					Drive screw, fixing lock assembly to door	2	AB604041	
					Locking pillar for catch	1	332434*	For early type
					Plain washer) Fixing pillar	1	3902	lock with hook
					Spring washer) to door	1	WM702001	catch.
					Nut (2 BA)	1	RTC608	
17					Waist rail lock handle protection strip	1	333037*	)For lock
					Bolt (¼" UNF x ½")) Fixing strip	2	255207	)with extended
					Spring washer) to door	2	GHF331	)inner handle
					Nut (¼" UNF)	1	GHF200	
18					Wheel stud plate	1	333435	Not part of Rear Door Complete Assembly

* NO LONGER SERVICED

2H 02

PLATE REF.	1 2 3 4 DESCRIPTION	QTY.	PART No.	REMARKS
19	Clamp plate for spare wheel stud plate	1	333446	)
	Bolt (¼" UNF x ⅞")) Fixing stud and	8	78210	)
	Spring washer) clamp plates to	8	GHF331	)
	Nut (¼" UNF)) rear door	8	GHF200	) Not part of
20	'U' bolt for spare wheel support	1	MRC1210	) Rear Door
	Nut (½" UNF) fixing bolt to door	4	NH608041	) Complete
21	Retaining plate for spare wheel	1	333439	) Assembly
22	Wheel nut 59/64" across flats	6	217361	) Alter-)
	Wheel nut, 1.1/16" across flats	6	576103	) natives)
23	Male dovetail for rear end door	1	332942	
	Screw (¼" UNF x 1")) Fixing	2	78389	
	Spring washer) male dovetail	2	GHF331	
	Nut (¼" UNF)) to door	2	GHF200	
24	Rod for check strap	1	333041	
25	Buffer for check strap, short	1	306295	
26	Buffer for check strap, long	1	333445	
27	Hinge for rear door, upper	1	333036	
28	Hinge for rear door, lower	1	346341	
	Bolt (5/16" UNF x 2")) Fixing hinge	4	BH605161	
	Spring washer) to door	4	GHF332	
	Nut (5/16" UNF)) frame	4	GHF201	
	Bolt (5/16" UNF x ⅞"))	4	255227	
	Plain washer) Fixing	4	3830	
	Spring washer) door hinges	4	GHF332	
	Nut (5/16" UNF)) to body	4	GHF201	
	Bolt (¼" UNF x 1½"))	1	SH604121	
	Spring washer) Fixing	1	GHF331	
	Plain washer, thick) check strap	2	4075	
	Plain washer, thin) rod to floor	2	3947	
	Nut (¼" UNF))	2	GHF200	
29	Striking plate	1	333140	
	Bolt (¼" UNF x 1")) Fixing	2	GHF101	
	Plain washer) striking	As reqd	3817	
	Spring washer) plate to	2	GHF331	
	Nut (¼" UNF)) rear of body	2	GHF200	
30	Female dovetail for rear door on body	1	332147	
31	Spacer for female dovetail	1	332943	
	Screw (¼" UNF x ⅝") fixing dovetail to spacer	2	78233	
	Screw (¼" UNF x ⅞"))	2	255207	
	Plain washer) Fixing spacer to	2	3900	
32	Shim) LH rear pillar	2	305232	
	Spring washer)	2	GHF331	
33	Seal for door sides	3	395674	
34	Seal for door side, LH bottom	1	332553	
35	End filler piece for seals	4	330850	
	Rivet fixing seals to body	22	302818	
36	Rubber seal, door, bottom	1	332564	
37	Seal retainer, door bottom seal	1	332566	
38	Protection strip for retainer	1	332565	
	Drive screw fixing retainer and strip	13	GHF421	

PLATE REF.	1 2 3 4 DESCRIPTION	QTY.	PART No.	REMARKS
39	Seal for rear door, top	1	396113	
	Rivet fixing seal	11	302818	
40	Retainer for rear door seal, top	1	332151	
	Screw (2BA x ½")) Fixing	9	77869	
	Plain washer) retainers	9	3902	
	Spring washer) to roof	9	WM702001	
	Nut (2BA)) panel	9	RTC608	
41	REAR STEP	1	501053*	Oblong step, overall width 19½"
42	Rubber mat for step	1	245137*	
43	Retainer for rear step mat, side	2	245136*	
44	Retainer for rear step mat, front	1	245135*	
45	Retainer for rear step mat, rear	1	245134*	
	Rivets fixing mat end cappings	16	4022	
46	Hinge centre for rear step	2	245131	
	Bolt (⅜" UNF x 4")) Fixing hinge centre	2	BH606321	
	Locknut (⅜" UNF)) to rear step	4	254852	
	Bolt (⅜" UNF x 1⅛")) Fixing	2	255248	
	Bolt (⅜" UNF x ⅞")) hinge centre	2	255246	
	Locker) to rear	2	235731	
	Plain washer) cross	2	2251	
	Packing washer) member	2	500588	
	Shakeproof washer) Fixing hinge centre	2	GHF323	
	Self-locking nut (⅜" UNF)) to rear crossmember	2	GHF243	
47	Spring for rear step	2	264362	
48	Buffer for rear step	1	304125	
	Plain washer) Fixing buffer to	1	4030	
	Drive screw) rear crossmember	1	GHF424	
	REAR STEP	1	508947*	Oblong step, overall width 11½"
	Rubber mat for rear step	1	508957*	
	Retainer for rear step mat, side	2	245136*	
	Retainer for rear step mat, front	1	508959*	
	Retainer for rear step mat, rear	1	508958*	
	Rivet fixing mat retainers	14	4022	
	Hinge, centre for rear step RH	1	526471*	
	Hinge, centre for rear step LH	1	526472*	
	Hinge pin for rear step	1	509120	
	Spring washer) Fixing	1	2286	
	Plain washer) hinge	2	3833	
	Split pin) pin	2	RTC600	
	Bolt (⅜" UNF x 1⅝")) Fixing	2	256042	
	Distance piece) centre	2	501070	
	Packing washer) hinges	2	500588	
	Plain washer) to rear	2	3933	
	Locknut (⅜" UNF)) crossmember	2	GHF223	
	Support bracket for rear step	1	526473*	
	Set bolt (⅜" UNF x 1")) Fixing support bracket) and centre hinge to) rear crossmember	2	GHF105	
	Spring for rear step	1	264362	

Continued ....

* NO LONGER SERVICED

GROUP L   REAR DOOR, 88IN STATION WAGON

PLATE REF.	1	2	3	4	DESCRIPTION	QTY.	PART No.	REMARKS
					Buffer for rear step	1	304125	
					Plain washer) Fixing buffer to	1	4030	
					Drive screw) rear cross-member	1	GHF424	
					Buffer for underside of rear step	1	304125	
					Plain washer) Fixing buffer	1	4030	
					Screw (2 BA x ⅜") to step	1	77758	
49					REAR STEP			
					Rubber mat for rear step	1	NRC2340	Semi-circular step opposite PTO apperture
					Rivet	7	517977	
					Screw (2 BA x ½")) Fixing mat	7	307840	
					Spring washer) to step	4	77869	
					Nut (2BA)	4	WM702001	
					Hinge, centre for rear step RH	1	RTC608	
					Hinge, centre for rear step LH	1	526471*	
					Bolt (¾" UNF x 1⅜")	1	526472*	
					Distance piece	2	256042	Fixing centre
					Packing washer	2	501070	hinges to rear
					Plain washer	2	500588	cross-member
					Locknut (¾" UNF)	2	3933	
					Support bracket for rear step	2	GHF223	
					Set bolt (¾" UNF x 1"), fixing support bracket and centre hinges to rear cross-member	1	526473*	
51					Spring for rear step	2	GHF105	
52					Buffer for rear step	1	264342	
					Plain washer) Fixing buffer to	1	304125	
					Drive screw) rear cross-member	1	GHF424	
53					Hinge pin for rear step	1	509120	
					Spring washer) Fixing hinge pin	2	WS600061	
54					Plain washer	2	WR110061	
55					Split pin	2	RTC600	
					REAR STEP			
					Rubber mat for rear step	1	NRC2340	Semi-circular step, offset to the left of PTO apperture
					Rivet	7	517977	
					Screw (2 BA x ½")) Fixing mat	7	307840	
					Spring washer) to step	4	77869	
					Nut (2BA)	4	WM702001	
56					Support bracket and hinge centre, LH	4	RTC608	
57					Anchor bracket for spring	1	552132	
					Bolt (5/16" UNF x 1⅜")) Fixing support	1	552133	
					Plain washer) bracket and anchor	2	255029	
					Self-locking nut (5/16" UNF)) bracket to rear	2	RTC610	
					crossmember	2	GHF242	

Continued ....

* NO LONGER SERVICED

2H 05

REAR DOOR - 88IN STATION WAGON

2H 05

PLATE REF.	DESCRIPTION 1 2 3 4	QTY.	PART No.	REMARKS
58	Hinge, centre RH	1	552129	
	Set bolt (⅜" UNF x 1")) Fixing RH	1	GHF105	
	Spring washer) centre hinge to	1	GHF333	
	Bolt (⅜" UNF x 1¼")) crossmember	1	255249	
	Distance piece)	1	501070	
	Self-locking nut (⅜" UNF))	1	GHF243	
	Spring for rear step	1	254362	
	Buffer for rear step	1	304125	
	Drive screw) Fixing buffer to	1	GHF424	
	Plain washer) rear crossmember	1	4030	
	Hinge pin for rear step	1	509120	
	Spring washer)	1	2286	
	Plain washer) Fixing hinge pin	2	3833	
	Split pin)	2	RTC600	

PLATE REF.	DESCRIPTION 1 2 3 4	QTY.	PART No.	REMARKS
	REAR DOOR COMPLETE ASSEMBLY	1	RTC1421	
1	Rear door	1	337781	
2	Glass for rear door	1	333031	
3	Retainer for glass, vertical	2	333033	
4	Retainer for glass, bottom	1	333032	
5	Retainer for glass, top	1	333034	
6	Retainer for glass, corners	2	333035	
	Drive screw, fixing retainers	32	AB606031	
7	DOOR LOCK, MOUNTING AND HANDLE ASSEMBLY	1	337789	Cam lever type lock with extended inner handle
8	DOOR LOCK, MOUNTING AND HANDLE ASSEMBLY	1	337801	Cam lever type lock with short inner handle
9	Mounting plate for door lock	1	333080	)For early type lock with
10	Washer, handle to cover	1	90302859	)detachable inner handle
11	Door handle with lock	1	332432*	)
12	Barrel lock	1	306036*	Early type with hook catch, locking pillar type) Alternatives
13	Barrel lock	1	320609	With plain catch, cam lever type) Alternatives
	Key for barrel lock, Zeni type	1	307289	State key no.) Alternatives
	Key blank, FP series	1	CD31709B	)
14	Bracket for door handle	1	302854	) For early type
	Screw (2BA x ½")) Fixing lock	6	313858*	) lock with detachable
	Spring washer) together	6	WM702001	) inner handle
	Plain washer)	4	WC702101	)
	Nut (2BA))	6	RTC608	)
	Rivet) Fixing	4	302222	
	Special screw) door lock	4	UFS1254R	2 off when screw retainer is fitted
15	Screw retainer, door lock, bottom) to cover	1	337806	
	Nut retainer)	1	345498	
	Spring washer)	4	GHF331	
	Nut (¼" UNF))	4	GHF200	
	Drive screw, fixing lock assembly to door	2	AB604041	
16	Locking pillar for catch	1	332434*	) For early type
	Plain washer)	1	3902	) lock with hook
	Spring washer) Fixing pillar to door	1	WM702001	) catch
	Nut (2BA))	1	RTC608	)
17	Waist rail lock handle protection strip	1	333037	)
	Bolt (¼" UNF x ¾")) Fixing	2	255207	)
	Spring washer) strip to	2	GHF331	) For lock with extended
	Nut (¼" UNF)) door	1	GHF200	) inner handle
18	Wheel stud plate	1	333435	Not part of Rear Door Complete Assembly

* NO LONGER SERVICED

REAR DOOR, 109IN STATION WAGON

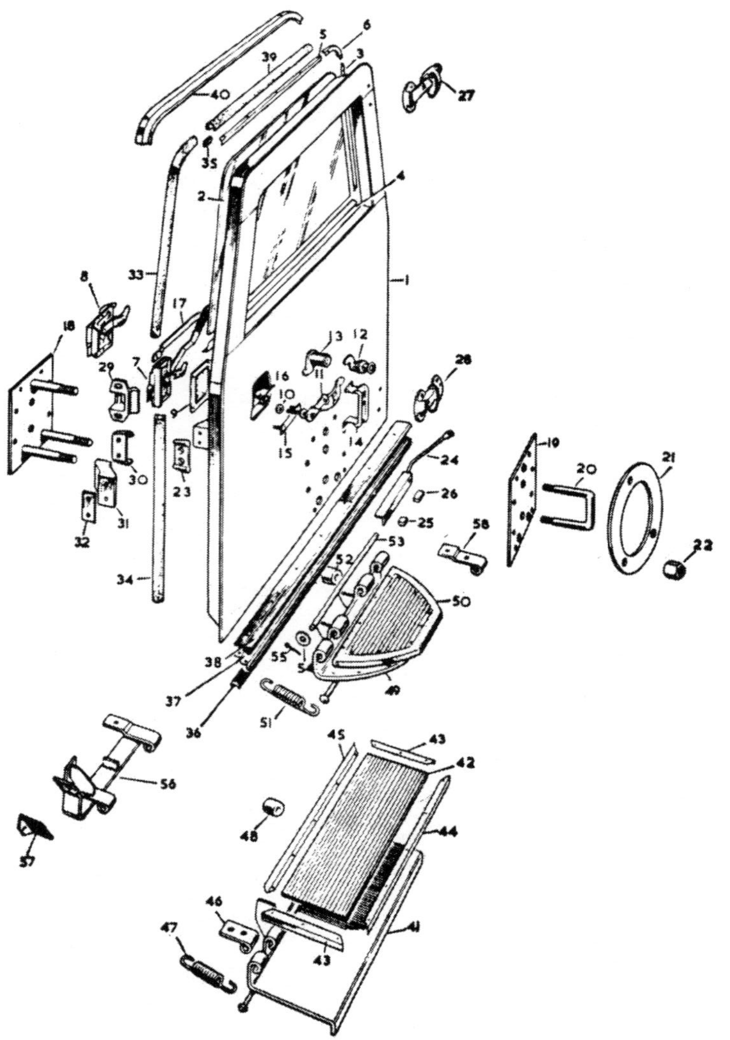

2H 08

PLATE REF.	1 2 3 4 DESCRIPTION	QTY.	PART No.	REMARKS
19	Clamp plate for spare wheel stud plate	1	333446	)
	Bolt (¼" UNF x ¾")) Fixing stud and	8	78210	) Not part of
	Spring washer) clamp plates	8	GHF311	) Rear Door
	Nut (¼" UNF)) to rear door	8	GHF200	) Complete
20	'U' bolt for spare wheel support	1	MRC1210	) Assembly
	Nut (¼" UNF) fixing 'U' bolt to door	2	NH608041	)
21	Retaining plate for spare wheel	1	333439	)
22	Wheel nut, 59/64" across flats	6	217361	) Alter-)
	Wheel nut, 1.16" across flats	6	576103	) natives)
	Male dovetail for rear end door	1	332942	
	Screw (¼" UNF x 1")) Fixing	2	78389	
	Spring washer) male dovetail	2	GHF331	
	Nut (¼" UNF)) to door	2	GHF200	
24	Rod for check strap	1	333041	
25	Buffer for check strap, short	1	306295	
26	Buffer for check strap, long	1	333445	
27	Hinge for rear door, upper	1	333036	
28	Hinge for rear door, lower	1	346341	
	Bolt (5/16" UNF x 2")) Fixing	4	BH605161	
	Spring washer) hinge to	4	GHF332	
	Nut (5/16" UNF))	4	GHF201	
	Bolt (5/16" UNF x ⅞"))	4	255227	
	Plain washer) Fixing door	4	3830	
	Spring washer) hinges to body	4	GHF332	
	Nut (5/16" UNF))	4	GHF201	
	Bolt (¼" UNF x 1½"))	1	SH604121	
	Spring washer) Fixing	1	GHF331	
	Plain washer, thick) check strap rod	2	4075	
	Plain washer, thin) to floor	2	3947	
	Nut (¼" UNF))	2	GHF200	
29	Striking plate	1	333140	
	Bolt (¼" UNF x 1"))	2	GHF101	
	Plain washer) Fixing striking	As reqd	3817	
	Spring washer) plate to rear	2	GHF331	
	Nut (¼" UNF)) of body	2	GHF200	
30	Female dovetail for rear door on body	1	332147	
31	Spacer for female dovetail	1	332943	
	Screw (¼" UNF x ⅝") fixing dovetail to spacer	2	78233	
	Set bolt (¼" UNF x ¾"))	2	255207	
	Plain washer) Fixing spacer to	2	3900	
32	Shim) LH rear pillar	2	305232	
	Spring washer) LH rear pillar	2	GHF331	
33	Seal for door sides	3	395674	
34	Seal for door side, LH bottom	1	332563	
35	End filler for seals	4	330850	
	Rivet fixing seals to body	22	302818	

2H 08

PLATE REF.	1 2 3 4 DESCRIPTION	QTY.	PART No.	REMARKS
36	Seal for rear door, bottom	1	332564	
37	Retainer fixing seal to rear door, bottom	1	332756	
38	Protection strip for rear door, bottom	1	333203	
	Drive screw (½" No.6), fixing seal and retainer to floor	13	GHF421	
39	Seal for rear door, top	1	396113	
	Rivet fixing seal	11	302818	
40	Retainer for rear door seal, top	1	332151	
	Screw (2BA x ¼"))	9	77869	
	Plain washer) Fixing retainers	9	3902	
	Spring washer) to roof panel	9	WM702001	
	Nut (2 BA))	9	RTC608	
41	REAR STEP	1	501053*	Oblong step, overall width 19½"
42	Rubber mat for step	1	245137*	
43	Retainer for rear step, side	2	245136*	
44	Retainer for rear step mat, front	1	245135*	
45	Retainer for rear step mat, rear	1	245134*	
	Rivets fixing mat end cappings	16	4022	
46	Hinge, centre for rear step	2	245131	
	Bolt (¼" UNF x 4")) Fixing hinge centre	2	BH606321	
	Locknut (⅜"UNF)) to rear step	4	NT606041	
	Bolt (⅜" UNF x ⅞")) Fixing hinge centre	2	SH606071	
	Locker) to rear cross-member	2	235731	
47	Spring for rear step	2	264362	
48	Buffer for rear step	1	304125	
	Plain washer) Fixing buffer to	1	4030	
	Drive screw) rear cross-member	1	GHF424	
	REAR STEP	1	508947*	Oblong step, overall width 11½"
	Rubber mat for rear step	1	508957*	
	Retainer for rear step mat, side	2	245136*	
	Retainer for rear step mat, front	1	508959*	
	Retainer for rear step mat, rear	1	508958*	
	Rivet, fixing mat end cappings	14	4022	
	Spring for rear step	1	264362	
	Buffer for rear step	1	304125	
	Plain washer) Fixing buffer	1	4030	
	Drive screw) rear cross-member	1	GHF424	
	Rubber buffer for underside of rear step	1	304125	
	Plain washer) Fixing buffer	1	4030	
	Screw (2 BA x ⅜" long)) to step	1	77758	
	Hinge pin for rear step	1	509120	
	Plain washer) Fixing	2	WB110061	
	Split pin) hinge pin	2	RTC600	

* NO LONGER SERVICED

PLATE REF.	1 2 3 4 DESCRIPTION	QTY.	PART No.	REMARKS
49	REAR STEP	1	523589	Semi-circular step.
	Rubber mat for rear step	1	517977	With hinge brackets
	Rivet)	7	307840	welded to rear cross-
	Screw (2 BA x ½")) Fixing mat	4	77869	member. Up to vehicle
	Spring washer) to step	4	WM702001	suffix 'C' inclusive.
	Nut (2 BA))	4	RTC608	
51	Spring for rear step	1	264362	
52	Buffer for rear step	1	304125	
	Plain washer) Fixing buffer to	1	4030	
	Drive screw) rear cross-member	1	GHF424	
53	Hinge pin for rear step	1	509120	
54	Plain washer) Fixing	2	WB110061	
55	Split pin) hinge pin	2	RTC600	
	REAR STEP	1	523589	Semi-circular step with
	Rubber mat for rear step	1	517977	hinge brackets bolted
	Rivet)	7	307840	to rear cross-member
	Screw (2 BA x ½")) Fixing mat	4	77869	From vehicle suffix 'D'
	Spring washer) to step	4	WM702001	onwards
	Nut (2 BA))	4	RTC608	
56	Support bracket and hinge centre, LH	1	552132	
57	Anchor bracket for spring	1	552133	
	Bolt (5/16" UNF x 1⅛")) Fixing support	2	255029	
	Plain washer) bracket and anchor	2	RTC610	
	Self-locking nut (5/16" UNF)) bracket to rear) cross-member	2	GHF242	
58	Hinge, centre RH	1	552129	
	Set bolt (⅜" UNF x 1")) Fixing RH	1	GHF105	
	Spring washer) centre hinge to) rear cross-member	1	GHF333	
	Spring for rear step	1	264362	
	Buffer for rear step	1	312027	
	Drive screw) Fixing buffer to	1	GHF423	
	Plain washer) rear cross-member	1	4030	
	Hinge pin for rear step	1	509120	
	Spring washer)	1	WS600061	
	Plain washer) Fixing hinge pin	2	WB110061	
	Split pin)	2	RTC600	

BODY TRIM - 88IN STATION WAGON

GROUP M   BODY TRIM - 88IN STATION WAGON

PLATE REF.	1	2	3	4	DESCRIPTION	QTY.	PART No.	REMARKS
1					Roof trim, front portion	1	331491	
2					Bracket, cant rail to roof frame	4	331168	} Alternatives
3					Bracket for roof trim, front portion	4	349218	}
					Drive screw (¼" No.6) fixing bracket to cant rail	8	GHF421	
					Drive screw (¼" No.6) } Fixing	9	GHF421	
					Plain washer, rear } roof frame	5	4592	
					Plain washer, front } to bracket	4	3852	
4					Centre bracket, canopy panel	1	331391	
5					Outer bracket, canopy panel	2	331390	
6					Canopy trim panel	1	331607	
					Plain washer } Fixing trim panel	3	3852	
					Drive screw (½" No.6) } to brackets	3	GHF421	
8					Head cloth, rear portion	1	331508*	
9					Fixing strip, head cloth, front and rear	2	331203	
					Drive screw (¾" No. 6) } Fixing	2	GHF421	
					Plain washer } strip to roof	6	4592	
					Retainer for roof trim	4	332240	
					Spire nut } Fixing retainer	12	GHF711	
					Drive screw } to vent	24	GHF421	
10					Side rail, head cloth, rear portion	2	331196	
					Plain washer } Fixing	2	4428	
					Drive screw (¾" No. 6) } side panel	2	GHF421	
					Bolt (10 UNF x ⅞") } Fixing	2	257015	
					Plain washer } side panel to	2	3902	
					Nut (10 UNF) } roof at rear	2	257023	
11					Fixing bracket, RH, sidelight casing, front	3	331192*	} Early
					Fixing bracket, LH, sidelight casing, front	3	331193*	} models
12					Sidelight casing, trimmed, RH, front GREY	1	331186*	
					Sidelight casing, trimmed, LH, front GREY	1	331187*	
					Sidelight casing, trimmed, RH, front BLACK	1	320682	
					Sidelight casing, trimmed, LH, front BLACK	1	320683	
					Plain washer } Fixing casing	6	GHF421	
					Drive screw } to bracket	6	4592	
13					Sidelight casing, trimmed, RH rear, GREY	1	331179*	
					Sidelight casing, trimmed, LH rear, GREY	1	331180*	
					Sidelight casing, trimmed, RH rear, BLACK	1	320684	
					Sidelight casing, trimmed, LH rear, BLACK	1	320685	
					Drive screw (¾" No. 6) } Fixing casing	2	GHF421	
					Plain washer } to panel	2	4592	
14					Roll trim for cant rail, RH, GREY	1	331497*	
					Roll trim for cant rail, LH, GREY	1	331498*	
					Roll trim for cant rail, RH, BLACK	1	320686	
					Roll trim for cant rail, LH, BLACK	1	320687	
					Drive screw (¾" No. 6) fixing roll trim to body	4	AB604041	

* NO LONGER SERVICED

2I 02

BODY TRIM - 88IN STATION WAGON

2I 02

BODY TRIM-88IN STATION WAGON

PLATE REF.	1	2	3	4	DESCRIPTION	QTY.	PART No.	REMARKS
15					Retaining clip) Fixing	8	331071	
16					Edge clip) roll trim	8	349899	
17					Rear door trim casing, GREY	1	331658*	When door lock with extended inner handle is fitted.
18					Rear door trim casing, GREY	1	345426*)	When door lock with short inner handle is fitted
					Rear door trim casing, BLACK	1	320679)	
					Drive screw (¼" No 6) fixing lock casing to door	4	GHF421	
19					Door pull handle	1	306460)	Alternative to
					Drive screw (¼" No. 10) fixing handle to door	2	AB610051)	grab handle
20					Door grab handle)Fixing grab	1	345450)	Alternative to
					Set bolt (¼" UNF x ½"))handle to door	2	255207)	pull handle
					Spring washer)	2	GHF331)	

* NO LONGER SERVICED

21 03

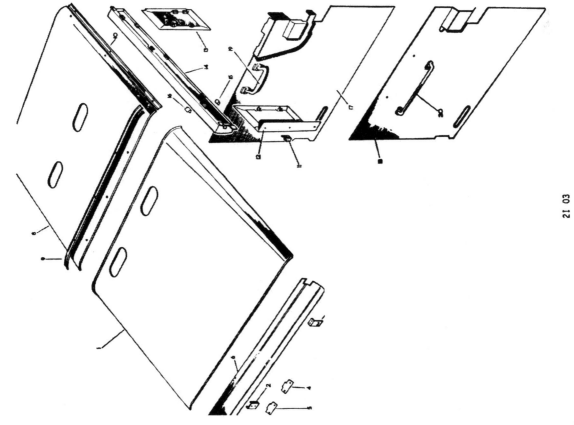

21 03

213

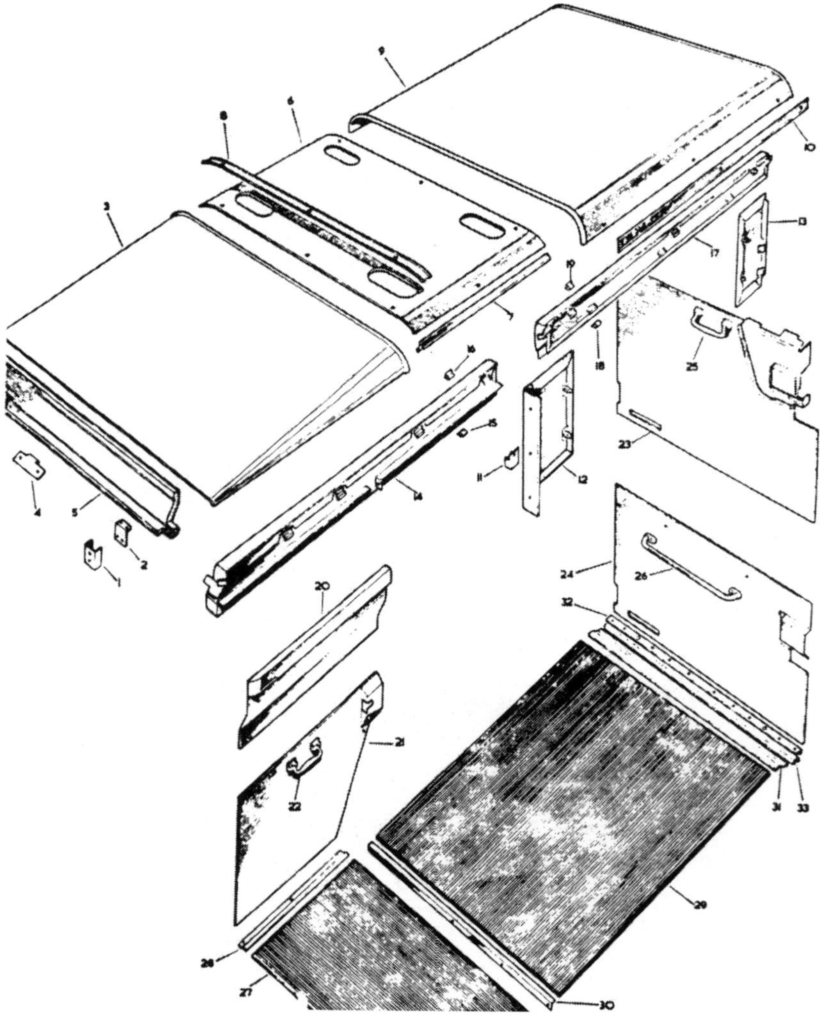

BODY TRIM, 109IN STATION WAGON

2I 04

GROUP M   BODY TRIM - 109IN STATION WAGON

PLATE REF.	1	2	3	4	DESCRIPTION	QTY.	PART No.	REMARKS
1					Bracket, cant rail to roof frame	4	331168	) Alternatives
2					Bracket for roof trim, front portion	4	34921R	)
3					Drive screw (¼" No.6), fixing bracket to cant rail	8	GHF421	
3					Roof trim, front portion	1	331491	
					Plain washer)	9	4592	
					Drive screw (¼" No.6)) to bracket	9	GHF421	
4					Centre bracket for canopy trim panel	1	331391	
5					Canopy trim panel	1	331607	
					Plain washer)	3	3852	
					Drive screw (¼" No.6)) Fixing trim panel	3	GHF421	
					) to centre bracket			
6					Headcloth, intermediate	1	331610	
7					Side rail for intermediate headcloth	2	331216	
8					Fixing strip for intermediate headcloth	2	331203	
					Drive screw (¼" No.6) fixing side rail to roof	10	GHF421	
9					Headcloth, rear	1	331605*	
10					Side strip for rear headcloth	2	331547	
					Drive screw (¼" No.6) fixing strip to roof	5	GHF421	
11					Fixing bracket, RH side light casing, front	1	331192*	) Early
11					Fixing bracket, LH side light casing, front	1	331193*	) models
12					Side light casing, front, RH GREY	1	331196*	
12					Side light casing, front, LH GREY	1	331187*	
12					Side light casing, front, RH BLACK	1	320682	
12					Side light casing, front, LH BLACK	1	320683	
					Drive screw (¼" No.6)) Fixing casing	6	GHF421	
					Plain washer) to bracket	6	4592	
13					Side light casing, rear, RH GREY	1	331179*	
13					Side light casing, rear, LH GREY	1	331180*	
13					Side light casing, rear, RH BLACK	1	320684	
13					Side light casing, rear, LH BLACK	1	320685	
					Drive screw (¼" No.6)) Fixing casing	2	GHF421	
					Plain washer) to panel	2	4592	
14					Roll trim, cant rail, RH front GREY	1	331589*	
14					Roll trim, cant rail, LH front GREY	1	331590*	
14					Roll trim, cant rail, RH front BLACK	1	320711	
14					Roll trim, cant rail, LH front BLACK	1	320712	
15					Retaining clip) Fixing roll	8	331071	
15					Edge clip) trim	8	349899	
16					Drive screw (¼" No.6) fixing roll trim to body	6	AB604041	
17					Roll trim, cant rail, RH rear GREY	1	331497*	
17					Roll trim, cant rail, LH rear GREY	1	331498*	
17					Roll trim, cant rail, RH rear BLACK	1	320686	
17					Roll trim, cant rail, LH rear BLACK	1	320687	
18					Retaining clip) Fixing roll	8	331071	
18					Edge clip) trim	8	349894	
19					Drive screw (¼" No.6) fixing roll trim to body	4	AB604041	

* NO LONGER SERVICED

2I 04

BODY TRIM, 109IN STATION WAGON

GROUP M   BODY TRIM - 109IN STATION WAGON

PLATE REF.	1	2	3	4	DESCRIPTION	QTY.	PART No.	REMARKS
20					Door trim upper, centre, RH GREY	1	339990	
					Door trim upper, centre, LH GREY	1	339991*	
					Door trim upper, centre, RH BLACK	1	320713*	
					Door trim upper, centre, LH BLACK	1	320714*	
					Drive screw (⅜" No.6), fixing trim to door	10	GHF421	
21					Door trim lower, centre, RH GREY	1	349974*	
					Door trim lower, centre, LH GREY	1	349975*	
					Door trim lower, centre, RH BLACK	1	320715	
					Door trim lower, centre, LH BLACK	1	320716	
22					Door pull handle for rear side door	2	306460	
					Drive screw (½" No.10), fixing handle to door	4	AB610051	
					Captive nut for drive screw	4	PFS510	
23					Rear door trim casing, GREY	1	331638*	When door lock with extended inner handle is fitted
24					Rear door trim casing, GREY	1	345426	When door lock with short inner handle is fitted
					Rear door trim casing, BLACK	1	320679	inner handle is fitted
					Drive screw (⅜" No.6), fixing door casing	5	GHF421	
25					Door pull handle for rear door	2	306460	Alternative to grab handle
					Drive screw (½" No.10), fixing handle to door	2	AB610051	
26					Door grab handle	1	345450	Alternative to pull handle
					Set bolt (¼" UNF x ¾")) Fixing grab handle	2	255207	
					Spring washer) to door	2	GHF331	
27					Intermediate floor rubber mat	1	331481	
28					Retainer for floor mat, Intermediate	2	331480	
29					Rear floor rubber mat	1	331670	
30					Retainer for rear floor mat, front end	1	331669*	
					Pop rivet fixing retainer	7	78248	
31					Retainer for seal and rear floor mat, rear end	1	332756	
32					Protection strip for rear door, bottom	1	333203	
33					Sealing rubber for rear door, bottom	1	332564	
					Drive screw, fixing retainer, strip and seal to floor	13	GHF421	

* NO LONGER SERVICED

GROUP M
FRONT SEAT SQUABS

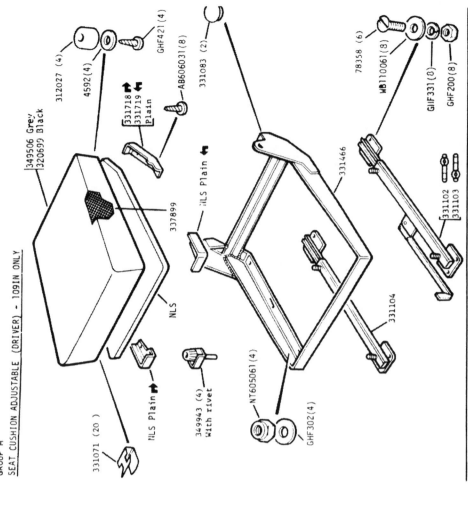

GROUP M
SEAT CUSHION ADJUSTABLE (DRIVER) - 109IN ONLY

312027 (4)
4592 (4)
GHF421 (4)
AB606031 (8)
331083 (2)
349506 Grey / 320699 Black
331718 / 331719 Plain
337899
NLS
NLS Plain
349943 (4) With rivet
331071 (20)
NT605061 (4)
GHF302 (4)
331466
331104
78358 (6)
WB110061 (8)
GHF331 (8)
GHF200 (8)
331102 / 331103

REMARKS

21 06

72628 (4)
RTC609 (4)
339986 (2)
337880 Interior
RTC521 (2)
RTC614 (6)
331170 (6)
331273 (3) 88 / 109
NLS
GHF421 (3) ③
78441 (3) ④
4034 (3) ④
349931 (2)
25520? (26)
RTC609 (28)
GHF331 (28)
GHF200 (28)
GHF421 (6) ③
RTC608 (6) ④
1H702001 (6) ④
304125 (6) ④
4030 (6) ④
77993 (6) ④
4592 (6) ③
312027 (6) ③
4032 (3) ③
78237 (3) ④
331008
331006 (2)
331818 (6)
331007
331709 (2) 109
RTC621 (2) 109
349931 (4) 109
37873 (2) interior

21 06

① Driver	① Passenger, outer	② Centre
349644 Grey 88	349644 Grey 88 and 109	NLS-349645 Grey 88 and 109
320698 Black 88	320698 Black 88 and 109	320701 Black 88 and 109
349562 Grey 109	NLS-349563 Grey 109SW	NLS-349564 Grey 109SW
320702 Black 109	320709 Black 109SW	320710 Black 109SW
NLS • 349565 Grey 109SW		
320708 Black 109SW		

③ For squab with spring interior
④ For squab with foam interior

GROUP M
SEAT CUSHION - NON ADJUSTABLE

320743 (2) Outer Grey
349967 (2) Outer Black

331071 (58)

337859

349503 Centre Grey
320726 Centre Black

AB606031(28)

337899 (2)

NLS
Plain

349943 (12)
With rivet

331973(2) Outer cushions
331974(1) Centre cushion
Nylon rivet fixing

NLS
Plain

GHF1083(3)

GHF421 (3)

4203 (3)

331272(2) Outer cushions
331273(1) Centre cushion
Drive screw fixing

RTC608(6)

WM702001(6)

348430 (6)

78120 (6)

Alternatives

78237 (6)

304125 (6)

4030 (6)

NLS

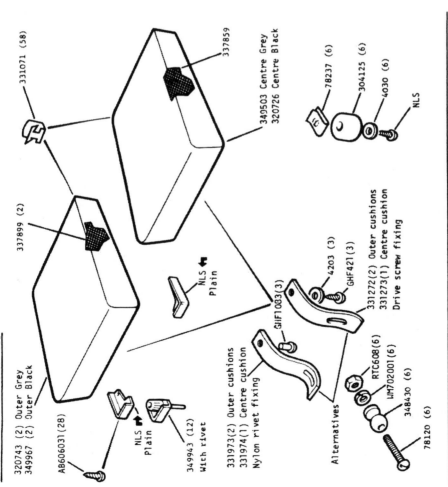

This page is intentionally left blank

21 07

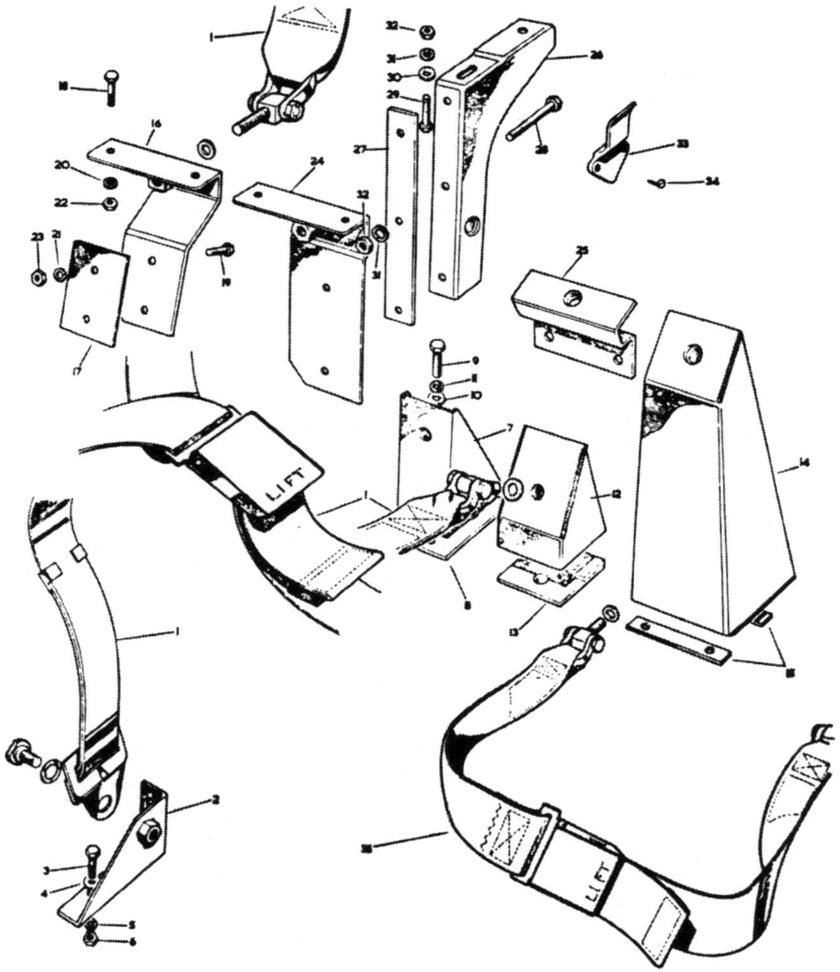

GROUP M   FRONT SEAT SAFETY HARNESS AND ANCHORAGE

PLATE REF.	1 2 3 4	PART No.	DESCRIPTION	REMARKS
1	2	347509	Safety harness for front seat, outer	All models
	1	320631*	ANCHORAGE KIT, RH	88. Except when
	1	320632*	ANCHORAGE KIT, LH	cab is fitted.
	1	320633	ANCHORAGE KIT, RH	88. With
	1	320634	ANCHORAGE KIT, LH	truck cab
	1	320635	ANCHORAGE KIT, RH	109 with hard top
	1	320636	ANCHORAGE KIT, LH	or full length hood
	1	320637	ANCHORAGE KIT, RH	109. With
	1	320638	ANCHORAGE KIT, LH	truck cab
	1	320639*	ANCHORAGE KIT, RH	109 Station
	1	320640*	ANCHORAGE KIT, LH	Wagon
2		345100	Sill gusset, RH	
		345101	Sill gusset, LH	
3	2	255208	Bolt (¼" UNF x ⅞")) Fixing	
4	2	WP8019	Plain washer) sill gusset	
5	2	GHF331	Spring washer) to seat	
6	2	GHF200	Nut (¼" UNF)) base	
			Self-locking nut (7/16" UNF) Fixing shackle bolt to cab rail	
7	1	252163	Gusset bracket at bulkhead	88. With truck cab
8	2	338752	Washer plate complete)	
9	4	255208	Set bolt (¼" UNF x ⅞")) Fixing	88. All models
10	4	WP8019	Plain washer) gusset	
11	2	GHF331	Spring washer) bracket	
12	2	345123	Gusset bracket at bulkhead) to floor	
13	2	345125	Clamp plate complete) Fixing	
	2	GHF103	Set bolt (5/16" UNF x 1")) gusset	109. Except
	2	GHF332	Spring washer) bracket	Station Wagon
	4	2266	Plain washer) to floor	
14	2	348788*	Gusset bracket at bulkhead	
15	2	336147*	Washer plate) Fixing gusset	109. Station Wagon
	8	255208	Bolt (¼" UNF x ⅞")) to bulkhead	
	8	GHF331	Spring washer	
	8	GHF200	Nut (¼" UNF)	
16	1	338753*	Shoulder bracket, RH	
	1	338754*	Shoulder bracket, LH	
17	2	336566*	Washer plate)	88.
18	4	255208	Bolt (¼" UNF x ⅞")) Fixing shoulder	Except when
19	4	255227	Bolt (5/16" UNF x ⅞")) bracket to	cab is fitted
20	4	GHF331	Spring washer) bulkhead	
21	4	GHF332	Spring washer	
22	4	GHF200	Nut (¼" UNF)	
23	4	GHF201	Nut (5/16" UNF)	
24	1	338759*	Shoulder bracket, RH	
	1	338760*	Shoulder bracket, LH	
	4	255208	Bolt (¼" UNF x ⅞")) Fixing	109. With hard
	4	255227	Bolt (5/16" UNF x ⅞")) shoulder bracket	top or full
	4	GHF331	Spring washer) to bulkhead	length hood
	4	GHF332	Spring washer	
	4	GHF200	Nut (¼" UNF)	
	4	GHF201	Nut (5/16" UNF)	
25	2	336577	Shoulder bracket and cab mounting	109. with cab

Fitted as standard on all Home Market models from vehicle suffix 'D' onwards optional on Export models

* NO LONGER SERVICED

2I 08

FRONT SEAT SAFETY HARNESS AND ANCHORAGE

2I 08

GROUP M   FRONT SEAT SAFETY HARNESS AND ANCHORAGE

PLATE REF.	1 2 3 4	DESCRIPTION	QTY.	PART No.	REMARKS
26		Shoulder bracket, RH	1	34R473	Fitted as standard on all Home Market Models from vehicle suffix 'D' onwards. Optional on Export models
		Shoulder bracket, LH	1	34847A	
27		Washer plate	2	34847	
28		Bolt (¼" UNF x 2½")	6	255219	Fixing shoulder bracket to door post and cant rail 109 Station Wagon
29		Bolt (¼" UNF x ⅝")	2	255206	
30		Plain washer	2	WP8019	
31		Spring washer	8	GHF331	
32		Nut (¼" UNF)	8	GHF200	
33		Stowage hook for safety harness	2	345117*	For lift latch
		Stowage hook for safety harness	2	346885*	For push button harness Irving
		Stowage hook for safety harness	?	347541	For press button harness Britax
34		Drive screw, fixing hook	4	AB604031	
35		Front seat safety harness, centre	1	MRC4350	All models
		Gusset bracket at bulkhead	2	338752	Fixing gusset bracket to floor
		Washer plate complete	2	336567	88
		Set bolt (¼" UNF x ½")	4	255208	
		Plain washer	4	WP8019	
		Spring washer	4	GHF331	
		Gusset bracket at bulkhead	?	345123	109
		Clamp plate complete	2	345125	Fixing clamp plate to bulkhead Except Station Wagon @
		Set bolt (5/16" UNF x 1")	4	GHF103	
		Spring washer	4	GHF332	
		Plain washer	4	2266	

@ Note: Anchorage point for centre harness is provided in normal build on late 109 Station Wagons.
To convert early models, fit the panel assembly 347807   See 2G07

* NO LONGER SERVICED

2I 09

2I 09

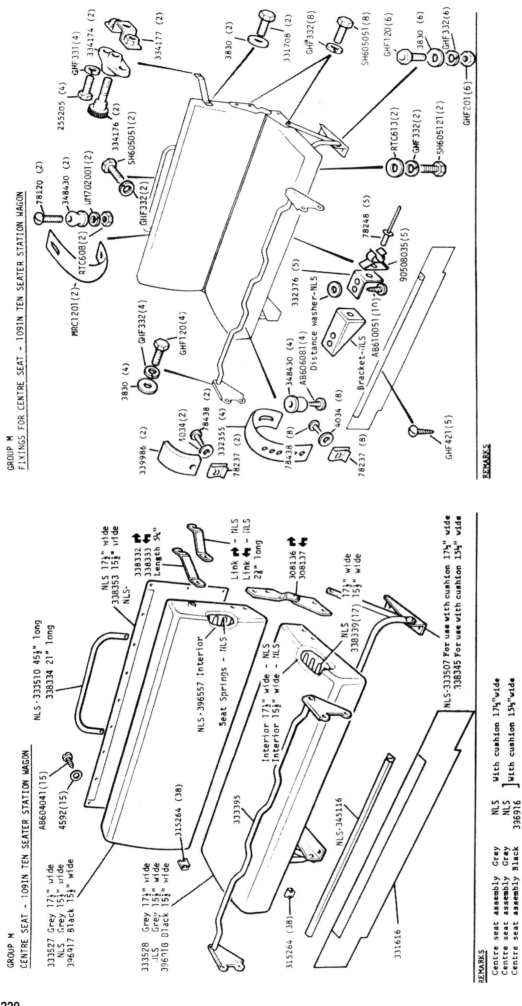

GROUP M
FIXINGS FOR CENTRE SEAT - 109IN TEN SEATER STATION WAGON

GHF331(4)
334174 (2)
334177 (2)
255205 (4)
334176 (2)
334175 (2)
3830 (2)
331708 (2)
GHF332(8)
SH605051(8)
GHF120(6)
3830 (6)
GHF332(6)
GHF201(6)
RTC613(2)
GHF332(2)
SH605121(2)
78120 (2)
348430 (2)
WM702001(2)
SH605051(2)
GHF332(2)
MRC1201(2)
RTC608(2)
GHF332(4)
GHF120(4)
3830 (4)
4034(2)
78438 (2)
332355 (4)
339986 (2)
78438 (8)
78237 (2)
4034 (8)
78237 (8)
GHF421(5)
348430 (4)
AB606081(4)
Distance washer-NLS
332376 (5)
Bracket-NLS
AB610051(10)
90508035(5)
78248 (5)

21 10

REMARKS

GROUP M
CENTRE SEAT - 109IN TEN SEATER STATION WAGON

333527 Grey 17½" wide
NLS Grey 15½" wide
396917 Black 15½" wide

333528 Grey 17½" wide
NLS Grey 15½" wide
396918 Black 15½" wide

AB604041(15)
4592(15)
315264 (38)

NLS-333510 45½" long
338334 21" long

338332 }
338353 15½" wide
NLS-

338332 Link - NLS
338333 Link - NLS
Length 5¼" 2⅛" long

308136
308137

NLS 17½" wide
338339(17) 15½" wide

NLS-396557 Interior
Seat Springs - NLS

Interior 17½" wide - NLS
Interior 15½" wide - NLS

333395
NLS-345116
331616
315264 (38)

NLS-333507 For use with cushion 17½" wide
338345 For use with cushion 15½" wide

21 10

REMARKS

Centre seat assembly Grey   NLS   With cushion 17½"wide
Centre seat assembly Grey   NLS } With cushion 15½"wide
Centre seat assembly Black   396916

220

GROUP M
CENTRE SEATS - 109IN TWELVE SEATER STATION WAGON

320826(3) Grey
349515(3) Black

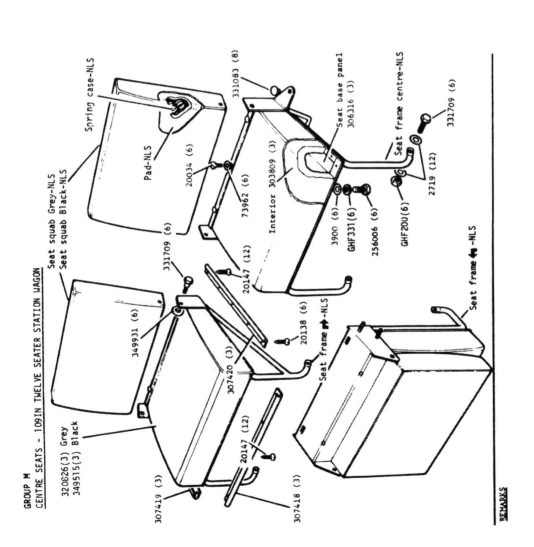

Seat squab Grey-NLS
Seat squab Black-NLS

Spring case-NLS

Pad-NLS

20034 (6)

73962 (6)

331083 (8)

Seat base panel
306316 (3)

Interior 303809 (3)

Seat frame centre-NLS

331709 (6)

2719 (12)

GHF200(6)

256006 (6)

GHF331(6)

3900 (6)

20147 (12)

331709 (6)

349931 (6)

331709 (6)

20138 (6)

Seat frame ➡-NLS

307420 (3)

20147 (12)

307419 (3)

307418 (3)

Seat frame ⬅ -NLS

This page is intentionally left blank

REAR SEATS AND MISCELLANEOUS FITTINGS-88IN STATION WAGON

2I 12

GROUP M   REAR SEATS AND MISCELLANEOUS FITTINGS 88IN STATION WAGON

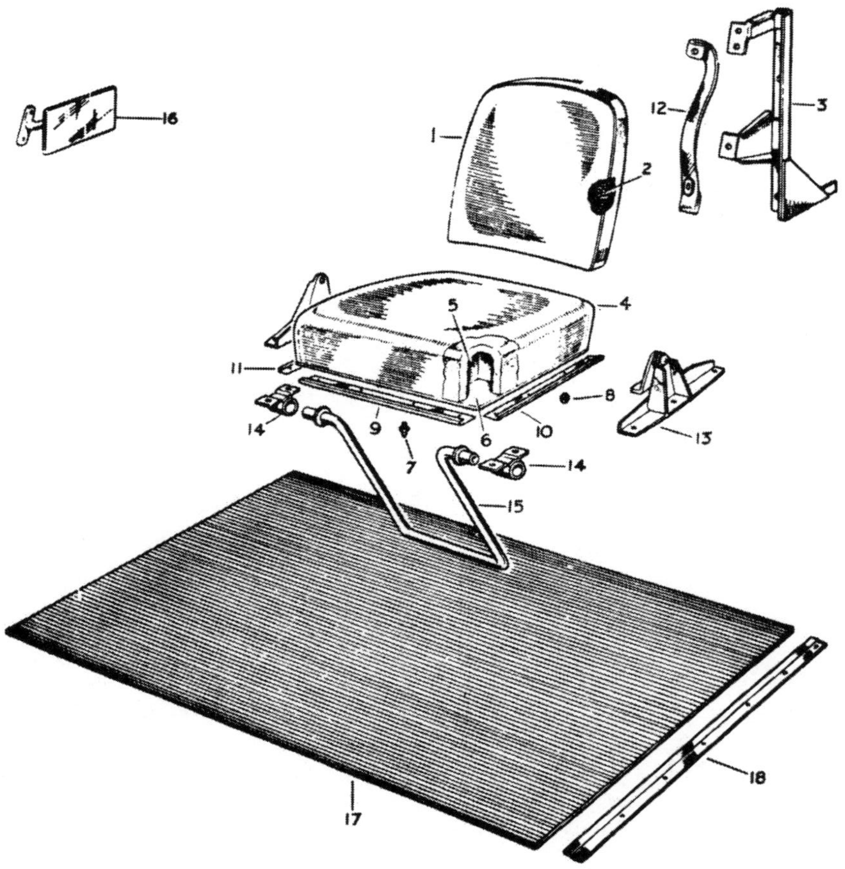

PLATE REF.	1	2	3	4	DESCRIPTION	QTY.	PART No.	REMARKS
1					Rear seat backrest complete, GREY	4	331149*	
					Rear seat backrest complete, BLACK	4	320703	
2					Pad for rear seat backrest	4	304054	
					Bolt (¼" UNF x ¾")	20	255204	
					Set bolt (¼" UNF x ⅜")	4	255208	Fixing backrests
					Plain washer	24	RTC617	to supports
					Spring washer	24	GHF331	
3					Support for backrest RH	4	331147R	
					Support for backrest LH	4	331479	
					Bolt (¼" UNF x ⅜")	6	255206	Fixing backrest support
					Plain washer, small	6	RTC617	to body capping
					Plain washer, large	6	3842	
					Spring washer	6	GHF331	
4					Rear seat cushion complete, GREY	4	320826	
					Rear seat cushion complete, BLACK	4	349515	
					Rubber interior for seat cushion	4	303809*	
6					Seat base panel	4	306316	
7					Fastener stud	4	24361R	
					Plain washer ⎱ Fixing stud	4	3852	
					Spring washer ⎰	4	WM702001	
					Nut (2BA)	4	RTC608	
8					Rubber buffer for rear seat cushion	4	317028	
					Woodscrew ⎱ Fixing base panel to	8	20034*	
					Cup washer ⎰ seat cushion frame	8	73962	
9					Front finishers for rear seats	4	307418	
10					Side finishers for rear seats RH	4	307419	
11					Side finishers for rear seats LH	4	307420	
					Woodscrew ⎱ Fixing finishers	8	2013P	
					Woodscrew ⎰ front and sides	16	20147	
12					Retaining strap complete for seat cushion	4	306326	
					Special nut ⎱ Fixing backrest and	4	GHF713	
					Special bolt ⎰ strap to upper body	4	78295	
13					Cushion pivot bracket complete	8	331122	
14					Support tube bearing ⎱ For rear seat	8	9030F199	
					Support tube ⎰ cushion	8	9030F200*	
					Bolt (¼" UNF x ⅝") ⎱ Fixing cushion pivot	24	255208	
					Bolt (¼" UNF x 1¼") ⎰ bracket and support	8	BH604101	
					Plain washer ⎱ tube bearings to seat	32	RTC617	
					Spring washer ⎰ cushion frame	32	GHF331	
					Bolt (¼" UNF x ⅞") ⎱ Fixing cushion	16	255206	
					Plain washer ⎰ pivot bracket	16	3900	
					Spring washer ⎱ to wheelarch box	20	GHF331	
					Nut (¼" UNF) ⎰	20	GHF200	
					Clamping bar ⎱ At centre squab	4	345804	
					Bolt (¼" UNF x ⅞") ⎰ brackets	4	255208	
					Packing block for roof lamp	1	332995*	
					Mounting pad for roof lamp	1	334111*	

* NO LONGER SERVICED

2I 12

PLATE REF.	1 2 3 4	DESCRIPTION	QTY.	PART No.	REMARKS
		Roof lamp complete	1	265295	
		Lens for roof lamp	1	320408	
		Bulb for roof lamp	1	GLB382	
		Drive screw, fixing lamp and block	2	AC606081 }	Alternatives
		Drive screw, fixing lamps and mounting pad	2	GHF421 }	
		Lead for roof lamp, roof portion	1	265492	
		Lead for roof lamp, chassis portion	1	90519976*	Up to vehicle suffix 'C' inclusive
		Lead for roof lamp, chassis portion	1	555879	From vehicle suffix 'D' onwards
		Grommet for roof lamp lead	1	312A56	
		Grommet for lead	2	233244	
		Cable clip	2	41379	
		Drive screw	2	AB608031	
16		Interior mirror	1	345188	
		Support bracket for interior mirror	1	338275	From vehicle suffix 'D' onwards
		Drive screw fixing mirror	2	AD606041	
17		Rubber mat for rear body floor	1	331801	
18		Protection strip for floor mat	1	332565	
		Drive screw fixing protection strip	7	GHF400	

* NO LONGER SERVICED

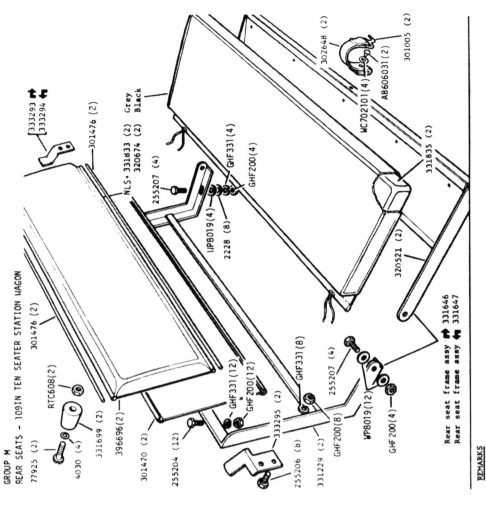

333293
333294

301476 (2)

302648 (2)

301005 (2)

AB606031(2)

WC702101(4)

NLS· 331833 (2) Grey
320674 (2) Black

255207 (4)

GHF331(4)

GHF200(4)

IIPB019(4)

2228 (8)

331835 (2)

320521 (2)

301476 (2)

77925 (2)

RTC608(2)

331699 (2)

396696(2)

301470 (2)

255204 (12)

333295 (2)

255206 (6)

331229 (2)

GHF200(8)

GHF331(12)

GHF200(12)

GHF331(8)

255207 (4)

WPB019(12)

GHF200(4)

4030 (4)

Rear seat frame assy 331646
Rear seat frame assy 331647

REMARKS

Rear seat backrest trimmed assembly, Grey 320084 (2)
Rear seat backrest trimmed assembly, Black 396739(2)

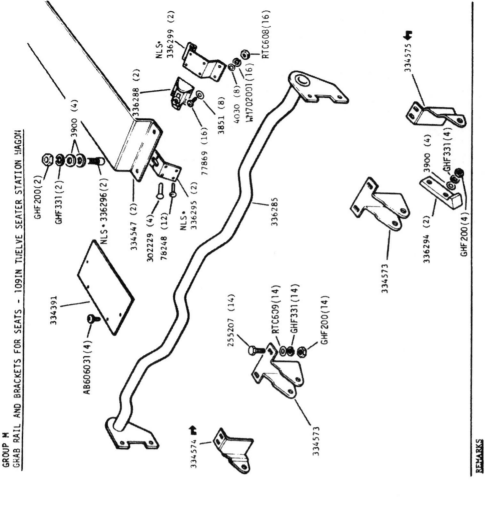

GROUP M
GRAB RAIL AND BRACKETS FOR SEATS - 109IN TWELVE SEATER STATION WAGON

REMARKS

21 15

GROUP M
REAR SEATS - 109IN TWELVE SEATER STATION WAGON

REMARKS

Rear seat backrest assembly, Trimmed Grey 334531 (2)•NLS

Rear seat backrest assembly, Trimmed Black 396698(2)

21 15

PLATE REF. 1 2 3 4	DESCRIPTION	QTY.	PART NO.	REMARKS
	Engine overhaul gasket set	1	608124	2½ litre)
	Decarbonising gasket set	1	GEG162	Petrol)
	Engine overhaul gasket set	1	606106	2.6 litre)
	Decarbonising gasket set	1	GEG1214	2½ litre)
	Engine overhaul gasket set	1	525520	Petrol)
	Decarbonising gasket set	1	GEG1200	Diesel)
	Gearbox gasket set	1	606603	
	Brake wheel cylinder overhaul kit, front	1	275744	88
	Brake wheel cylinder overhaul kit, front	1	266684	109 4-cylinder models
	Brake wheel cylinder overhaul kit, front	1	600210	109 6-cylinder models
	Brake wheel cylinder overhaul kit, rear	1	266687	88
	Brake wheel cylinder overhaul kit, rear	1	275744	109
	Brake master cylinder overhaul kit	1	502333	88 For CB type master cylinder G1 64067720 (GMC314)
	Brake master cylinder overhaul kit	1	868837	88 For CV type master cylinder G1 64068893 (GMC310)
	Brake master cylinder overhaul kit	1	50375A	109 4-cylinder models. For early CB type master cylinder G1 64067722
	Brake master cylinder overhaul kit	1	605127	109 4 cylinder models. For late CV type master cylinder G1 64068750 (GMC312)
	Brake master cylinder overhaul kit	1	90606023	109 4-cylinder models. For CV type master cylinder G1 64068830 (GMC311)
	Brake master cylinder overhaul kit	1	605127	109 6-cylinder models up to vehicle suffix 'F' inclusive
	Brake master cylinder overhaul kit	1	606415	109 6-cylinder models from vehicle suffix 'G' onwards
	Clutch master cylinder overhaul kit	1	868937	2.6 litre Petrol)
	Clutch slave cylinder overhaul kit	1	868900	up to vehicle suffix)
	Brake servo overhaul kit	1	600432	'F' inclusive)
	Brake servo poppet valve overhaul kit	1	600434	Export only)
	Brake servo non-return valve overhaul kit	1	600435	
	Brake servo overhaul kit	1	1RG8951	2.6 litre petrol from vehicle suffix 'G' onwards

PLATE REF. 1 2 3 4	DESCRIPTION	QTY.	PART NO.	REMARKS
	Repair kit for adjuster unit (transmission brake)	1	515924	
	Repair kit for expander unit (transmission brake)			
	Blue brake grease, tube	1	515923	
	Red brake rubber grease, tube	1	27H7946	
	Repair kit for fuel pump	1	514578	
	Overhaul kit for fuel pump	1	BG2030	2½ litre Petrol) models
	Repair kit for fuel pump	1	1RG824A	) models
	Overhaul kit for fuel pump	1	RG8844	Diesel) models
	Swivel pin overhaul kit	1	RG8845	) models
	Swivel pin overhaul kit	1	266752*	Cone and spring type.
	Swivel pin overhaul kit	1	532268	Pin and thrust washer type. Also suitable as conversion kit.
	Water pump overhaul kit	1	530590	2½ litre Petrol and all Diesel models
	Water pump overhaul kit	1	605716	2.6 litre Petrol
	Carburetter overhaul kit	1	507687	2½ litre Petrol For Solex carburetter
	Carburetter overhaul kit	1	605092	2½ litre petrol For Zenith carburetter
	Carburetter overhaul kit	1	606098	2.6 litre petrol For Zenith carburetter
	Carburetter gasket kit	1	507593	2½ litre petrol For Solex carburetter
	Carburetter gasket kit	1	605093	2½ litre petrol For Zenith carburetter
	Carburetter gasket kit	1	6S11574	2.6 litre petrol For SU carburetter
	Carburetter gasket kit	1	605867	2.6 litre petrol For Zenith carburetter
	Plastigauge strip, box of 20	1	605238	For checking bearing clearances
	'Loctite' Sealant, Grade AVV, 10 cc bottle,		600303	
	Coolant inhibitor, 18 oz bottle		605765	
	Brake fluid, 1 litre tin		GBF103	
	Brake cleaning fluid, ½ pint tin		AU115R2	
	'Hylomar' 4oz tube		GGC102	
	Radiator seal pellet		GAC148	* NO LONGER SERVICED

GROUP N   TRIMMING RAW MATERIALS

PLATE REF.	1	2	3	4	DESCRIPTION	QTY.	PART No.	REMARKS
					Cotton duck, 72" wide, khaki-green	As reqd	91957*	
					Cotton duck, 72" wide, blue	As reqd	91899*	
					Sheet wadding, 36" wide onen	As reqd	92496*	
					Cotton webbing, 1/32" x 1" khaki-green	As reqd	91878	
					Cotton webbing, ⅛" x 1" khaki-green	As reqd	91880*	
					Cotton webbing, 5/64" x 1" black	As reqd	92088	
					Seaming cord	As reqd	91171*	
					Black canvas, 54" wide	As reqd	91291*	
					Grey felt	As reqd	91414	
					Black felt, 50" wide	As reqd	91819*	
					Leather cloth, grey, 50" wide	As reqd	91979*	
					Leather cloth, black, 50" wide	As reqd	92616	
					White leather cloth, dull black, 50" wide	As reqd	92625	
					White leather cloth, 50" wide	As reqd	91950	
					Natural felt, 54" wide	As reqd	91890*	
					Felted plastic, black	As reqd	91965	
					Black cloth, 72" wide	As reqd	91913*	
					Fine fluted rubber matting, 36" wide	As reqd	261577*	
					Sealing strip, 'Prestik', ½" x ⅛" wide	As reqd	14617*	
					Sealing strip, 'Prestik', ⅜" x 1/16"	As reqd	13296*	

* NO LONGER SERVICED

2J 03

This page is intentionally left blank

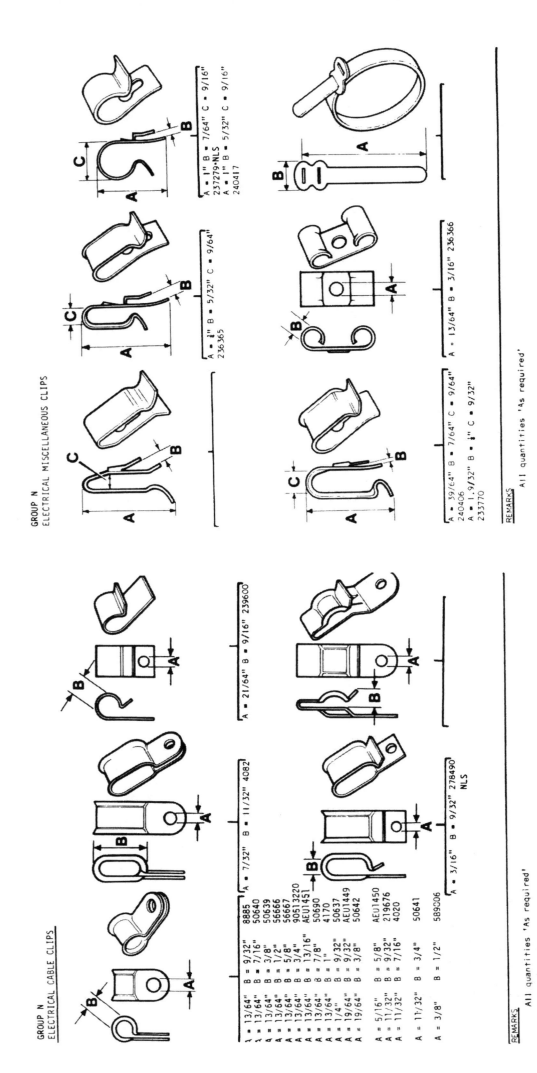

GROUP N
ELECTRICAL MISCELLANEOUS CLIPS

A = 1" B = 7/64" C = 9/16" 237279•NLS
A = 1" B = 5/32" C = 9/16" 240417

A = ¼" B = 5/32" C = 9/64" 236365

A = 13/64" B = 3/16" 236366

A = 39/64" B = 7/64" C = 9/64" 240406
A = 1.9/32" B = ¼" C = 9/32" 233770

REMARKS   All quantities 'As required'

2J 04

GROUP N
ELECTRICAL CABLE CLIPS

A = 13/64"	B = 9/32"	8885
A = 13/64"	B = 7/16"	50640
A = 13/64"	B = 3/8"	50639
A = 13/64"	B = 1/2"	56666
A = 13/64"	B = 5/8"	56667
A = 13/64"	B = 3/4"	90513220
A = 13/64"	B = 13/16"	AEU1451
A = 13/64"	B = 7/8"	50690
A = 13/64"	B = 1"	4170
A = 1/4"	B = 9/32"	50637
A = 19/64"	B = 9/32"	AEU1449
A = 19/64"	B = 3/8"	50642
A = 5/16"	B = 5/8"	AEU1450
A = 11/32"	B = 9/32"	219676
A = 11/32"	B = 7/16"	4020
A = 11/32"	B = 3/4"	50641
A = 3/8"	B = 1/2"	589006

A = 7/32" B = 11/32" 4082

A = 21/64" B = 9/16" 239600

A = 3/16" B = 9/32" 278490 NLS

REMARKS   All quantities 'As required'

2J 04

227

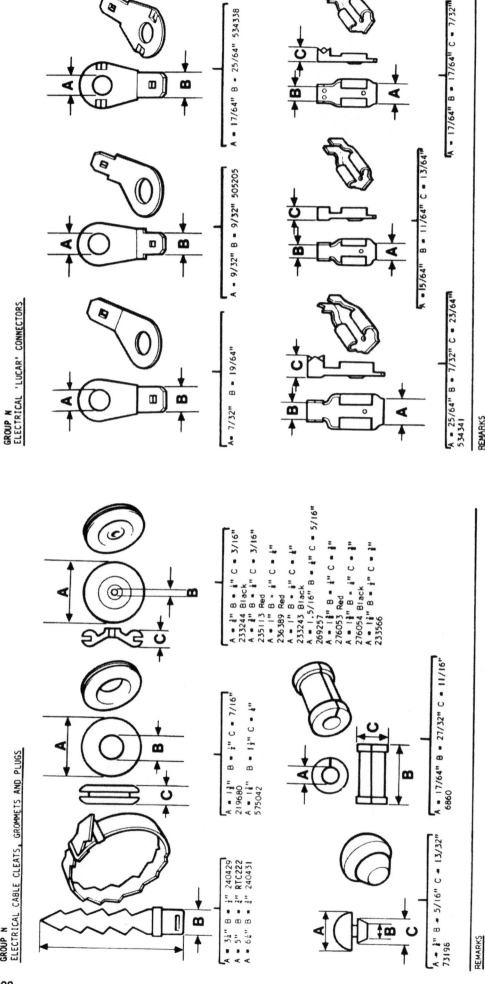

GROUP N
ELECTRICAL 'LUCAR' CONNECTORS

A = 7/32" B = 19/64"

A = 9/32" B = 9/32" 505205

A = 17/64" B = 25/64" 534338

A = 25/64" B = 7/32" C = 23/64" 534341

A = 15/64" B = 11/64" C = 13/64"

A = 17/64" B = 17/64" C = 7/32"

REMARKS

All quantities "As required"

2J 05

GROUP N
ELECTRICAL CABLE CLEATS, GROMMETS AND PLUGS

A = 3½" B = ½" 240429
A = 5" B = ½" RTC222
A = 6¼" B = ½" 240431

A = 1⅜" B = ⅞" C = 7/16" 219680
A = 1⅞" B = 1⅜" C = ¼" 575042

A = ¼" B = ¼" C = 3/16" 233244 Black
A = ¼" B = ¼" C = 3/16" 235113 Red
A = 1" B = ¼" C = ¼" 236389 Red
A = 1" B = ¼" C = ¼" 233243 Black
A = 1.5/16" B = ¼" C = 5/16" 269257
A = 1⅜" B = ¼" C = ⅜" 276053 Red
A = 1⅜" B = ¼" C = ⅜" 276054 Black
A = 1⅜" B = ¼" C = ⅜" 233566

A = 17/64" B = 27/32" C = 11/16" 6860

A = ¼" B = 5/16" C = 13/32" 73196

REMARKS

All quantities 'As required'

2J 05

Supplies of re-finishing paints are available in one litre cans from International Pinchin Johnson outlets. To obtain details of the service and facilities offered, or in the event of any difficulties please contact I.P.J. direct.

For Home and European Markets:

International Pinchin Johnson
Transport Paints Division
P O Box 359
Rotton Park Street
Ladywood
Birmingham B16 OAD

Telephone: 021-455-9066

Telex: 339266

For Overseas Markets:

International Pinchin Johnson
Export Division
380 Richmond Road
Kingston-upon-Thames
Surrey
England

Telephone: 01-546-1234

Telex: 27527

2J 06

GROUP N
PAINTS

UNIPART TOUCH UP

GTU405 Pastel Green
GTU406 Bronze Green
GTU407 Marine Blue
GTU408 Limestone
GTU409 Grey

UNIPART AEROSOL

GAP405 Pastel Green
GAP406 Bronze Green
GAP407 Marine Blue
GAP408 Limestone
GAP409 Grey

2J 06

GROUP N
TOOLS PART 1

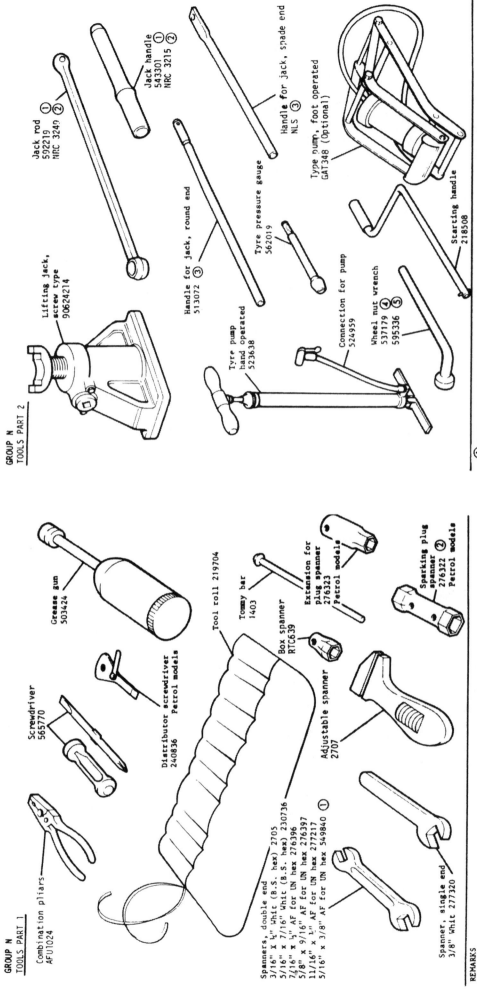

Grease gun
503424

Screwdriver
565770

Combination pliars
AFU1024

Distributor screwdriver
240836 Petrol models

Tool roll 219704

Tommy bar
1403

Box spanner
RTC639

Extension for
plug spanner
276323
Petrol models

Sparking plug
spanner ②
276322 Petrol models

Adjustable spanner
2707

Spanners, double end
3/16" x ¼" Whit (B.S. hex) 2705
5/16" x 7/16" Whit (B.S. hex) 230736
7/16" x ½" AF for UN hex 276396
5/8" x 9/16" AF for UN hex 276397
11/16" x ½" AF for UN hex 277217
5/16" x 3/8" AF for UN hex 549840 ①

Spanner, single end
3/8" Whit 277320

REMARKS
① For distributor pump bleed screw. Diesel models.
② Also required for radiator drain plug All models

2J 07

GROUP N
TOOLS PART 2

Jack rod ①
592219
NRC 3240 ②

Jack handle
543301 ①
NRC 3215 ②

Handle for jack, snade end
NLS ③

Handle for jack, round end
513072 ③

Tyre pressure gauge
562019

Type pump, foot operated
GAT348 (Optional)

Starting handle
218508

Lifting jack,
screw type
90624214

Tyre pump
hand operated
523638

Connection for pump
524959

Wheel nut wrench ④
537179
595336 ⑤

① Jack rod and jack handle - wooden handle type) Alternatives, for use
② Jack rod and jack handle - tommy bar handle type) with Jack 90624214
③ For early ratchet type jack
④ For wheel nuts 59/64" across flats.
⑤ For wheel nuts 1.1/16" across flats

2J 07

Vehicles to this specification are based on the normal 109 Three Quarter Ton models with 2¼ litre Petrol engine or 2.6 litre Petrol engine, the majority of parts are therefore identical to normal build, the variations on the 109 ONE TON LAND-ROVER are listed on the following pages.

The equipment listed below is also fitted, see Land-Rover Optional Equipment Parts Catalogue:

Truck cab
Private locks
Towing jaw (Export only)
Attachment bracket for towing jaw (Export only)
Interior mirror (Export only)

VEHICLE UNIT SERIAL NUMBERS

Vehicle:		2¼ litre Petrol	2.6 litre Petrol
Home,	RHStg ..	23100001G	22900001G
Export,	RHStg ..	23200001G	22200001G
Export,	RHStg CKD	23300001G	22400001G
Export,	LHStg	23400001G	22300001G
Export,	LHStg CKD	23500001G	22500001G

Engine: 2¼ litre Petrol, 8:1 compression ratio - Same as Three Quarter Ton 109, commencing suffix letter 'A' onwards

Engine: 2.6 litre Petrol 7.8:1 compression ratio-Same as Three Quarter Ton 109, commencing suffix letter 'B' onwards

Engine: 2.6 litre Petrol, 7:1 Compression ratio -Same as Three Quarter Ton 109, commencing suffix letter 'A' onwards

Gearbox: 2¼ litre Petrol, commencing 23800001A
Gearbox: 2.6 litre Petrol, commencing 22900001A

2K 02

LAND-ROVER Registered Trade Mark

SERIES IIA

PARTS CATALOGUE
SUPPLEMENT

FOR

109 ONE TON

2¼ Litre, 4 Cylinder Petrol Model
2·6 Litre, 6 Cylinder Petrol Model

2K 02

GROUP N   SUMMARY OF SPECIAL FEATURES

Engine, 2¼ litre Petrol
Inlet manifold and adaptor to suit servo vacuum pipe 9¼" diaphram spring clutch

Engine, 2.6 litre Petrol
As normal build

Gearbox
Easy change type gearbox with lower ratio transfer gears

Axles, front and rear
Heavy duty type, ENV manufacture, 51½" track

Differential, front and rear
ENV type to suit heavy duty axles

Propeller shafts, front and rear
To suit ENV axles

Steering unit
Lower steering ratio. Steering damper fitted between drag link and chassis frame

Chassis frame
Composite type to suit RH or LHStg. Extended shackle brackets. Additional support for fuel tank

Suspension
Heavy duty front springs, rear springs and shock absorbers. Two position shackle plates. Longer rebound check straps. Extension pads for axle buffers.

Wheels and tyres
Road wheel 6.50L x 16" (H" offset)
9.00 x 16" tyres

Brake pipes and servo
Brake pipes to suit ENV axles and servo unit. Hydraulic servo fitted to 2¼ litre Petrol models. Mechanical servo fitted to 2.6 litre Petrol models as normal build. Longer front brake hoses

Instruments
Speedometer to suit 9.00 x 16" tyres

Bonnet
Reinforced bonnet with spare wheel carrier to suit 9.00 x 16" tyre. Provision for spare wheel lock. Side fasteners for bonnet.

Tools
Extended wheel brace

GROUP N   ENGINE SECTION 2¼ LITRE, 4-CYLINDER, PETROL MODELS
109 ONE TON

PLATE REF. 1 2 3 4	Description	Qty.	Part No.	Remarks
	ENGINE ASSEMBLY, 0:1 Compression ratio	1	60730BH	Engine suffix 'A' onwards

MANIFOLD SECTION, 2¼ LITRE, 4-CYLINDER PETROL MODELS
109 ONE TON

PLATE REF. 1 2 3 4	Description	Qty.	Part No.	Remarks
	Adaptor, inlet manifold to servo pipe	1	90513171	Not part of engine assembly
	All other items as listed in main parts catalogue			

FLYWHEEL AND CLUTCH SECTION, 2¼ LITRE, 4-CYLINDER PETROL MODELS
109 ONE TON

PLATE REF. 1 2 3 4	Description	Qty.	Part No.	Remarks
	CLUTCH COVER, 9¼"	1	GCC112	
	Clutch plate complete	1	GCP129	
	Lining package for clutch plate	1	605997	Not part of engine assembly
	All other items as listed in main parts catalogue			

PLATE REF.	1 2 3 4	DESCRIPTION	QTY.	PART No.	REMARKS
1	CLUTCH WITHDRAWAL RACE HOUSING ASSEMBLY		1	528707	For gearbox with sealed clutch withdrawal unit
	CLUTCH WITHDRAWAL RACE HOUSING ASSEMBLY		1	591205	
2	Bush for cross-shaft, large		1	214793	
3	Bush for cross-shaft, small		2	214794	
4	Dowel locating housing		2	213700	
5	Bush for withdrawal race sleeve		1	231075	
	Bush for withdrawal race sleeve		1	591202	For gearbox with sealed clutch withdrawal unit
	Oil seal for bush		1	594224	
6	Clutch withdrawal sleeve		1	231074	
	Clutch withdrawal race sleeve assembly		1	591204	For gearbox with sealed clutch withdrawal unit
	Oil seal for sleeve		1	219768	
	Retaining bush for sleeve		1	265969	
7	Withdrawal race thrust bearing		1	GHB130	For gearbox with sealed clutch withdrawal unit
	Withdrawal race thrust bearing		1	268053	
8	Operating fork for clutch		1	264807	
9	Spring for operating fork		1	264806	
10	Cross-shaft for clutch operation		1	231943	
11	Thrust washer for cross-shaft		1	213660	
12	Oil seal for cross-shaft		1	90214787	
13	Cover plate for cross-shaft		1	213661	
14	Joint washer for cover plate or housing		1	90213662	
15	Spring washer		2	GHF331	
16	Set bolt (¼" Whit x 21/32")	Fixing cover plate or oil seal housing	2	90215593	
17	Joint washer for clutch withdrawal housing		1	528697	
18	Self-locking nut (¼" BSF)	Fixing withdrawal housing	3	251320	
19	Self-locking nut (5/16" BSF)	to bell housing	4	251321	

2K 04

109 ONE TON
CLUTCH SLAVE CYLINDER SECTION

PLATE REF.	1	2	3	4	DESCRIPTION	QTY.	PART No.	REMARKS
					Support bracket for clutch slave cylinder	1	561985*	4-cylinder models

ALL OTHER ITEMS AS LISTED IN MAIN PARTS CATALOGUE

* NO LONGER SERVICED

2K 05

This page is intentionally left blank

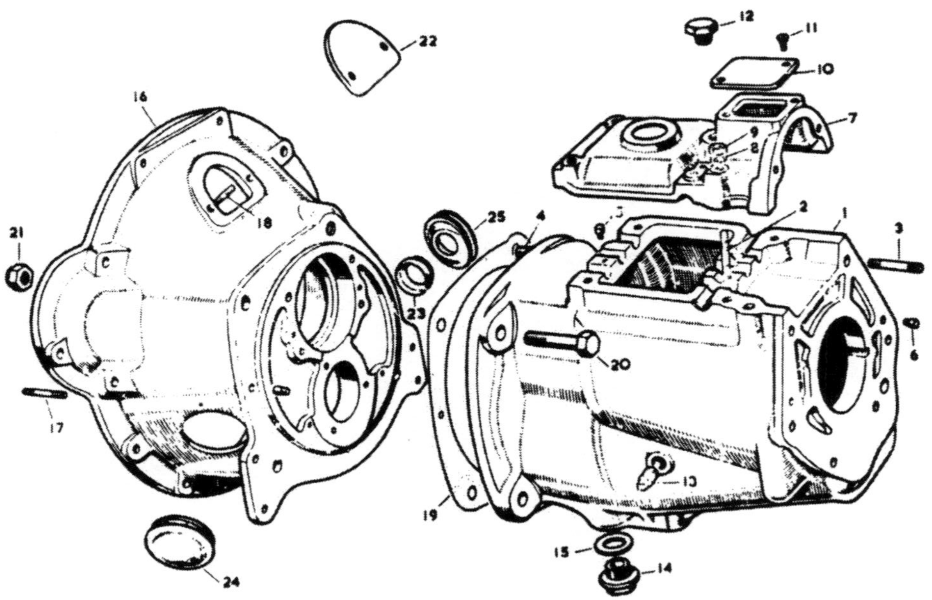

109 ONE TON
GEARBOX, MAIN CASING

GROUP N

PLATE REF.	1	2	3	4	DESCRIPTION	QTY.	PART No.	REMARKS
					GEARBOX COMPLETE ASSEMBLY	1	607908N	2¼ litre Petrol
					GEARBOX COMPLETE ASSEMBLY	1	607909N	2.6 litre Petrol
					GEARBOX CASING ASSEMBLY	1	605933	
1					Stud for top cover	2	3319	
2					Set bolt for top cover and gear change plate, front	2	561484	
					Stud, long)For transfer	2	55778	
3					Stud, short)casing	2	323R	
					Stud for transfer casing	1	528865	
4					Stud for bell housing	1	231341	
5					Dowel locating top cover	2	7289	
6					Dowel locating transfer casing	2	55636	
7					Top cover for gearbox			Not supplied separately
8					Spring washer)Fixing	2	GHF333	
9					Nut (⅜" BSF))top cover	2	2827	
10					Inspection cover plate for selectors	1	5843	
11					Set screw (¼" Whit x 7/16") fixing cover plate	2	52246	
12					Plug for retaining spring	1	556570	
13					Oil level and filler plug, ½" BSP	1	302	
14					Drain plug for gearbox	1	540R70	
15					Washer for plug	1	515590	
16					BELL HOUSING ASSEMBLY	1	556039	2¼ litre Petrol
					BELL HOUSING ASSEMBLY	1	556044	2.6 litre Petrol
17					Stud for withdrawal race housing	3	269413	
19					Joint washer, bell housing to gearbox	1	622045	
20					Fitting bolt (⅜" BSF x 2"))Fixing gearbox	3	2A720	
21					Self-locking nut (⅜" BSF))casing to bell)housing	4	251324	
22					Top cover for bell housing	1	512237	
					Rubber seal for top cover	1	512238	
					Spring washer)Fixing top	2	GHF331	
					Set bolt (⅜" Whit x 21/32"))cover to bell)housing	2	90215593	
					Grommet for bell housing shaft	1	553262	
					Plain washer) Fixing gearbox	8	WB110061	
					Nut (⅜" UNF)) to engine	12	GHF202	
					Gearbox gasket kit	1	600603	

109 ONE TON
GEARBOX, MAIN CASING

2K 06

109 ONE TON
GEARBOX, SHAFT AND GEARS

PLATE REF.	1	2	3	4	DESCRIPTION	QTY.	PART No.	REMARKS
1					Primary pinion and constant gear	1	542231	
					Primary pinion and constant gear	1	606099	For gearbox with sealed clutch withdrawal unit
2					Shield for primary pinion	1	RTC1954	
3					Ball bearing for primary pinion	1	55714	
4					Lockwasher) Fixing bearing	1	RTC1943	
					Locknut) to pinion	1	213416	
5					Retaining plate for primary pinion bearing	2	556379	
					Serrated bolt (5/16" BSF x 4") fixing retaining plate to bell housing	4	556147	
9					Layshaft	1	556040	
10					Mainshaft	1	521851	
11					Peg for 2nd gear thrust washer	1	6405	
12					Peg for mainshaft distance sleeve	1	RTC1979	
13					Thrust washer . 125"		257572	}
					Thrust washer . 128" For 2nd speed gear		257573	} As required
					Thrust washer . 130"		25757A	}
					Thrust washer . 135"		267575	}
14					1st speed layshaft gear	1	511189	
15					1st speed mainshaft gear	1	511205	
16					2nd speed layshaft and mainshaft gear	1	600916	
18					3rd speed layshaft and mainshaft gear	1	245767	
19					Distance sleeve for mainshaft	1	57171R	
20					Thrust washer . 125"		RTC1962	}
					Thrust washer . 128" For 3rd speed	1	50702	} As required
					Thrust washer . 130" mainshaft gear	1	50703	}
					Thrust washer . 135"		231737	}
21					Spring ring fixing 2nd and 3rd mainshaft gears	1	RTC1957	
22					Sleeve for layshaft	1	263878	
23					Bearing for layshaft, front	1	528701	
24					Plain washer) Fixing bearing to layshaft	1	528692	
25					Slotted nut)	1	528691	
26					Split pin	1	2766	
27					Bearing plate for layshaft	1	528685	
28					Distance piece, 0.405"	1	528720	}
					Distance piece, 0.425" For layshaft	1	528771	} As required
					Distance piece, 0.445"	1	528772	}
29					Retaining plate for layshaft front bearing	1	528690	
30					Lock washer) Fixing cap and bearing	1	528683	
31					Nut (5/16" BSF)) to bell housing	3	NT605041	
32					Bearing for layshaft, rear	1	55715	
33					Synchronising clutch	1	FRC1758	

2K 07

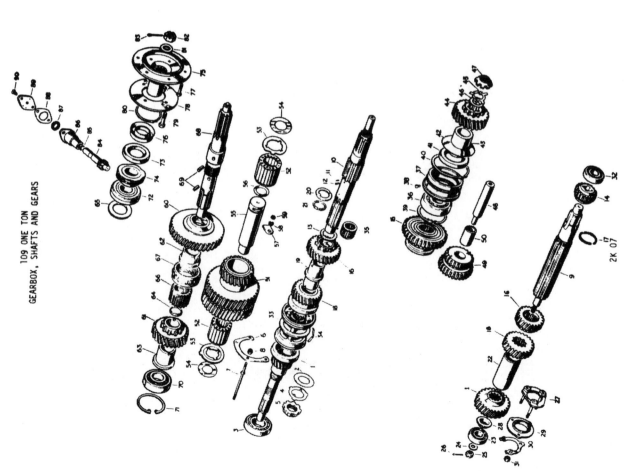

109 ONE TON
GEARBOX, SHAFTS AND GEARS

2K 07

GROUP N
109 ONE TON
GEARBOX, SHAFT AND GEARS

PLATE REF.	1 2 3 4 DESCRIPTION	QTY.	PART No.	REMARKS
34	Detent spring for clutch	3	RTC1956	
35	Roller bearing for mainshaft	1	6397	
36	Ball bearing for mainshaft	1	1645	
37	Housing for mainshaft bearing, rear	1	561877	
	'Loctite' compound Grade AVV for housing	1	600303	
			9960	
39	Circlip, bearing to housing	1	RTC1984	
40	Circlip, housing to casing	1	236305	
41	Oil seal for rear of mainshaft	1	232415	
42	Oil thrower for mainshaft	1	521852	
43	Distance piece, rear of mainshaft	1	522017	
44	Mainshaft gear for transfer box	1	521534	
45	Lock washer)	1	521636	
46	Shim washer) Fixing gear to mainshaft	1	521633	
47	Special nut)	1	561962	
48	Shaft for reverse gear	1	561960	
49	Reverse wheel assembly	1	561954	
50	Bush for reverse wheel	1	539928	
51	Gear, intermediate	2	599369	
52	Roller bearing for intermediate gear	2	521328	
53	Thrust washer for intermediate gear	1	561197	
54	Shim for intermediate gear	As reqd	594195	
55	Sealing ring for intermediate shaft	1	532323	
56	Retaining plate for shaft	1	217484	
57		1	GHF333	
58	Spring washer) Fixing plate	1	2827	
59	Nut (⅜" BSF)) to casing	1	576201	
60	Low gear wheel	1	521868	
61	High gear wheel	1	521864	
62	Bush for low gear wheel	1	90515855	
63	Bush for high gear wheel	1	513318	
64	Thrust washer for high gear wheel	1	515853	
65	Thrust washer for low gear wheel	1	571770	
66	Inner member for transfer change speed	1	576209	
67	Outer member for transfer change speed	1	515851	
68	Output shaft, rear drive	2	RTC1979	
69	Peg for output shaft	1	GHG159	
70	Bearing for output shaft, front	1	217330	
71	Circlip fixing bearing to case	1	90217512	
72	Bearing for output shaft, rear	1	FRC1780	
73	Oil seal for output shaft	1	540004	
74	Speedometer worm complete	1	236630	
75	Flange for output shaft, rear drive	1	236074	
76	Mudshield for flange	1	217564	
77	Fitting bolt for brake drum	6	217568	
78	Retaining flange for brake drum bolts	1		
79	Fitting bolt for propeller shaft	4	90512701	

GROUP N
109 ONE TON
GEARBOX, SHAFT AND GEARS

PLATE REF.	1 2 3 4 DESCRIPTION	QTY.	PART No.	REMARKS
80	Circlip retaining bolts and flange	1	217546	
81	Plain washer)	1	3300	
82	Slotted nut) Fixing flange to output shaft	1	3259	
83	Split pin)	1	PS608101	
84	Speedometer pinion	1	FRC1536	
85	Sealing ring for sleeve	1	267828	
86	Sleeve pinion	1	268791	
87	Oil seal for pinion	1	211502	
88	Joint washer for sleeve	1	267782	
89	Retaining plate for pinion	1	232565	
90	Screw fixing plate to housing	2	2529	

GROUP N

109 ONE TON — GEARBOX. TRANSFER CASING

PLATE REF.	1	2	3	4	DESCRIPTION	QTY.	PART No.	REMARKS
1					TRANSFER BOX CASING ASSEMBLY	1	539787	
2					Stud for intermediate shaft	1	217778	
3					Stud for speedometer housing, short	5	3650	
					Stud for speedometer housing, long	6	237251	
4					Stud for mainshaft housing	6	3650	
5					Stud for top cover plate	4	217978	
6					Stud, long) For transfer	4	232497	
					Stud, short) shaft housing	6	3200	
7					Stud for engine mounting	8	90217976	
8					Stud for bottom cover	10	90212104	
9					Dowel locating speedometer housing	4	55636	
11					HOUSING ASSEMBLY FOR SPEEDOMETER PINION	1	522318	
13					Insert for pinion	1	232846	
					Stud for transmission brake	1	217977	
					Shim .003"	As reqd	235455	
					Shim .005") For speedometer	As reqd	217622	
					Shim .010") pinion housing	As reqd	217623	
					Shim .015"	As reqd	217620	
					Shim .040"	As reqd	549200	
16					Spring washer) Fixing housing	6	GHF333	
17					Nut (⅜" BSF)) to transfer box	6	2827	
					HOUSING COMPLETE ASSEMBLY, REAR MAINSHAFT BEARING			
18					HOUSING ASSEMBLY, REAR MAINSHAFT BEARING	1	521857	
19					Bush for housing	1	539956	
20					Retaining plate, inner	1	521855	
21					Bearing for mainshaft	1	521853	
22					Retaining plate, outer	1	521856	
23					Circlip fixing bearing	1	214966	
24					Joint washer for bearing housing	1	622047	
25					Spring washer) Fixing housing to	6	GHF333	
26					Nut (⅜" BSF)) transfer box	6	2827	
27					Cover plate for PTO selector	1	217970	
28					Joint washer for cover plate	1	230140	
29					Spring washer) Fixing cover plate	4	GHF332	
					Nut (5/16" BSF)) to transfer box	4	2828	
31					Cover plate for transfer gear change	1	528235	
32					Joint washer for cover plate	1	219995	
33					Spring washer) Fixing	4	GHF331	
34					Set bolt (¼" Whit x ½")) plate	4	90215758	
35					Cover plate, bottom, for transfer box	1	533040	
36					Joint washer for bottom cover	1	FRC1516	
37					Spring washer) Fixing	10	GHF331	
38					Nut (¼" BSF)) cover	10	3819	
39					Drain plug for transfer box	1	235592	
40					Joint washer for plug	1	515599	
41					Oil level and filler plug. ½" BSP	1	3292	

2K 10

2K 10

109 ONE TON
GEARBOX, TRANSFER CASING

GROUP N

GEARBOX, TRANSFER CASING
109 ONE TON

PLATE REF.	1	2	3	4	DESCRIPTION	QTY.	PART No.	REMARKS
42					Rear mounting foot, LH	1	272185	
43					Rear mounting foot, RH	1	531104	
47					Locking plate) Fixing mounting feet	4	241839	
48					Nut (7/16" BSF)) to transfer box	8	2096	
49					Joint washer, transfer box to gearbox	1	622046	
50					Bolt (⅜" BSF x 1¼" long))	1	250544	
51					Spring washer) Fixing transfer	3	GHF333	
52					Nut (⅜" BSF)) box to gearbox	3	2827	
53					Self-locking nut (⅜" BSF)	3	50526	
53					Bolt (5/16" BSF x 1.29/32")) Fixing	2	215170	
54					Spring washer) transfer box	2	GHF332	
55					Nut (5/16" BSF)) to gearbox top cover	2	2820	

2K 11

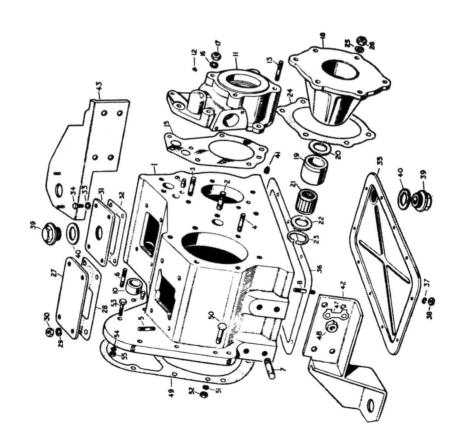

2K 11

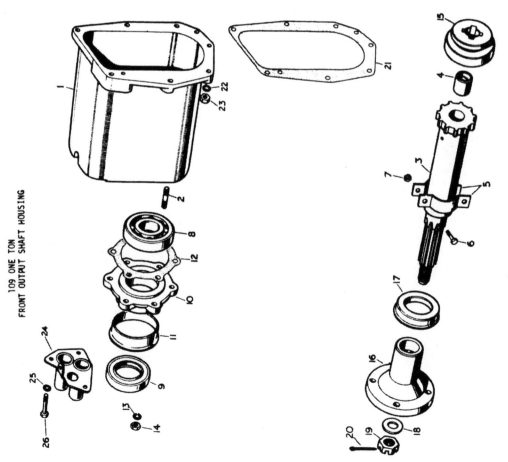

109 ONE TON
FRONT OUTPUT SHAFT HOUSING

GROUP N

PLATE REF.	1	2	3	4	DESCRIPTION	QTY.	PART No.	REMARKS
1					OUTPUT SHAFT HOUSING ASSEMBLY	1	268849	
2					Stud for oil seal retainer	6	21797R	
3					FRONT OUTPUT SHAFT ASSEMBLY	1	243611	
4					Bush for shaft	1	8566	
5					Oil thrower for output shaft	2	243873	
6					Bolt (2BA x ⅜") } Fixing oil thrower to	2	234603	
7					Self-locking nut (2BA) } front output shaft	2	251335	
8					Bearing for front output shaft	1	217325	
9					Oil seal for front output shaft	1	FRC1780	
10					Retainer for oil seal	1	236541	
11					Mudshield for retainer	1	236548	
12					Joint washer for retainer	1	FRC1511	
13					Spring washer } Fixing	6	GHF332	
14					Nut (5/16" BSF) } retainer	6	282R	
15					Locking dog, four-wheel drive	1	233241	
16					Flange for transfer shaft	1	539993	
17					Mudshield for flange	1	236074	
18					Plain washer } Fixing flange to transfer shaft	1	3300	
19					Slotted nut	1	3259	
20					Split pin	1	PS608101	
21					Joint washer for transfer housing	1	622048	
22					Spring washer } Fixing housing to	7	GHF332	
23					Nut (5/16" BSF) } transfer box	7	282R	
24					Dust cover plate for selector shafts	1	512760	
					Felt seal in plate for adjusting screw	1	512791	
25					Spring washer } Fixing dust	2	GHF331	
26					Set bolt (¼" Whit x 7/16") } cover plate	1	90215769	
					Set bolt (¼" Whit x ½") } to housing	2	90215758	

2K 12

240

109 ONE TON
MAIN GEAR LEVER

GROUP N

PLATE REF.	1	2	3	4	DESCRIPTION	QTY.	PART No.	REMARKS
					MAIN GEAR-CHANGE LEVER ASSEMBLY	1	FRC1836*	RHStg) 4-cylinder
					MAIN GEAR-CHANGE LEVER ASSEMBLY	1	FRC1837*	LHStg) models
					MAIN GEAR-CHANGE LEVER ASSEMBLY	1	622006	RHStg) 6 cylinder
					MAIN GEAR-CHANGE LEVER ASSEMBLY	1	622007*	LHStg) models
1					Gear-change lever	1	FRC1454	RHStg) 4 cylinder
1					Gear-change lever	1	FRC1455	LHStg) models
2					Gear-change lever	1	FRC1832	RHStg) 6 cylinder
2					Gear-change lever	1	FRC1833	LHStg) models
3					'O' ring for gear-change lever	1	540354	For early type gear-change lever
					'O' ring for gear-change lever	1	FRC13R7	For late type gear-change lever
4					Housing for lever	1	219714	
5					Locating pin for lever ball	1	507447	
6					Spherical seat for gear lever	1	219721	
7					Retaining spring for lever	1	219723	
8					Retaining plate for spring	1	219722	
9					Circlip fixing retaining plate	1	219797	
10					Knob for lever	1	217735	Screw-on type, for early type gear-change lever
10					Locknut (⅜" BSF) for knob	1	3905*	
10					Knob for lever	1	576316	Press-on type for late type gear-change lever
11					Star tolerance ring	1	571661	
12					Mounting plate for gear change	1	232608	
13					Set bolt (5/16" Whit x 13/16"))Fixing housing to mounting plate	4	215647	
14					Locker	4	2499	
15					Spring washer	2	GHF331	)Fixing mounting plate to bell housing
16					Set bolt (¼" Whit x 21/32")	2	90215593	
17					Reverse stop hinge complete	1	502202	
18					Adjusting screw) For	1	76653	
19					Locknut (2BA)) hinge	1	2247	
20					Bracket for reverse stop spring	1	502205	
21					Spring for reverse stop	2	514650	
22					Set bolt (¼" BSF x ½"))Fixing hinge and bracket to reverse selector shaft	2	237139	
23					Locker	1	FRC2469	

* NO LONGER SERVICED

2K 13

2K 13

GROUP N

PLATE REF.	1	2	3	4	DESCRIPTION	QTY.	PART No.	REMARKS
1					Selector fork, 3rd and 4th speed	1	RTC1953	
2					Shaft for fork, 3rd and 4th speed	1	90213636	
3					Selector fork, 1st and 2nd speed	1	6421	
4					SHAFT ASSEMBLY FOR FORK, 1st and 2nd SPEED	1	213637	
5					Interlocking pin	1	55697	
6					Peg fixing interlocking pin	1	55775	
7					Selector fork, reverse	1	90217391	
8					Shaft for fork, reverse	1	502201	
9					Set bolt (5/16" BSF x 1") fixing forks to shaft	3	237160	
10					Stop for 2nd speed	1	210203	
11					Locker Fixing stop to	1	210204	
12					Set bolt (¼" BSF x ⅜") selector shaft	1	250693	
13					Interlocking plunger	2	55638	
14					Steel ball for selectors	3	1643	
15					Selector spring, forward	2	3649	
16					Selector spring, reverse	1	56102	
17					Retaining plate LH	1	5853	
18					Retaining plate RH	1	5854	
19					Rubber grommet For selector springs, side	1	5852	
20					Spring washer Fixing	4	GHF331	
21					Set bolt (¼" Whit x 1") retaining plates	4	20215758	
22					Sealing ring, forward selector shaft	2	272596	
23					Sealing ring, reverse selector shaft	1	272597	
24					Retaining plate for sealing ring	2	241598	
25					Spring washer Fixing	4	GHF331	
26					Set bolt (¼" Whit x 7/16") retaining plate	4	90215769	
27					Set bolt (2 BA x 9/16") In cover for	1	251018	
28					Locknut (2 BA) 2nd gear stop	1	RTC608	
29					Bolt (½" BSF x 13/32") for reverse selector shaft	1	281033	

2K 14

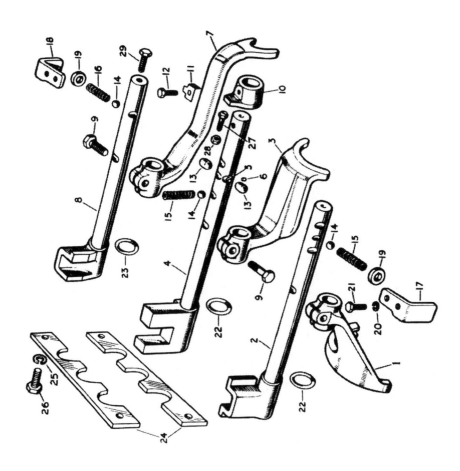

2K 14

GROUP N

PLATE REF.	DESCRIPTION	QTY.	PART No.	REMARKS
1	Selector shaft, four wheel drive	1	233416	
2	Selector fork complete, four wheel dirve	1	622155	
3	Bush for selector fork	2	90217521	For early type selector fork with replaceable bushes
4	Spring for selector fork	2	233449	
5	Block for selector shaft	2	233406	
6	Special screw ⎫ Fixing block	1	233409	
7	Castel nut (5/16" BSF) ⎬ to selector shaft	1	251601	
8	Split pin	1	2422	
9	Spring spacer for selector shaft	1	522308	
10	Selector shaft, transfer gear change	1	522303	
11	Sealing ring for transfer gear change shaft	1	515572	
12	Selector fork, transfer gear change	1	522334	
13	Set bolt (5/16" BSF x 1") Fixing fork	1	237160	
14	Distance tube for transfer selector shaft	1	233438	
15	Locating bush for selector shaft spring	1	233437	
16	Spring for selector shaft	1	217445	
17	Connector, gear change to pivot shaft	1	538536	
18	Block for selector shaft ⎫ Fixing block	1	233406	
19	Special screw ⎬ to selector	1	233409	
20	Castle nut (5/16" BSF) ⎭ shaft	1	251601	
21	Split pin	1	2422	
22	Pivot shaft for selector shafts	1	549201	
23	Coupling, selector shafts to pivot	1	233407	
24	Special screw ⎫ Fixing coupling	1	549169	
25	Castle nut 5/16" BSF) ⎬ to pivot shaft	1	251601	
26	Split pin	1	2422	
27	Shakeproof washer ⎫ Fixing pivot shaft	1	GHF323	
27	Nut (¼" BSF) ⎬ to connector	1	2827	
28	Plunger for transfer selector shaft	1	235416	
29	Spring for plunger	1	56102	
30	Plug retaining plunger	1	233441	
31	Link for selector shaft	1	539887	
32	Adjusting screw for link	1	532926	
33	Locknut (¼" UNF) for adjusting screw	1	NT606041	
34	Shakeproof washer ⎫ Fixing link to	1	77626	
35	Special nut ⎬ selector shaft	1	3764	
36	LEVER ASSEMBLY, FOUR WHEEL DRIVE	1	268847	
37	Bush for lever	1	230086	
38	Special bolt, hexagon head, lever to housing	1	540842	
39	Locking pin, four wheel drive lever	1	232464	
40	Sealing ring for four wheel drive locking pin	1	266992	
41	Plain washer ⎫ Fixing locking	1	2876	
42	Split pin ⎬ pin to lever	1	3958	
43	Selector rod, four wheel drive	1	571855	
44	Clevis complete for rod	1	215808	
45	Split pin for clevis	1	3958	
46	Spring for selector rod	1	561221	
47	Special bush for spring	1	234658	
	Control knob for rod	1	232813	
	Locknut (¼" BSF) for knob and clevis	2	3819	

2K 15

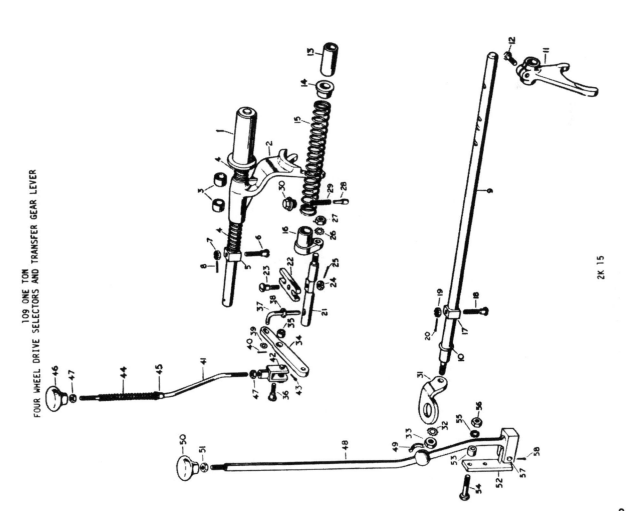

2K 15

109 ONE TON
FOUR WHEEL DRIVE SELECTORS AND TRANSFER GEAR LEVER

GROUP N   FOUR WHEEL DRIVE SELECTORS AND TRANSFER GEAR LEVER

109 ONE TON

PLATE REF.	1	2	3	4	DESCRIPTION	QTY.	PART No.	REMARKS
48					Transfer gear change lever	1	576210	
49					Spring for transfer gear change lever	1	243714	
50					Knob for gear change lever	1	219521	
51					Locknut for knob	1	3764	
52					Bracket for gear change lever	1	219709	
53					Distance piece for bracket, ⅞" long	2	266955	
54					Bolt (5/16" UNF x 1⅜" long)	2	BH605111	} Fixing bracket to
55					Spring washer	2	GHF332	} bell housing
55					Nut (5/16" UNF)	2	GHF201	}
56					Bolt (5/16" UNF x 1⅛" long)	1	BH605111	} Fixing transer gear
					Nut (5/16" UNF)	1	GHF222	} lever to bracket

2K 16

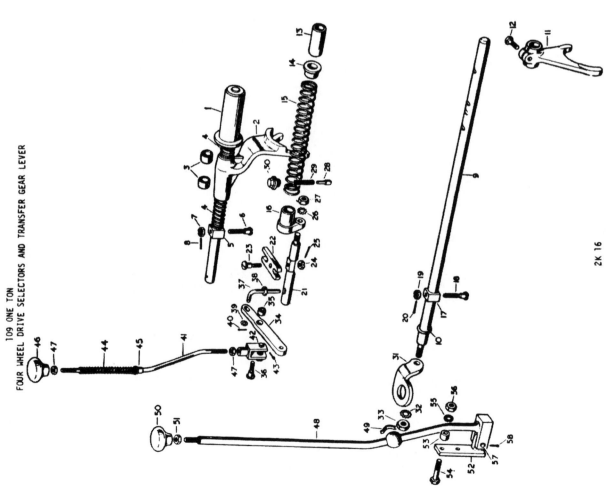

2K 16

109 ONE TON
FRONT AXLE AND PROPELLER SHAFT

GROUP N

PLATE REF.	1 2 3 4	DESCRIPTION	QTY.	PART No.	REMARKS
		FRONT AXLE ASSEMBLY, 4.7 RATIO, RH Stg	1	591314*	ENV type) See note at
		FRONT AXLE ASSEMBLY, 4.7 RATIO, LH Stg	1	591315*	ENV type) foot of page
1		Front axle casing complete	1	533570	
		Set bolt ($\frac{3}{8}$" UNF x 1$\frac{1}{8}$")) Fixing	10	255248	
		Spring washer) differential	10	GHF333	
		) to axle casing			
5		Oil seal in axle casing	2	217400	
6		Breather complete for front axle	1	515845	
7		Oil filler plug, front, for axle casing	1	3294	
8		Drain plug for front axle casing	1	235592	
9		Joint washer for drain plug	1	515599	
10		PROPELLER SHAFT ASSEMBLY, FRONT	1	533640	4-cylinder models
10		PROPELLER SHAFT ASSEMBLY, FRONT	1	576217	6-cylinder models
11		Splined stub shaft for propeller shaft	1	601790	Export only
12		Flange) Splined end) For) propeller shaft	2	600656	
13			2	GUJ117	
14		Circlip for universal joint	8	242522	
15		Universal joint	2	232557	) Alternatives
15		Grease nipple for universal joint, $\frac{1}{8}$" BSF	2	549229	)
16		Grease nipple for universal joint, $\frac{1}{4}$" UNF	1	276201	) Angled) Alternatives
16		Grease nipple for shaft sleeve	1	232037	) type)
17		Washer for nipple	1	234537	) Straight)
17		Grease nipple for shaft sleeve			) type
18		Bolt ($\frac{3}{8}$" UNF x 1.7/32")) Fixing	4	509046	
19		Self-locking nut ($\frac{3}{8}$" UNF)) propeller shaft	8	509751	
20		Rubber gaiter set for propeller shaft splines	1	275484	Part of front propeller shaft

NOTE: Replacement of Front Axle Assembly, ENV type

Use Front axle assembly, RH Stg   1   FRC3398) Salisbury type
     Front axle assembly, LH Stg   1   594416)

Also the following, which replace the existing parts fitted to the vehicles:
    Propeller shaft assembly, front   1   591278   4-cyl models
    Propeller shaft assembly, front   1   594361   6-cyl models
    'U' bolt   ) Fixing   1   592185
    'U' bolt   ) front springs   3   592184
    Bottom plate RH) to axle   1   598536
    Bottom plate LH   1   592177
    Nyloc nut 12mm   8   GHF234
    Track rod assembly   1   320903

2L 02

* NO LONGER SERVICED

109 ONE TON
FRONT AXLE AND PROPELLOR SHAFT

2L 02

GROUP N   109 ONE TON   UNIVERSAL JOINTS AND FRONT HUBS

PLATE REF.	1	2	3	4	DESCRIPTION	QTY.	PART No.	REMARKS
1					Half shaft complete for front axle, RH	1	540972	
1					Half shaft complete for front axle, LH	1	540973*	
3					Universal joint	2	GU3118	
4					Circlip for universal joint	8	247522	
5					Housing for swivel pin bearing	2	539741	
6					Distance piece for bearing	2	244151	
7					Bearing for half shaft	2	244150	
8					Retaining collar for bearing	2	90217398	
9					Joint washer for housing	2	GFG107	
10					Location stop for jack	1	90519206	
11					Bolt (½" BSF x 1¼")) Fixing stop and	2	576522	
12					Bolt (½" BSF x 1½")) housing to front	10	576521	
13					Self-locking nut (½" BSF)) axle casing	12	251322	
14					HOUSING ASSEMBLY FOR SWIVEL PIN, LH	1	FRC2074	
14					HOUSING ASSEMBLY FOR SWIVEL PIN, RH	1	FRC2075	
15					Special stud for steering lever and bracket	4	531043	
16					Stud for steering lever	4	531494	
16					Set bolt (7/16" BSF x 1?") for steering lever	8	237357	
17					Drain plug for housing	2	236070	
18					Joint washer for drain plug	2	230511	
19					Swivel pin and steering lever complete, RH	1	530988	RH Stg
19					Swivel pin and steering lever complete, LH	1	530989	RH Stg
19					Swivel pin and steering lever complete, RH	1	530990	LH Stg
19					Swivel pin and steering lever complete, LH	1	530991	LH Stg
					'O' ring for steering levers	2	531433	
20					Railko bush and housing	2	530742	
21					Thrust washer	2	528702	
22					Bearing for swivel pin, bottom	2	217268	
23					Swivel pin upper complete	2	565883	
24					Shim, .003")	As reqd	530984	
24					Shim, .005") For swivel	As reqd	530985	
24					Shim, .010") pin bearing	As reqd	530986	
24					Shim, .030")	As reqd	530987	
25					Locker) Fixing swivel pin to	8	531001	
26					Nut (7/16" BSF)) swivel pin housing	16	594104	
27					Oil seal for swivel pin bearing housing	2	GHS1003	

2L 03

109 ONE TON
UNIVERSAL JOINTS AND FRONT HUBS

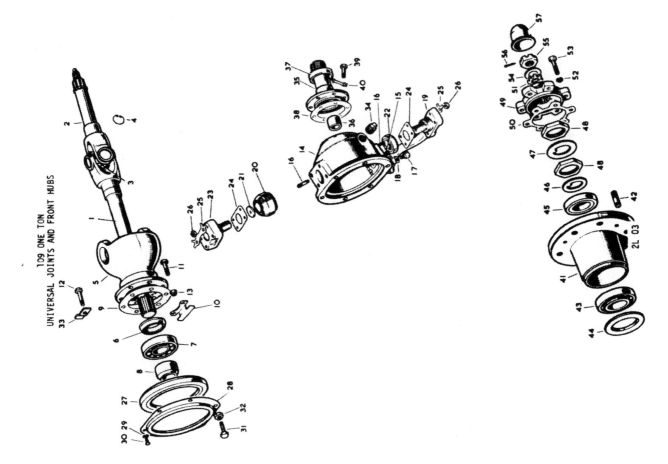

2L 03

PLATE REF.	1 2 3 4	DESCRIPTION	QTY.	PART No.	REMARKS
28		Retainer for oil seal	2	235568	
29		Spring washer	10	GHF331	
30		Set bolt (⅜" BSF x ½")	10	237139	} Fixing
		Plain washer	10	RTC609	} retainer to
31		Adjustable lock stop bolt	6	250696	} swivel pin
32		Locknut (⅜" BSF) for stop bolt	6	3819	} housing
33		Lock stop plate	2	508175	
34		Oil filler plug for swivel pin housing	2	3292	
35		STUB AXLE ASSEMBLY	2	599R27	
37		Distance piece for inner bearing	2	599R9R	
38		Joint washer, stub axle to swivel pin housing	2	GFG108	} Fixing stub axle to
39		Set bolt (⅜" BSF x 1")	12	237239	} swivel pin housing
40		Locker	6	277311	
41		FRONT HUB ASSEMBLY	2	561PR9	} Vehicle suffix 'G'
		Stud for road wheel, 9/16" BSF	10	561590	
		FRONT HUB ASSEMBLY	2	576844	} Vehicle suffix 'H' onwards
		Stud for road wheel, 16 mm	10	576925	
43		Bearing for front hub, inner	2	GHB162	
44		Oil seal for inner bearing	2	GHS202	
45		Bearing for front hub, outer	2	GHB163	
46		Key washer	2	217352	
47		Locker } Fixing front hub bearing	2	217353	
48		Special nut	4	90217355	
49		Driving member complete for front hub	2	571711	
50		Joint washer for driving member	2	GFG106	
51		Oil seal for stub shaft	2	549477	
52		Spring washer	12	GHF333	} Fixing driving
53		Set bolt (⅜" BSF x 1.19/32")	12	215331	} member to front hub
		Split pin	2	3177	} Fixing
		Split ring	5	549474	} driving member
		Spring clip	2	549399*	} to driving
		Slotted nut	2	549075	} shaft
57		Hub cap, front	2	219098	

2L 04

* NO LONGER SERVICED

UNIVERSAL JOINTS AND FRONT HUBS
109 ONE TON

2L 04

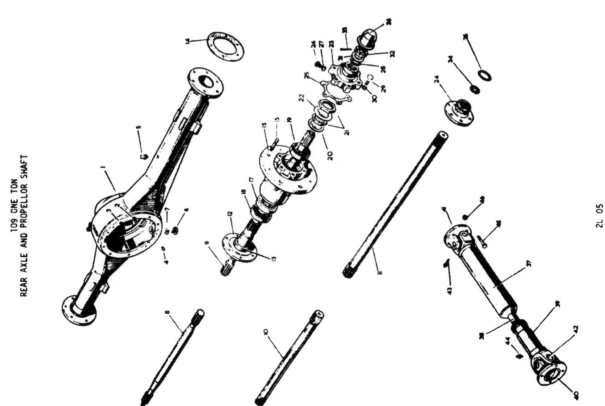

109 ONE TON
REAR AXLE AND PROPELLER SHAFT

GROUP N

PLATE REF. 1 2 3 4	DESCRIPTION	QTY.	PART No.	REMARKS
	REAR AXLE ASSEMBLY 4.7 RATIO	1	591316*	ENV type. See note at foot of page 2L06
1	Rear axle casing complete	1	533547	
3	Set bolt (⅜" UNF x 1¼")) Fixing differential	10	255248	
	Spring washer) housing to axle casing	10	GHF333	
	Oil filler plug for rear axle casing	1	3294	
5	Breather complete for rear axle	1	515845	
6	Drain plug for rear axle casing	1	235592	
7	Joint washer for drain plug	1	515509	
10	Rear axle shaft, RH	1	533579	
11	Rear axle shaft, LH	1	533580	
12	Rear hub bearing sleeve	2	599828	
13	Distance piece for bearing sleeve	2	599698	
14	Joint washer, bearing sleeve to axle casing	2	GFG103	
15	REAR HUB ASSEMBLY	2	561889	) Chassis suffix 'G'
	Stud for road wheel, 9/16" BSF	10	561590	)
16	REAR HUB ASSEMBLY	2	576844	) From chassis suffix
	Stud for road wheel, 16mm	10	576875	) 'H' onwards
17	Hub bearing, inner	2	GHB162	
18	Oil seal for inner bearing	2	GHS202	
19	Hub bearing, outer	2	GHB163	
20	Key washer) Fixing	2	217357	
21	Special nut) hub	4	90217355	
22	Locker) bearing	2	217353	
24	Driving member for rear hub	2	571711	
25	Joint washer for driving member	2	GFG106	
29	Set bolt (⅜" BSF x 1.19/32")) Fixing driving	12	215331	
30	Spring washer) member to rear hub	12	GHF333	
34	Circlip) Fixing axle shaft to	2	549473	
35	'O' ring) driving member	2	GHS1007	
36	Hub cap, rear	2	219098	
37	PROPELLER SHAFT ASSEMBLY, REAR	1	533639	4-cylinder models
	PROPELLER SHAFT ASSEMBLY, REAR	1	591279	6-cylinder models
38	Splined stub shaft for propeller shaft	1	601790	Export only
39	Splined end) For propeller	1	8407	
40	Flange) shaft	2	600656	
41	Universal joint	2	GUJ117	
42	Circlip for journal	8	242522	
43	Grease nipple for universal joint, ⅛" BSF	2	232557	) Alternatives
	Grease nipple for universal joint, ¼" UNF	2	549229	)

* NO LONGER SERVICED

2L 05

PLATE REF.	1 2 3 4	DESCRIPTION	QTY.	PART No.	REMARKS
44		Grease nipple for shaft sleeve	1	234532	Straight type ⎱ Alternatives
		Grease nipple for shaft sleeve	1	276701	Angled ⎰ type
		Washer for nipple	1	232037	
45		Bolt (⅜" UNF x 1⅛") ⎱ Fixing	8	509045P	
46		Self-locking nut (⅜" UNF) ⎰ propeller shaft	8	GHF273	

NOTE: Replacement of Rear Axle Assembly, ENV type

Use rear axle assembly   1   FRC2126   Salisbury type

Also the following, which replace the existing parts fitted to the vehicle:

Propeller shaft assembly, rear	1	591279	4-cylinder models
Propeller shaft assembly, rear	1	591283	6 cylinder models
'U' Bolt ⎱ Fixing	4	592183	
Bottom plate ⎰ rear springs	2	592179	
Nyloc nut 12mm ⎱ to axle	8	GHF234	
Rebound check strap	2	598598	
Brake pipe RH	1	592375	

2L 06

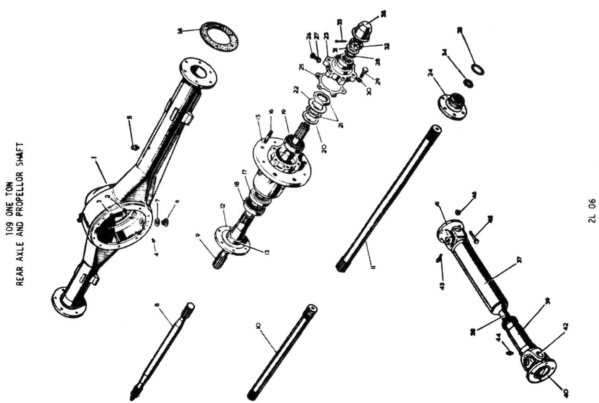

2L 06

109 ONE TON
DIFFERENTIAL, FRONT AND REAR, ENV-TYPE AXLE

2L 07

109 ONE TON
DIFFERENTIAL, FRONT AND REAR, ENV-TYPE AXLE

GROUP N

PLATE REF.	1	2	3	4	DESCRIPTION	QTY.	PART No.	REMARKS
					DIFFERENTIAL ASSEMBLY, 4.7 RATIO	2	533568	
1					Crown wheel and bevel pinion	2	549493	
2					Differential casing	2	600901	
3					Set bolt (7/16" UNF x 1") } Fixing crown wheel	24	SH607081	
4					Locking plate } to differential casing	12	549460*	
5					Set bolt (7/16" UNF x 1¼") } Fixing	16	BH607141	
6					Locking plate, double type } differential casing halves together	8	549464	
7					Differential wheel	4	549461	
8					Differential pinion	8	549462	
9					Spindle for pinion	2	549463	
10					Spherical differential pinion washer	8	549466	
11					Differential wheel washer	4	549465	
12					Taper roller bearings for differential	4	549457	
13					Differential bearing adjuster	4	549411*	
14					Locking plate } For bearing	4	549447*	
15					Set bolt (¼" UNC x ½") } adjuster	4	SH504041	
16					Nose piece and bearing cap complete	2	600902*	
17					Special set bolt fixing bearing cap	R	549409	
18					Bearing for bevel pinion, nose end	2	549417	
19					Retaining washer } Fixing bearing	2	2228	
					Alum rivet (⅛" dia x 1¼") } to nose piece and bevel pinion	2	4560	
20					Circlip	2	549419	
21					Bearing for bevel pinion	4	549420	
22					Spacer, .370" }	As reqd	549425	
					Spacer, .373" }	As reqd	549427	
					Spacer, .376" } For	As reqd	549429	
					Spacer, .379" } pinion	As reqd	549431	
					Spacer, .382" } shaft	As reqd	549433	
					Spacer, .385" } bearing	As reqd	549435	
					Spacer, .388" } adjustment	As reqd	549437	
					Spacer, .391" }	As reqd	549439	
					Spacer, .394" }	As reqd	549441	
					Spacer, .397" }	As reqd	549443	
					Spacer, .400" }	As reqd	549445	

* NO LONGER SERVICED

2L 07

GROUP N

PLATE REF.	1	2	3	4	DESCRIPTION	QTY.	PART No.	REMARKS
23					Bevel pinion housing complete	2	549413	
24					Oil seal for pinion	2	549412	
25					Mudshield for bevel pinion bearing housing	2	549454	
26					Mudshield for driving flange	2	549453*	
27					Driving flange for bevel pinion	2	549421*	
28					Special nut (¾" UNF), fixing driving flange to bevel pinion	2	549448*	
					Shim, .002" ⎫ For differential	As reqd	549414*	
29					Shim, .003" ⎬ bearing housing	As reqd	549415	
					Shim, .010" ⎭ adjustment	As reqd	549416	
30					Set bolt (⅜" UNF x 1⅜") ⎫ Fixing pinion	16	255248	
31					Shakeproof washer ⎬ housing to nose piece	16	GHF323	
32					Joint washer, differential to axle casing	2	533645*	
33					Set bolt (⅜" UNF x 1⅜") ⎫ Fixing differential	20	255248	
34					Spring washer ⎬ to axle casing	20	GHF333	

* NO LONGER SERVICED

2L 08

2L 08

PLATE REF. 1 2 3 4 — DESCRIPTION	QTY.	PART No.	REMARKS
CHASSIS FRAME			
CHASSIS FRAME			
Crossmember No.3 } For chassis	1	592472*	4-cylinder models
Crossmember No.4 } frame	1	592543*	6-cylinder models
Crossmember No.3)	1	90577407	} 4-cylinder
Crossmember No.4 For chassis frame	1	58394F	} models
Crossmember No.4)	1	90577407	
Crossmember No.8	1	592594	Welded type }6-cylinder
	1	90566017	Bolted type }models
Bolt (3/8" UNF x 3½") } Fixing crossmember	4	BH606281	} to frame
Self-locking nut (3/8" UNF)	4	GHF223	
ROAD SPRING COMPLETE, FRONT, DRIVER'S	1	276034	
ROAD SPRING COMPLETE, FRONT, PASSENGER'S	1	265627	
Main leaf	2	243121	
Second leaf	2	243126	
Bush	2	54P205	
Dowel and nut (5/16" UNF)	2	265461	} Alternatives
Dowel, 8 mm	2	RTC1920	}
Self-locking nut, 8 mm	2	GHF237	
Shackle plate, tapped	2	537735	
Shackle plate, plain	2	537780	
Distance piece for front shackle plates	2	504213	
Shim .003" } Fixing	As reqd	504213	
Shim .005" } distance	As reqd	504214	
Bolt (3/8" UNF x 5") } piece to	2	BH608401	
Spring washer } shackle	2	WM600081	
Nut (3/8" UNF) } plate	2	NH608061	
Bottom plate for front spring, LH	1	550802	
Bottom plate for front spring, RH	1	550801	
'U' bolt } Fixing	1	562771	
'U' bolt } front springs	3	562776	
Self-locking nut (½" UNF) } to axle	8	252164	
ROAD SPRING COMPLETE, REAR	2	535173	
Main leaf	2	537964	
Second leaf	4	600310	
Bush	4	54P205	
Dowel and nut	2	600311	} Alternatives
Dowel, 10 mm	2	RTC1921	}
Self-locking nut, 10 mm	2	GHF233	
Shackle plate, tanped	2	537736	
Shackle plate, plain	2	537778	
Distance tube for rear shackle plates	2	509218	
Shim .003" } Fixing	As reqd	504213	
Shim .005" } distance	As reqd	504214	
Bolt (3/8" UNF x 4½") } tube to	2	BH608361	
Spring washer } shackle	2	WM600081	
Nut (3/8" UNF) } plates	2	NH608061	
Bottom plate for rear spring	2	550786	
'U' bolt } Fixing rear springs	4	550791	
Self-locking nut (½" UNF) } to axle	8	252164	
Check strap for rear axle	2	543934	

* NO LONGER SERVICED

PLATE REF. 1 2 3 4 — DESCRIPTION	QTY.	PART No.	REMARKS
Pad for axle buffer	4	526608	
Bolt (1/4" UNF x ¾") } Fixing pad to	8	255207	
Spring washer } chassis frame	8	GHF331	
Nut (1/4" UNF)	8	GHF200	
Shock absorber, front	2	GSA411	
Shock absorber, rear	2	GSA412	
Bush for shock absorbers	12	552819	
Road wheel 6.50L x 16" (13/16" offset)	5	569204	
Tyre 9.00 x 16" Dunlop R.K. 2.A	5		}Alternatives
Tyre 9.00 x 16" Avon	5		
Inner tube 9.00 x 16" Dunlop	5		}Alternatives
Inner tube 9.00 x 16" Avon	5		

ALL OTHER ITEMS AS LISTED IN MAIN PARTS CATALOGUE

GROUP N

PLATE REF.	1 2 3 4	DESCRIPTION	QTY.	PART No.	REMARKS
		STEERING UNIT ASSEMBLY	1	552790	RH Stg
		STEERING UNIT ASSEMBLY	1	90577791	LH Stg
		STEERING BOX ASSEMBLY	1	541899	RH Stg
		STEERING BOX ASSEMBLY	1	541900	LH Stg
1		Bush for rocker shaft	1	261850	
2		Outer column	1	600984	
3		Joint washer, steel	As reqd	261858	
4		Joint washer, paper	As reqd	261857	
5		Joint washer, plastic	As reqd	271379	
		Bolt (5/16" UNC x 29/32") } Fixing outer	1	271380	
		Spring washer ⎬ column	4	GHF332	
6		Inner column	1	90577197	RH Stg
		Inner column	1	90577198	LH Stg
7		Ball bearing for inner column	1	RTC324	
8		MAIN NUT ASSEMBLY	1	600241	RH Stg
		MAIN NUT ASSEMBLY	1	600242	LH Stg
		Set bolt (2 BA x ⅜") } Fixing	2	234603	
		Lock washer for bolt } retainer	2	261865*	
9		Steel ball (⅜") for main nut	12	1643	
10		Roller for main nut	1	261869	
11		Adjustable ball race	2	271384	
12		Steel balls (9/32") for adjustable race	20	BLS109	
13		Rocker shaft	1	271372	
14		Adjuster screw for rocker shaft	1	261873	
15		Locknut for adjuster screw	1	261874	
16		Oil seal for rocker shaft	1	271013	
17		Washer for rocker shaft oil seal	1	271014	
18		End plate	1	271378	
19		Joint washer, steel	As reqd	261858	
		Joint washer, paper	As reqd	261857	
20		Joint washer, plastic	As reqd	271379	
21		Bolt (5/16" UNC x 29/32") } Fixing	4	271380	
22		Spring washer } end plate	4	GHF332	
23		Side cover plate	1	515848	
24		Joint washer for side cover plate	1	515849	
25		Bolt (5/16" UNC x 1.1/16") } Fixing side	4	271382	
26		Spring washer } cover plate	4	GHF332	
27		Oil filler plug	1	271386	
28		Special nut } Fixing	1	NT612061	
		Lock washer } drop arm	1	RTC673	
30		Steering drop arm	1	595123	
31		Rubber seal for steering column	1	303995	
32		Cover for steering column seal	1	303997	
33		Screw (2 BA x ⅜")	2	77861	
34		Special washer } Fixing cover and	2	303996	
35		Spring washer } seal to dash	2	WM702001	
36		Nut (2 BA)	2	RTC608	

* NO LONGER SERVICED

109 ONE TON
STEERING COLUMN

2L 10

2L 10

109 ONE TON
STEERING COLUMN

2L 11

109 ONE TON
STEERING COLUMN

GROUP N

PLATE REF.	1 2 3 4 DESCRIPTION	QTY.	PART No.	REMARKS
37	Steering wheel	1	NRC4346	
38	Special spring washer on inner column for wheel	1	551984	
39	Tag washer) Fixing steering	1	552572	
40	Special nut) wheel	1	552804	
41	Horn push and centre cover for steering wheel	1	90575201	
42	Dust cover and horn contact	1	552575	
	Screw (2 BA x ⅜")) Fixing dust cover to	2	77925	
	Plain washer) steering wheel	2	3902	
43	Slip ring complete for horn contact	1	519753	
44	Cable cleat on steering column	1	240431	
45	Dip switch, LU type 103SA	1	RTC432	
	Screw (2 BA x ⅜")) Fixing dip switch	2	78173	
	Spring washer	2	WM702001	
	Nut (2 BA)	2	RTC608	
46	Lead) Dip switch to	1	56096R*	RH Stg
	Lead) junction box	1	531501	LH Stg
47	Grommet for lead in toe box floor	2	236389	
48	Clip fixing dip switch lead to floor	2	50539	5 of on LH Stg
	Screw	2	77941	
	Spring washer) Fixing clip	2	WM702001	
	Nut (2 BA)	2	RTC608	
49	Support bracket on dash	1	349743*	
	Bolt (5/16" UNF x ¾"))	4	GHF120	
	Plain washer, small) Fixing	6	3830	
	Plain washer, large) support bracket	2	RTC604	
	Spring washer) to dash	4	GHF332	
	Nut (5/16" UNF)	4	GHF201	
50	Clamp, upper, for steering column	1	349744*	
	Bolt (5/16" UNF x ½")	3	GHF120	
	Plain washer	3	3830	
	Spring washer) Fixing upper clamp	3	GHF332	
	Nut (5/16" UNF)) to support bracket	3	GHF201	
51	Clamp, lower, for steering column	1	346715	
52	Rubber strip for clamp	1	348747	
	Bolt (¼" UNF x ⅞")) Fixing upper and	2	255209	
	Spring washer) lower clamps to	2	GHF331	
	Nut (¼" UNF)) steering column	2	GHF200	
53	Support bracket, RH) For steering box	1	537535*	
54	Support bracket, LH) on chassis	1	537533	
55	Bolt (5/16" UNF x 3½")	6	256233	
	Plain washer, thin) Fixing	6	3830	
	Plain washer, thick) brackets to	6	WP1R5	
56	Spring washer) chassis frame	6	GHF332	
57	Nut (5/16" UNF)	6	GHF201	
58	Stiffener bracket) For	1	90577264	RH Stg
	Stiffener bracket) steering box	1	537539*	LH Stg

* NO LONGER SERVICED

2L 11

109 ONE TON
STEERING COLUMN

PLATE REF.	1 2 3 4 DESCRIPTION		QTY.	PART No.	REMARKS
59	Bolt plate	) Fixing stiffener	2	395064	)
	Spring washer	) bracket to front	4	GHF331	) RH Stg
	Nut (¼" UNF)	) face of toe box	4	GHF200	)
	Bolt (¼" UNF x 1"))		1	GHF101	)
	Plain washer	) Fixing stiffener	1	RTC609	) 3 off on LH Stg
	Spring washer	) bracket to	1	GHF331	)
	Nut (¼" UNF)	) top face of	1	GHF200	)
60	Shim washer	) toe box	As reqd	504279	RH Stg
	Shim washer	)	As reqd	504275	LH Stg
	Bolt (⅜" UNF x 1⅜"))		2	255050	
	Set bolt (⅜" UNC x ¾"))		1	SH506061	Except 109 LH Stg
	Set bolt (⅜" UNC x ⅞")	) Fixing steering	1	SH506071	109 LH Stg
	Locking plate	) box to chassis	1	537543*	
61	Set bolt (⅜" UNC x ⅞")	) support bracket	1	SH506071	
62	Locking plate	)	1	537544	
63	Self-locking nut(⅜" UNF))		2	GHF243	

* NO LONGER SERVICED

109 ONE TON
STEERING RELAY AND LINKAGE SECTION

PLATE REF.	1 2 3 4 DESCRIPTION		QTY.	PART No.	REMARKS
	STEERING TRACK ROD ASSEMBLY		1	608465	
	Steering track rod only		1	526994	
	STEERING DRAG LINK AND DAMPER BRACKET ASSEMBLY		1	595468	
	Steering drag link tube		1	544581	
	Drag link and damper bracket		1	595469	
	Steering damper		1	NRC6474	
	Rubber sleeve for damper		1	544347	
	Inner stem cup washer	) Fixing damper	4	543819	
	Stem rubber	) to frame	4	568858	
	Outer stem cup washer	) bracket and	4	543818	
	Locknut (⅜" UNF)	) drag link	4	NT606041	
	Mounting bracket for steering damper, LH		1	552388	RH Stg
	Mounting bracket for steering damper, RH		1	552574	LH Stg
	Bolt (¼" UNF x ⅞")	) Fixing	4	SH606071	
	Spring washer	) damper bracket	4	GHF333	
	Nut (¼" UNF)	) to frame	4	GHF202	

ALL OTHER ITEMS AS LISTED IN MAIN PARTS CATALOGUE

* NO LONGER SERVICED

GROUP N   BRAKE PIPES AND SERVO, 4-CYLINDER MODELS

PLATE REF.	1 2 3 4	DESCRIPTION	QTY.	PART No.	REMARKS
1	BRAKE SERVO UNIT		1	562678	
2	Support bracket	) For brake	1	559646	
3	Stiffening plate	) servo	1	559647	
4	Bolt (5/16" UNF x ¾")	) Fixing support	1	GHF120	
5	Spring washer	) bracket to wing	1	GHF332	
6	Nut (5/16" UNF)	) valance and) stiffener	1	GHF201	
7	Set bolt (5/16" UNC x ½")) Fixing servo		2	SH505051	
8	Spring washer	) to bracket	2	GHF332	
9	Taper washer	) Fixing servo and	2	559648	
10	Spring washer	) stiffener plate	2	GHF332	
11	Nut (5/16" UNF)	) to wing valance	2	GHF201	
12	Adaptor pipe complete, inlet manifold to hose		1	559846	
13	Hose, adaptor pipe to servo		1	562795	
14	Clip fixing hose to servo and pipe		2	GHC507	
15	Pipe complete, brake servo to 4-way junction piece		1	562793	
16	Banjo for servo pipe		1	538618	
17	Banjo bolt		1	538615	
18	Gasket) Fixing banjo to brake servo		1	538616	
19	Gasket		1	538612*	
20	Pipe complete, master cylinder to servo		1	562791*	RH Stg
	Pipe complete, master cylinder to servo		1	504517	LH Stg
21	Adaptor for servo pipe		1	538613	
22	Joint washer for adaptor		1	538612*	
23	4-way junction piece for brake pipes		1	241690	
24	Bracket for junction piece		1	594938	
25	Drive screw, fixing bracket		2	72626	
26	Bolt (¼" UNF x 1¼")) Fixing		1	BH604101	
27	Spring washer) junction		1	GHF331	
28	Nut (¼" UNF)) piece		1	GHF200	
29	Brake pipe, junction piece to LH front		1	277922	
30	Brake pipe, junction piece to RH front		1	277923	
31	Bracket for LH front brake pipe		1	90508565*	
	Bolt (5/16" UNF x ½")) Fix		1	GHF120	
	Plain washer) bracket to		1	3830	
	Shakeproof washer) hose bracket on		1	GHF322	
	Nut (5/16" UNF)) chassis frame		1	GHF201	
32	Clip for LH front brake pipe		1	508565*	
	Bolt (2 BA x ½")) Fixing clip		1	234603	
	Plain washer		1	3902	
	Nut (2 BA)		1	RTC608	
33	Hose complete for front wheels		2	GBH302	
34	Hose complete to rear axle		1	GBH302	
35	Joint washer for hoses		3	233220	
36	Shakeproof washer) Fixing hose		3	GHF323	
37	Special nut (½" UNF)) to bracket		3	NT606041	
38	'T' piece on rear axle		1	537761	
39	Bolt (5/16" UNF x ½")) Fixing		1	GHF120	
40	Spring washer) 'T'		1	GHF332	
41	Nut (5/16" UNF)) piece		1	GHF201	

* NO LONGER SERVICED

2L 14

2L 14

GROUP N   109 ONE TON   BRAKE PIPES AND SERVO, 4-CYLINDER MODELS

PLATE REF.	1	2	3	4	DESCRIPTION	QTY.	PART No.	REMARKS
42					Bracket for rear axle 'T' piece	1	537R05	
					Bolt (5/16" UNF x ⅝")) Fixing 'T' piece	1	SH605051	
					Spring washer) bracket to rear	1	GHF332	
					Nut (5/16" UNF)) axle to bracket	1	GHF201	
43					Brake pipe to rear hose	1	279452	
44					Brake pipe, LH rear to 'T' piece	1	592374	
45					Brake pipe, RH rear to 'T' piece	1	551652	
46					Single clip) Fixing brake pipes to	As reqd	41379	
47					Double clip) chassis dash and wing	As reqd	233274	
					Drive screw	As reqd	72626	
					Screw (2 BA x ⅝")	As reqd	7775R	
					Plain washer) Fixing clips	As reqd	2260	
					Spring washer	As reqd	WM702001	
					Nut (2 BA)	As reqd	RTC608	
48					Clip on rear axle for LH pipe	4	11820	
49					Clip	4	56666	
50					Rubber grommet	4	6860	
					Bolt (2 BA x ½")) Fixing rear brake	4	234603	
					Plain washer) pipes to chassis frame	4	WC702101	
					Spring washer	4	WM702001	
					Nut (2 BA)	4	RTC608	
					Brake servo overhaul kit	1	600432	) Export only
					Brake servo poppet valve overhaul kit	1	600434	)
					Brake servo non-return valve overhaul kit	1	600435	)

2L 15

BRAKE PIPES, 6 CYLINDER MODELS SECTION
109 ONE TON

GROUP N

PLATE REF.	1	2	3	4	DESCRIPTION	QTY.	PART No.	REMARKS
					Hose for wheel cylinder, front	2	GBH302	
					Brake pipe rear LH to 'T' piece	1	592374	
					Brake pipe rear RH to 'T' piece	1	551652	
					'T' piece on rear axle	1	537761	
					Bracket for 'T' piece	1	537805	
					Bolt (5/16" UNF x ⅞") } Fixing 'T' piece	1	SH605051	
					Spring washer } bracket to rear axle	1	GHF332	
					Nut (5/16" UNF) } bracket	1	GHF201	

ALL OTHER ITEMS AS LISTED IN MAIN PARTS CATALOGUE

EXHAUST SYSTEM, 6 CYLINDER MODELS SECTION
109 ONE TON

GROUP N

PLATE REF.	1	2	3	4	DESCRIPTION	QTY.	PART No.	REMARKS
					Front exhaust pipe complete	1	GEX1564	

ALL OTHER ITEMS AS LISTED IN MAIN PARTS CATALOGUE

INSTRUMENT SECTION
109 ONE TON

GROUP N

PLATE REF.	1	2	3	4	DESCRIPTION	QTY.	PART No.	REMARKS
					Speedometer and warning lights miles	1	540119	} Non-trip
					Speedometer and warning lights kilometers	1	540120*	}
					Speedometer and warning lights miles	1	540131	} With trip.
					Speedometer and warning lights kilometers	1	540135	} Optional

ALL OTHER ITEMS AS LISTED IN MAIN PARTS CATALOGUE

* NO LONGER SERVICED

PLATE REF. 1 2 3 4	DESCRIPTION	QTY.	PART No.	REMARKS
Bonnet assembly, reinforced		1	320964*	
Bonnet fastener		2	300692	
Bolt (¼" UNF x ⅜")	) Fixing	4	255206	
Plain washer	) bonnet	4	2215	
Spring washer	) fastener	4	GHF331	
Nut (¼" UNF)	)	4	GHF200	
Staple for bonnet fastener		2	300693	
Screw (2 BA x ¾")		6	77861	
Packing washer		2	RTC615	
Plain washer	) Fixing staple to	6	WC702101	
Spring washer	) front wing	6	WM702001	
Nut (2 BA)		6	RTC608	
Clamp plate	) Spare wheel	1	334055	
Stud plate	) carrier	1	334055*	
Dowel for spare wheel lock		1	338414	
Bolt (¼" UNF x 1")	) Fixing plates	2	GHF101	
Bolt (¼" UNF x ½")	) and dowel	22	78210	
Spring washer	) to bonnet	24	GHF331	
Nut (¼" UNF)	)	24	GHF200	
Retaining plate for spare wheel		1	338827	
Nut for spare wheel		6	561254	
Cover plate for redundant spare wheel hole		2	330615	
Pop rivet fixing cover plate to wheelarch box		40	78248	

ALL OTHER ITEMS AS LISTED IN MAIN PARTS CATALOGUE

2L 17

PLATE REF. 1 2 3 4	DESCRIPTION	QTY.	PART No.	REMARKS
Wheel brace		1	569687	

ALL OTHER ITEMS AS LISTED IN MAIN PARTS CATALOGUE

2L 17

* NO LONGER SERVICED

LAND ROVER SERIES IIA
Bonneted Control Models

Numerical Index

PART NO	DESCRIPTION	REF.NO.
1035	Steel ball	1D 06
1384	Locking plate	1K 07
1403	Tommy bar	2J 07
1481	Ball end	1N 02
1510	Brake drum screw	1J 02
1564	Bolt 3/8in BSF X 1.11/16in	1H 06
1565	Bolt 3/8in BSF X 1.3/16in	1H 06
1645	Steel ball	1G 11
1664	Bearing	1G 04
2096	Key	2C 13
2208	Nut	1G 08
2215	Plain washer	1K 09
2219	Plain washer	2F 03
2228	Plain washer	1F 02
2258	Plain washer	1H 10
2260	Plain washer	1N 02
2265	Washer	2L 15
2266	Plain washer	1L 18
2284	Spring washer	2C 11
2388	Pin	2G 02
2390	Split pin	1K 07
2392	Pin	1N 08
2393	Split pin	1K 07
2422	Split pin	1I 07
2427	Split pin	1G 12
2499	Locker	1H 09
2504	Locker	1G 10
2529	Screw 1/4 in whit X 3/4 in	1D 07
2556	Split pin	1D 06
2630	Plain washer	1G 07
2705	Spanner	1D 06
2707	Adjustable spanner	2F 16
2719	Plain washer	2J 07
2764	Plain washer	2I 11
2765	Plain washer	1L 18
2766	Split pin	1N 03
2822	Castle nut (7/16in BSF)	1G 05
2827	Nut 3/8in BSF)	1I 07
2828	Nut 5/16 in BSF	1G 03
2851	Plain washer	1G 08
2876	Plain washer	2F 02
2974	Pin	1G 12
2986	Rivet	1K 07
2995	Locker	2G 07
3035	Pin	1E 06
3036	Plain washer	1J 13
3101	Washer	1N 03
3109	Washer	1L 18

PART NO	DESCRIPTION	REF.NO.
3127	Split pin	2L 04
3200	Stud	1G 08
3236	Stud	1G 03
3238	Stud	1G 03
3259	Slotted nut	1G 07
3279	Special screw	1I 04
3289	Plug	1G 08
3290	Plug	1F 05
3291	Plug	1G 03
3292	Filler plug	1H 05
3294	Plug	1H 02
3299	Plain washer	1J 06
3300	Washer	1G 07
3319	Stud	1G 03
3359	Split pin	1L 05
3466	Nut	2C 14
3467	Plain washer	1N 15
3649	Selector spring	1G 11
3650	Stud	1G 08
3739	Steel ball	1C 05
3748	Steel ball	1E 05
3764	Locknut 7/6in BSF	1G 13
3783	Nut	1C 12
3816	Plain washer	1N 09
3817	Plain washer	2F 11
3819	Nut 1/4 in BSF	1F 04
3829	Plain washer	2F 07
3830	Plain washer	1I 05
3831	Plain washer	1K 03
3842	Plain washer	2G 02
3852	Plain washer	2F 07
3890	Screw	1L 18
3895	Plain washer	2G 08
3900	Plain washer	2F 09
3902	Plain washer	1I 04
3905	Locknut 1/2 in BSF	1L 18
3933	Washer	1L 18
3947	Plain washer	2H 03
3958	Split pin	1G 12
3966	Plain washer	1I 05
3972	Screw	1L 18
3982	Plain washer	2G 02
3996	Plain washer	2F 15
4022	Rivet	2H 04
4024	Nut (4 BA)	2D 04
4030	Plain washer	1E 08
4032	Plain washer	2I 06
4034	Plain washer	2D 10
4035	Plain washer	2F 08
4047	Plain washer	1C 08
4063	Split pin	1H 14
4075	Plain washer	2H 03
4082	Cable clip	2J 04
4085	Washer	1F 04

PART NO	DESCRIPTION	REF.NO.
4170	Cable clip	2J 04
4172	Packing washer	1N 10
4203	Plain washer	2I 07
4428	Plain washer	1N 10
4433	Plain washer	2F 03
4514	Washer	1N 05
4560	Rivet 1/2in X 1.1/4in	1H 10
4574	Plain washer	1K 08
4592	Plain washer	2F 12
4594	Plain washer	1J 10
4870	Plain washer	2F 06
5804	Plate	1G 11
5832	Cap nut	1M 03
5843	Cover plate	1G 03
5852	Oil retainer	1G 11
5853	Plate	1G 11
5854	Plate	1G 11
6397	Race	1G 04
6405	Peg	1G 04
6419	Clip	1G 03
6421	Selector fork	1G 11
6860	Rubber grommet	1K 03
6993	Float chamber	1M 02
7015	Cup washer	1D 17
7289	Dowel	1H 03
7316	Joint washer	1H 09
7829	Screw (10 UNF X 3/8in)	2D 03
8185	Washer	1G 05
8407	Splined end	1H 07
8566	Bush	1F 05
8885	Clip	1J 13
9093	Washer	1E 06
9161	Clamp	1D 16
9210	Locker	1E 06
9225	Shield	1D 06
9927	Dowel	1G 04
9938	Sealing ring	2C 05
9960	Circlip	1G 05
10025	Lid for float chamber	1M 02
10713	Plug	1E 14
11820	Clip	1K 03
12882	Emission pack	1M 06
20034	Woodscrew	2F 15
20138	Woodscrew	2I 12
20147	Woodscrew	2I 12
36666	Clip	1K 05
40441	Washer	2C 06
40742	Bolt (7/6in BSF X 2.3/16in)	1H 08
40756	Nut	1H 08
41045	Roller bearing	1H 09
41049	Locker	1H 08
41379	Clip	1K 03
42537	Pin	1F 02
46032	Pressure plate	1F 02
50216	Joint washer	1F 05

PART NO	DESCRIPTION	REF.NO.
50235	Brake catch	1K 07
50301	Clip	1M 04
50309	Clip	1D 10
50322	Clip	1D 12
50446	Pin	1J 08
50453	Grooved pin	1H 03
50499	Elbow	1L 08
50526	Nut (3/8IN BSF)	2K 11
50552	Special drive screw	2E 03
50637	Cable clip	2J 04
50639	Clip	1I 05
50640	Cable clip	2J 04
50641	Cable clip	2J 04
50642	Clip	1K 04
50690	Cable clip	2J 04
50702	Thrust washer	1G 04
50703	Thrust washer	1G 04
52124	Dowel	1E 02
52246	Screw	1G 03
52278	Washer	2C 05
53491	Dished washer	1M 08
55636	Dowel	1G 03
55638	Plunger	1G 11
55697	Peg	1G 11
55705	Dowel	1G 07
55714	Bearing	1G 05
55775	Peg	1G 11
55778	Stud 3/8 in whit X 1.3/4 in	1G 03
56102	Selector spring	1G 11
56140	Cover plate	1F 04
56666	Clip	1K 03
56667	Cable clip	2J 04
59663	Spring	1J 04
68087	Rivet	1O 04
72085	Stowage clip	2G 02
72626	Drive screw No 8 X 3/8 in	1K 02
72628	Drive screw	2D 06
73198	Rubber plug	2F 06
73962	Cup washer	2I 12
73979	Bifurcated rivet	2G 02
74838	Screw 2BA X 1 in	1J 10
76653	Screw 2BA X 1.1/8 in	1G 13
77626	Star washer	1G 05
77700	Screw 2BA X 1/2 in	2D 02
77758	Screw 2BA X 5/8 in	1K 03
77784	Screw 2BA X 1/2 in	2F 10
77861	Screw (2 BA X 3/4 in)	1I 03
77869	Screw 2BA X 1/2 in	1N 10
77899	Screw (4 BA X 1/2 in)	2D 04
77925	Screw 2BA X 7/8 in	2I 14
77932	Drive screw no 6 X 1/2 in	2G 11
77941	Screw	1L 17
77993	Screw	2I 06
78114	Shakeproof washer	1I 04
78120	Screw	2I 07

2M 04

PART NO	DESCRIPTION	REF.NO.
78159	Glazing strip	2F 07
78159	Glazing strip	2G 09
78173	Screw (2 BA X 3/4in)	1I 04
78177	Screw 2BA X 5/8 in	1K 06
78208	Special set bolt	1O 04
78210	Bolt 1/4 in UNF X 3/4 in	2F 09
78226	Rivet fixing strip	1O 04
78227	Drive screw no 10 X 1/2 in	1J 10
78233	Screw 1/4 in UNF X 5/8 in	2H 03
78237	Spire nut	1O 03
78248	Pop rivet	2H 03
78256	Lockwasher	2F 10
78257	Pop rivet	1O 05
78274	Screw 1/4 in UNF X 2 in	2E 06
78291	Screw 10 UNF X 5/8 in	2G 11
78296	Bolt	2O 03
78316	Screw (10 UNF X 1 1/4in)	2I 12
78318	Screw	1I 04
78321	Rivet	1F 09
78331	Bolt 5/16 in UNF X 5/8 in	2G 03
78352	Bolt 5/16 in UNF X 3/4 in	2F 13
78358	Screw 1/4 in UNF X 2.1/4 in	2I 06
78382	Screw	2G 11
78384	Screw 1/4 in UNF X 1 in	1L 14
78389	Spire nut	2H 03
78393	Drive screw	2F 03
78401	Drive screw	2G 09
78402	Rivet	2G 03
78410	Drive screw no 8 X 3/4 in	2H 04
78430	Drive screw	1O 05
78438	Screw	2I 06
78441	Drive screw	2E 02
78443	Rivet	2F 09
78697	Screw (1/4in UNF X 1/2in)	2O 14
78755	Special screw	1O 04
78795	Special screw (1/4in UNC X 1/2in)	1O 05
78796	Taptite screw 10UNF X 1/2 in	2F 07
78808	Taptite screw	2G 09
78832	Screw 1/4 in UNF X 5/8 in	2D 15
78898	Screw	1J 13
78905	Screw 2BA X 1/4 in	2O 10
78924	Drive screw no 10 X 3/8 in	1G 05
78977	Special bolt	2F 10
79048	Nut	2F 09
79051	Screw 10 UNF X 1.3/8 in	2G 02
79054	Spire nut	2E 04
79175	Special nut	2F 11
79239	Spire nut	2E 04
79246	Drive screw no 8 X 1/2 in	1O 04
79307	Ht wire	2F 03
80603	Seaming cord	2C 03
91171	Black canvas	2J 03
91291	Grey felt	2J 03
91414	Black felt	2J 03

2M 04

PART NO	DESCRIPTION	REF.NO.
91878	Cotton webbing	2J 03
91890	Felt	2J 03
91913	Black cloth	2J 03
91950	Leather cloth	2J 03
91957	Cotton duck	2J 03
91965	Felted plastic	2J 03
91979	Leather cloth	2J 03
92088	Cotton webbing	2J 03
92496	Sheet wadding	2J 03
92616	Leathercloth	2J 03
92625	Leathercloth dull black	1H 08
100897	Pinion bearing	1M 02
108353	Taper pin	1L 09
108364	Union	1F 08
108771	Retainer	2D 02
139082	Adaptor	1D 10
142001	Rim	2D 15
149996	Flame trap	1G 11
150844	Mounting pad	1G 11
210203	Stop	1D 13
210204	Locker	1G 07
210492	Core plug	1D 08
211502	Seal	1D 08
212160	Cap	1D 06
212161	Circlip	1C 02
212309	Bush	1C 02
212430	Locker	1J 02
212919	Spring for piston	1J 02
212943	Spring for piston	1I 07
213340	Oil seal	1G 05
213416	Nut	1G 05
213417	Stud	1G 05
213419	Plate	1G 11
213637	Shaft	1F 07
213660	Thrust washer	1F 07
213661	Cover plate	1G 05
213666	Retaining plate	1C 02
213700	Dowel	1C 07
213744	Oil seal	1D 09
214058	Joint washer	2D 10
214090	Shouldered stud	1C 12
214223	Switch	1C 12
214228	Clip	2C 03
214229	Rubber grommet	1I 07
214262	Spark plug cover	1I 07
214649	Rubber cover	1G 05
214662	Retainer	1F 07
214685	Spring ring	1G 05
214792	Bearing plate	1F 07
214793	Bush	1G 05
214794	Bush	2K 10
214795	Circlip	1C 04
214965	Circlip	
214995	Bush oil pump	

2M 05

PART NO	DESCRIPTION	REF.NO.
215170	Bolt (5/16in BSF X 1 19/32in)	1G 08
215531	Bolt (3/8in BSF X 1 19/32in)	1H 07
215599	Bolt 1/4 in whit X 1.1/4 in	1G 03
215703	Bolt (3/8in whit X 1in)	2C 07
215808	Clevis complete	1G 12
215809	Clevis complete	1J 07
216421	Clevis pin	1G 13
216708	Clip	1L 16
216912	Nut	1F 08
216914	Gasket	1J 11
217268	Bearing for swivel pin	1H 04
217325	Bearing	1G 09
217330	Circlip	1G 07
217352	Key washer	1H 07
217353	Locker	1H 07
217354	Bush driving shaft	1H 05
217361	Wheel nut	2H 03
217400	Oil seal	1H 02
217421	Swivel pin & bracket	1H 04
217445	Spring	1G 13
217453	Shim .005in	1H 04
217454	Shim .010in	1H 04
217455	Shim .030in	1H 04
217476	Locker	1G 04
217477	Nut	1G 08
217478	Retaining plate	1G 07
217484	Bearing	1G 07
217490	Bearing	1H 08
217507	Oil seal	1G 08
217523	Plate	1G 07
217525	Circlip	1G 08
217546	Circlip	1G 07
217565	Bolt 5/16 in BSF X 29/32 in	1G 07
217568	Bolt 3/8 in BSF X 1.2 in	1G 07
217620	Retainer	1G 07
217622	Shim	1G 08
217623	Shim	1G 08
217694	Shim	1I 07
217735	Flange plate	1G 10
217778	Knob	1G 08
217781	Stud	2C 10
217811	Lockwasher	1G 04
217970	Housing	1G 08
217977	Plate	1G 08
217978	Stud	1G 08
217985	Stud	1K 09
218243	Felt ring	1G 07
218244	High gear	1G 04
218293	Mainshaft gear	1J 02
218382	Spring	1K 07
218386	Rachet	1J 06
218409	Bush	1K 09
218453	Plate	2F 02
218508	Crossmember	2J 07
	Starting handle	2M 05

PART NO	DESCRIPTION	REF.NO.
218983	Pull off spring	1J 02
219098	Hub cap	1H 07
219466	Bearing	1G 07
219468	Gear	1G 07
219469	Thrsut washer	1G 07
219521	Knob	1G 13
219544	Pinion bearing	1H 09
219547	Shim	1H 08
219548	Shim	1H 08
219549	Shim	1N 09
219673	Special screw	1O 03
219677	Clip	2J 05
219680	Grommet	2J 07
219704	Tool roll	1G 13
219709	Bracket	1G 10
219714	Lever housing	1G 10
219721	Seat	1G 10
219722	Plate	1G 10
219723	Spring	1F 07
219768	Seal	1G 10
219797	Circlip	1G 10
219995	Joint washer	1G 08
230007	Shim. 003	1H 04
230034	Distance piece	1D 09
230062	Washer	1D 13
230086	Bush	1G 12
230140	Joint washer	1G 08
230184	Distance piece	1I 07
230250	Core plug 11/16 in dia	1C 10
230251	Core plug	1D 13
230279	Pin and housing	1G 12
230294	Retainer for seal	1I 07
230313	Key	1C 05
230438	Shim	1H 09
230439	Shim	1H 09
230440	Shim	1H 03
230511	Joint washer for drain plug	1H 08
230696	Housing assy	1G 08
230736	Spanner	2J 07
230759	Spring	1I 07
230760	Washer	1I 07
230858	Cone seat	1H 04
230939	Lever	1N 05
231071	Housing	1F 07
231074	Sleeve	1F 07
231075	Sleeve	1F 07
231116	Spring	1G 10
231155	Piston ring	1D 05
231190	Chain	1L 17
231218	Cover	1D 03
231219	Joint washer	1D 03
231234	Harness carrier	2C 06
231242	Washer	1H 08
231318	Pin	1K 07
231341	Stud	1G 03
231343	Screw	1D 09
231344	Spacer	1D 09
		2M 06

PART NO	DESCRIPTION	REF.NO.
231348	Rocker shaft	1D 09
231349	Rocker shaft	1D 09
231352	Special washer	1D 09
231393	Return spring	1N 07
231576	Washer	1D 14
231577	Joint washer	1C 11
231601	Road wheel	1H 16
231737	Thrust washer	1H 09
231883	Spring	1G 04
231888	Cover plate	1F 03
231943	Shaft	1F 07
232006	Washer	1M 03
232037	Sealing washer	1C 11
232038	Joint washer	1H 07
232039	Joint washer	1C 11
232040	Washer	1C 11
232C44	Washer	1D 11
232074	Spring post	1C 04
232107	Washer	1J 02
232415	Oil thrower	1J 02
232425	Clip	1G 04
232464	Pin	1L 16
232497	Stud	1G 12
232557	Nipple	1G 08
222565	Retaining plate	1H 07
232566	Retaining plate	1G 07
232604	Grommet	2D 10
232608	Plate	1G 02
232647	Centre for dust cover	1G 10
232813	Knob	1G 02
232816	Pinion insert	1G 12
233017	Shakeproof washer	1G 08
233211	Spring	2D 10
233220	Washer	1J 03
233241	Locking dog	1K 02
233243	Rubber grommet	1G 09
233244	Grommet	2D 10
233274	Clip	2I 13
233326	Spring chain tensioner	1K 05
233328	Retainer	1C 05
233398	Shaft	1E 06
233406	Selector shaft block	1G 13
233407	Coupling	1G 12
233409	Shouldered pin	1G 12
233416	Shaft	1G 12
233419	Rubber ring	1G 12
233437	Bush	1D 13
233438	Tube	1G 13
233441	Plug	1G 13
233449	Spring	1G 12
233520	Banjo bolt	1G 12
233566	Grommet	2J 05
233625	Shackle pin	1H 15
233677	Shim	1H 08
233678	Shim	1H 09
233770	Clip	2D 07

2M 06

PART NO	DESCRIPTION	REF.NO.
234532	Nipple	1H 07
234603	Bolt (2BA X 1/2in)	1L 10
234658	Collar	1G 12
234835	Shim	1G 07
234889	Spring	1J 03
234928	T piece	1K 02
235113	Grommet	2D 11
235416	Plunger	1G 13
235438	Low gear	1G 07
235455	Shim	1G 08
235592	Plug	1G 08
235726	Chainwheel	1E 03
235731	Locker	2H 04
235770	Key	1C 03
235968	Retainer	1H 05
235985	Rear outpost shaft	1G 07
236022	Joint washer	1C 11
236060	Union	1C 08
236067	Idler wheel	1C 05
236070	Drain plug	1H 03
236072	Mudshield	1H 08
236074	Mudshield	1G 07
236173	Pistongring	1D 05
236174	Piston ring	1D 05
236175	Piston ring	1D 05
236176	Piston ring	1D 05
236257	Dowel	1D 06
236281	Grommet	1G 02
236305	Seal	1G 04
236365	Harness clip	2J 04
236366	Clip	2D 07
236389	Grommet	1I 05
236407	Union nut	1C 08
236408	Olive	1C 08
236541	Retainer	1G 09
236546	Mudshield	1H 08
236547	Retainer	1H 08
236548	Mudshield	1G 09
236630	Flange	1G 07
236632	Mudshield	1H 08
236658	Pedal shaft	1N 02
236665	Accelerator shaft bracket	1N 02
236891	Bowl	1L 09
236895	Joint washer for bowl	1M 11
236896	Bowl only	1M 11
236969	Shackle pin	1H 15
236993	Anchor for brake shoe	1J 02
236995	Locking plate	1J 02
236998	Accelerator shaft bracket	1N 02
237100	Check strap	2F 02
237119	Set bolt (2 BA X 3/8 in)	1C 11
237121	Bolt 2BA X 5/8 in long	1L 13
237138	Plug	1I 07
237139	Bolt 1/4 in BSF X 1/2 in	1G 10

2M 07

PART NO	DESCRIPTION	REF.NO.
237160	Bolt (5/16in BSF Xin)	1G 11
237161	Bolt (5/16in BSF X 5/8in)	1K 09
237179	Bolt (3/8in BSF X 1 1/8in)	1K 07
237251	Stud	1G 08
237279	Cable clip	2J 04
237324	Bolt (5/16in BSF X 7/8in)	1F 04
237339	Bolt 3/8in BSF X 1in	1H 09
237340	Bolt (3/8in BSF X 1 1/4in)	1H 03
237357	Set bolt (7/16in BSF X 1.3/8in)	1H 03
238180	Relay lever assy	1J 06
238329	Link	1G 13
238542	Special screw	1J 02
238553	Cone bearing for swivel pin top	1H 04
238793	Bearing	1N 06
238871	Retainer	1D 09
239017	Swivel pin	1H 03
239272	Split ring	1G 04
239449	Bracket	1D 03
239558	Cable battery to earth	2E 03
239564	Speedometer miles	2D 10
239565	Speedometer kilometres	2B 10
239600	Clip	2D 10
239673	Clip	1N 08
239688	Lead	2E 08
239716	Bracket	1N 13
240102	Acorn nut	2E 02
240234	Retainer for bowl	1M 11
240235	Screw cap for retainer	1M 11
240406	Clip	2D 07
240407	Clip	2D 10
240408	Rubber boot	2C 03
240417	Clip	2D 10
240428	Cleat	2C 06
240429	Cleat	2C 06
240431	Cable cleat	1I 04
240555	Driver gear - oil pump	1C 04
240708	Anchor for spring	1J 07
240829	Shaft hand brake lever	1J 06
240836	Screw driver	2J 07
240908	Panel light switch	2D 10
241090	Linings with rivets	1J 02
241223	Gauze for bowl	1M 11
241283	Spring	1H 15
241380	Rubber buffer	2F 02
241387	Felt washer	2D 10
241388	Thrust washer	1I 07
241445	Spring	1H 15
241446	Spring	1H 15
241598	Plate	1G 11
241649	Distance piece	1G 05
241650	Distance piece	1G 05
241651	Distance piece	1G 05
241690	4 way piece	1K 02
241839	Locker	1G 08

2M 07

PART NO	DESCRIPTION	REF.NO.
241958	Retaining ring	2K 14
242108	Plunger	1K 07
242109	Washer	1K 07
242117	Washer	1J 02
242127	U bolt	1H 15
242319	Adaptor	1M 04
242375	Joint washer	1M 04
242399	Filler cap for alternator	10 02
242520	Stub shafr	1H 03
242522	Circlip	1H 07
242669	Bracket	2C 10
242675	Bolt	2C 10
242742	Spring for cone bearing	1H 04
242863	Spring	1H 15
242958	Bush	2C 04
242996	Eyebolt	1F 02
243022	Plain washer	1H 14
243095	Grease cap	2C 04
243121	Main leaf	1H 15
243123	Main leaf	1H 15
243124	2nd leaf	1H 15
243126	2nd leaf	1H 15
243130	Dowel	1H 15
243131	Dowel	1H 15
243395	Clip=	1L 10
243611	Shaft	1G 09
243618	Stud	2I 12
243714	Spring	1G 13
243873	Oil thrower	1G 09
243958	Washer	1C 08
243959	Joint washer	1C 02
243960	Joint washer	1E 14
243967	Joint washer	1L 09
243968	Joint washer	1C 02
243970	Washer	1C 04
243971	Joint washer	1D 06
243972	Joint washer	1D 13
244150	Bearing for halfshaft	1H 03
244151	Distance piece for brg	1H 03
244162	Plate	1H 15
244163	Plate	1H 15
244487	Lock washer	1C 04
244488	Sealing ring	1C 04
244700	Bulb holder	2D 02
244705	Cover band	2C 04
244706	Bracket	2C 04
244709	Nut for pinion	2C 04
244711	Pinion & sleeve	2C 04
244713	Bracket	2C 04
244714	Bush	2C 04
244715	Armature	2C 04
244717	Bolt	2C 04
244718	Sundry parts kit	2C 04
245003	Clamping plate	2C 02
245008	Distributor cam	2C 02

2M 08

PART NO	DESCRIPTION	REF.NO.
245131	Hinge centre	2H 04
245258	Economiser union	1M 03
245261	Oil cap	1M 02
245266	Union	1M 03
245278	Union	1M 03
245279	Banjo	1M 03
245295	Union	1M 02
245384	Clip for condenser	1M 08
245766	2nd speed gear	1G 04
245767	3rd speed gear	1G 05
245940	Plunger	1D 06
246169	Seal ring	1F 02
246464	Dowel	1C 03
246565	Anchor plate	1J 03
246566	Anchor plate	1J 03
246569	Lining with rivets	1J 03
247040	Spring	1E 07
247051	Bolt (1/2in UNF X 4.9/16in)	1E 11
247070	Joint washer for cover	1C 05
247078	Special set bolt	1C 09
247121	Special nut	1C 10
247135	Plug	1C 02
247143	Bolt (7/16in UNF X 7/8in)	1F 02
247144	Stud	1E 11
247145	Stud	1C 10
247146	Stud	1F 05
247153	Washer	1F 02
247166	Special bolt	1E 07
247175	Stud	1F 05
247179	Stud	1F 02
247186	Joint washer	1L 10
247199	Sealing ring inlet valve guide	1C 10
247212	Special bolt	1C 05
247213	Joint washer	2C 03
247526	Clamp	1L 10
247554	Flywheel housing	1F 02
247555	Joint washer	1C 08
247583	Joint washer	1C 08
247607	Bush	1E 04
247614	Stud	1E 07
247624	Bush valve rocker	1C 06
247631	Cover for rubber washer	1C 10
247634	Engine breather filter	1C 11
247651	Tappet clearance plate	1C 10
247653	Exhaust manifold	1E 14
247664	Bush	1C 04
247665	Oil filter oil pump	1C 04
247683	Lockwasher	1C 04
247709	Bolt	1E 11
247715	Camshaft	1C 05
247723	Bracket	1E 12
247726	Bolt	1E 11
247737	Nozzle	1L 10
	Bush	1E 07

2M 08

PART NO	DESCRIPTION	REF.NO.
247738	Bush	1E 07
247742	Circlip	1C 04
247755	Set bolt (9/16in UNF X 3 1/4in)	1C 02
247758	Spring washer	1C 02
247766	Mud excluder	1C 07
247771	Locker	1C 03
247802	Joint washer	1L 09
247806	Driving shaft	2C 03
247811	Butterfly valve	1C 13
247818	Bi-metal spring	1C 13
247819	Stop pin	1C 13
247824	Joint washer	1C 13
247861	Plug	1C 02
247912	Piston chain adjuster	1E 06
247916	Impellor	1C 09
247929	Union	1L 09
247952	Lead	1E 12
247953	Lead	1E 12
247965	Plug	1C 02
248720	Bolt (1/2in BSF X 2 in)	1G 02
249473	Circlip	1H 13
250431	Wing nut	2F 02
250517	Bolt (1/4in BSF X 1 1/2in)	11 08
250543	Bolt (3/8in BSF X 1 1/2in)	2C 07
250544	Bolt (3/8in BSF X 1 3/4in)	1G 08
250551	Bolt (3/8in BSF X 3 1/2in)	1H 15
250693	Bolt (1/4in BSF X 5/8in)	1G 11
250696	Bolt (1/4in BSF X 1in)	1H 05
250830	Core plug	1C 10
250840	Core plug	1C 02
250962	Bolt (2BA X 7/8in)	1C 11
251002	Set bolt (2BA X 7/8in)	1G 11
251018	Bolt (2BA X 9/16in)	1F 07
251320	S.L. nut 1/4 in BSF	1J 02
251321	S.L. nut 5/16 in BSF	1F 02
251322	Nut (7/16in BSF)	1H 15
251323	Nut 3/8 in BSF	1G 02
251324	Nut (1/2in BSF)	1G 09
251335	S.L. nut 2BA	1G 12
251601	Nut (5/16in BSF)	1H 14
252164	Nyloc nut 1/2in UNF	1H 15
252165	Nut (9/16in UNF)	1L 08
252210	Self locking nut (1/4in UNF)	1N 12
252220	Nut (1/4in UNF)	1D 13
252497	Stud	1D 13
252500	Stud	1D 07
252501	Stud	1D 13
252514	Stud	1C 12
252515	Stud	1D 13
252621	Stud	1C 02
252622	Stud	1C 02
252623	Stud	1D 16
252627	Stud	1D 03
252638	Stud	1D 03

2M 09

PART NO	DESCRIPTION	REF.NO.
253003	Set bolt (1/4in UNC X 7/16in)	1D 13
253029	Bolt 5/16 in UNC X 1.1/8 in	1N 11
253205	Bolt (1/4in UNC X 9/16in)	2C 03
253405	Set bolt (3/8in UNC X 3/4in)	1N 12
253406	Set bolt (3/8in UNC X 7/8in)	1N 12
253817	Bolt 7/16in UNF X 6.1/2in	1H 14
253826	Bolt 7/16in UNF X 7.1/4in	1H 14
253905	Bolt (3/8in UNF X 5/8in)	1E 12
254823	Nut (7/16in UNF)	2C 09
254850	Special locknut 1/4 in UNF	1N 05
254852	Special nut (3/8in UNF)	1K 02
254911	Nut (5/16in UNF)	1E 08
255003	Bolt 1/4in UNF X 7/16in	1N 11
255029	Set bolt (5/16in UNF X 1.1/8in)	1C 13
255030	Bolt (5/6in UNF X 1/4in)	1F 08
255050	Bolt 3/8in UNF X 1.3/8in	11 06
255202	Bolt (1/4in UNF X 3.8in)	1J 08
255204	Set bolt (1/4in UNF X 1/2in)	1C 05
255205	Bolt (1/4in UNF X 9/16in)	1C 05
255206	Bolt (1/4in UNF X 5/8in)	1C 12
255207	Bolt (1/4in UNF X 3/4in)	1C 09
255208	Bolt (1/4in UNF X 7/8in)	1C 03
255211	Bolt (1/4in UNF X 1 1/4in)	1N 02
255219	Bolt 1/4 in UNF X 2.1/2 in	21 09
255220	Self locking nut (1/4in UNF)	1N 14
255223	Bolt (5/16in UNF X 1/2in)	1N 02
255227	Set bolt (5/16in UNF X 7/8in)	1C 04
255229	Bolt (5/16in UNF X 1.1/8in)	2G 10
255237	Bolt (5/16in UNF X 2 1/4in)	2C 13
255245	Bolt (3/8in UNF X 3/4in)	1N 15
255248	Bolt (3/8in UNF X 1.1/8in)	1F 02
255288	Bolt (3/8in UNF X 1.1/4in)	1K 08
255426	Screw 1/2 in UNF X 1.3/8 in	2F 07
255427	Bolt (5/16in UNF X 3/4in)	2C 13
256004	Bolt (5/16in UNF X 7/8in)	1F 02
256025	Bolt (1/4in UNF X 1in)	2C 13
256203	Bolt (5/16in UNF X 1.5/8in)	1D 12
256223	Bolt 1/4in UNF X 1.1/2 in	1N 10
256233	Bolt (5/16in UNF X 1.5/8in)	1F 10
256280	Bolt (5/16in UNF X 3.3/4in)	1C 09
256295	Bolt (1/2 in UNF X 1.5/8 in	2F 07
256410	Bolt (1/3in UNF X 5in)	2L 09
256421	Bolt (1/4in UNF X 2 3/4in)	1D 12
256429	Bolt (5/16in UNF X 2 3/4in)	2C 10
256801	Nut (5/16in UNC)	1C 13
257004	Bolt (10 UNF X 7/16in)	1N 06
257015	Bolt (10 UNF X 3/8in)	1E 08
257017	Bolt (10 UNF X 1/2in)	2E 05
257019	Bolt 10 UNF X 5/8 in	1M 04
257022	Bolt 10 UNF X 1 in	2E 04
257023	Nut 10 UNF	2F 11
		1M 04

2M 09

PART NO	DESCRIPTION	REF.NO.
260140	Special screw	1L 02
260166	Banjo union	1L 04
260167	Special bolt	1L 04
260585	End plate	1M 08
260707	Screwed union	1L 02
260708	Olive	1L 02
260714	Spring washer	1L 04
260725	Needle valve	1L 04
260823	Steel ball	1I 03
261238	Spring set	1I 03
261252	Rubber grommet	2C 10
261414	Seal	2D 02
261483	Brush set dynamo	1L 08
261503	Wiper arm	2C 10
261850	Bush for rocker shaft	2D 13
261857	Joint washer	1I 02
261858	Joint washer	1I 02
261862	Main nut assy	1I 03
261865	Main nut assy	1I 03
261869	Roller for main nut	1I 03
261873	Adjuster screw	1I 03
261874	Locknut	1I 03
262303	Spring washer	1M 08
262305	Lead washer	1M 08
262307	Terminal screw	1M 08
262309	Terminal nut	1M 09
262313	Special screw	1L 03
262342	Light unit	2D 02
262468	Splined end	1H 07
262469	Flange	1H 07
262703	Bush and spring	2C 02
262860	Field coil	2C 10
263878	Sleeve	1G 05
264024	Plain washer	1H 14
264250	Mainshaft	1G 04
264362	Spring restrictor	1N 02
264563	Spring	1H 15
264591	Gudgeon pin	1D 05
264767	Bulb	2I 13
264782	Sealing washer	1J 10
264806	Bulb holder	2D 02
264807	Spring	1F 07
265038	Fork	1F 07
265169	Banjo bolt	1D 06
265175	Gudgeon pin	1C 03
265295	Circlip	1C 03
265461	Roof lamp	2I 13
265482	Dowel	1H 15
265569	Lead	2I 13
265627	Bush	1F 07
265642	Spring	1H 15
265779	Plate	1C 03
265969	Bush	1F 07

PART NO	DESCRIPTION	REF.NO.
266321	Valve seat insert	1D 13
266661	Tensioner	1D 07
266662	Camshaft chain	1D 07
266684	Wheel cylinder kit	1J 03
266687	Wheel cylinder kit	1J 02
266694	Slave cylinder	1F 08
266752	Swivel pin kit	2J 02
266900	Oil strainer	1D 06
266945	Circlip	1E 04
266955	Distance piece	1G 13
266956	Dust cover	1G 09
266992	Seal	1G 12
267193	Shaft hand brake lever	1J 06
267412	Anchor for spring	1J 07
267451	Spring chain adjuster	1C 05
267494	Fuel sediment bowl complete	1M 11
267572	Thrust washer	1G 04
267573	Thrust washer	1G 04
267574	Thrust washer	1G 04
267575	Thrust washer	1G 04
267601	Banjo bolt	1J 11
267721	Joint washer for union	1M 12
267782	Joint washer	1G 07
267828	Sealing washer	1G 10
267829	Drive shaft	1D 06
267837	Joint washer	1L 18
268053	Bearing	1F 07
268292	Valve spring cap	1C 06
268293	Split cone for valve halves	1C 06
268791	Sleeve	1G 07
268793	Body only	1M 11
268847	Lever	1G 12
268849	Housing	2D 09
268883	Clip	2D 12
268887	Filter sealing ring	1C 11
269132	Stop clip	1N 02
269257	Grommet	2J 05
269265	Halfshaft complete for front axle R H	1H 03
269266	Halfshaft complete for front axle L H	1H 03
269267	Track rod assy	1I 07
269269	Track rod only	1I 07
269413	Stud	1G 02
269783	Distance piece	1C 08
269889	Rubber washer	1C 11
269960	Casing assy	1G 03
270105	Olive	1L 10
270115	Nut (1/4in BSP)	1L 10
270235	Circlip	2C 08
270251	Sundry parts kit	2C 08
270287	Rocker	1H 04
270297	Bracket	1L 13
270420	Battery bolt	2F 02
270520	Plate	1H 15
270521	Plate	1H 15
270656	Tube of silicone grease 1oz	1C 03

PART NO	DESCRIPTION	REF.NO.
270741	Shackle pin	1H 15
271013	O ring	1I 03
271014	Washer	1I 02
271367	Inner column	1I 03
271368	Inner column	1I 02
271372	Rocker shaft	1I 03
271378	End plate	1I 03
271379	Joint washer	1I 02
271380	Bolt (5/16in UNC X 29/32in)	1I 03
271382	Bolt (5/16in UNC X 1.1/16in)	1I 03
271384	Adjustable race	1I 03
271386	Plug	2C 10
271614	Bush	1L 18
271872	Elbow	1E 11
271881	Peg	2D 08
271931	Lens	1I 03
272181	Side cover plate	1G 08
272185	Bracket	1H 16
272309	Road wheel	1D 03
272451	Gallery pipe	1D 03
272452	Water pipe	1D 03
272474	Joint washer	1C 14
272498	Engine mounting	1C 14
272501	Engine mounting	1C 14
272506	Engine mounting	1C 14
272512	Grommet	1L 10
272539	Gasket - oil filter	1C 11
272596	Seal	1G 11
272597	Seal	1G 11
272632	Pedal bracket	1J 08
272712	Shaft pedal	1J 08
272713	Pedal bracket cover	1J 08
272714	Bush for pedal	1J 08
272729	Return spring	1J 10
272749	Bolt	1F 03
272784	Indicator	1N 02
272804	Bracket pedal shaft	1J 09
272819	Gasket	1H 09
272835	Joint washer	1H 09
272922	Locker	1H 09
272934	Set bolt	1F 10
273069	Sealing washer	1C 10
273077	Clutch shaft & lever	1F 02
273163	Bush	1D 05
273166	Plug	1C 02
273306	Rocker shaft	1D 09
273307	Rocker shaft	1D 09
273308	Spacing washer	1D 09
273309	Spacing washer	1D 09
273370	Split rubber grommet	2D 10
273441	Diff case assy	2D 10
273521	Banjo bolt	1H 09
273711	Plunger	1C 04
273883	Sleeve	1H 13

PART NO	DESCRIPTION	REF.NO.
273937	Inspection lamp socket red	2D 10
273964	Ball end	1M 03
274084	Housing assy	1D 06
274086	Special screw	1D 06
274089	Nut (5/16in UNF)	1D 10
274091	Special nut	1D 10
274093	Bolt (3/8in UNF X 29/32in)	1D 13
274100	Plate	1D 14
274104	Joint washer	1D 15
274115	Bearing	1D 07
274116	Bearing	1D 07
274117	Bearing	1D 07
274118	Special screw	1D 07
274145	Swivel pin & steering lever R H	1H 03
274146	Swivel pin & steering lever R H	1H 03
274147	Swivel pin & steering lever L H	1H 03
274148	Swivel pin & steering lever L H	1H 03
274378	Adaptor	2D 02
274379	Headlamp rim	2D 02
274423	Brake drum	1J 07
274469	Check strap	2F 02
274609	Joint washer	1D 15
274711	Camshaft	1E 06
274737	Distance piece	1D 12
274773	Rocker	1E 07
274774	Rocker	1E 07
274775	Rocker	1E 07
274928	Oil feed bolt	1D 06
274963	Throttle stop	1M 02
274964	Gland washer	1M 02
274965	Spring	1M 02
274966	Gland washer	1M 02
274967	Retainer cap	1M 02
274979	Spring	1M 03
274980	Top plate	1J 06
275199	Clevis fork end	1C 05
275234	Vibration damper	2K 08
275238	Flange	1L 10
275265	Joint washer	1L 10
275266	Banjo bolt	1L 09
275565	Joint washer	1E 12
275679	Pipe	1N 09
275706	Housing	1N 09
275709	Lever and ball end	1N 09
275713	Quadrant plate	1N 09
275714	Bush	1N 09
275715	Washer	1N 07
275744	Wheel cyl kit	1J 10
275769	Oil pipe	1C 11
275836	Oil pipe	1D 03
276013	Lever	1N 09
276014	Control rod	1N 09
276015	Joint pin	1N 09
276034	Spring	1H 15

2M 11

PART NO	DESCRIPTION	REF.NO.
276053	Grommet	2J 05
276054	Grommet	2J 05
276133	Chainwheel	1E 06
276201	Nipple	1H 07
276317	Stop tail lamp	2D 02
276322	Plug spanner	2J 07
276323	Plug spanner extension	2J 07
276396	Spanner	2J 07
276397	Spanner	2J 07
276426	Hose	1L 08
276482	Castle nut (7/16 UNF)	1I 07
276484	Rubber gaiter assy	1H 02
276511	Bracket	1F 02
276541	Joint washer	1D 07
276719	Halfshaft only R H	1H 03
276720	Halfshaft only L H	1H 03
276784	Steering tube	1H 08
277103	Accelerator shaft housing	1N 02
277105	Accelerator lever assy	1N 02
277106	Lever assy	1N 03
277120	Bush	1N 03
277153	Pedal shaft	1N 02
277154	Accelerator cross shaft	1N 02
277217	Spanner	2J 07
277259	Filler tube complete	1L 17
277260	Filler cap	1M 10
277261	Filler tube	1M 10
277262	Extension for filler tube	1M 10
277311	Locker	1H 05
277320	Spanner	2J 07
277388	Cylinder - chain adjuster	1C 05
277450	Bell crank	1N 08
277453	Bush	1N 08
277454	Pin - bell crank	1N 08
277455	Return spring	1N 03
277473	Acc lever	1N 07
277475	Accelerator lever	1N 02
277478	Engine stop control	1N 08
277490	Square nut (1/4in UNF)	1N 10
277491	Locking plate	1M 10
277502	Spring	1N 08
277532	Stud	1F 05
277565	Anchor	1N 08
277593	Inlet valve	1C 06
277612	Acc lever	1N 08
277778	Nut	1N 07
277779	Control rod	1N 07
277840	Support bracket reservoir tank	1J 10
277921	Brake rod	1J 06
277922	Brake pipe	2L 14
277923	Brake pipe	1K 02
277929	Pipe tank to master cylinder	1J 11
277930	Pipe 3/16 in clutch master cylinder to hose	1J 11
277956	Dowel	1C 06

2M 12

PART NO	DESCRIPTION	REF.NO.
277961	Bell housing	1G 02
277999	Bracket	2C 10
278000	Steady bracket	2C 10
278002	Strap	1L 10
278010	Clip	2D 10
278020	Brake rod	1J 06
278021	Strap	1K 07
278025	Shaft	1G 07
278109	Idler gear - oil pump	1C 04
278161	Liner	1C 13
278162	Packing	1C 12
278163	Joint washer	1C 13
278164	Plug	1D 13
278386	Special screw	1H 09
278490	Cable clip	2J 04
278690	Return spring	1F 10
278698	Check strap	2F 02
279014	Brake shoe starter	2C 08
279015	Driving washer	2C 09
279019	Bolt for starter motor	2C 09
279168	Spindle	1C 13
279169	Weight	1C 13
279340	Speedometer - miles	2D 10
279341	Speedometer - kilometres	2D 10
279412	5 way piece	1K 02
279413	Plug	1D 03
279415	Plug	1D 03
279418	Brake pipe	1K 03
279452	Brake pipe	1K 03
279648	Special set bolt	1C 10
279650	Set bolt (1/2in UNF X 6 11/16in)	1C 10
279651	Elbow	1L 08
279652	Air cleaner	1L 08
279653	Hose clip	1H 15
279678	Spring	1H 15
279679	Spring	1L 09
279702	Plugs	1H 15
279969	Plate	1H 15
279970	Plate	1M 10
300692	Bonnet fastener	2L 17
300693	Staple	2L 17
300715	Clip	1I 05
300716	Rubber strip	1I 08
300783	Rivet	2G 03
300784	Rivet	2G 08
300789	Rivet	2G 03
300816	Grab handle	2F 02
300824	Bonnet rest strip 35in long	1D 04
300851	Turnbuckle	2F 10
300924	Staple for hood	2G 03
301005	Hook	2I 14
301437	Seal	2F 09
301470	Panel	2I 14
301476	Rod	2I 14

2M 12

PART NO	DESCRIPTION	REF.NO.
301879	Rivet	2G 02
302177	Weather strip	2G 11
302178	Filler strip	2G 11
302186	Rivet	2G 03
302222	Rivet	2F 12
302229	Rivet	2I 15
302371	Rubber washer	2G 11
302373	Rubber washer	2G 11
302533	Bolt	2F 09
302648	Strap	2I 14
302818	Rivet	2G 11
302825	Chain bracket	2G 03
302828	Clevis pin	2G 03
302854	Bracket	2F 13
302933	Tie bar	2G 02
302934	Wing nut	2G 02
302954	Bracket	2G 08
302986	Support bracket	11 05
302987	Rubber seal	2D 13
303729	Wing nut	2F 08
303750	Special bolt	10 04
303809	Rubber interior	2I 12
303817	Retainer	2F 09
303828	Cover plate	2F 09
303847	Spare wheel clamp	2G 02
303875	Hinge complete	2F 10
303975	Sealing rubber	2G 08
303990	Cover panel	2F 05
303995	Rubber seal	11 03
303996	Special washer	11 03
303997	Cover steering column	11 03
304054	Pad	2I 12
304111	Cover panel	2F 05
304125	Buffer	2H 04
304401	Lid for locker	2G 04
304874	Tread plate	2G 08
305232	Shim	2H 04
306295	Buffer	2H 03
306316	Seat base panel	2I 12
306326	Retaining strap	2I 12
306407	Nameplate	2G 03
306460	Door pull handle	2I 03
306471	Buffer	2F 08
306474	Check strap assy	2F 08
306564	Clevis pin	2F 08
307220	Rubber plug	2F 06
307289	Key zeni type	2H 02
307418	Finisher	2I 12
307419	Finisher	2I 12
307420	Finisher	2I 12
307840	Rivet	2H 05
307977	Door handle	2F 13
308136	Hinge	2I 10
308137	Hinge	2I 10
308206	Tread plate	2G 05

2M 13

PART NO	DESCRIPTION	REF.NO.
310877	Rubber buffer for front apron panel	10 04
311373	Shakeproof washer	2E 02
312027	Buffer	2H 10
312028	Rubber buffer	2I 12
312856	Grommet	2I 13
312937	Grommet	1N 09
313385	Nut	1L 17
314203	Screw	2F 14
314394	Spire nut	2I 02
315264	Clip	2I 10
320045	Special bolt	2F 10
320084	Rear seat backrest assy	2I 14
320276	Diesel badge	10 05
320333	Fixing bracket for badge	10 05
320500	Circlip	2F 07
320521	Seat base	2I 14
320604	Tailboard	2F 03
320608	Lens	2I 13
320609	Barrel lock	2H 02
320633	Anchorage kit	2I 08
320634	Anchorage kit	2I 08
320635	Anchorage kit	2I 08
320636	Anchorage kit	2I 08
320638	Anchorage kit	2I 08
320658	Rear body complete assembly	2G 04
320674	Cushion	2I 14
320679	Trim casing	2I 03
320682	Sidelight casing	2I 02
320683	Sidelight casing	2I 02
320684	Sidelight casing	2I 02
320685	Sidelight casing	2I 02
320686	Cant rail trim	2I 02
320687	Cant rail trim	2I 02
320698	Seat squab	2I 06
320699	Cushion	2I 06
320701	Seat squab	2I 06
320702	Seat squab	2I 12
320703	Seat backrest	2I 06
320708	Seat squab	2I 06
320710	Seat squab	2I 06
320711	Cant rail trim	2I 04
320712	Cant rail trim	2I 05
320713	Door trim	2I 05
320714	Door trim	2I 05
320715	Door trim	2I 05
320716	Door trim	2I 05
320719	Cushion	2I 15
320726	Cushion	2I 07
320743	Seat cushion	2I 07
320826	Cushion	2I 12
320853	Sidescreen assy	2F 12
320854	Sidescreen assy	2F 12
320857	Rear side door assy	2F 14

2M 13

PART NO	DESCRIPTION	REF.NO.
320858	Rear side door assy	2F 14
320863	Rear body comp assy	2G 02
320864	Bonnet assy	2L 17
320902	Ball joint assy	11 07
320903	Track rod assy	2L 02
330037	Floor plate	2F 09
330038	Floor plate	2F 09
330061	Ventilator hinge	2F 06
330069	Gearbox cover	2F 09
330113	Door lock	2F 14
330122	Capping	2F 12
330123	Capping	2F 12
330143	Cover plate	2F 05
330144	Cover plate	2F 04
330145	Body capping	2G 05
330146	Support bracket	2E 13
330147	Fixing plate	2F 03
330149	Grille for radiator	10 05
330150	Support clip for grille mesh	10 04
330162	Buffer	2F 12
330163	Sealing strip	2F 12
330198	Retainer	2F 12
330202	Filler	2F 12
330203	Filler	2F 12
330208	Strengthening member	2G 02
330212	Rubber strip	2G 02
330214	Side and wheelarch	2G 02
330215	Side and wheelarch	2G 03
330237	Corner bracket	2G 03
330238	Corner bracket	2G 03
330245	Capping	2G 02
330248	End panel	2G 02
330249	End panel	2G 02
330265	Crossmember	2G 02
330267	Rear floor	2G 02
330271	Rear mounting angle	2G 03
330279	Strengthening angle	2G 02
330295	Side panel	2G 02
330296	Side panel	2G 02
330303	Stay	2G 02
330304	Stay	2G 03
330315	Rear corner capping	2G 03
330316	Rear corner capping	2G 03
330326	Sill panel	2F 11
330327	Sill panel	2F 11
330333	Fixing plate	2F 11
330336	Sill panel	2F 11
330337	Sill panel	2F 11
330347	Grommet	2F 10
330348	Retainer	2F 10
330349	Cover plate	2F 10
330366	Cowl	2G 02
330367	Cover plate	2G 03
330380	Sill channel	2F 11
330381	Sill channel	2F 11

2M 14

PART NO	DESCRIPTION	REF.NO.
330399	Chain	2G 03
330419	Buffer	2G 03
330422	Sleeve for chain	2G 03
330426	Outer panel	2F 03
330427	Outer panel	2F 03
330436	Front panel	2F 03
330437	Front panel	2F 03
330442	Strengthening angle	2G 05
330443	Panel	2G 03
330444	Mudshield	2F 04
330445	Mudshield	2F 04
330447	Mudshield	2F 04
330448	Mudshield	2F 04
330459	Cover box	2F 04
330460	Cover box	2F 04
330468	Mounting angle	2G 04
330534	Panel	2G 03
330548	Bracket for striker	2F 03
330582	Body side panel	2G 05
330585	Sill panel	2F 11
330586	Sill panel	2F 11
330602	Wheel housing	2G 04
330615	Tread plate	2G 05
330616	Cover plate	2G 04
330617	Rear floor	2G 04
330621	Sealing rubber	2F 07
330660	Sealing rubber	2F 12
330661	Channel	2F 12
330663	Side and wheelarch	2G 04
330667	Retainer	2F 07
330668	Retainer	2F 07
330669	Retainer	2F 07
330717	Tread plate	2G 05
330788	Retainer	2G 11
330789	Retainer	2G 11
330824	Nut plate	2G 05
330832	Capping	2G 03
330833	Capping	2G 03
330840	Capping	2G 05
330841	Runner	2G 09
330848	Filler piece	2F 08
330850	Special bolt	2F 13
330953	Cone bush	2F 13
330954	Spring	2F 13
330955	Lockwasher	2F 13
330956	Nut	2I 03
330957	Rear body complete assembly	2G 04
330958	Seat support	2I 06
331006	Seat support	2I 06
331007	Seat support	2I 06
331008	Clip	2I 03
331071	Plug	2I 06
331083	Seat slide	2I 06
331102	Seat slide	2I 06
331103	Seat slide	2I 06

PART NO	DESCRIPTION	REF.NO.
331104	Seat slide	2I 06
331122	Pivot bracket	2I 12
331149	Seat backrest	2I 12
331168	Bracket	2I 02
331170	Stud	2I 06
331179	Sidelight casing	2I 02
331180	Sidelight casing	2I 02
331186	Sidelight casing	2I 02
331187	Sidelight casing	2I 02
331193	Bracket	2I 02
331196	Side rail	2I 02
331203	Fixing strip	2I 02
331216	Siderail	2I 04
331229	Seat frame	2I 14
331272	Strap	2I 07
331273	Strap	2I 06
331390	Outer bracket	2I 02
331391	Centre bracket	2I 02
331401	Rubber mat	2I 13
331466	Frame	2I 06
331478	Support	2I 12
331479	Support	2I 12
331480	Retainer	2I 05
331481	Floor mat	2I 05
331491	Roof trim	2I 02
331497	Cant rail trim	2I 02
331498	Cant rail trim	2I 02
331508	Head cloth	2I 02
331547	Side strip	2I 04
331589	Cant rail trim	2I 04
331590	Cant rail trim	2I 04
331605	Headcloth	2I 04
331607	Trim panel	2I 02
331610	Headcloth	2I 04
331616	Cover	2I 10
331638	Door trim	2I 03
331646	Seat frame	2I 14
331647	Seat frame	2I 14
331669	Retainer	2I 05
331670	Floor mat	2I 05
331699	Buffer	2I 14
331708	Bolt (5/16in UNF)	2I 10
331709	Bolt	2I 06
331718	Bracket	2I 06
331719	Bracket	2I 06
331818	Bracket	2I 06
331833	Cushion	2I 14
331835	Pad	2I 14
331973	Strap	2I 07
331974	Strap	2I 07
332028	Stiffener	2G 11
332065	Stud plate	2G 09
332081	Nut plate	2G 09
332098	Wing nut	2F 08
332146	Buffer	2G 03

PART NO	DESCRIPTION	REF.NO.
332147	Dovetail	2H 03
332151	Retainer	2H 04
332194	Tropical roof	2G 11
332198	Roof and tropical roof assy	2G 11
332201	Bracket	2G 09
332215	Seal	2G 10
332216	Packing strip	2G 09
332230	Retainer	2G 09
332240	Retainer	2G 11
332280	Retainer	2G 09
332281	Retainer	2G 09
332282	Retainer	2G 09
332283	Retainer	2G 09
332284	Retainer	2G 09
332293	Special washer	2G 10
332306	Side panel assy	2G 09
332307	Side panel assy	2G 09
332324	Catch	2G 09
332325	Catch	2G 09
332327	Knob and screw	2F 07
332329	Tapped plate	2G 09
332355	Strap	2I 10
332376	Bracket	2I 10
332400	Washer plate	2F 03
332401	Bonnet control	2F 03
332435	Window catch	2F 15
332445	Hook for chain	2G 08
332446	Hook for chain	2G 08
332451	Nut plate	2G 02
332466	Instrument panel	2G 10
332484	Support bracket	2F 13
332485	Support bracket	2F 13
332503	Stud plate	2F 04
332521	Stay	2G 02
332524	Battery bolt	2F 02
332550	Buffer	2F 08
332563	Seal	2H 03
332564	Rubber seal	2H 03
332565	Protection strip	2G 03
332566	Seal retainer	2H 03
332581	Stay	2F 04
332582	Mounting pad	2G 02
332588	Tie bar	2F 08
332589	Fixing plate	2F 03
332603	Bolt plate	2F 11
332625	Striker pin	2F 03
332647	Buffer	2F 06
332670	Nameplate	2G 03
332672	Bracket assy	2G 05
332674	Rubber strip	2G 05
332715	Rod	2F 08
332729	Packing piece	11 05
332733	Retainer	2F 14
332756	Seal retainer	2H 09
332942	Male dovetail	2H 03

PART NO	DESCRIPTION	REF.NO.
332943	Spacer	2H 03
332983	Rear body complete assembly	2G 06
332985	Packing block	2I 12
333031	Glass	2H 02
333032	Retainer	2H 02
333033	Retainer	2H 02
333034	Retainer	2H 02
333035	Retainer	2H 02
333036	Door hinge upper	2H 03
333037	Waist rail	2H 02
333041	Rod	2H 03
333080	Mounting plate	2F 13
333081	Filler	2F 15
333082	Packing strip	2F 15
333089	Sliding window	2F 15
333096	Check bracket	2F 15
333140	Striking plate	2F 13
333144	Side panel	2G 06
333145	Side panel	2G 06
333159	Mounting angle	2G 04
333161	Sill panel	2F 11
333201	Cover plate	2G 07
333202	Cover plate	2G 07
333203	Protection strip	2H 09
333204	Rod	2F 15
333211	Roof assy	2G 11
333228	Rubber seal	2F 16
333229	Sealing rubber	2F 16
333233	Sealing rubber	2F 16
333234	Capping	2G 08
333235	Capping	2G 08
333243	Front extension	2G 06
333244	Front extension	2G 06
333246	Tropical roof panel	2G 11
333252	Stiffener	2G 11
333253	Protection angle	2G 03
333254	Protection angle	2G 03
333259	Bracket	2F 16
333261	Sealing rubber	2F 16
333262	Sealing rubber	2F 16
333263	Sealing rubber	2G 06
333266	Corner capping	2G 08
333267	Corner capping	2G 08
333272	Locking catch	2F 14
333293	Clip	2I 14
333294	Clip	2I 14
333295	Bracket	2I 14
333395	Grab rail	2I 10
333435	Stud plate	2H 02
333439	Retaining plate	2H 03
333445	Buffer	2H 03
333446	Clamp plate	2H 03
333452	Side and wheelarch	2G 06
333487	Sealing rubber	2G 10

2M 16

PART NO	DESCRIPTION	REF.NO.
333507	Support	2I 10
333510	Grab rail	2I 10
333527	Seat squab	2I 10
333528	Cushion	2I 10
333551	Retainer	2I 15
333560	Rear floor	2G 06
333562	Side and wheelarch	2G 06
333693	Panel	2F 10
333710	Nut plate	2F 15
333714	Nut plate	2G 07
333719	Waist moulding	2F 15
333720	Waist moulding	2F 15
333745	Sealing rubber	2G 06
333835	Front ventilator	2G 11
333836	Rear ventilator	2G 11
333882	Gearbox cover	2F 09
333972	Sealing rubber	2G 03
334055	Clamp plate	2L 17
334056	Stud plate	2L 17
334111	Mounting pad	2I 12
334121	Hinge pin	2F 07
334174	Plate	2I 10
334176	Bolt 5/16 UNF	2I 10
334177	Nut plate	2I 10
334179	Tread plate	2G 05
334189	Grommet	2F 09
334242	Rubber strip	2F 02
334391	Cover plate	2I 15
334523	Hasp	2F 10
334525	Turnbuckle	2F 10
334531	Backrest assy	2I 15
334532	Panel	2I 15
334535	Pad	2I 15
334540	Rod	2I 15
334541	Frame	2I 15
334542	Frame	2I 15
334547	Support angle	2I 15
334573	Bracket	2I 15
334574	Bracket	2I 15
334575	Bracket	2I 15
334601	Retaining bracket	2I 15
334612	Sealing rubber	2G 11
334613	Sealing rubber	2G 11
334615	Sealing rubber	2G 11
334617	Pad	2F 11
334845	Retainer	2I 15
334894	Stay	2F 11
334895	Stay	2G 04
334896	Stay	2G 05
334959	Check strap mounting bracket	2F 08
334960	Check strap mounting bracket	2F 08
334966	Panel	2F 10
336147	Washer plate	2I 08
336285	Grab rail	2I 15
336288	Locking catch	2I 15

2M 16

PART NO	DESCRIPTION	REF.NO.
336294	Striking plate	2I 15
336295	Reinforcing plate	2I 15
336296	Locking pin	2I 15
336299	Support bracket	2I 15
336411	Top capping	2G 08
336412	Locking plate	2G 08
336422	Cover	2F 07
336451	Channel	2F 12
336454	Channel	2F 12
336466	Radiator grille panel complete	10 04
336474	Hinge	2F 03
336476	Hinge	2F 03
336503	Distance piece	2G 11
336512	Tool tray	2F 11
336535	Pivot pin	2F 03
336536	Retainer clip	2F 03
336567	Washer plate	2I 08
336577	Shoulder bracket	2I 08
336738	Tie bolt	2F 06
336764	Drain channel	2G 09
336780	Retainer	2I 15
336781	Retainer	2I 15
336782	Bolt plate assy	2G 04
336786	Front apron panel	10 04
336872	Pivot bracket	2F 11
337290	Sealing rubber	2G 03
337643	Windscreen assy	2F 07
337644	Windscreen glass	2F 07
337710	Sill panel	2F 11
337711	Sill panel	2F 11
337735	Shackle plate	2L 09
337771	Stay	2F 11
337772	Stay	2F 11
337774	Bracket	2F 11
337781	Rear door	2H 02
337789	Door lock	2H 02
337801	Door lock complete	2H 02
337806	Screw retainer	2F 13
337859	Foam interior	2I 07
337873	Foam interior	2I 06
337880	Foam interior	2I 06
337899	Foam interior	2I 06
337932	Sill panel	2F 11
337933	Sill panel	2F 11
337938	Sill panel	2F 11
337939	Sill panel	2F 11
337942	Sill panel	2F 11
337943	Sill panel	2F 11
337969	Striker pin	2F 03
338009	Plastic plug	2F 06
338013	Small plug	2D 11
338014	Rubber plug	2F 06
338015	Plastic plug	2F 03
338016	Large plug	2D 11

2M 17

2M 17

PART NO	DESCRIPTION	REF.NO.
338017	Plastic plug	2F 06
338019	Plastic plug	2F 06
338020	Plastic plug	2F 06
338021	Plug	2F 16
338025	Grommet	2G 03
338027	Plastic plug	1J 13
338028	Plastic plug	1J 13
338029	Plug	2F 06
338035	Clip	1J 13
338085	Plate	1K 05
338086	Plate	2F 05
338088	Cover plate	2F 05
338091	Cover plate	2F 06
338194	Fastener	2F 06
338195	Fastener	2F 08
338240	Turret nut	2F 08
338248	Seat squab	2F 08
338275	Support bracket	21 10
338332	Bracket	21 13
338333	Bracket	21 10
338334	Grab rail	21 10
338339	Seat spring	21 10
338345	Support	21 10
338353	Trim board	21 10
338380	Spring clip fixing strip	10 04
338414	Dowel	2L 17
338428	Mounting box	2F 05
338430	Stud	21 07
338552	Rubber buffer	2G 10
338553	Rubber buffer	2G 09
338554	Bracket	2G 10
338617	Tailboard hinge	2G 09
338618	Tailboard hinge	2G 08
338636	Bonnet prop rod	2G 08
338652	Bracket	2G 06
338653	Bracket	2F 04
338740	Stud	2F 04
338741	Stud	2G 10
338743	Protection strip	2F 05
338752	Gusset bracket	2G 03
338754	Shoulder bracket	21 08
338780	Grommet	21 08
338827	Retaining plate	2F 10
338845	Windscreen assy	2L 17
338846	Rubber cover	2F 07
338871	Seal	2D 14
339986	Rubber packing	2F 09
339990	Door trim	21 06
339991	Door trim	21 05
340391	Washer	21 05
345052	Instrument panel	2G 09
345077	Finisher	2D 11
345100	Cover plate	2F 05

2M 18

PART NO	DESCRIPTION	REF.NO.
345101	Sill gusset	21 08
345116	Retainer	21 10
345120	Intermediate floor	2G 06
345123	Gusset bracket	21 08
345125	Clamp plate	21 08
345140	Grommet	2F 09
345188	Interior mirror	21 13
345192	Securing bracket for panel	10 04
345426	Trim casing	21 03
345433	Door lock assy	2F 13
345434	Door lock assy	2F 13
345435	Locking catch	2F 14
345436	Locking catch	2F 14
345442	Two piece door	2G 07
345450	Handle	21 03
345498	Nut retainer	2F 13
345549	Tie bar	2F 08
345552	Bracket	2F 04
345553	Bracket	2F 04
345573	Radiator grille panel complete	10 04
345591	Finisher	2F 05
345620	Mounting panel	2F 03
345621	Mounting panel	2F 03
345623	Front panel	2F 03
345624	Front panel	2F 03
345631	Lamp surround	2F 03
345636	Plate	2F 05
345637	Plate	2F 05
345658	Capping	2G 09
345659	Capping	2G 09
345666	Grille for radiator	10 05
345830	Heat shield	2F 11
345831	Spacer	2F 11
345832	Insulation washer	2F 07
345845	Lid and hinge	2F 07
345847	Lid and hinge	2F 05
345879	Dash complete	2F 05
345882	Mounting bracket	2F 05
345883	Blanking plate	2F 05
345915	Reinforcing panel	2G 08
345930	Nut (5/16in UNF)	21 06
346241	Nut plate	2F 15
346339	Door hinge upper	2F 13
346340	Door hinge upper	2F 13
346341	Door hinge lower	2F 13
346342	Door hinge lower	2F 13
346370	Tie bar	2F 08
346376	Door hinge upper	2F 13
346377	Door hinge upper	2G 08
346399	Grab handle	2F 12
346426	Plug	2F 12
346460	Packing strip	11 05
346715	Clamp lower	11 05
346804	Clamping bar	21 12

2M 18

PART NO	DESCRIPTION	REF.NO.
346885	Stowage hook	21 09
347035	Side panel	2G 04
347036	Side panel	2G 04
347436	Bracket	2F 11
347463	Strengthening member	2G 05
347464	Nut plate	2G 05
347488	Channel	2F 12
347489	Channel	2F 15
347509	Stowage hook	21 08
347541	Safety harness	21 09
347553	Bracket for buffer	2G 04
347594	Shim	2F 13
347595	Bonnet prop	2F 03
347637	Retainer	2F 07
347638	Retainer	2F 07
347807	Toe panel	2G 07
347808	Gusset bracket	2G 07
347810	Backing plate	2G 07
348182	Protection plate for headlamp	10 04
348370	Rubber finisher	2F 05
348371	Rubber finisher	2F 05
348393	Channel	2G 09
348394	Channel	2G 09
348396	Channel	2G 09
348430	Stud	21 07
348433	Warning label	2E 06
348447	Washer plate	21 09
348473	Shoulder bracket	21 09
348474	Shoulder bracket	21 09
348535	Rubber finisher top	1N 10
348537	Rubber seal	2D 14
348541	Rubber finisher	2D 14
348678	Rubber seal	2G 11
348738	Gusset bracket	21 08
348743	Support bracket	11 05
348744	Clamp	11 05
348747	Rubber strip	11 05
348748	Clamp	11 05
348800	Seat base assy	2F 10
348852	Seat base	2F 10
348854	Lid	2F 10
348855	Lid	2F 10
348859	Detachable lid	2F 10
348868	Gearbox cover	2F 09
348869	Gearbox cover	2F 09
348871	Side and wheelarch	2F 09
348872	Side panel	2G 04
348874	Rear floor	2G 04
348882	Cover plate	2G 04
348893	Floor plate	2F 09
348894	Floor plate	2F 09
349218	Bracket	21 02
349503	Cushion	21 07
349506	Cushion	21 06

PART NO	DESCRIPTION	REF.NO.
349515	Cushion	2I 12
349523	Cushion	2I 15
349562	Seat squab	2I 06
349563	Seat squab	2I 06
349564	Seat squab	2I 06
349565	Seat squab	2I 06
349644	Seat squab	2I 06
349645	Seat squab	2I 06
349899	Clip	2I 03
349931	Plastic washer	2F 03
349943	Bracket	2I 06
349967	Cushion	2I 07
349974	Door trim	2I 05
349975	Door trim	2I 05
364684	Rubber plug	2F 06
368427	Rubber grommet	2F 06
395014	Wing top	2F 03
395064	Bolt plate	11 06
395404	Front panel	2G 04
395409	Front panel	2G 02
395430	Sealing strip	2F 07
395431	Seal	2G 11
395459	Front apron panel	10 05
395529	Door	2F 12
395530	Door	2F 12
395598	Sealing rubber	2F 12
395599	Sealing rubber	2F 12
395652	Door lock assy	2F 14
395653	Door lock assy	2F 14
395670	Sealing rubber	2F 12
395671	Sealing rubber	2F 12
395672	Sealing rubber	2F 12
395673	Sealing rubber	2G 10
395674	Seal	2H 04
396113	Seal	10 04
396124	Protection plate	2I 10
396557	Squab interior	2I 14
396696	Pad	2I 15
396698	Rear seat backrest assy	2I 14
396739	Rear seat backrest assy	2I 10
396916	Centre seat assy	2I 10
396917	Seat squab	2I 10
396918	Cushion	1C 10
500144	Valve guide inlet & sealing ring	1C 10
500145	Valve guide exhaust & sealing ring	1C 10
500150	Lens	2D 02
500201	Filler cap	1J 10
500257	Accelerator pedal	1N 02
500419	Filter	1L 09
500432	Elbow	1L 18
500446	Distance tube	1M 11
500447	Mounting rubber	1M 11
500559	Lead	2E 03
500571	Cold start control	2D 10

PART NO	DESCRIPTION	REF.NO.
500588	Packing washer	2H 04
500609	Spring	1D 09
500710	Joint washer	1L 17
500729	Cover	2E 02
500746	Retainer	1H 14
500792	Stud	1C 08
500810	Elbow	1L 18
501070	Distance piece	2H 04
501198	Locking plate	2C 10
501211	Release lever	1F 02
501224	Riv-nut	1L 09
501245	Bush inner column	11 03
501246	Spring ring	11 03
501374	Lever	1M 03
501389	Dowel	1H 15
501390	Main leaf	1H 15
501391	2nd leaf	1H 15
501428	Clip	1L 16
501501	Washer	1G 04
501503	Step	2H 09
501593	Dowel	1C 02
501616	1st lay gear	1G 04
501617	Mainshaft gear	1G 04
501690	Cable battery to switch	2E 03
501691	Cable	2E 03
501769	Suction pipe	1M 03
501864	Screw	1L 07
502029	Gudgeon pin	1E 04
502067	Dip switch	11 04
502116	Dowel	1F 05
502201	Shaft	1G 11
502202	Reverse hinge	1G 10
502205	Bracket	1G 10
502248	Washer	1H 08
502266	Thrust ring scrapper .030 O/S	1C 03
502282	Base plate	2C 02
502283	Terminal bush & lead	2C 02
502286	Vacuum unit	2C 02
502287	Clip	1J 12
502333	Overhaul kit BR M Cyl	1E 07
502473	Tappet guide	1G 04
502482	Distance piece	1C 06
502656	Stud	1C 06
502898	Special washer	1N 03
502899	Spacer for spindle	1N 03
502900	Spindle bell crank	1N 03
502904	Valve spring	1D 08
502951	Fuel instruction plate	2G 02
502982	Torsion spring	1N 03
503160	Cylinder liner	1C 02
503266	Shaft	1E 05
503307	Clamp	1N 11
503309	Heat shield	1N 11
503310	Heat shield	1N 11

PART NO	DESCRIPTION	REF.NO.
503424	Grease gun	2J 07
503430	Bracket accelerator controls	1N 03
503492	Elbow	1L 18
503665	Starting dog	1E 03
503754	Overhaul kit BR M cyl	1J 12
503805	Spring	1G 06
503893	Throttle spindle	1L 02
503900	Joint washer	1L 02
503901	Diaphram assy	1L 03
503915	Special screw	1L 03
503919	Top cover	1L 04
503920	Special screw	1L 04
503921	Elbow	1L 05
503981	Screw	1J 02
504006	Spring	1E 02
504007	Washer	1E 02
504032	Set bolt	1C 08
504082	Tube	1M 02
504104	Adaptor	1J 11
504105	Gasket	1J 10
504106	Clutch/brake reservoit tank	1J 10
504130	Pipe	2D 02
504169	Lens	1D 13
504211	Valve guide	2L 09
504213	Distance piece	2L 09
504214	Shim	1L 17
504233	Shim	11 06
504272	Seal	11 06
504275	Stiffener bracket	11 06
504279	Shim washer	1E 06
504375	Shim washer	1H 08
504433	Chain	1D 07
504443	Washer	1K 03
504517	Washer	1J 02
504577	Brake pipe	1D 17
504606	Lining with rivets	1D 17
504607	Tie rod	1N 03
504619	Sleeve	1N 04
504620	Bell crank lever	1N 04
504655	Relay lever	1L 17
504656	Carburetter relay lever assy	1L 17
504657	Cap	1L 17
504673	Tube	1E 10
504736	Joint washer	1K 04
504765	Thermostat	1D 06
504995	Union	1D 06
504997	Cap	2D 02
505144	Spring	2D 02
505150	Side lamp	2E 02
505158	Nylon insert	2J 05
505205	Cover	2D 02
505244	Lucar blade	2E 02
505244	Joint washer	1L 17

PART NO	DESCRIPTION	REF.NO.
505597	Spacing washer	1D 09
505612	Liner	1M 03
505613	Distance piece	1M 03
505786	Spring	1M 03
505790	Seal	1J 03
506047	Stud	1D 13
506069	Rubber washer	1C 10
506679	Rubber boot	2E 02
506799	Ring gear	1F 04
506814	ADJ screw	1E 07
506816	Screw	1D 07
506817	Screw	1D 08
507001	Rubber boot	2C 03
507025	Special set bolt	1C 06
507026	Tappet	1E 07
507129	Bulb	2D 10
507447	Pin	1G 10
507687	Carburetter kit	2J 02
507693	Gasket kit	2J 02
507827	Tappet assy	1E 07
507829	Tappet guide assy	1C 06
508045	Rubber mounting	1L 18
508148	Brake pipe	1K 02
508175	Lock stop plate	1H 05
508565	Clip	1K 02
508581	Handbrake lever assy	1K 07
508895	Guide washer	1H 14
508945	Clip	1K 03
508962	Special washer	1N 02
509009	Lever	1L 09
509045P	Bolt	1H 07
509045P	Bolt	1H 02
509045P	Bolt "	2L 06
509046	Bolt (3/8in UNF X 1.7/32in)	1H 02
509120	Hinge pin	2H 04
509218	Distance tube	2L 09
509311	Armature	2C 10
509407	Restrictor lever	1N 02
509412	Clip	1L 16
509414	Double clip	1L 16
509415	Clip	1L 13
509448	Steering unit assy	1I 02
509449	Steering unit assy	1I 02
509769	Chain for filler cap	1O 02
509856	Slave cylinder bracket	1F 09
509885	Bush	1D 17
509909	Fuel pipe	1L 09
510078	Heater plug	1E 12
510170	Fan disc washer	2E 03
510176	Stop tail lamp	2O 02
510179	Side lamp	2O 02
510192	Washer	2E 03
510489	Ring gear	1F 05
511127	Bearing	1N 06

PART NO	DESCRIPTION	REF.NO.
511189	Layshaft gear	1G 04
511205	Mainshaft gear	1G 04
511652	Joint washer	1M 03
511680	Shaft	1E 05
511690	Joint washer	1M 03
511837	Valve guide, inlet	1E 11
511838	Valve guide, exhaust	1E 11
511956	Outlet pipe	1E 10
511957	Thermostat gasket	1C 09
512018	Fan blade	1C 09
512106	Correction jet	1L 04
512206	Valve rocker inlet RH	1C 06
512207	Valve rocker RH exhaust	1C 06
512235	Banjo bolt	1F 08
512237	Cover	1G 02
512238	Joint washer	1G 02
512287	Special locknut	1M 05
512307	Adjusting screw	1M 06
512308	O-ring	1M 06
512311	O ring	1M 06
512319	Special washer	1M 06
512352	Horn push	1I 04
512359	Dust cover	1I 04
512402	Special screw	1L 02
512412	Plug	1C 02
512458	Carburetter body	1M 02
512460	Pipe	1M 03
512646	Clip	1C 12
512760	Dust cover	2K 12
512791	Felt seal	2K 12
512828	Valve seat insert	1E 11
512838	Brake pipe	1K 02
512839	Pipe 3/16in clutch master cyl to hose	1J 11
513072	Handle for jack	2J 07
513282	Fan disc washer	2E 04
513639	Pump cover	1E 05
513641	Pump body	2C 02
513679	Driving dog	1L 10
513926	Pipe	1L 10
513927	Injector pipe	1L 07
513928	Pipe	2C 09
513929	Pipe	1L 10
513991	Lever	1M 03
514147	Grommet	2D 02
514193	Brush set	2C 14
514195	Bracket	2C 14
514224	Tube	1E 11
514472	Adjusting link	2C 14
514527	Stud	1E 02
514578	Red grease	2J 02
514560	Clip	1C 12
514650	Spring	1G 10
514840	Lead	1I 04
514929	Riv-nut	2E 02

PART NO	DESCRIPTION	REF. NO.
515060	Grommet	2D 04
515218	Rim for light unit	2D 03
515291	Screw	1E 12
515321	Spring retainer	1C 05
515325	Plug - spring retainer	1C 05
515331	Steady strip	1N 11
515365	Anchor plate	1J 07
515366	Expander unit assy	1J 06
515405	Anchor plate	1J 02
515406	Anchor plate	1J 02
515466	Dust cover	1J 02
515467	Locking plate	1J 06
515468	Retaining spring	1J 06
515470	Packing plate	1J 06
515505	Distance piece	1N 11
515506	Bracket	1N 11
515508	Steering box assy	1I 02
515509	Steering box assy	1I 02
515572	Seal	1G 13
515573	O ring	1E 11
515597	Shield	1N 11
515599	Joint washer	1G 03
515845	Breather	1H 06
515848	Side cover plate	1I 03
515849	Joint washer	1I 03
515851	Output shaft	2K 08
515853	Thrust washer	2K 08
515923	Expander repair kit	1J 06
515924	Adjuster repair kit	1J 06
515926	Brake rod	1J 06
515927	Retaining clip	1J 06
516059	Housing	1E 10
516133	Engine bracket RH	1C 02
516316	Knob	1G 10
516496	Shield	1N 13
516498	Cylinder liner	1D 03
516599	Brake drum	1J 03
516885	Large seal for oil filter	1D 15
516945	Shield	1N 13
516962	Clip	1L 07
517474	Solenoid	2C 09
517502	Bracket	1L 15
517588	Bracket	1H 15
517589	Spring	1H 15
517682	Filter	1L 11
517684	Clip	1L 10
517685	Pipe	1L 10
517686	Pipe	1L 10
517689	Plug	1L 10
517690	Nut	1L 10
517706	Joint washer	1L 09
517707	Valve	1L 11
517855	Plug	1L 09
517903	Hose	1L 08

PART NO	DESCRIPTION	REF NO.
517907	Support bracket reservoir tank	1J 10
517976	Joint wheel	1L 11
517977	Rubber mat	2H 05
518100	Bolt	1D 05
518146	Clip	1D 10
518272	Core plug	1D 13
518318	Thrust washer	2K 08
518676	Inner column	1I 02
518677	Inner column	1I 02
519008	Washer	2C 08
519009	Screw	2C 08
519011	Plunger spring	2C 08
519440	Special bolt	1C 03
519742	Warning light-fuel	2D 10
519743	Warning lamp-charging	2D 10
519753	Slip ring horn contact	1I 04
519782	Dash harness	2E 03
519763	Crossmember harness	2E 03
519784	Frame harness	2E 03
519838	Gauge unit	1L 18
519840	Ammeter	2D 10
521328	Thrust washer	1G 07
521330	Gear	1D 06
521583	Bush	1E 11
521600	Stud	2K 08
521634	Lockwasher	2K 08
521636	Shim	2K 07
521851	Main shaft	2K 08
521852	Distance piece	2K 10
521853	Bearing	2K 10
521855	Retaining plate	2K 10
521856	Bush	2K 10
521857	Housing	2K 08
521864	Bush	2K 08
521868	High gear wheel	2K 08
522017	Gear	2K 15
522303	Shaft	2K 15
522308	Spacer	1G 08
522318	Housing assy	2K 15
522334	Fork	2K 15
522567	Diff case	1H 09
522593	Brake drum	1J 04
522745	Bush	1C 04
522756	Fuel filter	1L 11
522882	Wheel for flasher switch	2D 06
522913	Pulley	2C 10
522939	Special bolt	1L 14
522940	Washer	1L 14
523139	Camshaft	1D 07
523181	Bracket	1E 07
523240	Split seal halves	1C 03
523637	Cold start control	2D 10
523638	Tyre pump	2J 07

PART NO	DESCRIPTION	REF.NO.
523655	Exhaust silencer	1A 13
523695	Pedal bracket	1J 08
523696	Pedal & bushes	1J 08
523916	Brake pedal bracket assy	1J 08
524114	Throttle chamber	1L 02
524115	Accelerator pump	1L 03
524210	Adjusting link	2C 14
524492	Connecting rod assy	1D 05
524636	Packing	1D 03
524680	Shroud	1E 11
524765	Cup plug	1E 02
524769	Screw	1E 05
524846	Rocker cover top assy	1C 10
524874	Housing assy for swivel pin LH	1H 03
524875	Housing assy for swivel pin RH	1H 03
524894	Nut pipe to filter or bowl	1M 12
524959	Pump connrction	2J 07
525124	Inlet valve	1D 08
525131	Bracket	1E 12
525168	Clip	1L 10
525389	Washer	1C 06
525390	Screw	1E 07
525428	Plug	1E 14
525497	Cup plug	1C 10
525500	Set bolt (5/16in UNF X 23/41n)	1C 06
525520	Gasket kit	2J 02
525530	Double ended union	1M 12
525852	Crankshaft assy. 010 U/S	1C 03
525853	Crankshaft assy. 020 U/S	1C 03
525910	Rocker	1D 09
525911	Rocker	1D 09
526161	Locker	1F 05
526225	Stud	2C 14
526258	Rivet	2C 08
526360	Dynamo harness	2E 03
526440	Frame harness	2E 03
526608	Pad	2L 09
526753	Road wheel	1H 16
526994	Track rod only	1I 07
527109	Water outlet pipe	1C 09
527164	Connecting rod assy	1C 03
527167	Crankshaft assy lid	1C 03
527169	Con rod assy	1E 04
527240	Inlet valve	1E 07
527269	Plug	1L 11
527272	Special screw	1L 03
527349	Suction pipe	1C 12
527351	Cylinder liner	1C 02
528004	Gudgeon pin bush	1C 03
528041	Accelerator pump	1L 03
528235	Plate	1G 08
528683	Locker	1G 05
528685	Plate	1G 05
528690	Plate	1G 05

PART NO	DESCRIPTION	REF.NO.
528691	Nut (3/4 UNF)	1G 05
526692	Washer	1G 05
528697	Joint washer	1F 07
528701	Bearing	1G 05
528702	Thrust washer	1H 04
528703	Layshaft	1G 04
528707	Housing	1F 07
528720	Distance piece	1G 05
528721	Distance piece	1G 05
528722	Distance piece	1G 05
528865	Stud	1G 03
528900	Frame harness	2E 03
528963	Cable-coil to distributor	2E 03
529141	Clamp plate	1M 09
529221	Bearing	2C 14
529394	Baffle plate	1C 08
529823	Sump	1E 09
529963	Dash harness	2E 03
529964	Frame harness	2E 03
529969	Gauge unit	1L 18
529970	Gauge unit	1L 18
529972	Lead	1E 12
530034	Starter switch	2D 10
530085	Cable battery to starter	2E 03
530135	Stud	1C 13
530175	Drive shaft assy	1C 04
530178	Thrust washer	1C 04
530179	Retaining ring	1D 04
530343	Oil thrower	1D 04
530C354	Dowel	1D 03
530476	Thermostat bypass	1E 10
530478	Pump casing	1E 10
530481	Sealing plate	1D 07
530585	Hose for radiator bottom	1D 05
530590	Water pump kit	2J 02
530746	Bypass pipe	1C 09
530884	Coil complete	1M 08
530885	Spring for armature	1M 08
530890	Pulley	1E 10
530966	Olive	1L 10
530984	Shim .003	1H 04
530985	Shim .005	1H 04
530986	Shim .010	1H 04
530987	Shim .030	1H 04
530988	Swivel pin & steering lever	1H 03
530989	Swivel pin & steering lever	1H 03
530990	Swivel pin & steering lever	1H 03
530991	Swivel pin & steering lever	1H 03
530992	Swivel pin & bracket	1H 04
531001	Locker	1H 04
531040	Relay lever upper	1I 07
531043	Stud 7/16in	1H 03
531104	Engine bracket	1G 08
531332	Steady strip for shroud	1G 03

PART NO	DESCRIPTION	REF.NO.
531388	Control rod	1N 03
531389	Control rod	1N 03
531390	Control rod	1N 03
531391	Control rod	1N 08
531392	Bell crank	1N 08
531394	Linkage clip	1N 03
531395	Cross shaft lever	1N 03
531433	O ring	1H 03
531439	Control rod	1N 04
531494	Stud 7/16in	1H 03
531501	Lead	1I 04
531586	Gasket for head lamp	2D 03
531591	Lead	2E 06
531684	Stop tail lamp	2D 05
531695	Battery cable	2E 03
531873	Valve rocker	1D 09
531874	Valve rocker	1D 09
531888	Anchor plate	1J 05
531889	Anchor plate	1J 05
531893	Spring	1J 05
531895	Stud	1E 11
531896	Stud	1E 11
531897	Clamp	1L 10
531906	Brake pipe	1K 03
532268	Swivel pin kit	2J 02
532319	Swivel pin kit	1H 05
532323	O ring	1G 07
532329	Swivel pin kit	1H 05
532387	Sealing ring	1D 11
532552	Bracket	2C 13
532566	Terminal	2C 14
532568	Bracket	2C 08
532571	Bracket	2C 08
532572	Bush	2C 08
532574	Bush	2C 08
532577	Locker	2C 08
532578	Solenoid	2C 08
532579	Base	2C 08
532580	Nut	2C 08
532587	Seal	1E 09
532806	Front flasher lamp	2D 08
532807	Rear flasher lamp	2D 09
532809	Stop tail lamp	2D 08
532810	Number plate lamp	2D 08
532848	Rivet	1L 14
532878	Bulb holder	2D 05
532879	Lamp base	2D 05
532880	Lens	2D 05
532881	Stop tail lamp	2D 05
532925	Screw	2K 15
532963	Swivel pin & bracket	1H 04
532979	Low gear	1G 07
533040	Bottom cover plate	1G 08

2N 06

PART NO	DESCRIPTION	REF.NO.
533080	Intermediate gear cluster	1G 07
533354	Plug	1G 03
533358	Plug	1H 08
533567	Axle casing	1H 06
533568	Differential assy 4.7 ratio	1H 10
533570	Axle casing	2L 02
533579	Axle shaft	1H 06
533580	Axle shaft	1H 06
533639	Prop shaft	1H 07
533640	Propeller shaft	2L 02
533645	Joint washer	1H 11
533731	Housing assy	1G 08
533777	Diff wheel	1H 09
533786	Thrust washer	1H 09
533787	Thrust washer	1H 09
533788	Thrust washer	1H 09
533794	Diff pinion	1H 09
533858	Casing assy	1G 08
533860	Washer	2C 14
534021	Spring dowel	1N 06
534098	Locker	1F 04
534200	Rubber strip	1M 09
534338	Lucar blade	2J 05
534341	Lucar connector	2J 05
534797	Olive	1L 16
534797	"	1M 12
535168	Carburetter lever ball end	1N 04
535173	Road spring rear	2L 09
535286	Relay lever	1I 07
535708	Stud & dowel kit	1D 03
535989	Valve spring	1D 08
536006	Head lamp complete RH stg	2D 03
536094	Flasher lamp	2D 06
536111	Head lamp complete LH stg	2D 03
536112	Head lamp complete LH stg	2D 03
536113	Head lamp complete LH stg	2D 03
536116	Adaptor & leads - headlamp	2D 03
536117	Sidelamp	2D 03
536148	Flasher lamp	2D 06
536151	Lens for sidelamp	2D 03
536152	Lens	2D 06
536269	Piston assy	1D 05
536270	Piston assy	1D 05
536272	Piston assy	1D 05
536273	Piston assy	1D 05
536275	Piston assy	1D 05
536514	Exhaust manifold	1E 14
536577	Plug	1E 12
536646	Plate	1C 13
536679	Strap	2C 14
536796	Sliding rod	1M 03
536803	Pin	1F 10
536872	Valve rocker	1D 09
536873	Valve rocker	1D 09

2N 07

PART NO	DESCRIPTION	REF.NO.
536913	Barrel lock	2D 10
537179	Nut wrench	2J 07
537229	Filter	1E 12
537269	Piston assy	1D 05
537271	Piston assy	1D 05
537284	Knob - ignition & lamp switch	2D 10
537297	Olive	1L 16
537533	Support bracket LH	1I 05
537535	Support bracket RH	1I 05
537539	Stiffener bracket	1I 06
537541	Steering unit assy	1I 02
537543	Locking plate	1I 06
537544	Locking plate	1I 06
537601	Push rod for slave cylinder	1F 08
537603	Clutch shaft & lever	1F 09
537685	Plate	1H 15
537686	Plate	1H 15
537687	Plate	1H 15
537707	Bracket accelerator controls	1N 03
537734	Shackle plate	2L 09
537735	Shackle plate tapped	2L 09
537740	Shackle pin	1H 15
537741	Shackle pin	1H 15
537742	Shackle pin	1H 15
537778	Shackle plate plain	2L 09
537780	Control rod	1N 07
537791	Control rod	1N 07
537792	Control rod	1N 07
537805	Bracket	1K 02
537877	Split bush	1I 07
537964	Main leaf	2L 09
538038	Joint washer	1E 08
538039	Joint washer	1E 08
538068	Banjo	1F 08
538073	Cover	1E 06
538130	Thrust washer	1E 03
538131	Thrust washer	1E 03
538132	Thrust washer	1E 03
538133	Thrust washer	1E 03
538134	Thrust washer	1E 03
538435	Throttle chamber	1L 02
538485	Body	1M 08
538489	Screw for valve assy	1M 08
538493	Bolt	1M 08
538496	Screw fixing air bottle cover	1M 08
538498	Union inlet & outlets	1M 08
538499	Joint washer diaphragm to body inner	1M 08
538502	Special screw	1M 08
538503	Spring washer	1M 08
538506	Screw	1M 08
538508	Washer for terminal screw	1M 08
538509	Cover black	1M 08
538510	Lucar connector	1M 08
538511	Insulating sleeve for terminal	1M 09

2N 07

PART NO	DESCRIPTION	REF.NO.
538536	Connector	1G 12
538612	Gasket	1K 04
538613	Adaptor	1K 04
538614	Banjo	1K 04
538615	Banjo bolt	1K 04
538616	Gasket	2C 13
538628	Bush	2C 13
538629	Bracket	2C 13
538631	Coil	2C 13
538632	Bolt	1E 10
538671	Joint washer	2C 02
539572	Weight	2C 05
539573	Vacuum unit	1H 09
539703	Cross shaft	1H 08
539706	Pinion bearing	1H 09
539707	Pinion bearing	1H 09
539711	Shim	1H 09
539713	Shim	1H 09
539715	Shim	1H 09
539717	Shim	1H 08
539718	Shim	1H 08
539720	Shim	1H 08
539722	Shim	1H 08
539724	Shim	1H 03
539741	Housing for swivel pin bearing	2L 03
539742	Housing for swivel pin bearing	1H 04
539745	Railko bush	1H 08
539756	Washer	2C 05
539787	Clip	1G 08
539828	Casing assy	2K 08
539687	Gear	2K 15
539955	Link	2K 10
539993	Housing	1G 09
540004	Flange	1G 07
540114	Speedo/warning lights MPH	2D 11
540115	Speedometer & warning lights kilometres	2D 11
540117	Speedometer & warning lights miles	2D 11
540118	Speedometer & warning lights kilometres	2L 16
540119	Speedometer miles	2L 16
540120	Speedometer kilometres	2L 16
540131	Speedometer miles	2L 16
540135	Speedometer kilometres	1G 10
540354	O ring	1G 12
540842	Shouldered bolt	1H 02
540870	Plug	2L 03
540972	Half shaft	2L 03
540973	Half shaft	1F 04
541195	Housing	1L 10
541229	Plate	1D 10
541291	Breather pipe	2C 13
541313	Bracket	2C 05
541492	Distributor	1M 04
541494	Stud	2D 05
541520	Stop tail lamp	

PART NO	DESCRIPTION	REF.NO.
541521	Lens	2D 05
541522	Stop tail lamp	2D 05
541523	Lead	1E 12
541755	Flashing indicator assy	2D 06
541760	Flywheel assy	1F 04
541860	Tube	1E 09
541899	Steering box assy	11 02
541900	Steering box assy	11 02
541910	Crankshaft std	1D 04
541921	Oil seal	1D 04
542036	Special screw	2D 05
542037	Bulb holder	2D 03
542038	Special screw	2D 03
542040	Bulb holder	2D 06
542041	Special screw	2D 05
542042	Special screw	2D 04
542043	Lens	2D 05
542044	Lens	2D 05
542045	Bulb holder	2D 05
542046	Bulb holder	2D 06
542048	Lens	2D 06
542049	Bulb holder	2D 03
542073	Mud excluder	1D 09
542231	Primary pinion	1G 06
542396	Oil pump body	1D 06
542425	Rocker cover	1D 10
542492	Oil seal	1C 03
542494	Oil seal	1E 03
542515	Tab washer	1J 06
542600	Side cover assy	1C 08
542601	Stud	1C 08
542622	Key	1D 04
542623	Key	1D 04
542762	Boss	1N 06
542776	Pin	1N 06
542783	Spiral pin	1N 06
542845	Nut	1M 12
542846	Olive	1M 12
542861	Spring	1N 05
543108	Main leaf	1H 15
543209	Air cleaner	1M 12
543254	Bracket	1D 17
543265	Brake lever	1K 08
543275	Distance piece	1K 08
543281	Pin	1K 08
543291	Plunger rod	1K 08
543292	Plunger rod	1K 08
543301	Jack handle	2J 07
543498	Anchor	1N 07
543546	Ratchet	1K 08
543629	Hose for radiator bottom	1D 05
543764	Hose	1L 17
543765	Hose	1L 17
543766	Pipe	1L 18

PART NO	DESCRIPTION	REF.NO.
543767	Pipe	1L 18
543782	Hose	1L 17
543803	Bolt (5/16 UNF X 11/2in)	1L 18
543808	Plate	1L 18
543818	Cup washer	2L 13
543819	Cup washer	2L 13
543934	Check strap	2L 09
543946	Crossmember	2F 02
543972	Housing for relay shaft	11 07
544337	Special bolt	11 07
544347	Rubber sleeve	2L 13
544389	Distance plate	1L 09
544391	Pipe	1L 11
544451	Bracket	1N 08
544573	Licence holder	2F 08
544581	Drag link tube	2L 13
544658	Elbow	1L 18
544674	Elbow	1L 18
544686	Packing piece	1F 08
544848	Cowl for fan	1D 02
544980	Clutch shaft & lever	1F 09
545149	Rim for headlamp	2D 03
545159	Rim for headlamp	2D 03
545218	Main harness	2E 03
545571	Bearing	1N 06
546026	ratchet	1E 06
546177	Adaptor	1E 13
546180	Carburetter	1L 02
546197	Locker	1F 04
546203	Breather filter	1D 14
546210	Clip	1D 14
546282	Sleeve	1L 12
546287	Pulley	2C 13
546324	Starting dog	1D 04
546333	Lockwasher	1D 04
546440	Filler cap	1E 09
546488	Joint washer	1L 18
546518	Flywheel assy	1F 05
546519	Flywheel assy	1F 05
546583	Guide tube	1D 11
546584	Adaptor	1D 11
546798	Tappet push rod	1C 06
546799	Push rod	1E 07
547346	Stop tail lamp	2D 05
547605	Breather filter	1D 14
548043	Turret nut 1/2 1n UNF	2F 07
548169	Spring	1J 05
548205	Flexible bush	1H 15
548262	Pipe	1L 09
549168	Pivot shaft	1G 12
549169	Shouldered bolt	1G 12
549200	Shim	1G 08
549201	Pivot shaft	2K 15
549229	Nipple	1H 07

PART NO	DESCRIPTION	REF.NO.
549230	Shim	1H 09
549232	Shim	1H 09
549234	Shim	1H 09
549236	Shim	1H 09
549238	Shim	1H 09
549240	Shim	1H 09
549242	Shim	1H 09
549244	Shim	1H 09
549246	Shim	1H 09
549248	Shim	1H 09
549250	Shim	1H 09
549252	Shim	1H 09
549399	Clip	2L 04
549409	Special bolt	1H 10
549411	Differential bearing adjuster	1H 10
549412	Oil seal for pinion	1H 10
549413	Bevel pinion housing complete	1H 10
549414	Shim .002	1H 10
549415	Shim .003	1H 10
549416	Shim .010	1H 10
549417	Bearing for bevel pinion nose end	1H 10
549419	Circlip	1H 10
549420	Bearing for bevel pinion	1H 10
549421	Driving flange for bevel pinion	1H 10
549425	Spacer .370	1H 10
549427	Spacer .373	1H 10
549429	Spacer .376	1H 10
549431	Spacer .379	1H 10
549433	Spacer .382	1H 10
549435	Spacer .385	1H 10
549437	Spacer .388	1H 10
549439	Spacer .391	1H 10
549441	Spacer .394	1H 10
549443	Spacer .397	1H 10
549445	Spacer .400	1H 10
549448	Special nut (7/8 UNF)	1H 10
549453	Mudshield for driving flange	1H 10
549454	Mudshield for bevel pinion bearing housing	1H 10
549457	Taper roller bearing for differential	1H 10
549460	Locking plate	1H 10
549461	Differential wheel	1H 10
549462	Differential pinion	1H 10
549463	Spindle for pinion	1H 10
549464	Locking plate double type	1H 10
549465	Differential wheel washer	1H 10
549466	Spherical differential pinion washer	1H 10
549473	Circlip	1H 07
549474	Split ring	2L 04
549475	Nut	2L 04
549477	Oil seal	2L 04
549493	Crown wheel and pinion	1H 10
549495	Axle shaft	1H 06
549496	Axle shaft	1H 06
549610	Adaptor	2C 02
549611	Distributor drive coupling	2C 03

2N 09

PART NO	DESCRIPTION	REF.NO.
549761	Mechanical fuel pump	1L 08
549840	Spanner	2J 07
549909	Plug	1E 05
550198	Exhaust valve	1E 07
550263	Inlet manifold	1E 14
550281	Washer	2C 15
550324	Pump	1L 09
550336	Fan	2C 15
550477	Pipe pump to carburetter	1L 16
550732	Master cylinder	1J 14
550786	Plate	1H 15
550791	U bolt	2L 09
550801	Bottom plate	2L 09
550802	Bottom plate	2L 09
551227	Wheel box	2D 14
551318	Cable	2E 06
551319	Cable	2E 06
551331	Strip	1N 13
551346	Cable	2E C6
551347	Cable	2E 06
551430	Special washer	2D 06
551436	Special screw	2D 05
551508	Switch	2D 11
551595	Red rear reflector	2D 05
551638	Cable	2E 06
551652	Brake pipe	1K 03
551702	Steering unit assy	1I 02
551703	Steering unit assy	1I 02
551714	Shroud for fan cowl	1O 03
551984	Special spring washer	1I 04
552057	Hose pipe to clutch slave cylinder	1F 08
552097	Bell crank lever assy	1N 03
552129	Hinge centre	2H 05
552132	Support bracket	2H 05
552133	Anchor bracket	2H 05
552174	Tank	1L 18
552175	Tank	1L 18
552223	Torsion spring	1N 03
552388	Mounting bracket	2L 13
552407	Brake rod	1J 06
552435	Pipe tank to pump	1L 16
552436	Pipe tank to pump	1L 16
552438	Pipe	1L 11
552517	Inlet pipe	1D 12
552520	Bracket - acc pedal	1N 05
552524	Bracket	1N 05
552526	Control rod	1N 06
552555	Nylon spacer	1N 09
552572	Tag washer	1I 04
552574	Mounting bracket	2L 13
552575	Dust cover	1I 04
552570	Cross shaft	1K 1C
552563	Ratchet	1K 10
552675	Petrol pipe nylon tank to pump	1M 12

2N 10

PART NO	DESCRIPTION	REF.NO.
552678	Clip	1K 06
552681	Clip	1M 12
552682	Cold start control complete	2D 11
552683	Cold start control complete	2D 11
552688	Engine stop-control	1N 08
552689	Engine stop-control	1N 09
552703	Lever knob	1N 14
552720	Heat shield	1J 06
552746	Shaft hand brake lever	1N 06
552784	Bracket assy	2L 10
552790	Steering unit	1I 04
552804	Special nut	1K 10
552805	Distancr piece	1H 14
552818	Rubber pad	1H 14
552819	Bush	1K 08
552856	Plunger	1K 08
552857	Washer	1K 05
552858	Bracket-acc pedal	1N 05
552975	Shaft & lever	1N 06
552980	Shaft & lever	1H 02
552989	Prop shaft	1H 07
553000	Prop shaft	1H 07
553001	Prop shaft	1G 06
553002	Block	2K 06
553084	Gearbox complete	1G 02
553164	Grommet	1H 08
553262	Joint washer	2C 13
553412	Dynamo fan	1C 06
554055	Rocker shaft	1E 07
554070	Rocker shaft	1C 12
554073	Suction pipe	1C 12
554145	Joint washer	1C 12
554163	Adaptor	1E 12
554175	Clip	1L 08
554260	Elbow	1L 08
554383	Hose	1E 02
554418	Bracket	1L 09
554434	Lever	1E 02
554525	Cover assy	1C 06
554541	Rocker bracket	1D 05
554602	Scraper ring	1C 10
554620	Set bolt (1/2in UNF X 5 3/16)	1E 11
554621	Sealing ring	1E 11
554727	Seal assy	1C 10
554728	Scraper ring	1D 05
554789	Scraper ring	1D 05
554790	Scraper ring	1D 05
554791	Union nut	1D 11
554792	Level rod tube	1D 11
554831	Bracket	1D 11
554832	Level rod	1E 08
554833	Cover assy	1D 11
554843	Level rod	1D 11
554852	Clip	1D 11

2N 10

PART NO	DESCRIPTION	REF.NO.
554917	Bracket	1D 10
554924	Front cover assy	1D 10
554925	Adaptor	1D 15
555661	Socket-inspection lamp-black	2D 11
555662	Socket-inspection lamp-red	2D 11
555702	Outer casing	2D 14
555754	Outer casing	2D 14
555762	Socket	2E 05
555776	Dash harness	2E 05
555778	Switch	2D 11
555798	Dynamo harness	2E 05
555800	Lead	2E 05
555835	Fuel gauge	2D 11
555837	Warning light lens	2D 11
555844	Gauge unit	1L 18
555845	Gauge unit	1L 18
555846	Gauge unit	1L 18
555847	Gauge unit	1L 18
555877	Switch	2D 11
555879	Lead	2I 13
556010	3rd speed gear	1G 05
556039	Bell housing	2K 06
556040	Layshaft	2K 07
556044	Bell housing	2K 06
556147	Bolt (5/16 BSF X 4in)	2K 07
556204	Plug	1H 07
556379	Retaining plate	1G 03
556449	Prop shaft	1H 02
556450	Prop shaft	1H 07
556508	Bleed screw	1F 10
556570	Plug	1G 03
556855	Nut (3/8 UNF)	2L 02
557432	Pipe pump to carburetter	1L 16
557498	Plug	1D 15
557523	Locker	1E 06
557693	Inlet adaptor	1M 04
557694	Hose	1M 04
557782	Banjo	1D 06
557967	Exhaust valve	1C 06
558168	Hot plug	1E 11
558190	Washer	1L 09
558302	Oil pipe	1D 06
559058	Dash & dynamo harness	2E 05
559140	Cable	2E 08
559141	Lead	2E 08
559150	Cable	2E 08
559159	Speedometer & warning lights-miles	2D 11
559160	Speedometer - kilometres	2D 11
559163	Cable	2E 08
559563	Pin	1K 08
559579	Cowl for fan	1O 02
559580	Shroud for fan cowl	1O 03
559646	Bracket	2L 14
559647	Plate	2L 14

2N 11

PART NO	DESCRIPTION	REF.NO.
559648	Taper washer	2L 14
559846	Adaptor pipe	2L 14
559884	Petrol pipe nylon filter bowl to carburetter	1M 12
559885	Petrol pipe nylon	1M 12
560103	Pin	1M 04
560233	Special bolt 5/16 in UNF X 1.3/8 in	1J 09
560404	Nameplate	2D 11
560405	Nameplate	2D 11
560407	Nameplate	2D 11
560410	Nameplate	2D 11
560411	Nameplate	2D 11
560412	Nameplate	2D 11
560532	Dynamo harness	2E 07
560533	Lead	1I 04
560555	Rear crossmember harness	2E 07
560557	Frame harness	2E 07
560566	Cable	2E 08
560567	Cable	2E 08
560744	Gauge panel complete	2D 11
560746	Water temperature gauge	2D 11
560749	Windtone horn	2E 07
560752	Cable-inner	2D 12
560753	Cable-outer	2D 12
560756	Warning light-blue	2D 11
560775	Switch	1K 02
560874	Terminal eyelet	2C 08
560875	Insulating boot	2C 08
560887	Wheelbox for wiper	2D 15
560898	Frame & cross member harness	2E 05
560899	Dash harness	2E 05
560901	Frame & crossmember harness	2E 05
560903	Frame & crossmember harness	2E 05
560904	Dash harness	2E 05
560910	Dash harness	2E 07
560941	Wiper blade	2D 14
560955	Headlamp-bulb type-LH stg	2D 03
560965	Cable	2E 06
560966	Outer casing	2D 15
560967	Nut plate	2D 15
560968	Lead	1I 04
560969	Engine harness	2E 05
560975	Frame & crossmember harness	2E 05
560976	Frame & crossmember harness	2E 05
560977	Frame & crossmember harness	2E 05
560992	Cable	2E 06
561195	Stud	1H 06
561196	Stud 3/8in UNF X 1.3/4in	1H 06
561197	Shim	1G 07
561221	Spring	1G 12
561242	Slave cylinder bracket	1F 09
561254	Wheel nut	1H 16
561368	Oil catcher	1J 06
561484	Bolt 3/8in whit X 1.29/32 in	1G 03
561590	Stud for road wheel	1H 06

2N 11

PART NO	DESCRIPTION	REF.NO.
561661	Connecting tube	1F 10
561762	Slave cylinder bracket	1F 09
561856	Joint washer	1J 06
561877	Housing	1G 04
561886	Stud	1H 06
561889	Hub assy	1H 06
561922	Slave cylinder bracket	1F 09
561954	Bush	1G 04
561960	Reverse wheel assy	1G 04
561962	Shaft	1G 04
561985	Support bracket	2K 05
562019	Pressure gauge	2J 07
562637	'U'bolt	1H 15
562641	Main leaf	1H 15
562654	Bracket	1D 03
562663	Bridge plate	2F 02
562666	Pipe	1K 04
562670	Bracket	1N 06
562675	Servo bracket	1K 04
562678	Servo unit	1K 04
562717	Spring	1N 05
562719	Support bracket	1M 09
562734	'U' bolt	1H 15
562735	Check strap	2F 02
562748	Sedimentor	1L 14
562758	Heat shield exhaust manifold	1N 15
562763	Support bracket	1N 15
562771	'U' bolt	2L 09
562776	'U' bolt	2L 09
562781	Heat shield	1N 14
562791	Pipe complete	2L 14
562793	Pipe complete	2L 14
562795	Hose	2L 14
562875	Shaft	1I 07
562905	Pipe	1K 04
562908	Pipe	1K 04
562912	Exterior mirror complete	2F 03
562919	Hose	1D 12
562928	Casing support	2F 02
562932	Pipe 3/16in	1J 11
562940	Gasket	1J 10
562943	Adaptor	1F 09
562944	Cowl for fan	1O 02
562947	Clip	1F 09
562953	Battery bolt	2F 02
562978	Pipe tank to master cylinder	1J 11
562979	Drive screw	1O 02
563037	Impellor	1D 12
563038	Joint washer	1D 12
563047	Water pipe	1D 03
563050	Wedgelok screw	1D 12
563121	Plug	1D 15
563145	Chain wheel	1D 07
563146	Fuel pump	1L 12

2N 12

PART NO	DESCRIPTION	REF.NO.
563154	Adaptor	1D 12
563165	Pipe	1L 12
563166	Pipe	1L 12
563167	Pipe	1L 12
563168	Pipe	1L 12
563181	Bracket	1M 04
563190	Fuel filter	1L 12
563195	Union	1L 13
563318	Switch	2D 11
564157	Joint washer	1D 12
564162	Adjusting link	2C 13
564163	Timing pointer	1D 10
564164	Tube	1D 12
564165	Connector	1D 12
564202	Cylinder head	1D 13
564206	Bracket	1D 13
564215	Crankcase sump	1D 10
564226	Control ring	1E 04
564231	Piston assy	1E 04
564233	Piston assy	1D 12
564267	Pulley	1D 12
564308	Hub	1E 14
564332	Injector complete	1L 12
564334	Oil pump assy	1D 06
564335	Oil pump assy	1D 06
564362	Timing pointer	1C 08
564375	Crnakshaft pulley	1C 03
564394	Flywheel housing	1F 02
564446	Adaptor	1M 07
564447	Washer	1M 07
564456	Spring	1C 04
564463	Chain wheel	1D 04
564467	Baffle plate	1E 08
564470	Timing pointer	1E 08
564495	Distributor pump	1L 12
564574	Stud	1C 10
564580	Union for petrol pipe	1M 12
564581	Petrol pipe nylon	1M 12
564602	Suction pipe	1M 07
564603	Pipe	1M 07
564704	Front bumper	2F 02
564718	Overflow bottle	1D 03
564719	Cap for overflow bottle	1D 03
564724	Hose radiator to overflow bottle	1D 03
564741	Flexible pipe overflow bottle outlet	1D 03
564785	Spring washer	1D 02
564786	Pipe tank to master cylinder	1J 11
564792	Brake pipe	1K 02
564793	Ext shaft and lever	1N 05
564794	Ext shaft and lever	1N 05
564797	Control rod	1N 06
564813	Control rod	1N 06
	Pedal shaft	1J 13

PART NO	DESCRIPTION	REF.NO.
564816	Pedal bush	1J 13
564825	Spring washer	1L 07
564898	Pipe	1L 13
564899	Pipe	1L 13
564902	Pipe	1L 13
564905	Pipe	1L 13
564907	Pipe	1L 13
564909	Valve	1L 12
564911	Bracket	1N 08
564936	Pipe tank to sedimentor	1L 08
564937	Pipe	1L 14
564944	Packing piece	1J 09
564962	Pipe	1L 13
564963	Pipe tank to sedimentor	1L 08
564999	Joint washer	1D 02
565770	Screw driver	2J 07
566462	Lever assy	2K 13
566761	Plate	2C 13
566813	Clip	1D 14
566851	Flywheel assy	1F 05
566957	Breather pipe	1D 10
567959	Mounting clip	2D 06
568005	Terminal sleeve	2D 02
568301	Carbon ring & seal unit	1C 09
568333	Chain wheel	1C 03
568363	Bracket	1D 13
568364	Joint washer	1M 07
568365	Joint washer	1M 07
568380	Adaptor	1M 07
568391	Hose	1D 14
568392	Clip	1D 14
568431	Ring gear	1F 05
568457	Adaptor	1C 11
568474	Chainwheel	1C 11
568475	Push rod	1C 05
568542	Cover	1D 08
568550	Valve spring	1E 08
568575	Olive	1C 06
568588	Piston ring	1M 12
568664	Stud	1E 04
568667	Front cover assy	1C 07
568686	Valve guide, inlet	1C 10
568687	Valve guide, exhaust	1C 10
568688	Valve guide, inlet	1E 11
568689	Valve guide, exhaust	1E 11
568725	Cover assy	1D 14
568766	Lead	2C 03
568786	Exhaust valve	1D 08
568802	Support for fuel tank	1M 10
568858	Stem rubber	2L 13
568866	Return spring	1D 10
568883	Trunnion	1J 08
568893	Pedal and bracket assy	1J 09
568894	Pedal and bracket assy	1J 08
568895	Pedal & bush	1J 13

PART NO	DESCRIPTION	REF.NO.
568896	Pedal and bushes	1J 08
568916	Cowl for fan	10 02
568917	Shroud for fan cowl	10 03
568922	Steady strip for shroud	10 03
568947	Pipe 1/4in	1H 11
569028	'U' bolt	1H 15
569047	Joint washer for plug	10 05
569054	Brake pedal bracket assy	1J 08
569055	Pedal bracket	1J 08
569057	Pesal bracket	1J 08
569058	Bracket	1J 08
569084	Brake pedal bracket assy	1J 08
569085	Pedal bracket	1J 08
569086	Pedal & bushes	1J 09
569096	Spacer	1J 09
569117	End stop	1J 09
569147	Pipe tank to master cylinder	1J 11
569149	Pipe tanktto master cylinder	1J 11
569201	Switch protector plate	2L 09
569204	Road wheel	1K 03
569212	Shroud for fan cowl	10 02
569223	Brake pipe	1N 10
569243	Housing & quadrant	1N 10
569250	Lever for control	1N 10
569291	Lever-cross shaft	1J 13
569338	Return spring	1J 13
569433	Servo unit	1K 06
569434	Pipe	1K 06
569462	Pipe	1F 08
569522	Mounting bracket	1J 05
569584	Packing piece	2J 13
569585	Switch lever	1L 14
569601	Mounting bracket	1J 13
569606	Pedal bracket	1J 13
569609	Bracket	1J 13
569652	Nylon bush	1J 13
569653	Pedal & bracket assy LH	1N 10
569654	Mounting panel LH	1N 10
569687	Mounting panel RH	1N 10
569689	Wheel brace	2L 17
569690	Casing support	2F 02
569701	Road wheel	1H 16
569702	Return spring	1J 10
569746	Pipe 1/4 in	1J 14
569769	Bush 1.187in O/D	1H 15
571059	Pipe	1K 06
571145	Oil seal	1G 03
571164	Peg	1G 11
571218	Cap for pivot pin	1G 03
571235	Distance piece	1G 04
571661	Driving member	1H 07
571711	Tolerance ring	1G 10
571770	Driving member	1H 07
571855	Inner member	2K 08
	Selector rod	1C 12

PART NO	DESCRIPTION	REF. NO.
571916	Set screw 5/16in BSF	1H 08
571922	Washer	1H 07
574044	Fan blade	1D 12
574048	Stud	1C 13
574144	Conversion set	2C 06
574217	Rubber boot	2E 02
574654	Clip	1E 12
574656	Connecting tube	1E 14
574658	Breather filter	1E 12
574661	Inlet manifold	1E 14
574871	Hose	1E 10
574878	Rubber sleeve for suction pipe	1M 07
575014	Spring washer	2E 04
575042	Grommet	2J 05
575047	Outer casing	2D 14
575081	Switch	2D 10
575082	Clip	2C 08
575099	Headlamp RH stg	2D 03
575101	Headlamp-LH stg	2D 03
575103	Light unit LH stg	2D 03
575114	Self-cancelling flasher switch	2D 06
575119	Sidelamp	2D 03
575123	Flasher lamp	2D 06
575125	Flasher lamp	2D 06
575166	Mechanical stop switch	1J 13
575801	Switch	2D 11
576103	Wheel nut	2H 03
576159	Pin	1H 08
576201	Low gear wheel	2K 08
576207	Bearing	1G 05
576209	Outer member	2K 08
576210	Transfer gear lever	1G 13
576217	Propeller shaft	2L 02
576236	Shim	1H 09
576237	Shim	1H 09
576238	Shim	1H 09
576239	Shim	1H 09
576302	Gearbox complete	2K 06
576316	Knob	1G 10
576521	Bolt (3/8 BSF X 1 3/8)	1H 03
576522	Bolt (3/8 BSF X 11/2in)	1H 03
576583	Swivel pin complete	1H 04
576686	Layshaft cluster	1G 06
576703	Fork	1G 11
576704	Fork	1G 11
576707	Reverse gear	1G 06
576714	Bell housing	1G 02
576717	Bolt 5/16 in BSF X 2 in	1G 03
576718	Frt cover G/box	1G 03
576720	Pivot pin clutch release	1G 03
576723	Clip	1F 10
576724	Joint washer G/box front cover	1G 03
576725	Mainshaft	1G 05
576727	Selector shaft	1G 11

PART NO	DESCRIPTION	REF. NO.
576729	Selector shaft	1G 11
576730N	Gearbox assy	1G 03
576734	Bush	1C 06
576735	Thrust washer	1G 06
576751	Push rod slave cylinder	1F 10
576761N	Gearbox assy	1G 03
576762	Bell housing	1G 02
576767	Half shaft	1H 13
576768	Half shaft	1H 13
576825	Stud for road wheel	1H 06
576836	Bearing housing	1G 06
576844	Hub and stud assy	1H 06
576895	Lock TAB	1H 08
576907	Distance piece for bearing	1G 06
576973	Brake drum	1J 03
576974	Brake drum	1J 04
577002	Battery frame	2F 02
577016	Bracket	1K 06
577137	Shaft hand brake lever	1J 06
577138	Washer plate	1J 06
577166	Brake pipe	1K 02
577331	Hand control housing	1N 10
577332	Distance tube	1N 10
577342	Cowl for fan	1D 02
577346	Bracket	1E 02
577354	Washer	1D 06
577383	Radiator block assy (less cowl)	1D 02
577414	Crossmember	2F 02
577609	Radiator block	1D 02
577874	Steady strip for shroud	1D 07
577898	Clip for ball joint	2F 02
577973	Check strap	2E 06
579243	Lead coil to distributor	2C 05
587001	Shield	1N 11
587095	Shield	1D 10
587104	Hose flame trap to carb	1D 10
587105	Hose	1D 13
587338	Set bolt 7/16 in UNF X 55/32 in	1D 13
587339	Plain washer	1E
587401	Manifold assy	1C 13
587405	Plain washer	1D 12
587463	Outlet pipe	1F 10
587622	Support plate	1C 02
587628	Cup plug	1C 12
587726	Stud	1C 12
587923	Plug	1D 09
589283	Lens for sidelamp	2D 04
589284	Lens for sidelamp	2D 04
589401	Sidelamp	2D 04
589403	Sidelamp	2D 06
589414	Front flasher lamp	2D 06
589448	Rear flasher lamp	2D 05
589806	Lens for stop/tail lamp	2J 04
589806	Cable clip	2J 04

PART NO	DESCRIPTION	REF. NO.
591039	Brake drum	1J 02
591202	Bush	1F 07
591204	Sleeve assy	1F 07
591205	Housing	1F 07
591231	Slave cylinder	1F 10
591278	Front propshaft	2L 02
591279	Rear propshaft	1H 07
591283	Rear propshaft	1H 07
591362	1st mainshaft gear	1G 06
591363	Second speed gear	1G 05
591364	Synchro cone	1G 05
591378	Axle shaft	1H 06
591379	Axle shaft	1H 06
591429	Rear output shaft	1G 07
591440	Gearbox assembly	1G 03
591441	Gearbox assembly	1G 03
591519	Spring pin	1G 06
591527	Shaft for reverse gear	1G 06
591544	Rear axle assy	1H 06
591661	Brake drum	1J 02
592177	Bottom plate	2L 02
592179	Bottom plate	1H 15
592182	U-bolt	2L 06
592183	U-bolt	2L 02
592184	U-bolt	2L 02
592185	U-bolt	2J 07
592219	Jack rod	1K 03
592374	Brake pipe	1K 03
592375	Brake pipe	2L 09
592472	Chassis frame	1J 11
592508	Clutch pipe	1J 14
592509	Clutch pipe	1F 10
592515	Jump hose	1K 02
592549	Brake pipe	2F 02
592594	Crossmember	1F 10
533664	Crossmember	1K 02
594018	Bracket	1G 05
594019	Shim	1G 05
594020	Shim	1G 05
594021	Shim	1H 04
594104	Nut (7/16 BSF)	1G 07
594195	Gear shaft	1F 07
594224	Seal	2L 02
594361	Front propshaft	2L 02
594416	Front axle assh LH strg	1H 08
594484N	Differential assy	2F 02
594683	Chassis frame 109 in 4 cyl SW	2F 02
594684	Chassis frame 109 in 6 cyl	2F 02
594698	Chassis frame 109 in 6 cyl SW	1L 08
594753	Hose clip	1F 10
594776	Bleed pipe	1M 10
594793	Clip for hose top	1F 10
594822	Adaptor	1M 10
594938	Bracket junction piece	1K 02

PART NO	DESCRIPTION	REF.NO.
595123	Drop arm	1L 03
595336	Wheel nut wrench	2J 07
595468	Strg drag link and damper brkt assy	2L 13
595469	Drag link and damper brkt	2L L3
596000	Inlet manifold	1C 12
596069	Plug	1C 12
596097	Stud 5/16 in UNF X 113/16 in long	1D 16
596495	Elbow	1M 07
597501	Piston assembly 020 O/S	1C 03
597503	Piston assembly 040 O/S	1C 03
597563	Banjo bolt	1C 11
598064	Hub for fan	1C 09
598086	Cylinder head assy	1C 10
598089	Cylinder head assy	1C 10
598110	Carburetter	1M 05
598214	Oil pump shaft	1D 06
598231	Oil filler cap	1D 10
598354	Joint washer	1C 11
598473	Exhaust manifold	1C 13
598531	Carrier bracket overflow bottle	1D 03
598536	Bottom plate	2L 02
598539	Exhaust silencer	1N 13
598598	Check strap	2L 06
599652	Bell crank lever and bush	1N 06
598854	Check strap	2F 02
599423	Chassis frame 109 in 4 cyl	2F 02
599698	Distancr piece	1H 06
599826	Stub axle assy	1H 05
599827	Stub axle assy	2L 04
599869	Bearing sleeve assy	1H 06
599869	Roller bearing	1G 07
600024	Screw	2D 03
600025	Spring for screw	2D 03
600026	Fibre washer	1D 04
600174	Thrust washer	1D 04
600175	Thrust washer	1D 04
600176	Thrust washer	1D 04
600177	Thrust washer	1D 04
600178	Thrust washer	1D 04
600179	Thrust washer	1D 04
600202	Anchor plate	1J 04
600203	Anchor plate	1J 04
600206	Pipe	1J 04
600210	Wheel cylinder kit	1J 04
600212	Spring	1J 03
600226	Adaptor & leads	2D 03
600241	Main nut assy	2L 10
600242	Main nut assy	2L 10
600243	Flywheel assy	1F 02
600245	Stud kit for cylinder block	1C 02
600310	Loctite compound	2J 03
600311	2nd leaf - rear	2L 09
600329	Dowel & nut-rear	2L 09
600334	Terminal bush & Lead	2C 02
	Bush	2C 02

2N 15

PART NO	DESCRIPTION	REF.NO.
600349	Grommet	20 08
600351	Throttle butterfly	1M 02
600401	Oil container	1M 12
600423	Special screw	20 04
600432	Servo overhaul kit	1K 05
600432	Servo overhaul kit	2J 02
600432	Servo overhaul kit	2L 15
600434	Poppet valve overhaul kit	1K 05
600435	Non return valve overhaul kit	1K 05
600468	Outer column	1L 02
600476	Springs set	2C 02
600603	Gearbox gasket set	2G 03
600613	Element for air cleaner	1M 12
600638	Contact set	2D 13
600645	Filler cap	1G 03
600656	Flange	1H 07
600851	Special screw	2D 02
600901	Diff casing	1H 10
600902	Nose piece	1H 10
600916	2nd speed gear	1G 04
600984	Outer column	1L 02
601313	Sealing pellet	2J 06
601316	Cylinder block assy	1C 02
601469	Cylinder head assy	1E 11
601521	Screw	1M 03
601543	Grommet	2D 07
601594	Washer	1M 02
601680	Servc kit major	1K 05
601689	Pivot pin	2C 08
601720	Lens	20 09
601721	Lens	20 02
601754	Spring set	2C 04
601790	Splined stub shaft	1H 07
601834	Carburetter body	1L 06
601835	Throttle spindle	1L 06
601836	Throttle lever	1L 06
601837	Throttle stop	1L 07
601838	Special nut	1L 06
601840	Relay lever	1L 06
601841	Split pin	1L 06
601842	Lever	1L 06
601843	Plain washer	1L 06
601844	Butterfly for throttle	1L 06
601845	Special screw	1L 06
601846	Special screw	1L 06
601850	'O' ring	1L 06
601851	Emulsion block	1L 06
601852	Ball for piston	1L 06
601853	Circlip	1L 06
601854	Plug for pump jet	1L 06
601855	Pump discharge valve	1L 06
601856	Accelerator pump	1L 06
601857	Special washer	1L 06
601858	Float	1L 06
601859	Spindle for float	1L 06

2N 16

PART NO	DESCRIPTION	REF.NO.
601860	Top cover	1L 07
601861	Lever & swivel	1L 07
601862	Spring	1L 07
601863	Circlip	1L 07
601865	Spindle and pin	1L 07
601866	Spring	1L 07
601867	Butterfly for choke	1L 07
601869	Plain washer	1L 07
601870	Bracket & clip	1L 07
601872	Special screw	1L 07
601873	Shakeproof washer	1L 07
601874	Spindle & lever	1L 07
601875	Spacing washer	1L 07
601876	Pump lever	1L 07
601877	Washer	1M 06
601878	Retaining ring	1L 07
601879	Diaphragm	1L 07
601880	Gasket	1L 07
601881	Spring	1L 07
601882	Cover	1L 07
601883	Screw	1L 07
601884	Spring washer	1L 07
601885	Spindle & pin	1L 07
601886	Special screw	1L 06
601887	Spring washer	1L 06
601888	Screw & washer	1L 07
601891	Split pin=	1L 07
601892	Plain washer	1L 07
601893	Link	1L 06
601894	Split pin	1L 06
601895	Main jet	1L 06
601896	Enrichment jet	1L 06
601897	Slow running jet	1L 06
601899	Screw & washer	1L 06
601900	Needle valve	1L 06
601954	Washer	1L 06
601999	Rim light unit	2D 03
602915	Drain tap	1C 02
603887	Clip fixing hose	1O 03
603888	Clip	1K 06
603896	Clip	1L 17
603897	Hose clip for air cleaner connection	1L 08
605010	Plug	1L 14
605011	Seal	1L 14
605012	Plug	1L 12
605013	Seal	1L 12
605047	Control ring	1E 04
605048	Control ring	1E 04
605049	Control ring	1E 04
605050	Control ring	1E 04
605056	Cover	2C 15
605061	Spring set	2C 15
605063	Bearing	2C 15
605063	Bracket	2C 15
605070	Headlamp	2D 02

2N 16

PART NO	DESCRIPTION	REF.NO.
605092	Carb overhaul kit	1L 05
605093	Carb gasket kit	1L 05
605106	Gasket kit	1D 03
605127	Overhaul kit Br M cylinder	1J 12
605157	Cylinder block assy	1D 03
605162	Jet housing	1M 02
605169	Gasket small	1D 15
605183	Joint washer for gauge unit	1M 10
605238	Plastigauge strip	2J 02
605280	Knob	2D 10
605322	Spring washer	1M 08
605484	Valve guide kit	1E 13
605539	Piston ring	1E 04
605540	Piston ring	1E 04
605541	Piston ring	1E 04
605542	Piston ring	1E 04
605560	Sedimentor	1L 14
605612	Cover	2C 09
605615	Pivot pin	2C 09
605621	Armature	2C 09
605622	Sundry parts	2C 05
605653	Spindle	2C 09
605683	Main jet	1L 07
605684	Main jet	1L 07
605685	Main jet	1L 07
605686	Main jet	1L 07
605687	Slow running jet	1L 07
605698	Lamp switch	2D 10
605699	Knob	2D 10
605705	Nut	2C 09
605716	Water pump kit	2J 02
605761	Valve guide oil control kit	1C 11
605765	Coolant inhibitor	2J 02
605793	Adaptor	1M 05
605794	Spindle	1M 05
605795	Lever	1M 05
605796	Throttle stop	1M 05
605797	Washer	1M 05
605799	Nut	1M 05
605800	Butterfly	1M 05
605801	Screw	1M 05
605802	Screw	1M 06
605803	Cover	1M 06
605804	Spindle	1M 06
605805	Spring	1M 06
605806	Washer	1M 06
605807	Screw	1M 06
605808	Lever	1M 06
605809	Washer	1M 06
605810	Washer	1M 06
605811	Screw	1M 06
605813	Bracket	1M 05
605815	Screw	1M 06
605816	Screw	1M 05
605817	Spring	1M 05
605818	Screw	1M 05
605820	Pin	1M 05
605821	Spring	1M 05
605822	Clip	1M 05
605827	Jet orifice	1M 05
605828	Spring	1M 06
605830	Carrier	1M 06
605833	Float	1M 06
605834	Spindle	1M 06
605835	Gasket	1M 06
605836	Float chamber	1M 06
605837	Screw	1M 06
605838	Screw	1M 06
605839	Washer	1M 06
605840	Washer	1M 06
605842	Retaining ring	1M 05
605843	Screw	1M 05
605844	Air cvalve	2C 09
605845	Screw	2C 09
605846	Top cover	2C 09
605847	Screw	2C 05
605848	Damper & cap	2C 09
605849	Washer	1L 07
605850	Bush	1L 07
605852	Washer	1M 06
605857	Gasket kit	1L 07
605904	Spindle & gear	2D 14
605933	Gearbox casing	2K 06
605997	Lining for clutch plate	1F 03
606098	Carburetter kit	2J 02
606099	Primary pinion	1G 05
606138	Enrichment jet	2E 03
606187	Mirror	1M 11
606207	Seal for centre bolt	2C 04
606220	Circlip	2E 02
606253	Fuse box	2E 02
606301	Washer	1M 06
606309	Wiper motor	2D 14
606314	Spark plug	2C 03
606318	Enrichment jet (150)	1L 06
606319	Emulsion block	1L 06
606329	End cap	1J 09
606330	Spacer	1J 09
606331	End cap	1J 09
606332	Spacer	1J 09
606404	Sealing washer	1J 13
606415	Overhaul kit Br M cylinder	1J 13
606486	Spring	1J 14
606487	Needle	1M 05
606499	Bulbholder	2D 03
606501	Bulb holder	2D 06
606502	Bulb holder	2D 09
606504	Bracket	2C 06
606505	Cover	2C 09
606507	Bracket	2C 09
606508	Pivot pin	2C 09
606577	Lamp switch	2D 10
606583	Vacuum unit	2C 02
606679	Gasket	1L 07
606700	Linkng c/w rivets	1J 04
606880	Pr pinion & const gear	1G 05
606881	Gear box casing	1G 03
606895	Bush	2C 02
606988	Exhaust manifold kit	1C 13
607125N	Gearbox assy	1G 03
607127N	Gearbox assy	1G 03
607141	Field coil	2C 15
607162	Gear carrier casing	1H 12
607163	Bolt	1H 12
607164	Diff case less gears	1H 12
607165	Bolt 12mm X 50mm	1H 12
607166	Diff pinion	1H 12
607167	Diff pinion	1H 12
607168	Thrust washer	1H 12
607169	Thrust washer	1H 12
607172	Plug	1H 12
607173	Bolt	1H 12
607175	Gasket	1H 12
607176	Washer for diff pinion	1H 12
607177	Shim	1H 12
607178	Shim	1H 12
607179	Shim	1H 12
607180	Pinion bearing	1H 12
607181	Pinion bearing	1H 12
607182	Oil thrower	1H 12
607183	Gasket	1H 12
607185	Flange	1H 12
607186	Bracket	1H 12
607187	Bearing	1H 12
607188	Shim	1H 12
607189	Shim	1H 12
607190	Shim	1H 12
607191	Shim	1H 12
607197	Spacer	1H 12
607247	Rear axle assy less hub brake & shafts	2C 09
607747	Bracket	2D 13
607808	Steady post and bush kit	1J 03
607815	Bush for jet orifiche	1M 06
607908N	Gearbox assy	2K 06
607909N	Gearbox assy	2K 06
607932	Pinion retaining kit	2D 13
607950	Bracket	2D 04
608004	Screw and washer	2D 04
608005	Screw and washer	2C 02
608111	Vacuum unit	2C 02
608124	Engine overhaul gasket kit	1C 04
608172	Bush kit	2C 04
608174	Bracket, drive end	2C 04
608246	Drain plug	1H 12
6082555	Piston assy	1C 03

2N 17   2N 17   2N 18

PART NO	DESCRIPTION	REF.NO.
608283	Inner and outer members	1G 06
608304	Bush kit for bracket	2C 09
608327	Cylinder block	1C 02
608388	Bolt kit	2C 08
608421	Spring set	2C 05
608457	Crown wheel and pinion	1H 09
608464	Ball joint assy	1I 07
608465	Strg track rod assy	1I 07
622006	Gear lever assy	1G 10
622007	Gear lever assy	1G 10
622042	Oil seal	1G 07
622045	Gasket for bell housing	1G 02
622046	Joint washer transfer box to gearbox	1G 08
622047	Joint washer for bearing housing	1G 08
622048	Joint washer for output shaft	1G 09
622155	Selector fork	1G 12
622195	Rear axle casing assy	1H 06
622197	Rear axle casing assy	1H 06
622199	Front axle casing	1H 02
622281	Bolt 1/4 in BSF X 13/32 in	1G 11
623065	Horn	2D 13
624077	Spring bottom plate	1H 15
624078	Spring bottom plate	1H 15
624079	Spring bottom plate	1H 15
624080	Spring bottom plate	1H 15
624084	Spring bottom plate	1H 15
624252	Handbrake lever assy	1K 08
626262	Handbrake lever assy	1K 10
850641	Plain washer M10	1C 14
AAU 1053	Swivel for stop lever	1L 09
AAU 1054	Clamp bolt	1L 03
AAU 1130	Sidelamp	2D 08
AAU 1484	Needle valve	1M 06
AAU 1582	Brake cleaning fluid	2J 02
AAU 1909	Outer casing	2D 15
AAU 2003	Socket for control rod	1N 03
AAU 2825	Spring washer	1H 12
AAU 3381	Oil seal	1H 12
AAU 4071	Heater / sealing switch	2D 10
AAU 8469	Lining with rivets	1J 04
AAU 8470	Lining with rivets	1J 05
AAU 8471	Lining with rivets	1J 03
AAU 9902	Seal, bottom	1L 09
AAU 9902	" "	1L 11
AAU 9903	Seal, top	1L 12
AAU 9903	" "	1L 14
AB 604021	Drive screw	1N 10
AB 604031	Drive screw	2F 07
AB 604031	" "	2G 09
AB 604031	" "	2I 09
AB 604041	Drive screw	2F 13
AB 604041	" "	2F 14
AB 604041	" "	2H 02
AB 604041	" "	2I 02
		2I 04

2N 18

PART NO	DESCRIPTION	REF.NO.
AB 604041	Drive screw	2I 10
AB 606021	Drive screw	1C 10
AB 606031	Drive screw	10 02
AB 606031	" "	2F 12
AB 606031	" "	2F 15
AB 606031	" "	2G 02
AB 606031	" "	2H 02
AB 606031	" "	2H 07
AB 606031	" "	2I 06
AB 606031	" "	2I 07
AB 606031	" "	2I 14
AB 606031	" "	2I 15
AB 606071	Drive screw	2F 12
AB 606071	" "	2F 15
AB 606081	Drive screw	2I 10
AB 608031	Drive screw	1L 10
AB 608031	" "	2G 02
AB 608031	" "	2G 05
AB 608031	" "	2G 07
AB 608031	" "	2I 09
AB 608031	" "	2I 13
AB 610031	Drive screw	1D 14
AB 610051	Drive screw	1L 14
AB 610051	" "	2I 03
AB 610051	" "	2I 05
ABU 5794	Headlamp	2D 02
AC 606081	Drive screw	2I 13
AD 604031	Drive screw	2G 04
AD 606041	Drive screw	2I 13
AEU 1022	Lining package	1F 03
AEU 1058	Lens	2D 06
AEU 1058	"	2D 07
AEU 1061	Headlamp	2D 02
AEU 1061	"	2D 03
AEU 1147	Centre seal, lower	1M 11
AEU 1367	Retention kit	2C 04
AEU 1428	Brush and spring	2C 02
AEU 1429	Vacuum unit	2C 02
AEU 1449	Clip	1L 16
AEU 1449	"	2J 04
AEU 1450	Clip	2J 04
AEU 1451	Clip	2J 04
AEU 1581	Clip	1F 09
AEU 1586	End cover bracket	2C 04
AFU 1024	Combination pliars	2J 07
AFU 1088	Drive screw	2D 02
AUA 573	Joint washer	1M 08
AUB 617	Filter	1M 08
AUB 654	Sealing ring	1M 08
AUB 656	Diaphragm	1M 08
AUB 657	Sealing ring	1M 08
AUB 676	Sealing washer	1M 08
AUB 795	Joint washer	1M 08
AUB 849	Joint washer	1M 08
AUB 6062	Valve assy	1M 08

20 02

PART NO	DESCRIPTION	REF.NO.
AUB 6106	Contact set, fuel pump	1M 08
AUB 6179	Condenser	1M 08
AUC 1123	Float	1M 02
AUC 1152	Pin	1M 02
AUC 1167	Spring	1M 02
AUC 1358	Screw	1M 02
AUC 1557	Aluminium washer	1M 03
AUC 1928	Fibre washer	1M 03
AUC 2001	Jet bearing	1M 02
AUC 2002	Jet screw	1M 02
AUC 2006	Jet spring	1M 02
AUC 2014	Gasket	1M 02
AUC 2027	Gland spring	1M 02
AUC 2028	Slow running valve	1M 02
AUC 2029	Gland washer	1M 02
AUC 2030	Brass washer	1M 02
AUC 2057	Special screw	1M 02
AUC 2110	Rolt	1M 02
AUC 2139	Filter and spring	1M 03
AUC 2175	Special screw	1M 02
AUC 2451	Spring	1M 03
AUC 8155	Jet complete	1M 02
AUD 247	Carburetter	1M 02
AUD 2285	Lever for float	1M 02
AUF 503	Fuel pump	1M 08
AXE 2070	Locker	1D 09
BAU 1689	Clip	1L 16
BH 505201	Bolt 5/16 in UNC X 2.1/2in	1M 07
BH 505241	Bolt 5/16 in UNC X 3in	1M 07
BH 604091	Bolt 1/4in UNF X 1.1/8in	1D 12
BH 604101	Set bolt	1D 12
BH 604101	" "	1K 02
BH 604101	" "	1K 04
BH 604101	" "	1K 06
BH 604101	" "	1N 02
BH 604101	" "	1N 03
BH 604101	" "	1N 05
BH 604101	" "	1N 07
BH 604101	" "	1N 09
BH 604101	" "	1N 10
BH 604101	" "	2I 12
BH 604101	" "	2L 14
BH 604111	Set bolt 1/4in UNF X 1.3/8 in	1D 07
BH 604161	Bolt	1I 08
BH 604181	Bolt 1/4in UNF X 2.1/4in	1D 12
BH 604201	Bolt 1/4in UNF X 2.1/2in	1C 09
BH 604221	Bolt	1C 09
BH 605101	Set bolt	1C 05
BH 605101	" "	1E 06
BH 605101	" "	1L 09
BH 605101	" "	1L 11
BH 605111	Bolt 5/16in UNF X 1.3/8in	2C 14
BH 605161	Bolt 5/16in UNF X 2in	1C 07
BH 605201	Bolt 5/16in UNF X 2.1/2 in	2F 15
BH 605221	Set bolt 5/16in UNF X 2.3/4in	1C 13

20 02

PART NO	DESCRIPTION	REF.NO.
BH 605241	Set bolt 5/16in UNF X 3in	1C 07
BH 605261	Bolt 5/16in UNF 3.1/4in	1C 07
BH 605281	Set bolt	1C 07
BH 605281	"	1E 08
BH 606141	Bolt 3/8in UNF X 1.3/4in	1F 02
BH 606201	Bolt 3/8in UNF X 2.1/2in	1L 18
BH 606281	Bolt 3/8in UNF X 3.1/2in	1D 17
BH 606321	Bolt 3/8in UNF X 4 in	1J 06
BH 607141	Bolt 7/16in UNF X 1.3/4in	1H 10
BH 607161	Set bolt 7/16in UNF X 2in	2C 08
BH 607241	Bolt 7/16in UNF X 3in	1D 15
BH 607281	Bolt 7/16in UNF X 3.1/2in	1D 15
BH 608361	Bolt 1/2 in UNF X 4.1/2in	2L 09
BHA 4602	Voltage regulator instruments	2E 04
BHA 4790	Mounting strap	2D 15
BHA 5252	Thermostat switch	1C 11
BHA 5252	"	1D 13
BLS 108	Ball	1G 06
BMK 1903	Locknut	1K 02
BTB 657	T - piece	2C 10
BX 605111	Bolt	2C 14
BX 605161	Special bolt	1C 13
BX 605281	Bolt	1I 07
BX 607181	Bolt	1D 05
C 3964	Circlip	1J 06
CCN 112	Circlip	1G 07
CCN 122	Key blank	2H 07
CD 31709B	Distributor complete	2C 05
ERC 545	Special nut for conn rod	1D 05
ERC 1027	Conn rod nut	1C 03
ERC 1029	Thrust plate	1C 05
ERC 1561	Support plate	1F 10
ERC 2060	Indicator	1F 05
ERC 2250	Piston assy	1D 05
ERC 2337S	Piston assy	1D 05
ERC 2339S	Piston assy	1E 04
ERC 2425	Control rod and joint	1N 04
ERC 2533	Lifting bracket	1C 11
ERC 2686	"	1E 12
ERC 2686	Carburetter	1L 06
ERC 2886	Spindle & bearing	1C 09
ERC 3978	"	1D 12
ERC 3978	"	1E 10
ERC 4110	Distributor	2C 02
ERC 4182	Vibration damper	1D 04
ERC 4199	Oil level rod	1C 08
ERC 4387	Lifting bracket	1D 13
ERC 4480	Leak off pipe	1L 13
ERC 4935	Insert	1D 03
ERC 5086	Seal	1C 02
ERC 5086	"	1E 02
ERC 6105	Drive shaft assy	1C 04
FRC 1387	C-ring	1G 10

20 03

PART NO	DESCRIPTION	REF.NO.
FRC 1454	Gear lever	1G 10
FRC 1455	Gear lever	1G 10
FRC 1511	Joint washer	1G 09
FRC 1516	Joint washer	1G 08
FRC 1516	"	2K 10
FRC 1536	Speedo spindle	1C 07
FRC 1758	Synchro clutch	1G 05
FRC 1780	Oil seal	1G 07
FRC 1832	Gear lever	1G 10
FRC 1833	Gear lever	1G 10
FRC 1836	Gear lever assy	1G 10
FRC 1837	Gear lever assy	1G 10
FRC 2060	Front axle assy	1H 02
FRC 2061	Front axle assy	1H 02
FRC 2074	Housing assy for swivel pin	1H 03/2L 03
FRC 2075	Housing assy for swivel pin	1H 03/2L 03
FRC 2135	Front axle assy	1H 02
FRC 2136	Rear axle assy	1H 06
FRC 2138	Front axle assy	1H 02
FRC 2216	Pinion housing	1G 10
FRC 2469	Locker	2K 13
FRC 3234	Brake spring	1J 06
FRC 3395	Front axle assy	1H 08
FRC 3398	Front axle assy	2L 02
FRC 4396	Front axle assy	1H 02
FRC 4398	Rear axle assy	1H 12
FRC 4835	Copper washer	1H 08
GAC 148	Radiator seal pellet	2J 02
GAP 405	Aerosol paint pastel green	2C 06
GAP 406	Aerosol paint bronze green	2C 06
GAP 407	Aerosol paint marine blue	2C 06
GAP 408	Aerosol paint limestone	2C 06
GAT 348	Aerosol paint grey	2C 07
GBF 103	Foot pump	2J 02
GBH 134	Brake fluid	1K 02
GBH 302	Brake hose	1K 02
GBS 728	Brake hose	1J 02
GBS 729	Brake shoe set	1J 03
GBS 730	Brake shoe set	1J 04
GBS 552	Brake shoe set	1J 06
GBS 793	Brake shoe assy	1J 05
GBY 2205	Brake shoe set	1J 06
GBY 2235	Activator 12volt	2E 02
GCC 112	Activator 6volt	2E 02
GCC 127	Clutch cover	1F 03
GCC 181	Clutch assy	1F 05
GCL 110	Clutch cover	2E 02
GCP 109	Ignition coil	1F 03
GCS 101	Clutch plate	1F 03
GCS 107	Clutch plate	2C 02
GCS 125	Contact points	2C 02
GDC 101	Contact set	2C 05
	Contact set	2C 05
	Distributor cap	

20 03

PART NO	DESCRIPTION	REF.NO.
GDC 103	Distributor cap	2C 02
GDC 107	Distributor cap	2C 02
GDC 115	Distributor cap	2C 05
GDC 226	Distributor cap	2J 02
GEG 162	Decarb gaskets	1C 02
GEG 240	Engine overhaul gasket set	1C 02
GEG 339	Cylinder head gasket	1D 13
GEG 393	Cylinder head gasket	1E 11
GEG 431	Joint washer top rocker cover	1C 1C
GEG 432	Joint washer for rocker cover	1C 1C
GEG 433	Joint washer for rocker cover	1D 14
GEG 452	Joint washer for rocker cover	1D 10
GEG 537	Joint washer for rocker cover	1E 12
GEG 538	Joint washer for sump	1C 08
GEG 639	Joint washer for sump	1D 10
GEG 640	Joint washer	1C 13
GEG 661	Joint washer for exhuast manifold	1D 16
GEG 685	Joint washer	1C 13
GEG 723	Manifold gasket	1E 14
GEG 1200	Gasket	1N 11
GEG 1214	Decarb gasket set	1E 02
GEG 3308	Decarb gasket set	1D 03
GEU 101	Cylinder head gasket	1C 10
GEU 104	Dynamo complete	2C 10
GEU 105	Dynamo complete	2C 12
GEU 419	Dynamo complete	2C 04
GEU 419	Starter motor	2C 06
GEU 430	Starter motor	2C 09
GEU 437	Starter motor	2C 08
GEU 603	Voltage regulator box	2E 02
GEU 605	Voltage regulator box	2E 02
GEU 607	Voltage regulator box	2E 07
GEU 701	Wiper motor	2D 13
GEU 708	Windscreen wiper motor	2D 14
GEU 714	Windscreen wiper motor	1N 11
GEX 1369	Front exhaust pipe	1N 12
GEX 1370	Intermediate exhaust pipe	1N 12
GEX 1372	Front exhaust pipe	1N 12
GEX 1373	Intermediate exhaust pipe	1N 12
GEX 1375	Intermediate ex pipe	2D 13
GEX 1376	Front exhaust pipe	2D 14
GEX 1377	Intermediate ex pipe	1N 11
GEX 1380	Front exhaust pipe complete	1N 12
GEX 1381	Intermediate exhaust pipe	1N 14
GEX 1383	Tail pipe complete	1N 14
GEX 1563	Front exhaust pipe	1N 11
GEX 1564	Front exhaust pipe	2L 16
GEX 3301	Exhaust silencer	1N 13
GEX 3302	Exhaust silencer	1N 13
GEX 3307	Exhaust silencer	1N 13
GEX 7325	Flexible mounting	1N 12
GEX 7513	Clamp	1N 14
GEX 7514	Saddle	1N 14
GEX 7515	Bracket	1N 12
CEX 7516	Packing plate	1N 13

20 04

Column 1 — plate 20 04

PART NO	DESCRIPTION	REF.NO.
GEX 7516	Packing plate	1N 14
GEX 7517	Saddle	1N 12
GEX 7517	"	1N 13
GEX 7518	Clamp plate	1N 12
GEX 7518	"	1N 13
GEX 7518	"	1N 14
GEX 7519	"	1N 13
GEX 7519	Clamp plate	1N 12
GEX 7521	"	1N 13
GEX 7521	Bracket	1N 13
GEX 7522	"	1N 12
GEX 7522	Distance piece	1N 13
GEX 7523	"	1N 14
GEX 7523	"	1N 12
GEX 7523	Mounting plate	1N 13
GEX 7523	"	1N 14
GEX 7524	"	1N 12
GFB 110	Clamp	1C 09
GFB 124	Fan belt	1E 10
GFB 189	Fan belt	1D 12
GFE 111	Fan belt	1D 15
GFE 130	Element for filter	1C 11
GFE 144	Oil filter element	1C 10
GFG 103	Oil filter element	1H 06
GFG 106	Axle flange gasket	1H 07
GFG 107	Axle flange gasket	1H 03
GFG 108	Axle flange gasket	1H 05
GFS 435	Joint washer	2E 02
GFU 103	Fuse	2D 06
GFU 116	Flasher unit	2D 05
GGB 101	Flasher unit	2C 13
GGC 102	Brushes set	2C 10
GGE 804	Dynamo brushes	1H 08
GHB 13C	Tube hylomar 4oz	2D 13
GHB 159	Horn	1F 07
GHB 162	Bearing	2K 08
GHB 163	Bearing	1H 06
GHC 406	Hub bearing inner	1H 06
GHC 507	Hub bearing outer	1L 17
GHC 811	Clip	2L 14
GHC 913	Hose clip	10 06
GHC 1217	Clip top and bottom radiator hoses	1E 10
GHF 101	Clip	1D 12
GHF 101	Clip	1I 06
GHF 101	Bolt	1J 09
GHF 101	"	1J 14
GHF 101	"	1N 12
GHF 101	"	1N 13
GHF 101	"	1N 14
GHF 101	"	1N 15
GHF 101	"	2G 02
GHF 101	"	2H 03
GHF 101	"	2L 12
GHF 101	"	2L 17

Column 2 — plate 20 05

PART NO	DESCRIPTION	REF.NO.
GHF 103	Set screw	1C 04
GHF 103	"	1C 08
GHF 103	"	1C 09
GHF 103	"	1E 05
GHF 103	"	1E 09
GHF 103	"	1E 10
GHF 103	"	1F 08
GHF 103	"	1F 10
GHF 103	"	1N 03
GHF 103	"	1N 09
GHF 103	"	1N 12
GHF 103	"	1N 13
GHF 103	"	1N 14
GHF 103	"	2F 15
GHF 103	"	2G 05
GHF 103	"	2I 08
GHF 104	"	2I 09
GHF 104	Bolt	1D 17
GHF 104	"	1J 09
GHF 104	"	1N 14
GHF 104	"	10 04
GHF 105	"	2C 13
GHF 105	Screw	2C 14
GHF 105	"	1D 18
GHF 105	"	1L 15
GHF 105	"	1L 14
GHF 105	"	1N 03
GHF 105	"	2F 02
GHF 106	Bolt	2H 04
GHF 120	Set bolt	2H 05
GHF 120	"	2H 10
GHF 120	"	1F 04
GHF 120	"	1C 08
GHF 120	"	1C 11
GHF 120	"	1D 10
GHF 120	"	1E 09
GHF 120	"	1E 12
GHF 120	"	1F 10
GHF 120	"	1I 05
GHF 120	"	1K 02
GHF 120	"	1K 04
GHF 120	"	1K 05
GHF 120	"	1K 06
GHF 120	"	1L 18
GHF 120	"	1M 12
GHF 120	"	1N 11
GHF 120	"	10 04
GHF 120	"	2E 03
GHF 120	"	2E 05
GHF 120	"	2E 08
GHF 120	"	2F 02
GHF 120	"	2F 03
GHF 120	"	2G 05
GHF 120	"	2I 10

Column 3 — plate 20 05

PART NO	DESCRIPTION	REF.NO.
GHF 120	Set bolt	2L 11
GHF 120	"	2L 14
GHF 161	Set bolt	1C 09
GHF 161	"	1E 10
GHF 200	Nut	1C 09
GHF 200	"	1C 12
GHF 200	"	1D 10
GHF 200	"	1D 11
GHF 200	"	1D 12
GHF 200	"	1E 10
GHF 200	"	1F 02
GHF 200	"	1F 05
GHF 200	"	1I 05
GHF 200	"	1I 06
GHF 200	"	1J 06
GHF 200	"	1J 10
GHF 200	"	1J 14
GHF 200	"	1K 02
GHF 200	"	1K 04
GHF 200	"	1K 06
GHF 200	"	1L 11
GHF 200	"	1L 12
GHF 200	"	1L 13
GHF 200	"	1L 16
GHF 200	"	1M 09
GHF 200	"	1M 10
GHF 200	"	1M 12
GHF 200	"	1N 02
GHF 200	"	1N 03
GHF 200	"	1N 04
GHF 200	"	1N 06
GHF 200	"	1N 07
GHF 200	"	1N 08
GHF 200	"	1N 09
GHF 200	"	1N 10
GHF 200	"	1N 11
GHF 200	"	1N 12
GHF 200	"	1N 13
GHF 200	"	1N 14
GHF 200	"	1N 15
GHF 200	"	10 03
GHF 200	"	10 04
GHF 200	"	2D 13
GHF 200	"	2D 14
GHF 200	"	2E 03
GHF 200	"	2E 04
GHF 200	"	2E 06
GHF 200	"	2E 07
GHF 200	"	2F 02
GHF 200	"	2F 03
GHF 200	"	2F 04
GHF 200	"	2F 05
GHF 200	"	2F 08
GHF 200	"	2F 09

PART NO	DESCRIPTION	REF.NO.
GHF 200	Nut	2F 10
GHF 200	"	2F 11
GHF 200	"	2F 13
GHF 200	"	2F 14
GHF 200	"	2F 16
GHF 200	"	2G 02
GHF 200	"	2G 03
GHF 200	"	2G 04
GHF 200	"	2G 06
GHF 200	"	2G 07
GHF 200	"	2G 08
GHF 200	"	2G 09
GHF 200	"	2G 10
GHF 200	"	2G 11
GHF 200	"	2H 02
GHF 200	"	2H 03
GHF 200	"	2H 07
GHF 200	"	2H 08
GHF 200	"	2I 06
GHF 200	"	2I 08
GHF 200	"	2I 09
GHF 200	"	2I 11
GHF 200	"	2I 12
GHF 200	"	2I 14
GHF 200	"	2I 15
GHF 200	"	2L 09
GHF 200	"	2L 11
GHF 200	"	2L 12
GHF 200	"	2L 14
GHF 200	"	2L 17
GHF 201	"	1C 05
GHF 202	"	1C 12
GHF 207	"	2C 05
GHF 214	Nut 10 mm	1C 14
GHF 221	Nyloc nut 1/4in UNF	1N 12
GHF 222	Nyloc nut 5/16 in UNF	1G 13
GHF 223	Nyloc nut 3/8in UNF	1L 18
GHF 224	Self lock nut	1H 14
GHF 224	"	1I 07
GHF 232	S.L. nut m8	1J 06
GHF 232	Self lock nut	1H 15
GHF 233	"	1C 14
GHF 233	"	1H 15
GHF 233	"	2L 09
GHF 234	S.L. nut 12mm	1H 15
GHF 242	Nut	1F 06
GHF 242	"	1I 06
GHF 242	"	1J 09
GHF 242	"	1J 14
GHF 242	"	1L 08
GHF 242	"	1L 09
GHF 242	"	1L 12
GHF 242	"	1N 03
GHF 242	"	1N 09

PART NO	DESCRIPTION	REF.NO.
GHF 242	Nut	2C 10
GHF 242	"	2C 11
GHF 242	"	2C 14
GHF 242	"	2F 06
GHF 242	"	2H 05
GHF 243	Phillidas nut 3/8in UNF	2H 10
GHF 273	Nut	1I 06
GHF 273	"	1H 07
GHF 300	Plain washer	2L 11
GHF 301	Plain washer	1C 13
GHF 301	"	1L 09
GHF 302	Plain washer	2I 06
GHF 321	Shakeproof washer	1C 11
GHF 322	Shakeproof washer	1D 09
GHF 323	Shakeproof washer	1G 12
GHF 331	Spring washer	1C 11
GHF 332	Spring washer	1C 12
GHF 333	Spring washer	1I 07
GHF 342	Fibre washer	1I 06
GHF 400	Drive screw	2I 08
GHF 400	"	2I 09
GHF 400	"	2I 11
GHF 400	"	2I 12
GHF 400	"	2I 14
GHF 400	"	2I 15
GHF 421	Drive screw	2L 09
GHF 421	"	2L 11
GHF 421	"	2L 12
GHF 421	"	2L 14
GHF 421	"	2L 17
GHF 421	"	1C 05
GHF 421	"	1C 12
GHF 421	"	2C 05
GHF 421	"	1C 14
GHF 421	"	1N 12
GHF 421	"	1G 13
GHF 421	"	1L 18
GHF 421	"	1H 14
GHF 421	"	1I 07
GHF 421	"	1J 06
GHF 421	"	1H 15
GHF 423	Drive screw	2D 06
GHF 423	"	2E 02
GHF 423	"	2E 07
GHF 423	"	2F 03
GHF 423	"	2F 11
GHF 423	"	2G 11
GHF 424	Drive screw	2H 10
GHF 713	Spire nut	1N 15
GHF 713	"	2I 12
GHF 1083	Plastic rivet	2I 07
GHS 202	Oil seal	1H 05

PART NO	DESCRIPTION	REF.NO.
GHS 202	Oil seal	1H 06
GHS 202	"	1H 13
GHS 202	"	2L 04
GHS 202	"	2L 05
GHS 1002	Oil seal	1H 07
GHS 1003	"	1H 05
GHS 1007	O ring	1H 07
GHT 127	Distributor lead set	2C 06
GHT 130	Distributor lead set	2C 03
GHT 173	Distributor lead set	2C 03
GLB 207	Bulb	2D 02
GLB 380	Bulb	2D 06
GLB 382	Bulb	2D 02
GLB 410	Bulb	2D 02
GLB 411	Bulb	2D 02
GLB 414	Bulb	2D 02
GLB 415	Bulb for headlamp	2D 06
GLB 643	Bulb	2D 10
GLB 987	Bulb	2D 02
GLB 989	Bulb	2D 02
GLR 303	Pedal pad	1N 05
GLU 104	Light unit sealed beam	2D 03
GLU 133	Light unit sealed beam	2D 03
GLU 513	Light unit bulb type	2D 02
GLU 517	Light unit	1J 13
GMC 309	Brake master cylinder	1J 09
GMC 310	Brake master cylinder	1J 09
GMC 311	Brake master cylinder	1J 09
GMC 312	Brake master cylinder	1J 09
GMC 314	Brake master cylinder	1C 11
GPS 102	Oil pressure switch	2C 02
GRA 101	Rotor arm	2C 05
GRA 102	Rotor arm	2C 02
GRC 123	Radiator cap	10 02
GRH 366	Hose for radiator top	10 05
GRH 369	Hose for radiator bottom	10 06
GRH 371	Hose for radiator bottom	10 05
GRH 439	Hose for radiator top	10 06
GRH 585	Hose radiator top	10 05
GRH 586	Hose radiator bottom	10 05
GSA 195	Front shock absorber	1H 14
GSA 196	Front shock absorber	1H 14
GSA 199	Rear shock absorber	1H 14
GSA 200	Rear shock absorber	1H 14
GSA 411	Shock absorber	2L 09
GSA 412	Shock absorber	2C 08
GSB 101	Brush set	2C 04
GSB 103	Starter brushes	1H 14
GSB 112	Brush set	2C 02
GSC 111	Condenser	2C 02
GSC 133	Condenser	2C 02
GSD 133	Speedo cable complete	2D 10
GSD 138	Speedometer cable complete	2D 12
GSU 102	Needle valve and seat	1M 02

PART NO	DESCRIPTION	REF.NO.
GSU 320	Oil cap	1M 02
GSU 524	Carb gasket kit	2J 02
GSU 551	Joint washer	1M 02
GTG 109	O ring	1C 09
GTG 110	Joint washer	1E 10
GTG 118	Joint washer	1D 12
GTG 119	Joint washer	1C 09
GTR 111	Water temp transm	1C 11
GTS 109	Thermostat	1E 10
GTS 114	Thermostat	1D 12
GTU 405	Touch up paint pastel green	2J 06
GTU 406	Touch up paint bronze green	2J 06
GTU 407	Touch up paint marine blue	2J 06
GTU 408	Touch up paint limestone	2J 06
GTU 409	Touch up paint grey	2J 06
GUJ 116	Universal joint	1H 07
GUJ 117	Universal joint	1H 07
GUJ 118	Universal joint	1H 03
GWB 127	Wiper blade	2D 13
GWB 128	Wiper blade	2D 13
GWB 195	Wiper blade	2D 15
GWC 301	Wheel cylinder	1J 04
GWC 302	Wheel cylinder	1J 04
GWC 303	Wheel cylinder	1J 03
GWC 304	Wheel cylinder	1J 03
GWC 305	Wheel cylinder	1J 02
GWC 306	Wheel cylinder	1J 02
GWC 1307	Wheel cylinder	1J 02
GWC 1308	Wheel cylinder	1J 02
GWP 305	Pump assy	1D 12
GWP 312	Water pump assy	1C 09
HB 913	Bolt	2H 04
JS 370	Bracket cover kit	2C 09
JS 499	Diaphragm	1M 05
JS 657	Centre seal upper	1M 11
JS 660	Element & seal	1M 11
MRC 1023	Bracket	2D 13
MRC 1201	Strap	2I 10
MRC 1210	U-bolt	2H 03
MRC 2178	Nut and retainer	2F 13
MRC 2237	Corner bracket	2G 03
MRC 2238	Corner bracket	2G 03
MRC 2244	Cover panel	2G 02
MRC 2245	Cover panel	2G 02
MRC 2381	Seal retainer	2F 16
MRC 2382	Seal retainer	2F 16
MRC 2440	Bonnet	2F 03
MRC 2479	Bonnet	2F 03
MRC 2595	Wing top	2F 03
MRC 3067	Mudshield	2F 04
MRC 3068	Mudshield	2F 04
MRC 3069	Mudshield	2F 04
MRC 3070	Mudshield	2F 04
MRC 3141	Frame	2F 16
MRC 4350	Safety harness	2I 09

20 07

PART NO	DESCRIPTION	REF.NO.
MRC 4753	Check bracket	2F 15
MRC 5740	Sealing rubber	2F 12
MRC 6483	Fixed window	2F 12
MRC 6484	Sliding window	2F 12
MRC 6485	Fixed window	2F 15
MRC 6490	Glass	2G 09
MRC 6493	Glass	2G 09
MRC 6499	Side light	2G 11
MRC 6526	Windscreen glass	2F 07
MRC 6950	Frame	2F 16
N 5	Sparking plug	2C 06
N 8	Sparking plug	2C 03
N 12Y	Sparking plug	2C 03
NC 112041	Castle nut	1I 07
NC 112041	" "	1I 08
ND 604041	" "	1D 06
NH 607041	Nut	2F 12
NH 608041	"	2F 06
NH 608061	"	1E 11
NH 608061	"	2L 09
NR 605090	"	1N 11
NR 605090	"	1N 14
NRC 62	Drain plug	1L 18
NRC 76	Bracket	1L 18
NRC 236	Rear crossmember	2F 02
NRC 1269	Steering relay	1I 07
NRC 1655	Clutch pipe	1F 10
NRC 2029	Mounting washer	1C 14
NRC 2052	Suspension rubber	1E 15
NRC 2053	Suspension rubber	1C 14
NRC 2054	Suspension rubber	1C 14
NRC 2130	Jump hose	1F 10
NRC 2340	Rear step	2H 05
NRC 2938	Engine bracket	1C 02
NRC 3215	Jack handle	2J 07
NRC 3249	Jack rod	2J 07
NRC 3448	Protection plate RH	2F 02
NRC 3449	Protection plate LH	2F 02
NRC 3812	Crossmember	2F 02
NRC 4346	Steering wheel	1I 04
NRC 4346	" "	2L 11
NRC 4354	Chassis frame	2F 02
NRC 4355	Chassis frame	2F 02
NRC 4356	Chassis frame	2F 02
NRC 4609	Drag link	1I 08
NRC 4642	Chassis frame	2F 02
NRC 5347	Pipe	1J 03
NRC 5829	Fuel tank	1L 18
NRC 5830	Fuel tank	1L 18
NRC 5830	" "	1M 10
NRC 6474	Steering damper	2L 13
NT 605061	Locknut	1C 06
NT 605061	"	1D 06
NT 605061	"	1D 08
NT 605061	"	1D 09
NT 605061	"	1D 17
NT 605061	"	1E 07
NT 605061	"	1G 05

20 08

PART NO	DESCRIPTION	REF.NO.
NT 605061	Locknut	1G 06
NT 605061	"	1J 03
NT 605061	"	1J 04
NT 605061	"	1J 09
NT 605061	"	1L 09
NT 605061	"	1L 11
NT 605061	"	2I 06
NT 605061	"	2K 07
NT 606041	Special nut	1F 08
NT 606041	" "	1F 10
NT 606041	" "	1K 02
NT 606041	" "	1K 04
NT 606041	" "	1K 06
NT 606041	" "	2H 09
NT 606041	" "	2L 14
NT 612061	Special nut	1I 03
NT 612061	" "	2L 10
PFS 510	Captive nut	2I 05
PRC 1716	Resistor	2E 02
PRC 1716	"	2E 05
PRC 2068	Lead	2E 03
PS 105281	Split pin	1I 07
PS 105281	" "	1I 08
PS 608101	Split pin	1G 07
PS 608101	" "	1G 09
PS 608101	" "	1H 05
PS 608101	" "	1H 07
PS 608101	" "	1H 08
PS 608101	" "	2K 09
PS 608101	" "	2K 12
PZJ 602	Screw	2D 02
RTC 162	Tab washer fixing throttle lever	1M 05
RTC 165	O ring for carburetter	1M 06
RTC 166	Lockwasher fixing throttle lever	1L 06
RTC 202	Flexible drive cable for wiper	2D 14
RTC 222	Cable cleat	2J 05
RTC 223	Strap	1M 12
RTC 253	Filler cap	1J 13
RTC 254	Drive for starter	2C 09
RTC 324	Bearing	1I 03
RTC 376	Wiper arm	2D 13
RTC 428	Dynamo	2C 12
RTC 430	Switch for panel lights	2D 11
RTC 432	Dip switch	1I 04
RTC 434	Voltage regulator box	2E 02
RTC 445	Headlamp	2D 02
RTC 465	Drive screw 7/8 in	2D 02
RTC 466	Spring set for brushes	2C 10
RTC 600	Split pin	2H 04
RTC 604	Plain washer fixing support bracket	1I 05
RTC 605	Plain washer	1I 07
RTC 607	Nipple for suction pipe	1C 12
RTC 608	Nut 2BA	1L 09
RTC 609	Plain washer fixing door check rod	2F 15

20 08

PART NO	DESCRIPTION	REF.NO.
RTC 610	Plain washer	1J 10
RTC 611	Plain washer for brake pedal pivot	1J 13
RTC 612	Plain washer	2G 07
RTC 613	Plain washer	2G 05
RTC 614	Split pin	2F 08
RTC 615	Plain washer	2L 17
RTC 617	Plain washer	2D 14
RTC 618	Plain washer	2D 13
RTC 621	Washer fixing squab	2I 06
RTC 622	Plain washer	2G 04
RTC 623	Lockwasher fixing drop arm	1I 03
RTC 626	Shim washer fixing dynamo	2C 11
RTC 631	Plain pin	1H 09
RTC 636	Plug for rocker shaft	1D 09
RTC 639	Box spanner	2J 07
RTC 640	Spring for plun-er rod	1K 07
RTC 643	Shim kit	2C 08
RTC 772	Cylinder head assy	1E 11
RTC 773	Bolt 12m	1H 12
RTC 819	Wiper arm	2D 15
RTC 822	Wiper arm	2D 15
RTC 840	Plain washer	1C 05
RTC 844	Cover	1H 12
RTC 845	Flitch plate	2C 08
RTC 1123	Pinion and barrel assy	1G 03
RTC 1215	Gearbox assy	1H 12
RTC 1392	Crown wheel and pinion	1G 04
RTC 1412	Rear door complete assy	2H 02
RTC 1443	Gearbox assy	1G 03
RTC 1720	Crankshaft bearing set std	1D 04
RTC 172010	Bearins set	1D 04
RTC 172020	Bearins set	1D 05
RTC 1721	Conn rod bearing set std	1D 05
RTC 172110	Bearins set	1D 05
RTC 172120	Bearins set	1C 03
RTC 1729	Main bearing set standard	1C 03
RTC 172910	Bearing set	1C 03
RTC 172920	Conn rod bearing set standard	1C 03
RTC 1730	Bearing set	1E 02
RTC 173010	Bearing set	2C 08
RTC 173020	Bearing set	1H 15
RTC 1813N	Engine assy	1H 15
RTC 1869	Retaining ring kit	1G 05
RTC 1920	Dowel m8	1G 05
RTC 1921	Dowel m10	1G 04
RTC 1954	Washer shield for primary pinion	1G 11
RTC 1956	Detent spring	1K 07
RTC 1957	Ring	1G 04
RTC 1958	Selector fork 3rd and 4th speed	1C 05
RTC 1961	Pin	1D 09
RTC 1962	Thrust washer	1D 12
RTC 1963	Locker	
RTC 1964	Screw	
RTC 1975	Seal	

20 09

PART NO	DESCRIPTION	REF.NO.
RTC 1979	Peg for distance sleeve	1G 04
RTC 1981	Lay shaft	1G 04
RTC 1982	Locker	1G 05
RTC 1983	Nut (1/2in BSF)	1G 05
RTC 1984	Seegar circlip 3.1/2in external	1G 04
RTC 1997N	Engine assy	1E 02
RTC 2038	Carb conversion kit	1L 02
RTC 2051	Wing top	2F 03
RTC 2052	Wing top	2F 03
RTC 2352N	Engine assembly	1C 02
RTC 2379N	Engine assembly	1C 02
RTC 2388N	Engine assy	1D 03
RTC 2407N	Engine assy	1D 03
RTC 2410	Piston ring set	1C 03
RTC 241020	Piston ring set	1C 03
RTC 241040	Piston ring set	1C 03
RTC 2411	Piston ring set	1D 05
RTC 241120	Piston ring set	1D 05
RTC 241140	Piston ring set	1D 05
RTC 2415	Piston ring set	1E 04
RTC 241520	Piston ring set	1E 04
RTC 241540	Piston ring set	1E 04
RTC 2547	Drag link assy	1I 08
RTC 2554	Oil pump assy	1E 05
RTC 2646	Control mechanism	2F 07
RTC 2664	Short engine	1E 02
SH 504041	Set bolt 1/4in UNC X 1/2in	1H 10
SH 505051	Bolt	1K 04
SH 505051	Set bolt 5/16in UNC X 3/4in	1K 11
SH 505061	Bolt 5/6in UNC X 7/8in	2C 11
SH 506061	Set bolt 3/8in UNC X 3/4in	1D 13
SH 506071	Set bolt 3/8in UNC X 7/8in	1I 06
SH 507101	Bolt 7/6in UNC X 1.1/4in	1D 15
SH 604101	Screw	1N 12
SH 604101	Screw	1N 13
SH 604121	Screw	2H 03
SH 605041	Special bolt 5/6 in UNF X 1/2 in	2H 08
SH 605051	Screw	1J 04
SH 605051	"	1I 05
SH 605051	"	1J 13
SH 605051	"	1K 02
SH 605051	"	2C 10
SH 605051	"	2F 08
SH 605051	"	2G 09
SH 605051	"	2I 10
SH 605051	"	2L 15
SH 605121	"	2I 10
SH 605201	Screw	1N 07
SH 606071	Bolt 5/16 in UNF X 2 1/2 in	1D 07
SH 606071	Set bolt	1D 07
SH 606071	" "	1E 06
SH 606071	" "	1K 07

20 09

PART NO	DESCRIPTION	REF.NO.
SH 606071	Set bolt	1K 08
SH 606071	"	1K 09
SH 606071	"	1K 10
SH 606071	"	2F 08
SH 606071	"	2H 04
SH 606071	"	2H 09
SH 606141	"	2L 13
SH 607081	Bolt 3/8 in UNF X 1 3/4 in	1K 10
SH 607101	Bolt 7/6in UNF X 11n	1H 10
SH 607101	Screw	1C 11
SH 608071	Set bolt 1/21n UNF X 7/81n	1G 06
SH 608081	Set bolt 1/21n UNF X 11n	1D 03
SH 608091	Screw	1C 02
SH 608091	"	1C 02
UFS 1254R	Screw 1/4 in UNF X 1/2 in	1E 02
UL 2806	Bolt 5/16 in X 3/4 in	2F 10
WB 106041	Plain washer	2F 03
WB 106041	"	1I 08
WB 106041	"	1N 02
KB 106041	"	1N 03
WB 106041	"	1N 05
KB 1C6041	"	1N 07
WB 1C6C41	"	1N 09
WB 106041	"	1N 10
WB 106041	"	1N 15
WB 106041	"	2C 03
WB 106041	"	2C 05
WB 108051	Plain washer	1J 09
WB 108051	"	1J 14
WB 108051	"	2C 11
WB 110061	Plain washer	1D 13
WB 110061	"	1F 04
WB 110061	"	1G 02
WB 110061	"	1G 06
WB 110061	"	1K 07
WB 110061	"	1K 08
WB 110061	"	1K 10
WB 110061	"	1L 14
WB 110061	"	1N 03
WB 110061	"	1N 15
WB 116101	"	2H 04
WB 116101	"	2H 05
WB 116101	"	2H 06
WB 116101	"	2H 09
WB 116101	"	2I 10
WB 116101	Plain washer	2K 06
WB 116101	"	1K 07
WB 116101	"	1K 09
WB 116101	"	1K 10
WB 116101	"	1L 18
WC 110061	Plain washer	1C 14

20 10

PART NO	DESCRIPTION	REF.NO.
WC 112081	Plain washer	1I 07
WC 112081	"	1I 08
WC 112081	Plain washer	2F 06
WC 702101	"	1K 03
WC 702101	"	1L 14
WC 702101	"	1N 09
WC 702101	"	1N 15
WC 702101	"	1O 03
WC 702101	"	2F 05
WC 702101	"	2F 07
WC 702101	"	2F 09
WC 702101	"	2F 11
WC 702101	"	2G 02
WC 702101	"	2C 05
WC 702101	"	2G 07
WC 702101	"	2H 02
WC 702101	"	2H 07
WC 702101	"	2I 14
WC 702101	"	2L 15
WC 702101	"	2L 17
WCX 600	Suppressor and cover	2C 03
WD 110061	Plain washer	1C 14
WD 110061	"	1D 18
WD 110061	"	1E 15
WD 110061	"	1M 10
WD 110061	"	2H 04
WE 702101	Shakeproof washer	1E 12
WE 702101	"	1K 03
WF 702101	"	2G 11
WL 110001	Shakeproof washer	1I 04
WL 110001	"	1C 14
WL 600050	Spring washer	1J 04
WM 600077	Spring washer	1C 11
WM 600081	"	1C 02
WM 702001	"	1C 11
WM 704001	Spring washer	1I 04
WP 185	Plain washer	1I 05
WP 8019	Plain washer	1N 02
WS 600041	Spring washer	2G 05
WS 600061	"	2H 04
WS 600061	"	2H 05
WS 600061	"	2H 06
WS 600061	"	2H 10
WS 600091	Spring washer	2G 08
WZX 1712	Diaphragm	1M 08
1H 9077	Switch	2D 11
7H 3006	Clutch spring	1F 03
7H 3006	"	1F 05
7H 5007	Main spring	2C 04
7H 5007	"	2C 06
7H 5483	Light unit	2D 02
13H 1515	Banjo bolt	1L 14
13H 3735	Stoplight switch	1J 08
13H 5952	Switch	2E 04

20 10

PART NO	DESCRIPTION	REF.NO.
17H 2475	Key blank	2D 10
17H 2475	"	2D 11
18G 8246	Overhaul kit for fuel pump	1L 08
18G 8951	Overhaul kit for br servo	1J 13
24G 8953	Non return valve	1J 14
24G 1345	Barrel lock	2D 10
27H 1330	Washer for bowl	1L 09
27H 3793	Brush set dynamo	2C 12
27H 5932	Spring set	2C 08
27H 7946	Blue grease	2J 02
27H 8207	Headlamp	2D 08
37H 575	Seal for element small	1L 11
37H 770	Seal, centre bolt	1L 09
37H 770	Seal, centre bolt	1L 11
37H 770	Seal, centre bolt	1L 12
37H 770	Seal, centre bolt	1L 14
37H 1581	Element, fuel filter	1L 09
37H 1581	"	1L 11
37H 1581	"	1L 12
37H 2736	Shaft and gear	2D 15
37H 3694	Ferrule	2D 14
37H 3694	"	2D 15
37H 5452	Bulb holder	2D 06
37H 6109	Lens	2D 08
37H 6134	Adjuster unit assy	1J 07
37H 6836	Sundry parts kit	2C 10
37H 6836	"	2C 12
37H 6836	"	2C 14
37H 6836	"	2C 15
37H 6928	Lens	2D 08
37H 7618	Sealing ring	2C 09
37H 7847	Wiper arm	2D 14
37H 7848	Wiper arm	2C 09
37H 8531	Bracket	1K 04
37H 8663	Hose	1K 06
47H 5394	Oiler	2C 14
47H 5531	Special nut	2D 02
57H 5398	Cover	2E 02
7H 3082	Clutch spring	1F 03
6G 2039	Repair kit for fule pump	1F 10
8G 8600	Overhaul kit cyl sl cyl	1J 12
8G 8837	Overhaul kit master cyl	1L 11
8G 8844	Fuel pump repair kit	1L 11
8G 8845	Fuel pump overhaul kit	1G 08
90 212104	Stud for bottom cover	2C 03
90 213172	Sealing ring for plug cover	1G 11
90 213636	Shaft for selector fork	1F 07
90 213662	Joint washer for clutch housing	1F 07
90 213663	Joint washer for clutch housing	1F 07
90 214684	Spring ring fixing cover	1F 07
90 214787	Oil seal	1F 07
90 215593	Bolt fixing cover plate	1G 08
90 215594	Set bolt 1/4 whit X 3/4 long	

20 11

PART NO	DESCRIPTION	REF.NO.
90 215647	Set bolt 5/16 whit X 13/16 long	1G 10
90 215758	Set bolt 1/4 whit X 1/2 long	1G 08
90 215769	Bolt 1/4 whit X 7/16 in	1G 11
90 216909	Banjo for brake pipe	1J 11
90 217279	Horn push	1H 04
90 217355	Special nut fixing hub bearing	1H 07
90 217389	Reverse wheel	1G 04
90 217391	Selector fork reverse	1G 11
90 217398	Retaining collar for bearing	1H 03
90 217448	Bush for shaft guide	1G 08
90 217488	Thrust washer for gearbox	1G 07
90 217512	Bearing for gearbox	1G 07
90 217521	Bush for selector fork	1G 12
90 217584	Selector fork	1G 13
90 217636	Clip for reservoir tank	1J 10
90 217787	Oil seal for clutch housing	1F 07
90 217843	Bush for housing	1G 08
90 217976	Stud for engine mounting	1G 08
90 217983	Housing for handbrake mounting	1K 09
90 217984	Spherical bearing handbrake mounting	1K 09
90 218402	Cross shaft for handbrake	1K 09
90 218408	Pin	1K 09
90 218410	Distance piece handbrake mounting	2F 13
90 302859	Sealing washer	21 12
90 306199	Support tube bearing	21 12
90 306200	Support tube	1O 04
90 306465	Rubber buffer for grille panel	2D 02
90 500411	Lens for stop tail lamp	2D 02
90 500514	Bezel for side lamp	1D 09
90 500610	Spring valve rocker	1L 04
90 602106	Correction jet 185	1E 05
90 602209	Spindle for idler gear	2H 03
90 502710	Swivel pin and steering lever	1H 03
90 502713	Swivel pin and steering lever	1H 04
90 502714	Swivel pin and bracket	1L 04
90 503916	Joint washer top cover on carburetter	2G 02
90 508035	Stowage clip	1H 03
90 508152	Stud 3/8 in	1H 03
90 508153	Special stud for steering lever	1D 17
90 508339	Bracket for engine tie rod	1L 1C
90 508544	Bush fixing fuel tank	1L 18
90 508545	Bush fixing fuel tank	1K 02
90 508566	Bracket for brake pipe	1K 02
90 509556	Control rod pedal shaft top cross shaft	1L 15
90 509730	Connection hose	1L 06
90 509970	Grommet for brake pedal bracket	1E 08
90 510730	Side cover and oil filler pipe	2E 03
90 510912	Fan disc washer	2E 03
90 511833	Valve guide exhaust	1D 03
90 511958	Joint washer thermostat housing	1C 09
90 512205	Valve rocker inlet LH	1C 06
90 512208	Valve rocker exhaust RH	1C 06
90 512305	Fan disc washer fixing earth lead	1E 12
90 512322	Steering wheel	1I 04

20 11

PART NO	DESCRIPTION	REF.NO.
90 512413	Core plu- for cylinder head	1E 11
90 512646	Clip for suction pipe	1C 12
90 512651	Shakeproof washer fixing brake hose	1F 08
90 512701	Bolt for flange	1G 07
90 513171	Adaptor	1K 04
90 513220	Clip for cable	2J 04
90 513454	Washer for flange	1H 08
90 513591	Oil filter	1D 15
90 513940	Clip fixing brake pipe	1K 03
90 514146	Gasket for stop tail lamp	2D 02
90 514148	Bezel for sidelamp	2D 02
90 514149	Screw fixing bezel	2D 02
90 514150	Lens for sidelamp	2D 02
90 514152	Lens for stop tail lamp	2D 02
90 514451	Front cover assembly	1E 08
90 515086	Flywheel housing	1F 05
90 515090	Fan blade	1E 10
90 515323	Piston chain adjuster	1C 05
90 515552	Injector complete	1L 10
90 515855	Bush for high gear wheel	2K 08
90 516028	Oil seal for front cover	1D 09
90 516914	Joint washer for filler cap	1O 02
90 517026	Linning park for clutch plate	1F 06
90 517429	Roller for cam follower	1D 09
90 517567	Clamp for tail pipe	1N 13
90 517878	Locking plate fixing steering box	1I 06
90 518100	Special bolt for conn rod	1D 05
90 518145	Filter for breather pipe	1D 10
90 518466	Stud for cylinder head	1E 11
90 518682	Filter for fluid reservoir	1J 10
90 518719	Rocker cover assembly	1E 12
90 519054	Bearing front for camshaft	1E 06
90 519055	Bearing centr and rear for camshaft	1E 06
90 519064	Dowel for rear amin oil seal	1C 03
90 519206	Locating stop for jack	1H 03
90 519775	Ignition and lighting switch	2D 10
90 519841	Fuel guage	2D 10
90 519857	Fan disc washer	2E 08
90 519865	Feed lead for flasher switch	2D 06
90 519866	Self cancelling switch	2D 06
90 519874	Fuel gauge	2D 10
90 519875	Gauge unit for fuel tank	1L 18
90 519897	Fan disc washer	2E 05
90 520940	Piston ring compression 010 O/S	1E 04
90 520941	Piston ring compression 020 O/S	1E 04
90 520942	Piston ring compression 030 O/S	1E 04
90 520943	Piston ring compression 040 O/S	1E 04
90 520978	Piston ring compression std	1E 04
90 545107	Headlamp	2D 03
90 552522	Lever for accelerator	1N 05
90 552791	Steering unit assy	2L 10
90 552971	Fuel tank	1M 10
90 560577	Cable fuel pump feed	2E 08
90 560612	Guage unit for fuel tank	1M 10

20 12

PART NO	DESCRIPTION	REF.NO.
90 562714	Shaft for accelerator pedal	1N 05
90 564216	Extension piece for oil pump	1D 06
90 564217	Stud for oil strainer	1D 06
90 564334	Oil pump assy	1D 06
90 564812	Pivot pin for brake pedal	1J 13
90 564832	Gasket brake pedal and bracket	1J 13
90 566617	Union fuel pipe connection	1L 12
90 568489	Banjo bolt for fuel pipe	1L 13
90 568525	Stop lever for distributor pump	1L 12
90 568526	Swivel clamp for stop lever	1L 12
90 569017	Crossmember no 4	2L 09
90 569251	Control for engine speed control	1N 10
90 569611	Brake pedal and bushes	1J 13
90 569612	Gasket for mounting bracket	1J 13
90 571227	Spacer for clutch plate	1F 06
90 574103	Special set bolt	1D 13
90 574104	Special set bolt	1D 13
90 574655	Hose breather filter to manifold	1E 12
90 574691	Plug for manifold	1E 14
90 575015	Nut for terminal post	2E 04
90 575150	Number plate lamp	2D 02
90 575183	Engine harness	2E 05
90 575201	Horn push and centre cover	1I 04
90 576693	Oil filler cap complete	1G 03
90 577060	Knob for lever	1N 10
90 577064	Fuel filter	1K 11
90 577065	Lever for control	1N 10
90 577082	Clip outlet pipe to bottle	1O 03
90 577143	Support plate	2F 02
90 577165	Brake pipe	1K 02
90 577193	Inner column RH steering	1I 02
90 577194	Inner column LH steering	1I 02
90 577197	Inner column RH stg	2L 10
90 577198	Inner column LH stg	2L 10
90 577264	Stiffener bracket for steering box	1I 06
90 577434	Bush 1.5in O/D	1H 15
90 577473	Wheel nut 16 mm	1H 16
90 577611	Plug for servo unit	1J 13
90 600400	Oil container	1L 08
90 601847	Spring for throttle stop	1L 06
90 601848	Volume control screw	1L 06
90 601849	Spring for control screw	1L 06
90 601890	Pin fixing relay lever	1L 07
90 601898	Ventilation screw for choke	1L 07
90 605057	Bearing for dynamo	2C 12
90 605561	Sedimentor complete	1L 14
90 605617	Bracket for starter	2C 09
90 605812	Shakeproof washer for carburetter	1M 06
90 605851	Retaining ring for carburetter damper	1M 05
90 606023	Overhaul kit Br M cyl	1J 12
90 606500	Bulbholder	2D 04
90 606892	Brake servo conversion kit	1J 12
90 607170	Cross shaft	1H 12
90 607193	Bolt fixing diff case	1H 12

20 12

PART NO	DESCRIPTION	REF.NO.
90 607607	Contact breaker base plate	2C 02
90 607809	Pr pinion and constant gear	1G 05
90 608175	Armature	2C 04
90 608178	Sundry parts kit	2C 04
90 608241	Roller for fuel pump diaphragm	1M 08
90 608307	Gear and con rod for wiper motor	2D 14
90 608462	Long strg tube assy	1I 08
90 608545	Locknut	1H 12
90 624083	Spring bottom plate	1H 15
90 624214	Lifting jack	2J 07
90 624436	Joint washer	1I 07

20 13

LAND ROVER OFFICIAL FACTORY PUBLICATIONS

Land Rover Series 1 Workshop Manual	4291
Land Rover Series 1 1948-53 Parts Catalogue	4051
Land Rover Series 1 1954-58 Parts Catalogue	4107
Land Rover Series 1 Instruction Manual	4277
Land Rover Series 1 & II Diesel Instruction Manual	4343
Land Rover Series II & IIA Workshop Manual	AKM8159
Land Rover Series II & Early IIA Bonneted Control Parts Catalogue	605957
Land Rover Series IIA Bonneted Control Parts Catalogue	RTC9840CC
Land Rover Series IIA, III & 109 V8 Optional Equipment Parts Catalogue	RTC9842CE
Land Rover Series IIA/IIB Instruction Manual	LSM64IM
Land Rover Series III Workshop Manual	AKM3648
Land Rover Series III Workshop Manual V8 Supplement (edn. 2)	AKM8022
Land Rover Series III 88, 109 & 109 V8 Parts Catalogue	RTC9841CE
Land Rover Series III Owners Manual 1971-1978	607324B
Land Rover Series III Owners Manual 1979-1985	AKM8155
Military Land Rover (Lightweight) Series III Parts Catalogue	61278
Military Land Rover Series III (L.W.B.) User Handbook	608179
Military Land Rover (Lightweight) Series III User Manual	608180
Land Rover 90/110 & Defender Workshop Manual 1983-1992	SLR621ENWM
Land Rover Defender Workshop Manual 1993-1995	LDAWMEN93
Land Rover Defender 300 Tdi & Supplements Workshop Manual 1996-1998	LRL0097ENGBB
Land Rover Defender Td5 Workshop Manual & Supplements 1999-2006	LRL0410BB
Land Rover Defender Electrical Manual Td5 1999-06 & 300Tdi 2002-2006	LRD5EHBB
Land Rover 110 Parts Catalogue 1983-1986	RTC9863CE
Land Rover Defender Parts Catalogue 1987-2006	STC9021CC
Land Rover 90 • 110 Handbook 1983-1990 MY	LSM0054
Land Rover Defender 90 • 110 • 130 Handbook 1991 MY - Feb. 1994	LHAHBEN93
Land Rover Defender 90 • 110 • 130 Handbook Mar. 1994 - 1998 MY	LRL0087ENG/2
Military Land Rover 90/110 All Variants (Excluding APV & SAS) User Manual	2320-D-122-201
Military Land Rover 90 & 110 2.5 Diesel Engine Versions User Handbook	SLR989WDHB
Military Land Rover Defender XD - Wolf Workshop Manual - 2320D128 -	302 522 523 524
Military Land Rover Defender XD - Wolf Parts Catalogue	2320D128711
Discovery Workshop Manual 1990-1994 (petrol 3.5, 3.9, Mpi & diesel 200 Tdi)	SJR900ENWM
Discovery Workshop Manual 1995-1998 (petrol 2.0 Mpi, 3.9, 4.0 V8 & diesel 300 Tdi)	LRL0079BB
Discovery Series II Workshop Manual 1999-2003 (petrol 4.0 V8 & diesel Td5 2.5)	VDR100090/6
Discovery Parts Catalogue 1989-1998 (2.0 Mpi, 3.5, 3.9 V8 & 200 Tdi & 300 Tdi)	RTC9947CF
Discovery Parts Catalogue 1999-2003 (petrol 4.0 V8 & diesel Td5 2.5)	STC9049CA
Discovery Owners Handbook 1990-1991 (petrol 3.5 V8 & diesel 200 Tdi)	SJR820ENHB90
Discovery Series II Handbook 1999-2004 MY (petrol 4.0 V8 & Td5 diesel)	LRL0459BB
Freelander Workshop Manual 1998-2000 (petrol 1.8 and diesel 2.0)	LRL0144
Freelander Workshop Manual 2001-2003 ON (petrol 1.8L, 2.5L & diesel Td4 2.0)	LRL0350ENG/4
Land Rover 101 1 Tonne Forward Control Workshop Manual	RTC9120
Land Rover 101 1 Tonne Forward Control Parts Catalogue	608294B
Land Rover 101 1 Tonne Forward Control User Manual	608239
Range Rover Workshop Manual 1970-1985 (petrol 3.5)	AKM3630
Range Rover Workshop Manual 1986-1989	SRR660ENWM &
(petrol 3.5 & diesel 2.4 Turbo VM)	LSM180WS4/2
Range Rover Workshop Manual 1990-1994	
(petrol 3.9, 4.2 & diesel 2.5 Turbo VM, 200 Tdi)	LHAWMENA02
Range Rover Workshop Manual 1995-2001 (petrol 4.0, 4.6 & BMW 2.5 diesel)	LRL0326ENGBB
Range Rover Workshop Manual 2002-2005 (BMW petrol 4.4 & BMW 3.0 diesel)	LRL0477
Range Rover Electrical Manual 2002-2005 UK version (petrol 4.4 & 3.0 diesel)	RR02KEMBB
Range Rover Electrical Manual 2002-2005 USA version (BMW petrol 4.4)	RR02AEMBB
Range Rover Parts Catalogue 1970-1985 (petrol 3.5)	RTC9846CH
Range Rover Parts Catalogue 1986-1991 (petrol 3.5, 3.9 & diesel 2.4 & 2.5 Turbo VM)	RTC9908CB
Range Rover Parts Catalogue 1992-1994 MY & 95 MY Classic	
(petrol 3.9, 4.2 & diesel 2.5 Turbo VM, 200 Tdi & 300 Tdi)	RTC9961CB
Range Rover Parts Catalogue 1995-2001 MY (petrol 4.0, 4.6 & BMW 2.5 diesel)	RTC9970CE
Range Rover Owners Handbook 1970-1980 (petrol 3.5)	606917
Range Rover Owners Handbook 1981-1982 (petrol 3.5)	AKM8139
Range Rover Owners Handbook 1983-1985 (petrol 3.5)	LSM0001HB
Range Rover Owners Handbook 1986-1987 (petrol 3.5 & diesel 2.4 Turbo VM)	LSM129HB

Engine Overhaul Manuals for Land Rover & Range Rover

300 Tdi Engine, R380 Manual Gearbox & LT230T Transfer Gearbox Overhaul Manuals	LRL003, 070 & 081
Petrol Engine V8 3.5, 3.9, 4.0, 4.2 & 4.6 Overhaul Manuals	LRL004 & 164
Land Rover/Range Rover Driving Techniques	LR369
Working in the Wild - Manual for Africa	SMR684MI
Winching in Safety - Complete guide to winching Land Rovers & Range Rovers	SMR699MI

Workshop Manual Owners Edition
Land Rover 2 / 2A / 3 Owners Workshop Manual 1959-1983
Land Rover 90, 110 & Defender Workshop Manual Owners Edition 1983-1995
Land Rover Discovery Workshop Manual Owners Edition 1990-1998

From Land Rover specialists or, in case of difficulty, direct from the distributors:
Brooklands Books Ltd., P.O. Box 146, Cobham, Surrey, KT11 1LG, England, UK
Phone: +44 (0) 1932 865051   info@brooklands-books.com   www.brooklands-books.com
Brooklands Books Australia, Renniks Publications, 3/37-39 Green Street, Banksmeadow, NSW, 2019, Australia
Phone: +61 (0) 2 9695 7055   info@renniks.com   www.renniks.com
CarTech, 39966 Grand Avenue, North Branch, MN 55056, USA
Phone: 1 800 551 4754 & +1 651 277 1200   info@cartechbooks.com   www.cartechbooks.com

Printed in Great Britain
by Amazon